PRIMA Official Game Guide

Written by Dan Birlew

Prima Games
A Division of Random House, Inc.
3000 Lava Ridge Court, Suite 100
Roseville, CA 95661
1-800-733-3000
www.primagames.com

Product Manager: Mario De Govia
Editor: Amanda Peckham
Design: José de Jesús Ramírez

ISBN: 0-7615-5287-1
Library of Congress Catalog Card Number: 2005910393
Printed in the United States of America

06 07 08 09 LL 10 9 8 7 6 5 4 3 2 1

Dan Birlew is a video game expert who has been writing official, published video game strategy guides since 1999. His original career goals included acting and directing. At the age of 26 he began honing his playing skills with the goal of becoming a video game expert. He enjoyed publishing online documents regarding games, known as "FAQs." Dan inadvertently created an online persona for himself when he wrote and self-published on the Internet a plot analysis of the highly popular survival horror video game, *Silent Hill.*

After some gentle nudging from his wife, Birlew decided to set aside his acting and directing activities and establish a career as a video game strategy guide author. He sent writing samples to several publishing companies. Based on the merits of his very first submission, he was hired by a major publisher within 24 hours. Birlew has authored over 40 published video game strategy guides.

Dan Birlew is a native of St. Louis, Missouri, and has lived in Pennsylvania, Texas, and California. He now resides with his wife of 12 years in Las Vegas. He graduated with a bachelor of fine arts from the University of Texas at Austin in 1993.

We want to hear from you! E-mail comments and feedback to **dbirlew@primagames.com.**

Special thanks to Fernando Bueno for Co-op contribution.

TABLE OF CONTENTS

01: PS2/GC
DOSSIERS

Sam Fisher

Occupation: Field Operative
Affiliation: Third Echelon, National Security Agency

Sam Fisher is the veteran of a hundred silent wars; he is part of covert operations aimed at sabotaging and dismantling terrorist organizations in various parts of the world that have plans for global terror. Sam's gruff attitude and numerous scars speak to his experience. A former Navy SEAL, Sam has now carried out several rough but successful operations under the NSA's top-secret Third Echelon department as a "splinter cell"—a lone operative working in the field with high-tech support.

After an infiltration mission in Iceland, Sam learns that his daughter, Sarah, has been killed in a hit-and-run accident. She was the last member of his family; his wife had died 10 years ago, and Sam took the loss hard. After diving into alcohol and self-abuse, Sam has reunited with Third Echelon for an important mission that only he is capable of carrying out. Will the training and experience of his years as a covert operative help him protect the United States? Or has the death of his daughter truly sent him over an edge from which he may not return?

Irving Lambert

Occupation: Operations Coordinator
Affiliation: Third Echelon, National Security Agency

Irving Lambert is a former CIA, former NSA administrator assigned to run Third Echelon. He has been Sam's handler on several tough assignments. The two have formed a deep bond over the years, and Lambert has seen Sam go through some rough times. After Sam loses his daughter, Sarah, Lambert does his best to rescue Sam by assigning him to a very hard mission. But as Sam works harder to convince the JBA that he is a real terrorist, Lambert may find that his old friend has gone too far off the cliff.

Emile Dufraisne

Occupation: Founder, Organizer
Affiliation: John Brown's Army

Emile Dufraisne is the megalomaniac founder and leader of John Brown's Army, named for the famous historical abolitionist who advocated guerrilla warfare as a means to abolish slavery and attempted to start a slave rebellion prior to the Civil War. Born and raised in New Orleans, Emile is a true Southern gentleman, minus the "gentle." Emile intends to use his inherited wealth to fund the JBA and purchase weapons of mass destruction, which will be deployed against the United States. He views the government as a corrupt and oppressive force that wants to suppress the people. His great distrust of the government makes him paranoid toward new recruits in the JBA. As a result, members such as Sam must go above and beyond to prove their loyalty to Dufraisne and must be willing to kill and murder innocent people at a whim.

Jamie Washington

Occupation: Electronics Expert
Affiliation: John Brown's Army

Jamie Washington is a volatile and unstable member of John Brown's Army. Caught stealing explosives from a military warehouse, he has recently been incarcerated at Ellsworth Penitentiary in Kansas. As a result, he may be Sam's ticket inside the JBA. If Sam can help him bust out of prison and rejoin the terrorist organization, then there's a good chance Sam will be accepted into the fold. But will Sam regret helping a violent-tempered fanatic like Jamie escape from incarceration?

Enrica Villablanca

Occupation: Weapons Designer
Affiliation: John Brown's Army

Enrica is the 30-year-old daughter of Cuban and German parents. While studying for a PhD in chemical engineering at Florida State University, she became active in campus protest groups. Following a "monkey-wrenching" protest at a Florida chemical plant—in which a security guard was accidentally killed—Enrica went underground. She joined the JBA as a consultant and has stayed only because of Emile Dufraisne's threats of exposure and arrest. She does not follow the JBA's ideology as closely as the other members and wants only to accomplish what Emile tells her in the hope of being released. She could make a good point of contact inside the JBA for Sam, but can he trust her?

02: PS2/GC

GAME BASICS

5'6"
5'3"
5'
Sam Fisher
D2334223424
Feb 5, 2008
llsworth Federal Penitentiary

Overview

Sam Fisher is an agent of Third Echelon, a top-secret branch of the CIA. Sam's usual job is to infiltrate high-security terrorist installations and prevent antigovernment factions from unleashing mass chaos or killing millions. But following the death of his daughter, Sam takes on the riskiest mission of his life. Posing as a convicted bank robber, Sam infiltrates the JBA (John Brown's Army) by befriending fellow convict Jamie Washington and helping him escape. Inside the JBA, Sam must carry out the terrorists' orders without betraying the government and the citizens he has sworn to defend.

Playing as Sam Fisher, the player must use shadows and high-tech gadgetry to take down enemies and law enforcement officials quietly and efficiently. The player must obtain data and complete objectives to keep both the JBA and NSA (National Security Agency) happy enough not to pull the plug on the mission. The Trust Level meter indicates how much faith each side has in Sam. If the meter leans too far to one side, the other side becomes suspicious and may require immediate action. Sam must maintain a balance of Trust and complete his objectives in order to prevent the JBA from unleashing global terror.

This section covers everything a splinter cell agent can do without weapons. For more information on using weapons and gadgetry, check out the "Equipment" section that's relevant to your platform.

Heads-Up Display

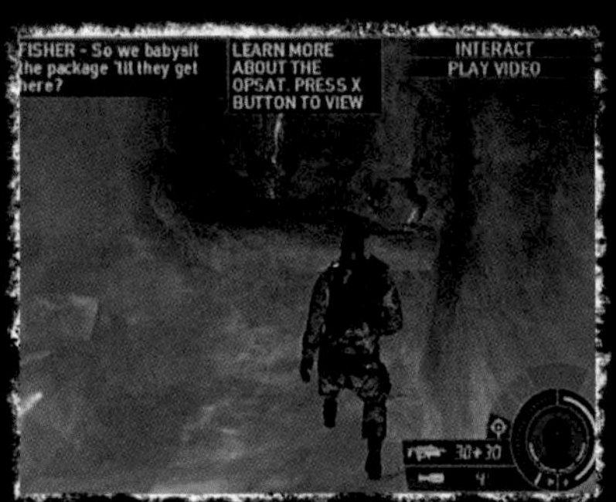

1. **Stealth Meter:** Indicates the amount of light striking Sam Fisher. When completely dark, Sam is fully immersed in shadow and cannot be seen by enemies if they look in his direction. When fully lit, Sam is clearly illuminated and all enemies in the area spot him immediately.
2. **Noise Meter:** The line across the meter indicates the amount of ambient sound in the environment. The curved meter indicates the amount of noise Sam's movements or actions are making. If the curved meter exceeds the ambient sound indicator, then Sam is making too much noise and could be detected.
3. **Life Bar:** Indicates the amount of damage the character can sustain before dying. Recover lost health by using a medkit.
4. **New Objective:** A new objective has been added to the Objectives menu on your OPSAT.
5. **New Note:** A new note has been added to the Note menu of your OPSAT.
6. **Co-op Action:** Mainly used in Co-op mode. A dot in this area indicates that your partner is waiting for you to complete a co-op action.
7. **Alarm Indicator:** Indicates the current alarm level. The alarm level rises each time Sam is detected, either by surveillance camera, laser trip wire, or when an enemy reaches an alarm panel and alerts the base. At higher alert levels, enemies may don protective armor and carry greater firepower. Alarm levels can be reduced by grabbing an enemy and forcing him to call in a false alarm.
8. **Selected Item:** The weapon or item currently equipped. Press the Equip button to activate the item shown.
9. **Ammo:** The quantity of ammo available for your equipped weapon. The first number shows the bullets remaining in the magazine, and the second number shows the quantity available for reload. If the item is an item such as a grenade, the quantity remaining in possession is shown.
10. **Secondary Function:** If the selected weapon is loaded with launcher gadgets such as the sticky shockers or airfoil rounds, an appropriate icon is displayed here. If the weapon is equipped with an OCP jamming device, the OCP Charge meter is displayed here.
11. **Communication Box:** When enabled through the Options menu, transcripts of incoming transmissions and Sam's responses are displayed in the screen's upper left corner.
12. **Objective Update:** When new or completed objectives are added to the Objectives menu of the OPSAT, a note is displayed in the screen's top center.
13. **Interaction Menu:** When Sam is near an object, door, or person he can interact with, the Interaction menu appears in the screen's upper right corner.

Default Controls for PS2 and GC versions

ACTION	PLAYSTATION 2	GAMECUBE
Move control	Left analog stick	Control stick
Back to wall/switch hand	L3	Z + A
Aim/camera	Right analog stick	C
EEV/zoom	R3	Z + C
Pause menu	START	START
OPSAT/PDA menu	SELECT	Z + START
Interact	×	A
Crouch/stand	●	X
Equip item	■	B
Jump	▲	Y
Night vision	D-pad (left)	←
EMF vision	D-pad (up)	↑
Thermal vision	D-pad (right)	→
Sticky camera	D-pad (down)	↓
Primary attack	R1	R
Quick inventory	R2	Z (hold) + ↑
Secondary attack	L1	L
Whistle/co-op action	L2	Z (hold) + ←

Control Functions

This section contains explanations of all control functions listed above.

Pause Menu

Press the Pause Menu button to pause the game and bring up the Pause menu. Here you can save your progress, load a previously saved game, or start a different mission, modify options, and restart or quit the current mission.

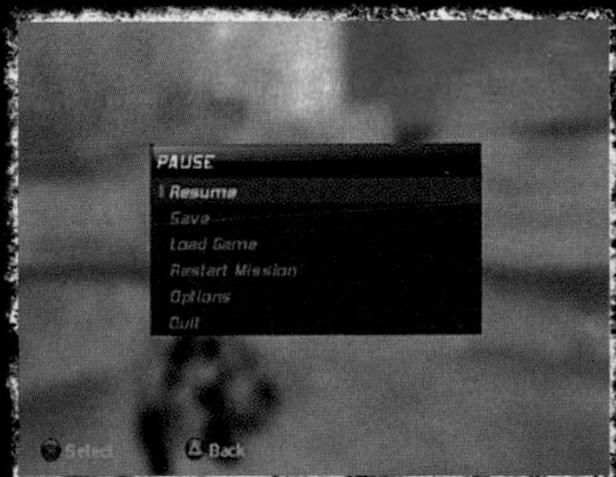

OPSAT/PDA Menu

Press the OPSAT/PDA Menu button to bring up Sam's OPSAT. The OPSAT shows how much time you have spent on the current mission and provides various functions to help serve in your situation.

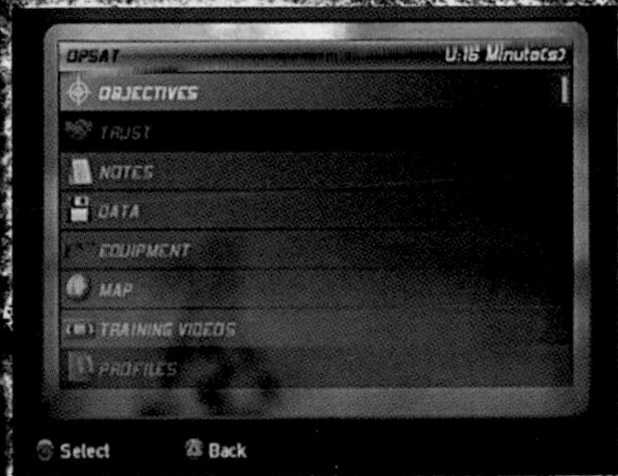

OBJECTIVES

This menu displays a list of the mission objectives and the current status of each objective. Use the cursor to highlight objectives and press the Details button to view more elaborate descriptions of objectives.

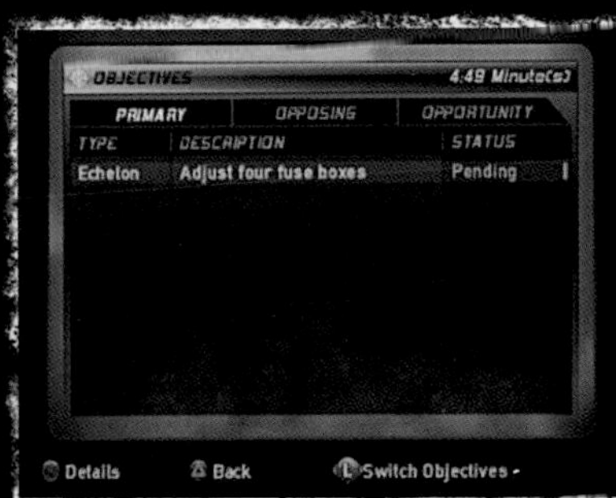

Objectives are divided into three categories: Primary, Opposing, and Opportunity. Primary Objectives must be completed in order to proceed in the mission and in the game. Failing a Primary Objective is often grounds for immediate mission failure.

Opposing Objectives come into play after the first mission. Any time Sam has Opposing Objectives, there are usually two. The Echelon or the NSA has issued one objective and the JBA the other. For instance, the NSA may want you to protect a key individual, whereas the JBA wants Sam to execute the person. You must choose whose side you are on and act accordingly. Completing an Opposing Objective garners Trust with that agency, and the opposing faction may become suspicious.

Opportunity Objectives are optional mission parameters. Completing Opportunity Objectives often allows Sam to score bonus points with Third Echelon or the NSA. Failure to complete Opportunity Objectives does not lead to instant mission failure.

Whenever Sam receives a new objective during a mission, the New Objective icon appears on the HUD display in the screen's lower right corner.

TRUST

The Trust Level meter indicates Sam's current level of Trust with the two opposing factions. Sam cannot engender great Trust with both the NSA and the JBA simultaneously. Any action that benefits the terrorists causes Sam to lose trust with the NSA. Any defiance of the terrorists' orders causes the JBA to become suspicious of Sam, throwing the entire mission into jeopardy.

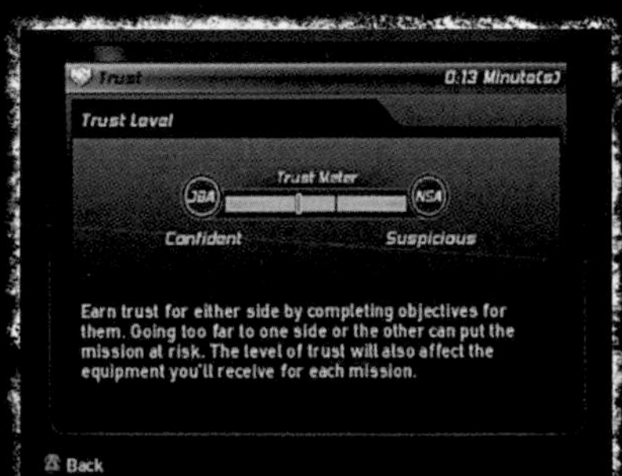

Trust also affects the type of equipment Sam receives at the start of each mission. If the NSA's Trust is high, then Sam receives more nonlethal gadgets such as sticky shockers and sticky cameras. If the JBA's Trust is high, Sam receives more lethal ammunition and fewer nonlethal gadgets.

The best strategy is to always keep the Trust meter in the Neutral zone (in the middle). This ensures that neither agency becomes too suspicious and starts demanding that Sam complete extra objectives such as sending e-mails from a computer or returning to the starting point of the mission. This also ensures that Sam receives a nice balance of lethal and nonlethal ammo at the start of each mission.

To maintain a Neutral Trust level, consider what is being asked of you and how it will affect the Trust meter. If the JBA wants something done and your Trust is extremely high on the NSA side, then you may have to kill someone. If the NSA is getting antsy and the JBA wants something stolen, you may have to drop the ball. Remember that you can always make up with the NSA by completing Opportunity Objectives.

NOTES

Whenever Sam uncovers useful information, you may store this news in the Notes directory on Sam's PDA. For instance, if Sam plants a certain number of bombs during a mission or finds the code for a certain door, this information is stored and can be viewed in the Notes directory. The New Note icon appears in the HUD whenever a new note is added to this menu.

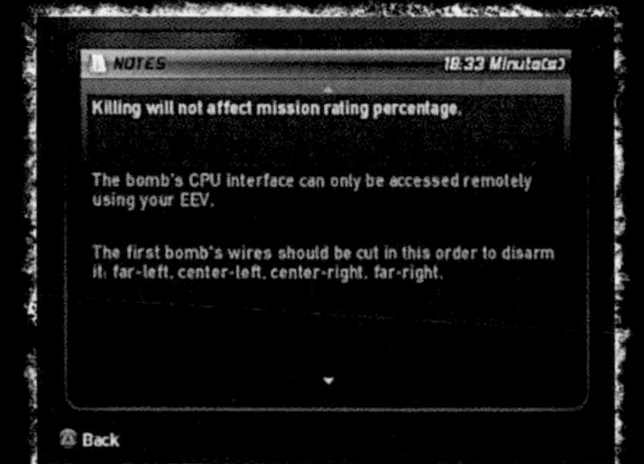

DATA

By accessing computers and laptops, Sam can download informative e-mails that may contain hints that certain areas might have extra security working against you. E-mails may also contain information that is extremely beneficial down the road. It is important to access computers and read e-mails to get a leg up on the mission.

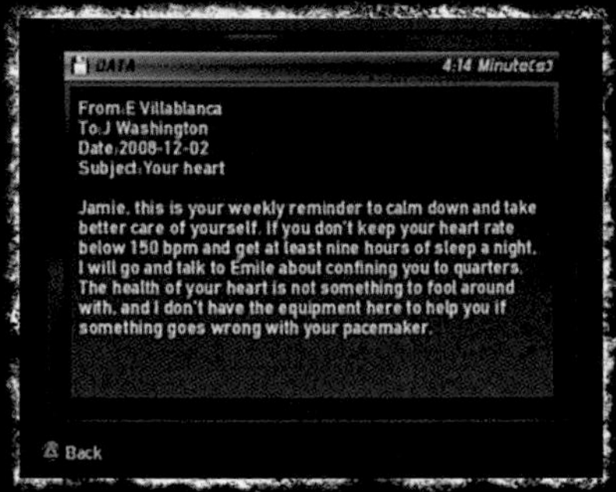

EQUIPMENT

This menu contains complete descriptions of all the equipment Sam currently carries and has valuable instructions and hints on how to use that equipment like a pro.

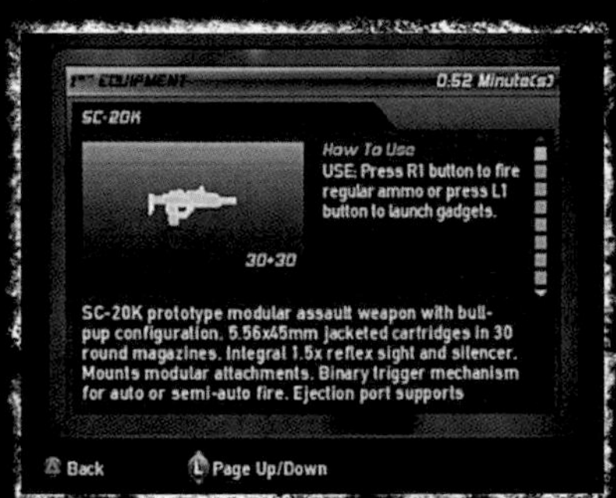

MAP

View a complete 3-D rendering of a satellite image of the stage. Also displayed are the name of the current area, the number of alarms triggered in the stage, Sam's current location, the locations of enemies, and the locations of Primary Objectives.

While viewing the map, use the Move control to zoom in or out. Use the Camera control to rotate the view, and press the Interact button to remove unexplored and previously explored areas from the view.

Depending on the satellite signal's strength, the tracker view depicting enemy positions refreshes every few seconds or minutes. The time required to refresh depends on how much structure interference is at work, which is different in each stage. Once the tracker view refreshes, you receive an updated image indicating where enemies have moved.

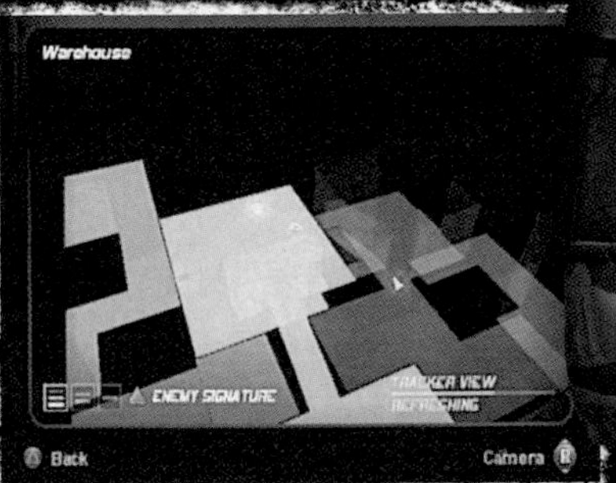

TRAINING VIDEOS

This menu allows you to view or review training videos shown during many of the early missions. While viewing training videos, press the buttons indicated during the pauses to practice controlling the game.

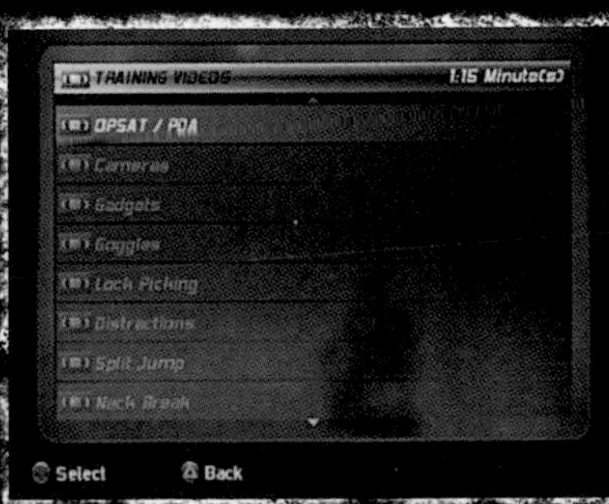

Training videos can also be viewed during missions whenever the Play Video option appears in the Interaction menu in the screen's upper right corner.

PROFILES

One of the Opportunity Objectives Sam has while sneaking through the JBA's headquarters is to scan the fingerprints of the key players in the organization. Successfully scanning a person's fingerprints allows Sam to download their profile from the NSA. Profiles give additional information on the key players in the terrorist organization.

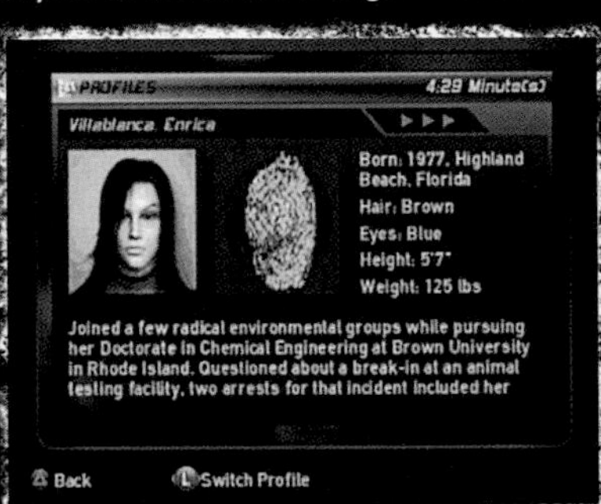

MOVEMENT

Use the Move control to move the character in the desired direction. Tilt the Move control only slightly to creep forward or tilt it all the way outward to run at full speed. Slower movement creates less noise and decreases the chances of detection. However, moving too slowly may allow patrolling guards to exit opportune striking locations. It is best to remain crouched at all times (by pressing the Crouch button) and tilt the Move control just less than halfway. This allows you to travel fast enough to sneak up behind moving enemies without being heard.

NARROW GAPS

To squeeze through a narrow gap, simply move toward the gap until Sam changes posture to slide through the opening. Continue moving through the narrow space until Sam emerges from the other end. Entering and exiting a narrow gap makes a small amount of noise and sometimes forces Sam to stand rather than crouch. Consider these things before entering a narrow gap.

Camera and Aim Control

Use the Camera/Aim control to change your angle of view. You can look in any direction, even ones in which Sam is not facing. Positioning the camera directly behind Sam is usually the best. However, sometimes you may want to position the camera in front of Sam to keep tabs on an enemy you might be trying to leave behind or who may be following you.

While equipping a gun or grenade, use the Camera/Aim control to point the crosshairs toward your desired target. The crosshairs widen out while you are changing aim or moving around to indicate lesser accuracy. When the crosshairs are the narrowest, Sam has the greatest chance of hitting the target.

Crouching

Press the Crouch button to crouch. As mentioned previously, crouching as you move is the best way to avoid being detected. Crouching also helps you to hide behind low cover such as boxes or counters. Sam moves more slowly while crouched and makes less noise.

ROLLING

To perform a roll, press and hold the Crouch button while moving in a crouched position. Rolling can help you avoid enemy gunfire, and it can help you move from cover to cover with less likelihood of being detected.

Sam can perform rolls to get past red laser mines in the New York mission near the game's end. By running toward a laser mine in a crouched position and rolling at just the right time, Sam can roll underneath the laser and continue. However, if you roll too soon or too late, you'll be singing "Good-bye Cruel World!"

DROPPING

Press the Crouch button to drop when hanging from a pipe, a ladder, a fence, or a ledge. Sam can drop from a height of roughly 12 feet without taking any damage. By dropping from greater heights, you risk inflicting damage to your character and making noise, which may alert enemies in the surroundings.

If you drop on top of a person, you automatically perform a "drop attack." If you are successful, your target is knocked unconscious. Perform a drop attack by dropping off a ledge that is taller than six feet high. You can also perform a drop attack by dropping from a Split Jump position.

In Co-op mode, avoid dropping on your partner or they suffer damage.

Jumping

Press the Jump button to leap roughly three feet off the ground. You can jump to grab higher ledges, or you can jump while running to clear small gaps. However, jumping creates noise. Make sure there are no active enemies nearby before risking any kind of jump.

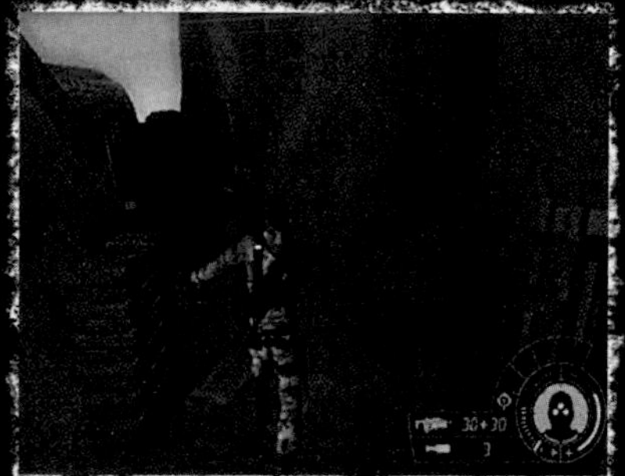

MANTLING

While facing any low ledge that is roughly waist height (when Sam is standing), such as a crate or a countertop, lightly tilt the Move control toward the ledge and press the Jump button to quietly mantle onto the ledge. Mantling properly allows you to climb around an area without rousing suspicion.

Press Back to Wall

When near a section of wall that is devoid of pipes, protruding panels, and the like, press down on the Move control to place Sam's back against the wall. Once Sam is attached to the wall, slide the Move control left or right to move Sam along the wall and around corners until he reaches a doorway.

At a doorway, Sam can peek into the room beyond if you hold the Move control toward the doorway. Sam is less likely to be detected peeking through a doorway if his back is pressed to the wall.

Equip Weapon or Item

Press the Equip button to draw and aim the selected weapon or item. Sam prepares the weapon or item, the camera changes to an over-the-shoulder perspective, and a crosshair appears onscreen. While equipping a weapon or item, use the Camera/Aim Control to move the crosshair over the intended target. When aimed and ready, press the Fire/Lethal Attack button to use the equipped item. Sam is more accurate with firearms when standing still and crouched. Moving while adjusting aim decreases accuracy.

ENVIRONMENTAL OBJECTS

Splinter cells can pick up noisy objects such as bottles and cans. Throw these objects (the same way you would throw a grenade) to create noise in some other part of the room and distract enemies from your current position. After throwing an object into the area behind an enemy, you can then sneak up behind the person and grab them. Or, you could use the opportunity to slip out of the room and continue your mission.

SWITCH HANDS

Splinter cells can fire accurately with either hand. While equipping a weapon, press down on the Move control to switch hands. Switching to your left hand can help you maximize cover at corners, as most of the character's body remains hidden while he fires a target. Splinter cells cannot switch hands while equipping a bottle, a can, or any type of grenade.

RELOAD WEAPON

While equipping a firearm, press the Interact button to reload. The character can only reload if the magazine is not filled to capacity and if additional ammo is available.

PRIMARY ATTACK

While equipping a firearm, press the Primary Attack button to open fire. Headshots kill instantly, so aim for the target's head every time.

When equipping a thrown weapon such as a grenade, bottle, or can, aim the crosshairs at the intended landing spot and press the Primary Attack button to throw the item in a short arc. Thrown items make noise upon landing, which may alert nearby enemies. If the item strikes an opponent, he becomes alerted instantly.

SECONDARY ATTACK

While equipping a firearm, press the Secondary Attack button to utilize the weapon's secondary function. The SC pistol is equipped with an OCP jamming device that allows splinter cells to jam surveillance cameras, lights, and electronic equipment for a short period of time. To use the OCP, press the Secondary Fire button when equipping the SC pistol. The SC-20K can be fitted with a variety of attachments, each with a different Secondary Attack function. The launcher attachment fires gadgets, and the shotgun attachment fires shotgun shells. When the sniper attachment is equipped and the player enters Zoom mode, hold the Secondary Fire button to make the character hold his breath, steadying his aim.

Lethal and Nonlethal Attacks

When not equipping a firearm or weapon, the character can attack enemies in unarmed, nonlethal ways and in lethal ways utilizing the SC combat knife.

When standing or moving within two feet of an enemy, press the Primary Attack button to perform a lethal attack against the enemy. Sam's attack style depends on whether he is in front of the character or behind them, and whether the enemy is aware of Sam's presence. Sam may slash the enemy's throat or stab them in the gut. If attacking from behind, Sam may stab the enemy in the spine or quickly slash their throat.

To perform a non-lethal attack, press the Secondary Attack button when standing close to an enemy. Sam steps toward the enemy and strikes them in the head with the palm of his hand, knocking the person unconscious. Nonlethal attacks may be more prudent in situations where Sam is infiltrating a bank or the JBA headquarters, where it is important not to leave a body count.

Both lethal and nonlethal attacks create quite a bit of noise, which may alert additional enemies in the area.

Whistle

Press the Co-op Action button to bring up an icon menu. Highlight the music note icon and release the Co-op Action button to whistle. Whistling can be used to draw the enemy toward your position. However, it is only useful if you can move through the dark around the enemy while they head toward your previous spot.

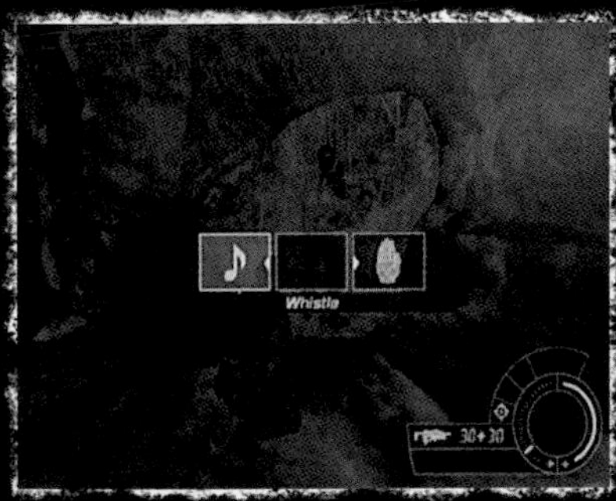

For instance, if you are in a room divided by a piece of machinery, you might stand at one side and whistle in order to draw an enemy around the corner. Meanwhile, you would move around the opposite side of the machinery and sneak up on the enemy from behind.

Co-op Action

When accompanied on a mission by a partner such as Hisham Hamza, Jamie Washington, or Enrica Villablanca, press the Co-op Action button to bring up an icon menu. Highlight the hand signal icon and release the Co-op button to signal to your partner. If your partner is following, you will command them to wait. If your partner is waiting, you will command them to catch up. Use the Co-op Action button to help your partner avoid detection by leaving them in a safe spot while you scout ahead.

Quick Inventory

Hold the Quick Inventory button to bring up the Inventory Icon menu. The icons of firearms, gadgets, and grenades currently in possession are displayed in the Quick Inventory menu.

While the Quick Inventory menu is open, use the Move control to cycle left or right, up or down through the icons. When the desired equipment is in the center, release the Quick Inventory button to equip the new item.

TIP

Briefly tap the Quick Inventory button to reequip the previous weapon. Use this function to switch quickly between the SC pistol and the SC-20K, or to switch between two types of launcher attachment ammo, and so on.

SC-20K LAUNCHER AMMO

To load the SC-20K's launcher attachment with a different type of gadget, cycle left or right through the Quick Inventory menu until the SC-20K with the launcher attachment icon is displayed in the center. Then cycle up or down through the launcher attachment ammo icons to load a device type, such as sticky shockers, airfoil rounds, sticky cameras, and so on.

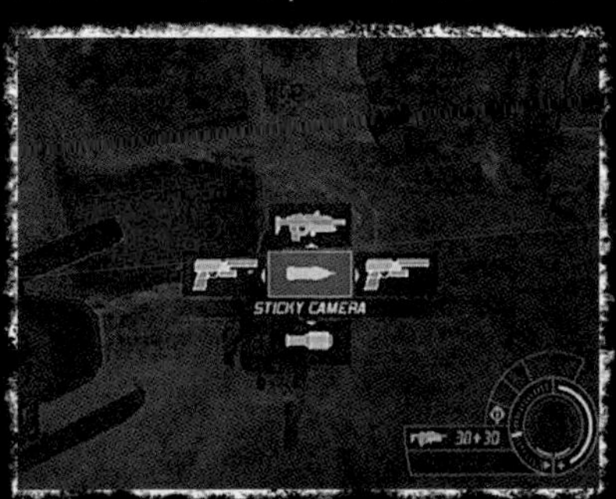

Night Vision

Press the Night Vision button to equip Sam's night vision goggles. In night vision, ambient light is collected and refracted to make the environment seem brighter. Night vision helps to delineate enemies that may be walking through shadowy areas or to spot surveillance equipment mounted in dark areas. However, the one drawback of night vision is that the user experiences a flattening effect, making distances between objects and/or people harder to judge. Avoid using night vision in brightly lit places, or the screen may grow so bright that the character becomes nearly blind for a few seconds.

Thermal Vision

Press the Thermal Vision button to turn thermal vision on or off. Thermal vision allows Sam to view heat signatures. In most areas, this should help Sam spot patrolling enemies more easily. However, thermal vision may be ineffective in some areas with lots of machinery.

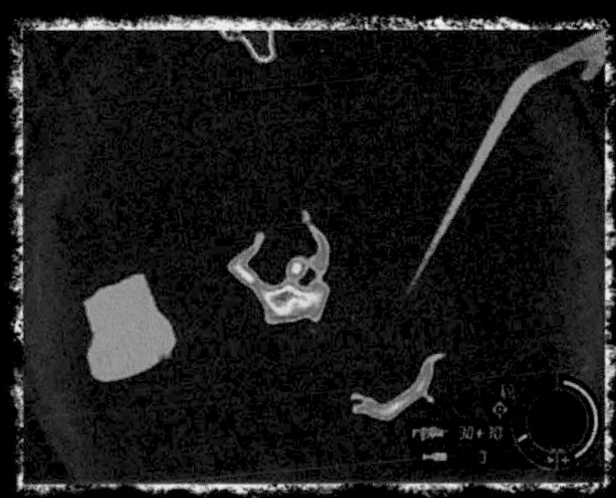

To ensure that you have killed an enemy, view them with thermal vision after inflicting a lethal attack. As their body temperature drops, they change colors and eventually become invisible in thermal vision.

EMF Vision

Electromagnetic field (EMF) vision highlights electronic devices in an area—colored bright white, while everything else is blue. EMF vision is extremely helpful in aiming at and disabling surveillance cameras and laser sensors. Disabled electronic devices disappear from EMF view as long as jamming is in effect. One drawback is that an enemy might walk right up on you unseen in EMF vision.

EEV

Press down on the Camera control to enter EEV (electronically enhanced vision). While in EEV, press down on the Move control to zoom in and out. EEV acts as a scope and allows you to access computer equipment by remote: Move the central cursor in the EEV view over a computer. Allow the EEV to scan the computer. When done, press the Interact button to access the computer's files. You may also hack computers and electronic gun turrets by remote using the EEV.

HACKING COMPUTERS AND EQUIPMENT

To open an encrypted file on a computer or laptop, choose the Security Access option. Sam's universal hacking device appears. Two frequency lines, one red and one green, appear on the hacking device. Three or four lights on the device's bottom portion indicate how many security levels you must overcome. You must hack all security levels before the green timer bar depletes, or the alarm stage rises. You may cancel at any time before the green timer bar turns red. If you attempt to cancel after the timer bar has changed colors, an alarm sounds.

To hack the encryption, move the left analog stick left or right, or up or down to adjust the green frequency wave's height and length, respectively. When the green frequency is touching the red frequency at all points, press the Interact button to hack one security stage. Repeat the process until you disable all security levels. The two lines do not have to overlap perfectly; the frequencies need only touch at all points. If you wait too long to press the Interact button, the frequencies fall out of alignment.

The player can also hack electronic devices such as gun turrets. Doing so allows you to disable friendly fire, causing the turret to open fire on enemies.

Doors that are electronically locked by security devices such as keypads, card readers, and retinal scanners can all be hacked.

Interaction Menu

The Interaction Menu appears whenever Sam Fisher or a splinter cell approaches a door, an object, a computer, or a character that he can interact with. While the menu is onscreen, press and hold the Interact button to access the Interaction Menu. While holding the button, use the Move control to cycle up and down through the options available. When the desired option is highlighted, release the Interact button to perform the desired action. If no action is desired, choose the "Back to Game" option always available at the top.

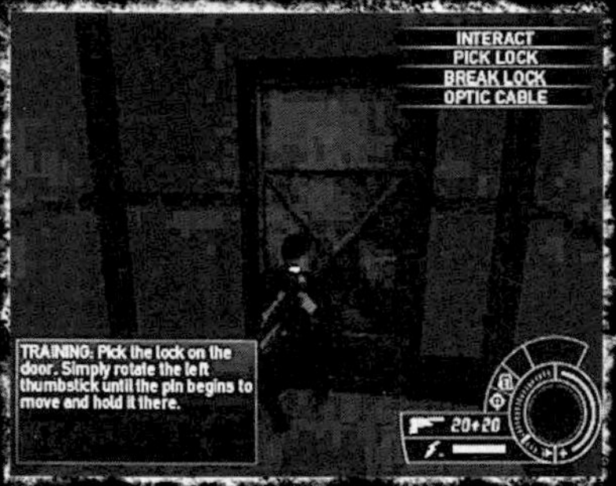

The following sections detail many of the actions available through the Interaction Menu.

Open Door or Trap

This option opens a door to a connecting room, a trapdoor in the floor, or any other type of door. This method is quick but may create a small amount of noise.

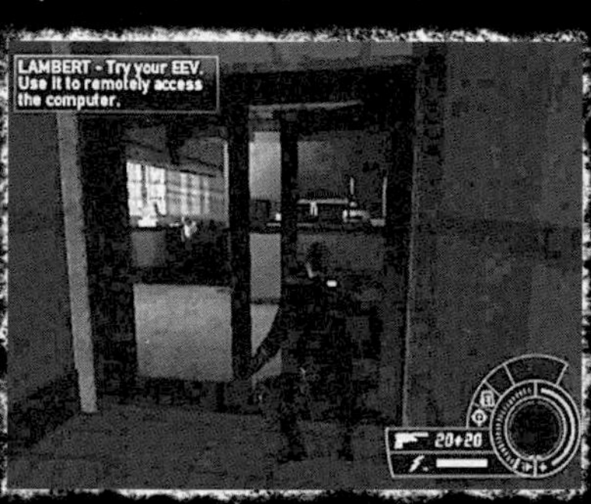

Open Door Stealth

This option allows the user to open a door without creating any noise. After choosing the Open Door Stealth option, the character merely turns the handle. Use the Move control to open the door slightly, halfway, or completely, depending on how far you tilt the Move Control. You may also close the door without opening it by tilting the Move Control downward. The only way characters inside the room will notice the door is opening or closing is if they see it move.

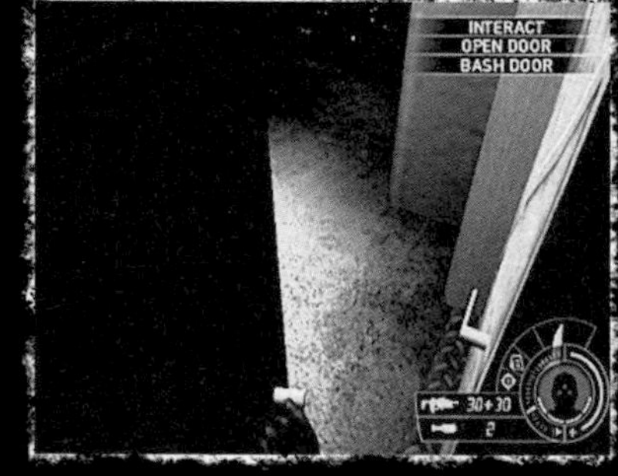

Open Door Stealth is even more useful in Co-op mode. For instance, one player can open a door halfway so that his partner can throw a grenade into the next room. Then the door can be closed, protecting both agents from the blast!

Close Door

The Close Door option appears as the character moves past an open door. Generally, it is better to close any doors you open. An open door arouses suspicion in anyone who sees it. However, if a door was previously open, closing it may also draw suspicion.

Optic Cable

Before opening any door, try to see what is on the other side first. Accomplish this by one of three methods: by opening the map in the OPSAT and viewing the tracker data, by activating thermal vision to see through the door, or by inserting the optic cable through the space under the door.

After inserting the optic cable through a door or trapdoor in the ceiling or floor, use the Move control to rotate the optic cable to view the surroundings. The optic cable can be used in combination with night vision, EMF, and thermal vision to determine what kind of hazards lie on the door's other side.

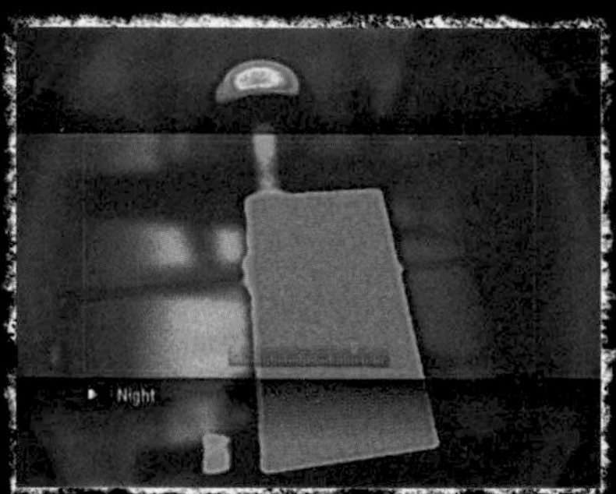

Bash Door

Use the Bash Door option to open a door forcefully enough to knock a person unconscious, should he be standing too close to the door. Use thermal vision to determine if a person is standing on the other side of a door. Note that bashing

doors creates a loud noise that draws the attention of any characters standing in either room the door connects.

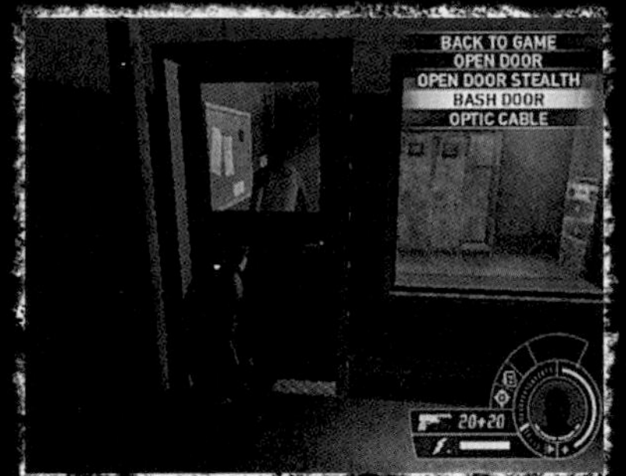

Pick Lock

Unlock doors using Sam's professional set of picks and tension rods. After you insert the lock picks, rotate the Move control until the pick begins to wiggle against the tumbler and the controller vibrates; this means you have hit the "sweet spot." Agitate the tumbler by moving the Move control from the center to the sweet spot until the tumbler sticks. Repeat the process for as many tumblers as necessary until the cylinder can be turned to unlock the door.

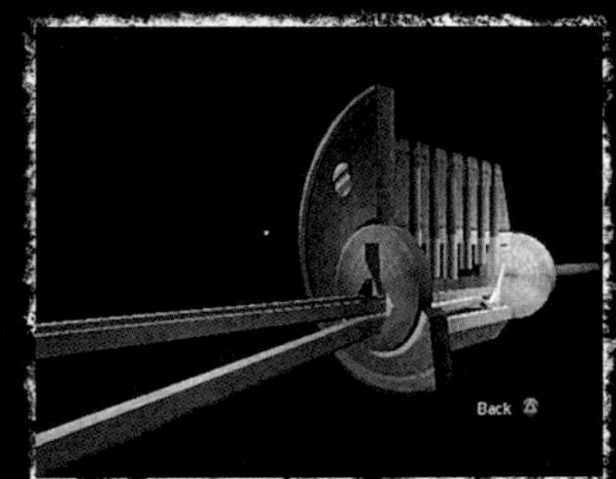

Picking a lock is quiet and should not alert anyone to your presence. However, the longer it takes to pick a lock, the more Sam grunts and groans, drawing attention to himself.

Break Lock

If after checking the current room and the adjoining room you are certain that no one is close enough to hear a rather loud noise, then choose the Break Lock option rather than picking the lock. When you choose Break Lock, Sam draws out a crowbar and jimmies the door open. The sound is loud enough to draw the attention of enemies either in your current area or in the next, so be sure the coast is clear before trying it. Many times the walkthroughs in this guide instruct you to break a lock rather than pick it to save time.

Use Keypad

To open electronically sealed doors, you must enter the correct code into the keypad to the door's left or right. Obtain keypad codes by reading e-mails stored on nearby computers or by grabbing a patrolling guard and asking him nicely for the code.

To input a code, use the Move control to highlight the keys on the keypad. Press the Interact button to enter a digit. When all digits are entered correctly, the door unlocks. You can hack keypads if the code is not available.

Swipe Card Reader

Some doors are electronically sealed and require you swipe a keycard through a card reader. Search the surrounding area to find a keycard—a small card the same size and shape as a credit card. Then return to the card reader and swipe the card through to unlock the door. You can hack card readers if the keycard cannot be found.

Retinal Scanner

Some doors and safes are prevented from easy access by a retinal scanner. This means that a staff member or security guard must stare into the retinal scanner in order to open the portal. To accomplish this, grab one of the characters in the immediate area of a retinal scanner. Drag the conscious person over to the retinal scanner until the Interaction Menu appears. Choose the appropriate option to force the person's face up to the retinal scanner. Afterward, dispose of the person as you wish.

Switch Object

If a wall switch controls the lights in the room, you may be able to conceal your position better by turning off the lights. However, if an enemy notices that the lights in a room are out, they may become suspicious and enter the room to investigate.

If an enemy is standing in the room when the lights go out, they immediately head for the wall switch to restore illumination. Use this to your advantage by circling around the person in the dark and grab them from behind.

Gas Generators

Spotlights in outdoor areas are typically powered by small gas generators located somewhere nearby. To deactivate the lights in an area, either flip the switch on the generator or pierce its gas tank to disable it permanently. If you only flip the switch on a generator, an enemy can easily turn it back on. But a punctured gas tank on a generator also tends to make a patrolling guard suspicious.

> **TIP**
>
> Generally speaking, avoid messing with the lights. Try to use available shadows to maneuver around guards and terrorists, and take them down while they walk through dark areas. When enemies perceive lights mysteriously going off and on, it only freaks them out, making infiltration that much harder.

Use Medkit

Use the medkits hanging on walls in certain locations to regain full health once or to restore partial health several times. Medkits are small white boxes with green medic symbols painted on them.

Grab Character

Grab Character is the most useful interaction in the game. By grabbing a character from behind, you can use that person to gain knowledge, use them as a human shield against other foes, and gain access to new areas.

Position yourself behind enemies by using shadows and silence to sneak up on them. Move close enough to the unsuspecting person's backside that the Grab Character interaction appears onscreen, and then press the Interact button to grab them. Once you have grabbed a character, you must either knock them out or kill them. Therefore, make sure you drag the person into the shadows for efficient disposal.

INTERROGATION

Some of the funniest lines of dialogue in the game can only be heard by grabbing and interrogating enemies. Interrogation is only possible if the Interrogate interaction appears in the Interaction Menu while a person is in a headlock. If the interaction does not appear while a hostage is held, then they have nothing to say. While interrogating a person, the dialogue can be advanced more quickly by choosing the Skip Ahead interaction. You may end a conversation at any time with a lethal or nonlethal attack.

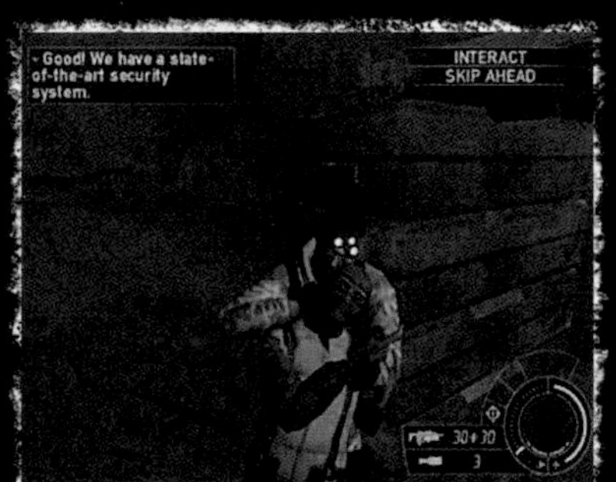

FORCE COOPERATION

Once you have hold of a person, you may be able to force them to do certain things. As mentioned previously, only someone on staff can activate a retinal scanner. Drag the person over to the scanner and force their eyes up to it in order to unlock the device.

You can also force a hostage to lower the alarm level. Whenever the alarm level is 1 or higher, drag a conscious guard or terrorist over to a small white speaker panel with a red button. When the Interact menu appears, force the person to call in a false alarm and lower the alarm level.

HUMAN SHIELD

If other enemies see that you hold a hostage, they will not open fire unless they have a clear shot at you from the side or behind. However, if you fire at them, they respond with deadly force, regardless of your hostage. Thus, use unsuspecting enemies as human shields during firefights if you can manage to grab them from behind. Once you have a hostage, press the Equip button to draw your SC pistol. A human shield can absorb roughly three or four bullets before dying, so be sure to kill your enemies with headshots quickly.

PLUNGE

When standing over a patch of thin ice and holding a hostage, the Plunge option becomes available. Sam breaks through the ice with his hostage and drowns the poor guy in freezing waters. Plunging is a lethal attack that may lower your Trust with the NSA at the end of a mission.

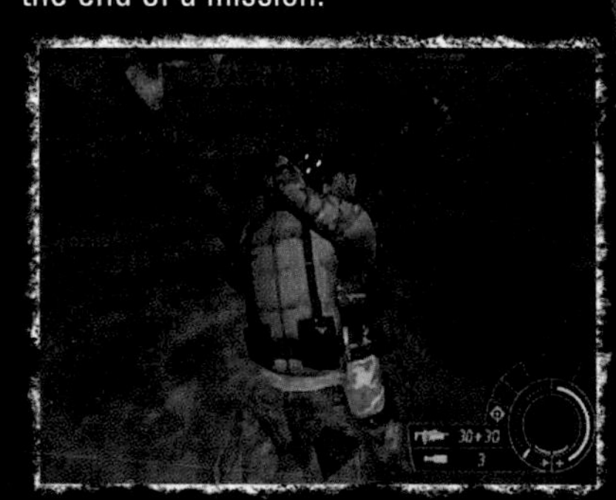

PULL INTO WATER

When wading through water, sneak up behind a character who is standing at the water's edge. When the Grab Character interaction appears, press the Interact button to seize the person and drag them into the water. After a violent thrashing, Sam drowns the person in the shallow depths. This is also considered a lethal kill that may affect your Trust level.

PULL OVER LEDGE

When hanging from the ledge underneath a rail, shimmy left or right until positioned directly under an enemy standing close to the rail. Use the Grab Character interaction to seize the person and pull them over the rail. Whether or not this action proves to be lethal depends on how far the person falls. If the victim falls less than 20 feet, they may only be knocked unconscious. However, if the distance is greater than 20 feet, the person will likely die in the bone-crunching impact.

CHOKE UNCONSCIOUS

After taking a person hostage, interrogating them, or forcing them to do stuff for you, you must silence that person. Press the Secondary Attack button to choke a hostage unconscious. Grabbing a person and then choking them unconscious is the stealthiest way of taking down an enemy. Any other method has a higher chance of drawing attention. Even while choking a person unconscious, you must be careful of where you drop the body. If the person falls on a metal grating, the sound of the body falling may be enough to make surrounding enemies suspicious.

Unconscious enemies can be awakened and reactivated by other enemies if their body is found. Before choking their lights out, drag the person somewhere dark and secluded where others do not patrol.

BREAK BACK

The lethal way to finish off a hostage is with a vertebrae-smashing knee to the back. Press the Primary Attack button to finish off a person for good. A back break attack is extremely loud and is sure to draw attention if other enemies are still active in the area.

Nothing frightens terrorists more than dead bodies. If an enemy finds a dead compadre, he begins exclaiming loudly and runs for the nearest alarm. If another enemy hears the commotion, they also run for the alarm.

Pick up Body

If you knock out a guard in an undesirable location, you must move the body to a safer hiding place where it will not be discovered. When standing over an unconscious or dead guard, select the Pick up Body interaction to sling the person over your shoulder. Sam moves bodies more quickly when standing upright.

Find a hiding spot that is both dark and away from another guard's patrol route. Then press the Interact button again to set the body down quietly. If you draw your weapon or drop off a ledge, the character drops the body with a loud thud.

Extract

The Extract interaction may appear when you approach a certain door in a stage. It may be the last door in the stage, or it may be the door you initially came through. Use the Extract interaction to complete the current mission. Just be sure that you have completed all objectives first, or Trust may be lost.

Special Abilities

Apart from the many controller functions, Sam Fisher and other splinter cell agents can perform some unique feats.

Climbing Pipes and Ladders

To begin climbing a ladder, simply move toward the ladder until Sam grabs the rungs and begins ascending. Jump to grab the ladder if the lowest rung is off the ground.

Pipes can be climbed in a similar fashion to ladders. Climbable pipes are almost as wide as Sam's head and are usually textured to stand out slightly from the environment. Sam grabs on to vertical pipes by simply walking into them. When vertical pipes connect with horizontal pipes, Sam automatically changes position and posture at the corners as applicable.

To grab hold of horizontal pipes running along the ceiling, position Sam directly under the pipe and jump up to grab hold. Press the Jump button while Sam hangs from a horizontal pipe to pull his legs up, making him harder to see and enabling him to move through small gaps in walls and fences. From this position, Sam can also grab characters from above and choke them unconscious with a nonlethal attack.

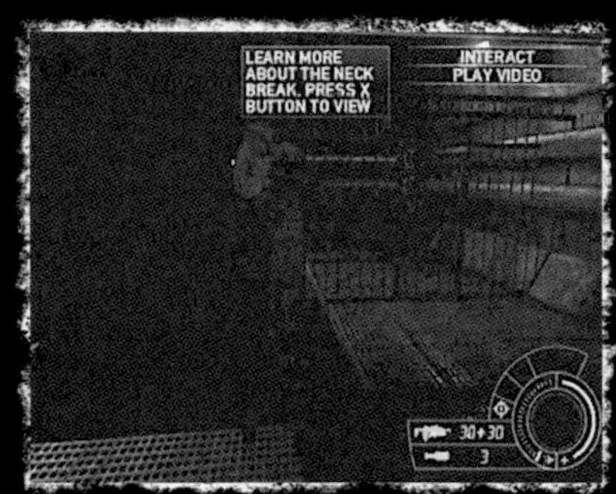

To draw the SC pistol while hanging from a ceiling pipe, press the Equip button. A hanging character can aim within 180 degrees in front of himself, but not to the sides or rear.

If a vertical pipe or ladder connects to the bottom of a rail rather than to an open space, move left or right at the top of the pipe or ladder to shimmy along the ledge under the rail. Then press the Move control up to climb over the rail.

Grab Ledge

While jumping, Sam grabs hold of any ledge situated less than three feet above his normal height. Sam can hang from a ledge for an unlimited amount of time, enabling him to wait for enemies to stop overhead or directly below.

While hanging from a ledge, shimmy to the left or right using the Move control. To climb onto a ledge or over a railing, tilt the Move control upward until Sam is standing on his feet.

Zip-line

A rope, a cable, or even a pipe with a tilted angle can be used as a zip-line to slide across areas quickly. Position Sam underneath a zip-line and then press the Jump button to leap up and grab hold. Sam automatically slides along the zip-line until he reaches the end. He then automatically drops to the ground.

Rappelling

When a small post or rock is positioned near the edge of a cliff or ledge, Sam can initiate rappelling by using the Interact menu. Sam hangs a spelunking line in the chasm and climbs down to a hanging position. Use the Move control to climb up or down the rope. Press the Jump button while descending to take a big leap downward. Jumping while rappelling is also useful in avoiding lighted areas on the wall. During a rappel, you cannot turn the Camera Control more than 90 degrees to the right or left.

While rappelling, press the Equip button to draw the SC pistolor SC-20K. You can aim and fire at enemies above, below, and to the sides. You can descend or ascend, but you cannot jump downward while aiming.

When descending an ice wall, you may encounter a thin patch and a Jump In interaction. Sam can break through thin ice walls to find hidden caves and passageways.

Climb Rope

Climbing a free-hanging rope is a bit different than rappelling. Sam does not have the support of his legs on the wall, so he cannot hasten his descent by jumping downward. However, you can equip the SC pistol while hanging motionless, and you can rotate the Camera control in any direction to view the surrounding area. Because Sam holds the rope only with his hands and is not fastened by spelunking hooks, he can drop from the rope and perform a drop attack by pressing the Crouch button. However, dropping from a height of more than 20 feet is not recommended.

Split Jump

Whenever Sam moves through a passage roughly two to three feet wide with solid walls on either side, he may start looking upward at the walls. This motion indicates that he can perform a Split Jump at that point.

To perform a Split Jump, face one wall in a narrow passage and press the Jump button. Sam scampers up the wall to a height of roughly 10 feet, his legs spread wide to anchor himself in the space. Sam can use this ability to hide in the shadows above a room or corridor with low-hanging lights.

Use the Split Jump to avoid patrolling enemies in narrow passages. Press the Crouch button while an enemy moves underneath Sam to perform a drop attack and knock the person out. Just be sure that no other enemies are nearby when dropping onto a foe from a Split Jump, or they may hear the noise.

While in a Split Jump stance, Sam has access to all his gear. He can equip the SC-20K, the SC pistol, and even grenades, bottles, and cans. There is no better sniping position than from above.

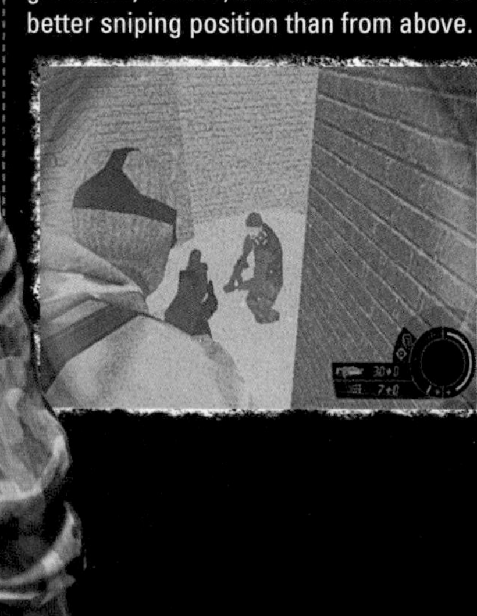

Traps

In addition to placing guards on patrol, terrorist factions utilize a wide variety of surveillance and security measures in their facilities. These devices act as a kind of trap for the unwary player. Most traps can be detected with EMF vision, so we recommend viewing each new area with EMF to detect security devices before taking any action.

Surveillance Cameras

Most often positioned high up on darkened walls, surveillance cameras monitor facilities for signs of intrusion and unauthorized personnel. Most cameras are equipped with night vision, meaning that a camera is more likely to spot a splinter cell than a human on patrol. If Sam or a splinter cell is spotted on a surveillance system, the alert level rises instantly. Typically, nearby guards and terrorists are immediately dispatched to Sam's position, leaving their usual locations and patrol routes.

Avoid being detected by surveillance cameras by jamming them with the OCP attached to the SC pistol. When the OCP is fired at a camera, the electronic device is disabled for roughly 30 seconds. Use EMF vision to help aim the SC pistol at the camera. Afterward, the surveillance camera returns to normal function. Make sure you are out of sight.

Another way to get past security cameras is to move through the blind spot directly beneath the camera. Cameras are mounted at an angle to view rooms or corridors and cannot rotate downward to spot an intruder sliding along the wall directly below.

Deploy smoke grenades at the base of the camera to enshroud it in phosphorus fumes. This may reduce the camera's viewing radius but is a finicky solution at best. The chances of being detected are reduced, but there is still a very good chance the camera might spot the player character entering or exiting the cloud of smoke.

Laser Sensors

Small electronic squares set into the wall on either side of a corridor emit thin green laser beams. If the beam is broken, intrusion is detected and the alarm level rises automatically. Personnel in the area may leave their normal patrol routes to investigate.

Laser sensors can be deactivated by firing the OCP at the small electronic square mounted on the wall at either end of a laser beam. Use EMF vision to help you aim and disable the lasers.

Lasers automatically deactivate whenever a person with a tracking device in their clothing moves through the laser. Therefore, any enemy can be used to deactivate a laser beam or laser grid array. Whether the enemy is conscious or alive during the process does not matter.

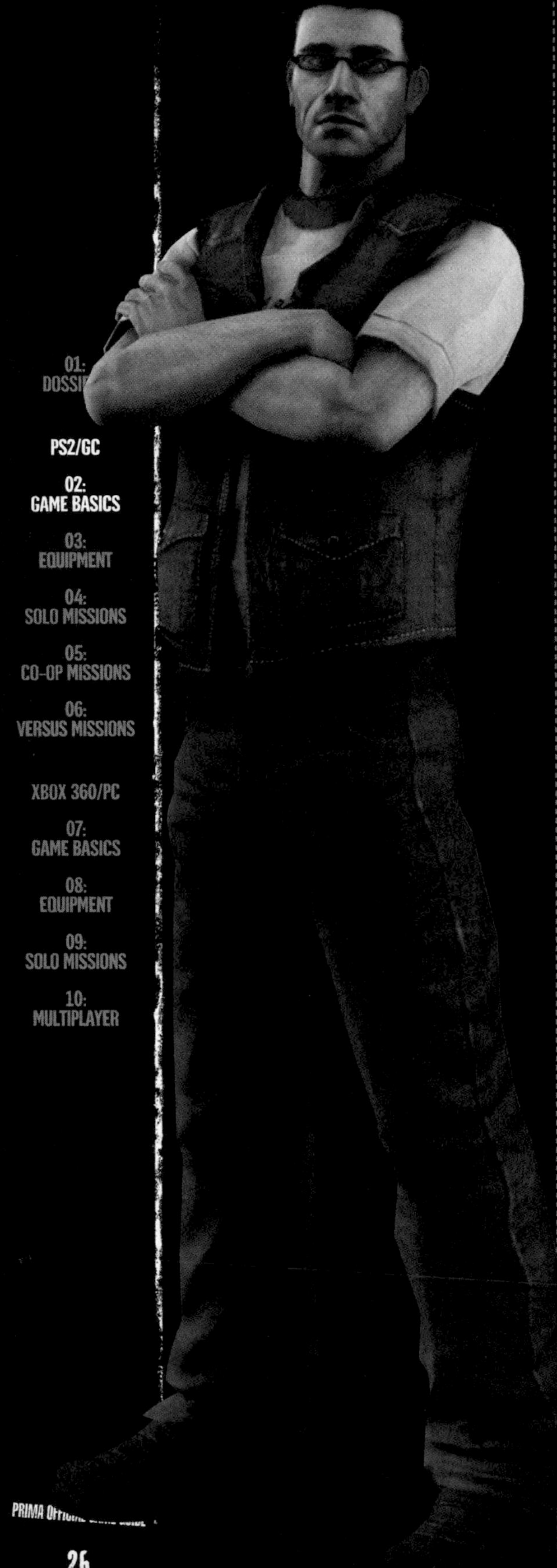

01: DOSSI

PS2/GC

02: GAME BASICS

03: EQUIPMENT

04: SOLO MISSIONS

05: CO-OP MISSIONS

06: VERSUS MISSIONS

XBOX 360/PC

07: GAME BASICS

08: EQUIPMENT

09: SOLO MISSIONS

10: MULTIPLAYER

Laser Trip Mines

Red laser beams in a room or corridor indicates the presence of laser trip mines. If the red laser beam is broken, explosives placed at either end of the area detonate, instantly killing intruders.

Deactivate laser mines the same as laser sensors by firing the OCP at the mine attached to the wall. Terrorist personnel are equipped with position-tracking devices that disable laser trip mines as they walk through the laser. Therefore, you can use a terrorist's body to deactivate laser mines, whether the person is conscious or not.

If neither of the above options is available, try dive-rolling underneath red laser beams. You must master the timing of rolling (hold the Crouch button while moving) in order to roll under a trip mine's laser without breaking it.

Wall Mines

A loud beeping sound in a passageway or room indicates the presence of an active wall mine. Wall mines are motion sensitive and are programmed to detonate if the character moves past at a rate any faster than a creep.

To bypass an active wall mine, move extremely slow or equip an item and crouch while moving. With a weapon drawn, Sam moves at just the right speed to avoid setting off the wall mine, even when you have the Move control tilted to full throttle.

To deactivate and acquire wall mines for personal use, approach them cautiously until the Deactivate Wall Mine interaction appears. Once Sam is in position, press and hold the Interact button and wait until the indicator light on the wall mine turns green. Then quickly release the Interact button to deactivate the wall mine, and slip it off the wall and into your pocket.

To place a wall mine, face a wall and equip the wall mine as an item. Use the crosshair to determine placement and then press the Primary Attack button to configure the mine on the wall. Once the trap is set, back off and whistle, or throw objects to lure enemies into the wall mine's area. Wall mines work best when set just inside a doorway in a tight passage, where enemies are unlikely to spot the wall mine until it is too late.

Gun Turrets

The telltale signs of active gun turrets are the loud mechanical noises they make as they scan the area. The other sign is the electronic signature it registers in EMF vision. Gun turrets are programmed to open fire upon any personnel not equipped with a friendly fire GPS tracking device, such as the kind that causes all enemies to be visible on Sam's OPSAT map.

Deactivate gun turrets just like surveillance cameras. Fire the OCP at a gun turret's body to disable it for up to 30 seconds. During that time, move behind the gun turret and deactivate it. If you cannot move behind the gun turret quickly because of additional security devices in the area, disable the gun turret permanently by firing EMP ammo from the SC-20K launcher attachment.

Gun turrets can also be turned against the terrorists by disabling the IFF (identify friend or foe) antifriendly fire program on the turret. To disable IFF, first hack the turret either from behind or by remote via the EEV. After successfully hacking the gun turret, get behind it and use the Disable IFF interaction to turn off friendly fire. With IFF off, the gun turret opens fire on the first person to cross its scanning zone, whether that be Sam or a terrorist.

03: PS2/GC

EQUIPMENT

SC-20K

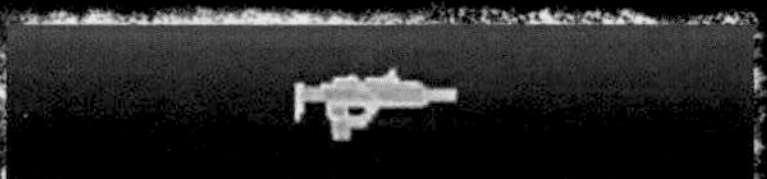

Magazine Capacity: 30 rounds
Maximum Ammunition: 120 rounds

The SC-20K is Fisher's most useful and versatile weapon, and it is only a prototype. The rifle is mounted with a 1.5x reflex sighting scope and a sound suppressor. The binary trigger mechanism allows Sam to fire a single round, by tapping the trigger, or to release a steady stream of bullets while the trigger is held down. The SC-20K is intended to combine the features of various SAR-21 (Singapore Assault Rifle 21st century) line models into one compact, multiuse bull-pup rifle.

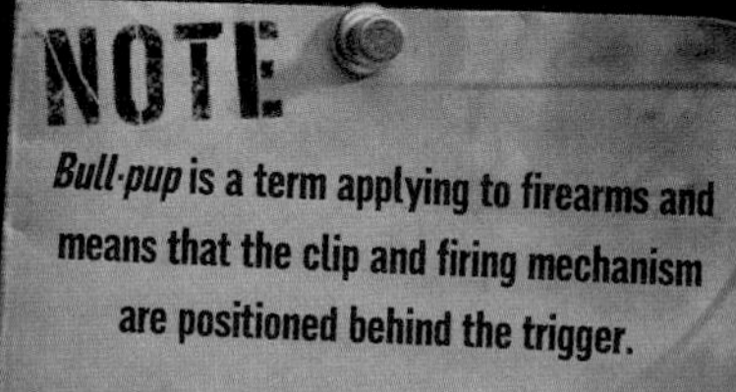

> Whether Sam fires from the shoulder or uses the scope to aim, he can activate his goggles any time and use the SC-20K in conjunction with night vision, thermal vision, or EMF.

> While aiming the SC-20K, press the Zoom button to enter Zoom mode. Without the sniper attachment, Sam can easily snipe enemies five to ten meters away. If the enemy is farther, try to move in closer, wait for the enemy to approach, or switch to the sniper attachment for closer zoom.

> While looking through the scope, Sam's breath gauge and health gauge appear near the bottom of the viewfinder. The zoom degree (1.5x) is displayed to the left and the estimated distance to the target is displayed on the right. Place the central crosshair over a target to get a distance reading. At the top of the display is a compass showing the direction Sam is facing.

> Hold the Secondary Attack button to make Sam hold his breath, steadying his aim. While Sam holds his breath, the breath gauge displayed at the screen's bottom gradually empties. When the breath gauge runs out, Sam automatically exhales and his aim becomes unsteady once again. Release the Alternate Fire button and then hold it again to try once more. Sam can hold his breath for approximately 27 seconds, which is longer than most people can manage.

GENERAL FIREARM TIPS

> Sam fires more accurately when standing still and when crouched.

> Most enemies wear some type of body armor or protective clothing, so always aim for the head.

> Try to kill with one shot to avoid excessive noise, ricochets, and bullet waste.

> Wait until the target stops moving or pauses, such as at the farthest or closest end of his patrol route.

LAUNCHER ATTACHMENT

The launcher attachment is a gas-powered 40 mm grenade launcher that mounts under the barrel and has been modified to deploy an array of nonlethal ammunition and devices. The launcher attachment fires silently, allowing the user to dispatch gadgetry without giving away his position.

To load the launcher attachment, open the Quick Inventory menu and scroll left or right until the launcher attachment icon is displayed. Then scroll up or down until the desired launcher ammunition is highlighted. Then release the Quick Inventory button to load the gadget.

> Fire the launcher attachment by pressing the Secondary Attack button.

> The launcher attachment cannot be used in Zoom mode.

> Ammo for the launcher attachment includes airfoil rounds, EMP ammunition, gas grenades, sticky cameras, and sticky shockers.

AIRFOIL ROUND

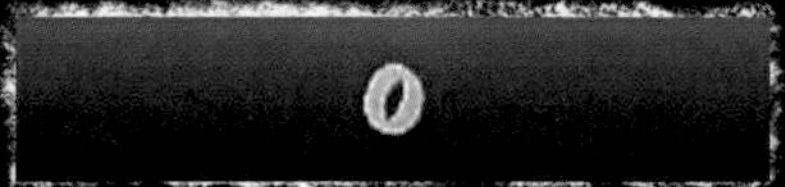

A launcher-compatible blunt round that can be fired from the SC-20K to stun and immobilize targets. Firing an airfoil round at the target's head may knock them out in a single shot. Striking the target anywhere else only stuns them momentarily, allowing you to approach and grab them or knock them out. Firing two rounds anywhere on any target should knock the person unconscious.

EMP AMMUNITION

A miniaturized magnetic device that attaches itself easily to metal-encased electronic devices such as surveillance cameras, gun turrets, laser beam sensors, wall mines, and laser trip mines. Upon contact, the EMP delivers an electromagnetic pulse of radiation that permanently disables electronic devices. Use EMP ammo to take out gun turrets and surveillance cameras that may prove problematic to neutralize repeatedly with the OCP.

GAS GRENADE

An SC-40 CS-gas (chlorobenzal-malononitrile) grenade. Three seconds after being fired from the launcher attachment, the gas grenade releases a cloud of nonlethal knockout gas roughly four feet in diameter. Any enemy within range automatically inhales the fumes and passes out within five seconds. If Sam passes through the gas cloud, he takes continuous damage until he leaves the area or passes out, resulting in mission failure.

For best results, fire a gas grenade at your opponent's feet. If two or more enemies stand less than four feet apart, aim the grenade at the ground between them to try and knock them both out with one grenade.

STICKY CAMERA

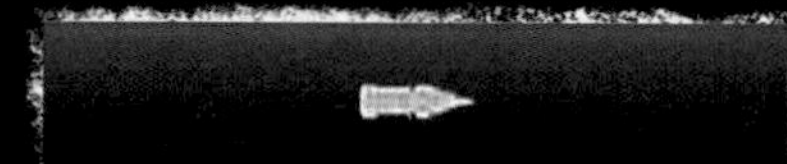

The "sticky camera" is the nickname for a launcher-compatible surveillance camera with a titanium anchor prong. The device can be fired at and anchored to any flat surface, including floors, walls, and boxes. The sticky camera may not anchor into certain metallic walls or objects.

After firing and successfully anchoring a sticky camera, the device links to the OPSAT PDA with a real-time wireless video signal relay. The sticky camera is capable of night vision, EMF, and thermal vision modes. While linked to the sticky camera, use the Camera control to pan and use the Move control to zoom.

If no signal is relaying from the sticky camera, there may be interference in the area. Sticky cameras generally do not work outdoors.

Multiple sticky cameras may be employed simultaneously. However, the OPSAT PDA can only link to sticky cameras in the player's immediate area. No link can be established if the sticky camera is out of range. If more than one active sticky camera is in the immediate area, press the Primary Attack or Secondary Attack buttons to cycle through the sticky cameras in range. Press the Jump button to disconnect the sticky camera link, and press the Sticky Camera button on the D-pad to reestablish signal relay with a device in range.

Sticky cameras can be used to distract and even knock out hostiles. While linked to a sticky camera, press the Equip button to make the sticky camera emit a clicking noise. This can draw enemies away from Sam's position or draw them *toward* the sticky camera. When enemies stand in close range of the sticky camera, press the Interact button to release knockout gas. The sticky camera disperses a fairly small cloud of gas, so the enemy must be in extremely close range. However, if an enemy gets too close to a sticky camera anchored in a fairly well-lit spot, they may detect it and blast it off the wall.

If the gas cylinder in a sticky camera has not been fired, you can retrieve the device from its anchor point. Simply approach a sticky camera and use the Interaction menu to retrieve the camera.

STICKY SHOCKER

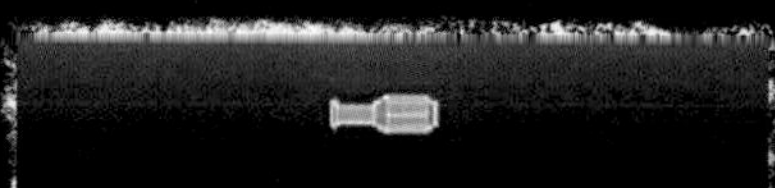

The "sticky shocker" is the nickname of a launcher-compatible high-voltage low-amperage adhesive shell. On impact, electrical discharge knocks the target unconscious. Water conducts the charge from a sticky shocker, so one sticky shocker effectively knocks out two or more enemies standing in a puddle.

To fire a sticky shocker, load them in the SC-20K, then aim at an opponent or puddle of water and press the Secondary Attack button to fire.

SHOTGUN ATTACHMENT

Magazine Capacity: 7 shells
Maximum Ammunition: 21 shells

The shotgun attachment is a pump-action module that mounts under the barrel of the SC-20K. It fires Triple-ought 9.1mm shells. Shell discharge spreads pellets in a cone-shaped blast, inflicting flesh-shredding damage even to individuals wearing bulletproof body armor.

> The shotgun attachment cannot fire in Zoom mode.

> Inflicts higher damage at close range.

> Emits a bright light and loud rapport, alerting all nearby enemies and civilians.

> The shotgun attachment is mainly useful in alarm situations where Sam has been located and must return fire.

> If you run out of shells, continue firing normal SC-20K ammo.

> After reloading standard SC-20K rounds, press the Reload button repeatedly to reload shells one by one into the magazine.

SNIPER ATTACHMENT

Magazine Capacity: 6 rounds
Maximum Ammunition: 18 rounds

This modular attachment enhances the sniping abilities of the standard SC-20K. It fires 20 mm APDS antimateriel armor-piercing discarding sabot rounds. A shot fired anywhere on the target's torso or head results in a one-shot kill, even when aimed at body armor.

> Cartridges must be reloaded individually. First reload the standard SC-20K magazine, and then load 20 mm sniper rounds one at a time.

> Press the Zoom button to use the sniper attachment.

> While zoomed in, steady your aim by pressing the Secondary Attack button to make Sam hold his breath.

> The sniper attachment is unsuppressed and makes a *very loud* noise. Only use the sniper attachment to take out lone enemies in otherwise empty areas.

> Press the Switch Shoulder button to cycle through zoom ratios, from 1.5x to 2.5x to 3.5x. The sniper attachment's default 1.5x zoom is quite a bit tighter on the subject than the SC-20K's standard scope.

> The heavy recoil knocks Sam out of Zoom mode.

SC PISTOL

Magazine Capacity: 20 rounds
Maximum Ammunition: 60 rounds

This prototype pistol designed specifically for Third Echelon splinter cell operatives is equipped with a nonremovable sound and muzzle flash suppressor. It fires 5.7x28 mm jacketed cartridges. The magazines are extended to carry 20 rounds. The grip is configured for ambidextrous use. A prototype optically channeled potentiator (OCP) is custom-mounted under the barrel.

- Press the Primary Attack button to fire a single shot.
- Even with the suppressor, the rapport is loud enough to be heard by enemies within a three-yard radius.
- If a bullet ricochets, the noise automatically alerts active enemies in the area.
- Aim for the head to ensure one-shot kills.
- Press the Secondary Attack button to use the OCP to disable electronic equipment or lights. The jamming effect lasts approximately 30 seconds.

SC-303 COMPACT LAUNCHER

A prototype gas-operated handgun-size .68 caliber compact launcher device designed to fire nonlethal ammunition. The compact launcher functions similarly to the SC-20K's launcher attachment, except that the Primary Attack button fires all ammunition types. The compact launcher is equipped with an OCP identical in function to the one mounted on the SC pistol.

- Operates silently. Firing does not give away the user's position.
- Only fires nonlethal ammunition. Ammunition types include rubber ammunition, tranquilizer ammunition, sticky cameras, and EMP ammunition. The latter two types operate identically to the SC-20K launcher attachment gadgets.

RUBBER AMMUNITION

A high-density rubber projectile designed to impact a target with blunt trauma. Targets struck by rubber bullets become stunned, waving their arms around briefly. Use the opportunity to grab the stunned target or knock them out. Two rubber bullets fired into a person's torso should knock them unconscious. However, a single shot to the head knocks out a person instantly.

TRANQUILIZER AMMUNITION

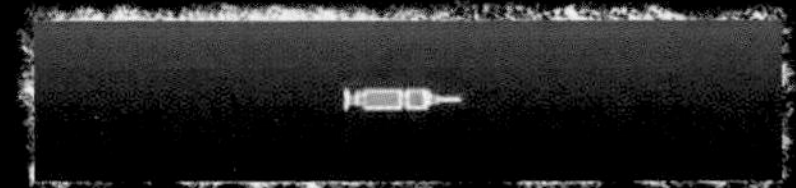

A remote injection disposable tranquilizer dart, fitted with a 3/4 inch needle. A small explosive inside the dart detonates on impact, forcing the inner plunger to close and deliver a concentrated dose of tranquilizer drug into the bloodstream. No matter where the dart is fired, the subject becomes stunned for approximately five seconds before collapsing in a heap. Extremely useful for long-distance, no-time-to-aim situations.

FINGERPRINT SCANNER

A dual-purpose folding tool combining an ultraviolet flashlight and high-resolution laser scanner in one sleek package. The flashlight enables the user to locate fingerprints left on objects, walls, and furniture. Once a fingerprint set is detected, the Scan Fingerprints interaction appears onscreen. Press the Interact button to scan the fingerprints and transmit them to Third Echelon headquarters for analysis. Fingerprint sets can only be identified in entirety at once, meaning that partial sets result in failure to identify the subject. For each complete set of fingerprints Sam scans, one of the JBA leaders' profiles appears in the Profile menu on the OPSAT.

FRAG GRENADE

An SC-60 series lightweight fragmentation grenade composed of a 5.5 cm steel sphere encasing comp B explosives and a fuse. The explosion casts fragments in a circular radius around the point of detonation, proving lethal to targets standing within two meters.

To toss a frag grenade, press the Equip button to aim. Mark the intended landing zone with the crosshair, and press the Primary Attack button to throw. Make sure Sam is at a safe distance from the intended target, unless you want to commit suicide. The resulting explosion is loud enough that enemies in adjoining rooms may radio in, raising the alarm level.

FLASHBANG GRENADE

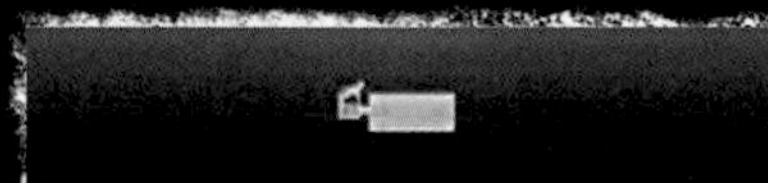

An SC-82 series nonlethal flashbang grenade emits a blinding burst of light upon detonation. The flare blinds all enemies within the room, stunning them for approximately 30 seconds. Unfortunately, many enemies are programmed to shield their eyes if they see a flashbang grenade about to detonate. If Sam is using night vision during a detonation and faces the blast, the screen may become whitewashed for a short period afterward.

To throw a flashbang grenade, press the Equip button to aim your throw. Direct the crosshair at the intended landing zone, and then press the Primary Attack button to let her fly. Try to throw flashbang grenades into shadows to prevent enemies from seeing them before they go off.

SMOKE GRENADE

An SC-81 series smoke grenade releases a cloud of sight-obscuring smoke. The fumes are harmless when inhaled and allow Sam to move through the smoke unseen by enemies.

To use a smoke grenade, press the Equip button to prepare to throw. Aim the crosshairs at the intended landing zone, and then press the Attack button to release it.

SC COMBAT KNIFE

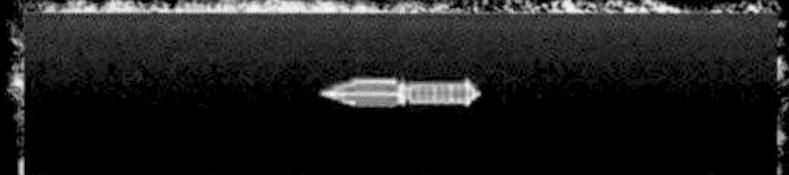

A custom knife employed by Third Echelon splinter cells. The blade is 3 3/8 inches and is made of high carbon steel with black oxidation to prevent reflections. With the black polymer rubber grip, the blade is 7.5 inches total.

Sam uses the SC knife whenever he grabs a character from behind. The threat of imminent throat slashing immobilizes the captive. If Sam performs a lethal attack against an enemy, he uses the SC knife to stab them in the guts or slash their throat, depending on Sam's angle of attack.

TRACKER DEVICE

A portable RFID (radio frequency identification) tracking device that connects to the OPSAT PDA wireless, enabling Sam to use satellite relay data to track enemy locations. Enemy locations are marked with yellow arrows on the 3-D map in the OPSAT menu. The tracking device updates regularly but may be slowed down due to environmental interference.

ADRENALINE SYRINGE

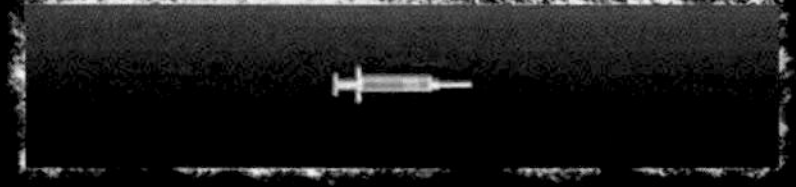

An experimental concentrated dose of a human DNA adrenaline compound. When a teammate is wounded and dying, injecting adrenaline into the heart increases their chances of recovery.

When a partner character such as Hisham Hamza, Jamie Washington, or Enrica Villablanca sustains too much damage while following Sam, they may collapse. Quickly approach them and use the Revive interaction to get them back on their feet.

UNIVERSAL HACKING DEVICE

A handheld dual-processor microcomputer outfitted with specialized code-breaking software. Readout appears in the form of twin frequency waves. Use the Move control to align the frequency waves as closely as possible and press the Interact button to lock in the appropriate signal to the device being hacked.

Attachable modules allow the universal hacking device to be utilized against a variety of security mechanisms:

Code Descrambling Module: Allows the user to hack number-input keypad security locks.

Retinal Override Module: Allows the user to hack retinal scanners.

Magstrip Decoding Module: Allows the user to hack card readers.

Ion Mobility Spectrometer: Allows the user to scan for hazardous chemicals and identify their properties.

04: PS2/GC

SOLO MISSIONS

01:
DOSSIERS

PS2/GC

02:
GAME BASICS

03:
EQUIPMENT

04:
SOLO MISSIONS

Iceland: Frozen Wilderness

05:
CO-OP MISSIONS

06:
VERSUS MISSIONS

XBOX 360/PC

07:
GAME BASICS

08:
EQUIPMENT

09:
SOLO MISSIONS

10:
MULTIPLAYER

Iceland: Frozen Wilderness

MAP KEY

Medkit

Ammo

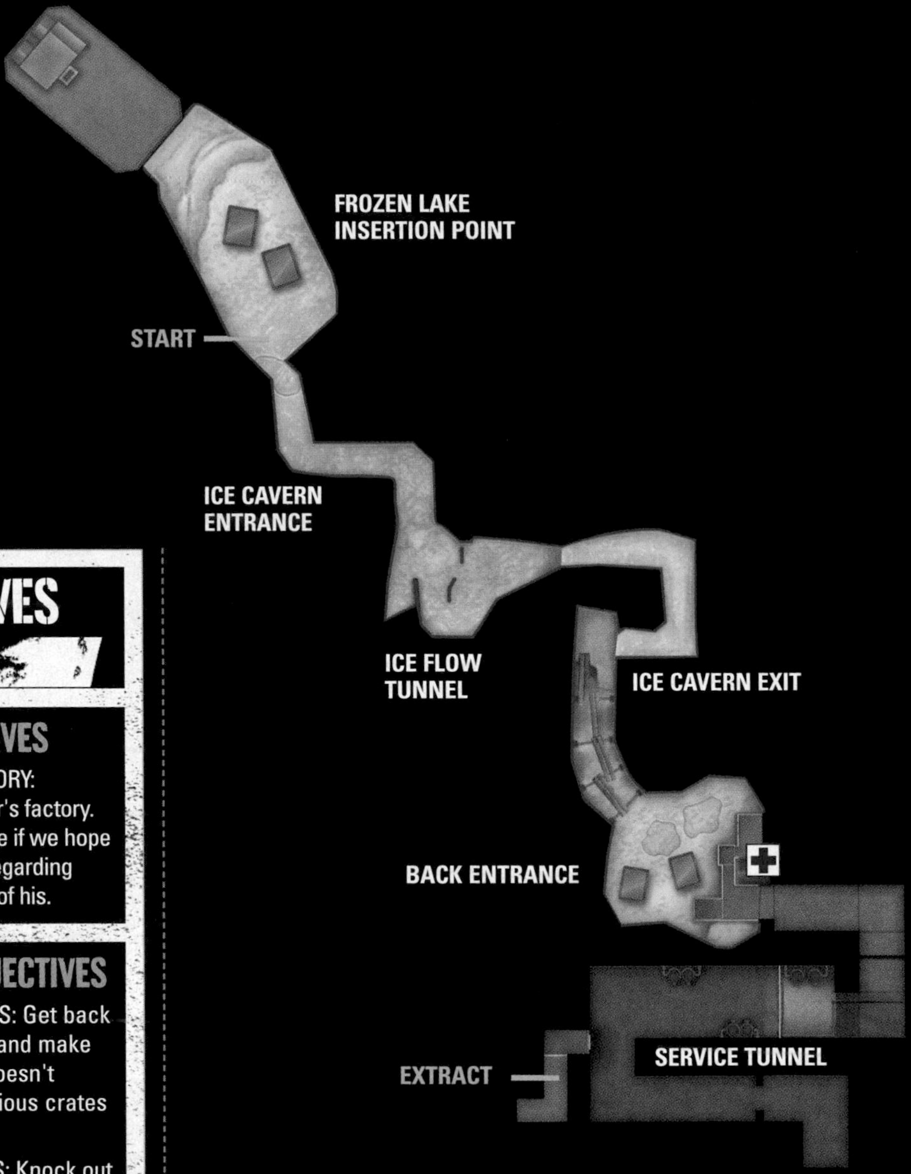

FROZEN LAKE INSERTION POINT

START

ICE CAVERN ENTRANCE

ICE FLOW TUNNEL

ICE CAVERN EXIT

BACK ENTRANCE

EXTRACT

SERVICE TUNNEL

OBJECTIVES

PRIMARY OBJECTIVES

> INFILTRATE THE FACTORY: Infiltrate Raheem Kadir's factory. We'll need to get inside if we hope to find any evidence regarding that rumored weapon of his.

OPPORTUNITY OBJECTIVES

> PROTECT THE CRATES: Get back to the insertion zone and make sure the helicopter doesn't leave with the suspicious crates Hisham found.

> NEUTRALIZE GUARDS: Knock out the two guards patrolling near the hovercraft so they can be retrieved by a Third Echelon recovery unit and interrogated.

LOADOUT: ICELAND MISSION

AVAILABLE WEAPONS
SC-20K/60
SC pistol/40
Sticky shocker/4
Sticky camera/4

Rumors point to Raheem Kadir, a notable arms trafficker, as the owner of a new type of weapon bought from the Russians. Search his base of operations in Iceland and prove or disprove the presence of such a weapon.

Frozen Lake Insertion Point/Ice Cavern Entrance

Enter the cavern. A video regarding Sam's OPSAT (Operational Satellite Uplink) becomes available; press the Interact button to view the footage. During the video briefing, press the displayed Action buttons to learn how to control the game. As you progress through the first few stages, you can view several more training videos.

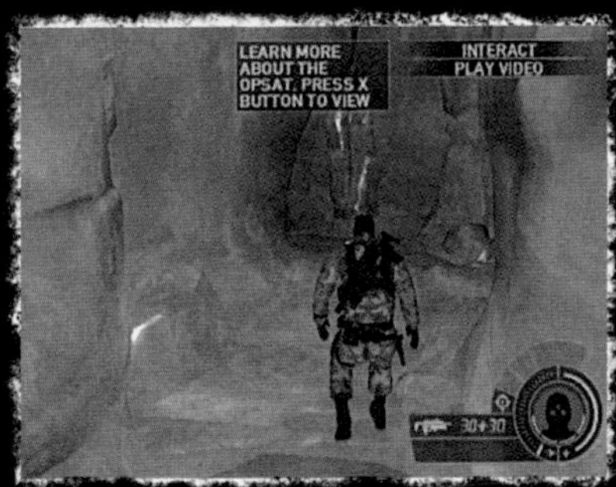

A training video becomes available after you enter the Ice Cavern.

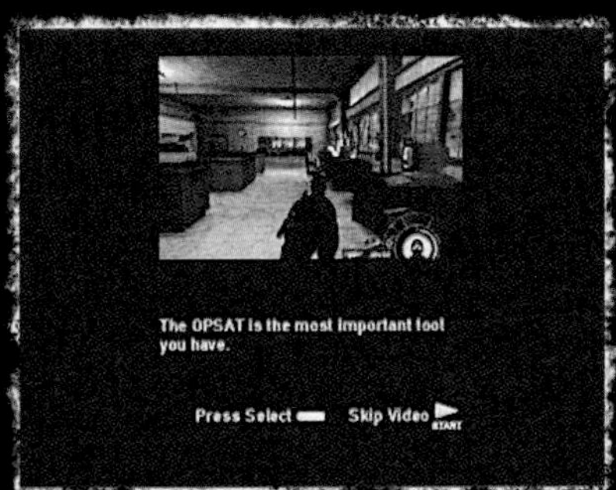

Press the buttons displayed during the playback to practice controlling the game.

Ice Flow Tunnel

Continue through the tunnel until you reach an open, red-lit cave. Notice the hostile standing on the opposite side of a thin ice wall, talking to his superior. Move up behind him until the Grab Character option appears. Then press the Interact button to smash through the ice wall and grab him.

Thin ice walls allow Sam to surprise enemies from behind.

Once Sam has hold of the hostile, press the Interact button to interrogate him. When the hostile is through spilling his guts (not literally), press the Nonlethal Attack button to choke him unconscious, or press the Lethal Attack button to break his spinal column, killing him.

The game has many enemies you can interrogate to learn important clues regarding what traps lie ahead.

Move past the wrecked snow sled to the tall ledge beyond. Hisham suggests that Sam give him a boost. Approach the high ledge until the Init Dynamic Hoist option appears onscreen. Press the Interact button to lift Hisham to the ledge. Hisham returns the favor by pulling Sam up.

Initiate a Dynamic Hoist co-op move to allow the duo to climb onto the steep ledge.

Proceed around the corner, where you hear a helicopter. Lambert orders the duo to head back to the starting point. The crates there are now in danger of falling into enemy hands.

Backtrack to the last corner just before the tunnel emerges to the Frozen Lake Insertion Point. Peek around the corner; Sam spots two enemy soldiers at the cave's mouth. Lambert wants both these men knocked unconscious. Equip the SC-20K and the sticky shockers—as it just so happens, both men stand in a puddle of water. Fire a sticky shocker at the ground directly between their feet to simultaneously electrocute both men unconscious.

Two enemies have found the weapon crates, and a chopper is hauling the cargo away. Quickly use a sticky shocker to knock out both men at the same time.

After you knock out both enemies, return to the Ice Flow Tunnel and repeat the Dynamic Hoist maneuver to climb the high ledge. Continue down the passage, and drop carefully into the Ice Cavern exit.

Walk slowly off the ledge so Sam automatically turns and grabs the wall for a safer and quieter fall.

Ice Cavern Exit

Use the Co-op Command button to make Hisham wait while you scout ahead. The passage is illuminated; traverse the planks lying across the support beams running down the passage. At the end, move across the beam a few steps to the left, then drop and hang from the beam. Drop to the ground, and move into the Back Entrance area.

The wooden boards connecting the tops of the supports allow Sam to move above the brightly lit passage.

Back Entrance

Move left and hide behind the tall stacks of crates. Gunfire erupts in the area as one of the terrorists turns on his two former comrades and kills them. Keep your wits during the battle and stay hidden behind the crates near the entrance.

The terrorist then climbs down from the high platform and patrols the area. Circle to the left around the crates stacked near the cave exit to maneuver behind the terrorist. Grab him from behind and interrogate him to find out why he shot the other two.

Capture and interrogate the lone guard near the Back Entrance to determine why surveillance is so heavy inside the factory.

Knock out or kill the lone guard, then climb the ladder and enter the small shack. Use the medkit if needed, and press the switch on the panel to open the doors to the Service Tunnel.

Press the switch inside the small shack to open the factory's rear entrance.

NOTE

There are always many options for dealing with enemy patrols and traps. For instance, instead of sneaking up behind the enemy in the Back Entrance area, you could simply draw a weapon and open fire. Or after grabbing him from behind, you could drag him onto any of the several thin ice patches in the area and then use the Plunge interaction to drown him.

We have chosen to outline only the stealth approach with regard to each enemy. This allows the player to minimize casualties and better manage the Trust Level (which comes into play in later stages). If sneaking up behind a hostile as described in the guide is proving too difficult, just pull out a gun and toe-tag the guy.

Service Tunnel

Proceed down the Service Tunnel and around the corner. When the Invite Boost Over option appears, press the Interact button and stand away from the gate barring the passage. Hisham moves to the gate and assumes a ready position. Move toward Hisham and press the Interact button to complete the boost-over. Looks like Sam can now complete the rest of the mission without the increased burden of Hisham's wisecracks.

Call upon Hisham to aid Sam in vaulting over the barrier in the Service Tunnel.

Move around the corner and use night vision to spot the pipe running down the ceiling's center. Stand directly under the pipe, then press the Jump button to leap up and grab it. While hanging from the pipe, press the Jump button again to make Sam pull his legs out of the way.

Jump to grab the overhead pipe, and pull Sam's legs up to avoid being seen by the nearby mechanic.

A mechanic inspecting the plumbing starts to move into the dark portion of the tunnel. He walks directly under the pipe. As he passes under Sam's position, the Grab Character option appears. Quickly press the Interact button to reach down, grab the man by the neck, and choke him unconscious.

When the mechanic moves underneath Sam, grab him from above and strangle him unconscious.

Climb along the pipe to the ceiling's edge, then move the left analog stick upward to continue climbing the vertical wall. At the top, move the left stick to Sam's right to start shimmying along the horizontal pipe. Continue shimmying around two corners until Sam is under a rail.

The same pipe that runs the length of the lower Service Tunnel bends upward and follows the wall to the ceiling. Climb up the pipe to reach the higher levels.

At the top, shimmy to Sam's right across the pipe, and around the room until positioned under a railing.

A guard soon moves to the edge above Sam and stops, looking over the rail. To dispose of him, climb up to the rail directly under the guard, then use the Grab Character interaction to pull him over the rail. The man falls to his death in the tunnel below.

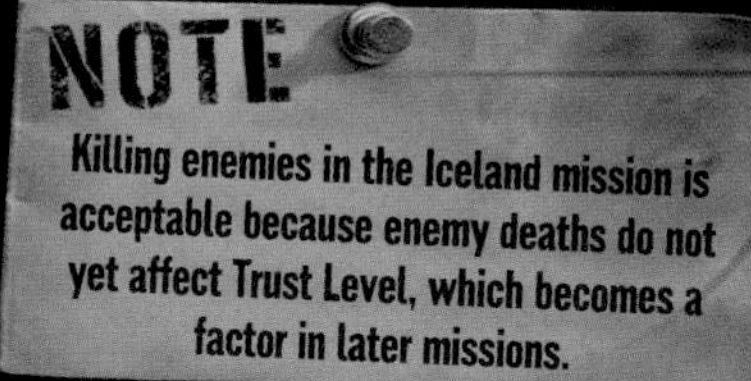

NOTE

Killing enemies in the Iceland mission is acceptable because enemy deaths do not yet affect Trust Level, which becomes a factor in later missions.

Move the left stick upward to make Sam climb to the rail's bottom. When the guard stops directly above Sam, use the Grab Character interaction to pull the man over the rail.

Take out the guard, then move forward to the edge of the shadows. A surveillance camera watches the area between Sam and the exit. If Sam steps into the lighted area in front of the camera, an alarm sounds. To disable a surveillance camera, do the following:

1. Press down on the D-pad to activate EMF (Electromagnetic Field) vision. This mode enables Sam to locate electronic devices such as the security camera.
2. Equip the SC pistol and use EMF to help aim at the camera.
3. Press down on the D-pad to deactivate the goggles, then press the Nonlethal Attack button to fire the SC pistol's OCP (Optically Channeled Potentiator).
4. Holster the pistol and move quickly through the area. The OCP jams the camera's circuitry for a short period of time, allowing Sam to pass through the area undetected.

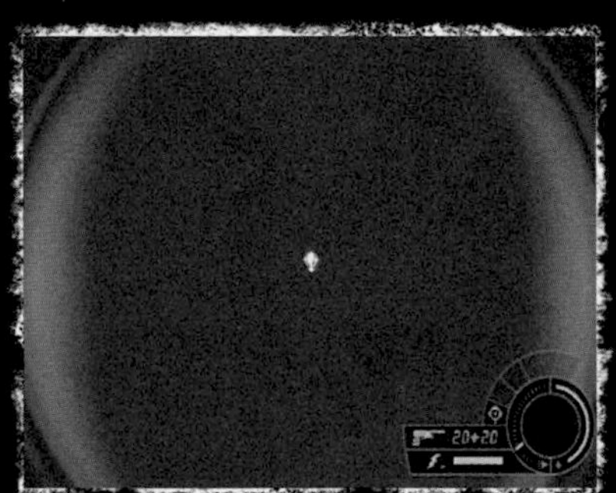

Use EMF vision to help aim the SC pistol at the surveillance camera on the wall...

...then deactivate the goggles and fire the OCP to disable the camera. Move through the area while the device remains jammed.

A medkit is located under the camera. Since there is a blind spot directly under the surveillance camera, using the medkit should not cause Sam to be detected should the camera resume function.

Climb up the small ladder to the camera's left. Cut the material blocking the narrow maintenance duct, and continue into the Munitions Factory.

Cut the material blocking the duct to proceed to the next stage.

ALTERNATIVE STRATEGY: NAVIGATE CAMERA BLIND SPOTS

Cameras cannot see in dark areas. Therefore, to get around the camera in this area easier, move through the darkness under the windows on Sam's right. After emerging from the narrow space behind the pipes, stick to the wall on the right and move down to the corner. Then turn left, move directly under the camera, and continue to the ladder. There is no need to stop and try to hit the camera with the OCP!

Iceland: Munitions Factory (A)

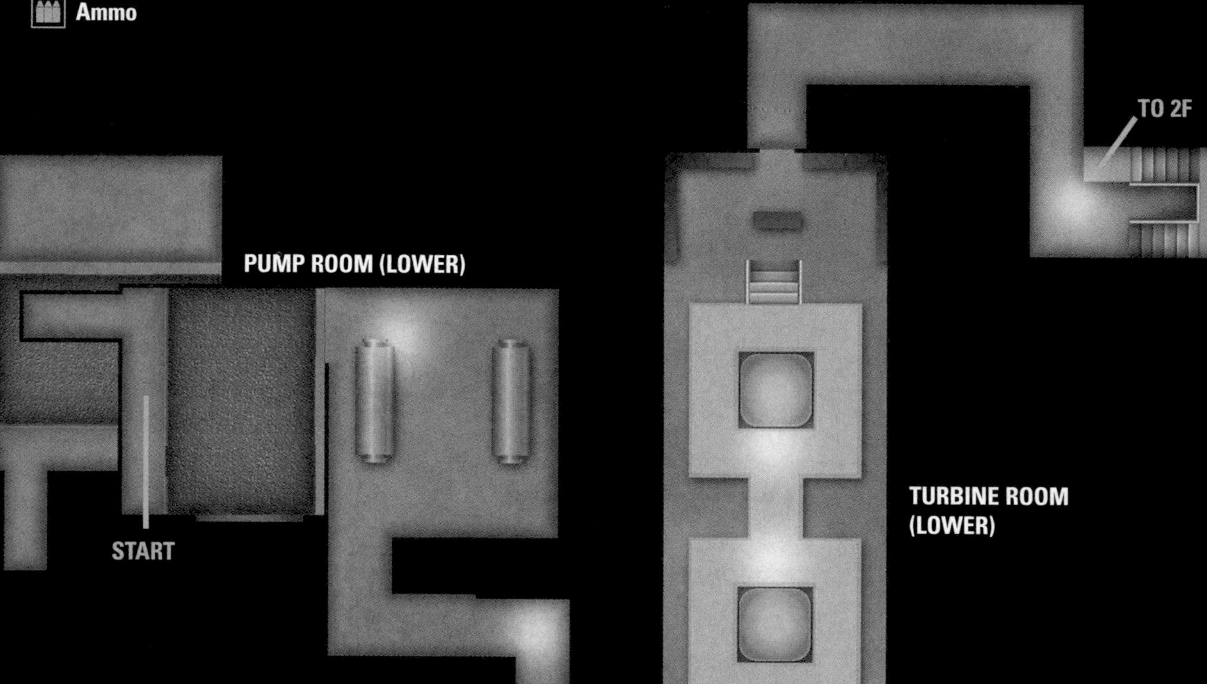

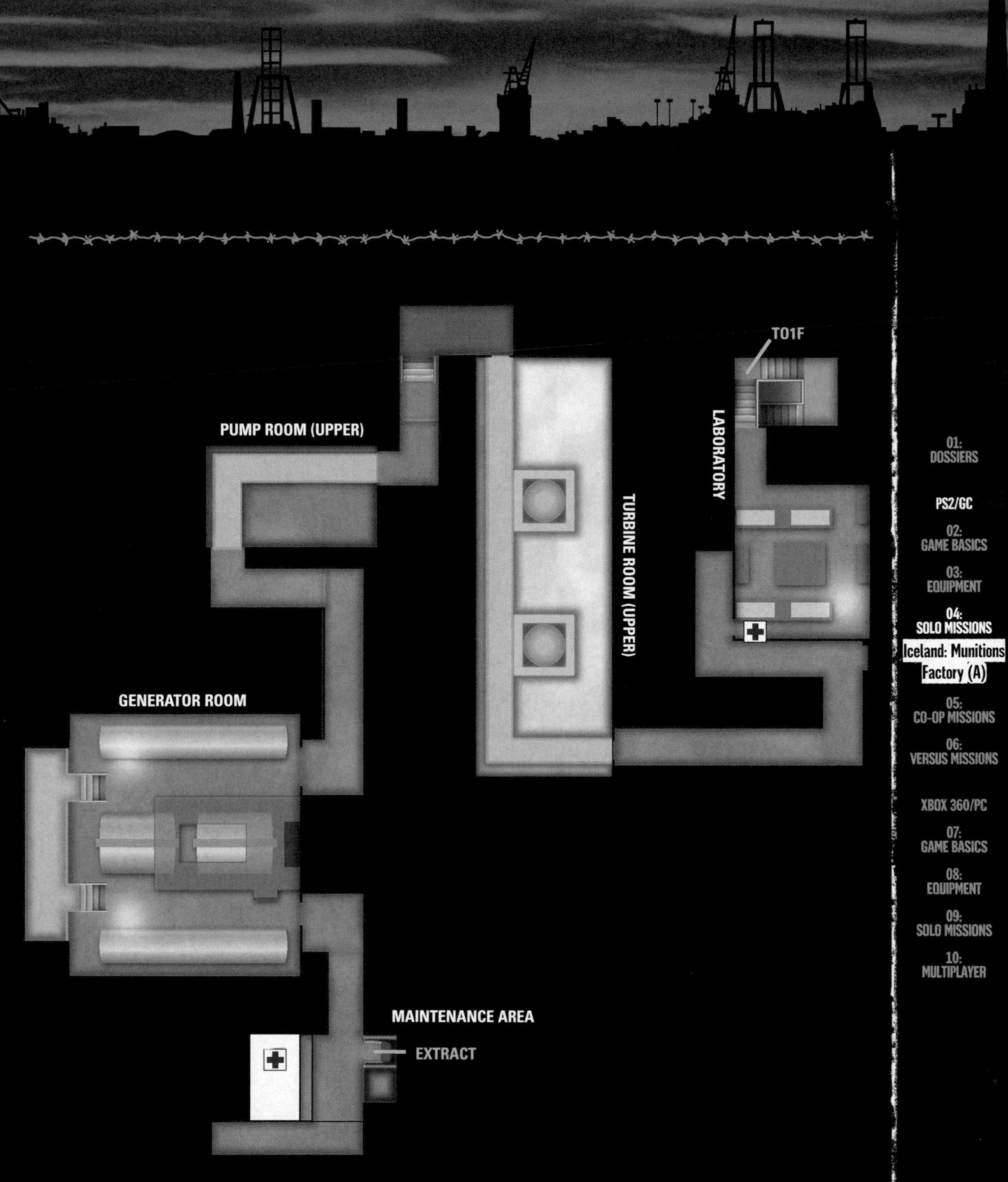
T01F
PUMP ROOM (UPPER)
LABORATORY
TURBINE ROOM (UPPER)
GENERATOR ROOM
MAINTENANCE AREA
EXTRACT

OBJECTIVES

PRIMARY OBJECTIVES

> ACQUIRE BUYERS LIST: Acquire a list of potential buyers for Raheem Kadir's alleged new weapon.

OPPORTUNITY OBJECTIVES

> RETRIEVE WEAPON SCHEMATICS: Obtain any schematics that might confirm the weapon's existence and purpose.

> PLANT EXPLOSIVE CHARGES: Plant explosive charges on the two production consoles located in this section of the factory.

Having infiltrated Raheem Kadir's arms factory, Sam must now reconnoiter for intelligence regarding the new type of weapon being produced here and determine to whom Kadir intends to sell it. Lambert soon orders Sam to prep the facility for demolition by installing explosives at key locations throughout the plant.

Pump Room (Lower)

Move to the right and turn the valve to open the sluice gate. Climb down the ladder into the water and go through the open gate; stick to the right to avoid being spotted by the mechanic on the platform. Quietly sneak around the corner and climb up the pipe.

Move from corner to corner through the waters to avoid drawing the attention of the mechanic on the platform above.

At the pipe's top, press left on the left stick to shimmy across the ledge under the rail. Wait until the mechanic steps up to the rail and stops. Shimmy under his location, then use the Grab Character option. Sam pulls the mechanic over the rail and throws him into the pit below.

Pull the mechanic over the rail to enable Sam to move through the Pump Room undetected.

Navigate to the lighted corridor—notice the green laser trip wire spanning the passage. Equip the SC pistol, and with the OCP, aim for the emitter on either wall to knock out the laser. These small emitters are difficult to hit, so move in close with the SC pistol drawn, and use EMF vision to help ensure knocking out the beam.

Practice knocking out laser trip wires with the OCP.

Move to the corner. Turn to Sam's left to face the next corner. A surveillance camera is mounted high on the wall. Use the OCP to knock it out, then move through the rest of the passage.

Stop well out of the camera's viewing range, and use the OCP to disable the device.

Turbine Room

Pause just outside the Turbine Room and wait for the two gentlemen to finish their conversation. While you wait, load the SC-20K with sticky shockers; both men are standing in a puddle of water. Before the two walk off to resume their duties, fire a single sticky shocker into the water. This simultaneously electrocutes both men.

Fire one sticky shocker into the puddle on the floor to wipe out security in the Turbine Room.

The Turbine Room is now clear of enemies. Head across the bridge to the other side. Lambert orders Sam to place charges on four important panels throughout the facility. The first of those panels stands in the spotlight on the Turbine Room's far side. Move up to the panel and press the Interact button to place the charges.

Fulfill an Opportunity Objective by placing bombs on four panels identical to the one shown here. Two panels are located in this stage, and two in the next.

Beyond the Turbine Room, move through the corridor and position Sam almost directly under the surveillance camera at the end. Use the OCP to disable the device, then head around the corner.

Disable another surveillance camera on your way to the lab.

Laboratory

At the passage's end, ascend the stairs and enter the Laboratory. Inside the lab, a lone guard dozes at the central desk near the wall. However, broken glass is scattered all around him. Sam may wake the guard by stepping on the glass. Instead of approaching the guard, climb onto the science table and move across the back of the room. Stop near the exit door in the southwest corner.

Climb onto the science table, and move through the dark portion of the lab to avoid waking the nearby guard.

Use the EEV (Electronically Enhanced Vision) to scan the computer behind the bulletproof glass inside the nearby sealed room. The computer contains an encrypted file.

To open the encrypted file, choose the Security Access option. Sam's universal hacking device appears. Two frequency lines, red and green, become visible on the hacking device. Three or four lights on the device's bottom portion indicate how many security levels you must overcome. You must hack all security levels before the green timer bar depletes, or the alarm stage rises. You may cancel at any time before the green timer bar turns red. If you attempt to cancel after the timer bar has changed colors, an alarm sounds.

To hack the encryption, move the left stick left or right, or up or down to adjust the green frequency wave's height and length. When the green frequency is touching the red frequency at all points, press the Interact button to overcome the security level. Repeat the process until you disable all security levels. The two lines do not have to overlap perfectly; the frequencies need only touch at all points. Waiting too long to press the Interact button causes the frequencies to fall out of alignment.

The decrypted e-mail describes Red Mercury, the weapon that Kadir may be trying to sell. In finding this information, Sam has fulfilled yet another Opportunity Objective. Use the medkit on the wall if needed, and head out to the corridor.

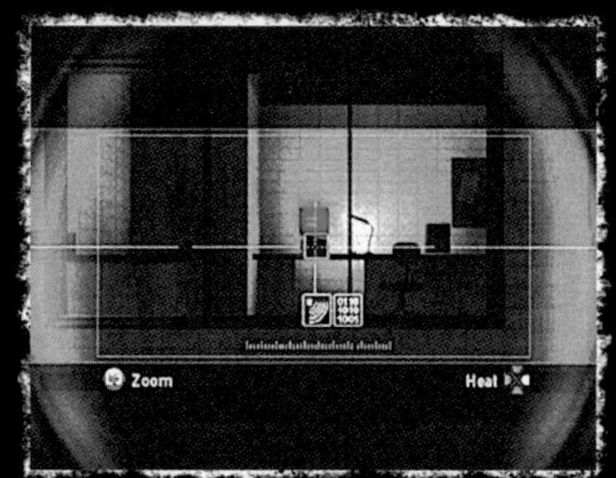

Aim the EEV at the computer behind the bulletproof glass and allow them to perform a scan...

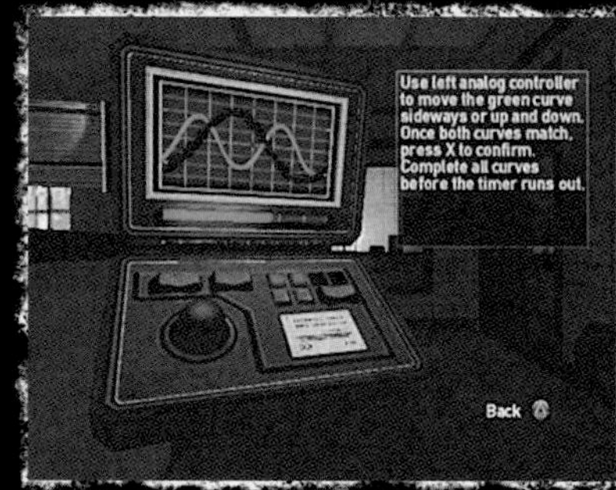

...disable the encryption levels by aligning the frequencies on the universal hacking device...

...then press the Interact button to view the computer's files, all without touching a single key!

Use the OCP to knock out the surveillance camera at the corner, and quickly move toward the opposite doorway. The door is locked; open it with the lock pick. You can also break the lock—no one is nearby to hear the noise.

To pick locks, simply move the left stick.

LOCK PICKING 101

Pick locks by rotating the left stick until you hear a clicking sound and feel a vibration. Allow the left stick to return to the center, and then move it out to the same point again to jostle the tumbler. Repeat until Sam lifts the tumbler. Continue this operation until you lift all tumblers and the cylinder rotates.

Turbine Room (Upper)

Move to the corner and stare down the passage. If you knocked out all the enemies on the level below, there should be only one guard on this level. Otherwise, there could be two or more. Move into the narrow space between two tall, yellow walls. Face either of the walls and press the Jump button to execute a Split Jump. Remain in the Split Jump until the guard moves directly under Sam. Then press the Crouch button to drop on top of him, knocking him out. If more than one enemy is on the catwalk, keep repeating this operation until you knock them all out. Continue across the Turbine Room and break the lock on the door at the opposite end.

Perform a Split Jump between the yellow walls to get the drop on the guard patrolling the catwalk.

In the corridor beyond the Turbine Room, move to the corner on Sam's left and use the OCP to knock out the surveillance camera watching the stairs. Head into the Pump Room's upper portion.

Knock out the surveillance camera with the OCP before proceeding through this well-lit zone.

Pump Room (Upper)

Move to the corner and peek into the Pump Room. A lone guard patrols the catwalk running across the area's top. Move to within a few feet of the catwalk, and wait for the guard to stop on his closest patrol point. When he turns his back to Sam and pauses for a moment, sneak up behind him and grab him. Knock him out, pick up his body, then cross the catwalk.

The guard patrolling the Pump Room's catwalk practically hands himself to Sam by placing his back to the shadows.

Generator Room

Several laser tripwires block the corridor just before the Generator Room. There are three ways to get across this passage:

1. Use the OCP to knock out two laser trip wires at a time (most difficult option).
2. Utilize a pipe that runs the corridor's length. Jump to grab it, pull Sam's legs up, and shimmy across the corridor on the pipe, past the sensors.
3. Pick up the unconscious guard from the upper Pump Room and carry him through the laser trip wires. The tracking device in his clothes disables the trip wires, allowing Sam to walk right through the corridor (easiest option).

Using the OCP to disable the many lasers barring this passage is hardly practical.

Shimmy along the ceiling pipe to bypass the lasers.

THE RECOMMENDED METHOD: Carry the unconscious catwalk guard through the lasers. The man's tracking implant deactivates the traps.

Enter the Generator Room proper. Two terrorists begin jawing about job transfers and vacation time. Ignore them and move to the right, behind the large gas tank. There is a narrow gap between the tank and the wall, which Sam can move through. Follow this gap to the room's other side.

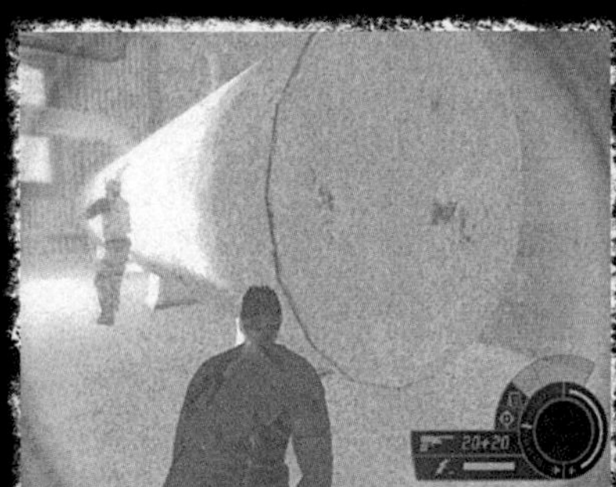

Search behind this big tank to find a narrow passage through the shadows, enabling Sam to circumnavigate the entire room.

Stop immediately after emerging near the bottom of the stairs. Allow the guard to pass by, and let him climb the ladder to the upper platform. A nearby mechanic changes his route and moves around the central generator. Catch up to him, grab him, and interrogate him. Then knock him out and leave his body behind the generator.

Follow the mechanic into the dark space under the ladder, grab him, and shake him down.

Step out from behind the central generator, move across the path to the opposite side of the path, and go behind the large tanks lined up along the south wall. Move to the room's bottom corner, and stop by the tank's corner. Glance up at the guard on the upper platform. If he is nowhere in sight, quickly climb the ladder. Stop on the ladder's top rung, just below the platform.

Sneak through the dark areas at the bottom of the steps to move from behind the tank to behind the generator to behind the tanks on the south wall.

Climb to the ladder's top rung and wait for the guard to stop nearby.

Wait until the guard patrols the upper platform again. When he stops with his back to the ladder, sneak up behind him. Press the Nonlethal Attack button to knock him unconscious.

When the guard stops in front of the equipment on the upper platform, climb onto the platform, sneak up behind him, and knock him out.

Press the switch to open the door and place the charge on the fuel regulator panel. Then climb back down the ladder and exit the room.

Accomplish both objectives here.

Maintenance Area

Proceed to the dark passage's end. The room on Sam's right contains a medkit. When at full health, move to the ladder and climb down to the factory's lower portion.

Descend into the Iceland mission's final stage.

Iceland: Munitions Factory (B)

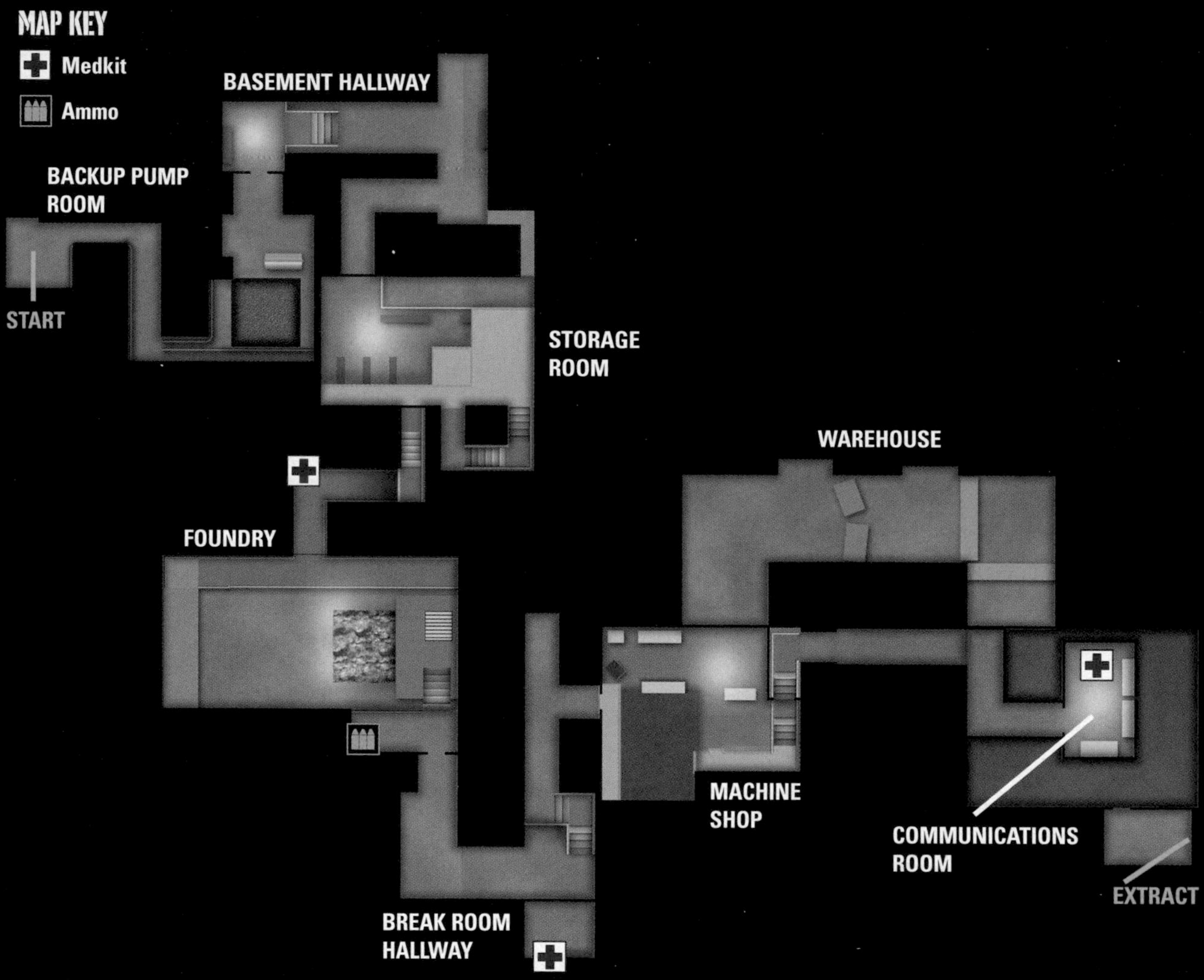

MAP KEY

Medkit

Ammo

BASEMENT HALLWAY

BACKUP PUMP ROOM

START

STORAGE ROOM

WAREHOUSE

FOUNDRY

MACHINE SHOP

COMMUNICATIONS ROOM

EXTRACT

BREAK ROOM HALLWAY

OBJECTIVES

PRIMARY OBJECTIVES

> ACQUIRE BUYERS LIST: Acquire a list of potential buyers for Raheem Kadir's alleged new weapon.

> EXTRACT THROUGH THE LOADING BAY: Lambert's helicopter will land near the factory's loading bay, which is close to your current location. Make your way there.

OPPORTUNITY OBJECTIVES

> PLANT EXPLOSIVE CHARGES: Plant explosive charges on two additional production consoles located in this section of the factory.

Backup Pump Room

Infiltrating into the deepest levels of the weapons factory, Sam is very close to determining what is transpiring in Iceland and how it may affect the world. Move into the area of narrow pipes. Crawl under the low pipe and emerge on the other side. Move down the narrow passage until you reach a pipe fastened to the wall on Sam's right. Climb the pipe to the ceiling, then follow it to the room's other side.

Maneuver through the pipes to the location shown here, then climb the pipe on the right. Shimmy hand over hand along the ceiling to the water's other side.

Climb down into the water and sneak up behind the mechanic working on the backup pump. Use the Grab Character option while standing in the water. Sam drags the man into the murk and drowns him. Go through the double doors to the Basement Hallway.

Sneak up on the mechanic from behind. Grab him and drown him in the water.

Basement Hallway

Move to the top of the stairs and use the OCP to knock out the surveillance camera overhead. Move downstairs and go right. Find the small vent in the corner, and enter the crawl space.

Find the ground-level vent in the corner, and crawl through it to the next area.

Storage Room

Sam emerges from the crawl space into the Storage Room, which is a fairly well-lit, two-level infiltrator's nightmare. Use extreme caution when moving through here. The trick is to leave the two men entirely alone, and get through this area unseen.

Move through the shadows along the wall to Sam's right, and climb up the fence. Descend over the fence's other side and into the Storage Room's main area.

Move to the fence's end and climb over quietly. A duct overhead blocks Sam from climbing over the portion of the fence to the right.

Cross the shadows toward the south wall. Move along the south wall and squeeze through the narrow gaps between the sides of two shelves and the wall. Sam emerges near a doorway.

Slip through the shadows by squeezing between the narrow gaps behind the ends of the shelves.

CAUTION

Move through this area steadily and stealthily, and you should be able to head directly upstairs. If you have been gradually feeling your way around the room, check to make sure that the man who walks around the floor is not headed toward the well-lit stairwell before you proceed.

On the upper level, avoid the pool of light and move along the wall to the left. Enter the left-hand passage and move up the stairs toward an impassable door.

Stay out of the light when moving through the upper level. It shines through to the level below. Any strange shadows may alert the enemies.

Climb over the railing and drop onto the platform below. A set of laser trip wires blocks the passage; you must use the OCP to dismantle them. Move as close to the trip wires as possible, with the SC pistol drawn. Use the EMF to help you take out one laser trip wire, then aim at the other trip wire and wait for the OCP to recharge. As soon as the OCP is recharged, knock out the other trip wire and run past the area. Use the medkit at the corner if needed.

Use the OCP to knock out the trip wires in the passage, one immediately after the other.

Foundry

Enter the Foundry and head right. Climb the ladder and wait for the moving bridge to arrive on Sam's side of the room. When ready, step onto the platform; it carries you to the room's southeast side.

Climb to the Foundry's upper levels and wait for the crucible platform to arrive.

Disembark the moving bridge and follow the narrow path out to a set of stairs. Take the stairs to the control center's roof. If necessary, use thermal vision to help sight an enemy standing at the rail of the opposite platform on the level below. Fire a sticky shocker at the terrorist to knock him out. His body falls into the molten steel and disintegrates.

Hit the guard near the rail with a sticky shocker or a single bullet. The body disposes of itself.

Head to the edge of the control booth on Sam's left, drop carefully over the side, and grab the edge; then drop and catch the rail at the control booth's floor level. Shimmy to the left under the window, and keep going until you reach the left side of the control booth's open viewport. The guard inside the booth moves toward the window and stops momentarily, staring out into the Foundry. Use the Grab Character option to pull him through the window and fling him into the molten steel below.

Drop over the side of the control booth and grab the ledge.

Shimmy left under the control booth window. Grab the man inside the control booth and pull him over the rail to a nasty death.

Place charges on the tall control panel inside the control booth, then break the lock on the nearby door. Climb the ladder to the highest level to find SC-20K ammo. Then slide down the ladders to the bottom level. Go through the double doors.

Rifle ammo is located on the uppermost platform above the Foundry's exit.

Break Room Hallway

Use the OCP to knock out the surveillance camera high up on the wall opposite the entrance. Then quickly move around the corner. Notice the man entering the break room on Sam's right. Position Sam in front of the door, press and hold the Interaction button, and select "Bash Door." Continue holding down the Interaction button until the man inside the break room returns to the door. Then release the Interaction button to slam the door open, knocking the man unconscious. This tactic is sickly amusing. Use the medkit in the break room if needed, and ascend the stairs opposite the break room to continue.

Prepare a little ambush for the man lounging in the break room.

Machine Shop

Use the OCP to disable the surveillance camera monitoring the door to the Machine Shop, then go inside.

Two mechanics toil away in the Machine Shop's lower portion. Take them down now to prevent problems later. The ladder is well lit and is not a stealthy way to drop to the lower level. Instead, climb over the rail opposite the entrance and move to the corner of the small building's roof.

Climb over the rail and move to the corner for a better view of the two workmen.

Drop over the side of the low structure onto the stack of pallets below, then descend to the ground. Grab the nearest workman from behind and drag him behind the pallets to interrogate him. Knock him out and then sneak up on the other mechanic. The second man is stationary and easy to capture and knock out.

Drop onto the pallets stacked near the corner, then sneak up behind the nearest tradesman for a little heart-to-heart.

Place charges on the panel in the corner near the garage door, then climb the ladder back to the catwalk. Head through the doorway into the passage leading to the Communications Room.

The final bombing point in the factory is located beside the large shutter door in the Machine Shop.

Communications Room

Proceed down the corridor to the halfway mark and stop in the shadowed area between the rays of light pouring through the two windows. Use the OCP to disable the surveillance camera high up on the wall, then proceed around the corner to the Communications Room.

Move in no farther than the location shown here before disabling the surveillance camera at the corner.

Use the EEV to scan the computer located in the room. One of the e-mails on the computer contains the garage door keypad code (7931). A medkit hangs on the far wall.

When Sam finishes reading the e-mail, Lambert orders him and Hisham to abort the mission. Remember to disable the surveillance camera in the corridor on your way back out.

Return to the Machine Shop and move to the right side of the garage door on the lower level. Input the keypad code—7931—to open the garage door.

Check the computer in the Communications Room to complete Sam's Primary Objective.

In the Machine Shop, input the code on the keypad to the shutter door's left.

Warehouse

Proceed through the Warehouse, climbing over the pallets and obstacles in Sam's way. Stick to the walls on Sam's left to avoid being spotted by the two guards inside the large area near the end. Then simply navigate undetected between the tall pallet stacks over to the door on the large room's opposite side. Make sure no one is standing near the exit door, then proceed. Open the door and move to the extraction point to complete the mission.

To slip through the Warehouse unseen, merely stick to the shadows and weave through obstacles with good timing.

Ellsworth Prison, Kansas: General Population (A)

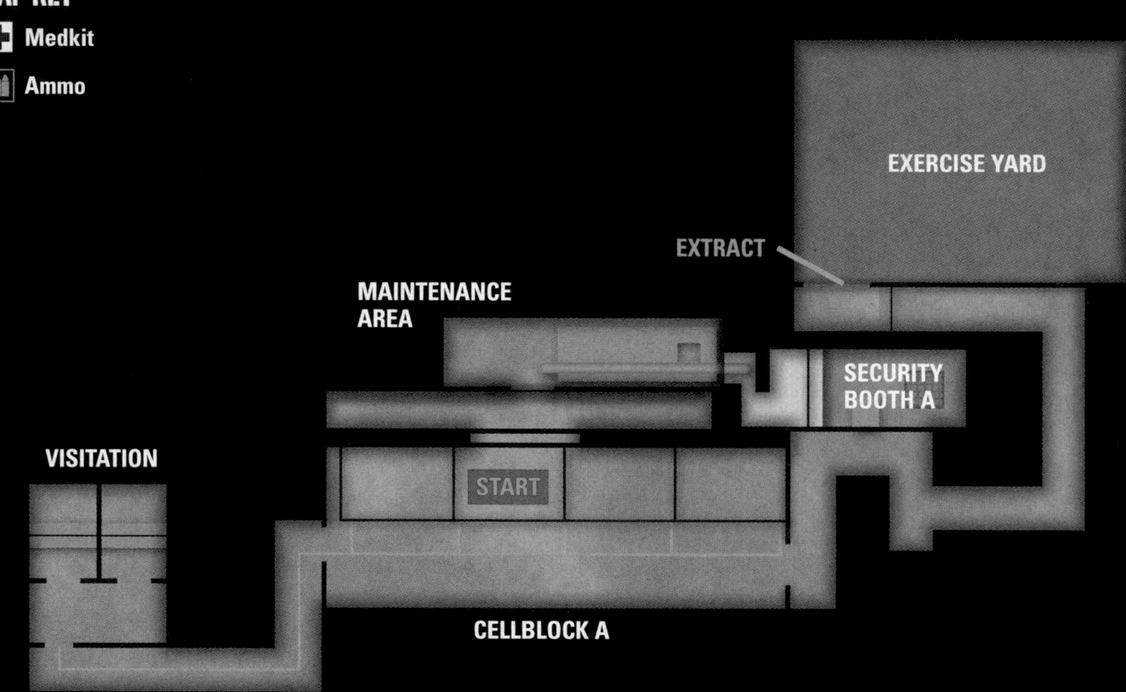

OBJECTIVES

PRIMARY OBJECTIVES

> ESCAPE ELLSWORTH PRISON WITH JAMIE WASHINGTON: Your escape is being staged by Third Echelon agents. You must proceed, with Jamie Washington, to the extraction point in the garage. It is crucial that Jamie Washington does not die.

> GET WALKIE-TALKIE FROM SECURITY BOOTH: Get walkie-talkie from security booth to help Jamie.

OPPOSING OBJECTIVES

> HELP JAMIE KILL BARNHAM: Jamie Washington and Barnham have been at odds ever since Jamie arrived at Ellsworth. Killing him would alleviate some of Jamie's suspicions and facilitate the infiltration of the JBA.

> DO NOT LET BARNHAM DIE: Barnham is an important witness for the DOJ. His death cannot be allowed.

OPPORTUNITY OBJECTIVES

> FIND HIDDEN INFORMATION DISK: Third Echelon agents have hidden a disk containing information about Jamie Washington that might prove useful later on.

Following the events in Iceland, several Red Mercury devices are on the loose. We have only one lead: Emile Dufraisne. Our only hope to infiltrate Dufraisne's operation is in Ellsworth prison. His name is Jamie Washington.

Cellblock A

After Sam hears Jamie speaking in the next cell, move to the back of Sam's cell and enter the crawlspace.

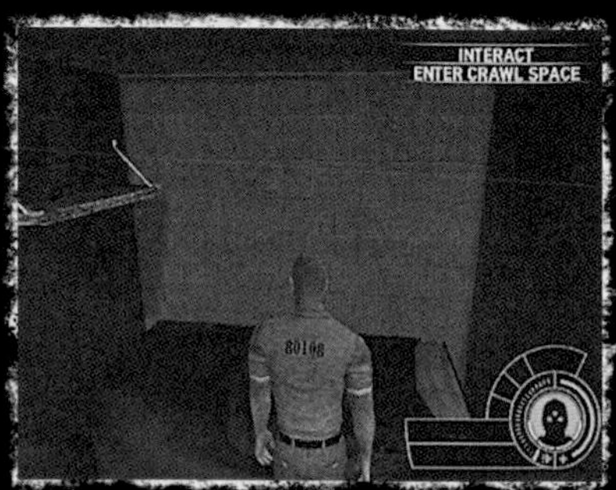

Sam has tunneled through the wall under his bunk.

Maintenance Area

Exit the crawlspace and move to the opposite wall. Jump to grab the bottom edge of a tall vent hole. Crawl through and drop to the ground to find Jamie Washington.

Crawl through the high vent hole to hook up with Jamie.

After Jamie speaks, he moves to the pipes at the far end of the area to initiate a Boost Over. Complete the co-op move and drop down on the other side of the pipes. Climb the ladder and open the trapdoor.

Jamie gives Sam a boost near the pipes.

Continue to the back of the area and climb up the ladder. Open the trapdoor at the top.

After stepping off the ladder, turn 180 degrees and look for a yellow pipe fastened to the wall at the corner. Climb the pipe to the ceiling, then follow the pipe across the ceiling and drop to the floor behind the fence.

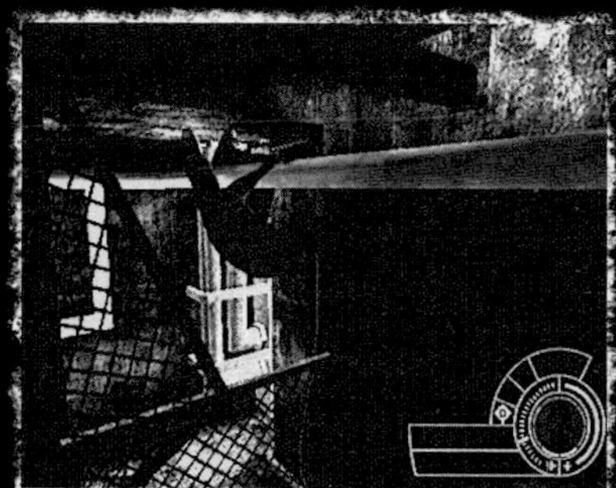

On the upper platform, climb along the yellow pipe to reach the next area.

Squeeze through the narrow gap between the pipes and the wall. Turn the corner, crouch, and squeeze through another tight passage.

Upon emerging, climb over the rail to Sam's right and drop from pipe to pipe until you reach the floor.

Drop carefully from pipe to pipe to reach the ground floor.

Squeeze through another narrow gap, and use the lock pick to open the trapdoor. Move toward the open trapdoor's left side and drop through the hole. Doing so should help Sam avoid detection if a prison guard is entering the booth.

After picking the trapdoor lock, move to the open door's left side and drop through. This should help Sam avoid discovery.

Security Booth A

Drop to the floor, sneak up behind the officer in the security booth, and knock him out. Grab the walkie-talkie off the table.

Sneak up behind the guard in Security Booth A. The walkie-talkie is on the table to the left.

Cell inspection is about to take place. You have one minute, forty-five seconds to return to your cell. Retrace your route before time expires, or the mission is a bust.

In the area where Sam met with Jamie, a guard now patrols. Move to the upper platform's edge, drop over the side, and hang. Wait until the guard moves underneath Sam, then drop to grab hold of a pipe. Drop again to fall on top of the guard and knock him out.

While returning through the Maintenance Area, drop from the upper platform's edge onto the patrolling guard.

Return to Sam's cell before the time limit expires. Soon a guard comes to escort Sam to the visiting area for a little face time with Lambert.

Sam has an important visitor.

Visitation

Lambert gives Sam his OPSAT/PDA. You now have access to your objectives and a map of the prison. Lambert also provides some interesting pointers regarding the Trust Level meter, so do not skip the scene.

Lambert has many wise words for Sam, as well as the OPSAT/PDA.

Exit the visiting area and follow the yellow line on the ground back to the cellblock. Continue to the cellblock's far end, and follow the corridor signs toward the "courtyard."

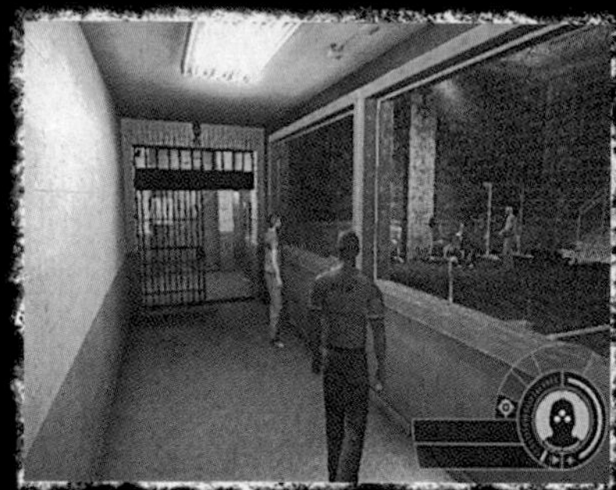

Move through the prison corridors until Sam stands outside the Exercise Yard, where a confrontation is brewing.

Exercise Yard

Barnham is attacking Jamie in the Exercise Yard. Sam pulls the guy off Jamie. Now you decide: either kill Barnham to gain Jamie's trust, or knock out Barnham to keep the NSA (National Security Agency) happy. If you kill the guy, Jamie allows Sam to have a firearm in the mission's next stage. If you knock him out, Sam is stuck with only a lock pick.

Press one of the buttons displayed to make a trustworthy choice.

Ellsworth Prison, Kansas: General Population (B)

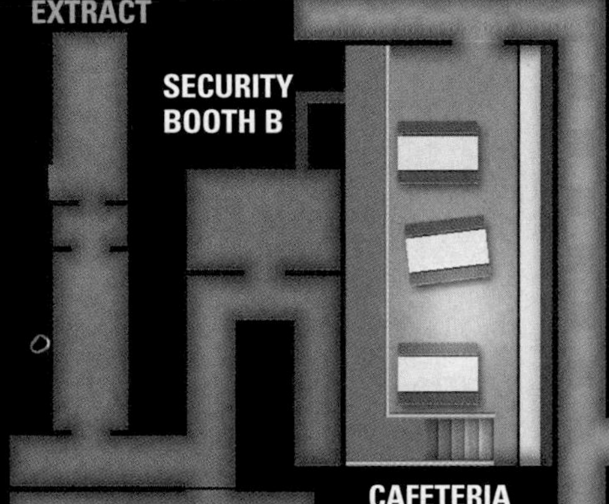

OBJECTIVES

PRIMARY OBJECTIVES

- ESCAPE ELLSWORTH PRISON WITH JAMIE WASHINGTON: Your escape is being staged by Third Echelon agents. You must proceed, with Jamie Washington, to the extraction point in the garage. It is crucial that Jamie Washington does not die.
- FIND AN ADRENALINE SYRINGE: An adrenaline syringe will allow you to keep Jamie alive if he's wounded.

OPPORTUNITY OBJECTIVES

- FIND HIDDEN INFORMATION DISK: Third Echelon agents have hidden a disk containing information about Jamie Washington that might prove useful later on.

After forming a bond with Jamie Washington, Sam must now help the convict escape from Ellsworth. While Jamie and Sam recuperate from knockout gas in the prison infirmary, an independent splinter cell team infiltrates Ellsworth and instigates a prison riot. Now is the time.

Infirmary

Sam and Jamie awaken in a holding cell inside the Infirmary. A full-scale riot is in progress. Soon, inmates chase a guard into the Infirmary. The guard mistakenly moves too close to the bars, and Jamie kills him.

After a moment, Jamie steps away and allows Sam to search the guard's body for items. Move to where the body lies on the other side of the bars, and search the guard. If you killed Barnham in the previous stage, you find the 9 mm handgun and the lock pick. If you chose to safely knock out the inmate, then only the lock pick is available.

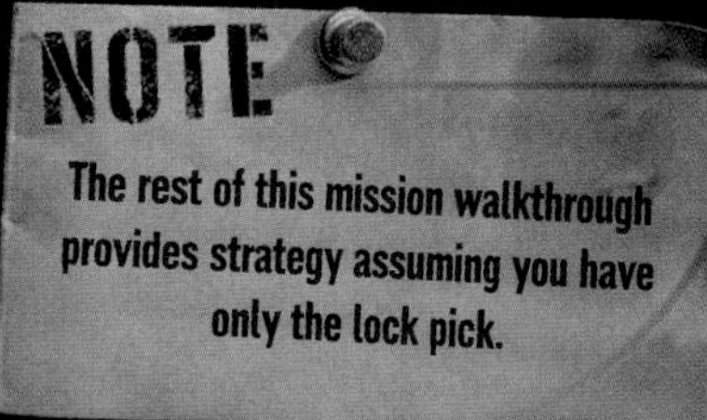

After Jamie kills the guard, search his body through the bars for items.

Pick the cell door lock and exit the holding area. Search the counter on Sam's right to find an adrenaline syringe. If the inmates or guards kill Jamie, you can revive him with the syringe before the time limit expires. Use the medkit located on the wall if needed.

The adrenaline syringe is located on the trashed countertop.

Cellblock B

Exit the infirmary and head down the passage to the left. Move toward the bars blocked by fire, and initiate a Dynamic Hoist.

Move to the opposite edge of the raised platform and look down. Notice the guard standing in the shadowed area on the left side. Drop over the side of the platform, and down to the ground within the shadows. Sneak up behind the guard, grab him, drag him back into the corner, and knock him out.

Seek Jamie's help in clearing the cellblock obstacle.

Drop from the raised platform's left side to enter the shadows behind the stationary guard.

Another guard patrolling the cellblock may notice this activity. If he moves toward your position, pick up the object on the ground and toss it at the opposite wall to draw him away from you and Jamie. As he moves to investigate, creep up behind him and knock him out.

The guard may instead patrol down the cellblock. Move to the opposite wall and pursue him. Sneak up behind him and knock him out with a nonlethal attack.

Take out the other cellblock guard through distraction.

Move toward the burning debris blocking the passage, and initiate a Hoist Split. On the level above, Jamie finds a control box and opens the stairwell gate for Sam. Head left to the gated area and go upstairs.

Find the spot where you can initiate a Hoist Split; lift Jamie to the level above. He returns the favor by opening the stairwell to the left.

Follow Jamie to the corner. At the point where the rail is demolished, drop to the level below. Head around the corner into the corridor.

Drop to the ground floor at the point where the rail is broken.

A guard holds a prisoner hostage and, in his panic, is about to wrongly execute him. You can either shoot him with the 9 mm, if you have it, or walk up behind him and knock him out.

Move steadily but quietly in order to get behind this guard and knock him out before he spots Sam or starts shooting.

Cafeteria

Continue following the passage past the Cafeteria windows. Notice the guards inside the Cafeteria, struggling with inmates. The end of the passage is engulfed in flames. Near the flames, initiate a Climb-On move, so that Sam stands on Jamie's shoulders. Turn the valve to activate the sprinkler system and put out the fire blocking the passage. Press the Interact button to drop from Jamie's shoulders.

Initiate a Climb-On in front of the valve handle, set high up on the wall, to extinguish the flames blocking the corridor.

Head around the corner and stop just outside the door. Two guards search the Cafeteria with flashlights. It's impossible to take down the closest one, because he patrols well-lit areas. Any attempt to grab him while the guard at the room's back is active results in failure.

Wait until the guard patrolling near the exit switches off his flashlight and moves into the bright area before entering.

Wait for the nearest prison guard to walk into the lighted area and turn off his flashlight. Then move into the room, sticking to your left and moving through the shadows. Head down the side of the Cafeteria until the shadows curve right, then cross the room. Continue following the shadows through the center of the area to the back wall.

Stick close to the lunch line on the left while moving into the room...

...then veer to the right and follow the shadow that runs across the room.

Move through the shadows on the back wall toward the guard standing behind his makeshift cover. Sneak up on him, grab him, and knock him out.

Follow the back wall behind the stationary guard's fortifications, and nab him.

By this point, the guard who usually patrols near the entrance may be standing near the bottom of the stairs leading to the catwalk. Sneak up behind him, grab him, interrogate him if you want, then knock him out.

Meet the other guard at the corner where the stairs meet the lunch line.

When the area is clear, Jamie moves through the room and opens the back exit. Follow him into the corridor, which is a dead end. Naturally, Sam is the one who must figure out a way around this roadblock.

Jamie and Sam must split up.

Return to the Cafeteria and follow the lunch line to where the protective fence is missing. A flashbang grenade lies near this spot. Climb over the service counter. Go to the right and upstairs. Follow the upper catwalk to its end, and enter the crawlspace.

Reach the stairs by climbing over the service counter where the protective fence is missing. Head upstairs and find a crawlspace into the Security Booth.

Security Booth B

Crawl through the vent duct into the Security Booth. Drop into the booth, sneak up on the guard, and knock him out. Then use the computer to find the door's access code (3190).

The guard in the booth is easy to knock out. Use the nearby computer to clear the passage and find the door code.

Press the button on the desk to open the cellblock; then use the access code 3190 to open the door. Follow Jamie down the passage and around the corner, then open the door on the right. Pass through the flames and enter the door into the Old Cellblock.

Hopefully Sam can reunite with Jamie in the Old Cellblock, because it is doubtful that Jamie can survive on his own.

Ellsworth Prison, Kansas: Old Cellblock

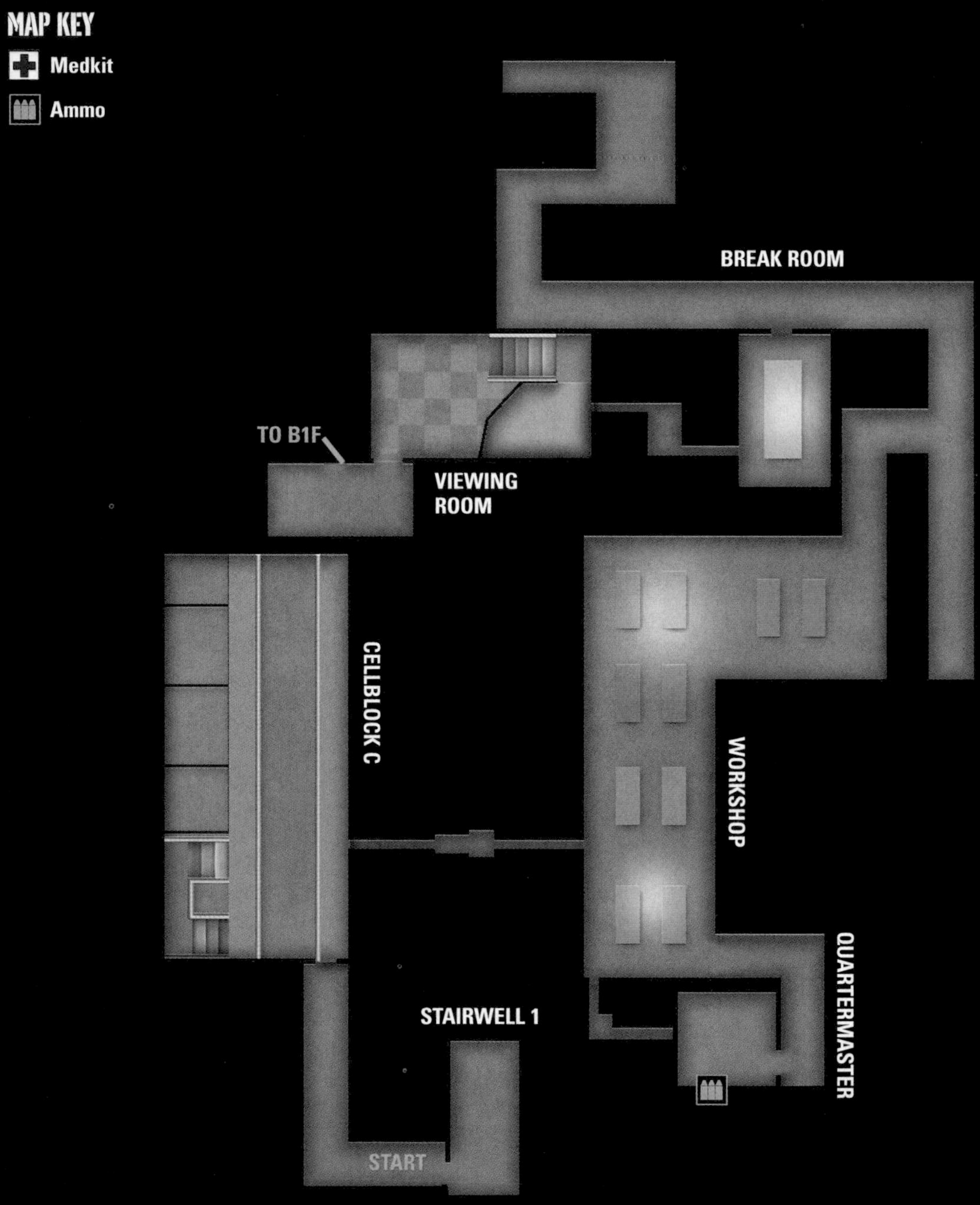

MAP KEY

Medkit

Ammo

BREAK ROOM
TO B1F
VIEWING ROOM
CELLBLOCK C
WORKSHOP
QUARTERMASTER
STAIRWELL 1
START

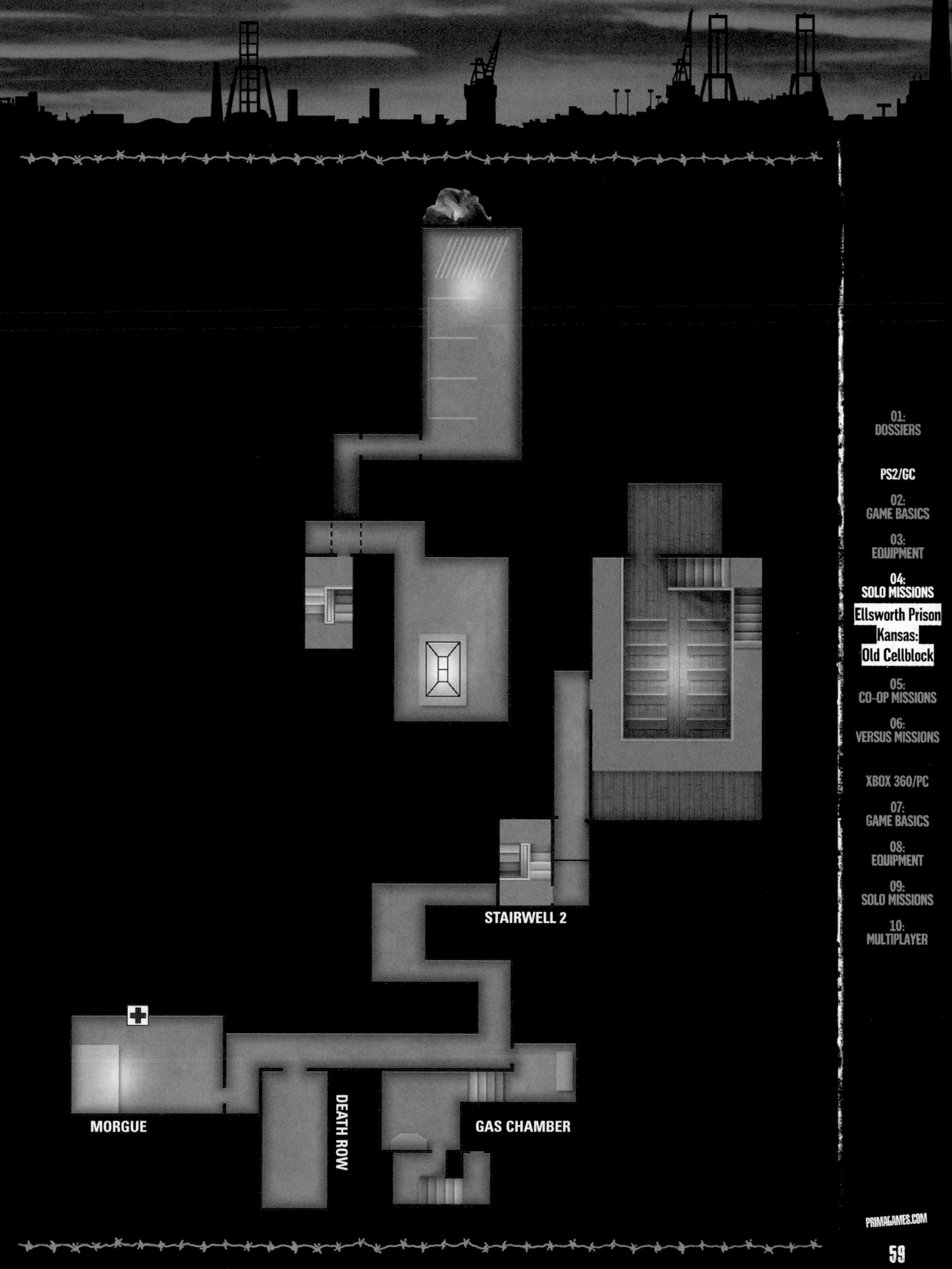
STAIRWELL 2
MORGUE
DEATH ROW
GAS CHAMBER

OBJECTIVES

PRIMARY OBJECTIVES

- > ESCAPE ELLSWORTH PRISON WITH JAMIE WASHINGTON: Your escape is being staged by Third Echelon agents. You must proceed, with Jamie Washington, to the extraction point in the garage. It is crucial that Jamie Washington does not die.
- > REGROUP WITH JAMIE WASHINGTON: You've been separated from your primary objective, Jamie Washington. It is imperative that you locate him quickly.
- > RELEASE LOCK TO GAS CHAMBER: Jamie Washington is locked in the prison's gas chamber. The chamber is most likely sealed from the viewing room upstairs.

OPPORTUNITY OBJECTIVES

- > FIND HIDDEN INFORMATION DISK: Third Echelon agents have hidden a disk containing information about Jamie Washington that might prove useful later on.

Jamie Washington has disappeared. His death would seriously compromise the mission. You must find him, and soon. Once Sam locates Jamie, the two must make their way toward the prison's exterior.

Stairwell 1

Move through the passage. Jamie radios in that he's been captured by other inmates and taken to the Gas Chamber. Sam must reunite with Jamie.

Allow Jamie to finish speaking so that you may proceed in silence.

Cellblock C

A guard patrols the bright central area. Upon entering, move to the left through the shadowed area by the wall. Find an object lying on the floor at the foot of the staircase. Wait for the ground floor guard to patrol near the stairs, and throw the object into the dark corner under the staircase. As the guard moves into the shadows to investigate the noise, sneak up behind him and knock him out.

Find an object at the base of the stairs. Wait until the ground floor guard reaches the position shown here, then throw the object at the wall under the stairs.

Flank the guard as he moves to investigate. Grab him and quietly strangle him unconscious by pressing the Nonlethal Attack button.

Ascend the stairs in the corner near the entrance and find the pipe near the top level. Climb the pipe to the ceiling, and then travel hand over hand across the cellblock to the opposite wall. Stop at the zigzag in the pipe so you can see the area.

As you cross the pipe's horizontal section, pull Sam's legs up so the upper-level guard doesn't detect you.

Survey the upper level. If the guard patrolling there is facing away from Sam's position, climb down the pipe and enter the crawlspace located directly next to the pipe. Conversely, if the guard is moving directly under Sam, drop on him and knock him out.

If possible, drop from the pipe onto the guard to knock him out.

The crawlspace entrance is beside the pipe's ending point.

Climb through the crawlspace. (You may need to stand upright to be able to enter the crawlspace.) Follow the crawlspace into an opening. Climb or slide down the ladder, and then search the opposite wall to find another crawlspace. Follow this into the Workshop.

Climb down the ladder, then turn around to find the crawlspace into the Workshop.

Workshop

Pick up the carving knife from the stool to the right of the spot where Sam drops out of the crawlspace.

Two guards patrol the Workshop. One guard stops near the crawlspace exit with his back to Sam. That guard is no problem to take down, but he patrols brightly lit areas. Therefore, deal with the other guard first. Follow him along his darkened path until you can overtake him, grab him, and knock him out.

Follow and overcome the guard patrolling the dark area to the left, then come back later to knock out the guard standing near the center.

At this point, tangling with the other guard is optional. If you prefer to be safe and cover all your bases, then sneak back to the area's center. Wait until the guard patrolling the bright areas returns to the center and stops with his back to Sam. Knock him out.

01: DOSSIERS
PS2/GC
02: GAME BASICS
03: EQUIPMENT
04: SOLO MISSIONS
Ellsworth Prison Kansas: Old Cellblock
05: CO-OP MISSIONS
06: VERSUS MISSIONS
XBOX 360/PC
07: GAME BASICS
08: EQUIPMENT
09: SOLO MISSIONS
10: MULTIPLAYER

Wait until the guard patrolling the lighted areas stops with his back to the shadows near the center, then sneak up on him.

Quartermaster

A metal detector guards the doorway nearby. Even if Sam has only the lock pick, he will set off the detector while trying to go through. This only alerts the guards inside the Workshop, so if you have taken them down already, there are no worries. You may proceed to the Quartermaster area; inside the office lies pistol ammo and a computer. Contact the NSA if necessary to dissuade their fears about the mission, or simply read the e-mail stored on the machine.

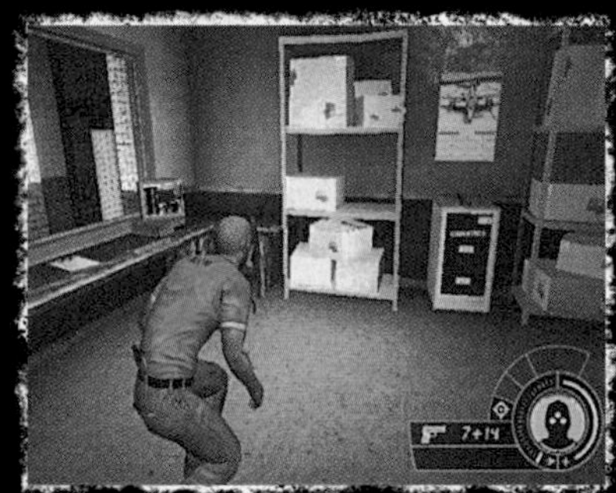

Pistol ammo is available in the Quartermaster room.

Go to the Workshop's opposite end. Another metal detector bars this doorway. If you have already taken out the guards, simply go through without worrying about the buzzer. But if guards remain in the Workshop, climb over the metal detector by using the yellow pipe mounted on the wall to the right.

If guards still patrol the Workshop, use the yellow pipe to climb over the metal detector.

Break Room

Follow the corridor, and go through the first door on Sam's left into the Break Room. At the back of the Break Room is an open vent. Enter the crawlspace and creep through. (You may need to stand upright in order to enter the crawlspace.)

Go through the open vent in the Break Room rather than face possible discovery in the corridor.

Viewing Room

Stop at the crawlspace's exit, but do not emerge just yet. Two guards chitchat just outside the security booth. Wait until their conversation ends and one guard moves back inside the booth. Exit the crawlspace, sneak up on him, and grab him. Drag him into the corner near the crawlspace entrance and interrogate him. Then knock him out and press the red button on the panel to unseal the gas chamber's magnetic lock.

Grab and knock out the guard in the control booth. Press the red button on the panel to unlock the gas chamber.

The guard patrolling the corridor outside the audience chamber can see through the window in the door. The safest bet is to open the OPSAT and look at the map. Make sure the guard is not right outside the door or moving toward you. If the coast is clear, head to the exit at the bottom of the audience chamber.

Use the lock pick to open the door at the bottom of the viewing room.

Gas Chamber

Pick the door's lock, then enter the short passage and descend the stairs. Quietly approach the doorway leading into the Gas Chamber. A single guard is posted inside the area. While he is distracted by taunting Jamie, sneak through the doorway and move up to his side. Use a Nonlethal Attack to knock him out.

Stay outside the Gas Chamber until the guard starts jeering at Jamie. Then slip inside and knock the guy out.

Turn the valve on the side of the gas chamber to free Jamie. He is greatly appreciative.

After freeing Jamie, descend the stairs and check the computer on the desk for a vital e-mail. If you have recently angered the NSA to the point where Sam needs to check in, then use the computer on the desk before time expires. You can read another e-mail on the computer as well.

Use the computer in the lower portion of the Gas Chamber as needed.

NOTE

There are two paths to the Chapel, Sam and Jamie's next destination. If you want to take the alternate route (although this is not recommended), return to the top of the Viewing Room and wait for the guard to pass in the corridor outside. Enter the passage, sneak up behind him, and knock him out. Then move past Security Booth D to the stairwell. First go downstairs and procure the information disk in the Morgue, then return to the stairwell and ascend to the top level. The guard in the Death Row corridor proves tricky to overcome when entering from the stairwell, so this is not a recommended route.

Death Row

Move to the left side of the door leading to the corridor and crouch. Rotate the camera angle using the right analog stick to see down the corridor beyond the door. Soon a guard emerges from the Morgue at the corridor's opposite end. When he follows the passage to the right, open the door and sneak up on him. He stops at the corner, where you can easily get the drop on him.

Stay inside the door and wait for the guard in the corridor to appear and move off to the right. Then enter the hallway and go after him.

Head down the passage in the direction the guard came from. Go past the Death Row area to the Morgue.

Morgue

At the back of the Morgue is an open body drawer. The information disk regarding Jamie Washington lies on the rack of the open drawer. Use the medkit in the room if needed and exit.

Find the information disk in the open body drawer to score points with the NSA.

Stairwell 2

Return down the passage toward the Gas Chamber, and follow the corridor to the left until you reach the stairwell door. Ascend the steps to the top level.

Open the door at the stairs' top, and give Jamie a boost over the gate barring the corridor. Jamie then uses the control panel to open the gate for you. Follow Jamie toward the Chapel.

Perform a Boost Over to help Jamie reach the gate control panel on the bars' other side.

Ellsworth Prison, Kansas: Chapel

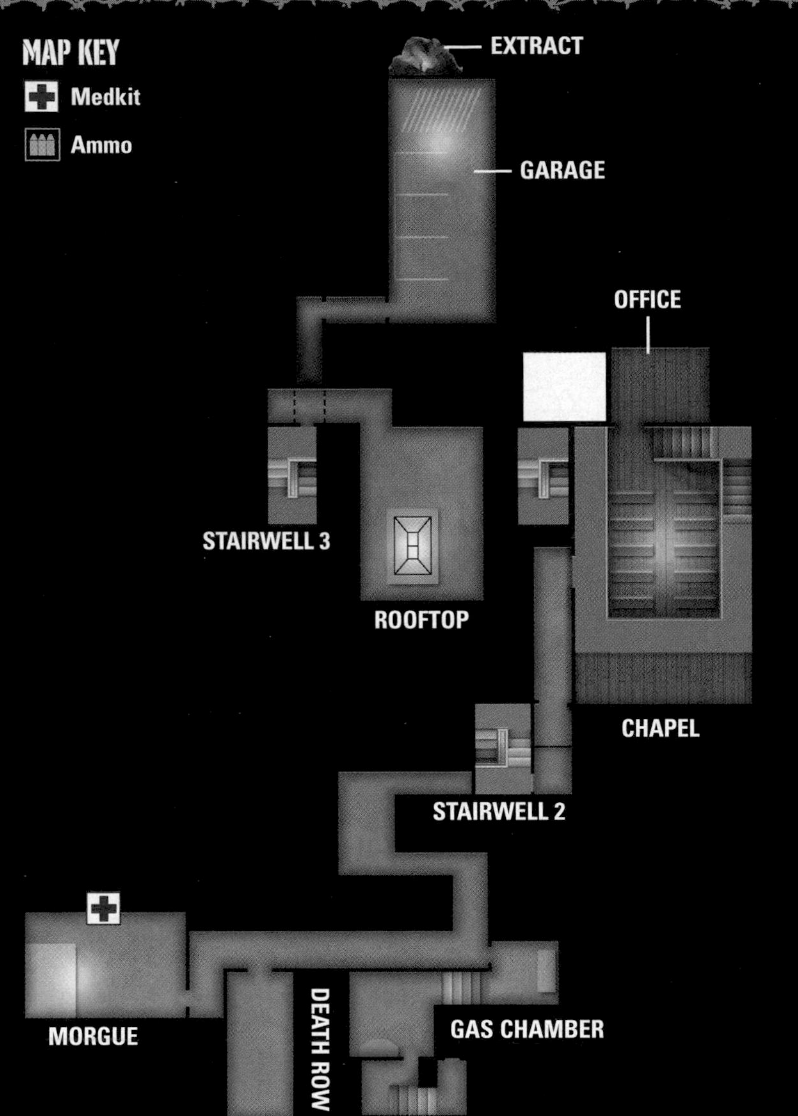

OBJECTIVES

PRIMARY OBJECTIVES

> ESCAPE ELLSWORTH PRISON WITH JAMIE WASHINGTON: Your escape is being staged by Third Echelon agents. You must proceed, with Jamie Washington, to the extraction point in the garage. It is crucial that Jamie Washington does not die.

OPPORTUNITY OBJECTIVES

> ALTER DEATH RECORDS: Find out where the death records are held and add Jamie's and your own.

A breach in the prison's outer wall has been created for your escape. You can reach it through the parking garage.

Chapel

Head down the passage until you reach a set of double doors. When Jamie finishes speaking, enter the Chapel. Move to Sam's left and stay within the shadowed area while the two guards patrolling the Chapel approach. One guard typically enters the door beneath the rear balcony while the other man turns and patrols the aisle between the office door and the top pew. Follow the officer down the aisle, grab him, and drag him into the corner to the door's left. Knock him out.

Stay in the shadows near the entrance, then follow the guard who moves down the aisle behind the pews. Grab him and knock him out.

Move to the door's left side. Stay back far enough that the guard inside the office can open the door. Wait for the other guard to emerge from the office. Follow him and take him down.

Wait for the other guard to emerge from the office, then knock him out and hide the body.

Use the computer in the chaplain's office to upload the fake death records for Sam and Jamie.

After faking Sam and Jamie's death records in the office, slip back out and turn toward the stairs. Move to the uppermost balcony. Climb up the first yellow pipe, then use the horizontal pipe to shimmy across the ceiling to the Chapel's opposite side. Drop onto the detached balcony.

Use the pipe that crosses the ceiling to reach the detached balcony.

A rope is tied to the rail's center. Detach the rope. Climb over the rail and drop to the ground. Climb up the rope through the shattered skylight.

Detach the rope from the balcony, then drop to the ground and climb the rope through the broken skylight.

Rooftop

On the Rooftop, a lone guard moves away from Sam's position. Move through the shadows along the wall to Sam's right. Move to the corner and wait for the guard to return to the area. As he heads back to the shattered skylight, grab him from behind and interrogate him. Knock him out.

If the Rooftop guard makes it to the corner near the exit, wait for him to return to ensure a grab.

Stairwell 3

Break the lock on the door to Stairwell 3, and descend to the level below. Open the door connecting to the Chapel, where Jamie waits. He follows you down the stairs to the bottom level.

Open the door on the second level to allow Jamie to enter the stairwell.

Garage

Proceed through the short passage and enter the Garage. Ignore the helicopter circling overhead, and move toward the back of the area. Initiate a Dynamic Hoist to enter the opening high up on the wall. To avoid falling damage, carefully drop down the narrow ledges outside the wall. With Jamie in tow, move across the exposed pipe toward the ladder to complete the mission.

Use co-op teamwork to reach the hole located high up in the Garage wall.

Carefully drop down the steep series of ledges to avoid damage. Head for the ladder in the background to escape Ellsworth Prison.

NOTE

Completion of the Ellsworth Prison mission unlocks the Ship bonus level in the PlayStation2 version. To play the bonus level, save your progress, then return to the Solo menu. Select "Load Game," then choose the Ship stage from the Bonus Levels menu.

JBA Headquarters: Part One

MAP KEY

Medkit

Ammo

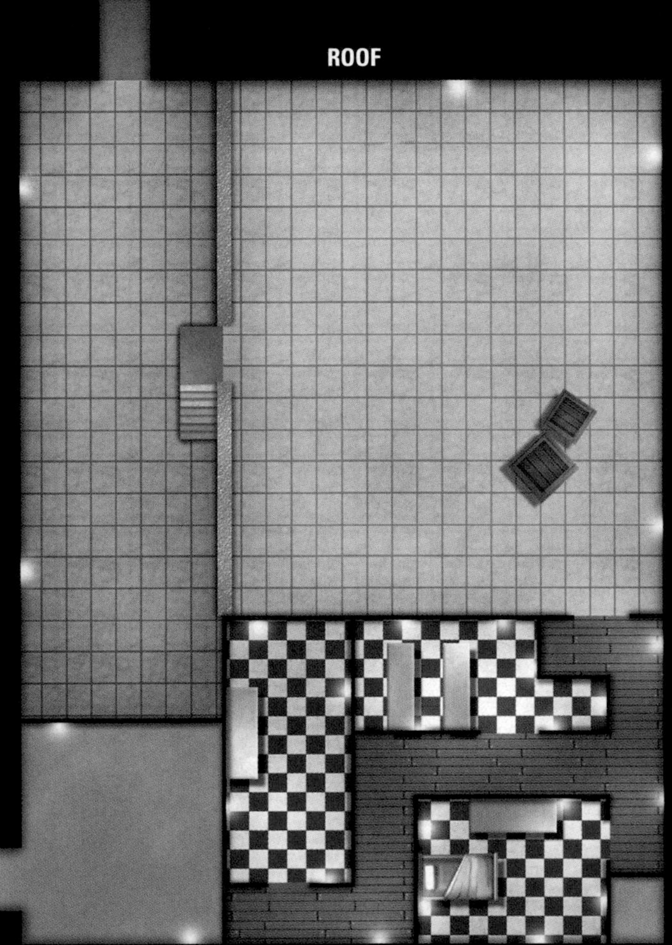

LOADOUT: JBA HQ 1 MISSION

JBA	NEUTRAL	NSA
SC-303 compact launcher	SC-303 compact launcher	SC-303 compact launcher
Rubber ammo / 10	Rubber ammo / 16	Rubber ammo / 24
Tranquilizer ammo / 1	Tranquilizer ammo / 2	Tranquilizer ammo / 4
Sticky cameras / 2	Sticky cameras / 3	Sticky cameras / 4
— —	Smoke grenades / 1	Smoke grenades / 1
— —	— —	Flashbang grenades / 1
Fingerprint scanner	Fingerprint scanner	Fingerprint scanner

OBJECTIVES

PRIMARY OBJECTIVES

> ADJUST FOUR FUSE BOXES: Circumvent the JBA's jamming by limiting electricity input at four fuse boxes—on the roof, near the entrance, in the warehouse, and on the docks. Use your mini-map to see their location.

> Find the JBA's server, then access it to open up a connection directly to Third Echelon.

> Return to public area.

OPPOSING OBJECTIVES

> SEND INFO TO LAMBERT ABOUT COLE YEAGHER: Lambert wants to know what Yeagher's plans are regarding Emile. They might prove useful to Third Echelon.

> SEND INFO TO EMILE ABOUT COLE YEAGHER: Emile Dufraisne suspects one of his men of plotting behind his back. Sending him info confirming his suspicions could increase Emile's trust.

OPPORTUNITY OBJECTIVES

> SCAN ENRICA'S FINGERPRINTS: Using your inventory's fingerprint scanner, locate and scan a set of fingerprints belonging to Enrica Villablanca, the JBA's weapons expert.

> PLANT FALSE INFORMATION ON CARSON MOSS'S COMPUTER: Plant false information propping up your cover on Carson Moss's computer. Moss is head of security and in charge of background checks.

Following the escape from Ellsworth Prison, Sam and Jamie traveled to New Orleans and rendezvoused with Emile Dufraisne and the JBA (John Brown's Army). Sam has been accepted into the terrorist organization, but the members remain skeptical of him.

When several JBA members leave the compound to run errands, Sam must utilize the opportunity to contact Lambert, gather intelligence on the JBA, and disable their scrambling devices. Lambert also wants Sam to patch a relay directly into the JBA's server. All of this must be accomplished without killing any of the JBA's members, or Sam's cover might be blown.

Alley

Head down the alley and enter the door on Sam's right. Adjust the first fuse box to reduce the jamming signal in the area. Sam's night vision, EMF, and thermal vision all suffer from electronic interference until he adjusts all four fuse boxes in the complex.

Sam's main objective is to locate and adjust four fuse boxes situated throughout the compound.

1. Press the Equip button to activate the ultraviolet flashlight.
2. Aim the fingerprint scanner at the center of the workbench to illuminate a set of prints.
3. When the fingerprints are revealed, the Scan Fingerprints interaction option appears in the screen's upper-right corner. Press the Interact button to scan the prints located in the bench's center.
4. Successfully scanning Yeagher's fingerprints adds his information to the Profile menu on Sam's OPSAT.

Continue around the corner. Head over to the workbench and use the fingerprint scanner to locate and scan Cole Yeagher's fingerprints, as follows:

Shine the fingerprint scanner on surfaces to reveal hidden fingerprints, then press the Interact button to scan and identify them.

Loading Bay

Follow the corridor past the pallet stacked with goods. Open one of the double doors and slip into the Loading Bay proper. Notice the surveillance camera directly over the door. Sam will be discovered if he moves too far into the Loading Bay. Set up a trap for local hostiles by opening both doors, then move a few steps back into the corridor.

Open the doors to the Loading Bay and stand back. Wait for flies to wander into your trap.

Meanwhile, two goons should be finishing up a short chat in the vicinity. Soon, one of the men comes around the corner and usually stops in front of the doors. If the doors are open, he moves in to investigate. He typically stops near the door and turns his back to the corridor. Grab him, pull him back into the corridor, and interrogate him. Knock him out when through.

The second guard patrols near the double doors on the lower level, so set the same trap for him. Knock him out and leave his body in the corridor as well.

The open doors lure one man and then the other into Sam's capable hands.

Equip the SC-303 and knock out the surveillance camera over the door. Move quietly up the metal stairs to the second level, and pause outside the doorway. JBA security chief Carson Moss paces around inside his office. Wait until he sits down at his desk or goes to the back corner, then sneak up behind him and grab him. Interrogate Moss for some laughs and knock him out.

Wait until Moss is seated at the computer desk or standing in the corner as shown. Then sneak in and grab him.

One e-mail on Moss's laptop reveals that the thug had been checking out Enrica's background. Choose the Security Access option to hack the device and plant Sam's false cover information.

Hack Moss's laptop to plant Sam's false cover information, increasing the JBA's trust level.

If necessary, use the medkit located in the corner of Moss's office. As you exit the office, use the fingerprint scanner on the rail next to the doorway to find Moss's fingerprints; scan them to obtain his profile.

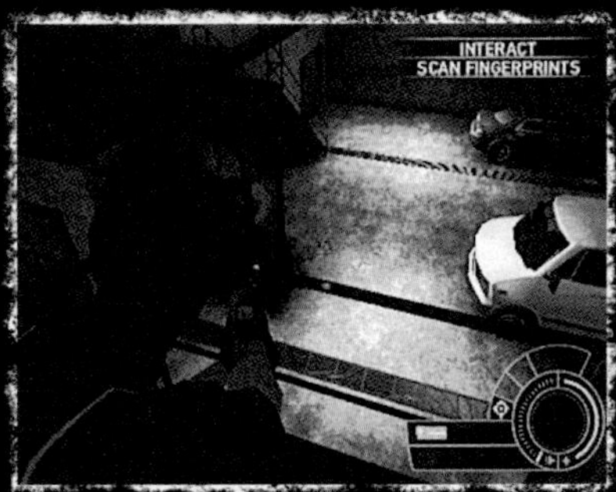

Download Moss's profile by scanning his fingerprints on the rail outside his office.

Follow the upper-level catwalk to the stairs at the north end of the Loading Bay. Stop at the top of the stairs and use the SC-303's OCP to knock out the surveillance camera above the doors. Exit to the Warehouse corridor.

Knock out the security camera over the door from above, then drop down and exit.

Move down the corridor's right-hand side, and use the OCP and EMF vision to help knock out the surveillance camera positioned a few feet from the corner. Go around the corner and move through the open door on Sam's right.

Use EMF vision to help detect the surveillance camera in the corridor beyond the Loading Bay.

Move down the passage, sticking to the left. Slowly creep under the surveillance camera, and use the OCP to knock out the laser blocking the corridor.

Follow the red brick corridor out to the Docks, using the OCP to knock out security equipment along the way.

Dock

Enter the Dock. To remain undetected in the shadows, climb over the rail rather than descend the stairs. Move across the area to the corner of a large cargo container.

Climb over the Dock's stair rail in order to remain in the shadows.

Sykes and another JBA henchman patrol the length of this area. When Sykes or the other guy moves into the shadowy area near the entrance, sneak out from behind the cargo container and grab him. Drag the victim behind the cargo container. If you've nabbed Sykes, interrogate him to learn something useful. Knock him out when done. Repeat this process with the remaining man who patrols the Docks.

Grab Sykes for a little chat, then take down the other guy as he moves into the strip of shadow lying between the entrance and the cargo container.

Adjust the fuse box at the area's west end.

Use the fingerprint scanner on the lighted side of the forklift parked near the fuse box to find and scan Jamie's fingerprints.

Warehouse

Return to the Warehouse corridor. This time, proceed toward the Warehouse. Open the right door and move through the shadows to Sam's left. Climb over the crate, and drop to the ground on the other side. Stay in this shadowed area until the guard moves past. He stops just shy of a pool of light near Sam. Sneak out and grab him. Drag him into the space between the crates for interrogation. Then knock him out.

Climbing over the crate near the entrance puts Sam in a prime position to take down the lone guard in the Warehouse.

When the guard stops near Sam's hiding spot, take him down.

Use the EEV to scan the Warehouse's north side. Scan the computer beneath the center shelves to read some e-mails.

Move through the shadows in the area's center to the back side of the center shelves, and slide to the left corner. Use the OCP to knock out the surveillance camera on the west wall, then climb the crates next to the camera. Adjust the fuse box atop the tall shelves.

Knock out the surveillance camera on the west wall before climbing the crates directly under it.

Adjust the fuse box located at the top of the shelves set against the west wall.

You can use an exit high on the south wall as a shortcut to the rooftop, but reaching it is challenging. Carefully drop from the shelves to the ground. Climb onto the crate placed at the corner, and move into the nook between the perpendicular shelves. Jump up to grab the edge of the shelves placed against the south wall. Carefully navigate over the boxes, and jump up into the exit.

Climb over crates and boxes to reach this tall vent hole above the shelves on the south wall.

Roof

Follow the tall vent into a small shack, and continue until you reach a crawlspace. Crawl through to the rooftop.

Move to the back side of the stairs. Jump and grab the top of the wall next to the stairs. Climb over.

Jump to grab the wall to the left of the stairs.

Climb over the wall and grab the lone enemy when he is near the fuse box.

One man patrols the Roof. Move to the satellite dish and wait for him to pass by on his way toward the stairs. When he stops near the top of the stairs, grab him, interrogate him, and knock him out. Sometimes this enemy merely stands at the fuse box, as if checking it over. If this happens, he is even easier to grab.

Adjust the fuse box on the rooftop. If you have adjusted all fuse boxes, Lambert contacts you and directs you to the server room inside the restricted area.

Adjusting the Rooftop fuse box last is easiest, since Sam can then proceed directly into the Off-limits Area without much backtracking.

Move toward the door at the back of the Rooftop, staying behind the crates to avoid the surveillance camera.

Off-Limits Area

After entering from the Rooftop, go around the corner. Press Sam's shoulder against the wall and move to the edge. If the guard turns the corner, he typically goes into Emile's room. Follow him inside and take him down there. If he goes around the corner toward the Rooftop, follow him and knock him out while he opens the door.

Follow the guard into Emile's room or out to the Rooftop before attempting to overtake him.

Enter the door marked "Emile." Use the fingerprint scanner to locate and verify Emile's prints on his laptop. Then use your EEV to view his e-mails.

Scan Emile's laptop with the fingerprint scanner to find his prints, then read his e-mails. There's no privacy with Sam around.

Return to the corridor and move down the passage. The server room is on Sam's right, but ignore it for now. Use the OCP to disable the surveillance camera, and go around the corner. Use the OCP again to disable the laser trip wire in the corridor. Go around the next corner and enter the door marked "Enrica."

Use the OCP to disable the security devices in the corridor.

Use the fingerprint scanner to detect and analyze BJ Sykes's fingerprints near the radio. Then scan Enrica's fingerprints off the laptop in the room. Use the EEV to view the e-mails on Enrica's laptop. In the process, you learn that Enrica has a crush on Sam and that Jamie Washington has a pacemaker.

BJ Sykes's fingerprints are located near the radio on the desk in Enrica's room.

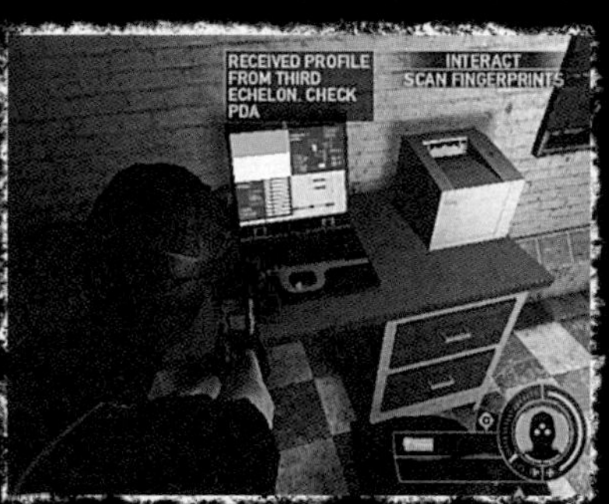

Scan Enrica's laptop to find her fingerprints and a somewhat humbling e-mail.

Return to the corridor, and use the OCP to knock out the laser trip wire and the surveillance camera again. Move down the passage and enter the server room. Use the OCP to knock out the two trip wires, and stop near the server access point. Avoid moving near the windows, or the surveillance camera outside might detect you.

Knock out the laser trip wires in the server room with the SC pistol's OCP.

Use the computer to open the connection to Third Echelon. Before exiting, hack the security access to open an e-mail from Yeagher to Massoud, which exposes Yeagher's intentions.

Upon exiting the computer's menu, you must make an important choice. The e-mail from Yeagher to Massoud must be sent to either Emile or Lambert. If Lambert gets the message, the NSA then extracts Yeagher and their trust in Sam is raised. If Sam passes the info along to Emile, then Yeagher is a dead man. However, Emile's confidence in Sam rises.

Yeagher's fate hinges on another of Sam's choices. Sometimes being a double agent is unsettling.

Return to the Alley. The shortest route is to go back to the Rooftop, then climb down the ladder to the Alley. Move onto the porch near the underground bunker entrance to extract. Remember to take out all laser trip wires along the way. Sam can exit the server room door without the surveillance camera in the hallway detecting him.

Return to the Alley and move toward the bunker door for extraction.

New York Underground: Bank Station (A)

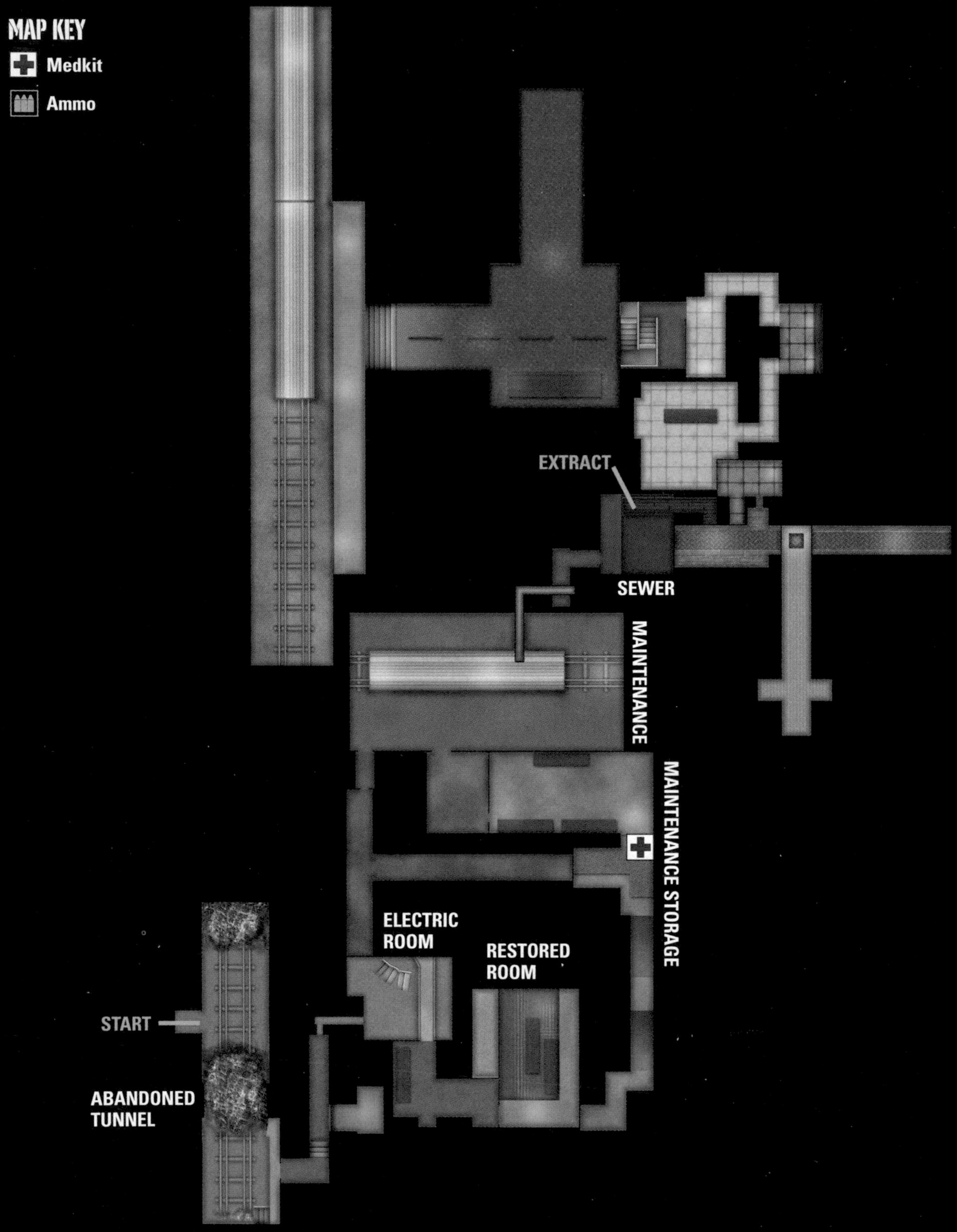

OBJECTIVES

PRIMARY OBJECTIVES

> GET THE VAULT'S CODE: The code to the armored train's vault is in the possession of the station chief. Get to him. Get the code.

LOADOUT: NEW YORK UNDERGROUND MISSION

JBA	NEUTRAL	NSA
SC-20K/90	SC-20K/60	SC-20K/30
SC pistol/60	SC pistol/40	SC pistol/20
Sticky shockers/2	Sticky shockers/4	Sticky shockers/6
Ring airfoils/2	Ring airfoils/4	Ring airfoils/8

Abandoned Tunnel

After Sam and Enrica converse, exit the small room and head toward the rubble to Sam's right. Initiate a Dynamic Hoist with Enrica. Cross the raised area and drop carefully from the other end, grabbing the ledge to avoid falling damage.

Work with Enrica to get past the rubble blocking the tunnel.

Go through the door on the platform and continue into the next passage. Stop and wait in front of a construction area blocked by red mesh for Enrica to catch up.

After you have a conversation with Enrica, initiate a Boost Over to get over the mesh blockade. Enrica moves to a control panel at the back of her area and turns off the fan spinning at the passage's end. Crawl into the vent duct behind the fan.

Boost Enrica over the mesh blocking the construction area.

Wait near the fan at the passage's end until Enrica switches it off. Then enter the crawlspace.

Electric Room

Crawl through the small vent, which leads to a room; notice a man in here. Drop from the vent duct and remain still until the electrician heads into the lighted area to Sam's left; then quietly sneak up behind him. Drag him into the nearby corner and put his lights out.

Wait for the electrician to pass to Sam's left and stop. Grab him while he talks to himself.

Instead of going through the well-lit lower corridor, look for a break in the rail on the catwalk overhead. Climb onto a fallen vent duct; from there, jump and grab the catwalk's lower edge. Pull yourself up and go through the nearby door.

You can also reach the catwalk by moving to the opposite wall, climbing up the pipe, and shimmying over to the rail. The pipe stops just short of the platform, so drop and catch the rail's bottom. Pull yourself up onto the catwalk.

Use your chosen route to climb onto the overhead catwalk.

Restored Room

Head through the ruined office and open the door. Close the door and quickly move to the platform's other side. Sam overlooks a larger room. One guard patrols the area while a welder works on the circuitry panel directly below Sam's emergence point. Carefully navigate the planks that connect across the top of the lower room.

Carefully cross the planks running over the open space below.

Follow the planks over to the center scaffold. Stay atop the scaffold until the patrolling guard is looking away from you. Then drop down a level, and drop again to the floor. Move into the shadows opposite the scaffold.

Follow the planks to the center scaffold, and drop to the ground on the far side.

Wait for the patrolling security guard to move near you and turn his back, facing the welder. Grab him, drag him into the dark, and knock him out. The welder should not notice if Sam sneaks quietly through the room to the exit.

The security guard in the Restored Room patrols a wide-sweeping and variable route, so stay in the shadows until he moves past, then knock him out.

Maintenance Storage

Proceed into the stairwell. A guard walks down the shadowy stairs and talks with a buddy near the fence. While they converse, move to the pipe fastened to the wall at the top of the stairs. Climb to the pipe's top and shimmy across its horizontal length.

Climb the pipe at the corner, then shimmy across the horizontal pipe fastened to the ceiling.

Continue until Sam automatically slides down the passage.

When Sam reaches the slope in the pipe, he automatically zip-lines down. Leaping the gap, he grabs hold of another horizontal pipe. Climb down this pipe to where it curves under the lower level's ceiling; continue moving hand over hand along the pipe as it leads into the area beyond the fence. Press the Jump button to pull up Sam's legs as you move through tighter territory.

Continue using the horizontal ceiling pipe to move past two station workers as they converse below.

Drop on top of the shelves where the pipe ends. Wait until the mechanic in the room below goes through the double doors, then drop to the ground and follow him.

Follow the shelves until they end, then drop to the floor and follow the mechanic through the double doors.

Maintenance

Move through the short passage, and use the optic cable to view the scene in the next room. Soon, a guard stops a few feet in front of the door, with his back turned. Open the door, grab him, drag him backward into the corridor, and knock him out.

Use the optic cable or thermal vision to determine when the guard in the next room stops in front of the door. Then go get him.

Wait until the mechanic climbs the stairs and begins welding on the train car. While he works, move from the entrance to your left, around the workbench, and to the back of the train car.

Jump to grab the car's back platform, and pull yourself up. Then jump to grab the car's top, and climb onto the roof.

Jump to grab the train car's back platform. Climb to the car's roof.

Sneak down the length of the train car's top. A vent opens to Sam's left. Enter the crawlspace. Crawl through and drop down into the corridor beyond the Maintenance room.

Enter the open vent above the train car. Crawl through and drop down into the passage beyond the Maintenance area.

Sewer

Move to the left along the rail to an opening, and rappel down the wall. Press the Jump button and tilt the left analog stick down to rappel more quickly.

Rappel down the wall toward the pipes at the bottom.

New York Underground: Bank Station (B)

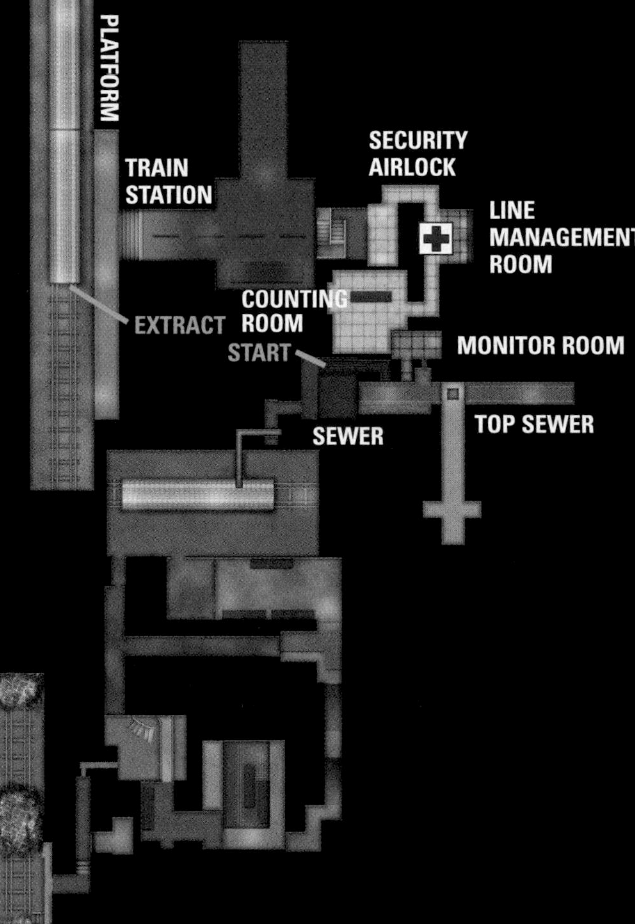

OBJECTIVES

PRIMARY OBJECTIVES

- GET THE VAULT'S CODE: The code to the armored train's vault is in the possession of the station chief. Get to him. Get the code.
- GET TO FRONT OF TRAIN: Reach the front of the train and take control of it.

OPPORTUNITY OBJECTIVES

- LEAVE STATION CHIEF ALIVE: During this mission, innocent lives must be spared. Killing the bank's personnel simply to please Emile cannot be allowed by Third Echelon.
- KILL STATION CHIEF: As a proof of loyalty, Emile has ordered you to kill the station chief after you've gotten the train vault's code from him.

Having penetrated the sewer system running between the dilapidated building and the bank, Sam is now ready to enter the facility and commence with the robbery. He must nab and coerce the station chief to obtain info. Then Sam must board the rear car of the underground money train.

Sewer

Sam stands on a cluster of pipes. Move forward and enter the crawlspace.

Emerging from the crawlspace, head down the drainage tunnel into the lighted area. Grab the reddish pipe on your right and climb to the level above.

Climb the red pipe to exit the Sewer.

Top Sewer

At the top, look for an extremely thin crevice on Sam's right. Despite the crevice's narrow appearance, Sam can slide through it into the next passage.

Slip through the crevice to continue.

Ignore the surveillance camera overhead, as Enrica has fed the system a twenty-second loop of clear video. Move to the right and enter the low crawlspace.

Find the low crawlspace in the corner.

Monitor Room

Two guards chat in the Monitor Room. Stay inside the crawlspace until one guard leaves. You must move quickly to neutralize the guard who remains in the Monitor Room before he notices that his buddy does not appear onscreen. While one guard walks out, emerge from the crawlspace and grab the remaining guard. Drag him into the dark area to the door's left and knock him out.

Stay in the crawlspace until one guard starts to exit the room...

...then exit the crawlspace and grab the remaining guard. Drag him into the passage to the door's left for disposal.

The other guard moves into the Counting Room and momentarily stares at a stack of money. Then he returns to the Monitor Room. Wait in the area's dark side until the guard enters and stops in the Monitor Room's center. Then go grab him. Drag him into the dark area and knock him unconscious. Close the door to the Monitor Room on your way out.

Wait until the other guard tours the Counting Room and returns, then grab him. Stow him with his buddy.

Counting Room

Return to the Counting Room and move into the short passage toward the Line Management Room door. Enrica spots oncoming trouble on the monitor, so retreat out of the passage and move to the Line Management Room door's left side.

After Enrica warns you of impending discovery, retreat from the Line Management Room corridor and hide at the corner just inside the Counting Room. Wait for a guard to emerge from the corridor.

Soon, a guard emerges from the Line Management Room. He heads directly for the Monitor Room. Pursue him toward the Monitor Room door, grab him, and knock him out. Otherwise, he might enter the security station and use his flashlight to discover any bodies tucked therein.

Grab the guard and knock him out; he drops a keycard.

If the guard dropped a keycard when you knocked him out, you may use it on the panel next to the Line Management Room door. Otherwise, you must hack it.

Use the keycard or hack the card reader to open the Line Management Room door.

Line Management Room

The station chief is typically on the room's opposite side, facing the console. Grab him before he starts to move around. Interrogate him *twice* to learn the vault code.

The station chief won't give up the goods unless you ask him twice.

NOTE

Emile orders Sam to kill the station chief, but Third Echelon has ordered Sam not to inflict casualties on this mission. You can either kill the station chief to increase trust with the JBA or merely knock him out to appease the NSA.

If necessary, use the medkit on the Line Management Room's back wall. Access the computer on the control console's left side. Read two e-mails; one contains the code to the vaulted exit from this room. If you had to knock out the station chief without a chance to interrogate him, accessing this computer reveals the vault code and fulfills the Primary Objective.

Enter the security code 2833 into the keypad next to the vault door to open it.

Access the computer in the Line Management Room for vital info, then input the security code into the vault door keypad to proceed.

Security Airlock

Proceed through the passage and around the corner. Head for the doorway, pressing your shoulder to the left wall. Stop at the doorway, and angle the camera to look into the next room. Wait until the two guards inside the room finish their conversation. One guard remains. Eventually he leans against the bars. The situation is not as dire as it appears. While the guard leans against the bars, simply sneak into the room and dash right, into the caged area. Find the crawlspace in the corner, and crawl through into the stairwell.

Wait in the corridor for the guard to lean against the bars to the right...

...then sneak past the guard into the caged area and enter the crawlspace in the corner.

If needed, use the EEV to scan the laptop under the stairs in order to check in with the NSA. There is also another e-mail of some small interest on the laptop.

A guard stands at the top of the stairs. Enter the room and move right. Find the pipe in the corner; climb it to the ceiling. Press the Jump button to pull Sam's legs up, and crawl across the ceiling until Sam hangs over the guard. Press the Interact button to grab him and knock him out. Make sure Sam does not fall over the rail in the process, or he may die.

Use the pipe in the corner to crawl up to the ceiling and position Sam over the guard near the door.

Take the guard down. Use the optic cable to scan the next room before proceeding.

Train Station

Use the optic cable on the door to determine whether the guard patrolling the Train Station is facing Sam's position. When the guard faces away, enter and head left. Hide in the dark corner behind the ticket booth and wait for the guard to pass. As he moves by, emerge from the corner, sneak up behind him, and knock him out. Alternatively, it is possible to sneak across the room's dark portion without alerting the guard. But this strategy is not nearly as easy.

Hide in the dark corner by the ticket booth and wait for the guard to approach. Then step out behind him and bash him unconscious.

Platform

Descend the stairs toward the Platform, sticking to the arched passage's left side. As you reach the stairs' bottom, a guard appears on the left. Another security guard enters from the right, and the two men speak briefly. *Do not wait* until they finish their conversation—immediately pass through the shadows behind the conductor on the left, and move to the back of the train. The money train soon departs upon its perilous course!

Money Train

OBJECTIVES

PRIMARY OBJECTIVES

- GET TO FRONT OF TRAIN: Reach the front of the train and take control of it.
- DISCONNECT COMMUNICATIONS SYSTEM: To keep the robbery a secret long enough to unload the cargo, the train communication system must be disabled. This will make the task of locating the train harder.

OPPORTUNITY OBJECTIVES

- ISOLATE REAR TRAIN CARS: The train has many bank security personnel onboard. Protect the lives of these men by uncoupling the rear train cars on your way to the train driver.

Having stolen aboard the money train, Sam must now head to the front car and take over the train. There are not many places to hide, so this may be Sam's toughest ride ever!

Rear Car

Climb the ladder to Sam's right. Remain crouched and move slowly across the train car's top. Occasionally a pipe swoops by, and Sam automatically ducks. This slows you down a bit, but it is acceptable for now. Drop into the gap between cars.

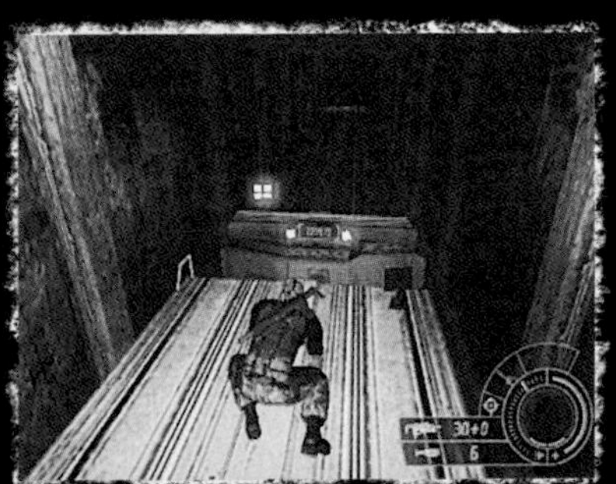

Move along the train car rooftop.

Enrica radios and instructs Sam to disconnect the communications system within eight minutes. A timer begins counting down the seconds. Sam must reach the second car and cut the communications system's wires before the timer elapses, or the mission is a bust.

Sixth Car

Open the rear door of the next train car, and close it behind you. The two guards traveling inside the car may react to Sam's entrance. If so, they both start moving toward the car's rear. Move to the car's right side, press Sam's shoulder to the wall, and allow the first guard to pass. Sneak up behind him and grab him before he opens the back door. Knock him out, and leave him in the shadows. The other guard takes a position directly under a surveillance camera. Use the SC pistol to knock out the lights, then quickly equip the SC-20K and airfoil rounds. Hit the remaining guard in the head with an airfoil round, then move forward and collect his body. Drag him to the back of the car before the light reactivates. Then use the OCP on the surveillance camera, and go to the car's front.

If the guards move to investigate Sam's entrance, stick to the wall on Sam's right and wait for the first man to pass.

Knock out the guard who moves near the door, then use the OCP on the light above the second guard.

Use an airfoil round to knock out the second guard, then move his body to the car's rear before the lights turn back on.

If the guards do not react to Sam's entrance, then sneak forward as much as possible while remaining in the shadows. Use the OCP to knock out the light overhead. This prevents both the guards and the surveillance camera from detecting Sam. Now you must move fast. Move up behind the central money carts and aim the SC pistol at the fire extinguisher between the two men. Shooting the fire extinguisher from this angle makes it release smoke, which knocks out both guys. Keep the SC pistol drawn, and use the OCP to knock out the surveillance camera behind and to Sam's left. This prevents you from being detected if the deactivated light comes back on. Quickly move to the car's front and exit.

If the guards remain seated, use the OCP on the overhead light and sneak forward.

Shoot the fire extinguisher to knock out both guards, then use the OCP on the surveillance camera to Sam's left for good measure.

Fifth Car

Close the last door behind you, and slide open the back door of the next train car. Squeeze through the narrow gap between the money carts, and crouch to walk under the first laser trip wire. Use the OCP to knock out the laser trip wire by the door, and pass into the next section.

Crouch and slip through the narrow gap between carts. Sam moves right under the two laser beams. Use the OCP on the next laser, and slide open the door.

Crouch and squeeze between the money cart and the pallets on the left. Upon emerging, use the OCP to knock out the laser trip wire that runs horizontally across the bottom of the shelves. Then move to the center of the shelves and enter the crawlspace beneath them. Crawl to the car's front, and proceed through the exit.

Use the OCP to disable the bottom laser trip wire, then enter the crawlspace beneath the shelves.

Stand on the back platform of the next train car, and detach the rear train cars. Any guards left alive in the train's rear portion now owe Sam a great deal of thanks.

Detaching the rear train cars increases the NSA's trust, but it also has other consequences....

Fourth Car

Climb the ladder up to the train car's top. If you detached the rear train cars, two guards appear on the roof, searching for the cause. Move forward as quickly as possible, past the roof's halfway point. Then move to Sam's left and drop over the car's side; Sam grabs the rail running along the side. Continue shimmying toward the car's front. Allow the two guards to pass, then climb back onto the roof. Move forward and drop between the cars before the guards notice.

Third Car

Climb the ladder to the next train car's top. Move to the car's front as quickly as possible.

If two guards patrol the train car's top, drop over the side and hang from the rail. Shimmy past the guards and climb back up to continue.

Second Car

Cargo blocks the rear door of the next car. Climb the ladder and move to the car's front, along the rooftop. Drop into the gap between cars, and enter the second car from the front door.

Cargo blocks the communications car's rear door. Enter from the front door.

For now, ignore the computer near the entrance, unless Lambert is demanding that Sam e-mail the NSA to reestablish trust. Move to the right side of the shelves blocking the car and enter the crawlspace. Drop down on the other side, and grab the guard standing nearby. Choke him unconscious to avoid alerting the other two guards.

NOTE

Clearing the Money Train mission unlocks the Bunker bonus mission! To play the bonus level, save your progress and return to the Solo menu. Select "Load Game," then choose the Ship stage from the Bonus Levels menu. This level is unique to the PlayStation2 version of the game.

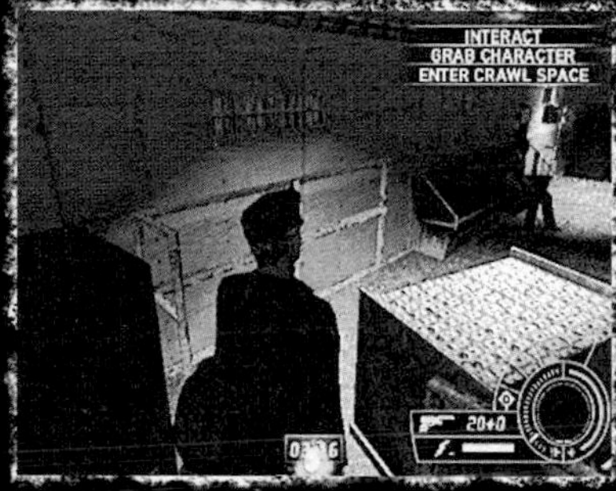

Crawl through the shelves blocking the passage and grab the nearest guard. Use a nonlethal attack on him and drop his body in the shadows.

Use the OCP to knock out the closest overhead light, then quickly equip the SC-20K, which is loaded with sticky shockers. Knock out the seated guard, then the standing guard.

Disable the overhead lights and move in close. Taser each guard with a sticky shocker before the lights come back on.

Move to the car's rear and access the panel on Sam's left. If you bypass the circuit in time, the countdown ends and the mission can continue.

To continue the mission, bypass the circuit box before the time runs out.

Return to the car's front. Use the computer to contact NSA if Williams is demanding as much. Otherwise, open the sliding doors and proceed to the front car.

Front Car

There is a slight possibility that the two guards in the engineer's car may notice Sam's entrance. If so, consider it a blessing. Move to the car's left side, crouch, and hide behind the first small cart on the left. Wait for the two guards to pass, then use the OCP to take out the closest light. Head for the front of the train and use the OCP to disable the light near the engineer's compartment. Open the sliding door to take control of the train.

If Sam's entrance draws the two guards to the back of the car, use the OCP to leave them in the dark while you race for the front.

If the guards do not approach Sam's entry point, use the OCP to knock out the closest overhead light. Move forward as far as possible, staying out of the light. Position Sam near the right-hand wall and equip the SC-20K. Zoom in on the fire extinguisher near the engineer's door. Aim for the extinguisher's bottom right corner, and tap the Fire button to release a single shot. When released from the proper height and angle, the fumes inside the extinguisher knock out both guards simultaneously. Slide open the door of the engineer compartment. Mission complete!

Without stepping into the light, move as close as possible to the two seated guards, then shoot the fire extinguisher at a low angle to knock them out.

Cozumel, Mexico: Honeymoon Cruise

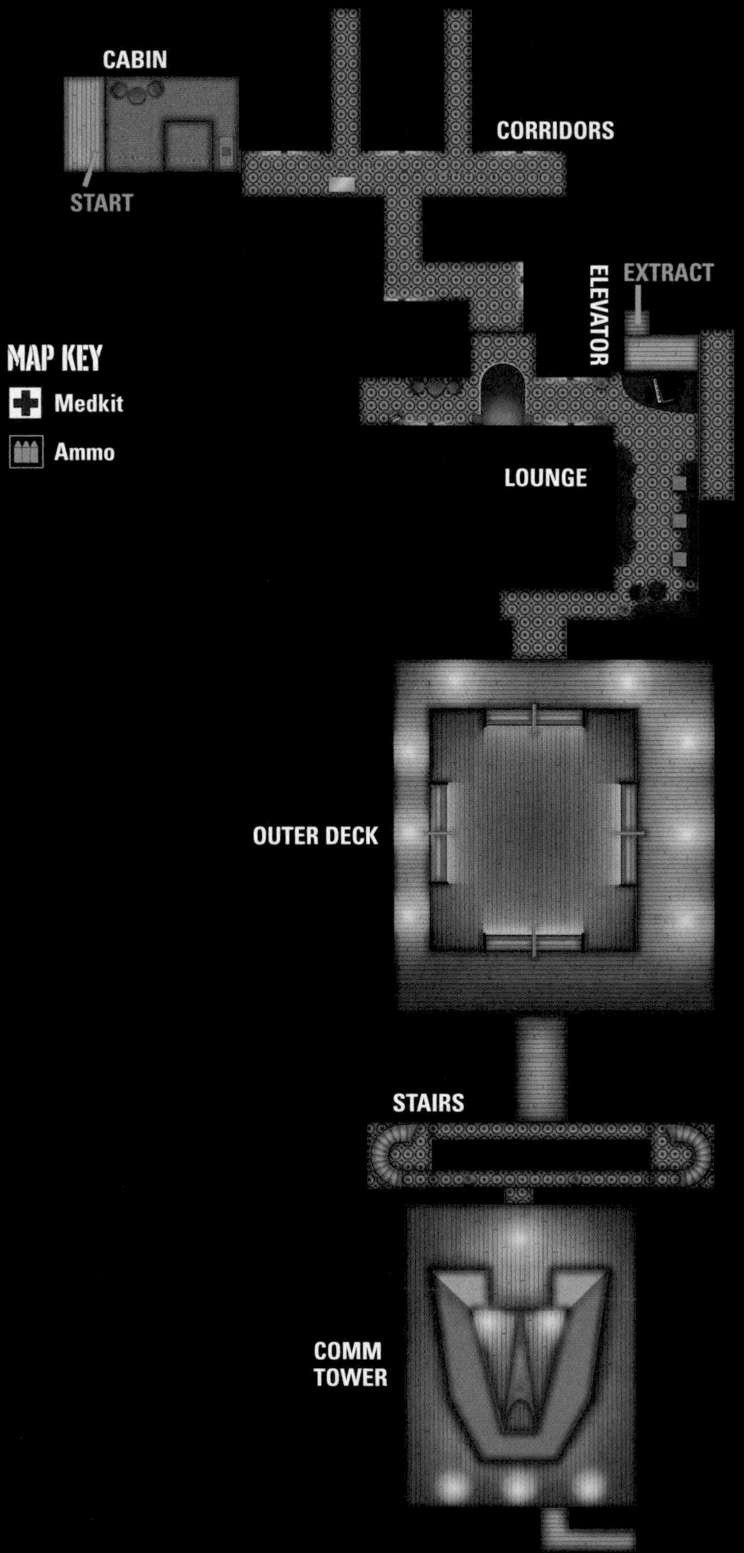

CABIN
START
CORRIDORS
EXTRACT
ELEVATOR
LOUNGE
OUTER DECK
STAIRS
COMM TOWER

MAP KEY
- Medkit
- Ammo

OBJECTIVES

PRIMARY OBJECTIVES

> HELP ENRICA INSTALL COMM RELAY: Enrica has set the bomb to be triggered via a call from her cell phone. For that call to be received, a relay must be placed on the ship. With all the police crawling around, Enrica cannot risk doing it alone.

> HELP ENRICA REACH THE COMM ROOM: For the communication relay to function, Enrica must patch it in the ship's radio console. Help Enrica reach the communications room.

> RECOVER THE BOMB: The JBA has managed to smuggle the Red Mercury device aboard by hiding it on a small service boat currently anchored in the ship's interior dock.

OPPOSING OBJECTIVES

> DISABLE ENRICA'S CELL PHONE: Enrica's cell phone is the trigger mechanism for the Red Mercury device. Plant a virus on it to scramble the ignition sequence it will send to the bomb's relay. This will prevent detonation.

> PROTECT ENRICA'S CELL PHONE: Enrica's cell phone is the trigger mechanism for the Red Mercury device. If anything happens to it, the bomb may not go off.

OPPORTUNITY OBJECTIVES

> OBTAIN PASSENGER MANIFEST: If the mission goes wrong and the boat explodes, the passenger manifest will help identify the victims.

LOADOUT: COZUMEL MISSION

JBA	NEUTRAL	NSA
SC-20K/90	SC-20K/60	SC-20K/30
SC pistol/60	SC pistol/40	SC pistol/20
Sticky shockers/2	Sticky shockers/4	Sticky shockers/6
Ring airfoils/2	Ring airfoils/4	Ring airfoils/8
EMP ammo/1	EMP ammo/2	EMP ammo/3
Sticky cameras/2	Sticky cameras/4	Sticky cameras/6
—	Gas grenades/1	Gas grenades/2
Frag grenades/2	Frag grenades/1	—
—	Smoke grenades/1	Smoke grenades/1
—	—	Flashbang grenades/2

Dufraisne finally determines what group stole the Red Mercury from Iceland, and uses the money stolen from New York to bargain with them. He has obtained a sample Red Mercury bomb and smuggled it onboard a passenger cruiser. Fisher and Enrica have stowed onboard the cruiser and have been ordered to arm and detonate the device by remote. Two thousand lives now rest in Sam's hands.

Cabin

Stay on the patio outside the cabin while Lambert briefs Sam on the mission. Soon an announcement from the marina police plays over the ship's PA system.

Enter the Cabin and move toward the front door. Press Sam's shoulder against the wall to the left and move toward the door. Use thermal vision to see the marina police in the Corridors area. As one officer approaches the door, slide back about halfway down the wall.

Hide in the shadows near the Cabin door. Wait for a guard to enter and pass, then slip out quietly.

Soon, the officer enters the Cabin and walks past Sam's position. Slip out the door while he searches the Cabin.

Corridors

A guard leans against the service cart on the corridor's right side. To slip past him, move from the Cabin door to the wall on Sam's right. Follow this wall to the service cart. Slip through the narrow gap between the cart and the wall. Upon emerging from the other side, sneak around the corner.

Bypass the guard in the Corridors by slipping behind the food cart parked in the aisle.

Follow the Corridors to the door at the end. Lambert radios in a new objective: Obtain the passenger manifest. However, that is the least of your concerns for now, as you are about to enter one of the trickiest areas of the game. Save the game now before proceeding.

Lounge

Open the door and move just beyond the doorjamb. Move right to allow the door to close behind you, but stay in the shadows. Move back in front of the door to ensure that Sam remains in shadow.

On your right, two guards finish a little chat. Directly in front of Sam is a surveillance camera. Equip the SC-20K loaded with EMP(Electromagnetic Pulse) ammunition. Use EMF vision to help you aim and fire an EMP disrupter at the surveillance camera, permanently disabling it.

Fire EMP ammo to permanently disable the surveillance camera on the wall.

This action is not without consequences. The two guards located here become suspicious and begin searching the area. The entrance is one of the first places they check, so move a few steps to the left or right. Watch the guards patrol the area back and forth at least once.

Step out of the way as the guards search for the person who disabled the camera.

Both of the guards patrol near the door, each in their turn. One stops and stares at the door for a moment, then turns around. When he turns, grab him from behind and interrogate him. Knock him out with a choke hold so as not to alert the other guard.

The guard with the assault rifle patrols everywhere, rarely stopping in any location for long. However, he sometimes makes a circle near the door. Use this opportunity to fall in line behind him, grab him, and knock him out.

Grab the guards as they patrol near the shadowy area by the entrance.

Use the EEV goggles to zoom in on the laptop on the table. Hack the security access on the laptop to obtain the passenger manifest, completing an Opportunity Objective.

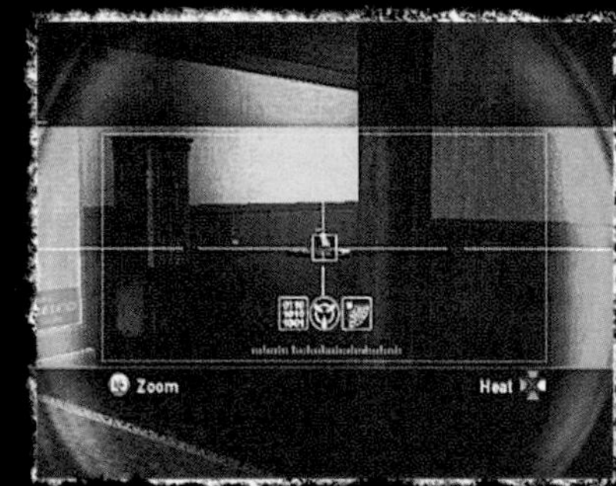

Obtain the passenger manifest from the laptop in the corner.

Head through the Lounge. Sam radios Enrica for an update along the way. The two decide to meet at the Comm Tower on the central promenade. Continue navigating toward the Outer Deck.

Outer Deck

To get through the heavily patrolled Outer Deck area, it is best not to mess with any of the guards. Instead, head left from the entrance and wait at the corner of the depression. Wait until a guard patrols the area with a flashlight, then walks away. Drop down into the lower area, and move along the left wall. Climb onto the pony wall and move across the steps' dark center portion. Jump to navigate over the stair banister blocking the path, and continue through the next dark corner. Climb onto the raised area near the exit.

Move through the shadows to avoid detection by the guards.

Move only one or two steps down the corridor leading to the Stairs. Turn the camera around to view the Outer Deck, and make sure that none of the guards are approaching or standing nearby. Then rotate the camera back, equip the SC pistol, and use the OCP to take out the light overhead. Proceed quickly into the Stairs area.

Stop just inside the exit corridor and use the OCP to knock out the light. Then exit the Outer Deck.

Stairs

Head to Sam's left and go up the darkened stairs. On the upper level, two guards stand directly beneath a surveillance camera, talking. Wait until they are done. The two men take up stationary positions on either side of the door leading to the Comm Tower area. Load the SC-20K with sticky shockers, and move as far onto the upper level as possible while remaining in the shadows. Use thermal vision to aim and fire a sticky shocker at the closest guard, then the other.

Use sticky shockers to avoid an all-out firefight against the two guards blocking the exit.

Before proceeding, hide the two guards' bodies. The best location is in the dark at the bottom of the southern spiral staircase. If you fail to hide their bodies, reinforcements may find and wake them, returning them to active duty. This would prove catastrophic to the mission! Also, remember to knock out the surveillance camera above the door each time you pass underneath.

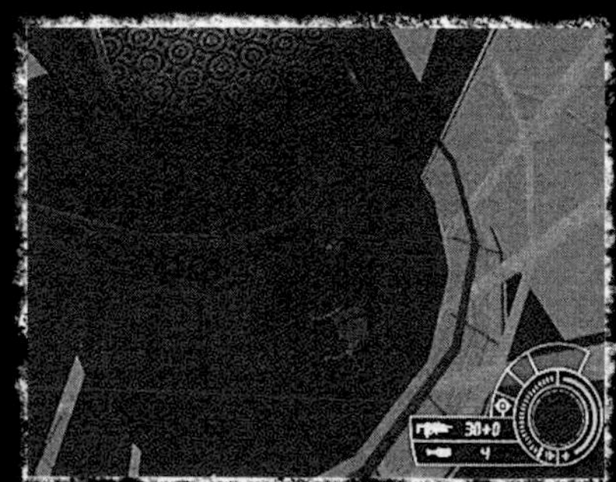

Move the guards' bodies to the bottom of the south staircase to avoid discovery.

Comm Tower

When the scene at the Stairs is set, proceed to the promenade. Enrica stands near the Comm Tower overhead. Move to the ledge underneath her, jump up to grab it, and climb to greet her.

Display your monkey-man skills by climbing up the back side of the Comm Tower to meet Enrica.

Initiate a Shoulder Climb so that Enrica can place the relay on the Comm Tower. Then follow her into the corridor at the forward part of the promenade.

Work with Enrica to place the relay on the Comm Tower uplink.

Move toward the fence in the corridor and initiate a Boost Over. Sam and Enrica separate for now, and agree to meet in the Engine Room. Sam must head back to the Lounge and use the Elevator to reach the belowdecks area.

Give Enrica a boost over the fence in the small corridor at the front of the Comm Tower area.

Three new marina police officers appear in the Stairs area. If you left the two guards previously stationed there in plain sight, these new officers find the bodies and will be alerted to foul play. But if you hid the bodies well, there should be no problem. Two of the men immediately proceed onto the promenade and start patrolling. Avoid them by moving aft along the Comm Tower's shadowed south side. Stop at the rear portion of the raised area.

Wait in the shadows for three police officers to enter the Comm Tower area before heading back through the Stairs area.

One man continues patrolling the upper Stairs area a few moments longer, then eventually heads out onto the promenade. Wait until he moves several paces away from the door, then head back inside. Upon entering the door, head left. Avoid stepping too far into the Stairs area so the still-active surveillance camera overhead doesn't detect you.

Return to the Outer Decks, moving through the shadowed areas to avoid detection. Even if Sam catches a little light and the guards do a double-take, continue moving through the area smoothly and you should avoid detection. If you previously knocked out or killed all three guards in this area, replacements appear.

Sneak back through the Outer Deck to the Lounge, moving through the shadows.

Elevator

Head through the Lounge toward the grand piano. On Sam's right is a door. Go through the door, head down the passage, and go through the double doors on Sam's left. Enrica overrides the elevator just in time.

Go through the side door in the Lounge area.

Drop onto the elevator car, and move to the rear. Open the trapdoor and drop inside the elevator. Use the control panel on the side wall to go to the ship's lower section.

Drop onto the elevator car, open the top hatch, and drop inside. Use the control panel in the car to descend.

Cozumel, Mexico: Bomb Drill

MAP KEY

Medkit

Ammo

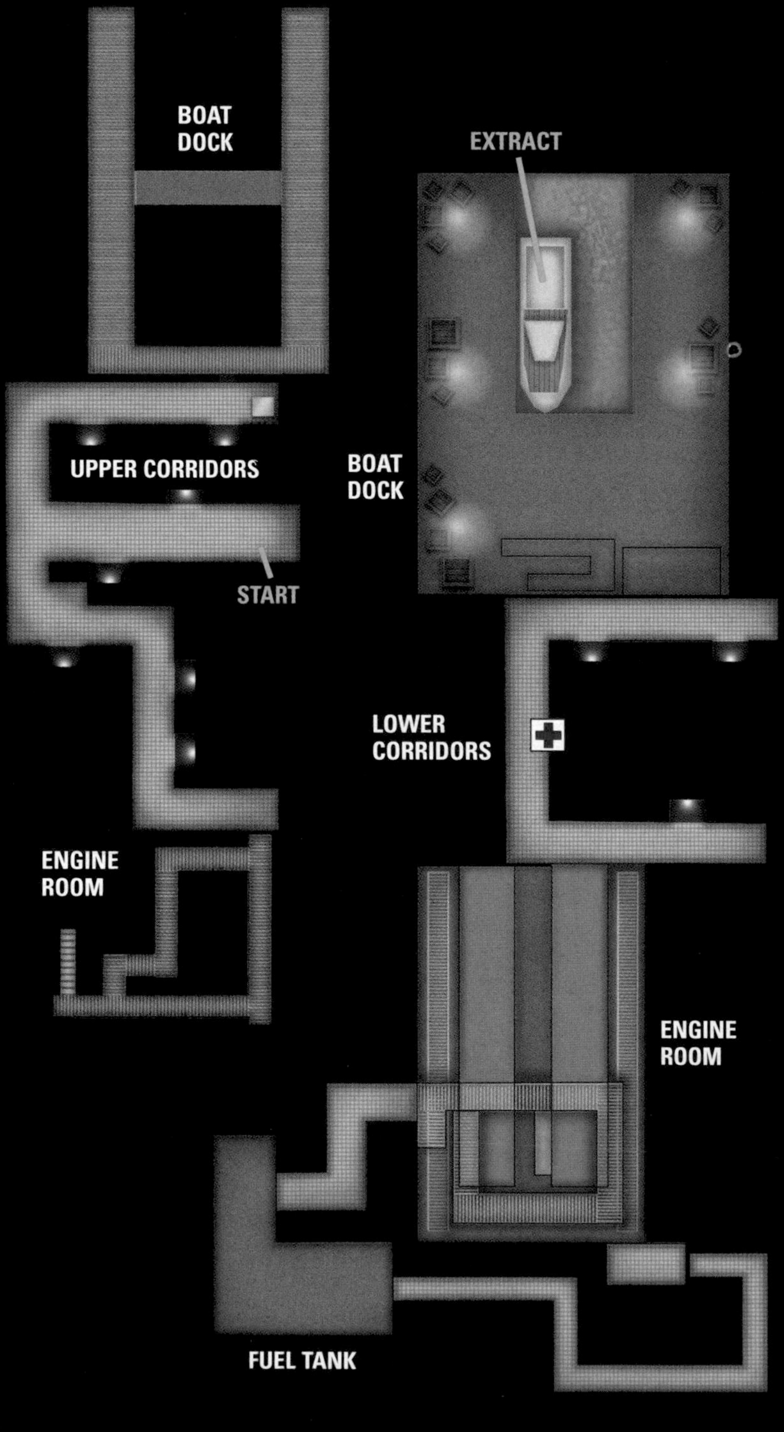

BOAT DOCK

EXTRACT

UPPER CORRIDORS

BOAT DOCK

START

LOWER CORRIDORS

ENGINE ROOM

ENGINE ROOM

FUEL TANK

OBJECTIVES

PRIMARY OBJECTIVES

> RECOVER THE BOMB: The JBA has managed to smuggle the Red Mercury device aboard by hiding it on a small service boat currently anchored in the ship's interior dock.

> DELIVER THE BOMB AND HELP ENRICA REACH THE FUEL TANK: Hand over the bomb to Enrica and then help her reach the fuel tank so she can install the bomb.

OPPOSING OBJECTIVES

> DISABLE ENRICA'S CELL PHONE: Enrica's cell phone is the trigger mechanism for the Red Mercury device. Plant a virus on it to scramble the ignition sequence it will send to the bomb's relay. This will prevent detonation.

> PROTECT ENRICA'S CELL PHONE: Enrica's cell phone is the trigger mechanism for the Red Mercury device. If anything happens to it, the bomb may not go off.

OPPORTUNITY OBJECTIVES

> DISABLE SHIP'S ENGINES: Disabling the ship's engines will prevent it from being too close to shore if it explodes. This might save thousands of lives.

> DELETE CAMERA RECORDS: Your presence on board this ship must never be known. Erase any evidence.

After completing their objectives in the passenger areas, Sam and Enrica agree to meet up in the Engine Room to set the bomb. Sam must find the bomb detonator and rendezvous with Enrica in the area behind the Engine Room. He has one opportunity to thwart mass murder. Can he do so without blowing his cover?

Upper Corridors

Move about halfway down the corridor, past the pool of light on Sam's right. Jump to grab the pipe running down the corridor's center, and pull Sam's legs up. Soon, a guard enters the corridor and moves directly under you. As he moves underneath, grab him and choke him unconscious. He moves quickly, so be ready on the Interact button.

Strike from above to take down a guard patrolling the corridor near Sam's entry point.

Head east from the intersection to the corner, and angle the camera to peek down the connecting passage. If all has gone well so far and no alarms have been triggered, a guard should be asleep in a chair. If things have not gone well up to this point, he may be patrolling the corridor and you must find a way to sneak up behind him. Try using the shadows. If he is asleep in his chair, sneak up behind him and grab him. Drag him out of the light and choke him unconscious. Then return to his chair to find an important keycard.

Sneak up quietly behind the snoozing guard to seize him. Search the chair afterward to find his keycard.

Follow the west corridor until it ends, taking out the surveillance camera at the first corner. Lambert radios in. He wants the ship's engines disabled so that any resulting explosions will not affect oceanfront population.

Engine Room

Use the optic cable to peek through the Upper Corridor's western door and into the Engine Room. Soon, a guard appears on the upper level beyond the door. He approaches the door, then moves right. As he passes, open the door and pursue him. Overtake him before he rounds the next corner, and grab him. Drag him to a dark location, and choke him unconscious.

Allow the guard patrolling the Engine Room's upper level to move past the door before you enter. Then catch up to him and take him down.

Follow the catwalk to the corner. Climb over the rail and hang. Shimmy until you are directly over the rail of the catwalk below. Drop onto the rail, and stay there until the guard patrolling the midlevel passes by you. Drop quietly off the rail, sneak up behind him, and grab him. Drag him toward the dark area at the top of the stairs that lead to the ground floor, and knock him out.

Drop from the upper level to the rail of the midlevel catwalk, as shown. Then follow the passing guard and grab him.

Descend the stairs, and wait at the bottom. Allow the guard patrolling the lower level to pass by. His patrol route leads him down either the center aisle or one of the side aisles. Avoid following him into the well-lit south aisle. If he goes down the center aisle or heads for the Engine Room's north side, follow him and grab him, then knock him out.

Stay at the bottom of the lower-level stairs until the guard passes, then take him out.

Move to the northwest corner of the lowest level in the Engine Room. Use the Interact option to disable the ship's engines.

Disable the engines using the machine in the room's corner.

Exit the Engine Room via the door in the southeast corner.

> **CAUTION**
> Although it is possible to slip through this room undetected and without attacking any of the guards, it is unwise. You risk being detected on your return trip(s) through the Engine Room.

Lower Corridors

Move quietly through the entire Lower Corridor area. A guard leans against the wall in the middle section and may be alerted by any footsteps.

As you reach the middle section, Lambert radios that he wants you to erase the ship's surveillance camera recordings. Ignore the laptop and medkit in the center aisle for the moment to avoid rousing the guard leaning against the wall. If Sam urgently needs to e-mail the NSA, use the EEV to access the laptop.

Sneak up beside the guard. There should be just enough room for Sam to squeeze in between the guard and the inside of the support column on the right. Knock out the guard from the side.

Quietly sneak up beside the guard leaning against the wall, and sock him from the side to knock him unconscious.

Boat Dock

Continue to the Lower Corridor's end and enter the Boat Dock. A security cage encloses the entrance. Move to the gate and use the keycard. If you failed to obtain the keycard, you must hack the card reader, which is not easy!

Use the keycard to open the gate.

Proceed into the room. The guard patrolling the lower level follows a variable route. He may patrol close to the water, or he may patrol the dark area near the security cage. No matter which route he patrols, he always goes to the lower level's northwest corner and stops, facing inward. Therefore, move directly to the northwest corner, press your back against the wall, and wait for him to come to you. He does not stay in the northwest corner long, so knock him out soon. Use a choke hold to ensure the least amount of noise in the action.

Take out the guard patrolling the lower level by waiting for him in the corner.

The room's north side is too well lit. Head back across the room's west part to the security cage. From there, head east along the wall to its end. Climb the ladder to the top level, and move into the corner of the catwalk to Sam's left.

Move behind the boxes stacked along the room's south side to avoid detection.

If you have had good timing up to this point, the guard patrolling the upper level should be walking away. If he is moving toward you, get out of his way. He moves to the corner and stops, facing inward. Grab him and choke him unconscious.

If he is walking away toward the other side, use night vision to spot the beam running between the upper level's two sides. Climb over the rail, move across the beam, and jump off on the upper level's other side. Move to the outside corner near the ladder and wait. The guard eventually moves to the upper level's inside corner and stops, facing inward. Grab him and choke him unconscious.

Allow the guard patrolling the upper level to move to a corner and stop, facing inward, for an easy takedown.

Climb down the ladder and move to the boat parked at the dock. Climb over the boat's side.

Use the lock pick to open the trapdoor in the floor below the steering wheel. Pick up the object lying there, which is the bomb. Time to rendezvous with Enrica, but there is still one last detail to take care of in this area.

Climb into the boat to search for the detonator.

Climb over the boat's south side, and slide into the water. Sneak up behind the guard standing near the dock's edge. To drown him, use the Grab Character interaction while standing in the water. For a nonlethal takedown, climb out of the water to the man's left, face him, and press the Nonlethal Attack button to smack him.

From the water, approach the guard standing near the boat to take him down, one way or another.

Ascend the central stairs to the upper level. Go through the portal into the enclosed end segment of the Upper Corridors. Access the computer there and hack the security access to erase the ship's camera records.

Be sure all guards in the Boat Dock are incapacitated before attempting to erase the security records in this well-lit corridor.

Return to the Boat Dock and head to Sam's right. At the corner, climb over the rail and drop onto the security cage's roof. Move forward to the opening and drop to the floor.

Return to the Engine Room. If the NSA is steamed at Sam's recent actions, use the laptop in the Lower Corridors to contact them.

Move to the north wall of the Engine Room's lower level. Crouch and move into the small opening to the right of a bright light. Follow this passage to meet up with Enrica.

Enter the low passage in the Engine Room to reach Enrica's location.

Fuel Tank

Move toward Enrica and give her the bomb. Then initiate a Boost Over.

Enrica drops her cell phone. This is Sam's chance to upload a virus to the phone and prevent the bomb from going off. Thousands of lives depend on your actions. If you upload the virus, you gain trust with the NSA. However, Emile will be furious with both Sam and Enrica. If you cancel, then the bomb goes off and all the passengers die. However, the JBA's faith in Sam rises to new heights.

Help Enrica reach her destination by giving her some help over the pipes.

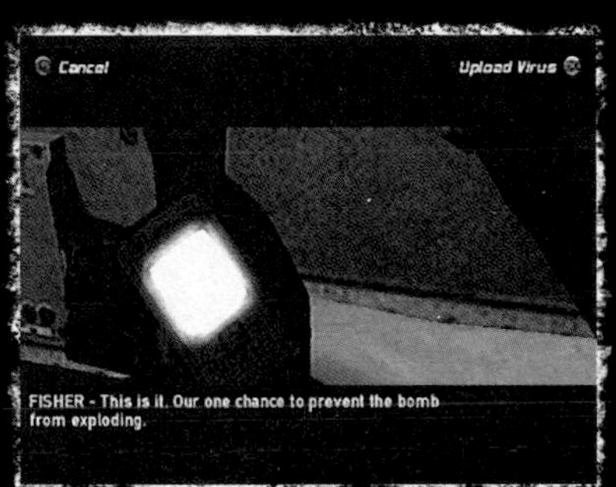

Will two thousand people die? Fate is in Sam's hands once again.

After handling the cell phone situation, it's time to extract. Return to the Boat Dock, board the small boat, and exfiltrate to complete the mission.

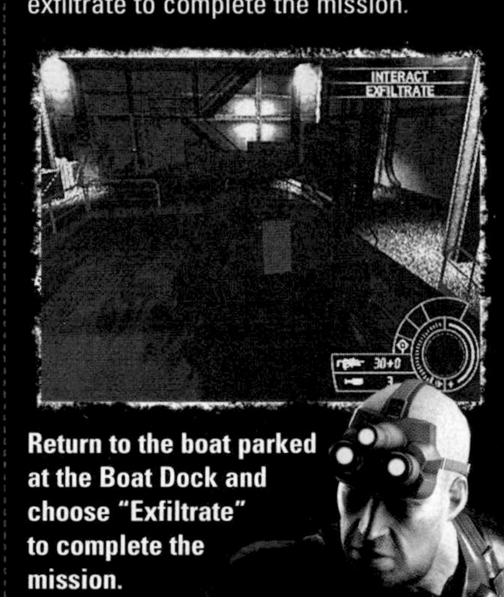

Return to the boat parked at the Boat Dock and choose "Exfiltrate" to complete the mission.

Sea of Okhotsk, Russia: Mercenary Camp

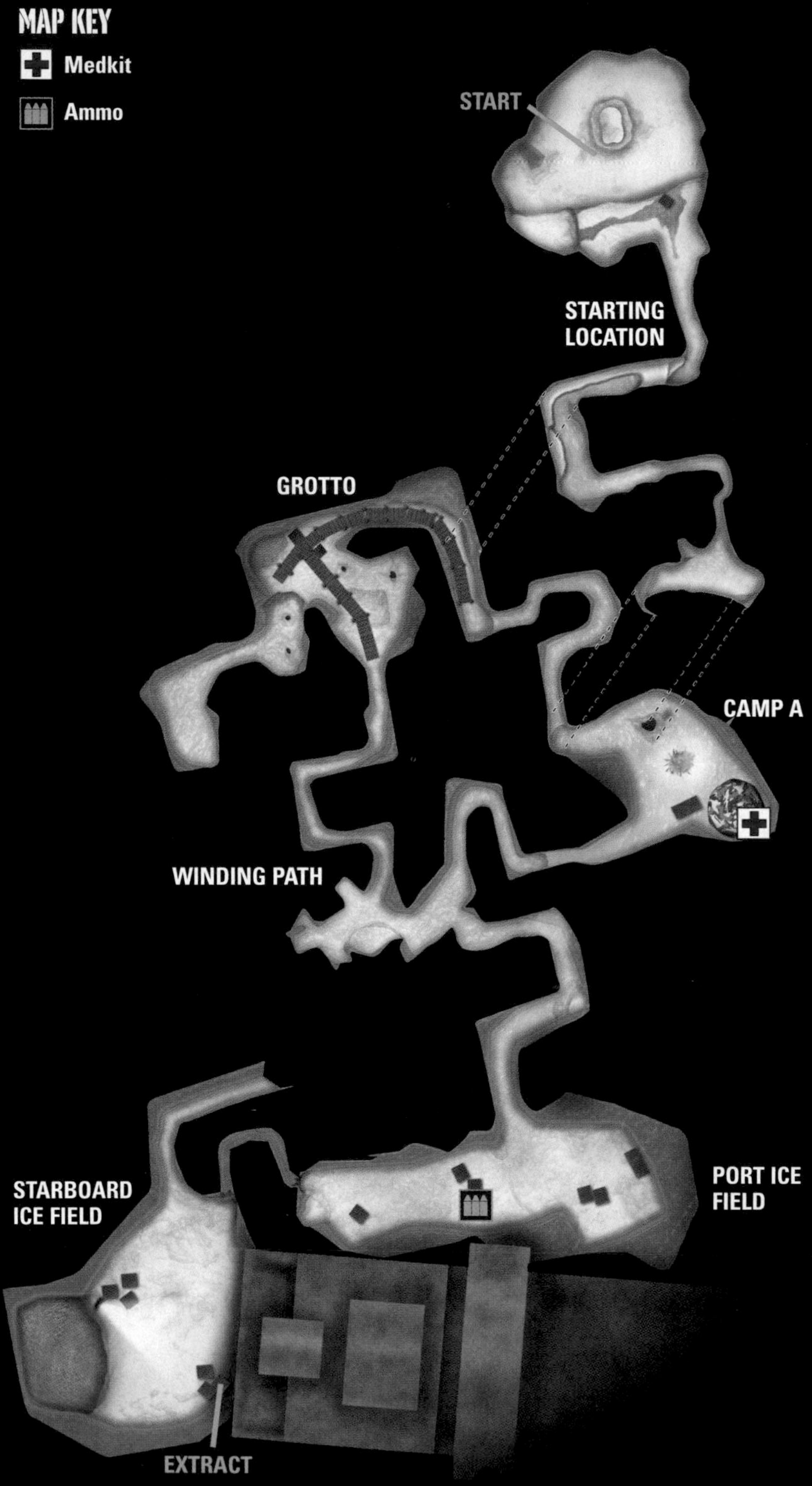

OBJECTIVES

PRIMARY OBJECTIVES

> NEUTRALIZE ALL MERCENARIES: Clear the area, by killing or knocking out all mercenaries, so Emile's allies can safely board the ship. Your mini-map's tracker feature should be useful here.

> DISABLE ALL FIVE COMMUNICATIONS RADARS: There are five communications radars in the entire area. Some can be hacked, others can be destroyed.

OPPORTUNITY OBJECTIVES

> LOCATE ENCRYPTION KEY: The mercenaries are using a sophisticated encryption algorithm for all their communications. Because we (Echelon) want to keep monitoring their network, we'll need the encryption key they are using to decipher the transmissions. The key is unlikely to be in electronic form and is probably printed on a piece of paper or in a ledger.

> DISABLE BOMBS PLACED AROUND SHIP: The tanker must stay stuck in the ice until it is secure. Defuse all the bombs before they explode.

LOADOUT: OKHOTSK MISSION

JBA	NEUTRAL	NSA
SC-20K/90	SC-20K/60	SC-20K/30
SC pistol/60	SC pistol/40	SC pistol/20
Sniper attachment/18	Sniper attachment/12	Sniper attachment/6
Shotgun attachment/21	Shotgun attachment/14	Shotgun attachment/7
Sticky shockers/2	Sticky shockers/4	Sticky shockers/6
Airfoil round/2	Airfoil round/4	Airfoil round/6
EMP ammo/1	EMP ammo/2	EMP ammo/3
— —	Gas grenades/1	Gas grenades/2
Frag grenades/2	Frag grenades/1	— —
— —	Smoke grenades/1	Smoke grenades/1
— —	— —	Flashbang grenades/2

Starting Location

Sam inserts via helicopter near the mercenary camp. Quickly move forward to the ridgeline and climb onto the ledge. Stay clear of the light cast by the gas lantern.

Prepare for the first enemy by quickly climbing onto the tallest ledge.

A mercenary soon comes around the corner, shining a flashlight toward Sam's insertion point. Sneak up behind him and grab him. Emile wants all the mercenaries in this camp dead. Lambert forbids it. Killing all the mercenaries engenders trust with the JBA, while merely knocking them out pleases the NSA. Your call. Either way, all mercenaries must be killed or incapacitated before Sam can enter the tanker.

When a merc shines his flashlight toward Sam's insertion point, sneak up behind him.

Use the EEV to access the satellite controls on the lower ridge.

Hack the satellite controls in the area. Then follow the narrow passage and slip around the corner. A mercenary patrols the passage, moving through an area illuminated by flares. Wait until he patrols near the entrance and turns his back. Then follow him down the passage, grab him, and knock him out.

Wait in the passage until a merc patrols near, then turns back. Grab him.

Moving through a narrow, flare-lit passage just is not the *Splinter Cell* way. Find the low ledge on the right side of the passage, and climb onto it. Continue climbing ledges until you reach the top. Follow the path around the area's upper part as it curves left. At the path's end, drop until Sam is just one ledge off the ground.

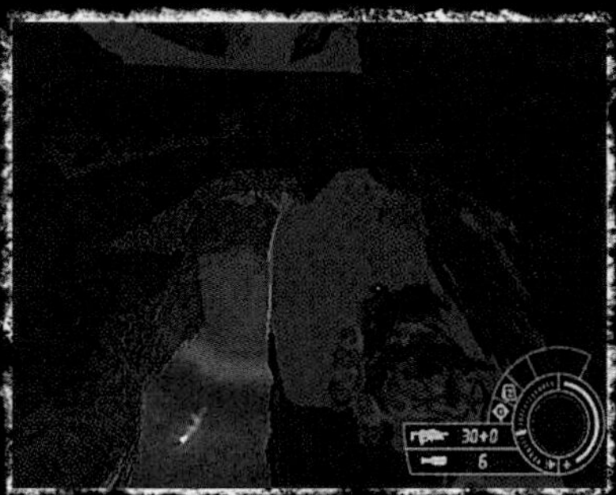

Use the ledges running alongside the passage to get the drop on the merc patrolling the passage's rear segment.

A mercenary with a flashlight patrols the area near the Crawlspace that leads to Camp A. Stay on the ledge until he passes, then drop behind him and knock him out.

Navigating along the raised ledges allows Sam to get the drop on the last merc in the area.

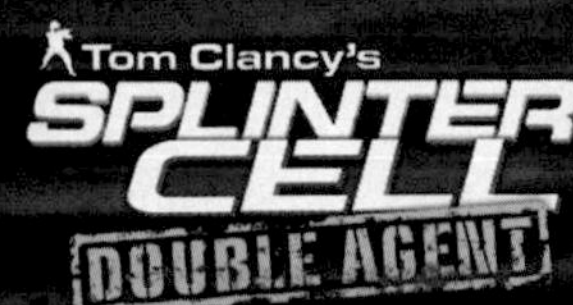

Camp A

Follow the second flare to a crawlspace. Crawl through the tiny passage. As you approach the exit, a guard searches the area with a flashlight. Stay a few feet back from the crawlspace's exit until he moves away. Then emerge from the crawlspace and follow the guard. He stops in front of a thin sheet of ice. Move behind the ice sheet, and use the Grab Character interaction to punch through the ice and grab him. Interrogate the mercenary, then strangle him unconscious.

Stay a few feet away from the crawlspace exit while the guard searches. Emerge only after he turns away.

Slip behind the thin sheet of ice and smash through it to grab the merc from behind. It's time for some questions.

The best way to get off the cliff and into Camp A is to move to the southeast corner and climb down the rope. While descending, survey the situation below. A mercenary patrols the area directly under the rope. If he is walking toward the rope, do not climb to the ground until he passes.

Pause while climbing down the rope to survey the scene below. Wait for a merc to stop just past the rope's bottom before climbing to the ground.

The mercenary stops with his back to the rope. Because campfire illuminates the mercenary, wait to grab him until he heads toward the other side of the ice column that divides the area near the rope landing. As he moves around the ice column to the right, go around the column to the left. The merc stops and turns inward on the column's other side. Sneak up behind him while he remains in this position, then grab him and drag him behind the ice column for strangulation.

Move behind the tall ice column to sneak up on the mercenary while he stands in the dark.

From behind the ice column, move east to find a narrow gap in the rock. Slip through the gap, then squeeze through another narrow gap to come out the other side. Sam is now behind the mercenaries' tent.

Sneak through the narrow passages to get behind the enemy camp.

Go through the open flap at the tent's rear. Use the medkit if necessary. Then use thermal vision to watch the scene outside the tent. The mercenary who patrols around the campfire sometimes moves in front of the tent's front entrance and stops, his back to the flaps. When he stops in front of the tent, move to the entrance and grab him. Drag him into the tent and knock him out.

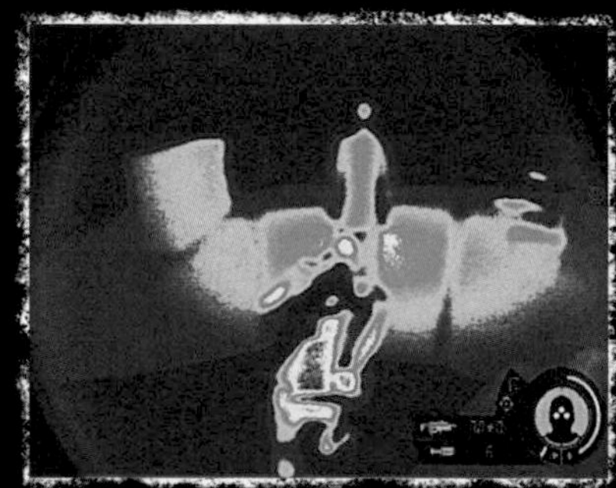

Use thermal vision to grab the hostile who stops in front of the tent's entrance.

Use the computer to hack the satellite equipment. On top of the container on the tent's other side lies the mercenaries' code book. Procure it to fulfill an Opportunity Objective.

The code book lies in the tent, along with another satellite computer that needs hacking.

Sam has two options at this point: to either go to the Winding Path or to the Grotto. We recommend going to the Grotto first; therefore, that is the path this guide follows. To access the Grotto, climb back up the rope to the high ledge. Move to the ledge's other side and rappel down the wall until the Jump In interaction appears. Sam smashes through an ice wall and lands in the tunnel leading to the Grotto.

Enter the Grotto by rappelling down the cliff wall, then jumping through the thin ice.

Grotto

Follow the tunnel into the Grotto until you spot two laser trip wires blocking the passage. Move to the first laser's left and crouch to pass under it. Equip the SC pistol, and use the OCP to knock out the second laser by aiming at the square emitter on the wall.

Using the OCP, disable the lasers barring the cave exit.

Two wall mines are located on the walls near the edge of a curving wooden walkway that leads deeper into the Grotto. Neither wall mine is active, so walk up and take them.

Make sure that no one is patrolling the curved walkway. Move onto the wooden platform and follow it until you reach a gap in the rail to Sam's right. Step off the ledge and hang from the underside of the walkway. Soon, a mercenary holding a flashlight patrols along the suspension. He stops directly in front of this gap. You may grab him from below to inflict a lethal kill. For a quieter, nonlethal approach, wait until the guard starts to move away, then climb up. Sneak up behind the man, grab him, and knock him out.

At the first gap in the rail, hang from the walkway's side. Wait for a merc to stop and search the area. As he walks away, climb up behind him and grab him.

Hang from the walkway's side and drop onto a small rock ledge that runs under the walkway. Follow the path to a crawlspace that runs under the walkway, and navigate to the other side. Use the EEV to access the satellite computer and hack the communications.

Navigate along the thin ledge running under the wooden walkway. Enter the crawlspace at the end.

Move to the crawlspace's end and use the EEV to hack this area's satellite computer.

Beyond the satellite computer is a small pond; on the pond's other side, a mercenary occasionally stops and stares at the computer. Wait until he turns away from the pond and check the mercenary who patrols to the far left. When neither man is facing your position, exit the crawlspace. Slip into the pond and move to the other side. Stay underwater until the mercenary returns. When he walks away from the pond, climb out and follow him until he stops in the darkness. Grab him and choke him unconscious.

Move through the water until Sam is under the mercenary who patrols near the pond. When he walks off, climb out and go after him.

After knocking out the second mercenary in the Grotto, the next is easy to deal with. Wait in the darkness at the bottom of the stairs near the pond until the mercenary patrols the walkway. When he moves past, follow him and grab him. Drag him toward the Grotto's south exit, and knock him out.

Wait at the bottom of the stairs leading off the walkway until the last mercenary moves past. Follow him to the right and nab him.

Pick up the last mercenary's body and carry it through the tunnel toward the Winding Path area. The merc's tracker device deactivates the many laser trip wires blocking the passage. After passing the trip wires, set down the mercenary's body.

Carry one of the mercs through the array of laser trip wires in the passage between the Grotto and the Winding Path areas.

Winding Path

Proceed to the corner just beyond the green flare, and stop at the corner. One of the two mercenaries patrolling the Winding Path area moves into the tunnel and stops. Move to within two feet of him. When he turns and walks away, sneak up behind him and grab him. Drag him back to the corner, and choke him unconscious.

Wait just beyond the guard's stopping point. When he turns away, grab him and drag him around the corner for disposal.

Move toward the area at the slope's bottom, lit by a red flare. Follow the wall to Sam's left, and stop just short of the corner. The second merc patrolling the Winding Path area enters from the left and stops just inside the red flare's area. Equip the SC-20K and airfoil rounds. Hit him in the head with an airfoil round to knock him out immediately.

Use an airfoil round to knock out the mercenary who walks into the flare-lit area.

Use the satellite computer on the Winding Path's west side to hack the mercenaries' communications.

Head east toward the Port Ice Field, proceeding cautiously. There are two active wall mines in the passage. Slowly approach them with your weapon drawn; to disable them, take them off the walls when the top light is green.

Approach the wall mines slowly, and deactivate them when the light is green.

TIP

Another wall mine is active in the passage leading back to Camp A. Carry the body of one of the guards from the Winding Path through the laser trip wires to deactivate them; then slowly approach the mine and take it off the wall when the top light is green.

Port Ice Field

As you emerge into the Port Ice Field, you see two mercenaries at the corner of a transport truck straight ahead, conversing. When their little chat ends, one of the guards turns on his flashlight and searches near the entrance. Move forward until Sam is just out of the light's range. Hit the guard in the head with an airfoil round.

Stay just out of flashlight range as one merc patrols near the entrance. Hit him in the head with an airfoil round.

As you navigate southeast, stay out of the pool of light surrounding the truck. At the area's rear is the detonator for one of two explosive charges set around the ship. Bypass the circuitry to deactivate it.

Deactivate the detonator located at the back of the area to prevent the mercenaries from freeing the ship from the ice.

Climb on top of the crates directly opposite the detonator. Wait for the second merc to pass by, then drop to the ground behind him and knock him out. Hide his body out of the light.

Wait on top of the crates near the detonator for the guard to pass, then drop to the ground behind him.

Retrace your steps to the area's starting point and head west. If the mercenary patrolling the west area is standing near the two crates, wait until he turns and goes away. Press Sam's shoulder against the dark eastern side of the crates, and wait for the merc to patrol his route again. After he pauses near the crates and turns away, sneak up on him and knock him out.

Wait behind the crates near the satellite computer in the area until the guard patrols near them and turns away. Then go take him down.

Collect the SC-20K ammo from the top of the crate near the satellite equipment. Use the computer to hack the communications system, completing your Primary Objective.

Head west toward a red flare. To the right is a crawlspace entrance.

Starboard Ice Field

Navigate through the crawlspace to the Starboard Ice Field, and stop at the exit. Two men patrol the area near Sam's entrance point. Wait until the closest turns and moves away. Then exit the crawlspace and head for the three crates in the area's center.

Remain inside the crawlspace exit until the two guards move away.

Climb on top of the crates. One mercenary patrols north to south, while the other patrols east to west. Focus on the guard patrolling east to west first. He barely stops at the western point of his route. Stay on top of the crates until he passes and stops at the corner of the three crates. Drop to the ground, sneak up on him, and grab him. Drag him behind the three crates and strangle him unconscious.

Climb over the crates to get behind the mercenary patrolling out to the water's edge and back.

Climb back onto the crates. Wait until the mercenary patrolling near the entrance passes by and stops at the crates' east corner. Drop down behind him, grab him, and knock him out.

This tactic also works on the other merc patrolling near the crates.

Move to the small ledge just left of the gas generator and drop into the shadowy area below. Move through the shadows toward the crate near the water's edge. Press Sam's shoulder against the crate's dark side.

Wait for the guard to pass by, heading east. Step out behind him and knock him out with a lethal or nonlethal attack, your choice.

Use the shadowy area along the water's edge to maneuver into a position beside the remaining guard, and knock him out.

Bypass the circuit on the second detonator to prevent explosives surrounding the ship from being set off. Climb onto the crates stacked near the base of the ship's hull. Provided you have killed or knocked out every mercenary in the camp, climb up the rope to enter the tanker.

Climb up the rope to continue the Okhotsk mission inside the mercenaries' tanker.

Sea of Okhotsk, Russia: Icebound Tanker

MAP KEY

Medkit

Ammo

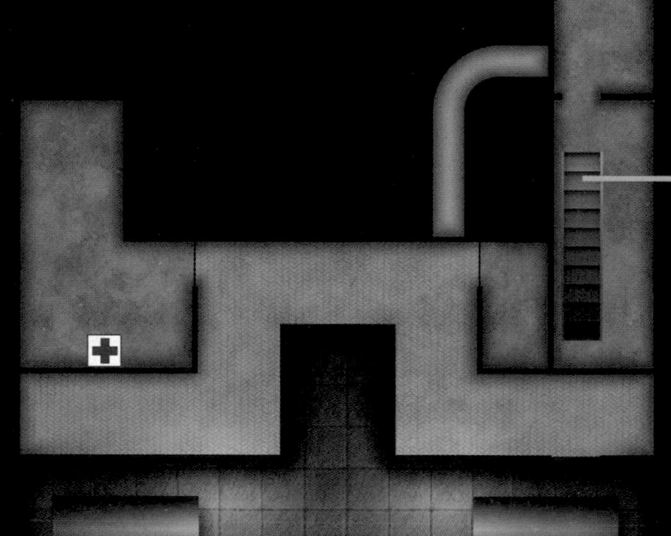

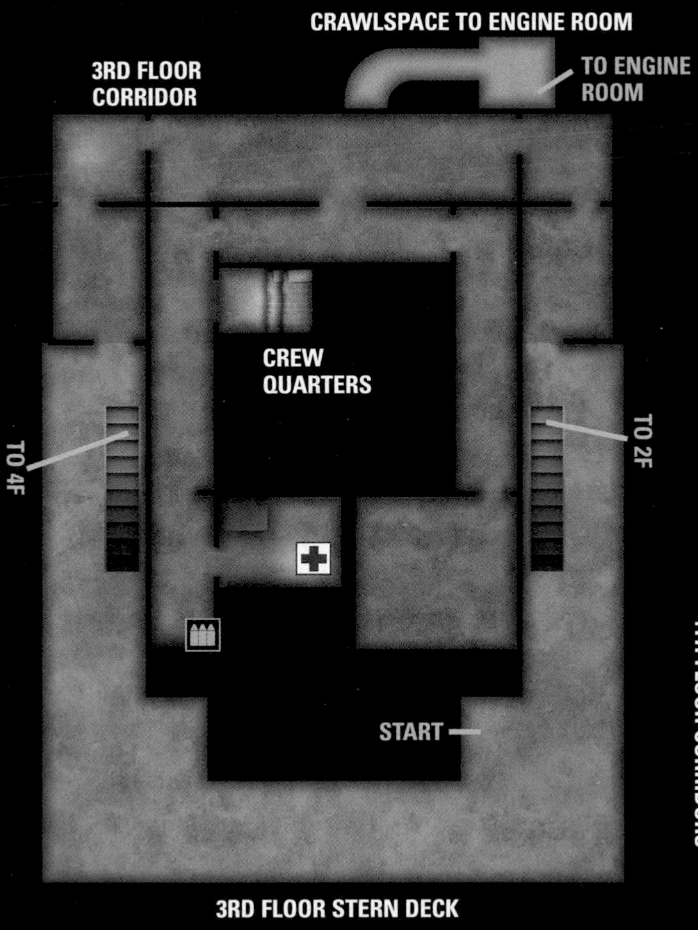

CRAWLSPACE TO ENGINE ROOM

3RD FLOOR CORRIDOR

TO ENGINE ROOM

CREW QUARTERS

TO 4F

TO 2F

START

3RD FLOOR STERN DECK

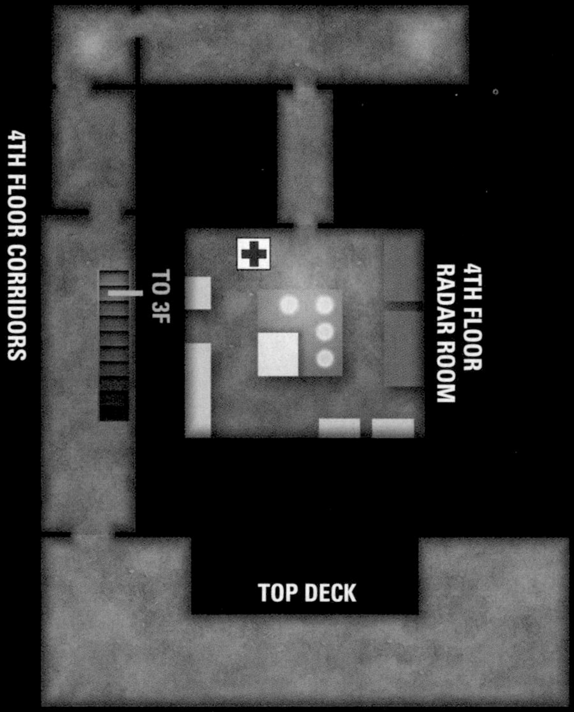

4TH FLOOR CORRIDORS

TO 3F

4TH FLOOR RADAR ROOM

TOP DECK

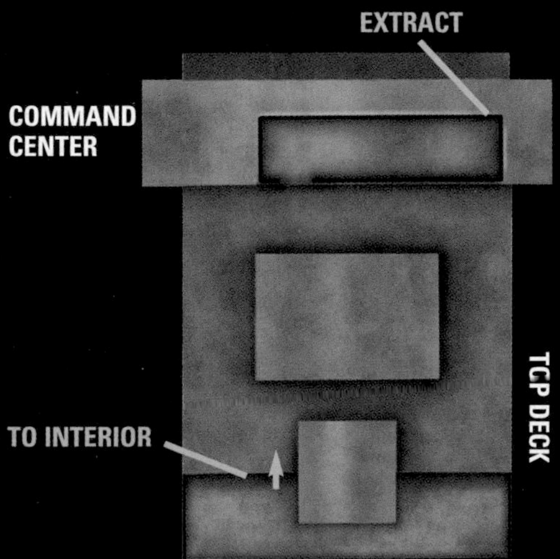

EXTRACT

COMMAND CENTER

TCP DECK

TO INTERIOR

OBJECTIVES

PRIMARY OBJECTIVES

> BOARD THE TANKER AND NEUTRALIZE THE CAPTAIN: A rope waits for you at the rear of the tanker. Use it to get aboard the ship, then make your way to the captain's chambers and neutralize him. Once the captain is out of the picture, the rest of the crew will be easily subdued.

OPPORTUNITY OBJECTIVES

> IDENTIFY THE SHIP'S CARGO: The tanker is operated by a group of smugglers posing as merchants. Identify what they are carrying and make sure the cargo cannot be used for nefarious purposes once the JBA gets its hands on it.

> INSTALL TRACKER IN COMMUNICATIONS ROOM: We want to be able to track the tanker while it is in the JBA's possession. For this, we need you to install a tracker in the communications room, which is located on the upper decks, below the command center.

Third-Floor Stern Deck

While Dufraisne and Lambert spell out Sam's objectives, adjust your viewpoint to the left. Notice the mercenary who stops at the corner on his patrol route. Creep out to the corner, and wait for the man to turn and walk away. Move in behind him, grab him, and drag him back to your starting position. Interrogate him to find out about the captain's surly nature. Then press the Nonlethal Attack button to knock him unconscious; leave him there in the shadows.

Wait at the corner for the nearest guard to patrol his route, and then turn back. Grab him and interrogate him.

There are two more enemies to neutralize on the Third-Floor Stern Deck. Head in the opposite direction around the deck, move around the corner, and hide behind the barrels in the aisle. Another mercenary stops beside the barrels. When he turns to walk away, sneak up behind him and capture him. Take him around the corner toward Sam's starting position and knock him out.

Continue from corner to corner until you spot the last guard, who patrols near a brightly lit door. Wait until the guard stops near the corner, then turns around and walks away. Sneak up behind him, grab him, and knock him out. Stow his body around the corner in the shadows just to be safe. Go through the door behind him.

Use the barrels to hide in close proximity to the end of the second guard's patrol route.

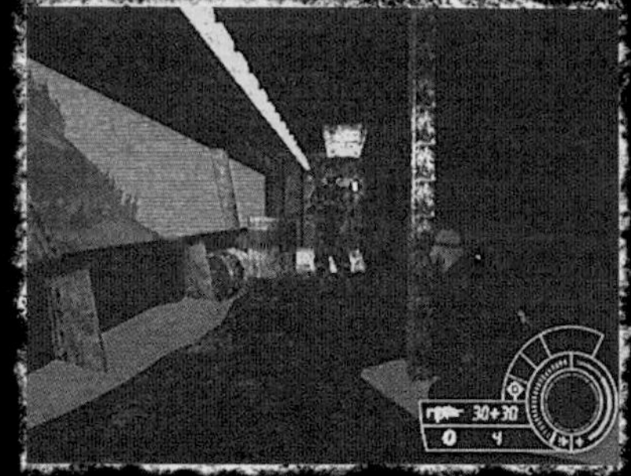

Pull the "corner maneuver" against the last mercenary on the deck as well. Go through the door behind him.

Third-Floor Corridor

Move through the small room and slide open a hatch. Press Sam's back against the wall to the right of the next

portal and peek into the corridor. Soon a merc appears in the corridor. Wait until he searches near the doorway and then turns away. Sneak into the room and follow him. Grab the mercenary and drag him out of sight before silencing him.

Stay out of sight until the mercenary in the corridor moves away. Then grab him and drag him into the darkness.

Crew Quarters

Sam's shoulder against the opposite wall and slide to the right. Stop at the doorway, and angle the camera to see down the dark corridor. One mercenary patrols up and down the corridor; however, a crew member sits in the open quarters right next door, and if anything happens to the merc or if Sam passes the doorway, the crew member attacks immediately.

Hide at the corner to spy on the merc who patrols the adjacent passage.

Equip the SC-20K and sticky shockers. As the patrolling merc turns away from the doorway and moves down the corridor, enter the passage and remain at the corner. Allow the mercenary to reach the corridor's end, and then hit him with a sticky shocker.

If a crew member inside the tanker gets the drop on Sam, they use a taser to capture him. Identify crew members by their dress, which is like that of mechanics or workmen. Mercenaries wear camouflage.

After being captured, Sam wakes up in the storage room in the Hold. Use the lock pick to take off the handcuffs. Picking the lock is difficult since you can't see the tumblers, but just keep rotating the left analog stick until you find the next sweet spot, and jiggle the left stick until each tumbler lifts.

Sam is left with minimal health, so use the medkit to recover. Check the crate in the corner to determine what the mercenaries are transporting, and then collect Sam's gear.

Use the lock pick on the door while two mercenaries discuss Sam in the corridor outside. When the door is unlocked, use the optic cable to make sure they have left the area. Exit the storage room, and wait near the door for the merc who patrols the upper level to pass. Grab

him, drag him to the corner, and knock him out. Climb over the rail at the middle point and drop onto the engine. Wait for the merc who patrols the lower level to move into shadow, and then sneak up behind him.

At this point, climb back up to the upper level and return to the Crew Quarters on the third level. Resume the mission using the rest of the walkthrough as described next. Do not let Sam be captured again. All crew members are now armed with pistols and shoot on sight.

Step into the passage as the merc moves away, and allow him to reach the corridor's other end before hitting him with a sticky shocker.

Keep the SC-20K equipped. Head toward the wall on the right, and slowly move forward in a crouched position, with weapon drawn. Aim into the open and lighted compartment on Sam's left. When you can see the seated crewman's knee, shoot him in the leg with a sticky shocker to knock him out. Check the laptop in the crewman's quarters to view an e-mail that could prove dangerous for Lambert.

From an angle outside the door, use a sticky shocker to attack the crew member sitting in his quarters.

Check the open locker at the corridor's far end to find SC-20K ammo. Use the medkit in the nearby bathroom if needed.

Find rifle ammo in the open locker at the hall's end.

Explore the other side of the Crew Quarters. The door at the far end is the captain's quarters. The door is locked, so talk to the captain through the door. The captain has rigged the entire vessel with a series of bombs set to go off in 10 minutes. Sam must reach the engine room and defuse the four bombs placed there before time elapses!

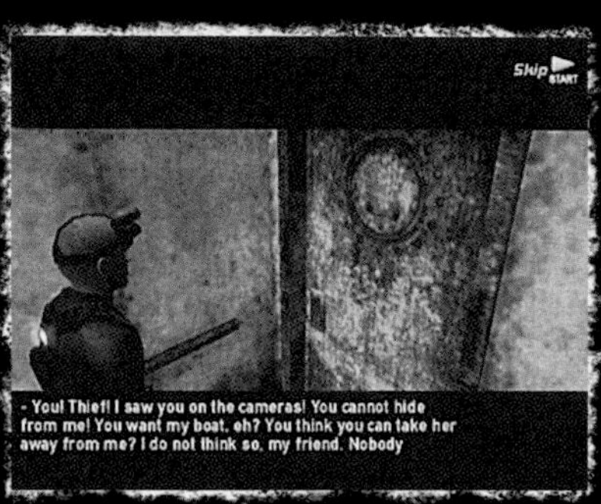

Speak with the captain through his door to learn of a dangerous situation.

Crawlspace to Engine Room

Head back out to the Second-Floor Corridor. Enter the crawlspace on the opposite wall. Go through the crawlspace into the vent shaft, and climb down the ladder.

Climb down the ladder in the crawlspace to reach the Engine Room.

First-Floor Engine Room

A surveillance camera and a light are next to Sam's landing spot. Use the OCP to take out the light and proceed down the platform until you find the first bomb planted on the pipe. Select the Defuse option to begin disarming it.

The first bomb is planted roughly halfway down the upper platform.

Sam must cut the correct wires to defuse the bomb. After you cut the first wire, a 20-second timer begins counting down. Sam must cut the remaining wires before time elapses or the ship explodes. To determine which wire to cut, move the left analog stick to select the wires. If the controller vibrates, then cut the selected wire. Highlight another wire, and if it vibrates, cut it. Repeat the process until you cut all four wires.

> **TIP**
>
> **You can also determine which wire to cut by switching to EMF vision. The "hot wire" is the one that registers electricity. Cut the wires in the order they become "hot." Combining this method with the vibration technique is the surest way to defuse the bomb in time. To defuse the first bomb, cut the third wire from the left, then the first wire, then the fourth wire, then the second wire.**

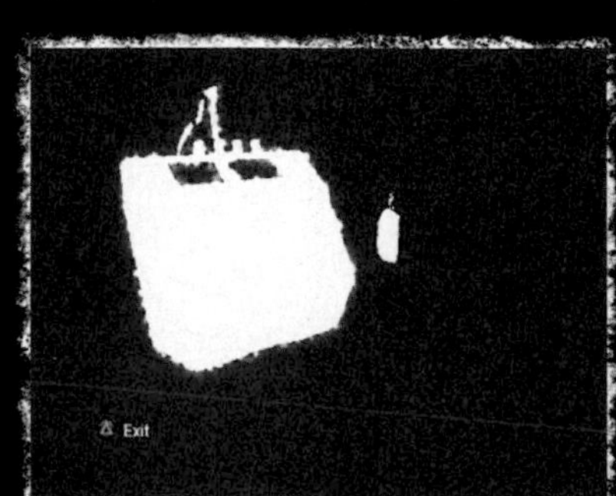

Use EMF vision and controller vibration to help cut the wires on the bomb in the proper order.

After defusing the first bomb, the captain resets the timer to only three minutes!

01: DOSSIERS
PS2/GC
02: GAME BASICS
03: EQUIPMENT
04: SOLO MISSIONS
Sea of Okhotsk, Russia: Icebound Tanker
05: CO-OP MISSIONS
06: VERSUS MISSIONS
XBOX 360/PC
07: GAME BASICS
08: EQUIPMENT
09: SOLO MISSIONS
10: MULTIPLAYER

Climb down the ladder to the lower level. Slowly move toward the guard standing in the light. Another guard soon enters from the right and stands near the stationary guard for a moment. Then he turns around and moves back down the middle aisle. Follow him, grab him, and drag him back into the shadows. Use a nonlethal attack to choke him unconscious.

Sneak up behind the guard patrolling the middle aisle. Grab him, drag him into the dark, and knock him out quietly.

Sneak up to the side of the guard standing in the light. Grab him and drag him into the shadows, then knock him out quietly.

Sam needs to get only a few inches behind the stationary guard in the corner to be able to grab him.

Move to the bomb placed on the engine's side. Cut the first wire from the left, then the third, the second, and the fourth to defuse the bomb.

Defuse the second bomb, then go through the crawlspace below the engine to find the next bomb.

Use the crawlspace located under the second bomb to crawl under the engine. Sam comes out right next to the third bomb. Defuse it by cutting the wires in order from left to right.

The third bomb is located on the back side of the engine where the second bomb was located.

If you killed or knocked out the first three men, defusing the third bomb may cause additional forces to enter the area. However, if one member from the first group remains active, the second wave does not appear.

Move to the machine opposite the third bomb's location and enter the crawlspace under it. This crawlspace emerges near the ladder up to the second platform. Climb up there, use the OCP on the far surveillance camera, and approach the final bomb. To defuse it, cut the wires from the right to the left. The captain makes one final threat after you defuse the fourth bomb.

Crawl under the adjacent machine to reach the ladder to the upper platform.

Use the OCP to knock out the camera at the far end, and then defuse the bomb planted on the left wall.

Head to the hatch on the upper level's far side, then exit. Close the hatch behind you to prevent active crew members and mercenaries from following.

Second-Floor Corridor

Head through the doorway on Sam's left. Go to the corridor's end and open another hatch. Move toward the next hatch; there's a crawlspace near the floor on the right. Enter this and head through into the Hold.

Find the crawlspace in the Second-Floor Corridor for easy access to the Hold.

Hold

> **NOTE**
> The following walkthrough applies only if Sam has not been captured and previously held in this area.

Exit the crawlspace but stay in the corner where you emerge. Soon a mercenary patrols past. Grab the merc and interrogate him to determine the ship's cargo. If you knock out the merc, there is no need to mess with the other individual patrolling the lower level. Go back out through the crawlspace.

Grab the guard who patrols near the crawlspace exit and shake him down for valuable info.

Starboard Stairs

Equip the SC pistol. Ascend the first flight of stairs, and quickly use the OCP to take out the light at the top. Use your night vision to spot a mercenary descending the next staircase from the third level. Press Sam's shoulder against the wall to the left, and slide down the corridor. The mercenary walks to the second level's midpoint. Continue sliding along the wall until Sam is behind him. Then step away from the wall and grab him. Quietly strangle the mercenary unconscious, because another merc waits in ambush on the level above.

Carefully pass the mercenary who descends the stairs to investigate the failing light. Fall in behind him and knock him out.

Use the OCP to disable the light at the top of the stairs on the third level. Equip the SC-20K with sticky shockers, and move quickly to the top. Turn 180 degrees and use thermal vision to spot a merc standing behind the barrels at the deck's other end. Fire a sticky shocker to take him out quietly, or use the sniper rifle attachment if preferred. Either way, take him down before the light regains its function!

Afterward, head to the ship's north side and go upstairs.

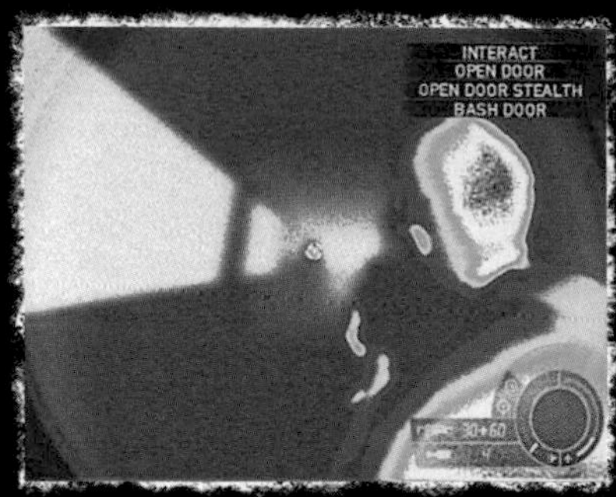

Under the cover of darkness, go upstairs and use thermal vision to help take out a mercenary waiting in ambush on the third floor.

Portside Stairs

Ascend the stairs. Stop at the bottom of the stairs that lead to the fourth floor. An active turret is ready to kill Sam. Jump from the bottom of the stairs and grab the edge of the floor above. This places you safely behind the turret. Deactivate it, and then head through the east door.

Jump from the bottom of the fourth-floor stairs to grab the lip of the upper floor. Then climb up and deactivate the turret gun.

Fourth-Floor Corridors

Slide open the hatch and close it behind you. Move to the right of the next doorway. Wait for the merc in the next corridor to patrol near the doorway and then move away. Pursue him and take him down.

Take down another merc on the fourth floor just as you did on the third floor.

Move down the corridor leading to the Radar Room. Use the OCP to take out the light overhead and then slide open the door. Enter the room, closing the door behind you.

To avoid detection, disable the light outside the Radar Room before sliding open the door.

Fourth-Floor Radar Room

Stay near the door until one man seats himself in the chair on the room's left side. Fire an airfoil round at his head to knock him unconscious.

Wait until the man on the left is seated, and then hit him with an airfoil round.

Sneak up on the man who occasionally crouches in the aisle, and knock him unconscious from the side or rear. Use the computer on the room's far side to view e-mail or check in with the

NSA if necessary. Then install the tracking device in the narrow space between the machinery at the room's rear. Use the medkit near the door if necessary and return to the corridor. Head back across the Portside Stairs and go through the western door.

Knock out the technician in the aisle from the side.

Install the tracker on the communications equipment located in the narrowest spot in the room.

Top Deck

Close the door behind you and head for the deck's south side. The guards have congregated here to discuss recent rumors. Press Sam's back against the wall and wait for them to finish. As the guard on the lower deck resumes his patrol route and passes by, step out behind him and grab him. Choke him unconscious.

Wait by the dark wall for the guards to finish their discussion, then grab the visible guard when he passes by.

Return to the deck's north side, close to where you entered. Use the OCP to disable the light on the wall, and then climb the ladder to the upper deck.

To ensure Sam the full cover of darkness, disable the light on the wall before climbing the ladder.

Move to the nearest corner and press Sam's back against it. Wait for the guard to move into the area. He walks over to the railing and stops, staring out at the sea. Grab him and choke him unconscious.

Wait at the corner for the guard shown here to move past Sam and to the railing. When he stops, grab him and strangle him unconscious.

Move a few steps down the passage toward the turret; stick to the left wall to avoid being detected and shot. Use the OCP to scramble the turret's sensors. While the machine is in chaos, sneak behind it and deactivate it.

For the mercenary standing near the rail, either fire an airfoil round at his head to knock him unconscious, or leave him alone.

Take out the turret gun before heading down the passage, using EMF vision to assist your aiming.

Deactivate the turret gun from behind. The last guard by the rail is easy to knock out, or you can just leave him alone.

Move toward the Command Center, but avoid going around the last corner. An active turret guards the passage, and wall mines are set to either side. Load EMP ammunition in the SC-20K, and fire it at the turret to permanently disable it. Then slowly creep down the passage with weapon drawn until you're clear of the wall mines. Open the door at the passage's far end.

Use EMP ammo to permanently knock out the turret so Sam can move as slowly as needed to get past the wall mines.

Command Center

Enter the door at the corridor's far end to complete the mission.

Kinshasa, Congo: Hotel Suites

MAP KEY

Medkit

MAINTENANCE

START

9TH FLOOR WEST

9TH FLOOR EAST

9TH FLOOR NORTH

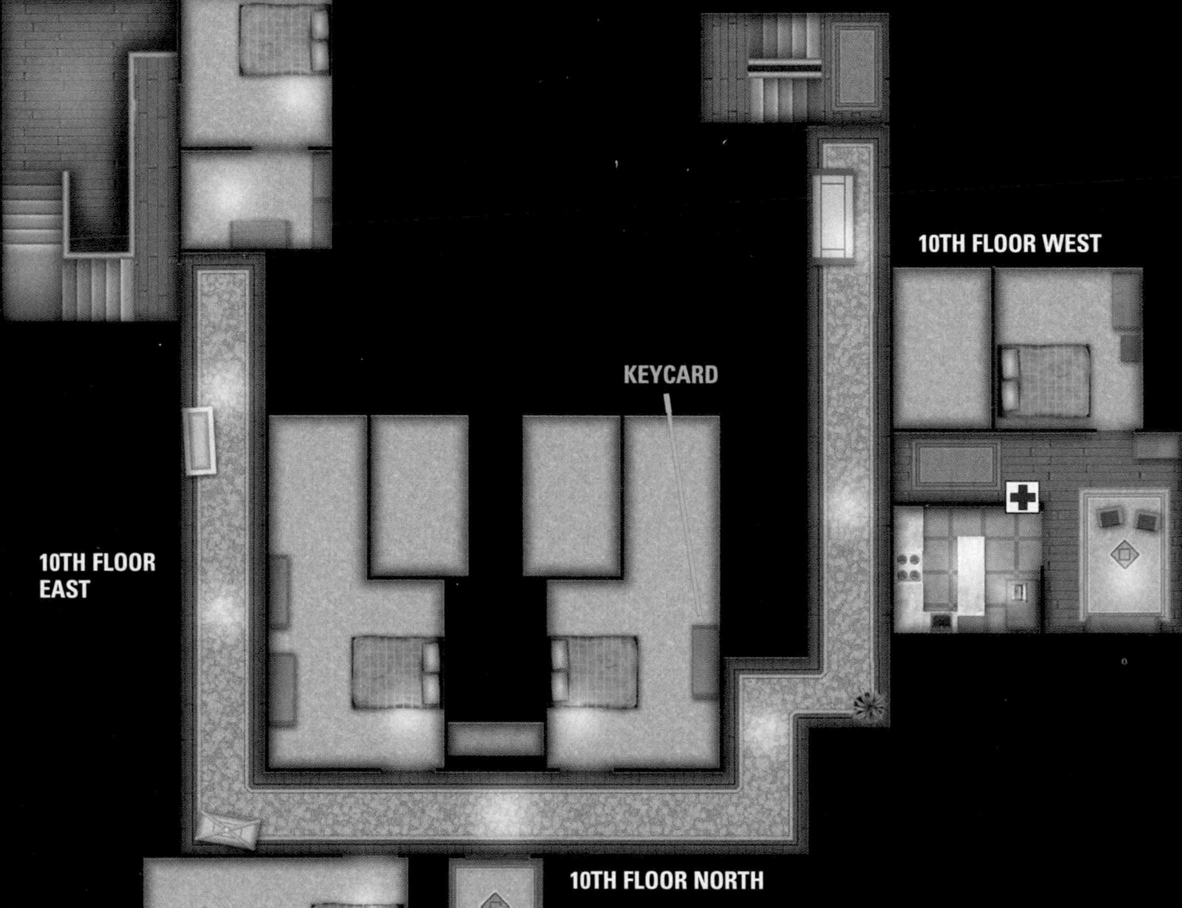

OBJECTIVES

PRIMARY OBJECTIVES

> CONFIRM INTENTIONS OF OTHER 2 GROUPS: Emile needs to know that the two other groups are on schedule and are loyal to his cause.

> MEET EMILE IN ROOM 901: Emile sounded urgent; you must meet with him in room 901.

> FIND YOUR EQUIPMENT IN THE MAIN ELEVATOR AND GO TO LOBBY: Find your equipment in the main elevator and go to lobby.

OPPORTUNITY OBJECTIVES

> FIND ADDITIONAL INFORMATION ABOUT TAKFIR'S GROUP: Documents found on a computer show the location of a Congolese rebel bunker which Takfir's group is currently borrowing. Echelon will most probably be very interested in raiding that location.

> FIND ADDITIONAL INFORMATION ABOUT MASSOUD'S GROUP: Any information you can get to Echelon will help them bring down Massoud.

Select members of the JBA's leadership are journeying to Kinshasa to close a deal for the purchase of all the Red Mercury devices stolen in Iceland. Sam accompanies Emile Dufraisne to a hotel situated in a battle-stricken area. Rebel fighters are skirmishing against corrupt government forces. Sam's initial objective was to monitor the meeting between Dufraisne, Takfir, and Massoud, but the meeting is abruptly cut short, and Dufraisne intends to take advantage of the opportunity.

Maintenance

Sam inserts inside an underground floor duct. He has no equipment other than his hacking devices and his knife. Emile has Sam's equipment. Therefore, Sam must complete the mission's entire first stage without weapons.

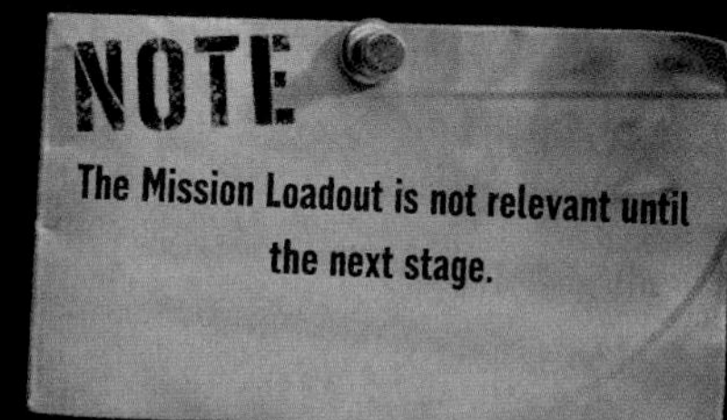

NOTE

The Mission Loadout is not relevant until the next stage.

Move forward along the underground duct until you reach the first open grate. Stand up so Sam's head pokes out of the floor. A soldier walks from the room and into the adjoining chamber, and speaks to the soldier working on the machinery there. Climb out of the floor duct and sneak quietly across the room. Go through the door, and take the precaution of closing it behind you.

Peek out of the floor duct and watch the soldier leave the room. Then climb out and go through the double doors.

A guard is asleep in the corridor. Leave him unmolested, and sneak past him. Continue to the hall's end and slip through the narrow gap. Call the elevator.

Careful not to step too loudly.

Board the elevator and use the control panel on Sam's left to reach the upper levels. The elevator rises most of the way up the shaft, but then artillery fire knocks out the power. The elevator stops just below the ninth floor. Move toward the gate and jump up to grab the edge of an open trapdoor above. Quickly climb through the trap onto the elevator car's roof. Hurry! Otherwise the lights may come back on, and a soldier on the ninth floor may spot Sam when he leans into the shaft to inspect the elevator.

Climb up through the open trapdoor before the soldier on the level above spots Sam in the elevator.

To the left side of the open elevator door above is a tall, open vent duct. Climb into the duct and follow it into the main room.

Climb into the open vent duct on the elevator shaft's side. Move through the duct to enter the maintenance room.

Ninth Floor West

The duct exits into a dark corner of the room behind tall machinery. Press Sam's shoulder against the machinery, and slide out to the corner. One soldier paces the room, while another works on the machinery. Wait at the corner until the next round of artillery fire impacts, knocking out the power. Then slip around the corner and grab the soldier working on the machinery. Drag him into the dark corner near the vent duct opening, and interrogate him to learn about the full political situation at work here. When finished, choke him unconscious.

Wait at the corner of the machinery for the lights to go out, then grab this mechanic and drag him into the shadows for a little one-on-one.

Again, press Sam's shoulder to the machinery's side, and slide out to the corner. Wait until the soldier who patrols the room stops in front of the open elevator doors. Step out beside him and press the Nonlethal Attack button to knock him unconscious.

Knock out the second soldier during a blackout.

Go through the door into the hotel corridor. Immediately, the door down the corridor to Sam's right opens and a rebel enters the hallway. Whether the hotel is currently in blackout or not, move quickly down the hall to the left. Stop behind a cart placed against the wall to the right. Even if the lights come back on, this spot remains in shadow.

After entering the corridor, race to this dark point in the hallway to avoid being seen.

Allow the fast-moving rebel to patrol past, pause at the end of the corridor, and return. Then step out from behind the cart and grab him. Interrogate him, then strangle him unconscious.

A rebel enters the corridor late; allow him to patrol to the far end. Catch him on

Ninth Floor North

Head down the corridor and around the bend. Press Sam's shoulder against the shadowed wall and move out to the corner. A rebel patrols the stretch of the Ninth Floor North. He moves directly under a surveillance camera mounted between the elevator doors. Following the rebel past the midpoint of the corridor leads to detection.

Press Sam's shoulder to the wall near the corner, then peek into the area beyond.

Stay at the corner until the power comes back on, then study the pattern of light and shadow in the corridor. About 10 feet up from the corner, a patch of shadow stretches across the corridor just before the first elevator door. When the rebel is patrolling down the corridor, facing away, move quickly to that spot.

During the next blackout, or as the rebel in the corridor moves away, head to this well-shadowed point in the passage.

Press Sam's shoulder to the wall on his left, and wait until the rebel returns. As he turns around and starts heading back down the corridor, step out and grab him before he moves into the camera's surveillance zone.

Grab the rebel patrolling the corridor before he moves under the surveillance camera by the elevators.

Drag the guard back to the shadowy area, and choke him unconscious. Pick up his body and wait. The rebel patrolling the east corridor appears at the opposite corner. Wait until he turns and moves out of sight, or wait until the next blackout. Then head back to the previous corner with the body. Dump the rebel's body in the shadowed corner.

Watch the far corner to make sure the guard patrolling the adjacent passage does not spot Sam carrying the guard's body.

The rebel patrolling the Ninth Floor East corridor is too difficult to approach from this vector. Therefore, return to the Ninth Floor West passage and go through the door at the far end. Ascend the stairs.

Return to the stairwell at the far end of

Use the optic cable to look beyond the door at the top of the stairs. Soon a rebel appears in the corridor. He heads down the hall and enters the stairwell. As you see him approaching, move to the rail, climb over it, and hang. When the rebel enters and moves to the rail, use the Grab Character interaction to pull him over the rail. The fall merely knocks him out, so you don't lose any Trust points.

Hang from the rail just inside the top stairwell door. Wait for the rebel patrolling the next corridor to enter the stairwell and stop near the rail. Pull him over the rail to knock him out.

Tenth Floor West

With the patrol cleared, head down the corridor and stop at the first door on Sam's left, labeled "Suite de l'Ambassador." To unlock the suite door at this point, you must hack the card reader. The frequency lines move extremely fast, so your hacking skills are tested.

Access the door to the Ambassador Suite.

TIP

A much easier way to open the door is to obtain the keycard from room 1003. Refer to the "Tenth Floor North" section for strategy about procuring the keycard.

Enter the suite and close the door behind you. Turn out the lights using the switch on Sam's right. Use the medkit at the corner if health recovery if necessary. Head around the corner to Sam's right, into the kitchen.

Turn out the lights near the entrance to delay any rebels who might follow Sam into the suite.

Use the wall switch to turn out the kitchen lights, and use the laptop on the table. Hack the "Security Access" to view an encrypted e-mail about "Agency Activity." A few Trust points are gained with the NSA.

Hack the "Security Access" on the laptop to fulfill an Opportunity Objective and swing the Trust Level meter.

Hacking the laptop prompts two rebels to enter the Ambassador Suite. One heads to the bedroom while the other either sits on the couch or searches the kitchen. Either way, move to the wall near the light switch and press Sam's shoulder against the wall to prepare for the situation. If the rebel sits on the couch, sneak out of the kitchen and move behind the couch. The rebel soon stands and moves a few steps toward the kitchen. Steal up to his side and use a nonlethal attack to take him down.

Alternatively, this rebel may notice that the kitchen lights are off. If so, he moves into the kitchen and starts heading toward the laptop. Sneak up behind him, grab him, and choke him unconscious. The situation depends on whether the rebel enters the area during a blackout or not.

The rebel who heads toward the kitchen may notice the lights are off. If so, allow him to enter the dark kitchen and seize him from behind.

Go to the bedroom door and use the optic cable to spy on the rebel inside. He sits for long periods at the desk, then moves toward the doorway and quickly returns to the desk. The next time the lights go out, enter the room and sneak up beside him when he's seated. Use a nonlethal attack to knock him out from the side.

Enter the bedroom during a blackout and knock out the rebel seated at the desk. Search the cabinet for information on Massoud's group.

Search the cabinet to find information about Massoud's group. Now you must find information about Takfir's group in order to complete the Primary Objective. Exit the suite and continue down the corridor to the next corner.

Tenth Floor North

Move to the corner and angle your camera to peer down the passage. A rebel patrols up and down the corridor, moving in front of a surveillance camera. Handle the situation exactly as you did on the Ninth Floor. When the rebel turns his back or when the lights go out, move down the passage and stop in the shadowy area near the first elevator door. Press Sam's back to the wall on the left, and wait for the guard to pass. Sneak up behind him and grab him. Drag him around the corner and interrogate him for information about where Takfir stores his group's plans. Then knock the guy out.

Seem familiar? The tactical situation on this rebel is the same as previously encountered on the Ninth Floor.

Move to the door of room 1003. Pick the door's lock and enter quietly. A rebel is asleep on the bed. Move beyond the entertainment center on Sam's right. Pick up the keycard from the small table. You can swipe the keycard at all card readers on this floor, including the Ambassador Suite and the Presidential Suite.

The keycard in room 1003 allows instant access to the hotel suites.

Quietly sneak past the dozing rebel to the door in the corner. Move through the passage to the adjoining room, and exit to the corridor. Head around the corner to the right.

Be careful not to wake the sleeping rebel!

Tenth Floor East

A surveillance camera monitors the area in front of the door to the "Presidentille Suite" at the corridor's far end. Move up the corridor, hugging the left wall. Stop behind a small service cart near the wall, and wait for the next blackout. Move quickly to the suite door and swipe the keycard to gain access.

Wait behind the cart on the left wall until the next power blackout. Then move to the far door and swipe the keycard while the camera is blind.

Two rebels converse in the suite, one on the upper level and one in the living area below. Move behind the open door and close it while they talk. Remain at the corner until the two rebels finish speaking; one goes inside the room at the balcony's end. Move down the balcony toward the doorway, hugging the wall to Sam's right.

Remain at the corner until the rebel on the upper level goes through the doorway behind him.

Enter the bedroom and go through the door toward the adjoining room. The rebel sits at the table. During the next blackout, move into the room and follow the wall to Sam's right. To keep the room in darkness, flip the light switch before the power comes back on.

Wait until the next blackout to enter the room with the wall safe, then move to the far right and turn off the light switch to maintain darkness.

Soon, the suspicious rebel stands and moves toward the door. Follow him and grab him. Drag him to the painting on the wall, and force his eyes up to the retinal scanner, which opens the wall safe. When the wall safe is open, knock out the guard.

Wait for the rebel to stand, then grab him and drag him to the retinal scanner. Use the rebel's eyes to open the wall safe.

Copy the plans in the safe to complete the Primary Objective. Emile intermittently radios and demands that Sam head to room 901, on the floor below. Do not let Emile rush you. Maintain a slow and stealthy pace.

Copy the plans in the safe to complete the Primary Objective.

Head back through the bedroom to the balcony. Close the bedroom door, and climb over the railing to the right. A rebel stands directly below. Drop to the ground behind the rebel and knock him out.

Drop from the balcony to the floor behind the rebel on the lower level, and ambush him from behind.

Enter the kitchen and use the laptop on the table to check e-mail. Hack the Security Access to decrypt an e-mail about "chemical operations"; this fulfills an Opportunity Objective for the NSA.

Use the laptop in the kitchen to fulfill another Opportunity Objective, if needed.

Ninth Floor East

Move to the Ninth Floor exit of the Presidential Suite and use the optic cable to survey the corridor. Wait for the rebel in the hallway to patrol near the door, and turn away. Enter the corridor behind him, follow him down the passage, and knock him out. Then enter room 901, which is next door to the Presidential Suite.

Use the optic cable to watch the guard in the corridor. Enter the corridor and sneak up behind the guard as he moves away.

Massoud ended the meeting early because he learned of an infiltrator in his organization. Hisham Hamza's cover has been blown, and Emile orders Sam to kill him.

Emile has a troubling request.

After Emile leaves, return to the corridor and head to Ninth Floor North. Move down the passage while hugging the wall to the right. Press the Call Elevator button between the elevator doors. Enter the elevator and pick up Sam's equipment.

Find Sam's equipment in the elevator. Equipping it transports Sam to the mission's next stage.

Kinshasa, Congo: Hotel Suites

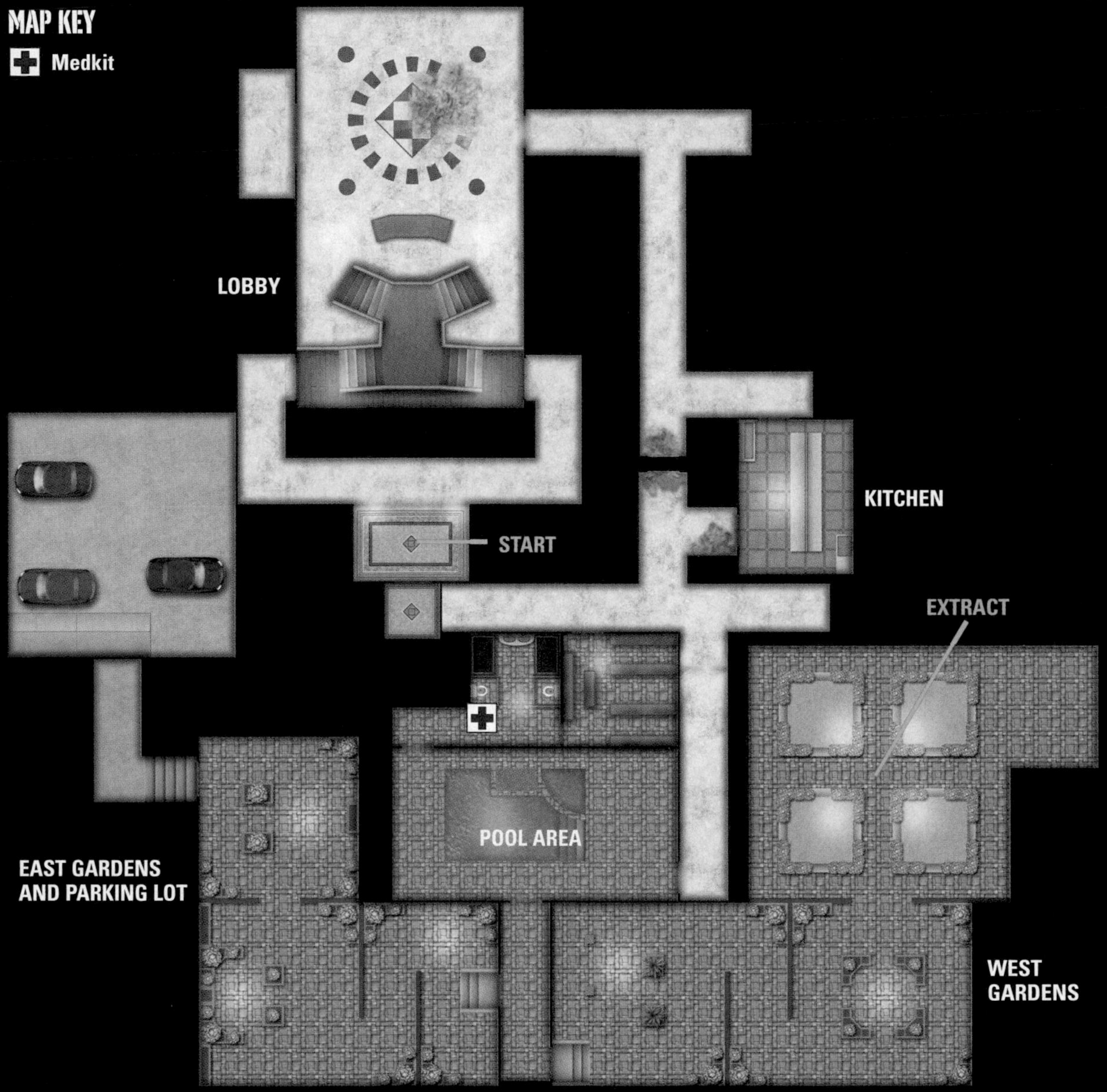

MAP KEY
Medkit
LOBBY
KITCHEN
START
EXTRACT
POOL AREA
EAST GARDENS AND PARKING LOT
WEST GARDENS

OBJECTIVES

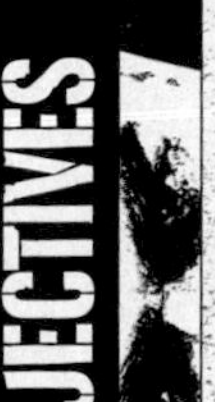

PRIMARY OBJECTIVES

- CLEAR EXTRACTION AREA: Clear extraction area of all hostiles and AA gun.
- EXTRACT FROM HOTEL: Extract from the hotel grounds.

OPPOSING OBJECTIVES

- SAVE HISHAM: Help Hisham to safety by extracting him through the parking garage. Clear the garage of any hostiles first so there are no witnesses.
- KILL HISHAM: Emile wants Hisham dead. Find him and put a bullet in him.

OPPORTUNITY OBJECTIVES

- DISPOSE OF HISHAM'S BODY: Place Hisham's body back in his SUV and detonate it using an explosive charge.

LOADOUT: KINSHASA MISSION

JBA	NEUTRAL	NSA
SC-20K/90	SC-20K/60	SC-20K/30
Sniper attachment/18	Sniper attachment/12	Sniper attachment/6
Shotgun attachment/21	Shotgun attachment/14	Shotgun attachment/7
Sticky shockers/2	Sticky shockers/4	Sticky shockers/6
Airfoil round/2	Airfoil round/4	Airfoil round/6
EMP ammo/1	EMP ammo/2	EMP ammo/3
Sticky cameras/2	Sticky cameras/4	Sticky cameras/6
—	Gas grenades/1	Gas grenades/2
Frag grenades/2	Frag grenades/1	—
—	Smoke grenades/1	Smoke grenades/1
—	—	Flashbang grenades/2

Sam has determined the JBA's ultimate plan: to simultaneously detonate Red Mercury bombs in three major cities. The president is set to be in Nashville, one of the target cities. Never before have so many lives depended on Sam Fisher.

Massoud and Takfir have uncovered Hisham Hamza's infiltration. Emile wants Massoud in his debt and orders Sam to kill Hisham. Whether Sam's former partner dies is completely in your hands.

Lobby

Head to Sam's left and go around two corners to enter the Lobby. Soldiers are fighting rebels just outside the door. The fighting soon ends.

Navigate out of the elevator corridor toward the stairs.

The stairs are extremely well lit, and descending them leads to instant detection. Therefore, move to the middle of the upper level. Climb over the rail and drop into the dark area between the two staircases. Move down the middle level, stop behind the railing, and use the right analog stick to angle your camera to view the area below.

Rather than descend the well-lit stairs, climb over the center railing and drop to the midlevel.

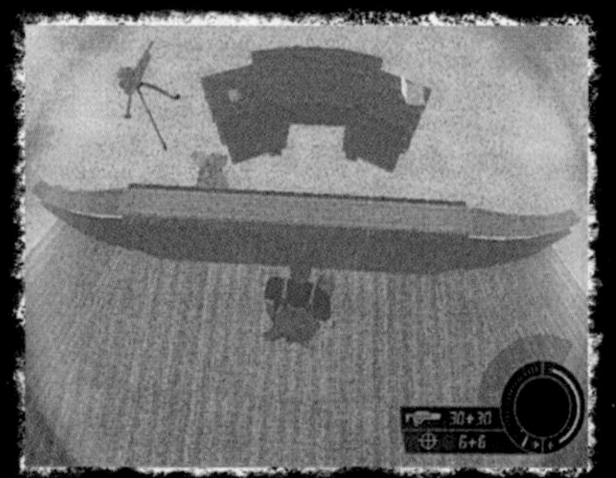

Move up behind the lower rail and angle your camera down to spot a guard near the security desk.

Wait for the soldier to move out from behind the security desk on the ground level. Then climb over the rail and drop to the ground. Move to the desk's left side and deactivate the turret.

Deactivate the turret; otherwise, any movement beyond the security desk draws gunfire.

Slip between the turret and the desk's side. Move across the Lobby and hide behind a potted palm next to a tall column. Wait for a soldier to patrol past and move through the area in front of the security desk. Sneak up behind him, grab him, and quietly choke him unconscious. Leave his body in the shadows in front of the desk.

Hide behind the palm tree near the exit and wait for a soldier to pass close by. Follow him and grab him.

Climb on top of the security desk. When the other soldier moves through the area behind the security desk, drop down behind him and follow him. Knock him unconscious at the first opportunity. Use the laptop on the security desk to read e-mail or check in with the NSA if needed, then head into the passage to the south.

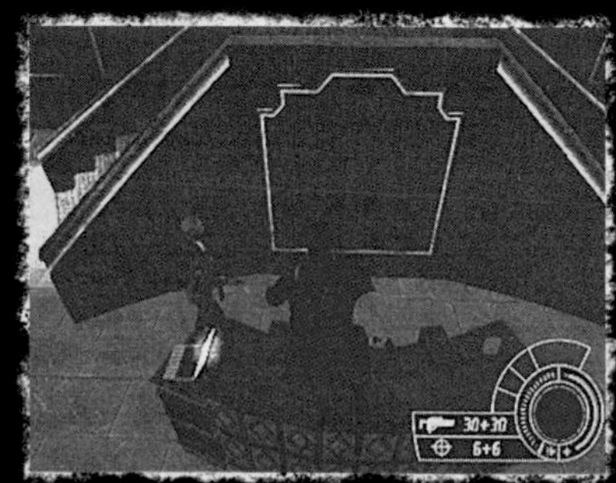

Wait for the other soldier to move behind the security desk, then drop down behind him and knock him out.

Stop at the corner and peek into the corridor beyond. A soldier patrols to the corridor's midpoint. There he stops and stares at the wall for a moment. Move into the corridor and stick to the wall to the right. Stop across from the aquarium, and press Sam's shoulder to the wall. Wait for the soldier to return and stop in front of the fish tank again. Step out and knock him unconscious. Continue around the corner.

Stick to the right wall and slide down to the corridor's midpoint. Wait for the soldier to stop nearby, and grab him.

Kitchen

Stop outside the double doors, and use thermal vision to view the kitchen interior. One rebel patrols the kitchen, while another occasionally steps through the exit door. Wait for the rebel who circles the kitchen to move past Sam's position and stop. Open the left door, sneak up behind him, and grab him. Drag him out into the corridor and interrogate him.

When the rebel stops just inside the kitchen doors, open the left door and sneak in behind him. Grab him and drag him out to the corridor.

Press your shoulder against the doorjamb of the open kitchen door. Wait as the rebel comes through the opposite door, stops a moment, looks around, then goes back outside. He stops just outside the exit door. Cross the kitchen, go through the open door, and grab the rebel. Interrogate him, then choke him. Follow the corridor to the Pool Area.

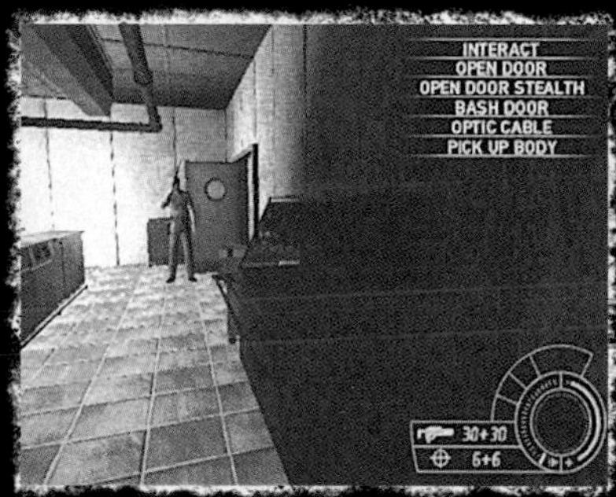

Watch from outside the kitchen as a second rebel enters the opposite doors. When he exits...

...follow him through the door he leaves open. He stands in the dark corridor just outside the kitchen. Grab him!

Pool Area

Sam enters the Pool Area via the locker room, where he reunites with Hisham Hamza. To carry out Emile's orders, simply point a gun at Hisham's head and execute him. The rest of the mission certainly becomes much easier! However, the NSA wants Sam to extract Hisham via the parking lot. (If you decide to kill Hisham, then simply head through the West Gardens and clear the extraction point to complete the mission.)

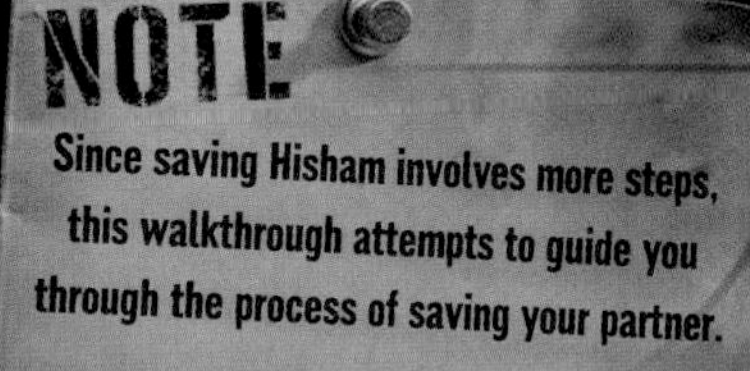

NOTE

Since saving Hisham involves more steps, this walkthrough attempts to guide you through the process of saving your partner.

Kill Hisham now to please Emile, or rescue him for NSA brownie points.

Exit the locker room through the north door. Ignore the Climb-On option near the window—using the option draws the attention of the rebel patrolling the pool's far side. If necessary, use the medkit hanging on the side of the toilet stall, then head for the northwest door.

Ignore the Climb-On option near the window. The rebel in the next room may spot Sam peeking through the opening.

Command Hisham to wait, and enter the Pool Area proper. Stay in the shadows near the door, and close it behind you. Wait until the rebel patrolling the pool's opposite side walks away from Sam's position. Cross the area to the opposite corner. Enter the shadowed area next to the overturned table, and press Sam's shoulder against the wall. Wait for the guard to stop near Sam and turn around. Dislodge from the wall, face the guard, and press the Nonlethal Attack button to knock him out.

Wait near the door until the rebel on the far side walks away to the left...

...then move to the opposite corner. Press Sam's shoulder against the wall near the corner and wait for the rebel to patrol nearby. Sneak up behind him and knock him out.

Use the Co-op command to signal Hisham to follow you into the next area. Go through the west door. Move down the corridor and go through the first door on Sam's right into the East Gardens.

Lead Hisham toward the East Gardens entrance.

East Gardens and Parking Lot

Proceed into the gardens and through a dark, narrow passage. Stop at the passage's corner and signal for Hisham to wait here. Watch the two soldiers patrolling the open area. At some point on their respective routes, the men move through the dark area near the entrance. As one moves past, sneak up behind him and grab him. Drag him behind the wall, and choke him unconscious. Consider using a sticky shocker to take down the remaining soldier.

Stop at the corner and signal for Hisham to hold position. Survey the patrol patterns of the soldiers in the next area.

The dark area near the entry point is a good vector from which to sneak up and grab the soldiers.

Command Hisham to follow, and lead him to the northeast exit. Descend the stairs yourself, but command Hisham to wait on the stairs. Carefully creep forward into the Parking Lot.

Command Hisham to wait on the stairs just inside the parking area while you scout ahead.

Two rebels lie in ambush in the Parking Lot. One is behind the black car to the right, and the other crouches behind Hisham's red SUV in the back. Follow the strip of dark shadow that runs from the entrance to the black car's rear corner. Then turn right and move around the car's front. Stop when you can see both rebels in their hiding places.

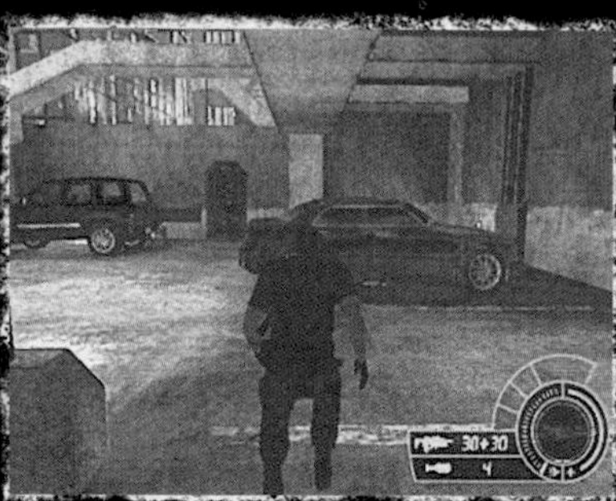

Follow the strip of shadow from the entrance to the rear of the parked car. Then move right, around to the car's front.

Load the SC-20K with sticky shockers. First use a sticky shocker to knock out the rebel hiding behind Hisham's SUV in the far corner. Then sneak up behind the man hiding at the black car's tail end, and knock him out.

Use a sticky shocker to knock out the farthest rebel. Then the closest rebel is safe to approach.

Command Hisham to come out and meet you, and move to the Parking Lot's back gate. Boost Hisham over the gate. In reward for saving him, Hisham gives Sam a nearly useless adrenaline syringe.

Give Hisham a boost over the gate to set him free.

NOTE

To score a little extra credit with the JBA, you can place Hisham's dead body in the back of his SUV and blow it up. Simply move to the SUV's open back door while carrying Hisham's corpse. Press the Interact button to toss the body into the SUV. Then plant the charges and go back toward the entrance. Move several steps down the passageway to avoid explosion damage, then detonate the charges on the SUV.

West Gardens

Return to the corridor behind the Pool Area, and head to the southwest door. Open the door, take a few steps in, and close it behind you.

Stay near the dark entrance after entering the West Gardens.

Two soldiers patrol the extremely well-lit area near the entrance. The best option here is to load the SC-20K with EMP ammo and permanently disable the central light. Then you may sneak around the area's edges, taking your time and remaining silent.

Knock out the central light with EMP ammo. Then sneak around the perimeter to proceed to the next area.

In the area's second sector, notice a soldier patrolling through both the lighted and dark areas of the south side. Move along the wall to Sam's right, follow the curve to the southern wall, and stop somewhere near the middle. No matter which direction he walks, the soldier always momentarily stops near this position. Step out and knock him unconscious. Make sure his body is hidden by shadow, and proceed to the next area.

This vantage point on the southern wall places Sam near the soldier's one stopping point.

Upon entering the sector where the antiaircraft (AA) gun is located, move along the wall to Sam's right. Follow this wall to the corner. Equip the SC-20K with sticky shockers, and aim at the opposite corner. When a soldier comes around the opposite corner, hit him with a sticky shocker in order to drop him in the dark area.

From the corner south of the entry point, aim north and wait for a soldier to come into view. Hit him with a sticky shocker to drop him in the shadows.

Now head east toward the AA gun. Stop at the next corner, and watch the remaining guard patrol his route. He momentarily pauses near the AA gun, then emerges from between the hedges on Sam's right. Gun him down or hit him with a sticky shocker.

Wait for the other soldier to emerge from between the hedges on the right, then hit him with a sticky shocker.

Move up to the AA gun and place charges under it. Deactivate the nearby turret gun, then head back toward the entrance. Detonate the charges from a safe distance to blow up the antiaircraft gun. Then call for extraction.

Place charges on the AA gun. Return to the entrance and detonate them to destroy the gun. Clearing the landing zone allows Sam to call for extraction while standing anywhere in this area.

JBA Headquarters: Part Two

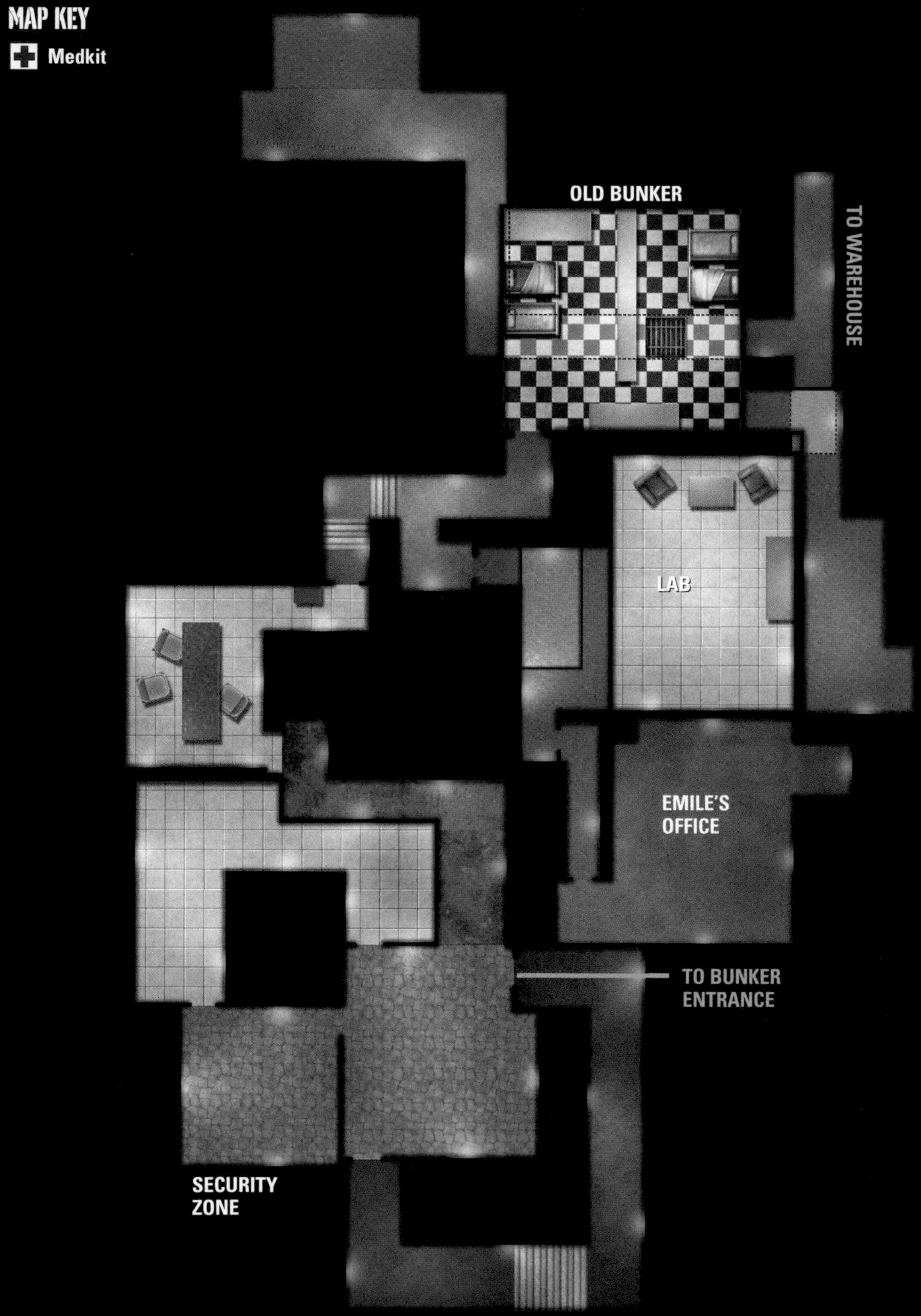

MAP KEY

Medkit

BOMB
DOCK
WAREHOUSE
TO OLD BUNKER
TO ROOF
ALLEY
START/EXTRACT
BUNKER ENTRANCE
TO B1F
LOADING BAY
TO WAREHOUSE
ROOF
BOMB
TO ALLEY
OFF-LIMITS AREA

OBJECTIVES

PRIMARY OBJECTIVES

> STEAL EMILE'S CONTACT LIST: Access Emile's office located in the bunker underneath the warehouse and steal his list of contacts.

> SAMPLE RED MERCURY: Locate the JBA's stash of Red Mercury. Use the IMS on a sample of the substance to confirm that it is indeed Red Mercury.

> RETURN TO PUBLIC AREA: Return to public area via the alley.

OPPOSING OBJECTIVES

> STRENGTHEN LAMBERT'S FALSE IDENTITY: Strengthening Lambert's identity will save his life but will only increase Emile's suspicions that someone else near him is a mole.

> REVEAL LAMBERT'S TRUE IDENTITY: Revealing Lambert's true identity to Emile will appease his suspicions. By eliminating Lambert, Emile will feel confident his operation is now secure.

> DISABLE LA BOMB: Disable the LA bomb on the roof of the warehouse.

> DISABLE NASHVILLE BOMB: Disable Nashville bomb on the docks.

> PREVENT THE BOMBS' DEFUSAL: Use the computer in the bunker's communications room to contact Emile's men and tell them to leave with the bombs right away using an alternate route. This will make it harder for Third Echelon to locate the bombs in transit and may prevent them from defusing them before they reach their destination.

LOADOUT: JBA HQ 2 MISSION

JBA	NEUTRAL	NSA
SC-303 compact launcher	SC-303 compact launcher	SC-303 compact launcher
Rubber ammo/10	Rubber ammo/16	Rubber ammo/24
Tranquilizer ammo/1	Tranquilizer ammo/2	Tranquilizer ammo/4
Sticky cameras/2	Sticky cameras/4	Sticky cameras/6
EMP ammo/1	EMP ammo/2	EMP ammo/4
— —	Smoke grenade/1	Smoke grenade/1
— —	— —	Flashbang grenade/1

The Red Mercury devices have been shipped to the JBA using a shell shipping company. The devices are about to be transferred to their final destination. Sam has one last opportunity to infiltrate the JBA headquarters and secure the bombs.

Once the Red Mercury devices have been secured, Third Echelon will dismantle the JBA and any of its affiliates. For that to happen, a list of Emile Dufraisne's contacts is needed.

Bunker Entrance

Sam starts the mission in the Alley, near the starting point of the previous JBA HQ mission. Enter the "bunker" through the door closest to the starting point.

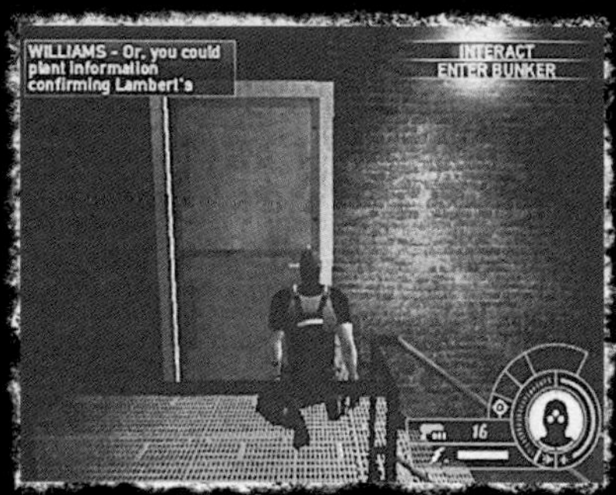

Go through the door into the previously unexplored building.

Move through the short passage and go through the door. Descend the stairs in the second area. Cross the gravel area slowly to avoid making loud noise and alerting the terrorist patrolling the corridor behind the door.

Cross the gravel area slowly to avoid being heard.

Approach the door and use thermal vision to see the corridor beyond. On his normal patrol route, the aforementioned terrorist moves directly up to the door and stops for several seconds. At that moment, use the Bash Door interaction to knock him out.

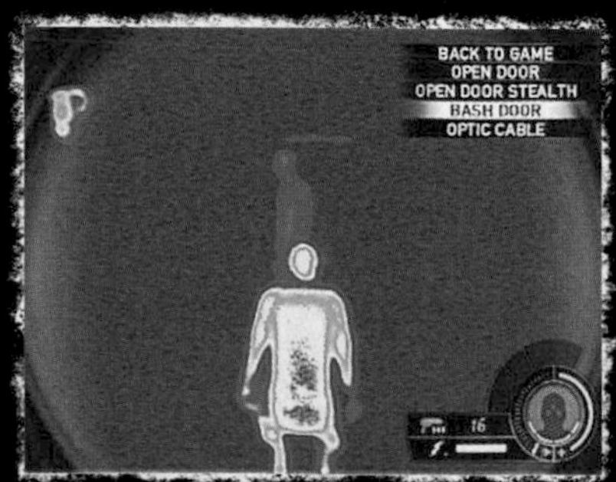

Surprise the terrorist patrolling the corridor.

The corridor beyond is filled with laser trip wires and surveyed by a camera at the end. Pick up the unconscious terrorist's body and carry him down the corridor to deactivate the lasers. Stop just after the final laser to avoid moving within the camera's range. Set down the terrorist's body and use the SC-303's OCP to disable the camera. Continue to the passage's end and hack the card reader next to the door.

Carry the terrorist's body through the laser trip wires. Then set him down and disable the camera at the corner.

Security Zone

Upon opening the door, use the EEV to look through the window into the room on Sam's left. Hack the security access of the computer where the terrorist is seated to upload the information concerning Lambert. If you reveal Lambert's true identity to Emile, the JBA begins to trust Sam almost completely. If you plant false cover information bolstering Lambert's fake identity, Lambert lives. However, the Trust Level meter goes almost completely over to NSA.

Look through the window on Sam's left and use the EEV to hack the computer. Does Lambert live or die?

If at any point during this mission the Trust Level meter goes completely over to NSA, you must return to the bunker entrance in the Alley and check in with Emile before a three-minute timer expires. Otherwise, the JBA scrubs the entire operation and the mission fails.

After deciding Lambert's fate, press Sam's shoulder against the wall to his left and slide under the window. Upon reaching the central door, detach from the wall and follow the strip of shadow running across the floor to Sam's right. Hide behind the boxes and wait.

Move along the wall under the window to avoid being seen by the terrorist inside.

Several minutes may pass, but eventually a lone terrorist enters the room on patrol. He moves past the window, then returns to the door of the office where the other terrorist is seated. Grab him before he goes through the door. Drag him behind the crates and choke him unconscious.

Grab the patrolling terrorist as he prepares to enter the central door.

Go through the door into the corridor. A laser sensor sweeps the corridor in a circular arc. When the sensor is sweeping the corridor's other side, move through the passage and go through the door into the communications center.

When the laser sensor searches the passage's other side, quickly move across the area to the door.

From the corner, use the EEV to access the computer on the central table to read a funny e-mail, if desired. Use the OCP to disable the surveillance camera high up on the back wall, then navigate through the room. Hack the card reader to unlock the exit door.

Knock out the surveillance camera on the back wall before moving through the communications center.

In the well-lit passage, Sam can either go right, to the Lab, or go left, to the Old Bunker farther down the hallway. Clear out the Old Bunker first, which makes later time-sensitive objectives far easier to accomplish. Just remember to take out the surveillance camera in the corridor before going in any direction.

Disable the surveillance camera in the bright corridor before proceeding to either the Old Bunker or the Lab.

Old Bunker

Use the optic cable to survey the scene inside the Old Bunker before entering. The two JBA members inside meet near the door to discuss Moss's recent lack of work ethics.

Wait until the two men inside the Old Bunker move away from the door before entering.

When they finish talking, one terrorist goes back to his computer while the other man stands near the door for a moment. When he moves away, open the door and follow him. He walks down the length of the room under a surveillance camera. As you follow him, stick close to the wall on the right to avoid the camera detecting you. The terrorist turns the corner and goes into a tiny room. Catch up to him as he opens the door, grab him, and drag him into the small room. Choke him unconscious.

Follow the patrolling terrorist along the room's length. Stick to the wall on the right to avoid detection by the surveillance camera.

Seize the terrorist just as he enters the small room at the far end of the short passage.

Return to the main room. Stick to the wall to avoid the surveillance camera. Once you are past the column, navigate quietly toward the terrorist seated at the computer. Grab him from behind, drag him off to the side, and knock him out. Access the computer to read e-mail, if desired.

Sneak up on the man seated at the computer and knock him out.

Use the OCP to knock out the surveillance camera. Directly across from the camera is a trapdoor. Open the trapdoor to "set the stage" for a quick escape at a later time. Exit the Old Bunker via the door you came in.

Set the stage by opening the trapdoor in the floor across from the surveillance camera.

In the corridor, use the OCP to deactivate the surveillance camera overhead. Go down the corridor and take the first left into the Lab.

Lab

Enter the Lab and stop at the first corner on Sam's right. Equip the SC-303 with rubber ammo, switch the gun to Sam's left hand, and aim at the door in the far corner. Wait for a terrorist to emerge from Emile's Office, and hit him in the head with a rubber bullet to knock him out. Shoot him twice if necessary. If your aiming abilities aren't great, load the SC-303 with tranquilizer ammo, and aim for the center of his chest.

Aim at the door in the far corner and take out the terrorist who emerges into the Lab.

Remove the subdued hostile's body from in front of the door, then head up to Emile's Office. Complete your objectives there before scanning the Red Mercury in the lab. Otherwise, you may lose valuable time later.

Move the terrorist's body to avoid complications in opening and closing the door to Emile's Office.

Emile's Office

Ascend the stairs and enter the office. Search the file cabinet on Sam's right to find the complete list of Emile's contacts. Scan the computer on the desk to read e-mail, then head back down to the Lab.

Search the cabinet in Emile's Office to find his list of contacts.

Hack the card reader on the Red Mercury containment chamber and enter. Read the e-mail on the laptop on the desk to the right. Sam must release some Red Mercury in order to scan and identify it. When the Red Mercury is released, the door automatically closes and the room begins filling with poisonous gas that reduces Sam's life in increments every second. Prepare to escape via the vent, which is atop the shelves set against the wall to the side.

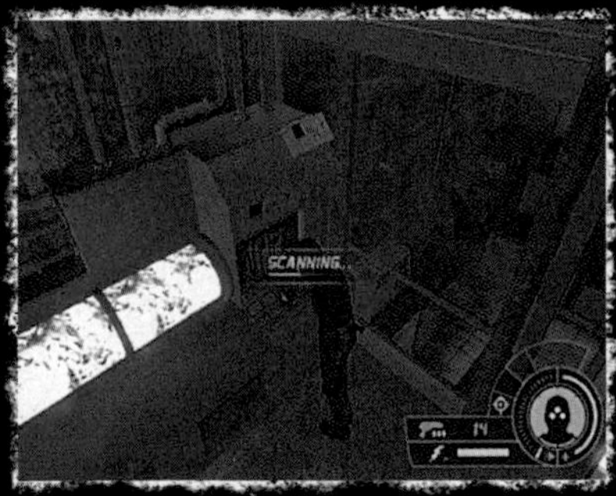

Prepare to escape the small chamber quickly after scanning the Red Mercury.

With your escape route identified, move to the machinery at the back of the containment chamber and scan the Red Mercury. Then quickly climb onto the small box next to the shelves. Jump up and grab the shelf's side, and pull yourself onto the top. Move to the shelves' end and enter the vent. Crawl through and drop down on the other side to escape the Red Mercury chamber and stop losing life.

To escape the chamber, climb onto the tall shelves and crawl through the vent.

An announcement indicates that the Nashville and LA Bombs will ship out for their target destinations in eight minutes. The time remaining is displayed at the screen's bottom. If you can reach the bombs and defuse them in time, you save Nashville, LA, and the president of the United States. However, this portion of the mission is optional. If you do not wish to save Los Angeles or Nashville, then backtrack to the communications center (where the large map, several security monitors, a surveillance camera, and a computer are located) and use the computer to warn Emile's men to depart with the bombs immediately. Doing so engenders a massive amount of trust with the JBA.

If you do not want to defuse the Los Angeles and Nashville bombs, then return to the communications center and use the computer there to warn Emile.

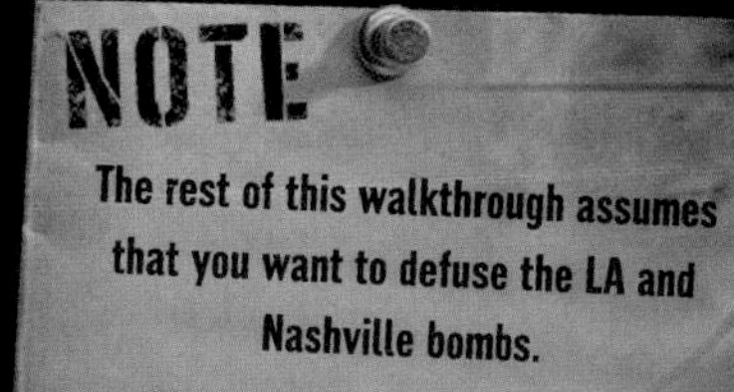

NOTE

The rest of this walkthrough assumes that you want to defuse the LA and Nashville bombs.

Return to the Old Bunker. Disable the surveillance camera on the wall and drop down through the trapdoor in the floor. Stand up and run to the other end of the subterranean passage. Climb up the pipe.

Climb through the trapdoor in the Old Bunker to drop into a subterranean tunnel. Navigate through the tunnel and climb the pipe at the end.

Warehouse

Sam emerges from the subterranean passage into a small room below the Warehouse. Climb up the ladder and use the lock pick on the trapdoor. Then use the optic cable to make sure no one is nearby. Open the trapdoor and climb out. Sam emerges near the middle of the Warehouse. Two men patrol the area. The sound of the trapdoor opening invariably draws attention. Quickly head through the shadows to the exit. Enter the double doors in the corner.

Pick the trapdoor and emerge into the Warehouse. Quickly make your way through the shadows before the guards in the room find the open trapdoor.

Follow the corridor toward the Docks. Stick to the left wall to navigate through the surveillance camera's blind spot, then knock out the laser trip wire with your OCP.

Remember to perform this old routine.

Dock

Close the door behind you upon entering. A terrorist patrols near the entrance. He will probably hear or see Sam enter the area. Move down the steps quietly and move in behind him as he crosses to the left. Grab him and strangle him unconscious with a nonlethal attack.

Quietly take down the guard near the entrance.

Move to the corner of the large shipping container and jump up to grab the edge. Climb onto the container and move to its opposite end. Drop down the side quietly.

Use the large shipping container to get close to the bomb.

Sam is now near the Nashville bomb. So are BJ Sykes and another man. The two enemies' positions depend on whether or not Sam raised any suspicion while entering the area. In their default positions, BJ Sykes stands a few feet down in the shadows, while the other man works on the Red Mercury bomb. If they are in these locations, use rubber bullets to take out BJ Sykes. You *must* hit him in the head, or he and the other man counterattack.

With Sykes successfully down, use the OCP on the surveillance camera. Then sneak up beside the man near the bomb and perform a nonlethal attack to knock him out. Pick up his body and move it a few feet back into the shadows.

Sykes typically stands nearby while another man works on the bomb. Take down Sykes, then the surveillance camera, then the man near the bomb.

If you raised the suspicion of the terrorist near the entrance, Sykes possibly stands under the surveillance camera, making your task much harder. Hit Sykes in the head with a rubber bullet, which knocks him into the surveillance camera's blind spot. Then use the OCP on the camera and knock out the guy near the bomb.

Sykes may also be standing at the Dock's far end, near the fuse box. If so, ignore him completely and focus on the bomb.

Defuse the bomb by cutting the wires in the order they become hot. Use the same method as employed on the tanker in the Okhotsk mission (see screen caption below).

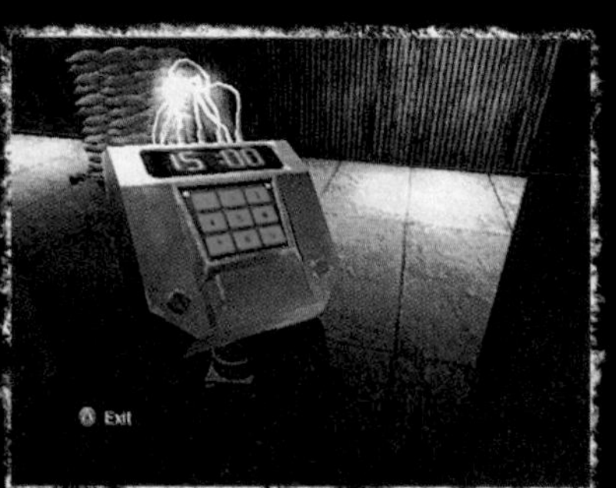

To defuse the Nashville bomb, cut the third wire from the left, then the first wire, then the fourth wire, and finally the second wire.

> **TIP**
>
> If defusing the Nashville bomb swings the Trust Level meter over to the NSA's side, Emile may order Sam to report it. Disregard this order until you find and defuse the Los Angeles bomb or until it is sent to its destination. After you handle the bomb situation, a four-minute time gauge appears. You must reach the bunker entrance and use the interaction to report to Emile.

Stand up and run full speed back to the entrance. Disable the trip wire and sneak along the passage's right side to avoid the surveillance camera.

Return to the Warehouse. Upon entering, climb over the crates to Sam's left. Drop down quietly and navigate through the shadows toward the shelves in the room's center. One terrorist patrols this side of the Warehouse. As he moves through shadows, sneak up behind him and grab him. Drag him a little farther into the darkness and choke him unconscious.

To enable safe access, grab and knock out the guard who patrols near the corner where the crates are stacked.

When the other guard is not facing Sam's direction, climb onto the crate in the corner between the two shelves. Move back into the niche and climb onto the shelves. Crawl over the boxes dividing the top shelf, and climb into the tall, open vent. Run quickly through the vent into the small shack on the Roof. Find the crawlspace in the corner of the shack and crawl through to the exterior.

Climb up to the tall, open vent in the Warehouse.

Roof

Move to the side of the stairs, jump up and grab the ledge above, and climb over. Move toward the back of the Roof, where the Los Angeles bomb sits. Moss and another man converse near the bomb. Shoot them both with tranquilizer darts. After they both pass out, quickly move in and defuse the bomb.

No time to analyze patrol routes! Depending on your loadout, shoot Moss and the other man near the LA bomb with tranquilizer darts or rubber bullets.

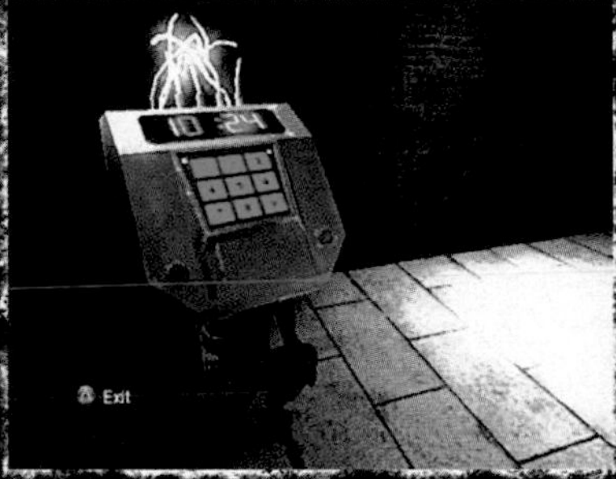

To defuse the Los Angeles bomb, cut the second wire from the left, then the fourth wire, then the third wire, and finally the first wire.

Emile orders Sam to report in. Head out to the Roof's edge and descend the ladder into the Alley. Move toward the bunker door. Choose the option to exfiltrate.

Return to the bunker's back porch and choose to exfiltrate.

NOTE

We have provided only one of two possible walkthroughs for this mission. The other option is to first clear the entire Warehouse of terrorists, then climb down through the open floor hatch and enter the bunker area through the Old Bunker. This basically reverses the order of every step. We feel our walkthrough is the most efficient.

New York City: Snowbound Rooftop

MAP KEY
- Medkit
- Ammo
- Frag Grenade

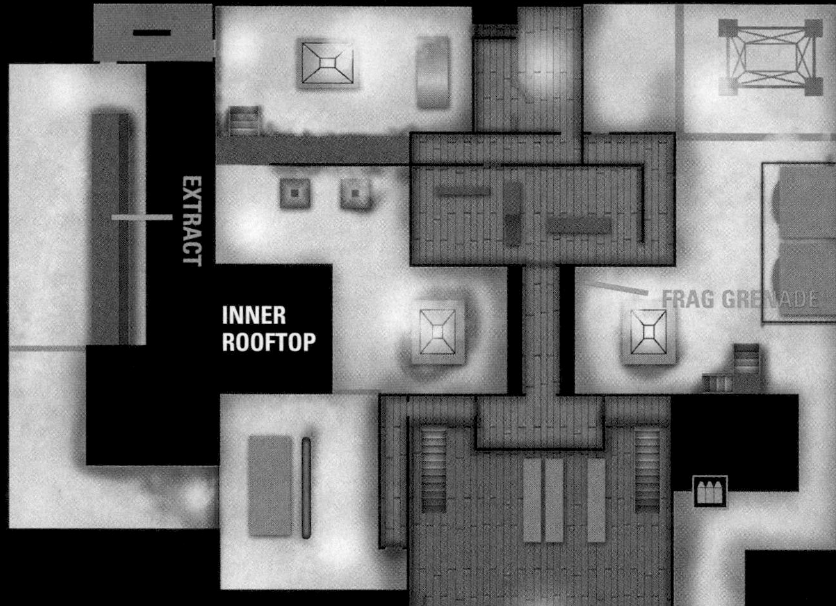

OBJECTIVES

PRIMARY OBJECTIVES

> DEFUSE FIRST BOMB: Find and disarm first of three bombs located somewhere on upper floor of old tower.

> KILL BJ SYKES AND JAMIE: Find and eliminate both BJ Sykes and Jamie, guarding first bomb.

> MAKE YOUR WAY TO SIDE OF TOWER: Make your way to side of tower using cable now present on lower roof section.

OPPORTUNITY OBJECTIVES

> NEUTRALIZE SYKES'S MEN: Sykes and Washington have set up their men to protect the first tower's roof. Find these men and eliminate them.

LOADOUT: NEW YORK CITY MISSION

JBA	NEUTRAL	NSA
SC pistol/60	SC pistol/40	SC pistol/20
SC-20K/90	SC-20K/60	SC-20K/30
Sniper attachment/18	Sniper attachment/12	Sniper attachment/6
Shotgun attachment/21	Shotgun attachment/14	Shotgun attachment/7
Sticky shockers/2	Sticky shockers/4	Sticky shockers/6
Airfoil round/2	Airfoil round/4	Airfoil round/6
EMP ammo/1	EMP ammo/2	EMP ammo/3
Sticky cameras/2	Sticky cameras/4	Sticky cameras/6
— —	Gas grenade/1	Gas grenade/2
Frag grenade/2	Frag grenade/1	— —
— —	Smoke grenade/1	Smoke grenade/1
— —	— —	— Flash grenade/2

Members of the JBA have deployed three Red Mercury devices on two of New York's towers. You must secure these devices at all costs.

The bluff is up and all cards are on the table! Sam's cover is blown, and his sole remaining objective is to eliminate every terrorist. The Fifth Freedom is in full force; killing enemies is in fact Sam's Opportunity Objective! Therefore, this mission's walkthrough explains how to eliminate each terrorist without being spotted.

Rooftop

Move forward from the starting point and hide at the brick wall's corner. Two terrorists discuss Sam's treason momentarily, then turn and begin to walk off. Sneak up behind the second of the two men as they move away. Grab him and interrogate him. Afterward, drag him around the corner, toward the red laser beam emitting from a wall-mounted laser mine. The terrorist's tracking device disables the laser. While the lasers are deactivated, silence the hostile's protests with a lethal jab in the back. That's right, *lethal*.

As the two men move back around the corner, follow and grab the closest man for a little Q&A.

At the corner, near a backpack, is sniper ammo for the sniper rifle attachment.

Sneak down the narrow passage past the corner. Continue to the back corner of a gated area and wait in the darkness for a terrorist to come within range. Sneak up close to his back and press the Lethal Attack button to kill him.

Wait near this fenced area until a guard moves close by. Stab him in the spinal column.

The last terrorist in the area moves through a narrow passage behind a large chimney. As he enters the passage's right side, go to the left entrance. Face the wall to Sam's left or right and Split Jump between the walls. When the terrorist comes around the corner and moves under Sam, drop on him. Equip the SC-20K and carefully tap the Fire button to put a single bullet in his brain. Use thermal vision to make sure his vitals cease.

Use a Split Jump to get the drop on the guard who patrols behind the chimney.

Check the snow at the chimney's far side to find a frag grenade.

Continue to the roof's other side. Equip the SC pistol and use the OCP to disable the laser trip mine. Enter the door around the corner. Move through the narrow passage until you reach a door.

Use the OCP to disable laser mines.

Warehouse

Rotate the camera angle to look through the door's window and spot a terrorist patrolling in the next room. When he moves up a ramp to the left, enter the room, sneak up behind him, and kill him.

The man patrolling the chicken coop may go directly to the ramp, or he may circle the entire room first. Either way, kill him on the ramp.

Pick up the dead body and carry it to the ramp's top. The terrorist's tracking device deactivates the laser mine. Drop the man's body near the laser mine to keep it inactive and go through the door into the next room.

01:
DOSSIERS

PS2/GC

02:
GAME BASICS

03:
EQUIPMENT

04:
SOLO MISSIONS

New York City:
Snowbound
Rooftop

05:
CO-OP MISSIONS

06:
VERSUS MISSIONS

XBOX 360/PC

07:
GAME BASICS

08:
EQUIPMENT

09:
SOLO MISSIONS

10:
MULTIPLAYER

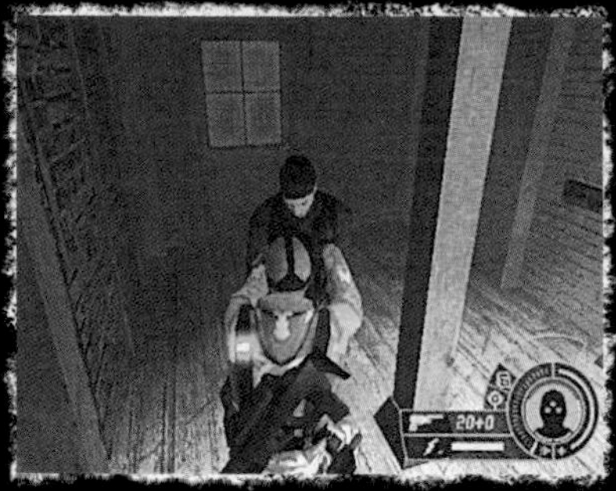

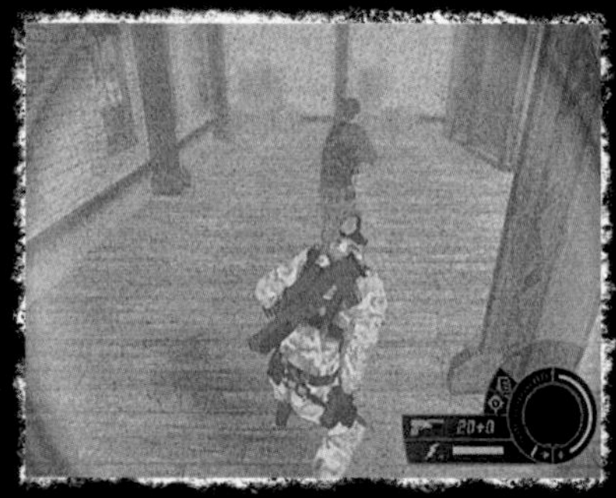

Use the dead guard's tracking device to turn off the laser mine.

One terrorist patrols the lower level while another moves back and forth in the rafters high above. Quietly but quickly, sneak downstairs and pursue the lower-level terrorist, who just starts to move away. Sneak up on him and grab him before he moves through the lighted area near the inoperative lift. Grab him, drag him back into the shadows near the south wall, and use a lethal attack.

Quickly overtake the lower-level guard before he moves into well-lit territory.

Equip the SC-20K and use the sniper attachment to take out the terrorist patrolling in the rafters. With the sniper attachment equipped, Sam can zoom in up to 3.5 times. Wait until the terrorist pauses at the end of his patrol route, then shoot him.

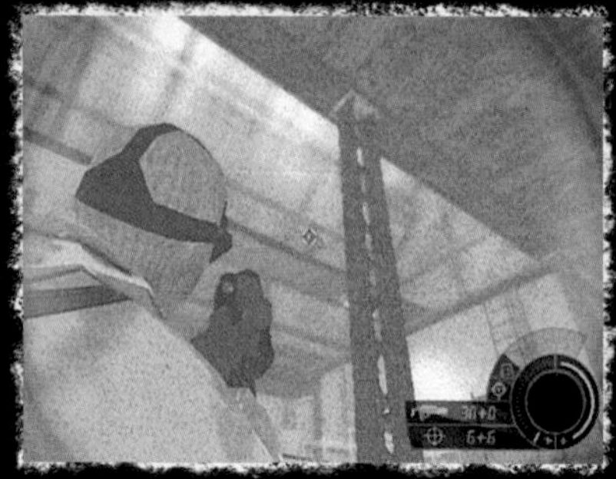

After neutralizing the lower-level terrorist, use the sniper attachment to take out the man on the upper level.

All the guards in the Warehouse are now dead. The best way to breach the next area, the Inner Rooftop, is to return through the Warehouse chicken coop area. Break the lock on the door in the east wall. No one is in the next room to notice you. Move carefully down the corridor to avoid setting off the wall mine mounted at the corner. Disable and collect the wall mine if you desire.

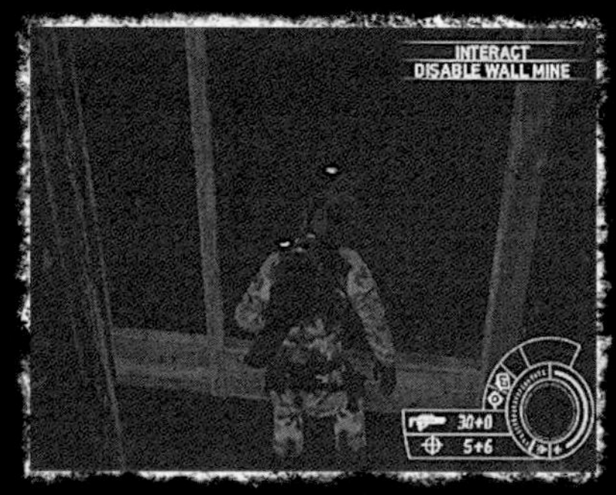

Slowly approach the wall mine in the corridor to avoid setting it off.

Around the corner to Sam's left, flip the wall switch to turn out the lights in the room. Do not proceed to the back of the room without dousing the lights, or Sam might be spotted through the open vent. Find the crawlspace in the corner and crawl through to the Inner Rooftop.

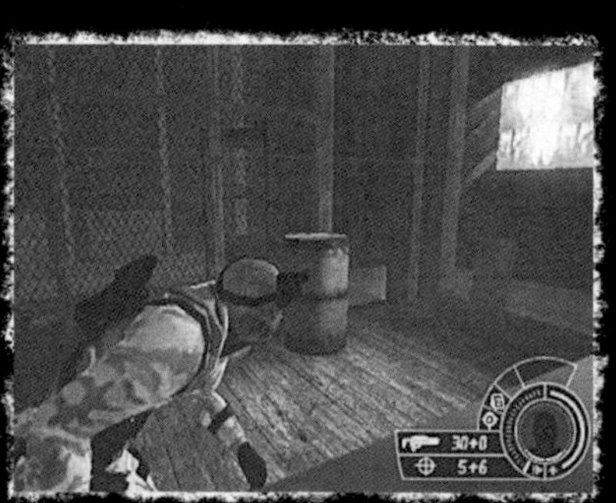

The crawlspace is the best way to breach the Inner Rooftop area.

Inner Rooftop

Three terrorists patrol this area. Two are visible at first—one heads off to patrol around the corner while one remains stationary near the door. Climb out of the vent and move left, to the air-conditioning unit's other side. Stop at the foremost corner, between the air-con unit and the railing, facing the stationary guard. Soon, the third terrorist enters the area and moves along the inside of the railed area. He stops just in front of Sam's position. Stand up, equip the SC pistol, and shoot him in the head. If done correctly, the stationary guard never notices a thing.

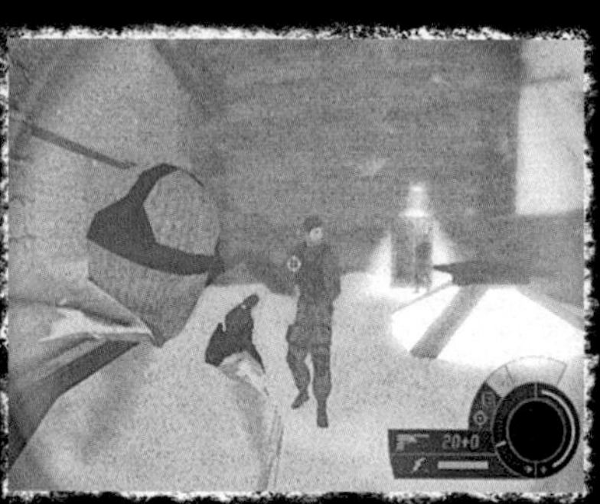

Move to the air conditioner's forward right corner and wait until a terrorist stops just feet away. Take him out with a single pistol shot to the head.

Climb over the railing on your left and carefully move along the brick wall to the corner. Go around the corner, and head across the passage to the side of one of two small structures. Wait until the other patrolling guard returns and moves past the corner. Step out and grab him. Drag him back behind the small structure and smash his spinal column.

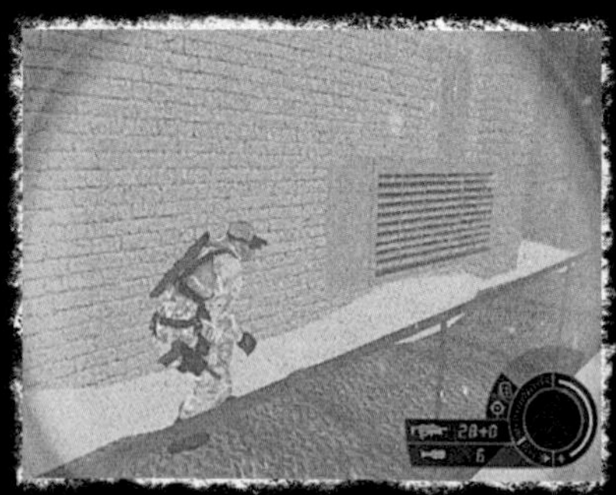

Climb over the railing near the brick wall. Move down the wall and around the corner.

Hide behind the small structure shown here and wait for the returning patrol to move past. Step out behind him and stab him.

Equip the SC-20K with the sniper attachment. Take out the terrorist standing in front of the door to the stairs. All of Sykes's men should now be neutralized.

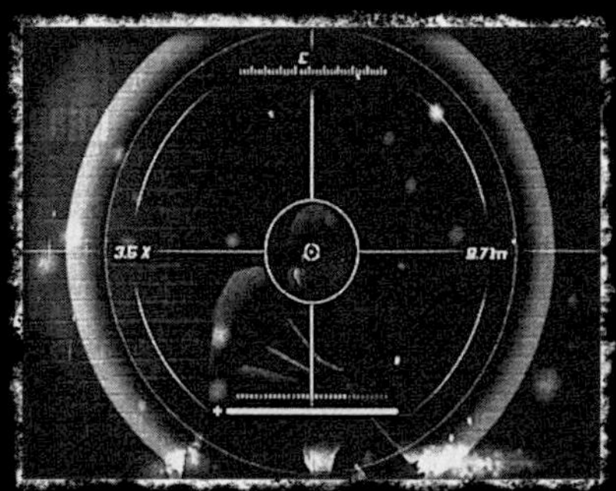

Take out the stationary guard near the door with a sniper shot.

Head west along the Inner Rooftop, deactivating the turret gun at the inside corner of the second area. Continue into the well-lit area, and head right. Go out to the roof's edge and rappel down the wall to the Billboard area.

Rappelling from the Inner Rooftop down to the Billboard area is the best way to get the drop on Sykes and Washington.

Billboard

Move slowly down the narrow passage to avoid setting off a wall mine. Jamie and Sykes patrol the area in front of a large billboard. The first Red Mercury device is near the wall, in the area's center.

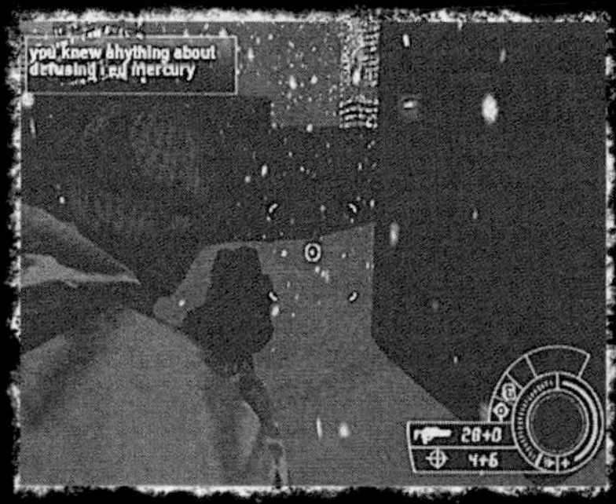

Avoid setting off the wall mine as you move toward the main area.

There are two ways to defuse the bomb: initiate the bomb's countdown to force Jamie and Sykes to disarm it, or defuse it yourself. The first method (initiating the bomb's countdown) is available only while Jamie and Sykes are still alive. Use the EEV to scan the bomb, then choose the Initiate Countdown Sequence option. Jamie shouts to Sykes, and they both converge on the bomb. Jamie convinces Sykes to disarm the device. Looks like they took care of that objective!

Use the EEV to scan the bomb and initiate the countdown sequence.

Jamie and Sykes defuse the bomb in a panic.

Jamie patrols closest to Sam, and therefore he is the first to die. To kill him, you can sneak up behind him and grab him; interrogate him to exchange a few heartfelt good-byes, then break his back in half. To kill him another way, first view him with EMF vision—Jamie wears a pacemaker, which shows up on the EMF. Equip the SC pistol and use the OCP to interrupt his pacemaker. Jamie groans and dies within five seconds.

Either grab Jamie and interrogate him one last time before killing him, or...

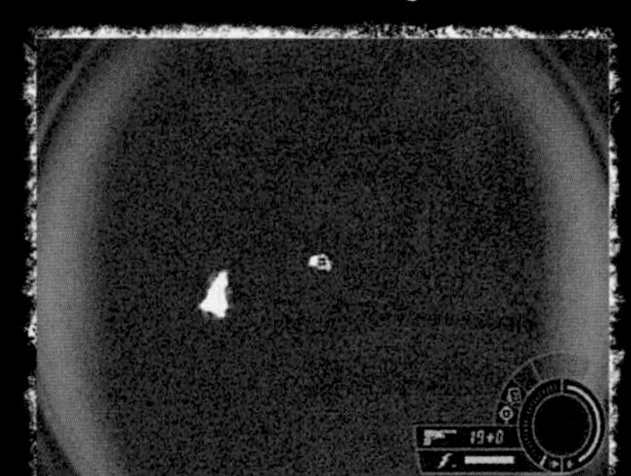

...use the OCP and EMF vision to locate Jamie's pacemaker and stop his heart.

If Sykes is just climbing up to the billboard's catwalk, follow him to the top. Sneak up behind him and grab him for a little interrogation, then dispose of him. If Sykes climbed up to the billboard a while ago and Jamie died a fairly silent death, then Sykes could be facing in any direction if you try to climb the billboard's ladder. Instead, move to the bomb and defuse it. Defusing the bomb alerts Sykes, who then climbs down from the billboard to see what's going on. Move through the support beams into the dark area under the billboard, sneak up behind Sykes, and kill him.

Sneak up on Sykes using the best method possible. End his sniveling with a hard chop to the back.

If you chose any strategy that leaves the bomb for Sam to defuse, then move to the bomb and do so. Download via the EEV complete schematics on the bomb—simply scan the bomb with the EEV and hack the security access. The frequency lines move extremely fast, and hacking it is not easy. However, there is no alert or penalty for not aligning all the frequencies in time. Once you successfully hack the security access, choose the new Download Bomb Specs option. Then open your OPSAT and look at the Notes menu. The Notes list the order in which you should cut the bomb's wires!

Downloading the bomb's specs gives you the cutting order for the wires.

A much easier way to defuse the bomb it to simply cut the wires in order from left to right. Enrica fires a cable from the next tower. Climb up the ladder to the billboard and use the zip line to slide over to the next tower.

Use the zip line Enrica provides to reach the next tower.

New York City: Darkened Offices

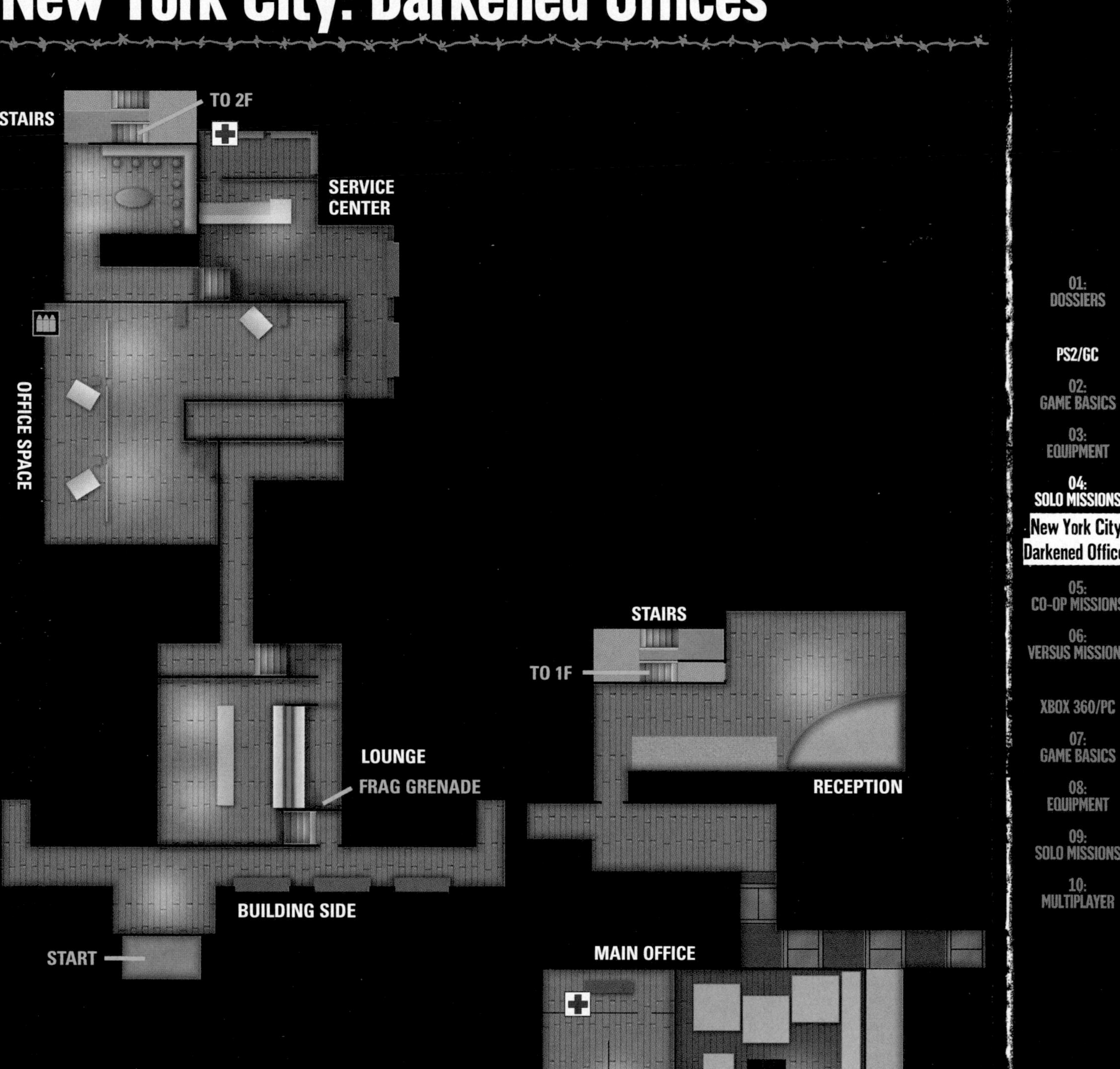

OBJECTIVES

PRIMARY OBJECTIVES

- DEFUSE SECOND BOMB: Find and disarm the second of three bombs located somewhere on upper floor of the tower.
- KILL MOSS: Find and eliminate Moss, who is guarding the second bomb.
- MAKE YOUR WAY TO ROOF: Make your way to the roof of the tower through the ventilation shaft, using a charge to enter it.

OPPORTUNITY OBJECTIVES

- NEUTRALIZE MOSS'S MEN: Moss has spread his team out on one of the floors of this building. Locate these men and eliminate them.

Carson Moss and his team are protecting the second Red Mercury device. All of them are equipped with night-vision goggles and may turn off the lights if their security is threatened. Sam cannot hide so easily in the shadows during this stage of the mission.

Building Side

Ascend the ramp and climb the ladder to a small platform. Go through the open vent hole into the elevator shaft. Pick the lock on the elevator roof's trapdoor and drop into the car.

Use the lock pick to open the elevator's trapdoor.

Lounge

When the elevator stops, exit and head down the corridor to the right. Open the door at the end of the corridor and close it behind you. Press Sam's shoulder against the opposite wall and slide down toward the corner. Stop roughly at the middle of the steps, and equip the SC-20K with sticky shockers. Two men in the room below complain about the sprinklers coming on. When they finish speaking, one of them moves into sight. Take him down quietly with a sticky shocker. Hitting him with the shocker is not hard, but shooting the sticky shocker into the water puddle he's standing in is even easier. Afterward, move over to his body and place a single bullet in his head.

Hide behind the corner near the entrance and fire a sticky shocker into the water puddle below this man's feet.

A waterfall pours into the drain on top of a stone bench. Climb over the bench and through the waterfall into the small room behind. Move to the room's door and use the optic cable to view the passage beyond. Wait patiently for several moments until the second terrorist comes around the corner. As he heads past the door on the left, open the door and sneak up behind him. Grab him and interrogate him for a bit of funny dialog, then silence him with a lethal blow. A frag grenade lies in the corner of this area next to a backpack.

Climb through the waterfall to reach the back room.

Wait for the guard to move around the corner before emerging from the room behind the waterfall. This gives Sam the drop on the guard.

Return to the door and close it. Then head around the corner and up the stairs. Press Sam's back against the wall at the next corner and peek down the long corridor. Soon, another terrorist comes into view. Retreat back to the corner and hide on the other side of the dividing wall. The terrorist emerges from the corridor and starts down the opposite steps. Sneak up behind him and stab him in the back.

Wait near the corner leading into the hallway. When the terrorist appears at the other end, retreat to the next position.

Hide as shown here and wait for the guard with night vision to start down the other stairs.

Sneak up behind the guard as he moves around the opposite corner.

Move down the long corridor, using the OCP to disable the laser mine in the passage. Continue around the corner to the Office Space door, but do not go in just yet.

Stop just outside the Office Space entrance and use the optic cable to survey the next room.

Office Space

Stop outside this room's door. Use the optic cable to spy into the Office Space, and twist the cable hard to the right. Wait until a terrorist starts to walk past. Quickly enter and move up the stairs. Sneak up behind the guard and grab him. Time is crucial, because you must nab him before he turns around. Drag him back toward the entrance, and quietly choke him unconscious for now.

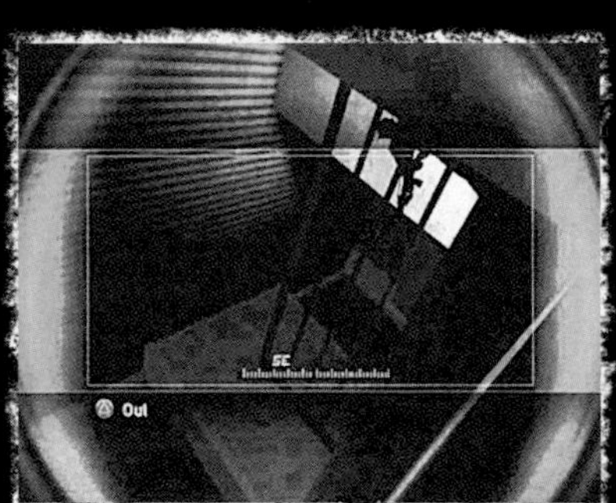

When the terrorist appears as shown here, remove the optic cable and enter the room.

Sneak up behind the terrorist and grab him. Drag him back to the door and quietly choke him unconscious to avoid alerting the other guard in the room.

Move to the corner where the rail meets the doorjamb, and angle your camera to peer west. Wait for another terrorist to appear as he patrols the room's other side. When he turns and starts to go behind the corner, climb over the rail. Sneak up behind him and press the Lethal Attack button to stab him in the spine.

Wait near the corner until the terrorist in the back area moves around the corner. Then climb over the rail and go after him.

Return to the Office Space entrance and kill the unconscious guard with a bullet. Search the room's southwest corner to find SC-20K ammo near a backpack.

Rifle ammo is located in this area's back corner.

Service Center

Open the door and proceed slowly through the corridor into the Service Center. Try not to set off the wall mine to the left. Use the medkit in the small room behind the counter to regain lost health if needed.

Disable the wall mine while entering the Service Center.

Ascend the short flight of steps and disable the laser mine with the OCP. Continue down the passage. As you near the corner, press Sam's back against the wall to the right and peek around the corner.

Use the OCP to take out the laser mine.

This situation is extremely tricky; one terrorist patrols very close to Sam's corner. Take this enemy down first. The other man patrols far into the break room to the right, into an area you cannot see. Therefore it is difficult to know whether the second man is facing Sam's position.

Wait through several patrols until both guards are visible at the same time. One man moves toward the exit door, while the other is nearly back at the corner by Sam's position. When the nearest guard stops and turns his back to Sam, slip out of hiding and quickly go after him. Grab him before he moves too far into the room. Drag him back around the corner just past the laser mine, and quietly choke him unconscious with a nonlethal attack. Leave his body close enough to the mine to keep the laser inactive. If done with the proper timing, the second guard will never notice.

Retaining stealth here is difficult. Before moving, wait near the corner until you see the men patrolling, as shown here.

Then move quickly up behind the closest guard and grab him. Drag him far out of the room before choking him unconscious.

Return to the corner, and slide down to the next corner with Sam's back against the wall. Wait for the second guard to patrol past the corner. Sneak up behind him and stab him in the back. Go back and kill the other guy as well.

The second man is easy to sneak up behind and kill.

Stairs

Enter the Stairs cautiously, moving slowly enough not to make much noise. A terrorist patrols the level above. He soon goes into the Reception area and closes the door behind him. When you hear the door close or see his tracker go back into the Reception area on the map, quietly ascend to the door.

To avoid detection from above, stay very close to the inside rail while quietly ascending the stairs.

Reception

Stop outside this room's door, and use the optic cable to watch the guards patrol their routes. A guard circles the Reception area's wide portion, then returns to the door and stops with his back to it. Remove the optic cable and switch to thermal vision. As the guard moves away from the door, open the door, sneak up on him, and grab him. Do not allow him to move too far into the room, or you risk being detected by the guard around the corner to Sam's right. Drag the guard into the Stairs area and choke him unconscious.

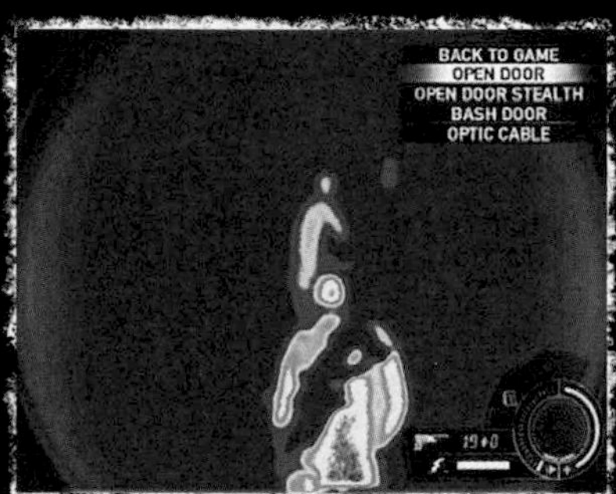

Wait in the Stairs area until the guard stops on the door's other side.

As the guard moves away, go through the door and grab him. Drag him out into the Stairs area and strangle him unconscious.

Stay in the Stairs area and close the stairwell door. Then use the optic cable on the door again. Wait until the second guard appears on the right and then goes back around the corner. Open the door and go after him. Stab him in the back, then return to the stairwell and execute the man you left there.

Insert the optic cable through the Stair door to spy on the guard who patrols the Reception area.

When the guard moves back around the corner, enter the room and go after him.

Approach the door at the Reception area's far end. Use the EEV to scan the computer inside the adjacent room to read three e-mails. The second one reveals the door code (4869). Enter the code into the keypad to open the door.

Scan the computer in the room behind the glass to determine the door's keypad code.

Sneak up behind the terrorist standing in the passageway. Sever his spinal column from behind.

The last terrorist standing between Sam and Moss is literally a pushover.

Proceed down the passage until you reach a ladder at the top of a short flight of stairs. The passage continues down the steps to the right. However, above the corridor runs a maintenance space. Jump up from the bottom step to grab a board. Then climb up from the board into the maintenance space. Moving through the small space above the corridor allows you to avoid detection by the wall mine and gun turret protecting Moss.

Jump up from the bottom step to grab the board overhead; climb from there into the maintenance space running above the passage.

Main Office

Follow the maintenance space into the rafters above a large gallery. Two of Moss's men patrol the area below. Moss is located in the upper-level office on the gallery's opposite side. He stands before the second bomb. Another terrorist patrols back and forth through the office.

Sam emerges from the maintenance space into the Main Office. Moss and the bomb are on the upper level on the room's opposite side.

After stepping onto the rafters, turn right and quietly head along the gallery's back wall. Watch Sam's Light meter, and stop moving when you reach a completely dark spot. Use the EEV to locate Moss and the bomb in the upper-level office. Scan the bomb and initiate its countdown sequence. After a few seconds, all the men, except Moss, leave the room!

Follow the rafters to this corner.

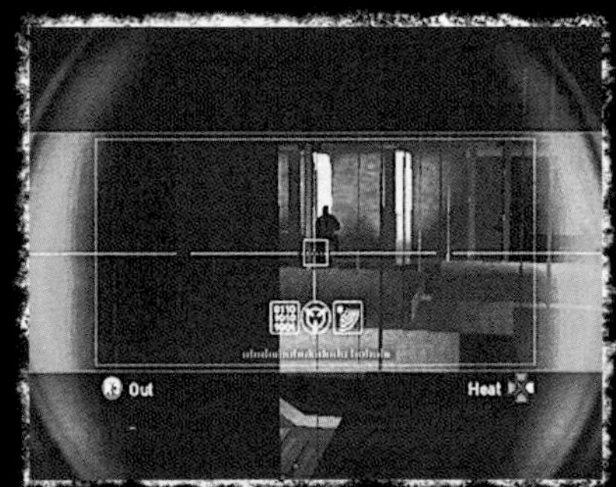

Use the EEV to initiate the bomb's countdown sequence.

When the last man has fled to the corridor, move quickly to the rafters' end, near Moss's position. Pull out the SC-20K, zoom in, and press the Nonlethal Attack button to hold your breath and steady your aim. Shoot Moss in the head to kill him. No big loss to humanity, there.

After everyone but Moss flees, move to the corner nearest Moss and execute him with a silenced shot.

The timer continues counting down. Quickly drop from the rafters near the stairs and race up into the office. Approach and defuse the bomb by cutting, in order from left to right, the first wire, then the third wire, then the second wire, then the fourth wire.

Quickly defuse the bomb before the timer you set off triggers an explosion!

Now take care of the three men cowering in the hallway. Approach their location and move toward the door's right side—without moving too close to the turret gun. Equip the frag grenade garnered earlier, and aim down the corridor toward the plant set against the wall. Throw the frag grenade just past the plant's base, then whip out the SC-20K. If the grenade doesn't kill all three men, gun down any survivors who charge around the corner.

Aim a frag grenade down the corridor to take out the three men who bailed on Moss.

Head to the door in the lower level's southwest corner. Use the medkit near the door to recover lost life, then break the lock on the door.

Recover from battle before moving on.

Ventilation Room

Place charges on the panel at the end of the short passage. Then retreat out of the corridor and detonate the charges. Head through the opening the blast created to the final stage.

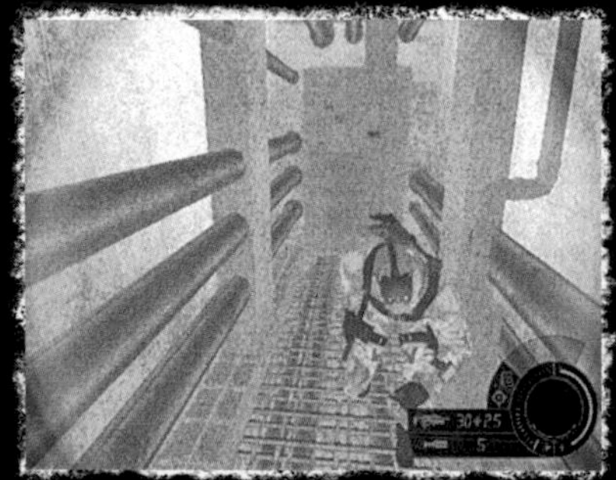

Detonate charges on the back panel of this tiny passage in order to reach the tower's upper levels.

New York City: The Fifth Freedom

MAP KEY

Medkit

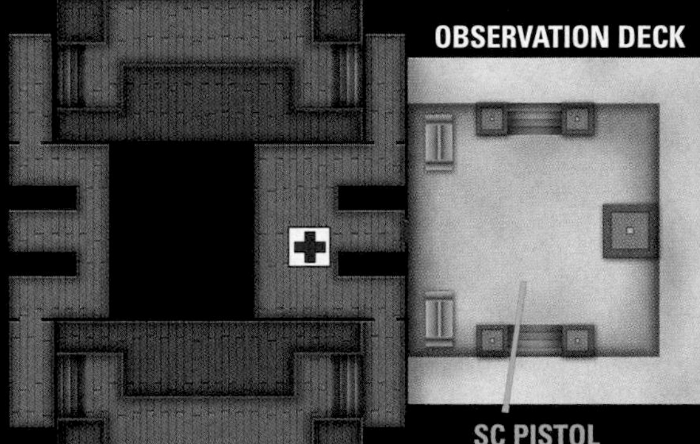

OBJECTIVES

PRIMARY OBJECTIVES

> DEFUSE THIRD BOMB: Find and disarm the last of three bombs located on tower roof.

> KILL EMILE: Find and eliminate Emile, who is guarding the last bomb.

OPPORTUNITY OBJECTIVES

> NEUTRALIZE EMILE'S MEN: Emile's men are patrolling the full top section of the tower. Get rid of them.

Emile Dufraisne is guarding the last Red Mercury device. Take him out and defuse the bomb.

Ventilation Shaft

Move forward along the pipe until you reach a horizontal beam. Follow the beam to Sam's left. Near the wall, jump up and grab a pipe. Climb to the area's top, then shimmy hand over hand across the horizontal pipe until Sam is positioned above a catwalk. Press the Crouch button to drop from the pipe onto the catwalk. Head north to the catwalk's end, then turn right and move across the last horizontal beam. Bypass the circuit on the open breaker box, then return to the catwalk.

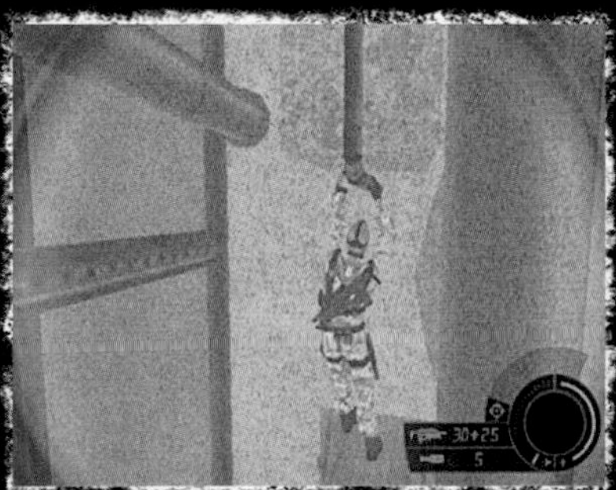

Jump to grab the pipe above the beam.

Climb along the pipe until Sam is over a catwalk, then drop onto the iron grating.

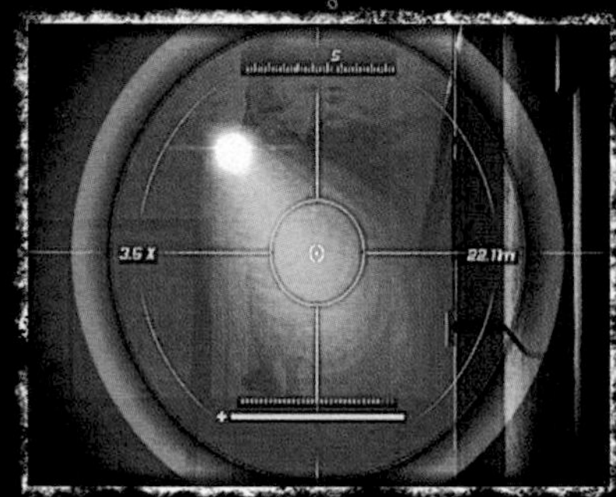

Bypass the circuitry on the breaker box at the area's far end.

At the catwalk's far end, a terrorist searches for Sam with a flashlight. Use the sniper attachment to take him out.

Use a sniper shot to take out the guard who enters the area.

Move to the catwalk's other end. The door to the top of the stairs is now open. Behind the machinery to the left is a narrow passage running behind the wall. Follow the narrow passage to a turbine room. Move slowly past a wall mine and continue to the far end of the room.

Navigate through the machinery area, being careful of the wall mine set on the wall to Sam's right.

Pick the lock on the exit door. Then use the optic cable at the door to monitor the two men in the next room. Wait until both terrorists patrol near Sam's position and turn away. Then open the door and enter.

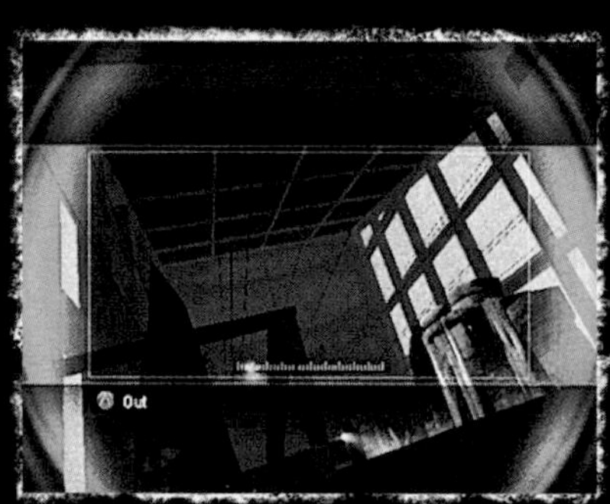

Use the optic cable to make sure neither man in the next room is facing your direction before entering.

Central Greenhouse

Close the door behind you and turn right. Run to the room's south side. Climb over the low wall and behind the tall rock before either terrorist turns around.

Climb over the low wall near the windows to get behind the cover of the tall rocks.

Move along the rock toward the corner. However, stay about a foot back from the rock's corner to remain out of sight. Use the EEV to hack the turret gun at the top of the stairs.

Use the EEV to hack the turret gun at the top of the stairs.

Angle your camera view to see the terrorists patrolling the central aisle. Wait until both men pause near the gun turret and then turn and walk away. When the coast is clear, drop into the pool of water below. Quickly wade through the water and jump up to grab the rail near the back wall. Climb over the rail and move behind the turret gun.

When the patrolling terrorists aren't looking, move through the low pool and climb over the rail on the opposite end of the pool.

Watch the terrorists patrol the room. When one man is nearly at the gun turret and the second guy is on his way back, turn off the machine's friendly-fire inhibitor mechanism. The turret gun opens fire on the two terrorists, eliminating them. Wait until the background music dies down and the suspicion level returns to normal before proceeding.

When both guards are headed back toward the turret, turn off the friendly-fire inhibitor.

Move around either corner of the dividing wall and quietly approach the central door. Use thermal vision to see two men patrol the Central Deck area. Load the SC-20K with sticky shockers, then open the door.

Central Deck

Before the two men finish their conversation, hit the man on the midlevel catwalk with a sticky shocker. Switch the gun to Sam's left hand, use the door as cover, and aim at the other guy. Take him down with a sticky shocker too.

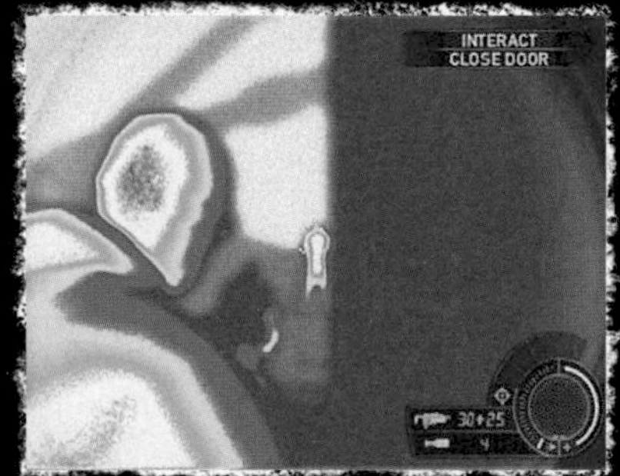

Use the entrance door as cover while using sticky shockers to knock out both men patrolling this area. Execute them later.

On the catwalk in the southwest corner are two flashbang grenades. Take these, and before leaving the area, remember to put bullets in both men's heads to complete the Opportunity Objective.

Find two flashbang grenades in the area's lower corner.

Go through the door on the uppermost deck. A guard equipped with thermal vision is setting a wall mine around the corner to Sam's left. Take him out with a single shot to the head to avoid alarming the men in the surrounding rooms. Don't hit the wall mine or you die as well.

Aim around the corner to the left and take out the guy installing a wall mine.

At this point, you may go either through the East or West Greenhouse. To complete the Opportunity Objective, you must eliminate the soldiers in both areas.

West Greenhouse

Open the door, move inside, go right a few steps, and close the door behind you. Although the entry point is dark, the rest of the West Greenhouse is extremely well lit and infiltration is nearly impossible.

When the nearest guard is facing away from you, move quietly across the top of the stairs toward the exterior wall. Hide behind the low pony wall and equip the SC-20K with the sniper attachment. Wait for the nearest terrorist to stop close to Sam's position. Tap the Fire button to suppress the closest terrorist with a single shot to the head. Quickly zoom in on the terrorist patrolling the room's opposite side and snipe him.

Snipe the two men in the room from cover behind the low pony wall.

The back doors in both the West Greenhouse and the East Greenhouse are locked. To enter the East Greenhouse, return through the Central Deck corridor and go through the unlocked door.

East Greenhouse

As in the West Greenhouse, wait until the terrorist patrolling closest to Sam's entry point turns and walks away. Then sneak over to the exterior wall and hide behind the low pony wall. Looking toward the back of the room, Sam can hit both men as they move along the walkway near the window. Remove the sniper attachment from the SC-20K and zoom in. First snipe the farthest terrorist, then hit the closest when he returns to the portion of walkway near the windows.

Move to the low pony wall near the windows and snipe the two men in the room from behind cover.

Use the OCP to deactivate the laser mine blocking the walkway. Proceed to the room's back door and break the lock.

Observation Deck

Use the medkit near the passage's center to fully recover, then proceed through the central door to confront Emile.

Be sure to heal up and save your game before heading toward the final showdown.

Emile forces Sam to drop all his weapons so he cannot shoot back. The SC pistol falls near the area's center. Laser mines are set up in a grid formation to prevent Sam from approaching Emile or the final bomb. They also prevent Sam from reaching his gun.

Emile sprays the area with machine-gun fire. Occasionally he stops shooting to change mags. Wait to move or take any action until he reloads.

There are two ways to maneuver around the benches and reach the SC pistol. Both methods are tricky. The first strategy is to wait until Emile reloads, then run from the starting point to the bench to Sam's left. Farther to your left is another laser mine. Wait until Emile relocates to the left, deactivating the laser. Run around the bench and hold the Crouch button to roll behind the central bench.

One method of retrieving Sam's weapon is to move from bench to bench between Emile's machine-gun volleys.

Wait for Emile to move to Sam's right, deactivating the next laser. This allows Sam to run to the area's south side. Stand up and run to avoid as much damage as possible. Hide behind a large column near the area's east edge.

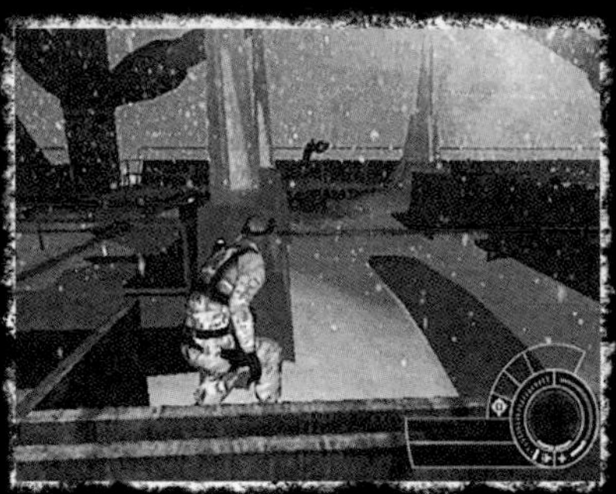

Emile's tracking device disables laser mines when he changes positions. Use the opportunity to advance toward the column on the area's far side.

Use the EEV to look toward the area's center. Spot the laptop sitting on the back side of a bench. Use the EEV to access the laptop and deactivate all the laser sensors. At this point, Emile initiates the bomb's countdown sequence.

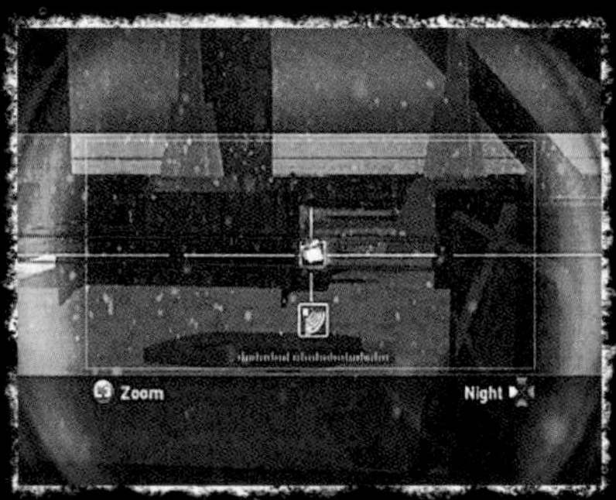

Use the EEV to scan the center laptop and disable all the laser mines.

The next time Emile reloads, run out and grab Sam's SC pistol and find cover behind the central bench. Move out to the edge of the bench closest to Emile's position. Draw the SC pistol and wait for Emile to reload. Move beyond the bench's corner and shoot Emile repeatedly until he falls.

Hide behind the central bench with the SC pistol ready. When Emile stops firing, step out and shoot him dead.

If you have any skill at rolling, consider a different strategy. Between Emile's volleys, move and hold the Crouch button to roll under the laser beams and cut down on the amount of time Sam is exposed without cover. From the starting point, wait until Emile takes his first break in firing, then roll under the laser beam spanning between the two closest benches. If successful, Sam winds up unscathed near the back of the central bench. If unsuccessful, Sam hits the laser and triggers the mine, dying instantly. From behind the central bench, you can then dive roll under the laser beam to the right. Although this places you on top of Sam's pistol, immediately run forward and seek cover behind the bench nearest the laptop. During the next break in machinegun fire, run back and pick up the pistol. Take cover behind the bench near the laptop once again, and kill Emile when you have the chance. Then use the laptop to deactivate the laser array, and defuse the bomb. This strategy prevents Emile from ever initializing the bomb's final countdown!

Dive-rolling under the lasers may save you time and prevent some damage.

With Emile dead, quickly go to the bomb and defuse it by cutting, in order from left to right, the fourth wire from the left, then the first wire, then the third wire, then the second. Operation complete.

Defuse the final bomb to complete the game!

Harbor, Washington, DC: Cargo Ship

OBJECTIVES

PRIMARY OBJECTIVES

> NEUTRALIZE ALL KIDNAPPERS ON BOARD SHIP: Sarah's been kidnapped with two other young women and is being held on this ship. She must not see you saving her. Neutralize everyone on the ship while making sure she is unaware of your involvement.

OPPORTUNITY OBJECTIVES

> FIND OUT WHO ORDERED THE KIDNAPPING: Third Echelon wants to know who is behind the kidnapping.

LOADOUT: SHIP MISSION

AVAILABLE WEAPONS
SC pistol/40
SC-20K/60
Sticky shockers/2
Sticky cameras/4

Kidnappers have taken over a cargo vessel in the Washington, DC harbor and are now holding the crew hostage. Secure the location by neutralizing every kidnapper. One of the hostages is Sam's daughter, Sarah Fisher.

Cargo Storage Area A

As Sam communicates with Lambert, a kidnapper searches the back of the insertion area with a flashlight. Move to Sam's left and follow the wall to a stack of metallic boxes. Climb on top of the boxes and move to the edge. When the kidnapper stops under Sam's position, drop on top of him, knocking him out.

Climb onto the boxes in the area, then drop onto the kidnapper to knock him out.

NOTE

This is a very basic mission, originally intended as a training excursion and a prelude to the Iceland mission. Trust Level is not a factor. Use lethal or nonlethal force to take out the kidnappers, whatever you prefer.

Climb down the ladder at the back of the area and move through the low passage. Climb up the next ladder into the back of a cargo container. Move to the container's end and stop to survey the next area.

Follow the low passage to the next ladder and climb up. The open cargo containers serve as corridors between areas.

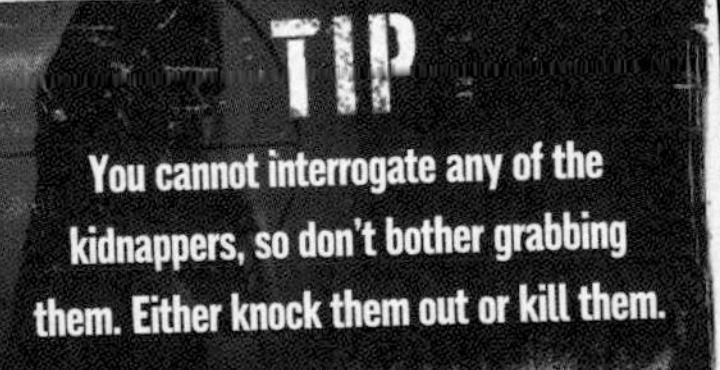

TIP

You cannot interrogate any of the kidnappers, so don't bother grabbing them. Either knock them out or kill them.

Cargo Storage Area B

Initially two kidnappers are visible in the area. Soon, one man exits. The remaining kidnapper heads over to the fence on the left to relieve himself. Intercept him and knock him unconscious.

When one kidnapper leaves the other alone, follow the man over to the fence and interrupt his "business."

Follow the kidnapper who left by going through the open cargo container into the area's second portion. Stop near the end of the cargo container and wait for the kidnapper to approach. When he turns his back to Sam, step up behind him and knock him out.

Wait near the cargo container's exit until the guard patrolling the next area stops nearby and turns his back to Sam, practically begging to be smacked.

Head around the corner and squeeze through the narrow gap between the stack of crates and the cargo container. Head to the passage's end and go around the corner to Sam's left. Follow another kidnapper into the next area.

Squeeze through the narrow gap between the crates and the cargo container to reach the next area.

Cargo Storage Area C

One man paces the area while another sits on a crate. Wait near the entrance until the pacing kidnapper walks past Sam, to the left. Step up behind him and grab him. Press the Nonlethal Attack button to choke him unconscious quietly, so as not to disturb the other kidnapper. Then move behind the seated man and karate-chop him from behind.

Take out the pacing kidnapper quietly to avoid alerting the other.

Sneak up behind the seated kidnapper and knock him out.

Head to the corner the seated man was staring at, then go through the narrow gap, past a floodlight, and into an open cargo container. Move to the container's end, and head around the corner to Sam's right. Two kidnappers stand near a table at the back of the area. To the right is a stack of boxes. Climb on top of the boxes and wait. Soon, one of the kidnappers edges around the boxes on patrol. Let him pass, then drop to the ground behind him. Sneak up behind him and knock him out.

Climb on top of the boxes near the two kidnappers' position. Wait until one man patrols near Sam, then drop down behind him and knock him out.

Creep up on the kidnapper bent over the map, and knock him unconscious. To the table's left is a small box. Pick up the keycard that's lying on the box and swipe it through the card reader on the nearby door. Enter the ship's interior.

Find the keycard for the nearby door on the small box next to the map table.

Crew's Quarters

Sneak over to the man dozing in the chair on the left, near a medkit. Knock him unconscious, then rummage through the file cabinet in the far corner to uncover the identity of the group responsible for the kidnapping. As we well know, Raheem Kadir shall soon receive a little visit from Sam.

Search the file cabinet in the infirmary to find out who is behind the kidnapping.

Head through the doorway and descend the stairs. A kidnapper is approaching, so quickly move about halfway down the corridor and then jump up to grab a pipe running along the ceiling. Press the Jump button again to pull Sam's legs up. Wait for the kidnapper to walk underneath Sam. When the Grab Character interaction appears, press the Interact button to grab the kidnapper and strangle him unconscious. Do this immediately, or you may miss the opportunity.

Hang from the pipe in the corridor to take out the patrolling kidnapper from above.

Speak to Sam's daughter through the last door in the passage.

Stop at the last portal on the left and speak to Sarah through the door. Then turn around and head through the short passage to the stairwell. Two kidnappers stand just inside the doorway to the right. While they talk, load the SC-20K with sticky shockers. Aim at the man standing on the ground

but I don't work for you," wait a beat and then hit him with a sticky shocker.

When the two men near the stairs stop talking, knock out the man on the ground level.

The other kidnapper moves up the stairs and stops in the middle of the balcony, leaning on the rail. Move through the room's dark portion to the balcony's left end, where the rail is broken. Jump to grab the balcony ledge, and climb up. Approach the kidnapper from the side and knock him out or stab him.

Climb up through the railing's broken section in order to stealthily approach the kidnapper leaning on the balcony rail.

Cargo Storage Area D

Cross the area and enter the open cargo container. Find the crawlspace beneath the shelves and crawl through.

The crawlspace to the area's next section is located behind the tarp covering the opening of the cargo container.

In the next passageway, climb atop the two metal containers stacked on the left. A kidnapper leans against the wall just behind the stack. Drop off the containers onto him, knocking him unconscious. Five more hostiles to go.

Climb onto the stack of two containers, and drop off the other side to knock out a hidden kidnapper.

Slide through the narrow space in the corner to reach the next area.

Cargo Storage Area E

Quickly move around the corner to Sam's right. A kidnapper approaches on patrol. Face the wall to the left or right and press the Jump button to initiate a Split-Jump. Allow the kidnapper to approach. As he moves underneath Sam, press the Crouch button to drop on top of him, knocking him out.

Perform a Split-Jump in the next passage to get the drop on the man patrolling the passage.

Continue following the passage south. At the corner, head left around the cargo containers. Take another left at the row's end, then head toward two kidnappers standing in the middle of the deck, shooting the breeze.

Approach the two kidnappers standing in the deck's middle from the south vector for the greatest chance of success.

Stay close to the wall on Sam's right and move in close to the two men as they talk. Between Sam and the kidnappers is a low support beam. Jump up to grab the beam and climb on top of it.

Use the beam in the area's center to get the drop on one of the guards.

Wait for the two men to finish talking and start patrolling the area. One man stops under the beam. Walk off the beam and drop onto him, knocking him out.

The second kidnapper hears the noise. This area of the deck is rather dark, so as the suspicious man approaches, quietly circle around behind him. As the kidnapper reaches his comrade's body, knock him unconscious.

If this kidnapper fails to respond to the noise, simply use a sticky shocker to knock him out, or snipe him with the SC-20K.

Just two more kidnappers left. Open your OPSAT and find "Cargo Storage Area F." Navigate toward there now.

Cargo Storage Area F

A floodlight just inside the entrance lights the area. One man patrols back and forth while another leans against the wall behind the stack of crates to the left. Wait until the kidnapper on patrol stops near the entrance and pauses. Hit him with a sticky shocker.

Electrocute the kidnapper that stops in front of the area's entrance.

Reenter the area and move up behind the stack of crates on the left. Climb on top of the crates, then drop from the other side to knock out the last kidnapper.

Climb over the crates and drop off them to knock out the remaining kidnapper.

With all the kidnappers dead or unconscious, return to the Crew's Quarters and speak to Sarah again to complete the mission.

To complete the mission, reassure Sarah that she will be okay.

Location Unknown: Underground Bunker

OBJECTIVES

PRIMARY OBJECTIVES

> ESCAPE BUNKER: It's been swell, but you really can't stay. Unless they have cake.... No. It might not have a file in it.

LOADOUT: BUNKER MISSION

AVAILABLE WEAPONS
SC-303 compact launcher/6

Following a raid, Sam is captured and being held in an undisclosed facility. Find a way to escape and report back to Third Echelon.

The guards in this mission are equipped with Tasers. If they shoot you, you will be knocked out instantly. This results in instant mission failure. Further complicating matters, Sam has been drugged. Occasionally his vision grows blurry, to the point of complete disorientation.

Cells

Sam awakens in a prison cell deep within a bunker, possibly located in Normandy, France. He is equipped only with a compact launcher and six rubber bullets.

Turn around and locate the pipe attached to the wall near the corner. Climb to the pipe's top, shimmy to the left across a ledge to its end, then climb into an open vent.

Climb the pipe in the corner to reach the opening high in the cell.

Boilers

Turn left and squeeze through the narrow gap into the next area. Jump up to grab a horizontal pipe, then shimmy through a small hole into a guard post.

Use the pipe to exit the boiler area.

Bunker Corridor A

Continue shimmying along the pipe until Sam is directly above the lone man in the room, who stands bent over a map table. When the Grab Character option becomes available, reach down and choke him unconscious.

Use the pipe to grab the lone man from above.

Open the door and proceed into the corridor. Close the door behind you. Move into the dark area in the passage's middle, then jump to grab the pipe overhead. Press the Jump button again to pull Sam's legs up, and wait. After a few moments, a guard walks around the corner and moves under Sam. Strangle him from above.

While hanging from the pipe above, grab the guard patrolling the corridor.

Drop to the ground and follow the corridor around the corner and to its end. Enter the crawlspace and head into the next room.

Find the crawlspace exit at the corridor's far end.

Storage Area A

Two guards stand watch in this room; one man blocks the ground floor exit while another patrols on the catwalk above. Take out the guard on the catwalk first. That way you are free to approach the ground floor guard and do whatever you want to him. After exiting the crawlspace, turn left and move through the shadows behind the crates stacked on pallets.

Exit the crawlspace and move along the crates stacked at the catwalk's base.

Jump and climb on top of the tall crate that is directly under the catwalk. Then jump to grab the catwalk's ledge. Shimmy a few inches to Sam's left, then climb up through the rail's broken section.

Jump up and climb onto the catwalk at the break in the rail.

Wait until the guard patrolling the catwalk approaches the sawhorses blocking the path and then walks away. Then climb over the sawhorses and sneak up behind the guard. Grab him from behind and interrogate him to learn about a secret stash of grenades in the next room. Choke him unconscious.

The guard on the catwalk reveals a secret hiding place.

Follow the catwalk to its end, climbing over the barrels blocking the path. Slide down the ladder to the ground floor. Follow the wall to the corner, then sneak toward the stationary guard's position. Creep up to the guard's side and knock him out.

Use the shadows to sneak up on the guard blocking the exit.

01: DOSSIERS
PS2/GC
02: GAME BASICS
03: EQUIPMENT
04: SOLO MISSIONS
Location Unknown: Underground Bunker
05: CO-OP MISSIONS
06: VERSUS MISSIONS
XBOX 360/PC
07: GAME BASICS
08: EQUIPMENT
09: SOLO MISSIONS
10: MULTIPLAYER

TIP

Without night vision, you may have serious trouble locating objects and enemies in the environment. If so, visit the Options menu and change the Shadow Calibration to increase the brightness of your display.

Storeroom

Go through the door and follow the passage to the right. At the end of the locker row, one locker is slightly removed from the wall. Search behind this locker to find flashbang and smoke grenades.

Nonlethal grenades are stored behind the detached locker at the row's end.

Machine Room

Enter the passage behind the broken vent and wade into the water. Continue through the passage until Sam passes out. When he awakens, continue through the watery passage into a maintenance room. Move to the inside corner and climb out onto the platform. Find the pipe bolted to the wall in the corner, and climb to the ceiling. Pull Sam's legs up, and shimmy along the ceiling using the horizontal pipe. A single mechanic works in the maintenance room. Drop to the floor behind him and knock him out.

Climb out of the water, and climb up the pipe to the ceiling.

Drop to the floor behind the mechanic, and knock him out.

Enter the corridor and prepare to move fast. Two men patrol past the intersection ahead. Fall in line and follow them. As you all move through a dark area, grab the second man and drag him toward the next passage intersection. When you reach the wall, choke him unconscious. When the first guard reaches the end of his patrol route, he turns around and immediately notices that his buddy is missing. As he moves back through the corridor to search for the missing guard, equip the SC-303 and hit him in the head with a rubber bullet. Climb over the sawhorses and go through the door into the next passage.

Pursue the two men into the dark area.

Grab the second man and drag him toward the wall. Choke him unconscious, then fire the SC-303 from this position to knock out the other guard.

Bunker Corridor B

To Sam's left is a door. But as you head toward the door, it suddenly disappears. Sam was hallucinating, and it turns out there is no door. Turn around and go to the passage's other end; climb the iron rungs set into the wall.

Appearances can be deceiving while under the influence.

Weapon Storage

Go through the door into the next room. Sam enters a catwalk. A guard and a mechanic stand directly below Sam's position, finishing a conversation.

Move along the rail to the left. Climb

Move a few steps to Sam's left, and climb over the rail. Hang from the catwalk's bottom. While the guard patrols the room's well-lit portion, the mechanic makes a close circle and eventually moves back under the catwalk. As he moves underneath Sam's position, drop to the ground beside him and knock him out.

When the mechanic passes under the catwalk, drop to the ground and knock him out.

If you grab the mechanic and interrogate him, the results are somewhat bizarre.

Move to the tail end of the corroded missile and check the central area. If the guard is not there, go through the door in the corner.

When the coast is clear, sneak from the tail end of the missile over to the exit.

As Sam enters the narrow, well-lit passage full of jail cells, his vision begins to blur. The guard at the corridor's other end immediately becomes suspicious and begins to approach. You must equip the SC-303 and fire two rubber bullets at the guard. Do not aim for a headshot, since the screen is too blurry to rely on. Aim the first shot center mass, and then lower your aim a bit to fire the second shot while the guard is stunned.

Sam's vision is compromised. Draw the SC-303 and fire upon the dark blur that is slowly approaching. Otherwise, the guard may taser Sam.

Continue to the corridor's far end, and climb the iron rungs set into the wall.

Storage Area B

Enter the crawlspace and crawl through to the next area. Upon exiting from the front of the crawlspace, Sam's vision soon clears up. Move out of the lighted passage into the main room. Stop at the corner of a caged area. Jump to grab the cage's top ledge, and pull yourself on top. Move across the cage's top and drop down from the other side.

Climb across the top of the cage to reach the dark corner on the far side, which provides Sam the best point of attack.

While you move across the cage, two guards enter the room. Drop to the ground floor. Both guards patrol the room. Remain in the shadowed corner with your back pressed against the wall until one of the men patrols around the cage's edge. As he moves away from the corner, follow him and grab him. Drag him back into the corner and quietly choke him unconscious. Now simply pursue the other guard on his patrol route and knock him out at the first opportunity.

Pursue one of the guards away from the corner. Grab him, drag him into the shadows, and knock him out.

Climb onto the cage again. Face the corner lit by a bluish light, and jump up while moving the left analog stick forward—Sam grabs the ledge of the upside-down catwalk and pulls himself up. Jump to grab the bottom of the inverted doorway, and climb up through it.

Exit through the inverted doorway on the upper level.

Flooded Corridor

Move through the flooded passage. Sam drops into a partially collapsed area. Go through the door at the end to complete the mission.

Been nice seeing ya!

05: PS2/GC

CO-OP MISSIONS

Co-op Introduction

Co-op mode enables two players to partake in a series of missions specially designed for team play. The story line in these missions runs parallel to Sam Fisher's Solo missions. Only the Xbox version of the game allows two players to connect online. In the PlayStation 2 and GameCube versions, Co-op mode can only be played offline.

NOTE

This Co-op mode walkthrough is drawn from the PlayStation 2 version of the game. Minor differences may arise in the GameCube and Xbox versions. However, for the most part, the strategy presented here should be comprehensive across all last-generation versions.

Co-op mode is very different from Solo mode in many respects:

> The EEV is not available. You must access all computers and electronic devices by hand. To zoom in for surveillance purposes, use the SC-20K's scope.

> You can use the OCP to jam electronic devices, but jamming is effective only while you hold down the Nonlethal Attack button and while charge remains in the battery. If charge runs low, tap the Nonlethal Attack button rapidly to extend the OCP's use.

> Whistling is not available.

> Both players can utilize additional Co-op actions, such as the Boost, the Hang Over, the Human Ladder, cutting surveillance camera wires, and so on. These actions are explained in the following walkthrough, mainly in the Iceland—The Ruins mission.

> If one player is killed, the other player can revive him by moving in close and pressing the Interact button. The dead player must be revived within 30 seconds, or the mission ends. No Adrenaline Syringe items are necessary for this action.

Please note that we have written this walkthrough in a generalized manner. Rather than telling you how to move through a section of clear corridor, we have focused on major hurdles that require teamwork and tactics to overcome. The walkthrough provides help for Normal difficulty, although many strategies would also apply to Elite (no ammo) mode.

To clarify actions and co-op moves, we illustrate a hypothetical situation by assigning specific tasks to the two operatives. We named them based on the color of their electronic goggles: "Blue" and "Red." However, the roles can be switched in your game. We merely hope this approach illustrates co-op moves and strategy more clearly in this narrative.

The best way to prepare for Co-op mode is to complete the Solo missions. Two players with a thorough understanding of infiltration, sneaking, grabbing characters, and gadgetry functions are more likely to work well as a team.

Iceland—The Ruins

Simultaneous Action

Blue and Red start the mission in a dilapidated warehouse. They must restore the power before they can open the door at the room's far end. Both players move to the crates stacked under the catwalk on the room's left side. Blue crouches near the boxes, faces into the room, and presses the Co-op button to prepare for a Boost maneuver. Red moves toward Blue and crouches. When Red presses the Co-op button, Blue flings him upward, where he automatically grabs the catwalk overhead. Red pulls himself up onto the catwalk and waits for Blue to get into position on the room's other side. If Red becomes bored while waiting, there are snowball objects on the catwalk. Try to hit your partner with snowballs for some mean-spirited fun!

One player can Boost the other onto the catwalk with the broken rail.

Blue, still on ground level, should move to the room's back corner, where a vertical pipe is bolted to the wall. Climb up the pipe toward the ceiling, then shimmy across the horizontal pipe. Press the Jump button to raise Blue's legs in order to get over the rail. When positioned over the catwalk, press the Crouch button twice to drop to the platform.

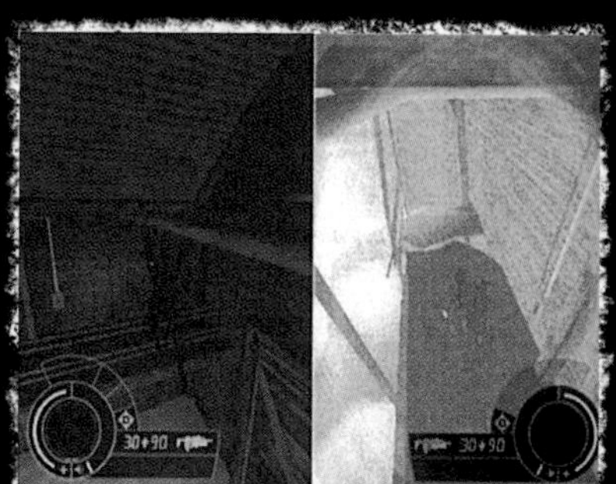

Blue climbs up and across the pipe to reach the catwalk on the room's other side.

Both players position themselves near the breaker boxes on their respective catwalks. In order to restore the power, both breaker boxes must be activated at the same time. Coordinate your efforts by saying a countdown out loud (for example, "three, two, one, GO!").

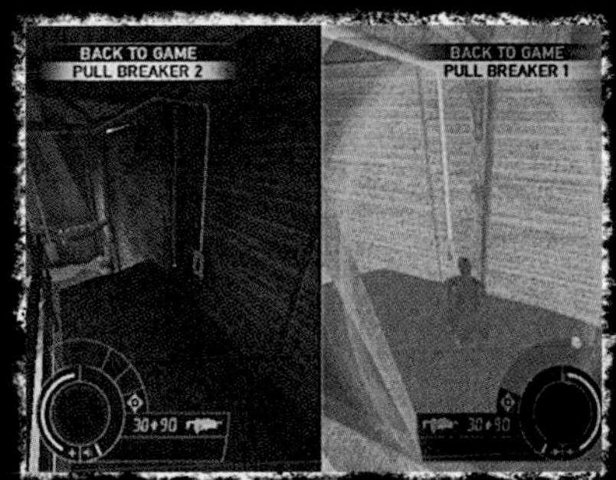

Throw both breaker switches simultaneously to restore power.

Opening Doors

After restoring the power, both players drop to the ground floor. Collect the two keycards located on the crate near the exit door. Each player moves to one of the card readers on either side of the door. To open the door, both keycards must be swiped simultaneously.

Find the keycards on the crate near the exit door. Each operative gets one.

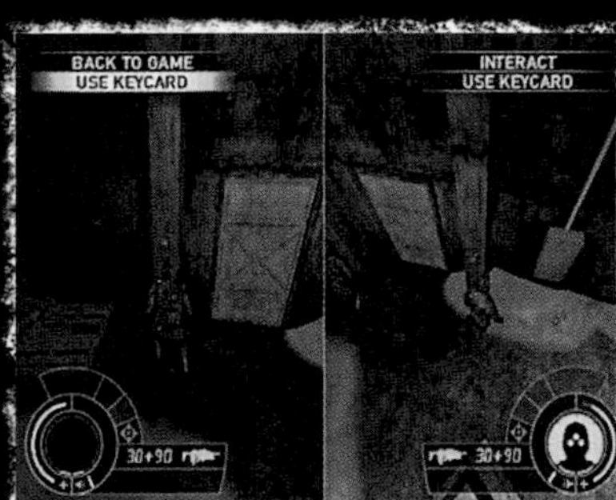

Both players must swipe the keycards simultaneously to open this door and most of the doors in Co-op mode.

CAUTION

As Lambert warns, the splinter cells must evacuate the ruins before an avalanche destroys the area. There is not a set time limit on this, but if the players spend too long in one area, the mission abruptly ends.

The Horizontal Partner Toss

Move through the corridor into the next room. The players must get across a chasm dividing the room, but there is a pane of glass in the way. Break the glass by throwing a snowball at it or firing a single shot.

In order for one player to cross the chasm, the players must coordinate a Tomoe Nage throw. The Tomoe Nage is a Judo throw from Japanese martial arts. To initiate a Tomoe Nage, have Blue stand, facing away from the chasm. *The Tomoe Nage cannot be initiated while crouching.*

When Blue presses the Co-op button, the onscreen character gets into position and a green crosshair appears at the landing zone. The target can be adjusted, but it shouldn't be necessary. However, if the crosshair target ever turns red, use the right analog stick to readjust the landing zone aim. When Blue is in position, Red approaches Blue and presses the Co-op button to complete the Tomoe Nage. Blue flings Red horizontally to the chasm's other side.

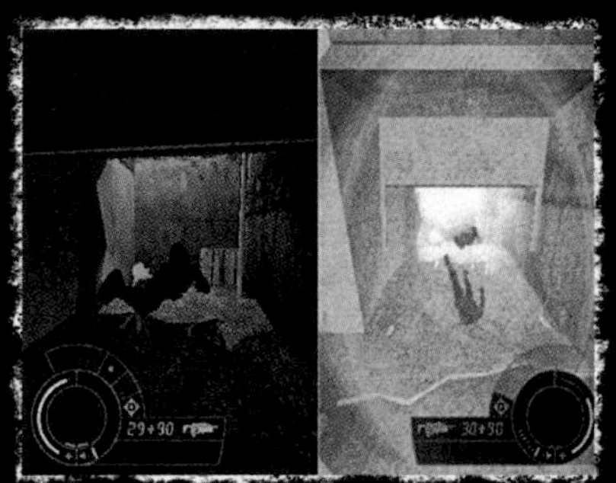

Stand and face away from the chasm to initiate a Tomoe Nage.

Red climbs up the vertical pipe fastened to the wall, then shimmies to the right over to the upper-level platform. Red then moves to the doorway in the area's far corner, where the Init Rappelling interaction appears onscreen. Press the Interact button to drop a rope over the ledge into the area below. Blue then moves to the bottom of the rope and presses the Interact button to grab it. Climb the rope by moving the left analog stick upward. If the climbing player ever becomes stuck and can't ascend while rappelling, the player holding the rope can step left or right by pressing R1 or L1 (in PS2 version) or the left trigger or right trigger (in GC or Xbox version).

Use rappelling to leave no man behind.

Back-to-Back

When both players have reached the upper levels, cross the wooden planks and descend the slope. Jump to grab the bottom ledge of a raised doorway, and climb up. Although this area appears to be a dead end, one player can initiate a Back Climb by facing the wall to either side and pressing the Interact button. When one player is ready, the other player should approach him and press the Interact button to get into position. The two players link arms back-to-back, with their feet pressed to the walls. When both players tilt the left stick upward simultaneously, Blue and Red begin to ascend in the shaft.

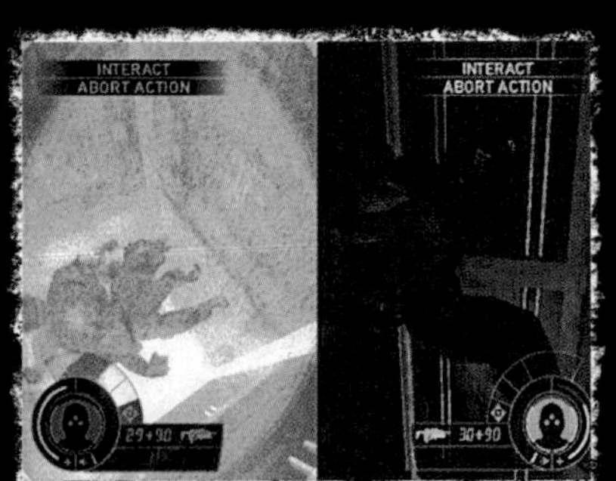

Use the Back Climb co-op action to ascend tall, narrow shafts.

Squeeze through a narrow fissure in the wall to reach the next room, then slide through another fissure into a large room

A Little Persuasion

A lone terrorist stands near the edge of a deep chasm. Have Blue quietly sneak up behind the terrorist and use the Grab Character interaction to seize him in a chokehold. The Interrogate interaction appears onscreen, but when Blue attempts to interrogate the guy, he laughs it off. Blue drags the terrorist a few steps away from the chasm, and Red moves in front of the terrorist. Red can then press the Interact button to "Persuade" the hostile to talk. The two operatives learn that the terrorist is looking for important lists scattered around the room. Blue drags the terrorist off to a corner and presses the Nonlethal Attack button to choke him unconscious. Avoid killing hostiles to avert lowering mission ranking.

Splinter cells must work together to persuade the bad guys to talk.

The Three Inventory Lists

To complete an Opportunity Objective and maintain a high mission ranking, find the three important documents scattered around the room. The first inventory list is located near the chasm's edge, by the wall to the far left.

The second is located at the chasm's bottom. To reach it, have Blue move to the chasm's edge, where the Init Hang Over interaction appears. Blue presses the Interact button to get ready. Red approaches Blue and presses the Interact button to complete the Hang Over. Red connects a rope to Blue, who then drops, upside down, over the chasm's side. Red may then lower Blue by pressing L1 (in PS2) or the left trigger (in GC and Xbox versions). Continue lowering Blue until he reaches the inventory list on the ledge near the chasm's bottom. Blue can then press the Interact button to pick up the second inventory list. Red must raise Blue back up to solid ground by holding R1 (in PS2) or right trigger (in GC and Xbox).

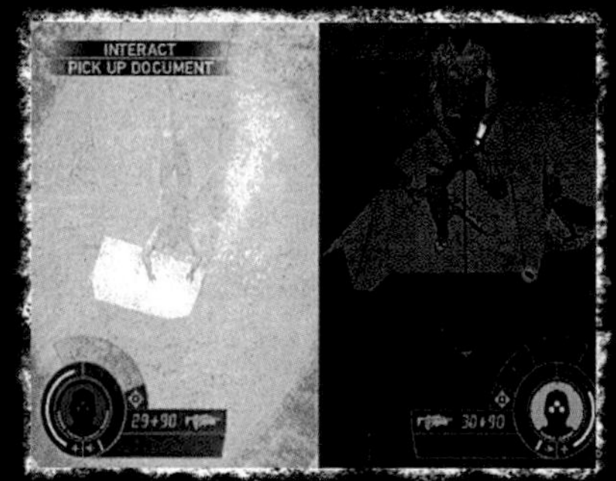

Perform a Hang Over at the chasm's edge to reach the document that has fallen to the ledge near the bottom.

The chasm is too wide to cross with a Tomoe Nage, so the players must cross the room using the shelves fastened to the wall. Have Blue crouch on the pallet at the base of the shelves and press the Co-op button to initiate a Boost. Once Blue boosts Red to the higher level, he moves to the end of the shelves and presses the Interact button to initiate rappelling. Blue can then climb up Red's rope to reach the upper level.

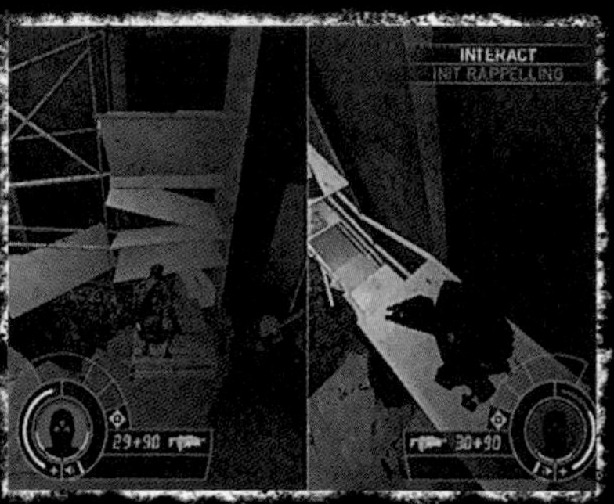

Use a Boost to place one player atop the shelves, then bring the other man up by rappelling.

Both players move across the collapsing shelves toward the room's opposite side. The final inventory list lies near the end of the shelves.

Have both players jump up to grab the bottom edge of the raised doorway, and proceed through the low passageway until they reach a dead end. Work together to perform a Back Climb to the shaft's top, then press the Interact button to "Extract."

Iceland—The Thermal Base

One Man for the Job

Blue and Red begin the mission in a dark corner of a machine room. Ahead and to the right is a fence, and an armed terrorist patrols the well-lit area beyond. Have Blue slip around the corner and climb over the fence while Red waits at the starting point. This reduces the chances of the patrol detecting you.

Blue stops behind the turbine nearest the fence. The terrorist typically starts near the control panel in a bright zone, then he moves over and examines the turbine. When he turns his back and starts to walk back into the area, follow him and grab him.

To reduce the risk of discovery, only one player should sneak into the fenced area while the enemy patrols.

Interrogating the enemy alone does nothing. Red must climb over the fence, stop in front of the terrorist, and Persuade him to speak. He reveals specifics on the security in this area.

The Human Ladder

At the back of the area, have Blue crouch near the center of the brick wall and press the Co-op button to initiate a Boost. After Red completes the Boost and is hanging from the ledge above, have Red press the Co-op button to initiate a Human Ladder; then Blue can face Red and press the Co-op button to climb up Red to the level above.

Boost one man up so that he may form a Human Ladder, allowing both men to reach the upper level together.

Ambush the Guard

Drop down through the hole in the ceiling. There is no need to use the ladder. Have Blue race to the room's opposite end and hide in the shadows on the right side of the exit door. Red should stay in the shadows at the ladder's base. Wait until another terrorist enters the room on patrol. Blue, near the door, sneaks up behind him and knocks him out with a Nonlethal Attack from the side or rear.

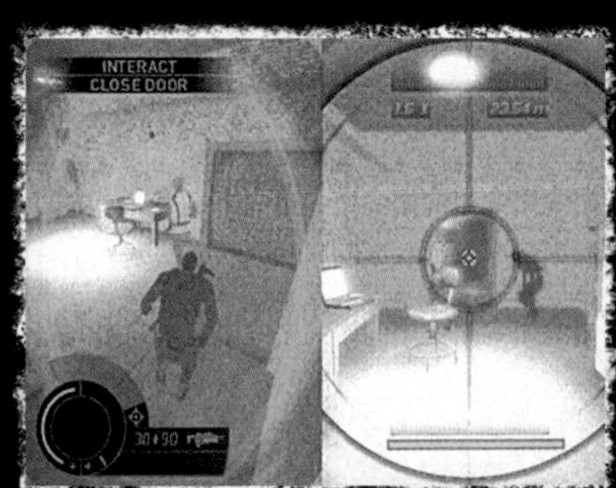

One player should hide on the door's right side and wait for the enemy to enter the room.

Two keycards are on the desk in the room's center. Have one player use the laptop and hack the security access. (Hacking is accomplished by aligning the frequency lines, as in Solo mode.) Decrypting the security access gives the splinter cells the laser grid access code (4759).

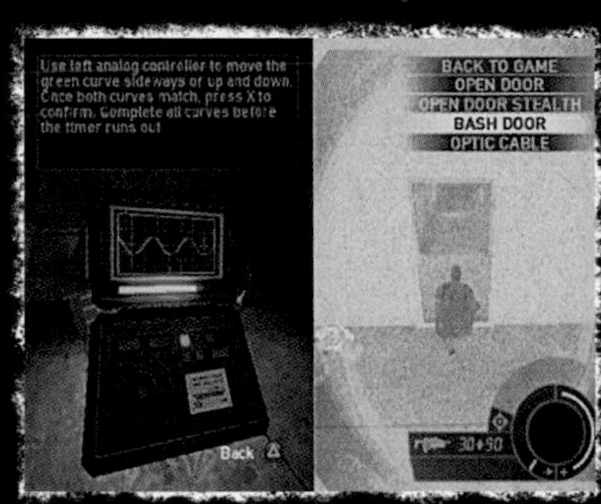

Hack the laptop in the room to learn a vital security code.

Jamming the Camera

Exit the room and follow the connecting cave through an open doorway. Move a few steps to the left and stop. Roughly halfway down the corridor to the left is a surveillance camera. The OCP mounted on either player's SC pistol allows for disabling the camera. However, the function is different than in Solo mode; the OCP only works if one of the players presses the Nonlethal Attack button, and if there is battery charge remaining in the OCP. This means that Blue must use his OCP and EMF vision to disable the camera while Red runs through the camera's area of vision. Once Red is a safe distance beyond the camera and well-hidden in the dark, he must turn around and use his OCP to jam the camera while Blue runs through the area.

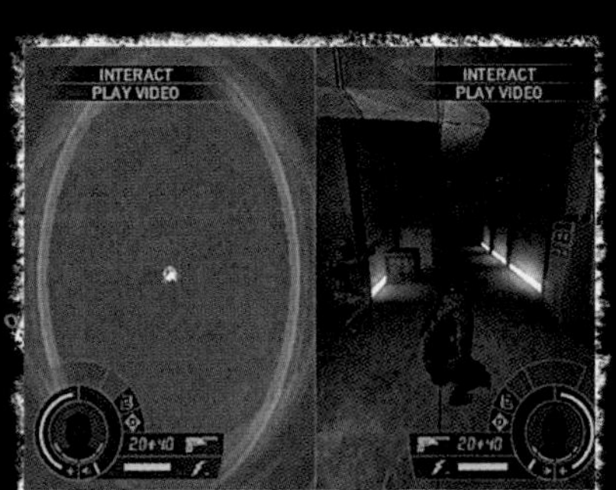

Take turns jamming the surveillance camera with the OCP while your partner moves through the area.

Remember that you can also move unseen through a camera's blind spot. In this instance, it is possible for both splinter cells to move down the corridor by sticking to the left wall and moving directly under the camera, with no need for tag-team jamming.

Mission Possible

Around the corner in the same corridor, an array of lasers blocks the passage. Have Blue stand up, face away from the lasers, and press the Co-op button to initiate a Tomoe Nage. After Red completes the Tomoe Nage and flies to the corridor's end, he should enter 4759 on the keypad on the wall to disable the laser array. Then Blue can join Red near the sealed door.

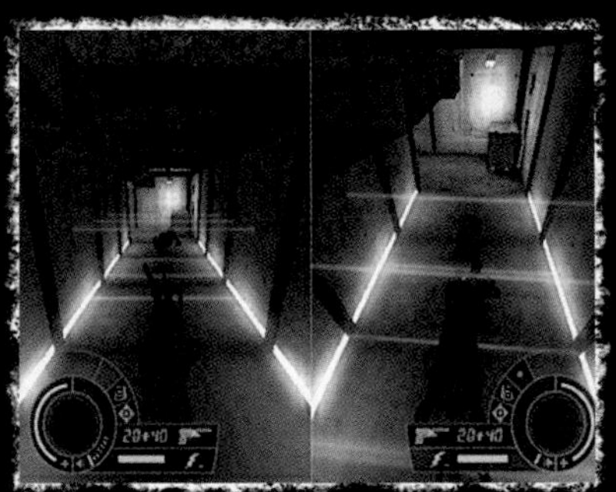

Perform a Tomoe Nage to throw one man clear past the laser array.

Pipe Tactics

Both splinter cells must swipe their keycards simultaneously to open the door to the break room. Inside, one guard patrols the room's entire length while another sits in a brightly lit cubicle, watching television. When the patrolling terrorist is not in the vicinity of the entrance, have the splinter cells enter one at a time and stop just inside the doorway. Two pipes run the length of the ceiling, but only the pipe closest to the entrance allows the splinter cells to move through the room completely unseen. After Blue jumps, grabs the pipe, pulls his legs up, and shimmies toward the exit, Red should follow suit.

Use the first pipe in the break room to navigate undetected across the ceiling.

Continue shimmying down the pipe until both splinter cells are near the exit. When the patrolling terrorist heads for the door, have one splinter cell use the Grab Character interaction to knock him out from above. Then both splinter cells can drop to the floor and exit through the open doorway.

Move down the corridor stacked with boxes. A surveillance camera is posted at a brightly lit corner, so stop beside the last box placed against the wall to the right. Have Blue use his OCP on the camera so that Red can move down to the corner and a few steps to the right. Red positions himself close to the wall from which the camera hangs and uses his OCP to return the favor.

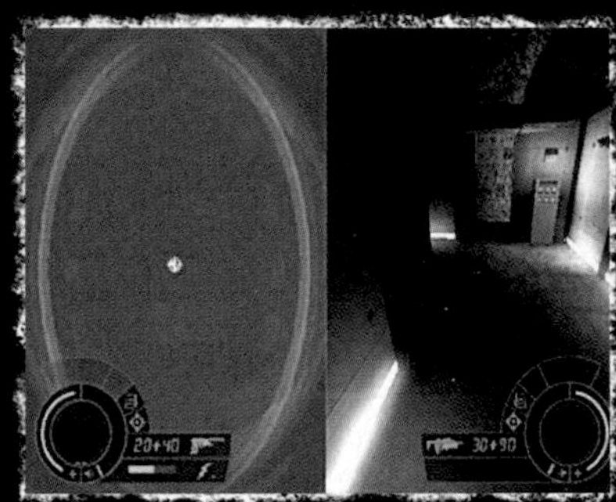

Cameras posted in brightly lit areas should be handled with greater caution.

Making the Elevator Arrive

Swipe your keycards simultaneously to open the door to the engine room. Head left from the doorway and up the dark stairs to the upper level. One terrorist patrols the entire catwalk. Wait at the top of the stairs for him to pass by, then knock him out. Access the two computer terminals on the upper level to read e-mails bearing clues for making the elevator to the second floor available.

Wait in the shadows at the top of the stairs for the guard patrolling the catwalk to walk by. Then knock him out.

Drop from the catwalk's sides to the lower level near the elevator. In the corner to each side of the elevator shaft is a pump valve. Have each player position himself in front of a valve and turn the wheels simultaneously. This prompts a terrorist from the level above to ride down in the elevator to see what is going on. After turning the valves, Blue and Red immediately hide in the shadows on each side of the elevator's landing point. When the terrorist steps out of the elevator, sneak up behind him and knock him out.

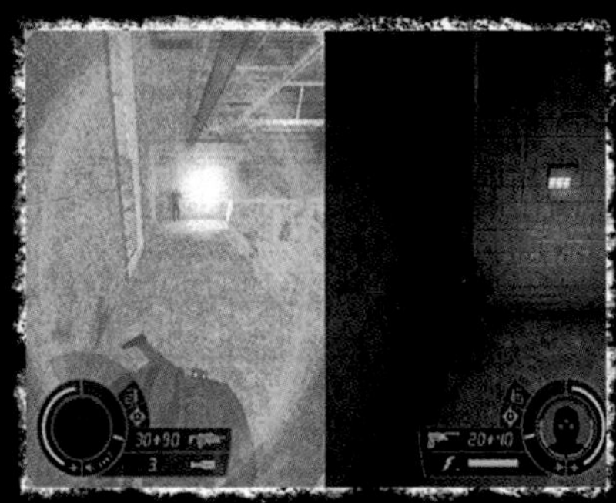

Turn both valve handles simultaneously to anger a terrorist on the level above. The intemperate guard soon arrives in the elevator.

Hide in the shadows to either side of the elevator. Take out the guard as he emerges from the lift.

To raise the elevator to the second floor, both splinter cells must swipe their keycards simultaneously at the two card readers.

The Next Level

When the elevator reaches the second level, exit the car and hide in the shadows. A guard soon approaches the elevator from the side corridor. As he enters the area, the nearest splinter cell should grab him and choke him unconscious.

Hide in the shadows of the corner across from the elevator entrance. Wait for a guard to appear. One player should take him out.

Head down the corridor the terrorist emerged from. The laser beams in the passage can be bypassed by one of three methods:

1. Perform a Tomoe Nage so that one player can reach the keypad at the corner and input the code 4759, deactivating the lasers.
2. Carry the unconscious terrorist's body through the array. The tracking device in the man's clothing disables the lasers. If the splinter cells move together at the same speed, both can pass through the lasers undetected while carrying the guard.
3. One player disables the lower laser with his OCP while the other player crouches and moves through the area in order to disable the lasers from the keypad at the next corner.

While one man carries the guard's body to disable the lasers, walk together to move through the passage while the grid is down.

Work as a team to disable the surveillance camera at the next brightly lit corner so that both players can pass through the area. Swipe keycards simultaneously to open the next door.

Fan Controls

A laser grid and a surveillance camera protect the computer that controls the vent fan. However, the computer is not protected from above. From the doorway, head to the right to find a yellow pipe that ascends into the ceiling. Both players should climb up the pipe and move to the open skylights. Have Blue initiate a Hang Over so that Red can lower him into the room below. Once Blue is in range of the computer, press the Interact button to disable the vent fan.

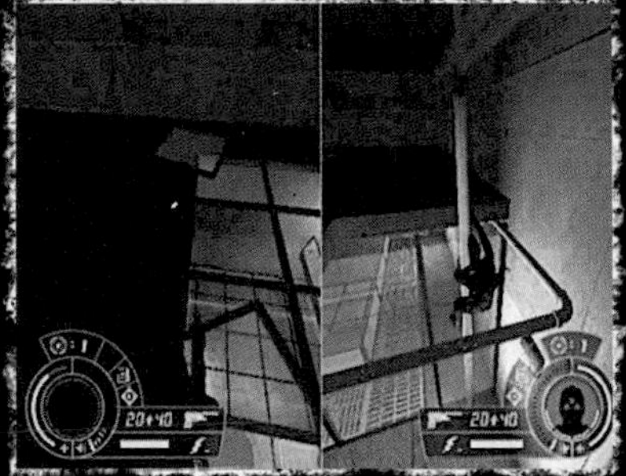

Climb up the yellow pipe in the corner of the fan control room to reach the space above the ceiling.

Perform a Hang Over from the open skylights to reach the computer undetected.

Extract through the Fan

Both players should now return to the area near the elevator. One player must use his OCP to jam the gun turret at the passage's far end. Meanwhile, the other player runs down the corridor and behind the gun turret, where he can deactivate the device.

Jam the gun turret with the OCP while your partner moves behind the turret to deactivate it.

Then have Blue move to the wall to the turret's right, then crouch and prepare to Boost the other player. As Red hangs from the ledge above, he should press the Co-op button to form a Human Ladder so that Blue may climb up. Have both players move in range of the inoperative fan in order to exfiltrate.

Perform a Boost and then a Human Ladder to extract through the deactivated fan.

Iceland—The Foundry

Reach the Top

Blue and Red start this mission at the bottom of an elevator shaft. Have Blue crouch near the wall to the left of the yellow pipe and press the Co-op button to initiate a Boost in order to lift Red to the horizontal railing overhead. Red hangs from the rail, then climbs to the next railing above and shimmies right around the corner and grabs on to the yellow pipe. From there, Red climbs to the shaft's top and initiates rappelling so that Blue may climb up the shaft.

Boost one player up to the rails to the left of the yellow pipe.

Shimmy left across the rails to reach the yellow pipe, then climb to the shaft's top.

The Two Cameras

The splinter cells now stand outside an occupied room. Just beyond the door to the left, a terrorist sits at a desk typing on a computer. A surveillance camera is mounted on the wall directly above his head, monitoring the bright area surrounding him. Use caution and move silently here.

Another surveillance camera hangs on the far wall. This camera can be permanently disabled by cutting the wires underneath it. Therefore, move around the room's dark edges while sticking to the right-hand wall, squeezing through the small space behind the crates stacked in the corner. Have Blue position himself under the camera and initiate a Shoulder Climb. Red can then move behind Blue and complete the move. Blue lifts Red into place directly under the camera, where he can cut the wires, permanently disabling the device. Have one player sneak over to the nearby desk and pick up the first of three important blueprints.

Work together to deactivate the camera on the room's far side.

Collect the first set of blueprints on the desk. They are easy to miss.

To take out the seated guard, backtrack to the elevator shaft opening. Have Blue equip the SC-20K and airfoil rounds, while Red equips his SC pistol. Blue moves in close to the desk, but not so close as to arouse suspicion. In a coordinated strike, Red uses his OCP to disable the surveillance camera while Blue fires an airfoil round at the seated man's head. While Red continues to jam the surveillance camera, Blue moves in and moves the guard's body into the blind spot directly under the camera, if needed. Blue then positions himself near the wall directly under the camera before Red's OCP runs out of power.

One player jams the camera while the other person takes out the guard.

Procure New Keycards

Blue should now be able to hack the desktop computer in order to obtain the server room access code (1985). When he is finished, Red should use his OCP to jam the camera once again while Blue moves out to the desk's corner and picks up a second keycard. Then Blue should quickly move toward the exit in the room's far corner. Once Blue is out of range, he must use his OCP to jam the camera while Red runs across the room to join him. Have Red pick up the second keycard located on the shelves to the left of the exit door. One player must swipe their keycard at the card reader so that both may leave.

Work together to pick up the keycards, located in conspicuous places.

Disable the Mines

In the next corridor, two laser mines divide the corridor. Have Blue use his OCP to deactivate the lower laser mine while Red crouches and moves beyond the laser beams. Red should then return the favor, allowing Blue to catch up. At the corridor's far end, both players must simultaneously swipe their keycards through the dual card readers in order to open the door.

Take turns disabling the lower laser mine so that your partner can do the limbo under the upper laser.

Shimmy 'n' Shake

Across from the entrance inside the first foundry area, a horizontal pipe runs from the wall across the entire room. Have Blue jump up and grab the pipe. After pulling his legs up, Blue then shimmies across to the room's midpoint, where he is positioned over the catwalk's middle aisle. Have him wait there until a terrorist on patrol moves underneath him; Blue grabs the character from above and strangles him unconscious. Meanwhile, Red stays near the entrance and waits for the second terrorist to patrol past the door. Grab him from behind and choke his lights out. Head through the open doorway at the back of the room.

Coordinate to take out the two terrorists patrolling the foundry catwalk almost simultaneously.

Dark Doorway

At the corridor's far end, swipe both keycards simultaneously to open the door, but *do not enter the room*. Stay outside the doorway until a terrorist on patrol stops directly in front of the door. One player should move through the doorway and perform a nonlethal attack from the side to knock the man out.

Wait until a guard stops in front of the doorway, then give him a tap on the chin.

Two Turret Guns

Follow the catwalk into the room, but avoid stepping into the first pool of light. Instead, look for a horizontal pipe near the ceiling. Have Blue jump, grab the pipe, pull his legs up, and shimmy along the pipe's length. The pipe curves and leads Blue over a platform to the side of an active gun turret; he can then move behind the gun turret and disable it, enabling Red to penetrate the room as far as Blue's position.

Use the ceiling pipe at the first corner to navigate to a position beside the first turret gun.

Blue should use EMF vision to help him spot another gun turret on the catwalk near the far wall. Disabling this turret requires teamwork. While Blue positions himself near the railing closest to the active turret, Red should move to the corner nearest the path leading down to the turret. Be careful that Red does not move close enough to cause the turret to open fire. When both players are in position and ready, have Blue use his OCP to disable the gun turret while Red runs all the way down the catwalk. Blue can stop jamming the device when Red is safely behind it. Red can then deactivate the turret, and both players can swipe their keycards at the exit door in the opposite corner.

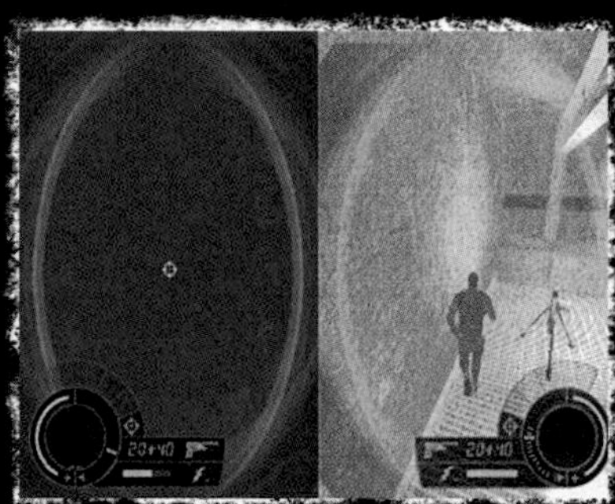

Classic teamwork; one player jams the turret gun while the other moves behind the device to take control.

The Long Bright Stretch

Red should stay back in the shadows near the entrance while Blue moves up to the nearest corner and peeks down the hallway. Wait patiently until a terrorist patrols down the corridor and stops at the corner near your position. When he turns to walk back down the corridor, have Blue sneak up behind him and knock him out.

Stay at the corner near the entrance as long as needed to get the drop on the patrolling guard.

A little more than halfway down the long corridor is a surveillance camera. A pallet leaning against the wall under the jack prevents the players from moving down the corridor through the camera's blind spot. Therefore, the players must take turns jamming the camera with the OCP until both have crossed the corridor.

The Second Blueprint Set

Open the door at the corridor's far end and enter the lab. On the desk to the door's right is the second blueprint. One player should hack the security access on the nearby computer to retrieve the arsenal information from the server, completing a major objective. Doing so sets off a silent alarm (not related to the Alarm Level), which opens the double doors at the corridor's midpoint. The splinter cells must take turns jamming the camera in the corridor directly across from the double doors so that both may move into the new area.

Find the second set of blueprints in the lab. Use the computer in the corner to complete an objective and access a new area.

Secured Extract

Head down the corridor and around the corner. There are two ways to enter the security office on the right: either through the door, or through the crawlspace situated above the cargo container in the corner. Use the route most applicable to your selected difficulty level and current Alarm Level. The third set of blueprints is located on the central table. Hack the nearby computer to determine the security code (1985), if you failed to do so earlier.

Use the crawlspace atop the boxes to access the security station if necessary.

Find the third set of blueprints in the security station near the exit.

Return to the corridor. Perform a Tomoe Nage to throw one player beyond the laser mines to the passage's end, where he can input the code 1985 into the keypad to deactivate the grid. One player must then use their keycard to activate the elevator for extraction.

Perform a Tomoe Nage and disable the laser mines to reach the extraction point.

Iceland—Sabotage

The Hot Zone

Blue and Red commence the sabotage leg of the mission on a platform above the second foundry. Two guards patrol this area. One patrols the area directly to the left of the players' starting point. When he turns to walk away, one player should grab him and the other should persuade him to talk. The guard divulges the master code for the elevators in this area (090980). This completes an Opportunity Objective. Choke the man unconscious.

Grab an enemy and make him talk to learn an important code.

The second guard patrols near the stairs at the back of the area on the right. When he is standing nearer to the starting point, facing inward, sneak up beside him and knock him out.

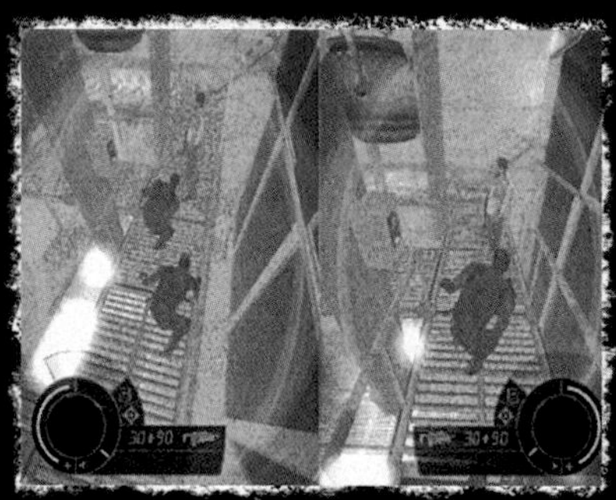
The other guard in the first area stops in this convenient position. Sneak up beside him and punch his lights out.

Ascend the stairs and use the computer in the corner to read an e-mail divulging an important extraction clue. If you failed to obtain the elevator code from one of the guards, hack the security access to obtain it now.

A wired surveillance camera is on the wall above the next corner. One player should lift the other player up to cut the wires, disabling the device.

Work together to disable the security cam at the corner facing the elevator.

Proceed to the elevator at the end of the passageway. To operate the elevator, both players must simultaneously input the elevator code 090980—both players should input the first five digits at their own pace, then input the final zero at the same time.

Coordinate your timing to simultaneously input the code's last digit at the elevator keypads.

The Tricky Patrol

When the elevator stops, move down the passage and around the corner. Red should use his OCP to jam the camera while Blue moves around the corner. Have Red maintain his position while Blue moves to the next corner in order to overhear the conversation between the two terrorists. When the men finish, one starts walking toward Blue's position. Have Blue retreat to the shadows of the two crates stacked near the surveillance camera. The guard on patrol stops under the surveillance camera for a long moment, at which time Red can knock him out by firing an airfoil round at his head. His body is perfectly concealed in the camera's blind spot. Or, Blue can wait until the guard starts to return to his normal patrol route on the catwalk and grab him there at an

opportune time. Afterward, Blue can stand behind the stack of crates and jam the security camera so that Red may pass.

Allow one man to pass beyond the surveillance camera's area. Then hold position until one enemy steps between you two.

The other terrorist remains seated at the computer console inside the security station. Use the crawlspace to the left of the station's windows to enter the security station. Sneak up behind the seated man and knock him out.

Access the crawlspace leading into the security office via the vent at the corner. Use this to get the jump on the guard inside the room.

Across from the security station door is a ladder. One player should climb down the ladder and obtain the keycard lying on the ground on the lower level. The other keycard lies on the central table inside the security station. Hack the security access on the computer in the corner to view the rest of the stage using the security cameras. Watch the patrol patterns of the remaining guards. Use the medkit in the station if necessary before swiping one keycard at the door to proceed.

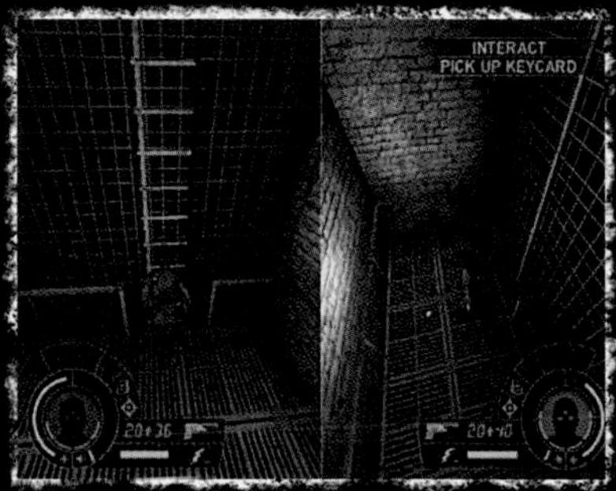

One keycard is located in the security office, the other on the floor below the catwalk.

Control Center

Move through the corridor, disabling laser mines and surveillance cameras as needed. In the elevator at the end of the corridor, swipe both keycards simultaneously to take the elevator down another level.

Take turns disabling the surveillance camera in the corridor. When both players are through, proceed toward the room at the corridor's end. One player, Blue, should wait in the shadows near the end of the corridor while the other player, Red, moves into the room and to the right. Red should stop just outside the doorway. Hold these positions until one of the guards stops near the hallway entrance and stares down the corridor for a long moment. While he is stationary, Red can move behind the guard, grab him, drag him into the corridor, and choke him unconscious.

One player should breach the control room and step to the door's right to lay a trap for this patrolling guard.

Both players should now enter the room and move down the catwalk to the right. Stop near the gap in the rail. Wait until the guard patrolling the level below stops directly beneath the gap in the rail, then quickly perform a Hang Over. The

Use a Hang Over from the upper level to get the drop on the lower-level guard.

Return to the center of the upper catwalk. One player must use his OCP to disable the gun turret at the upper level's far end while the other player races down behind the turret and deactivates it.

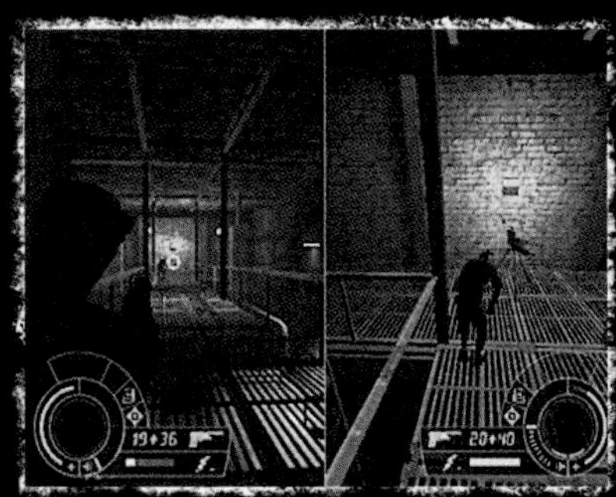

Work together to neutralize and bypass the gun turret.

There are two computers on either side of the turret. Use them both to shut down two controls for the cooling system. One player should then climb over the portion of the rail between the turret and the computer. He should drop to the level below and hack the security access on the computer in order to disable the laser grid and all the security cameras. Both players can then move to the lower level's north side. Use the two computers located there to disable the last two controls of the cooling system.

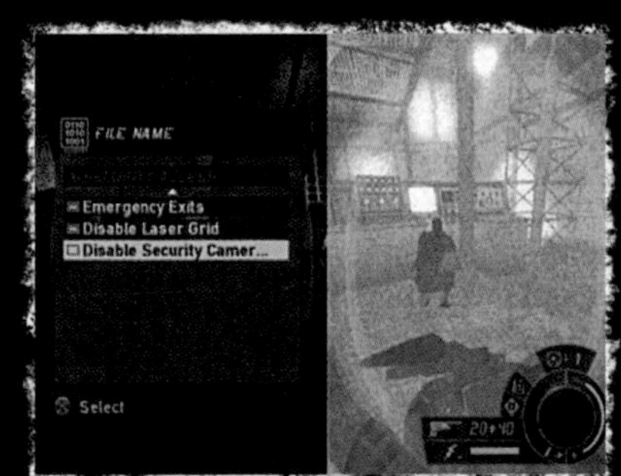

Drop to the lower level and disable the

Escape!

Return to the elevator and swipe both keycards simultaneously to ascend to the level above. The security cameras are no longer of any concern, so make your way quickly back to the elevator on the second level and simultaneously enter the code (090980) on the keypad to reach the top floor.

Run through the foundry toward the starting point, then climb down the ladder on the left. A three-minute timer begins counting down. You must evacuate the factory in time, or the mission fails.

Climb to the foundry's lower level.

Head to the back corner of the foundry's lower level and enter the corridor. Venting steam makes crossing the corridor impossible. Perform a Tomoe Nage to throw one player to the corridor's other end. He lands near a valve that he can turn to deactivate the steam.

Now Blue must crouch near the fence and give a Boost to Red. Red must then move around the corner to the right and turn another valve to deactivate the steam emanating from the pipes near the end of a crawlspace. Blue can then crawl through the crawlspace to join Red.

Boost one player over the fence so that he may clear the crawlspace for the other player.

Crouch and run under the next gout of steam. Vapors emanate from the pipe beyond. Blue must Boost Red up to the horizontal pipe hanging from the ceiling. Red then pulls his legs up and shimmies well past the steam before dropping back to the ground. Red turns the valve on the wall to deactivate the steam, allowing Blue to catch up.

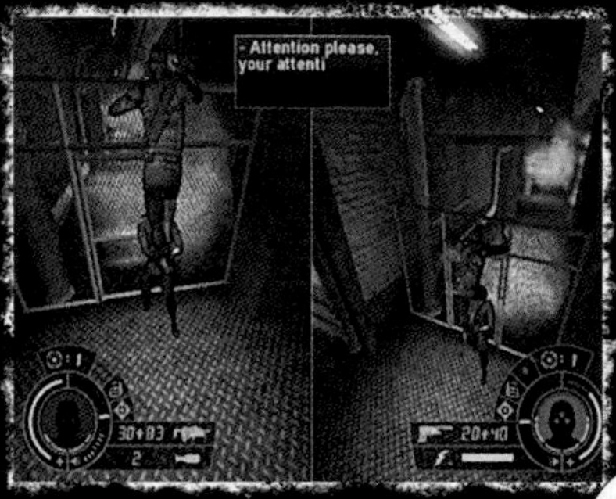

Boost one player up to the ceiling pipe so that he may shimmy beyond the steam barrier and use the valve to turn it off.

Slide through the narrow gap between the pipes and the wall on the right. Stop just before a small gout of steam and allow it to pour out for a few seconds. When it ceases momentarily, continue sliding through the narrow passage and exit. If the second man is caught in the steam and dies, the first man through can then move to the side of the bars and revive his teammate. However, if the first man through collapses from steam damage, there is no solution. After the downed agent screams in agony for thirty seconds, the players must restart the mission or load the last saved game.

Slide through the narrow gap between the pipes and wall, being careful of steam intermittently emanating near the middle of the pass.

Both players should move to the door at the passage's end. When both are in close range of the door, extract.

NOTE

Completion of all four Iceland missions unlocks a Co-op bonus mission. The "Tanker on the Way" mission is covered later in this section.

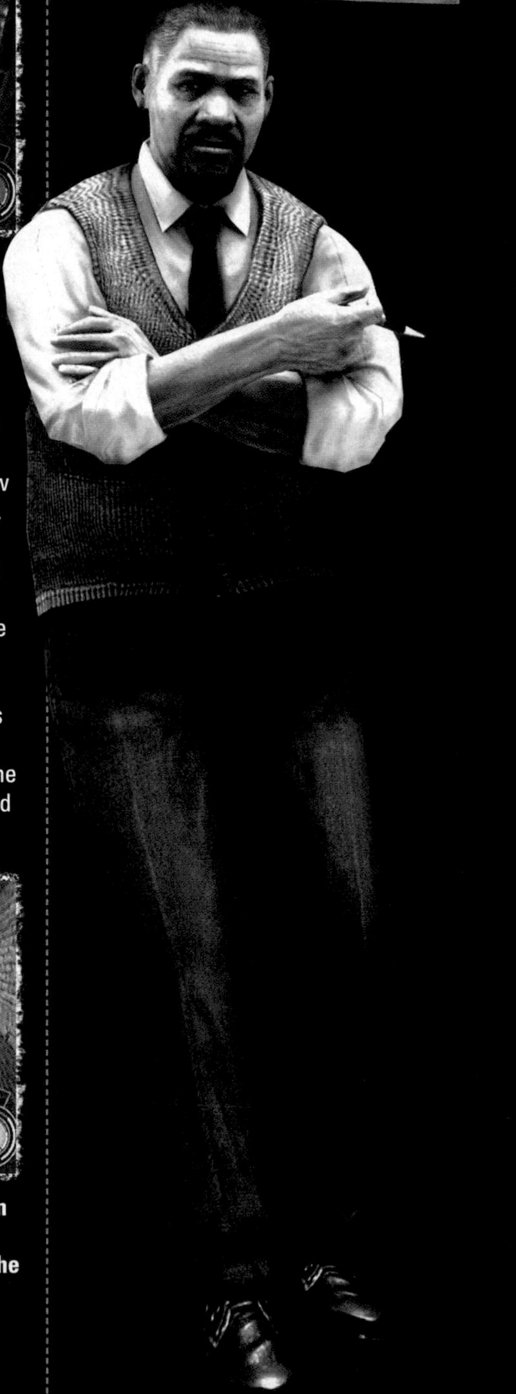

Ellsworth—The Insertion

Rooftop Insertion

Blue and Red start the mission on the rooftop of a company that delivers supplies to Ellsworth Penitentiary. To achieve a 100 percent mission ranking, no guards may be killed during any of the Ellsworth missions.

From the starting point, have Blue move forward and go around the corner to the left. Pick the lock on the door. Enter the door and stop at the top of the stairs to survey the situation. The stairs descend through several well-lit areas, so climb over the railing near the entrance and drop into the dark area below. Wait outside the arched passage until a prison guard enters the area on patrol. Grab him from behind before he enters the well-lit area surrounding the surveillance camera in the corner. The guard can be interrogated, but to no avail.

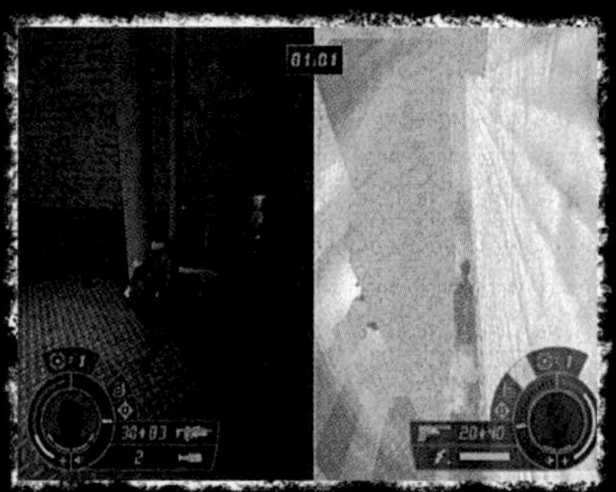

Grab the guard in the stairwell before he moves too close to the pool of light below the surveillance camera.

Now have Red rendezvous with Blue. Red must climb over the rail instead of taking the stairs. Approach the captive guard from the front and Persuade him to talk. The guard divulges the truck's delivery time, and the agents accomplish an Opportunity Objective.

Only team persuasion can make this tough guy talk.

The cables on the nearby surveillance camera are exposed and can be cut. However, do not approach the camera from the front. Climb over the stair railing and enter the camera's blind spot from the side. When both agents are in the blind spot, initiate a Shoulder Climb so that one man can cut the wires. This makes leaving the building a little easier.

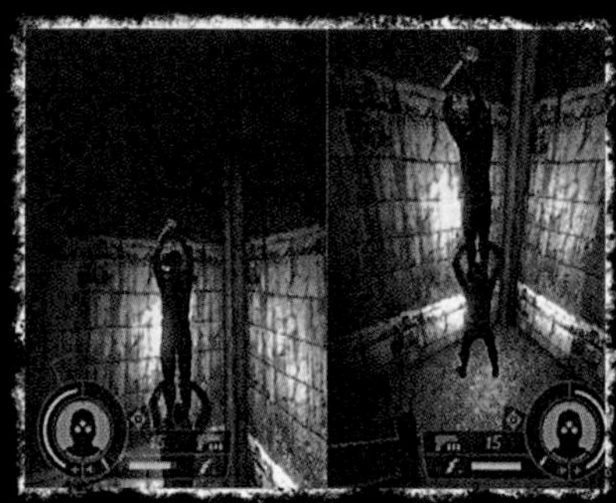

Clip the wires of the surveillance camera.

The Cooling System Generator

Both players should proceed through the archway and down the stairs to the left. In the next room, a guard stands with his back to the doorway, bouncing his leg to the music. Grab him from behind and interrogate him to find out that the nearby generator runs the cooling system. Choke him unconscious.

Sneaking up on the distracted guard is easy.

You must shut down the generator in this room, either by turning off the breaker on the wall near the entrance, or by piercing the machine itself. Through the door in the far corner of this area is a small room containing a medkit.

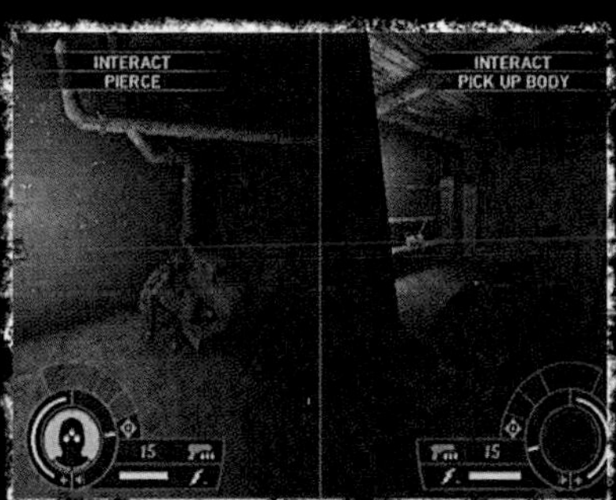

Shut off or destroy the generator for the cooling system.

The Cold Chamber

Both agents should now return to the starting point. In the far corner is an open hatch. Now that you've disabled the cooling engine, it is safe to climb down the vertical shaft using the pipe. Have Blue move to the vent's other end and place a charge while Red stays near the bottom of the vertical shaft and out of harm's way. When the charge is set, Blue should retreat toward Red before detonating the explosive to avoid damage.

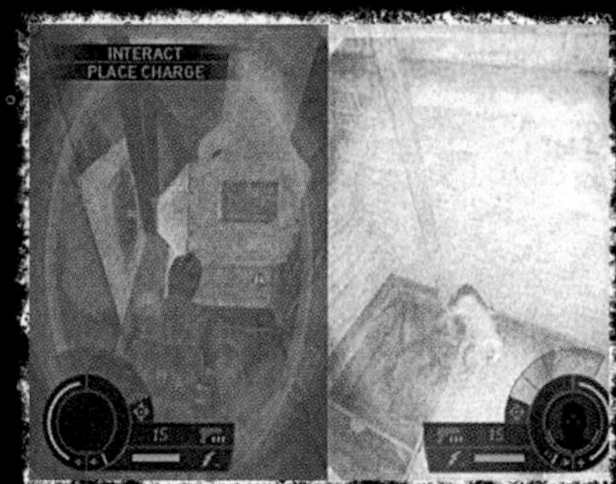

Climb down the vent shaft. Set a charge on the machinery at the shaft's end.

Both agents should proceed through the vent into the cold chamber. A piece of hanging meat blocks the exit. There are two switches on the wall. Press the right-hand switch to "Activate Conveyor B"; this moves the carcass out of the way and you can continue.

Press the wall switch to move the hanging meat out of your path.

Shattered Glass

Follow the passage to a set of double doors. You cannot open the doors, but there is a tall window above them. One agent should initiate a Shoulder Climb in front of the doors so the other agent can plant charges on the glass. Both agents should then retreat around the corner before detonating the charges. The window is tall enough and wide enough that Blue and Red can jump up to grab the opening's lower ledge and climb through, even simultaneously.

Plant charges on the large window above the door, then climb through the opening.

The Steal

Have Blue and Red enter the first door on the left in the corridor. One keycard lies on the desk. Have Blue pick it up. To obtain the other keycard, Red should move into the small space in the back corner and initiate a Hang Over. Blue can then quickly lower his partner into an office far below so that Red can snatch the second keycard from the desk beneath the vertical vent. (Do not worry about the guard you hear talking.) After Red takes the item, have Blue quickly raise Red back up before the guard speaking loudly finishes his phone call.

Perform a Hang Over to lower one agent through the office vent in order to obtain the second keycard from the level below.

Bait and Drop

Return to the corridor and move into the shadows near the window you previously destroyed. Have Blue jam the laser sweeper overhead while Red moves down the corridor past the tall crates. Red should then turn around and return the favor for Blue.

Take turns jamming the laser sweeper overhead so that both players may move to the corridor's end.

Blue should move quietly around the corner and use the optic cable on the door. A guard stands at the top of the stairwell in the next room. To draw his attention, use the Open Door Stealth interaction. Then shift the move control upward just a bit to open the door a crack. When the guard notices, shift the move control down to close the door. Quickly retreat to the dark corner opposite the door. The guard comes through the door; seeing nothing, he turns around with his back to your position. Sneak up behind him and knock him out.

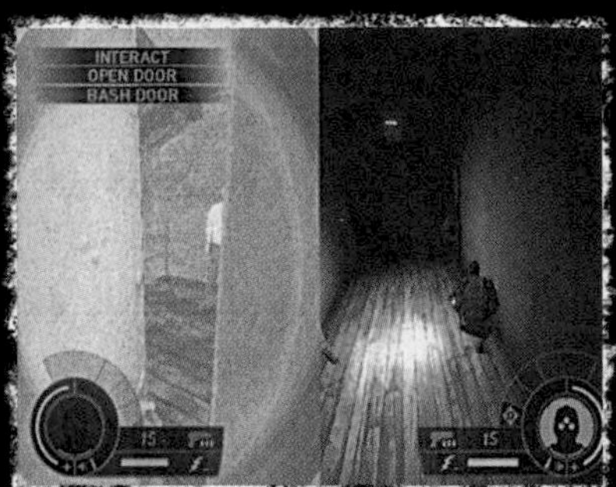

In stealth mode, open the door just a crack to draw the guard out into the corridor.

Have both players move to the top of the stairwell. A surveillance camera monitors the level below. Blue should jam the camera while Red moves down to the corner to the camera's left. Then Red should return the favor by jamming the camera while Blue moves directly under the camera and initiates a Shoulder Climb. Red should then complete the Shoulder Climb and cut the wires on the device.

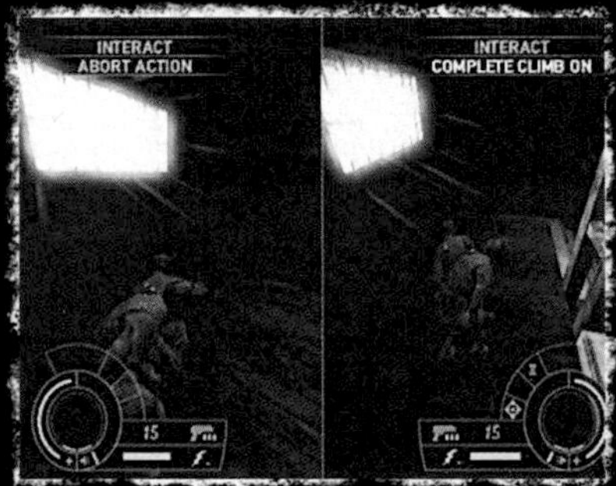

Cut the wires on the surveillance camera in the stairwell.

The Garage

Sneak downstairs and peek through the doorway into the garage. One guard patrols the area while another stands near the garage door. The patrolling guard eventually moves in front of the door. Enter the room behind him, grab him, and drag him out to the corridor. Choke him unconscious.

Wait at the doorway until a guard walks past. Follow him and take him out.

Have Blue sneak into the garage and down the stairs beside the blaring radio. Fire a tranquilizer dart at the guard standing in front of the garage door. Both players should then simultaneously swipe their keycards at the card readers on each side of the garage door to proceed. Head down the corridor and enter the back of the truck to extract.

After neutralizing the guard, simultaneously swipe both keycards to open the garage door and complete this mission.

Ellsworth—The Break-in

Supply Depot

Wait at the starting point until Lambert finishes his briefing. Then two guards standing in the room's center begin talking. While they speak, turn to the right and climb over the railing. Follow the railed-off platform to the next corner and wait for the men to finish talking. One guard leaves the area and enters a small room down the hall. The remaining guard starts moving back and forth between two cargo stacks. One player should climb over the railing and wait at the corner for the guard to stop at the cargo nearest the starting point. While he faces the cargo, grab him from behind, drag him back to the starting point, and choke him unconscious. Then climb back over the railing.

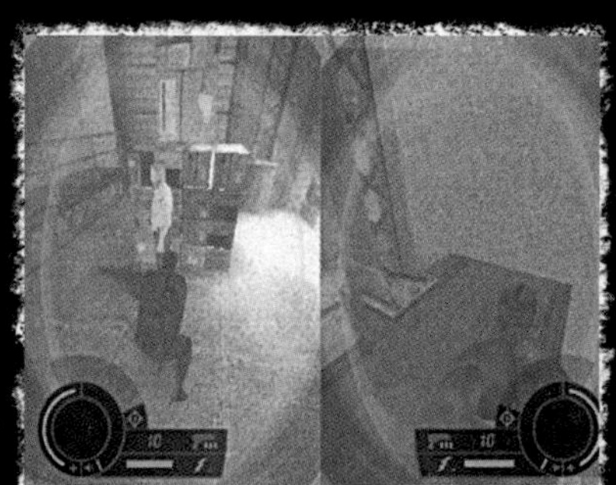

Wait until all chatter subsides before moving into position to get the drop on the first guard.

Both players should move along the dark, railed-off area toward the doorway. This allows them to avoid being spotted by the camera overhead.

Another camera monitors the area near the exit. Have Blue climb on top of the stack of supplies on the corridor's left side. When Blue drops down on the other side, he is in an optimal position to jam the surveillance camera with his OCP. Red can then move down the corridor and search the shelves against the right wall to find a keycard. After procuring the card, Red should move into the

shadows behind Blue.

One player should jam the camera while the other player snags the keycard from the shelves on the right and then hides in the shadows.

Blue should allow his OCP to recharge, and then he can jam the camera again. Red can then sneak over to the dark corner beside the camera. However, moving too quickly could create noise that might alert the guard in the next room. If the guard exclaims and then moves into the corridor to investigate, Red should remain hidden in the dark corner opposite the door while Blue holds position. Wait until the guard satisfies his suspicions and returns to the next room.

Blue should then jam the camera again so that Red may sneak over to the door, open it, and slip inside. The guard stands in front of the desk inside the room. Red should knock him unconscious, then move to the left side of the open door and jam the camera so Blue can enter the small room.

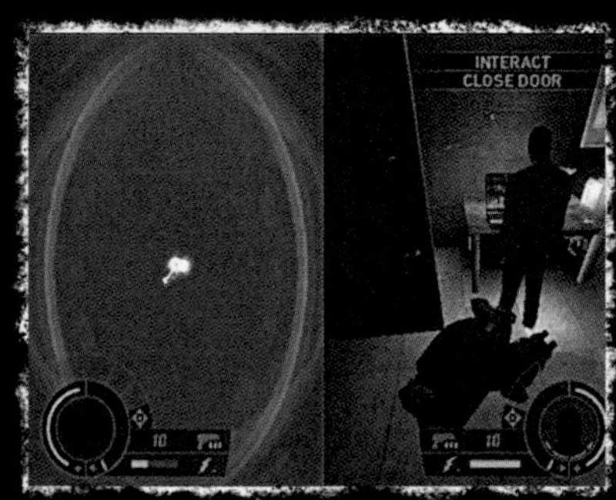

One man jams the camera so the other may sneak into the next room and knock out the guard.

Blue can procure his own keycard from the desk. Read the e-mail on the laptop to learn that the door code has changed to 1612. Proceed to the exit and input the code into the keypad to unlock the door.

The Bars Before the Eye

Bars block the corridor and a surveillance camera watches the area beyond. One player should load their compact launcher with EMP ammo and permanently disable the camera. Use EMF vision to make sure not to miss. Then have Blue crouch in front of the bars and press the Co-op button to initiate a Boost. Red can then complete the move and grab the pipe overhead. While hanging from the pipe, Red should press the Co-op button to become a Human Ladder. Blue can then press the Co-op

button to climb up Red and grab the pipe. Both players can then pull their legs up and shimmy along the horizontal pipe to the other side of the bars. Head down the corridor to the right, and simultaneously swipe both keycards to unlock the door.

Form a Human Ladder so that both players can bypass the bars by shimmying along the horizontal pipe.

Coordinated Strike

Both players should move through the corridor until they reach an open doorway. Blue should go through the doorway while Red holds position in the dark shadows on the door's left side. Have Blue move through the open security gate and then head directly to the wall on his left. By pressing his shoulder to the wall under the windows, Blue becomes invisible in the shadows. Hold this position while two guards in the adjacent room finish their conversation. The two men then proceed into the corridor.

One guard moves to the open door and eventually turns his back to Red's position. Red should grab the man and start dragging him into the shadows while Blue detaches from the wall. If Red is slick enough, the second guard will never notice. If not, the second guard may start to move in. Whether or not the second guard notices him, Blue should sneak up behind him and grab him. The guard who stops near the door can be Persuaded to divulge a clue about the vent in the next room. Choke both guards unconscious.

The key to taking down these guards successfully is to strike from both ends of the corridor, simultaneously if needed.

The Air-Con Duct

Proceed into the room the two guards emerged from and go around the corner to the right. Use EMP ammo to permanently disable the camera mounted over the door. Have Blue go through the door and pick up two smoke grenades on the desk to the right. Use the controls for the air-conditioning access to open the vent across from the surveillance camera located in the main room. Blue can then exit the small side room and give a smoke grenade to Red.

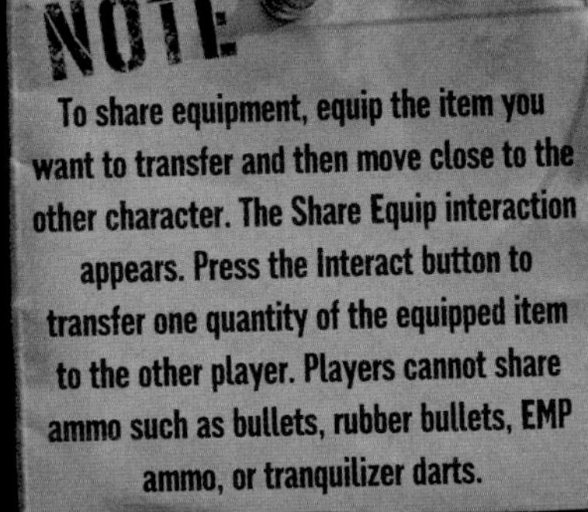

NOTE

To share equipment, equip the item you want to transfer and then move close to the other character. The Share Equip interaction appears. Press the Interact button to transfer one quantity of the equipped item to the other player. Players cannot share ammo such as bullets, rubber bullets, EMP ammo, or tranquilizer darts.

Blue should Boost Red up to the open vent. Then Red should press the Co-op button to form a Human Ladder so that Blue may climb into the vent.

Use the air-conditioning controls to open the vent in the main room.

Disk Drop

The vent leads into a small room. Lambert orders the agents to approach the grill across from the emergence point and drop a disk there.

The agents must drop the disk Sam Fisher finds in the Morgue during his escape.

Short Circuit

Now both agents should slide down the ladder to find another vent opening. The second vent leads into a small room containing a medkit. Heal up if needed, then proceed through the door into the corridor.

One player should move to the side of the bars blocking the passage and initiate a Shoulder Climb so the other player can plant an electric charge on the gate's circuitry box. Both players should then move into shadowy areas before detonating the charges.

Plant a short circuit charge on the electric panel above the gate.

Watch the area beyond the bars; a guard starts to patrol the area. One player should wait in the shadows on the gate's right side until the guard moves up the stairs and enters the players' area. Then he can sneak up behind the guard and knock him out.

When the guard enters the area to see what happened to the gate, take him down.

Both players should go through the gate and descend to the bottom of the steps. A laser sweeper in the ceiling scans the corridor in front of the exit. Have one player jam the device while the other player goes through the door. Then that player can turn around and do the same for his partner.

Move the Lift

Take turns jamming the surveillance camera in the turbine room so that both players can reach the other side. Go through the connecting corridor into a small warehouse. Blue and Red stand on a balcony overlooking the industrial zone. Use the small control panel on the left to move the lift in the warehouse. Both players should then climb over the rail and move into the small space between the lift and the wall. Blue and Red can then perform a Back Climb to reach the top of the high shelves. Follow the shelves to the left and climb onto the small boxes at the end to find a hole in the ceiling. Face the wall and jump up to grab the hole's ledge, then shimmy around to the right and climb into a short maintenance passage.

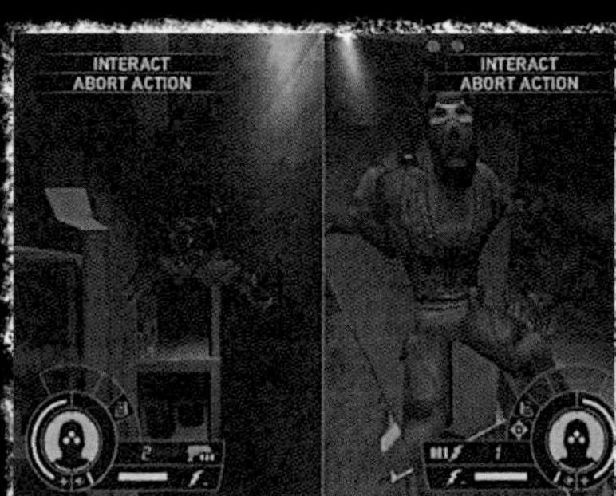

Move the lift closer to the wall, then perform a Back Climb to reach the top of the shelves.

High Beams

Follow the passage into a large room patrolled by two guards far below. Blue should head to the second thick beam connecting the support columns to the room's far corner. Move to the beam's left end and drop over the side so the agent hangs over the dark portion of the raised platform below. Wait until one of the guards moves under your position, then drop on him to knock him out.

The guard on the lower level hears the noise and comes to investigate. Quickly pick up the body and move into the niche behind the power generator to avoid discovery. When the guard gives up and moves away, leave the body in the niche and move out to the railing. Climb over the railing's dark section and drop to the level below. The guard patrolling the lowest level moves around very quickly. The best strategy is to wait until he moves under the platform close to Blue's position, then shoot him in the head with a rubber bullet. Blue can then move through the shadows up the central stairs and initiate a Shoulder Climb under the surveillance camera.

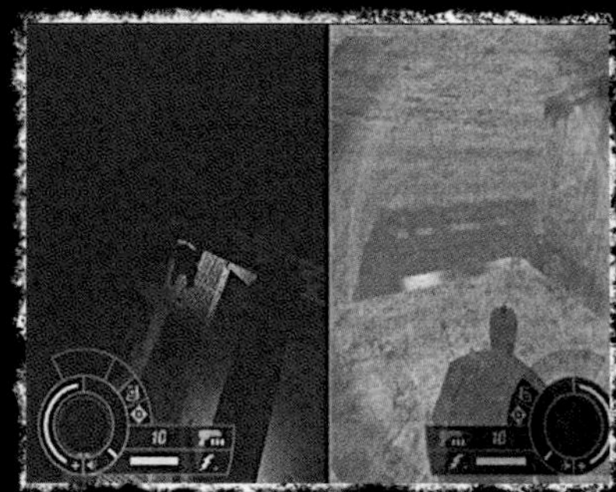

Drop from the ceiling beams onto a guard in order to knock him out. Just be sure to hide the body quickly.

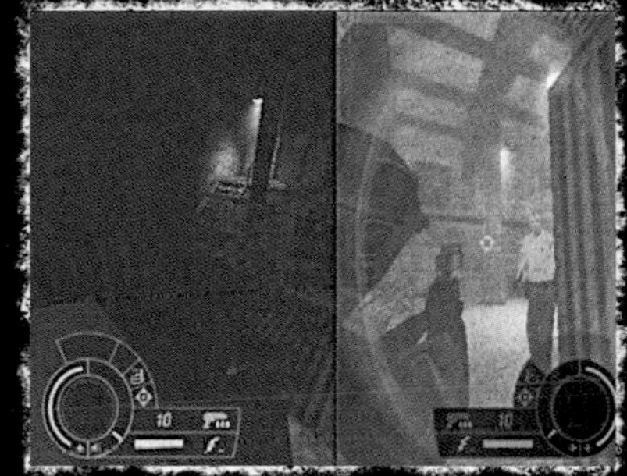

Climb over the rail to the lower level and hide in the shadows. When the patrolling guard moves near, hit him with a rubber bullet.

Red can now drop from the ceiling beams to the raised platform. He should work his way around the room's outer wall to Blue's position, complete the Shoulder Climb, and cut the wires on the surveillance camera.

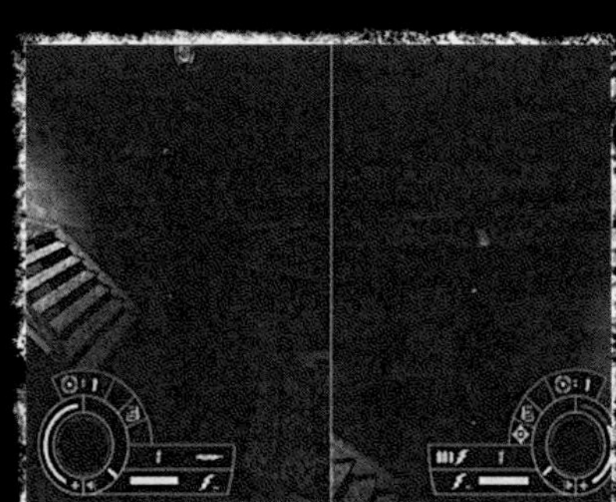

Permanently disable the surveillance camera mounted above the shadowy stairs.

Now Blue and Red can safely move down to the lowest level and take positions in front of the breakers on either side of the main power conduit. Both players must turn off the breakers simultaneously to cut the power to the prison and complete the mission.

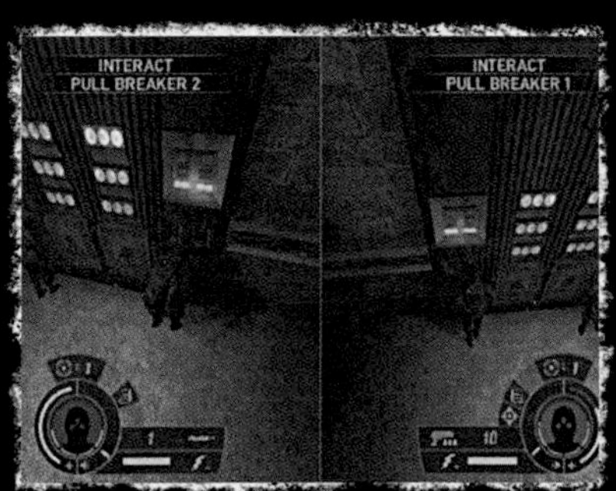

Turn off both breakers simultaneously to cut the power and complete the mission.

Ellsworth—The Blackout

Bathroom Strike

"The Blackout" is an extremely tricky mission from start to finish, and advanced tactics are required. Blue and Red start the mission in the space over the restroom's ceiling. Two holes allow the players to drop into the toilet stalls below. Red starts the mission equipped with tranquilizer ammo in his loadout. Therefore, he should move to the corner and drop through the hole near Blue's starting position, landing in the dark toilet stall at the row's end. Red should then move to the corner, load his compact launcher with tranquilizer ammo, and wait for a guard and an inmate to enter.

Red should get into position and wait for the guard and inmate to finish their conversation. Then he should fire a tranquilizer dart at the guard.

When the guard and the inmate finish their terse conversation, have Red shoot the patrolling guard with a tranquilizer dart. Although the inmate is startled, he surrenders immediately. Blue can then drop through the ceiling hole into the stall behind the inmate and knock him out without being seen.

Elevator Crash

A laser sweeper in the ceiling scans the corridor outside the bathroom. Blue can jam the device with his OCP while Red moves down the corridor and hides behind the column jutting from the right-hand wall. Red can then disable the device so that Blue can pass through the area.

Both players can squeeze through the narrow gap in the elevator doors to drop on top of the elevator car stopped on the level below. Use your EMF goggles to spot the fuse box high on the wall in the corner. One player should crouch below the fuse box and initiate a Shoulder climb so the other agent can place an electric charge on the fuse box. Move away from the box and detonate the charge to cause the elevator to drop several stories.

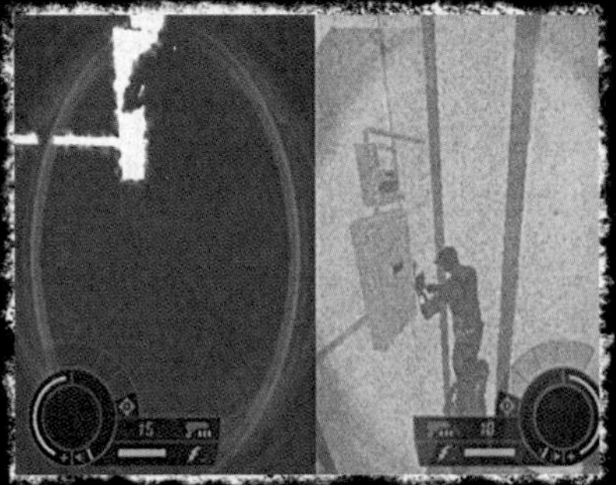

Plant a short circuit charge on the electric breaker box high in the elevator shaft's corner to trigger a sharp descent.

When the players crash-land at their destination, a guard peers out from the open elevator door overhead. Although the shaft is completely dark, move slowly to avoid making noise or he may open fire. Blue should move to the wall below the elevator door and initiate a Boost. When Red completes the move and hangs from the door's bottom ledge, he should press the Co-op button to form a Human Ladder so that Blue may climb up.

Work together to climb out of the shaft.

Another laser sweeper scans the room. As soon as Blue is on his feet, have him move a few steps to the side so Red may climb into the room. Then Blue should jam the sweeper with his OCP while Red moves through the doorway on the room's opposite side. From outside the doorway, Red should jam the sweeper so Blue may follow.

Office Politics

A laser sensor blocks the corridor. However, there is a second laser sensor that only activates when someone is near. Therefore, Red should stand and face away from the first laser and press the Co-op button to initiate a Tomoe Nage. Blue can then complete the throw. When Blue lands in the corridor beyond the lasers, two guards can be heard talking nearby. Blue should quickly move toward the corner, hiding in the shadows with his shoulder pressed against the wall to the right. Soon, a guard strolls past Blue's position. Have Blue grab the guard, then drag him toward Red until both lasers are deactivated. Red can then move into the passage beyond the lasers, and Blue can choke the guard unconscious.

Perform a Tomoe Nage to put one agent on the other side of the laser grid so he may intercept the patrolling guard.

Approach the next corner and peek into the next room to observe the guard inside. A surveillance camera on the wall to the right makes it difficult to go after the guard. As the guard moves away, Blue should enter the room, staying close to the left wall. When the guard returns and then starts to head back through the lasers monitoring the stairs, Blue should sneak up behind him and capture him while the lasers are deactivated. Blue can then hold the guard in place while Red joins Blue on the stairs. Blue can choke the man unconscious and leave his body on the stairs so the lasers remain disabled.

01:
DOSSIERS

PS2/GC

02:
GAME BASICS

03:
EQUIPMENT

04:
SOLO MISSIONS

05:
CO-OP MISSIONS

Ellsworth—The Blackout

06:
VERSUS MISSIONS

XBOX 360/PC

07:
GAME BASICS

08:
EQUIPMENT

09:
SOLO MISSIONS

10:
MULTIPLAYER

One player must grab the patrolling guard while he is on the stairs.

Use EMP ammo to permanently disable the camera positioned above the laptop on the desk. One player should hack the laptop's security access in order to disable all security cameras in this area. One player should pick up the keycard on the desk to the laptop's left while the other player obtains the other keycard from the desk monitored by the camera mounted on the column.

Disable the cameras, then pick up both keycards in the office.

Use the medkit near the exit if necessary, then simultaneously swipe both keycards to unlock the exit door. Move through the long passage and swipe both keycards again to proceed to the next area.

Cell Block

Wait inside the barred area until the guard on the upper catwalk moves away. Then enter the large area and initiate a Shoulder Climb under the camera. Cut the camera's wires, then retreat to the darkness near the entrance.

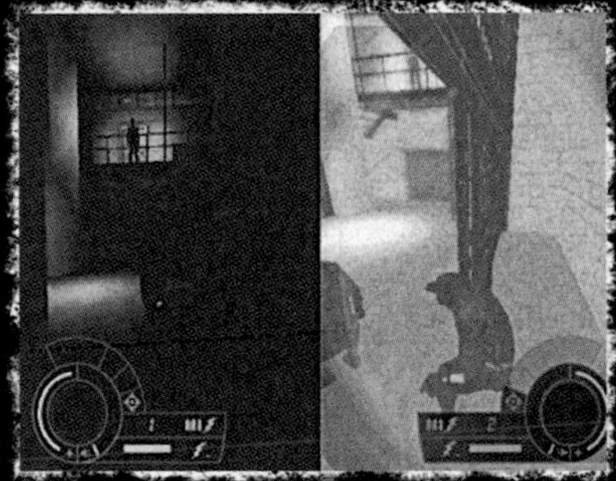

Wait for the guard on the upper level to leave the catwalk before clipping the camera's wires.

Wait for the guard to patrol the upper catwalk again. When he leaves, move through the shadows to the cage below the catwalk. Blue should Boost Red up, then Red should initiate a Human Ladder while hanging. Blue can then climb over the rail to the catwalk. While Red holds position, hanging off the cage's side, Blue should sneak up to the control booth door where the guard went, sticking to the right-hand wall. There is a small corner to the door's right. Have Blue hide there and wait for the guard to emerge again. The guard may notice the door is open, but that is okay. As the guard passes, Blue can grab him and quietly choke him unconscious. Both Blue and Red may enter the control booth.

Perform a Boost and a Human Ladder at the cage's base to reach the catwalk.

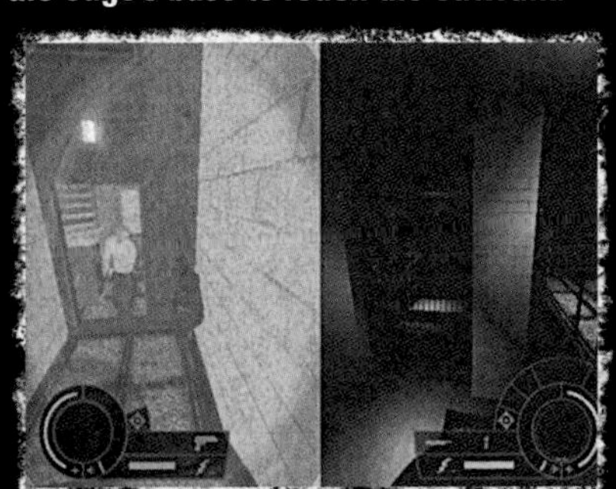

One player should hang from the cage's side while the other hides just outside the doorway, waiting for the guard to patrol past.

A guard patrols the catwalk outside the booth windows; both players should crouch while moving through the control booth to avoid detection. Two keyboards are on the console. Each player should move to a keyboard and use them to simultaneously unlock both Cell Block A and Cell Block B.

Unlock both cell blocks simultaneously.

Watch through the control booth windows as the guard patrols his route on the catwalk outside. When the guard is walking away, Blue should quietly exit the booth and follow him. As the guard descends some stairs, have Blue wait near the railing at the stairs' top until the guard comes back up. Blue can then get the drop on the guard easily.

Take out the guard who patrols both levels.

Both players should descend the stairs and go through the exit door in the corner. At the short passage's end, one player must Boost the other into the vent opening high up on the wall. The hanging player can then form a Human Ladder so his partner may climb into the vent.

Two Pairs of Eyes

The situation in the last room is extremely tricky; it may take a few attempts to get right, so save now. There are two ways to reach the extraction point: (1) knock out both guards with rubber bullets, then hack the dual retinal scanners at the exit

door; or (2) figure out a way to grab both conscious guards, drag them over to the doors, and force their heads to the scanners simultaneously. We shall elaborate on the second method—using the guard's eyes at the retinal scanners.

Blue should move to the vent opening's far end while Red stays near the entrance. Red can easily drop down from the vent into the room and still be well concealed in the shadows. Have Red run around in the corner so the guard nearest the exit hears the noise. He signals to his partner, and both men move in to investigate. Red should then hide near the wall and wait for both guards to search the area. As they start moving away, have Red grab the second guard in line and drag him back into the shadows.

When the two guards move to investigate the noise in the corner, Red can seize a guard.

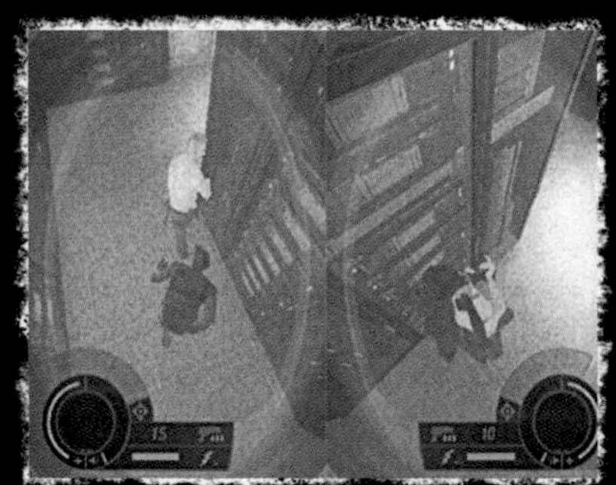

As the remaining guard searches for his missing buddy, he becomes vulnerable to capture.

The remaining guard soon notices that his partner has disappeared. As the remaining guard returns to Red's side to investigate, Blue should drop into the room on the central server's other side. Blue should quickly but quietly navigate around the central server and grab the remaining guard from behind. Both players may then drag their men over to the retinal scanners and simultaneously force their heads up to the oculars to complete the mission.

Use both retinal scanners simultaneously to proceed.

Ellsworth—The Riot

Low Down the Doors

Around the corner from the starting position, two armed and anxious inmates shout threats into the dark. Blue should sneak up behind the closest inmate while Red moves to the opposite corner. Have Blue seize the closest inmate and drag him around the corner toward the starting point before choking him unconscious. As the second inmate becomes suspicious and moves in to investigate, Red can sneak up on him and knock him out with a nonlethal attack.

Seize the inmates near the starting point before they start to patrol.

Blue should get on top of the table near the area's center, standing with his back to the kitchen. Have him press the Co-op button to initiate a Tomoe Nage. Red can then complete the move to be thrown into the kitchen, where he can enter the crawlspace in the corner and crawl to the corridor outside.

Perform a Tomoe Nage to fling one player into the kitchen area.

There are no enemies in the corridor. Red should follow the passageways until he stands outside the double doors of the room where Blue is trapped. Red must place charges on the door and then move away before detonating them.

Blast the door open from the corridor.

Blue and Red may now reunite in the corridor. Both players should return to the area near the crawlspace exit. To the left is an open elevator shaft. Blue can Boost Red to the ledge above. Red can then form a Human Ladder so Blue may climb into a narrow shaft. Both players can perform a Back Climb in the narrow elevator shaft to reach the top.

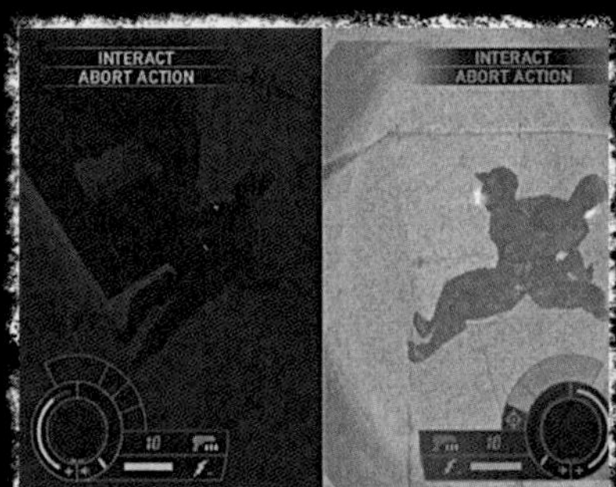

Perform a Back Climb to reach the top of the elevator shaft.

Upon reaching the small ledge at the top, both players can jump up to grab a rail that runs around the elevator shaft. Have Blue and Red shimmy to the left and drop onto the platform in front of the open elevator doors.

Grab the ledge that runs horizontally around the elevator shaft and shimmy over to the doorway.

Hang and Jam

As the players move down the corridor, the voices of guards can be heard from the passage on the right. Bars block this corridor. Blue should Boost Red up to a horizontal pipe that runs behind the bars. Red must then press the Co-op button to form a Human ladder so Blue can grab the pipe. Have Red then pull his legs up and shimmy to the other side of the bars. Before he can drop, Blue must use his OCP while hanging to jam the gun turret in the corridor; then Red can drop to the ground, move behind the turret, and deactivate it. Blue may then follow Red into the area.

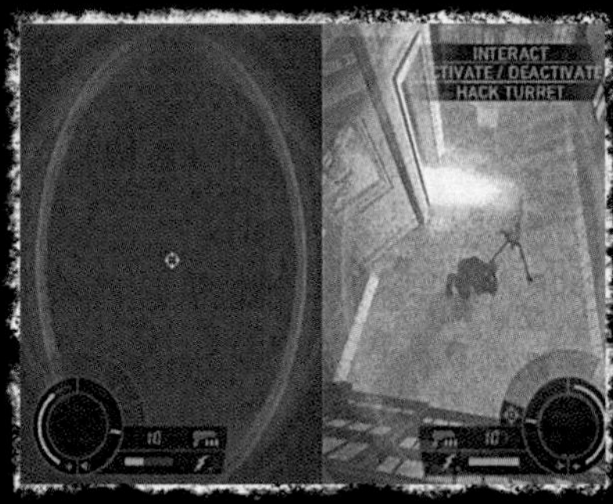

One player must jam the gun turret while hanging so the other may deactivate the turret.

The Guard Station

Pick the lock on the gate to avoid alerting guards who may be lingering in the vicinity. After opening the gate, go through the door on the left. Go through the short corridor and another door to reach the exterior of a guard station. Both players must activate both switches outside the guard booth simultaneously. The sounds of gunfire between guards and the inmates can be station to find a keycard and a medkit.

Throw both switches outside the guard station to unlock the doors in the other

Inmate Showdown

Both players must return to the area where the gun turret is located. Go through the other door and approach the next door quietly. Two inmates are arguing in the next room. Blue should approach the door while Red remains in the shadows near the corridor's entrance. Have Blue choose the Open Door Stealth interaction and open the door a little way. When the inmates notice, Blue must close the door and retreat to the shadows near the entrance.

Draw the inmates toward the door by opening it only slightly.

The inmates open the door to check out the corridor. When they give up searching, they leave the door open. Blue can then enter the room more easily, sneak across the area to the opposite corner, and hide in the shadows. The inmates become suspicious again and move toward the door. Blue can then grab one of the inmates and drag him over to the corner to choke him. Meanwhile, Red should creep up to the doorway. When the remaining inmate turns away from the open door to find his partner missing, Red can then sneak into the room and knock the second inmate unconscious.

One player can slip into the room and seize one of the inmates while the other player grabs the man near the entrance.

The player who picked up a keycard can swipe it at the card reader to access the small power room. Blue should crouch under the open ceiling vent and press the Co-op button to initiate a Boost. Red can then return the favor by forming a Human Ladder so Blue may climb into the vent. Both players may then exfiltrate.

Work together to get into the ceiling vent and exfiltrate.

Ellsworth—The Breach

Tactics in the Ruins

When the mission starts, Blue stands directly under a horizontal pipe. Blue should jump to grab the pipe, pull his legs up, and shimmy to the bright passage's end. Soon a guard emerges from the doorway on the right. As he passes underneath, Blue should grab him and strangle him from above. Red can then sneak into the next room where a guard stands at the edge of a pool of light. Red must sneak around the room's shadowy edge to maneuver behind the guard and knock him out.

Quickly grab the guard who enters the corridor at the insertion point.

Sneak under the light of the window on the right to get behind the guard at the room's rear.

Follow the tunnel dug through the room's corner. The tunnel ends at a brick wall, where Red can Boost Blue up to a high vent. When Red grasps the vent's bottom ledge, he can then form a Human Ladder so Blue may climb up.

Form a Human Ladder so both operatives may climb into the vent.

Spinning Death

Carefully cross over the spinning fan by navigating along the narrow beam. Jump to cross over the central obstacle and continue to the other side. Then move to the left corner, shut down the fan, and rappel down the wall one at a time.

Press the Jump button to get over the central obstacle on the fan.

At the bottom of the fan shaft, go through the small hole in the wall into a tunnel. Move Blue to the right to get out of Red's way. Blue should use his EMF vision to locate the gun turret at the tunnel's far end, then jam the turret while Red runs down the tunnel and deactivates the device.

CAUTION

Avoid moving too far into the tunnel behind the fan shaft or the gun turret may open fire.

Follow the passage beside the gun turret. One at a time, the players should drop into the pit spanning the center of the corridor, then climb out the other side. Head around the corner to the right and climb up through the hole conveniently ripped in the fence.

The Sewers

Approach the door quietly to avoid alarming the inmates in the next passage. Use the optic cable to spy on them until they move out of sight. Blue should go through the door and close it behind him. Have him wait until the inmate patrolling the area near the entrance draws near; then he can grab the inmate. Drag the prisoner back through the open entrance and choke him unconscious.

Wait until the inmate patrolling near the door stops on the bridge, then sneak up behind him and knock him out.

Check your left to make sure the other inmate is not staring in your direction, then cross the small bridge to the tunnel's far side. Where the rail ends, a narrow ledge allows Blue to move down the tunnel while remaining concealed in darkness. Blue should stop near the area where the second inmate patrols. When the inmate stops and peers toward the entrance, Blue should sneak up beside him and knock him out.

One player can follow the thin ledge down the tunnel's side to reach a flanking position on the second inmate.

Head down the long corridor. Near the end on the right is a narrow shaft. Both players can work together to perform a Back Climb to reach the shaft's top.

The Final Blow

At the top of the tall shaft is a mechanic's bay. Blue should head right, to where the hydraulic lift has been raised. Using the right analog stick, angle the camera to see around the pit's edges. Blue should climb out at the corner nearest the control booth, which is the darkest spot. If Blue makes it undetected, he can sneak under the window and into the booth to knock out the guard who is listening to music. Under the window are two switches. Press the switch to activate car lift 1, which raises the hydraulic lift on the other side of the fenced area.

Climb out of the mechanic's pit into the shadows.

Blue can now drop back into the pit and rendezvous with Red. Red can then climb out of the newly opened pit and place a charge on the tank standing in the corner, which is marked with an explosion warning label. After placing the charge, Red and Blue should take cover in the pit, then detonate the charge to complete the Ellsworth missions.

Set charges on the large tank to blast a hole in the wall.

Kinshasa—The Front

Loud Entrance

Both players start in a subterranean cave. Follow the cave to the end, where one player must place charges on the brick wall. Back out of harm's way, then detonate the charges to blow through the wall.

Plant charges on the brick wall and back away before detonating them.

Enter the sewer junction and go left until you find a ladder. One at a time, simultaneously jump and shift the move control upward at the same time to grab the ladder's lower rungs. Climb to the catwalk above. More than halfway down the catwalk, the bridge to the left has collapsed. Blue should stand with his back to the gap in the rail and press the Co-op button to initiate a Tomoe Nage. Red can then complete the move to be thrown across the top of the area to the catwalk running along the room's other side.

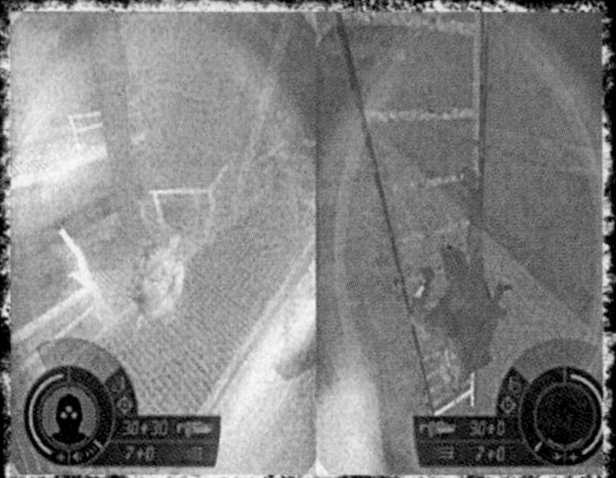

Climb up the ladder in the corner.

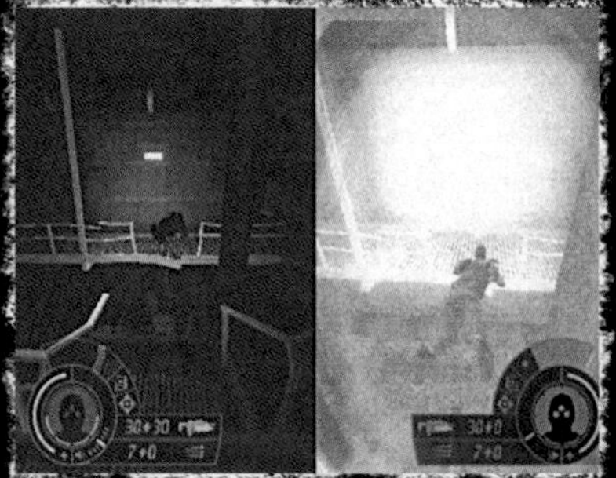

Perform a Tomoe Nage to send one player to the upper level's other side.

Separate Paths

While Red heads down the corridor to the left to find the exit, have Blue locate a vent opening in the nearby wall and enter the crawlspace, then crawl through to the server room. Meanwhile, Red must navigate through the passageway to an intersection and head left to reach the server room door. Feel free to break the lock rather than pick it, since no enemies are close enough to hear. After Red reunites with Blue in the server room, Blue should crouch near the enclosed area and press the Co-op button to initiate a Boost. Red can then complete the move and jump into the server area. Use the computer on the right to read e-mail if desired, then move a little farther down the panel to find the surveillance camera system's controls. By deactivating the system, many of the security cameras in the next several missions should be inoperative. Red can climb out of the enclosure by jumping to grab the top of one of the small servers near the fence, then hopping over the barrier.

Boost one player into the enclosed area to access the servers.

Both players should exit the server room and move down the corridor to the intersection. Just past the intersection, a dual laser mine blocks the passage. There are two ways to get past the laser mine:

1. Defuse the bombs on both walls simultaneously to deactivate the beam. Each player should move to a separate bomb and choose the Defuse interaction. Switch to EMF vision to determine which wire is hot—it is glowing in EMF vision. Then shift the move control left or right to highlight that wire, whereupon the controller may vibrate. When both players have the hotwire selected, they must simultaneously cut the wires on their bomb. A countdown begins. Both players must then simultaneously cut another hotwire before the time displayed on the bomb's timer elapses, or the bomb detonates. When the players have cut two wires simultaneously, the bombs are defused and the laser sensor is deactivated.
2. Dive-roll under the laser beam. One at a time, players should crouch, run toward the beam from a distance, then hold the Crouch button to dive-roll under the laser. Practice dive-rolling in the corridor away from the bomb for a while in order to learn the timing and the movement. When you think you have mastered the skill, dive-roll under the laser beam one at a time.

Dual laser mines are difficult to defuse.

TIP

Defusing the bombs is tricky, and detonation will occur several times. Do not become frustrated. Persevere in defusing this first bomb, and the bomb in the next Kinshasa mission will be defused as well!

Coercion Cry

Enter the warehouse. If you previously deactivated the camera system, you will have no problem moving through this area. Sneak between the covered vehicles to the warehouse's other side and watch the guard patrol back and forth between the two lighted areas. When he stops near the pool of light on the left, sneak up behind him and grab him. The players together can make this guard radio in for another guard to open the exit door. He is one tough cookie to crack; one agent alone cannot coerce him into calling for the door to open, so the other player must approach the guard from the front and Persuade him. When finally persuaded, the guard radios a soldier elsewhere, who opens the door in the warehouse's corner. Choke the guard unconscious and leave his body in the shadows.

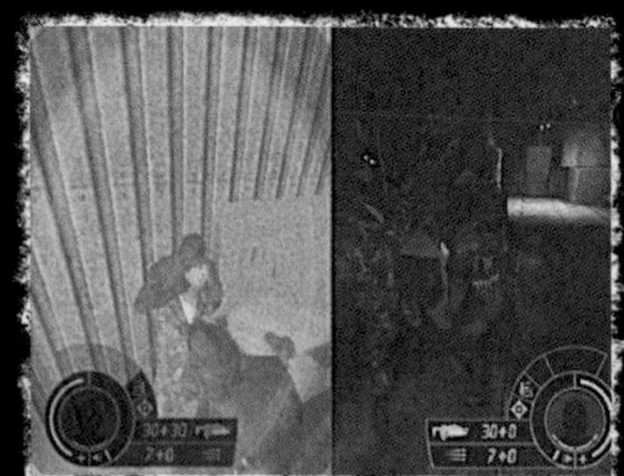

Persuade the guard in the warehouse to call for the opening of the door in the corner.

Blue can collect the keycard on the desk in the brightly lit area. Red should move through the shadows toward the crates near the open door. Even though you've deactivated the camera system, EMF shows that the two cameras nearest the exit continue to actively survey the area. The crates stacked directly below the camera to the door's right side block its view. Therefore, have Blue use his OCP to jam the camera to the door's left so Red may pass through the exit and go a few steps into the corridor beyond. Red may then turn around and use his OCP to jam the camera while Blue follows the same route into the passage.

Jam the cameras surrounding the door so that both players can pass into the corridor.

Desk Job

Red, or the player without a keycard at this point, should quietly enter the first door on the passageway's left. A guard is seated at a desk in this room. Sneak up behind him and knock him out. Then pick up the keycard on the desk. Use the desktop computer to access the camera system and hack the security access to obtain the security log, completing an Opportunity Objective. Use the server in the corner to unlock the elevator security door at the corridor's far end.

Knock out the guard and use the computers in the security office to override the locks on the exit door.

Return to the corridor and proceed to its end. Both players must swipe both keycards simultaneously to unlock the elevator and extract.

Swipe both keycards simultaneously to open the extraction point.

Kinshasa—The Chemical Depot

High Surveillance

Both players start the mission facing a corridor. Two cameras survey the corridor's first corner; the two agents can maneuver past the cameras unseen by sticking to the shadowed left wall and moving carefully around the dark corner.

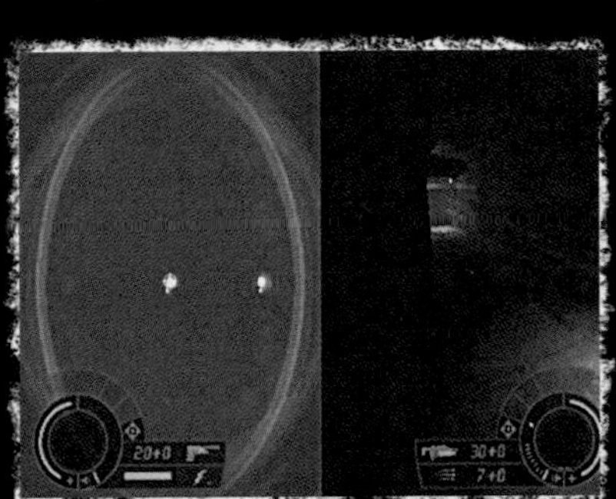

Stick to the corner to bypass the first

Follow the passage to the next corner. Two active security cameras survey the door at the passage's end. The camera on the left surveys the corridor's right portion while the camera on the right surveys the passage's left side. Blue should stay near the corner and use his OCP to deactivate the camera on the passage's *left* side while Red moves down the passage's *right* side. Red may then pick up the first keycard lying on the ground near the door. The door itself cannot be opened, although Red can use the optic cable to peek into the next room. Blue should jam the left camera again so that Red may return to the safety of the shadows.

Jam the left camera so your partner can move down the passage's right side to snag the keycard.

The Refrigerated Element

Both players should now return to the starting point, using the same caution as before when passing the cameras in the corridor. To the starting point's left is a

the Co-op button to initiate a Boost. While Red is hanging from the top of the machinery, he should press the Co-op button to form a Human Ladder. Blue may then climb onto the machinery and enter the crawlspace, which emerges in a tight area. Turn to the left and jump to climb onto a higher ledge, then crawl through another crawlspace into the sample storage room.

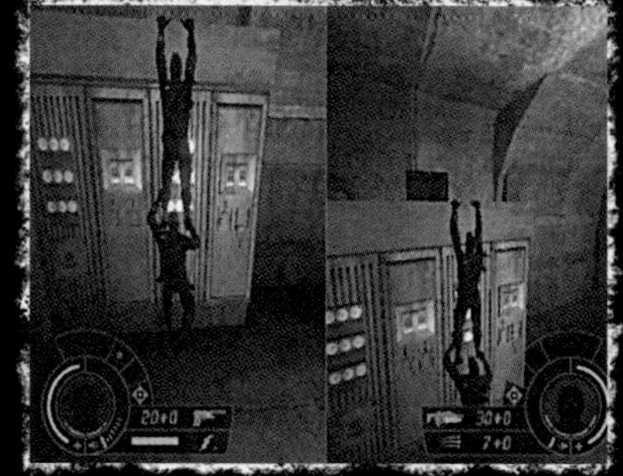

Use co-op moves to reach the crawlspace on top of the machinery near the starting point.

A surveillance camera watches the well-lit refrigerated room. Too bad neither player has any EMP ammo handy. The player who does not yet have a keycard (Blue in our game) should move along the right-hand wall until he is positioned under the security camera. Red should stay near the crawlspace exit and use his OCP to jam the camera. Blue can then move over to the shelves on the room's left side to pick up his own keycard, then quickly move across the room and hide in the shadows near the storage case on the back wall. Red can take a break while Blue inputs the code 5268 into the keypad on the refrigerated case to open it. (We tell you later how to obtain this code.) Inside the storage case is a sample. Scan the sample to obtain the first chemical element. Red should then use his OCP to jam the camera so that Blue may move over to the door, open it, and go through. Red should follow Blue out to the corridor.

The player who already has a keycard must jam the surveillance camera so his partner can procure one.

Surprise!

Defuse the bomb in the corridor if needed, then head to the right around two corners to a door. Approach the door quietly. One player should use his optic cable on the door to survey the scene inside. One guard patrols the level below, while another guard patrols every portion of the upper-level catwalk; he even briefly goes down the stairs opposite the door. He stops in front of the door for a long moment. When he does, use the Bash Door interaction. The guard on the door's other side is knocked unconscious. The guard on the level below becomes suspicious for several moments thereafter, so wait in the corridor until the intense music fades off before entering.

Use the Bash Door option to surprise the guard who stops in front of the door.

One player should descend the stairs to the midlevel. Wait until the guard patrolling the ground floor moves over to the door in the corner. Climb over the rail and drop to the ground. Wait until the guard moves back toward the center. Get behind him and knock him out.

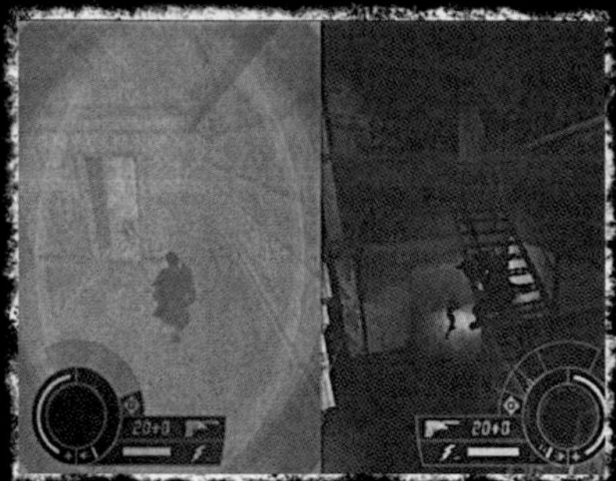

Drop from the midlevel stair platform to get the jump on the guard patrolling the lower level.

Use EMF vision to find the surveillance camera in the corner. If the surveillance camera detects an intruder, the machine-gun turret next to the camera activates and fires. Blue should use his OCP to deactivate the camera while Red moves through the doorway directly under the camera into a storage area. Scan the silver container in this area to locate the second element.

Jam the camera protecting the second element so that your partner can scan the substance.

Both agents should ascend the stairs to the upper level and move toward the collapsed portion of the catwalk. Blue should stand near the platform's edge and initiate a Tomoe Nage. Once Red is across, he can move to the platform's other end and initiate rappelling. Blue can then descend to the lower level and climb up the rope to reunite with Red.

Perform a Tomoe Nage to fling one player to the disconnected catwalk...

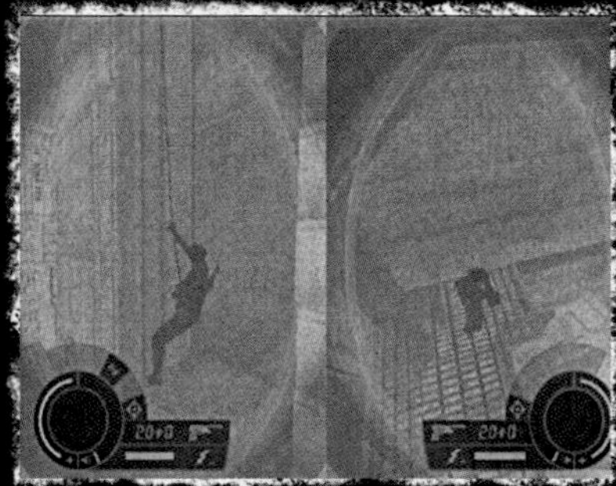

...then move to the lower level so that player can allow you to rappel.

Gun on a Rail

A machine gun moves slowly along a rail, guarding the next long passage. Use your EMF vision to locate the machine gun, which is motion-sensitive. If an agent moves across its field of vision, it opens fire. However, if the agent stands still while the machine gun passes, it fails to detect him. There is also a guard patrolling in a booth at the passageway's far end. To avoid the guard spotting you, stick close to the right-hand wall without actually pressing your shoulder to it.

When the mobile machine gun is not scanning your vicinity, move down the long passage while sticking to the right-hand wall.

Furthermore, the agents must avoid alarms at all costs. Triggering even a level-one alarm at this time activates backup security devices, making advancement beyond this area impossible.

The bridge between the catwalk and a nearby office is retracted. First, draw the guard out of his booth by shooting out the glass covering the gap's far side. Wait until he emerges from his office and moves toward the wall at the back of the area. If he returns to his booth without stopping near the back wall, it means he did not hear the bullet strike the wall. Simply fire another shot at the wall to draw him out of his booth. Knock him out with a sticky shocker while he stands near the back wall; he should fall in such a way that the nearby surveillance camera fails to spot his body.

Perform a Tomoe Nage to throw Red across the gap. Then Blue should jam the security camera while Red goes into the booth. Red can use the computer to obtain the access code 5268 for the door back in the refrigerated room and to extend the bridge across the gap. Now Blue can move forward and use his OCP again so that Red may safely leave the booth and move to one of the card readers on the back wall. Have Red jam the camera with his OCP so Blue may move to the other card reader. Swipe both keycards simultaneously to open the door.

Shoot out the glass to draw the guard out of his booth. Use bullets if necessary to draw his attention to the back wall (as shown). Then hit him with a sticky shocker.

If you triggered even a level-one alarm by this point, additional security, including laser sensors and a ceiling turret, may be active in this corridor. Take out the turret with machine-gun fire only if necessary. Otherwise, simply move to the other end and go through the door.

The Final Three Elements

Blue and Red emerge in a large warehouse with two patrolling guards. The three final samples to be scanned are located in this area. First, take out the guards. Both Blue and Red should move to the right along the catwalk rail until positioned over a dark spot on the level below, between two shelves. One of the guards on the level below stops directly under this portion of the rail. When he does, Blue should climb over the rail and drop on top of him to knock him out. The action may attract the attention of the other guard, who moves in quickly to investigate. Blue should quickly pick up the unconscious guard's body and hide in the low dark space under the shelves. As the suspicious guard moves under the catwalk, Red can climb over and drop onto the guard to knock him unconscious. Tangos down, area clear.

TIP

If the second guard does not hear the first guard getting knocked out and does not move in to investigate, then one player must simply sneak up behind this guard while he patrols and knock him out.

Take down the guards by dropping from the middle of the catwalk.

Now to scan the samples and destroy them. A vertical pipe hangs on the wall near the stairs. Both players should jump up from the floor to grab the pipe and climb to the ceiling. Shimmy along the horizontal pipe until positioned over a beam. Drop to the beam and carefully maneuver onto the suspended platform. Work together to perform a Hang Over at the available point so that one player may scan the first of the three elements.

Climb the vertical pipe near the stairs by the entrance to reach the suspended platform overhead.

Perform a Hang Over from the suspended platform to scan the first of the three elements.

Now the players should split up to scan the remaining two elements. One player can jump up to grab the pipe and shimmy back over to the catwalk. From there, he can descend to the lower level and find the forklift in the corner, diagonally opposite the stairs. Lower the forklift's payload to scan the second element.

Meanwhile, the other player should navigate along the rear ceiling beam until positioned over a shiny silver box that registers on EMF. Drop from the beam onto the shelf's top and scan the third and final element.

One player drops onto the shelves near the element container while the other lowers the forklift payload.

Before destroying the elements, both players should locate the emergency shutter door in the corner. One agent should move beyond the emergency shutter into the safe area while the other agent sets off the sprinkler system (by using their sniper attachment to shoot the sprinkler head on the thin pipe on the ceiling). Thereafter, both players have 20 seconds to move beyond the closing shutter door. If both players do not make it beyond the door, the mission is a failure. Once both players are inside the safe area, they can extract.

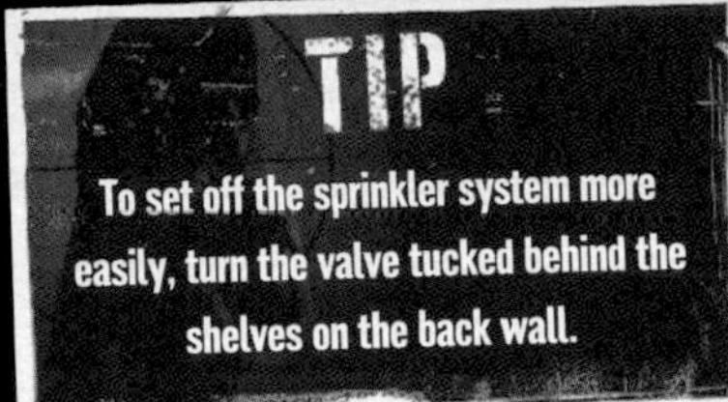

Turn the valve behind the shelves to set off the sprinkler systems. Then hurry to the extraction point before the shutter door closes!

Kinshasa—The Old Mine

The Plunge

Time to escape. From the starting point, first one player and then the other should turn left and climb up the vertical pipe. Shimmy along the horizontal ceiling pipe to the roof of the central elevator. There are two rappel points on the elevator's roof, allowing both agents to rappel down the sides of the elevator simultaneously. Rappel downward until you are just above a brightly lit spot on the wall, often indicated by emanating steam. To jump through this area very quickly and avoid detection by the guards patrolling on the surrounding cliffs, press the Jump button and shift the move control downward.

Use the pipe near the starting point to reach the central elevator's rooftop.

Rappel down the elevator's sides, jumping while descending to avoid lighted spots.

Upon reaching the cavern floor, move along the fence to the end nearest the elevator engine and climb over. Move through the cave opening on the open area's far side, avoiding the pool of light on the ground.

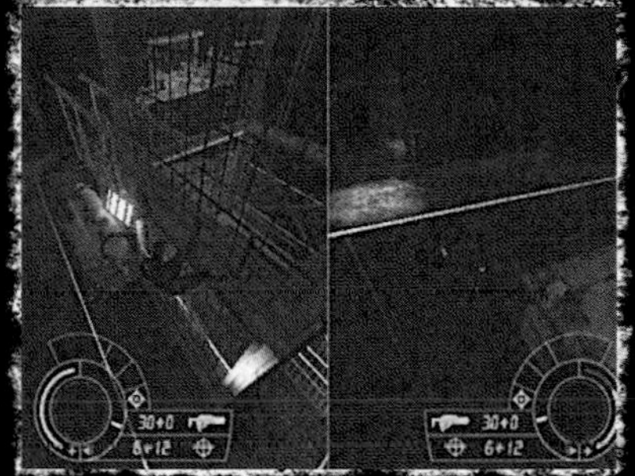

Climb over the fence near the engine to avoid being spotted.

Detour

Defuse the dual laser mines in the next cavern, or perform dive-rolls under the laser beam. Farther back in the cavern, the floor collapses. Both agents suffer minor damage, which is unavoidable but soon treatable. Enter the tunnel to the left and proceed with caution, detaching a wall mine on the right-hand wall. At the path's end, use the medkit to heal up.

Defuse the bomb blocking the tunnel.

On the ledge high overhead, an active gun turret monitors the gap in the railing. Blue should crouch below the gap in the railing and press the Co-op button to initiate a Boost. While Red hangs from the ledge, Blue should back up and move down the slope a little until he can clearly see the turret on the level above. Blue can then jam the turret with his OCP while Red climbs up and deactivates the turret. Red should then resume a hanging position over the ledge and press the Co-op button to form a Human Ladder. Blue and Red can then climb to the upper level, and both players can move down the tunnel to the left.

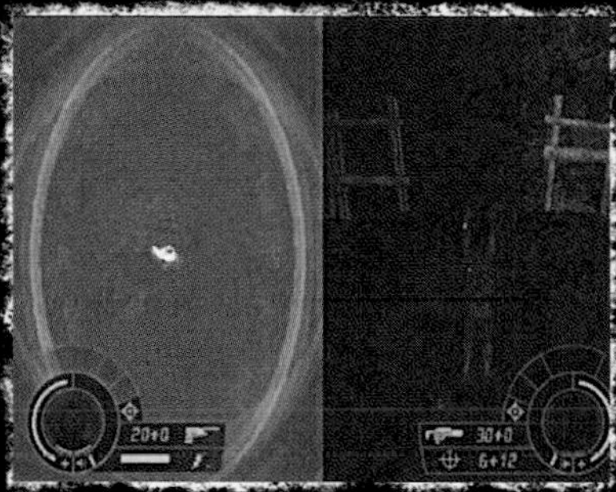

While one player hangs from the ledge, the other must jam the gun turret with the OCP.

The Great Pit

While moving through the tunnel, watch out for another wall mine placed on the wall to the right. At the tunnel's end, both players emerge in a huge mining pit. Head left through a tunnel to find a platform with a ladder. Climb down the ladder to the ledge below. At this ledge's other end, climb up a vertical pipe. Shimmy left from the pipe's top until you can go no farther, then drop onto a small ledge. At this point, carefully watch the movement of the spotlight scouring the pit's lower portion. When the searchlight is pointed at the pit's far side, drop to the next ledge below; quickly jump to grab the rope and use it as a zip-line to the area directly beneath the searchlight. If your timing is bad, the searchlight may pass across the low ledge and reveal your location.

Navigate down the ledges inside the pit.

Once both players are safely hidden at the base of the searchlight, they should face the open area and watch the searchlight's pattern. When the searchlight scours the area to the right, one player should run to the left along the back wall toward a brightly lit exit tunnel. This may arouse some suspicion from guards on the level above, so the second player should wait near the searchlight until the suspicion music fades away. Then the second player can run across the ground level when it's dark and go through the bright doorway.

One at a time, run from the searchlight's base to the exit.

Around the first corner in the corridor are a gun turret and two wall mines. This situation is extremely tricky. One player should stay at the corner and use his OCP to jam the turret while the other player, with gun drawn, moves slowly into the area behind the turret to deactivate it. The player doing the jamming can prolong his OCP's battery life by rapidly tapping the Nonlethal Attack button rather than holding it. Once the gun turret is disabled, the second player can move through the area with gun drawn to avoid setting off the wall mines. Both players can then approach the double doors at the passage's end for extraction.

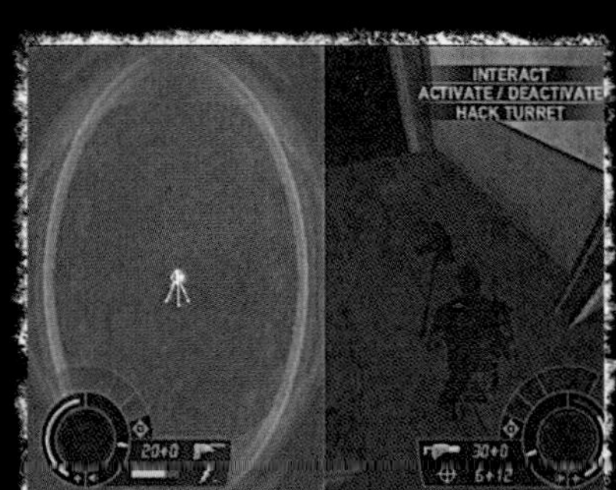

Two wall mines and a gun turret block the exit.

Kinshasa—The Canyon

Extraction Pressure

The agents must reach the helicopter waiting for them at the extraction zone within 30 minutes. All instructions in this walkthrough must be carried out with extreme precision and no hesitancy, or the players have no hope of completing Co-op mode.

From the starting point, both players should drop off the ledge to the left and follow the lower ledge to the base of a tall embankment. One player should crouch at the embankment's base and Boost the other player up, who then returns the favor by forming a Human Ladder so both players may climb to the upper level.

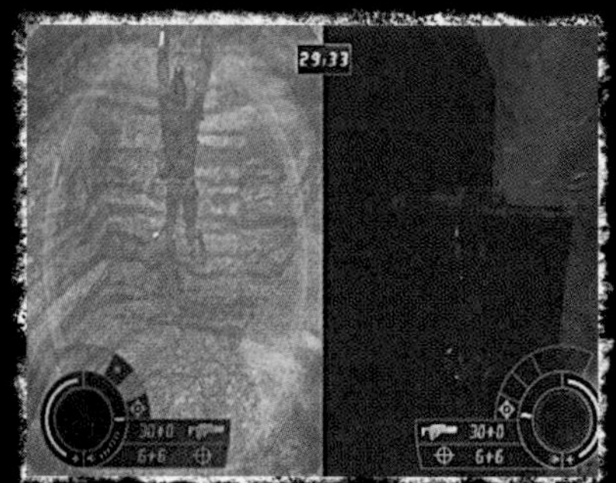

Work together to surmount the obstacles near the starting point.

At this point, Blue should remain near the ledge's top while Red runs to the ledge's far end and jumps up to grab the thin crack in the rock face in order to shimmy around the corner. Blue waits near the ledge because, while Red is moving through the area, an enemy helicopter appears and begins searching the region. If the helicopter's spotlight falls on either agent at any time during the rest of the mission, the helicopter opens fire. Blue should wait until the helicopter moves off before following Red.

The helicopter pursues the players throughout this mission, but this is the only location where it opens fire.

The Bridges

Once both players have shimmied to the end of the ledge, they must drop down two levels to another long stretch running alongside a river. Blue should move to the edge of the small ledge jutting off the cliff's right side and initiate a Tomoe Nage. Red can then complete the move and be thrown to the river's other side. Blue should hide in the small depression in the rock face opposite the Tomoe Nage point while Red moves along the river's other side. Red must jump up three levels to reach a natural rock bridge. If necessary, wait for the helicopter to fly away, then move to the bridge's other end and initiate rappelling off the left side. Blue must climb up the rope quickly to avoid leaving either agent exposed to the helicopter's searchlights.

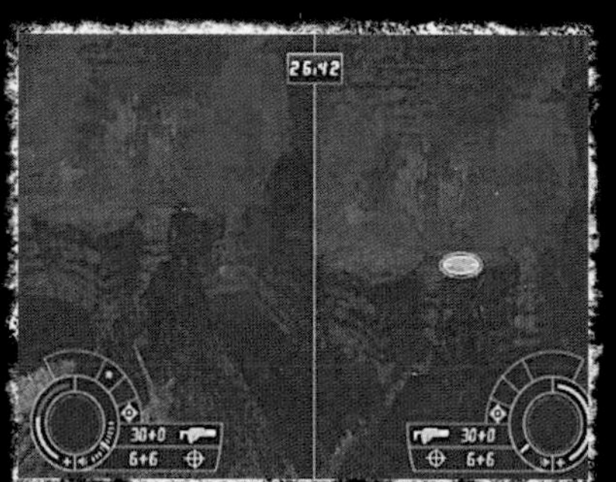

Perform a Tomoe Nage to throw one player to the opposite riverbank.

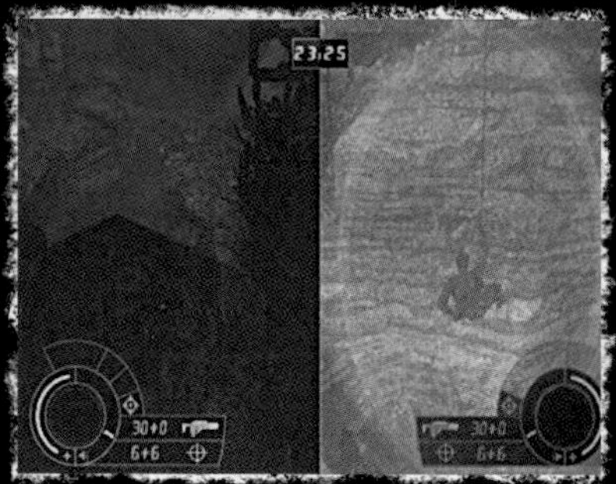

When the searchlights point elsewhere, the player on the bridge must lower the rope so that his partner may rappel.

Drop from the back side of the rock bridge, opposite the rappelling point. Run quickly along the long ledge before one of the guards on the level above spots either of you. At the end, jump up and grab another rock face crevice, and shimmy to the right around two corners to reach a new area.

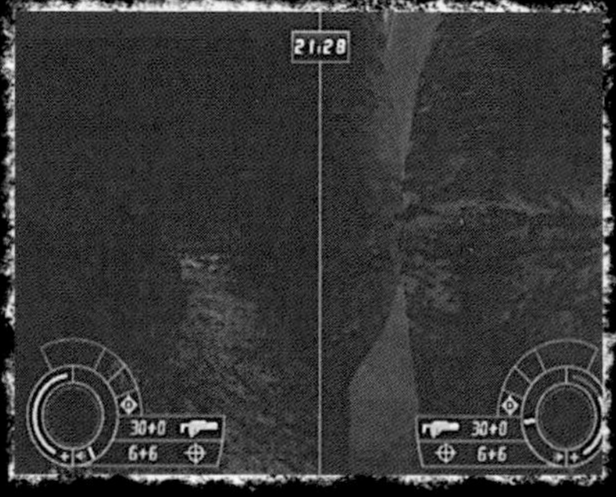

Shimmy around two corners to escape from this dangerous area.

The Tunnels

After dropping from the crevice, move through a long canyon until you reach a narrow area where the players can perform a Back Climb to reach the top. Head down the tunnel to the right and enter a crawlspace that's big enough for two to crawl through simultaneously.

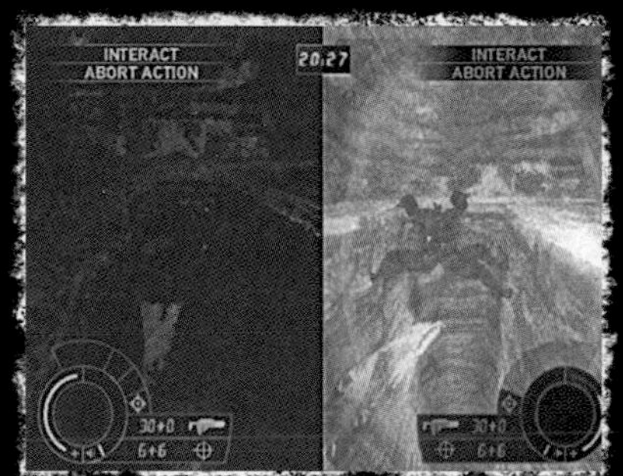

Work together to reach the gorge's top.

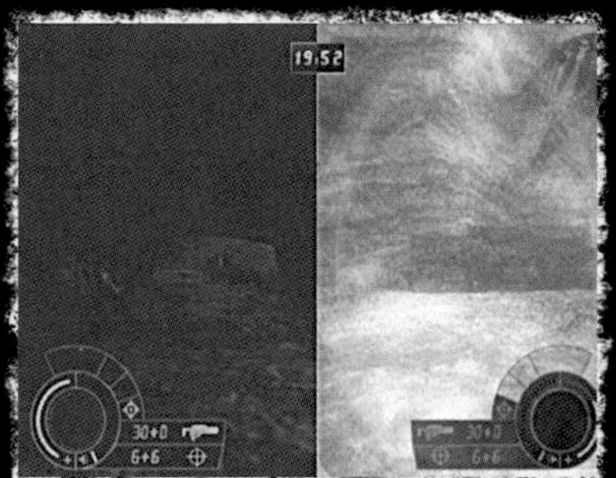

Both players should crawl through the crawlspace simultaneously.

Crisscrossing the River

Emerging from the crawlspace, head right. Blue must position himself under the higher of two ropes, then crouch and press the Co-op button to initiate a Boost. When Red hangs from the branch overhead, he must then press the Co-op button so that Blue may climb up to grab the branch also. If both players are not on the branch at this point, one becomes stuck on the river's other side and you must restart the mission.

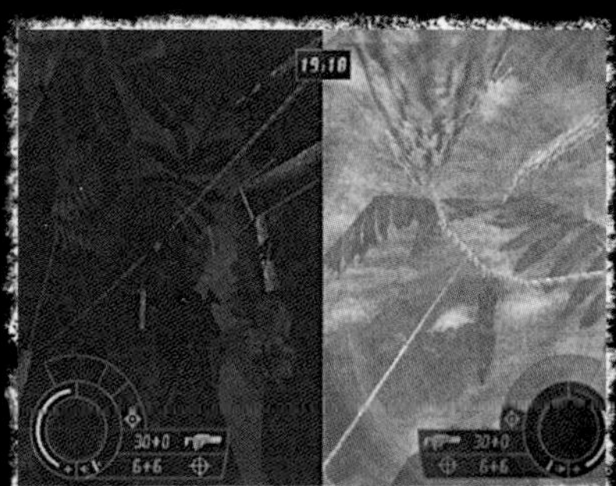

Use the rope to zip-line over the river.

Climb out a little on the branch until the character begins to zip-line across the ravine on a rope. After dropping on the other side, both characters should head right and jump up to climb onto another natural bridge. Cross the bridge and use the cave in this area to hide from the helicopter and the snipers on the bridge high overhead. When the coast is clear, both players should jump and climb onto the ledge near the cave. One player, preferably the one with the most health, must initiate rappelling from the ledge's steep side. The other player may then move in front of the player holding the rope to complete the rappelling. When the weaker player has made it to the bottom, the other player may then drop over the side and grab the ledge, then drop to the ledge below. This character takes some heavy damage from the fall.

The player with the most health remaining must lower the other from the high ledge via rappelling. The straggler's only option is to jump and take damage.

Both players should move quickly along the ledge. Reaching the edge, both must jump to grab a crevice in the rock face to the right, and shimmy across the gap until positioned over an extremely thin rock bridge. Drop onto the rock bridge, cross to the other side, and hide in the cave located there until the helicopter passes or until the soldiers high above stop being suspicious. Then drop from the bridge's side and continue down the path.

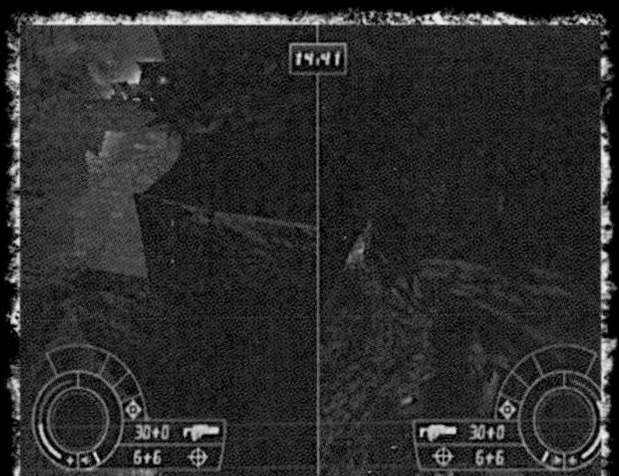

Carefully and quietly work your way through the area under the snipers' bridge.

Once you move past the sniper's bridge and get fairly far down the canyon, you no longer need to hide. Run down the path to beat the timer. Eventually both players arrive at a high cliff overlooking a waiting chopper. One at a time, drop carefully down the cliff to the bottom, then run toward the cliff's edge and jump to leap into the helicopter. When both agents are aboard, the mission is complete.

Leap into the waiting helicopter to escape Kinshasa!

Bonus Map—Tanker on the Way

The "Tanker on the Way" mission becomes available only after you complete all Iceland co-op missions. This mission can be started from the Bonus Map menu, or the mission starts immediately after the players have completed all other missions.

Bound for Los Angeles

Blue and Red start the mission in the tanker's central hold. Both agents stand atop a massive stack of crates. Red stands near a ledge, with a door on the gap's other side. Red must move a few feet to his right and press the Co-op button to initiate a Tomoe Nage. Blue can then complete the move to be thrown across the gap, where he can initiate rappelling at the ledge. Red must drop carefully off the side of the cargo onto a stack of crates, and drop down again to the floor. Red can then complete the rappelling move and rejoin Blue.

Throw one player across the gap with a Tomoe Nage.

Hold 1

Both players should go through the door and climb down the ladder one at a time. Follow the passage to a sliding hatchway. The sign next to the hatchway should read "Hold 1"; if not, you are in the wrong place. Have the first player slide open the hatchway and the second player close it behind him to avoid drawing suspicion.

While two guards can be heard talking overhead, both players should sneak to the corner. A surveillance camera scans the middle of the next area, and an overhead light casts a bright pool of luminescence around the device. Maneuver around it by dropping over the ledge into the lower area. Then move through the lower area to the camera's other side. Blue should crouch near the wall's base by the corner, face inward, and press the Co-op button to initiate a Boost. Then Red can complete the move and hang from the wall. While hanging, Red should press the Co-op button to become a Human Ladder so Blue may climb back up.

Drop into the low area in order to move past the surveillance camera.

Only one player should navigate around the lower level to the ladder in the corner. Climb up and notice the patrolling guards' patterns: One moves quickly back and forth between the top of the ladder and the corner. The other guard patrols the entire upper level, stopping momentarily to look over the rail into the hold's center. Depending on which guard is closer, grab him when he is in the dark area near the ladder's top and quietly choke him unconscious. Wait as long as necessary for the guard who patrols the entire upper level to stop in the area near the ladder so that you can grab him quietly.

One player can effectively take out both guards patrolling the upper level with less chance of discovery.

The Engine Room

When the coast is clear, both players can go through the doorway on the upper level. Follow the passage to the right. Beyond the next doorway, the players find two valves, one on either side of the door. Both players must turn the valves simultaneously to open the other door in this area.

Turn both valves simultaneously to open the passage to the engine room.

Enter the next area. The door is locked, and there is a high crawlspace to the left. Have Blue navigate through the crawlspace. Upon dropping out of the crawlspace, hide behind the nearest piece of machinery and peek into the room. One guard patrols the engine room. Typically, if he does not see anything suspicious, he stops in front of the farthest engine and stares at its control panel. When he stops in front of the engine, climb over the nearest engine and drop quietly from the other side. Then climb over the next engine, and prepare to climb over the last. Use your night vision to perceive a cone-shaped light emanating from the security camera mounted on the central post; you can see what direction the camera is looking. While the camera scans the room's other side, quickly climb over the third engine and drop from the other side. Sneak across the room, moving directly under the surveillance camera, and grab the guard. Drag him behind the camera's location and choke him unconscious.

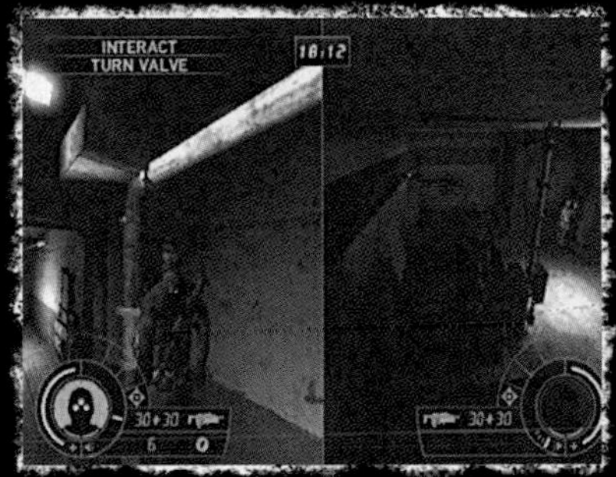

Climb over the engines to avoid being spotted by the guard or the security camera.

Red can now break the lock on the door. Blue should use his OCP to jam the camera so that Red can safely cross the room. Then Blue should move under the surveillance camera and initiate a Shoulder Climb. Red can follow suit and cut the camera's wires. With security neutralized, it is now safe to turn off all six engines and complete the Opportunity Objective.

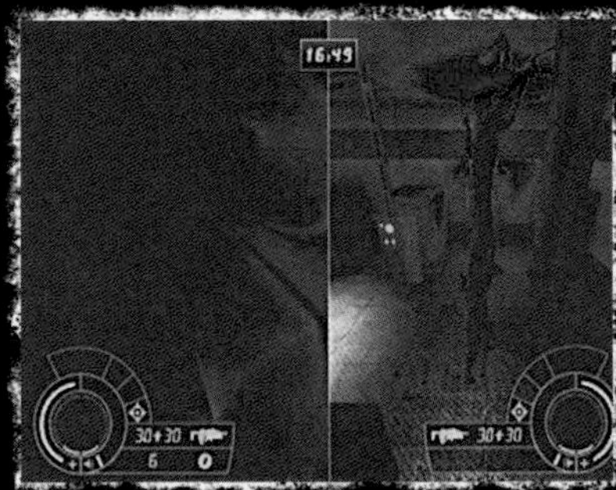

Cut the wires on the security camera, then turn off the engines.

Captain's Quarters

Open the door in the opposite corner of the engine room from where you entered. Proceed only a few steps into the corridor, because a gun turret monitors the corridor from the opposite end. Have Blue enter the corridor and move into the corner on the right; he can jam the turret while Red races to the corridor's other end and deactivates the device.

Jam the turret so your partner may deactivate it.

Head left from the deactivated turret into a short passageway. Load the SC-20K with airfoil rounds and aim through the open hatchway into the captain's quarters. When the guard moves behind the desk and stops for a long moment, hit him in the head with an airfoil round and knock him out. Hack the security access on the laptop in the room's back corner. This unlocks the shipping container ID log and an e-mail that states that you must use your EMF to determine which crates carry the three red mercury bombs.

Fire an airfoil round from outside the doorway to knock out the guard in the captain's quarters.

The First Red Mercury Bomb

Both players must now return to the room with the two valves. When last they were turned, the valves closed the hatchway to the hold. Turn both valves simultaneously to reopen the hatchway. Return to the hold and use EMF vision to locate the crate carrying the bomb. In this area, the crate may be in one of five randomly determined locations. If the crate is in either of the positions on the hold's far side, then simply move to the tall ladder in the area's opposite corner, climb all the way down to the lowest level, and perform a Shoulder Climb to reach the crate and plant a charge. If not, disable the appropriate surveillance cameras on the wall before moving into the hold area. Cut the wires on the camera on the upper and lower level if necessary. If the bomb's crate is located in the stacks on top of the large cargo containers, then run and jump from the top level to land on the containers, and go from there.

Use EMF vision to locate the crate containing a red mercury device in Hold 1, then act appropriately.

Back to the Starting Point

After you plant the charges in Hold 1, backtrack to the starting point. The second two crates are always located in the same positions. Move down the balcony to the left, climb over the rail, and drop onto a stack of crates. Use your EMF to spot the red mercury device crate directly under your feet. Drop to the ground floor and perform a Shoulder Climb to reach the crate and plant a charge on it.

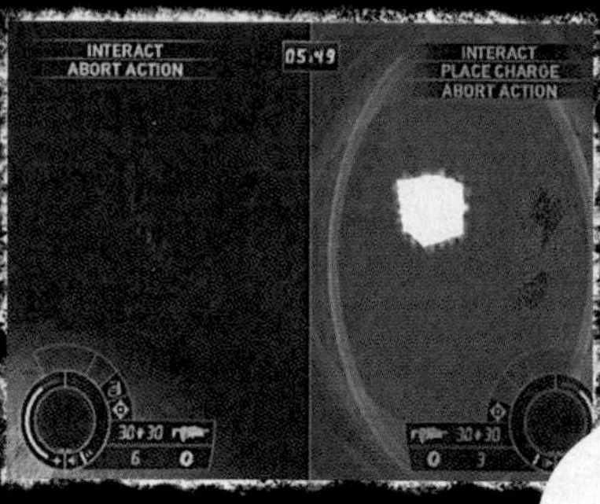

Place charges on the red mercury crate near your starting point.

Move to the opposite corner of the ground level. The space in the corner is narrow enough that both players can perform a Back Climb to reach the upper balcony. Both players should then move down the balcony and go through the portal.

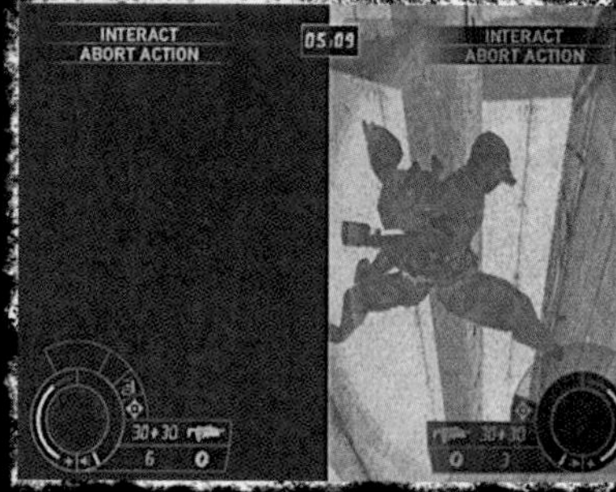

Perform a Back Climb in the area's opposite corner.

The Final Bomb

Climb down the ladder one at a time and go through the hatchway. After entering the last hold, close the hatch behind you to avoid suspicion. Moving quickly but stealthily, Red, whose loadout includes gas grenades, should move down to the corner and into the central area. Use night vision to determine when the surveillance camera on the wall is not facing your direction, then move behind the closest tall crate. Two guards in this area should be making the final checks on the crates. While they stand fairly close together, fire a gas grenade between them to knock them both out.

Sneak into the last hold and use one or two gas grenades to knock out the two guards.

Have Blue move under the surveillance camera mounted on the wall and initiate a Shoulder Climb. Red can climb onto Blue's shoulders and cut the camera's wires. Then use EMF vision to locate the crate containing the third red mercury bomb. It is always located on the top of the tallest crate stack, to the right of the surveillance camera. Move behind the stack and climb onto the small crate at the stack's base. One player must Boost the other up to grab the ledge. That player can then form a Human Ladder so the other player may climb to the bomb crate's level and plant the charges. Los Angeles is saved!

Perform a Boost and then a Human Ladder so that one player may plant the last charge and save the day.

06: PS2/GC

VERSUS MISSIONS

Multiplayer Overview

DEFAULT CONTROLS

Action	PLAYSTATION2	GAMECUBE
Move Control	Left Stick	Control stick
Back to Wall	R3	Z + A
Aim/Camera	Right Stick	C
Rear View/Weapon View Type	L3	Z + ◀C/C▶
In-game Menu	START	START
Help Text Display	SELECT	Z (hold) + ↑
Interact	×	A
Crouch/Roll/Drop	●	X
Weapon Mode	■	B
Jump/Reload	▲	Y
Night Vision	✥	←
Laser Sight On/Off	✥	↑
Return to Sticky Camera	✥	↓
Close Combat/Fire	↑	R
Gadget	↖, L2	L

Move Control

Use the Move Control to move your character onscreen. Tilt the Move Control only slightly to move at a slow, quiet pace, or tilt the Move Control all the way in any direction to run at full speed. Running causes the character to make more noise, and may give away his or her position to the enemy.

Back to wall

Press the Back to Wall button when near a suitably flat surface to place a spy's back against the wall. Move out to a corner or edge of a doorframe to peek into the next area.

Aim/Camera

Move the Aim/Camera control to change the camera's angle of view. Tilt the camera left or right, up or down. You may invert the Y axis or X axis control of the camera by opening the In-game Menu and changing the controller settings.

In Weapon Mode, use the Aim/Camera control to aim your weapon. Check your aim either by using the laser sight in normal view or align the center of the crosshairs on your target when looking through the weapon scope.

Rear View

When not in Weapon Mode, press and hold the Rear View/Weapon View Type button to move the camera 180 degrees opposite of it current position. This allows you to take a quick peek behind to see if someone is sneaking up on you.

Weapon View Type

While in Weapon Mode, press the Rear View/Weapon View Type button to switch from normal aiming view to scoped aiming view. Aiming in normal view allows you to aim and shoot with optional laser sighting. The player maintains greater peripheral vision in this mode.

Normal aiming view can be modified to third person view, where the character remains visible onscreen, by opening the In-game Menu and changing the appropriate controller setting.

Aiming through the scope allows you to shoot vulnerable body parts such as the head or heart with greater accuracy, doing greater damage to enemies.

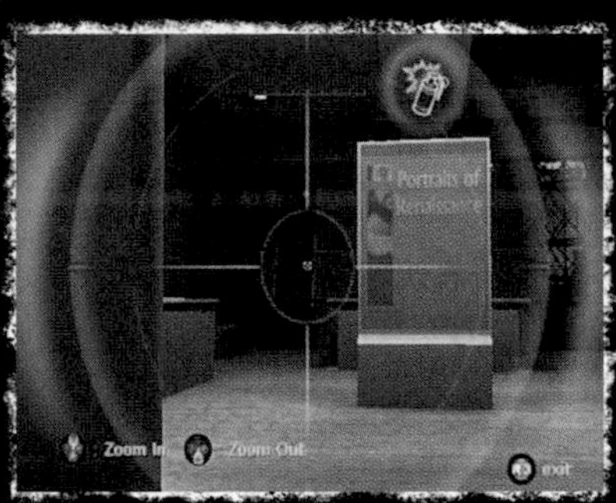

In-Game Menu

Press the In-Game Menu button to change playing configuration options or quit the current game. If you created the session, other players will be kicked from the session if you quit.

The Options menu allows the player to change various settings, such as controller settings, audio settings, video settings and headset settings.

Note that the game is not paused while the In-game Menu is open. Other players can take advantage while you are trying to alter settings.

Help Text Display

In certain game types, objectives may be displayed in the corner of the screen. Press the Help Text Display button to toggle help text on or off.

Interact

Press the Interact button when the Interact button icon is displayed onscreen to perform certain actions in the environment. Many multiplayer maps have switches that can be pressed to open and close doors or turn lights on and off. In game types requiring teams to hack terminals, press the Interact button to begin hacking. The context of the Interaction button changes depending on the type of device the character is standing near, and the function is labeled with text.

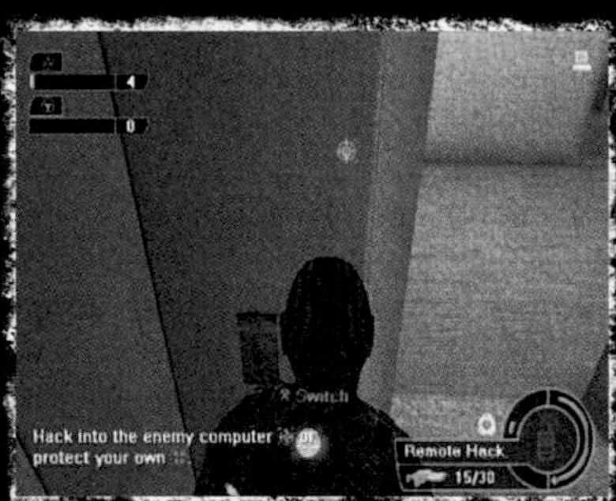

Crouch/Roll/Drop

Press the Crouch button to assume a crouching stance. Crouching can help spies to hide behind boxes or crates, or to move through low crawlspaces.

While moving, press the Crouch button to perform a roll. This is an effective evasive maneuver for characters being fired upon. If the character is crouched, he performs a shoulder roll. If the character is standing and running, he performs a dive roll.

When hanging from a ledge or beam, press the Crouch button to drop to the level below. Just make sure that the character doesn't fall too far, or damage could be sustained. Dropping on top of an enemy character kills them instantly. Be careful not to drop onto allies, or they will take severe damage as well.

Weapon Mode

Press the Weapon Mode button to draw the character's weapon. The character aims in normal view with laser sighting. However, laser sighting tends to give away your position. Use laser sighting sparingly.

While Weapon Mode is active, the character moves more slowly. The best way to attack with your weapon is to leave it holstered until ready. Then draw, aim, and fire as quickly as possible.

Jump/Reload

Press the Jump button to leap roughly five feet off the ground. Jump up to grab high ledges, beams, and zip-line cables. Jump while running to clear short gaps of less than four feet.

While your weapon is drawn, press the Jump button to reload the weapon if your magazine is shy a few bullets.

Night Vision

Press the Night Vision button to toggle night vision on or off. Night vision collects available light and focuses it for the user's vision. Unlike solo mode, Night Vision runs on a battery. When the battery charge runs out, Night Vision switches off automatically.

Laser Sight On/Off

Press the Laser Sight button while in Weapon Mode to toggle the gun's laser aiming beam off or on. While the laser beam is helpful in aiming, a laser beam emanating from a dark corner tends to give away its user's position.

Return to Sticky Camera

After deploying a sticky camera gadget, it is possible to quit the sticky camera. If the player did not release the gas from the sticky camera's canister, then the signal can be reacquired when the player is within range (inside the same room). Press the sticky camera button to reacquire the signal from a sticky cam.

Primary Attack/Fire

Press the Primary Attack button while unarmed to strike an opponent at close range. If striking from behind, your character will grab the enemy in a chokehold. Then press the Primary Attack button again to knock them out.

In Weapon Mode, press the Fire button to shoot. Ammunition must be remaining in the magazine in order to fire. Many maps have an ammo dump where ammunition can be refilled.

Gadget

Press the Gadget button to use the device indicated in the HUD. You may have to pick up a gadget from the environment first, depending on the game type. Many gadgets hang in space over beams or zip-lines, requiring some acrobatics on the part of the player in order to reach them.

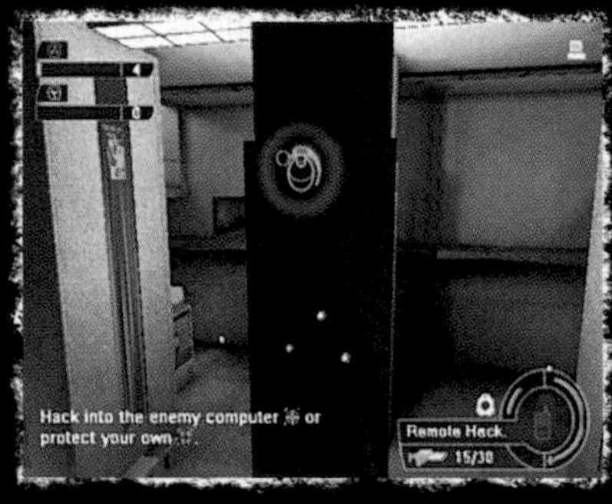

Frag Grenade: A great device to use against pursuing enemies. While running away from a foe, press the Gadget button to drop a frag grenade at your feet. Continue running, or you'll be caught in the blast and killed as well. The frag grenade detonates after three seconds.

Flash Grenade: A fragmentation device that temporarily blinds individuals using night vision at the time. The user is not affected.

Smoke Grenade: A smoke-emitting device. Use when running away from enemies. The player throws the smoke grenade at his or her own feet. The device detonates instantaneously, spreading a cloud of disorienting tear gas. Individuals passing through the gas, including the user, suffer from blurred double vision for a short period of time.

Shocker Battery: A battery for the shocking device mounted on the underside of the weapon barrel. Allows the user to fire an electrical charge at a foe, knocking them out.

Sticky Camera: A device almost identical to the one used by Sam Fisher in Solo mode. Press the Primary Attack button to dispense a cloud of knockout gas to take out enemies.

Mine: A wall-mounted, motion-detecting, friendly-fire, inhibited explosive device. Face a wall or smooth vertical surface and press the Gadget button to place the device. Detonates upon detecting enemies moving within range. Will not explode when teammates pass by. Remains fixed and active even if the player picks up a different gadget type. Plant these near computer terminals you wish to protect from being hacked.

Presence Detector: A wall-mounted, motion-detecting alarm device. Makes a direction-oriented alarm sound when an enemy player moves within range of the device. Mount these on walls near locations you wish to protect.

Remote Hacker: A short-range automatic hacking device that allows the user to hack a computer for fifteen percent of total data without actually touching the computer. The user must be inside the same room as the computer, and can hack while hiding.

General Tips

> The Tutorials menu contains a great explanation of controls and the heads-up display. This menu also contains a Tips section which every player should consult before playing. You can also visit maps and get the hang of game types before playing others.

> To perform a split jump in a narrow passage, face the direction you wish to face when in the split jump (not the wall). Then press the Jump button twice to leap up into a split jump.

> Take the high ground. Dropping onto enemies and knocking them out is a much more efficient way of racking up kills than trying to shoot people.

> Use gadgets like they're going out of style.

> Unless you are psychic, communicate with your teammates via a headset. If you don't have one, *buy one!* No one can play this game with a silent partner.

> Look for players that are low on health, approach them, and press the Interact button to heal them.

> If you find yourself alone near a computer terminal, hacking it will only give your position away. Call for your teammates to come and cover you before attempting to download data.

Game Types

Team DeathMatch

Kill as many of the other team's members as possible. First team to reach 30 kills wins.

Deathmatch

Kill as many enemies as possible, regardless of team or character type. First player to reach 20 kills wins.

TeamHack

Hack into the enemy team's computer, and protect your own computer from being hacked. Approach the computer and press the Interact button to begin hacking. If a remote hacking device is available, press the Gadget button to begin hacking the terminal from within a few feet of range. When discovered near the computer or attacked, simply move away from the terminal to quit hacking. The first team to complete hacking the other team's computer wins.

Key Run

Teams must fight to acquire the lone access key item, the position of which is indicated onscreen by a cardkey icon. Only the team with the access key can hack the other team's computer. The person with the access key cannot return to their insertion point, or the key is lost. Once the data is completely downloaded from the enemies' computer, the person must find a safe place to hide and press the Interact button to begin uploading to the satellite. The first team to complete an upload wins.

Blitz

Players must race to reach the other team's computer, hack it, and then upload as much data as possible, all within three minutes!

Sam vs. All

One player plays as Sam Fisher, and everyone else plays as mercenaries. The objective is to completely hack the two enemy team's computers. Each player gets only one life, so if Sam dies then the enemies win. If Sam kills the mercenaries, then he is more certain to win. If Sam does not make any progress within three minutes, the game is over. To reset the timer to three full minutes, Sam must kill an enemy or hack a computer.

Disk Hunt

In this altered version of deathmatch, the player squares off against all others to rack up the highest kill count. However, players drop disks when they are killed. Thus, it is possible to "steal" other players' frags. Try to keep all your combat close quarters, and pick up disks quickly after they are dropped. The player to collect the most disks within the five-minute time limit is the winner.

Survival

The goal is to kill all other players. Every player gets five lives, and the person with one or more life left wins.

Countdown

Each player has four minutes to live. Additional time is gained by killing other players. Think of this as a modified version of Survival where players end up killing themselves through inaction. The last player whose time expires is the winner.

07: 360/PC

GAME BASICS

Overview

The high-definition, next-generation version of *Splinter Cell: Double Agent* is completely different from the PlayStation2/GameCube/Xbox versions, and it is quite unlike any game that has ever come out before. Over the course of a dozen solo missions, series hero Sam Fisher breaks from the status quo and goes undercover inside a terrorist organization. To garner the trust of the nefarious JBA (John Brown's Army), Sam may have to lie, steal, and even murder innocent people in order to prevent the terrorists from unleashing global chaos and destruction. But the safety of the population outweighs the lives of a few. Sometimes Sam must carry out these actions in *broad daylight*, as he cannot always depend on finding a shadow and lying low until the coast is clear.

More than ever before, Sam must take down opponents with extreme cunning and rely on alternate methods of infiltration. He must also perform new activities such as skydiving and helicopter piloting. Never before has Sam Fisher been required to do so much for his country. Never before has Sam Fisher come so close to the edge.

This section covers everything a splinter cell agent is capable of doing without weapons. For more information on using weapons and gadgetry, check out the "360/PC Equipment" section.

Heads-Up Display

1. **Visibility System:** Indicates the amount of light striking Sam Fisher. Color-coded system is explained further in the "Visibility System" section.
2. **Update Bar:** Text regarding current objectives, new objectives, urgent messages, Trust level changes, and items procured are displayed here. Also serves as a timer bar and upload gauge when certain equipment is used.
3. **Selected Item:** The firearm or item currently equipped, including ammunition in the magazine/total ammunition data. Fire with Primary Attack button.
4. **Secondary Item:** Displays icon and information regarding Secondary Attack functions of weapon. Used mainly to display Charge bar of SC pistol's OCP and gadgetry loaded in the SC-20K.
5. **Quick OPSAT:** Aerial satellite display. Little green dots indicate personnel positions. Press the Quick OPSAT button to display this function. SATCOM function may be deactivated if NSA Trust level falls too low.

Visibility System

The Visibility System is brand new to the *Splinter Cell* series. The large dot in the Status bar changes to indicate Sam's level of visibility.

Green: Situation optimal. Sam is hidden in the shadows and has not been detected.

Flashing green: Sam is hidden, but enemies are suspicious of noise or visible bodies and are moving in to investigate.

Yellow: Visibility. Enemies looking in Sam's direction will spot him. Could also mean enemies have spotted visible bodies.

Flashing yellow: Detection. Enemies are actively searching for Sam. Find a hiding spot or neutralize all enemies.

Flashing red: Combat! Find cover and return fire.

Health System

Sam's health is no longer displayed onscreen. Instead, the screen indicates when Sam is taking damage by flashing red at the edges. As Sam takes continuous damage, the screen image loses color until the scene becomes completely grayscale, at which point Sam dies.

Sam naturally regenerates health when not in a combat situation. To regain health, try to hide from enemies so that the Visibility meter changes from red to yellow or green.

Quick OPSAT Map

Press the Quick OPSAT button to activate the Quick OPSAT map. A small satellite photo appears above the Update bar in the heads-up display. Tracker device, signal-intercept technology allows the OPSAT to create several marks on the display. Sam's position is in the map's center. Enemies and characters unaware of Sam's presence are displayed as green dots. Red dots represent enemies that are suspicious or aware of Sam's presence. Brown dots depict the locations of unconscious or dead bodies. The Quick OPSAT map rotates as Sam's view rotates.

The Quick OPSAT image is lost when Sam moves. Activate the OPSAT only while hiding in a safe spot; otherwise, it is just a waste of screen space.

The Quick OPSAT may become unavailable if the NSA Trust meter becomes low. Try accomplishing Secondary Objectives in order to appease the NSA and regain usage of satellite radar imaging. The Quick OPSAT cannot be used while Sam is holding a person hostage.

Default Controls for Xbox 360 and PC versions

ACTION	XBOX 360	PC
Move control	Left analog stick	W A S D
Back to wall/Switch hand	Click left analog stick	Q
Aim/camera	Right analog stick	[mouse]
First-person view/zoom	Click right analog stick	1 / [mouse]
Pause menu	START	ESC
OPSAT Watch menu	BACK	F1
Interact	[A]	Spacebar
Crouch/stand	[B]	C
Equip item	[X]	E / [mouse] (click)
Jump	[Y]	Shift
Night vision	[D-pad left]	2
Wave vision	[D-pad up]	4
Thermo vision	[D-pad right]	3
Whistle	[D-pad down]	X
Primary attack	RT	[mouse]
Quick Inventory	RB	CTRL
Secondary attack	LT	[mouse]
Quick OPSAT map	LB	Z

Control Functions

This section details the control functions listed in the preceding table.

Pause Menu

Press the Pause Menu button to pause the game and bring up the Pause menu. The selection choices on this menu allow you to save your progress, load a previously saved game, restart from the last checkpoint or save, modify options, and restart or quit the current mission. The Pause menu also contains the "Equipment Guide" option, allowing you to view the equipment available in the game, including equipment upgrades and additions not yet obtained.

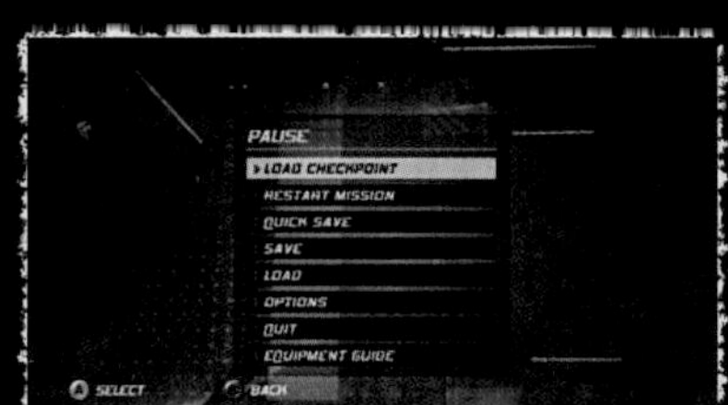

The Quick Save option creates a quick save slot on your hard drive or memory unit. This save is overwritten each time you perform a Quick Save. To create a permanent save that will not be overwritten unless you intentionally do so, use the Save function.

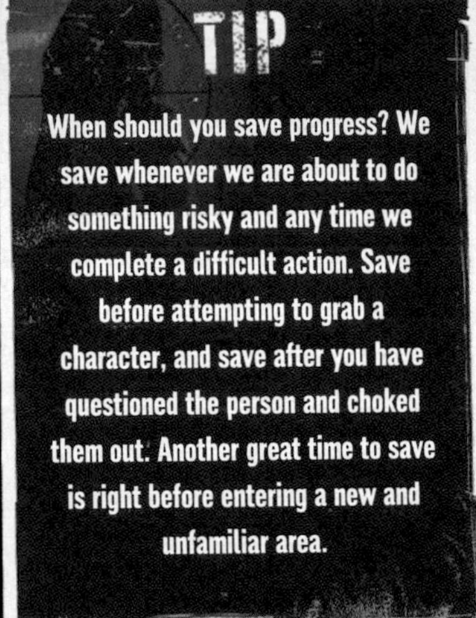

TIP

When should you save progress? We save whenever we are about to do something risky and any time we complete a difficult action. Save before attempting to grab a character, and save after you have questioned the person and choked them out. Another great time to save is right before entering a new and unfamiliar area.

OPSAT Watch Menu

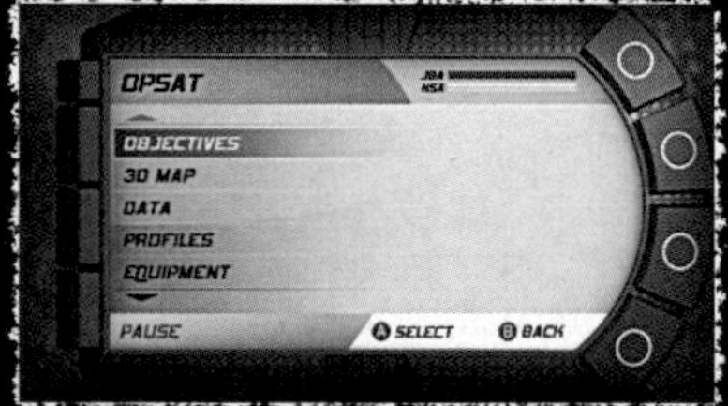

Press the OPSAT Watch Menu button to bring up Sam's OPSAT. The OPSAT provides various data to help serve in your mission.

OBJECTIVE

This menu displays a list of the mission objectives and each objective's current status. Use the cursor to highlight objectives and press Ⓐ to view more elaborate descriptions of objectives. The objectives describe how to complete the mission. The amount of Trust to be garnered via objective completion or lost through objective failure is indicated in the upper right corner of the OPSAT watch face.

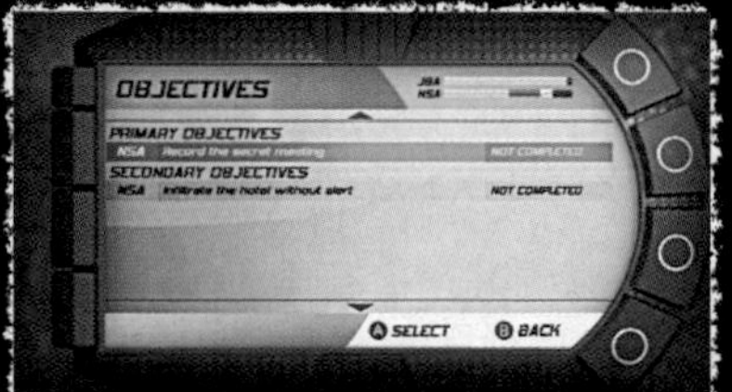

Later in the game, both the NSA (National Security Agency) and the JBA provide Sam with objectives. Completing NSA objectives raises Trust with the government, and completing JBA objectives raises Trust with the terrorists. Failure to complete main assignments or Primary Objectives may cause Trust to decrease. The player does not have to complete all objectives before the end of the mission.

3-D MAP

View a complete 3-D rendering of a satellite view of the stage. Sam's current location and the locations of enemies are also displayed.

While viewing the map, use the Move control to zoom in or out. Use the Camera control to rotate the view, and

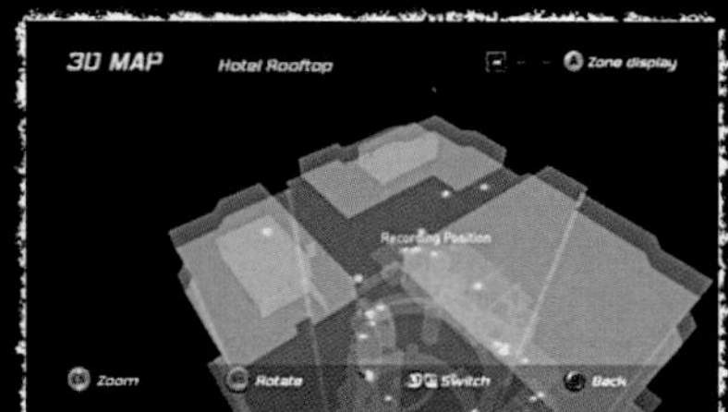

press the Interact button to toggle the display of the current area and the next. Press the Primary Attack button to highlight the next area, or press the Secondary Attack button to highlight the previous area. Press either button repeatedly to cycle through areas.

DATA

By accessing computers and laptops, Sam can download informative e-mails. Sometimes e-mails may contain hints that certain areas might have extra security working against you. E-mails may also contain information that is extremely beneficial down the road. It is important to access computers and read e-mails to get a leg up on the mission. All e-mails accessed are stored in this menu on the OPSAT watch.

PROFILE

While sneaking through the JBA's headquarters, Sam may optionally steal the medical, personal, and activity files of the JBA's leaders. Upon successfully stealing their files, new data regarding the JBA members can be viewed through this menu. The icons on the screen's left side indicate when Sam has obtained the person's vocal sample, fingerprint scan, and retinal scan.

EQUIPMENT

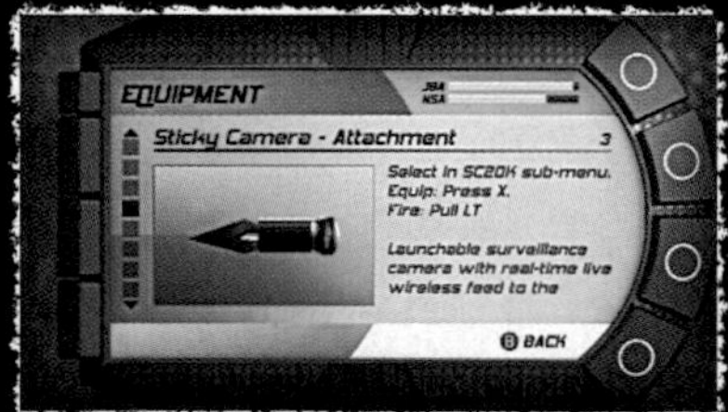

This menu contains pictures and complete descriptions of all the equipment Sam currently carries. The menu also contains valuable instructions and hints on how to use equipment like a pro.

Movement

Use the Move control to move the character. Tilt the Move control only slightly to creep forward at a slow pace, or tilt the Move control all the way outward to run at full speed. Slower movement creates less noise and decreases the chances of detection. However, moving too slowly may allow patrolling guards to exit opportune striking locations. The best strategy is to remain in a crouched stance at all times (press the Crouch button) and tilt the Move control just less than halfway of what it will go. This allows you to move fast enough to sneak up behind moving enemies without being heard.

NARROW GAPS

To squeeze through a narrow gap, simply move toward the gap until Sam changes posture to slide through the opening. Continue moving through the narrow space until Sam emerges from the other end. Entering and exiting a narrow gap causes Sam to make a small amount of noise and sometimes forces him to stand rather than crouch. Consider these things before entering a narrow gap

The same control method works with crawlspaces. To enter an open ventilation shaft, simply move toward it until Sam crawls through the opening. Crawl through the shaft and emerge from the other end.

Camera and Aim Control

Use the Camera/Aim control to change your angle of view. You can look in any direction, even directions Sam is not facing. While equipping a firearm or grenade, use the Camera/Aim control to point the crosshairs toward your desired target. The crosshairs widen out while you are changing aim or moving around to indicate lesser accuracy. When the crosshairs are the narrowest, Sam has the greatest chance of hitting the target.

Crouching

Press the Crouch button to assume a crouching stance. As previously indicated, crouching while moving is the best way to avoid being detected. Crouching also helps you to hide behind low cover such as boxes or counters. Sam moves more slowly while crouched and makes less noise.

ROLLING

While moving in a crouched position, press and hold the Crouch button to perform a roll. Rolling can help you avoid enemy gunfire, and it can also help you move from cover to cover with less likelihood of being detected.

DROPPING

Press the Crouch button to drop when hanging from a pipe, a ladder, a fence, or a ledge. Sam can drop from a height of roughly 12 feet without taking any damage. By dropping from greater heights, you risk inflicting damage on your character and making noise, which may alert nearby enemies.

To perform a "drop attack," drop on top of a person. If successful, you knock the person unconscious in the process. You can perform a drop attack by dropping off a ledge that is taller than six feet. You can also perform a drop attack by dropping from a Split Jump position.

Jumping

Press the Jump button to leap roughly three feet off the ground. You can jump up to grab higher ledges, or you can jump while running to clear small gaps. Jumping is a good way to get up a ladder or vertical pipe more quickly. However, landing from a jump creates noise. Make sure there are no active enemies nearby before risking any kind of jump.

MANTLING

While facing any low ledge that is roughly waist height when Sam is standing, such as a crate or a countertop, lightly tilt the Move control toward the ledge and press the Jump button to quietly mantle onto the ledge. Mantling properly allows you to climb around an area without rousing suspicion.

Press Back to Wall

When near a fairly smooth section of wall or a flat surface devoid of pipes, protruding panels, and the like, press down on the Move control to press Sam's back against the wall. Once Sam is attached to the wall, use the Move control to slide left or right along the wall and around corners until Sam reaches a doorway.

At a doorway, Sam can peek into the room beyond if you hold the Move control toward the doorway. In dark areas, Sam is less likely to be detected peeking through a doorway if his back is pressed to the wall. However, in broad daylight, Sam might be spotted while peeking around a corner.

Equip Weapon or Item

Press the Equip button to draw and aim the selected weapon or item. Sam prepares the weapon or item, the camera changes to an over-the-shoulder perspective, and a crosshair appears onscreen. While equipping a weapon or item, use the Camera/Aim Control to move the crosshair over the intended target. When aimed and ready, press the Primary Attack button to use the equipped item. Press the Secondary Attack button to perform alternative, nonlethal actions if available. As indicated previously, Sam is more accurate with firearms when standing still and crouched. Moving and adjusting aim decreases accuracy.

ENVIRONMENTAL OBJECTS

Splinter cells can pick up objects such as bottles and cans. You can throw these objects—the same way you would throw a grenade—to create noise in some other part of the room and distract enemies from your current position. After throwing a bottle or can into the area behind an enemy, you might then be able to sneak up behind the person and grab them. Or, you could use the opportunity to slip from the room and continue your mission.

SWITCH HANDS

Splinter cells can fire accurately with either hand. While equipping a weapon, press the Switch Hands button to change the shoulder Sam aims from. Switching to your left hand can help you maximize cover at corners so that most of Sam's body remains hidden behind cover while still being able to fire on a target. Splinter cells cannot switch hands while equipping a bottle, a can, or any type of grenade.

RELOAD WEAPON

While equipping a firearm, press the Interact button to reload. Sam can reload only if the magazine is not filled to capacity and if additional ammo is available.

PRIMARY ATTACK

While equipping a firearm, press the Primary Attack button to open fire. Headshots kill instantly, so aim for the target's head every time.

While equipping a thrown weapon such as a grenade, bottle, or can, aim the crosshairs at your target and press the Primary Attack button to throw the item in a short arc. Thrown items make noise upon landing, which may alert nearby enemies. If the item strikes an opponent, he becomes alerted instantly.

SECONDARY ATTACK

While equipping a firearm, press the Secondary Attack button to utilize the weapon's secondary function. The SC pistol is equipped with an OCP jamming device that allows splinter cells to jam surveillance cameras, lights, and electronic equipment for a short period of time. To use the OCP, press the Secondary Fire button when equipping the SC pistol. The SC-20K can be fitted with a variety of attachments, each with a different Secondary Attack function. The launcher attachment fires gadgets, and the shotgun attachment fires shotgun shells. When you equip the sniper attachment and enter Zoom mode, holding the Secondary Fire button causes Sam to hold his breath, steadying aiming.

Lethal and Nonlethal Attacks

When not equipping a firearm or weapon, Sam can attack enemies in unarmed, nonlethal ways; he can also attack in lethal ways utilizing the SC combat knife.

When standing or moving within two feet of an enemy, press the Primary Attack button to perform a lethal attack against the enemy. Sam's attack style depends on whether he is in front of the character or behind them, and whether the enemy is aware of Sam's presence or not. As a result, Sam may slash the enemy's throat or stab them in the gut. If attacking from behind, Sam may stab the enemy in the spine or quickly slash their throat.

Press the Secondary Attack button when standing close to an enemy character to perform a nonlethal attack. Sam steps toward the enemy and strikes them in the head with the palm of his hand, knocking the person unconscious. Nonlethal attacks may be more prudent in situations where Sam is infiltrating a prison or cruise ship, where it is important not to leave a civilian body count.

Both lethal and nonlethal attacks create quite a bit of noise, which may alert additional enemies in the area.

Quick Inventory

Hold the Quick Inventory button to bring up the Inventory Icon menu. The icons and names of firearms, gadgets, and grenades currently in possession are displayed in the Quick Inventory menu.

While the Quick Inventory menu is open, use the Move control to cycle left or right, up or down through the icons. When the desired equipment is in the center, release the Quick Inventory button to equip the new item.

> **TIP**
>
> Briefly tap the Quick Inventory button to reequip the previous weapon. Use this function to switch quickly between the SC pistol and the SC-20K, or to switch back to using the fingerprint scanner, and so on.

SC-20K LAUNCHER AMMO

To load the SC-20K's launcher attachment with a different type of gadget, cycle left or right through the Quick Inventory menu until the SC-20K icon is displayed. Then cycle up or down through the available gadget icons to load a device type, such as sticky shockers, airfoil rounds, sticky cameras.

Night Vision

Press the Night Vision button to equip Sam's night vision goggles. In night vision, ambient light is collected and refracted to make the environment seem brighter. Night vision helps to delineate enemies who may be walking through shadowy areas or to spot items and equipment hidden in the darkness. However, the one drawback of night vision is that the user experiences a flattening effect, making distances between objects and/or people harder to judge. Avoid wearing night vision in brightly lit places, or the screen grows so bright that Sam is nearly blind for a few seconds.

Thermo Vision

Press the Thermo Vision button to turn thermo vision on or off. Thermo vision allows Sam to view heat signatures. In most areas, this helps Sam spot patrolling enemies more easily. However, in some areas with lots of machinery, thermo vision may be ineffective.

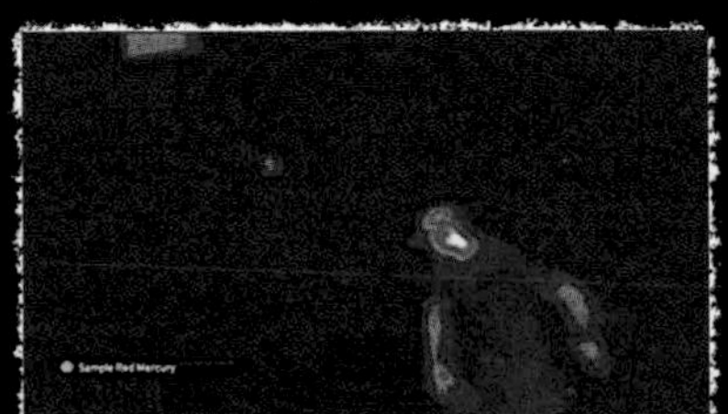

To ensure that you have killed an enemy, view them with thermo vision after inflicting a lethal attack. As their body temperature drops, they change colors and eventually become invisible in thermo vision.

Wave Vision

Wave vision filters background and highlights sound and harmonic wave resonance, thus giving the viewer a picture of electronic devices in an area. Electronic devices are bright white, while everything else is pink. Wave vision is extremely helpful for aiming at and disabling surveillance cameras and laser sensors. Disabled electronic devices disappear in wave vision as long as jamming is in effect.

Whistle

Press the Whistle button to whistle. Whistling can be used to draw the enemy toward your position. However, it is only useful if you can move through the dark around the enemy while they head toward your previous spot.

For instance, if you are in a room divided by a piece of machinery, you might stand at one side and whistle in order to draw an enemy around the corner. Meanwhile, you would move around the opposite side of the machinery and sneak up on the enemy from behind.

First-Person View

Press down on the Camera control to enter first-person view. The camera moves to the character's eye level. While in first-person view, press down on the Move control to zoom in and out.

Interaction Icon Menu

Whenever Sam Fisher or a splinter cell approaches a door, an object, a computer, or a character that he can interact with, the Interaction Icon menu appears. While the menu is onscreen, press and hold the Interact button to interface with the Interaction menu. While holding the button, use the Move control to cycle up and down through the icons available. Text appearing underneath each icon describes the action to be performed. When the desired option is highlighted, release the Interact button to perform the desired action. If no action is desired, choose the cancel icon.

NOTE

If you are unsure of the function of various interactions, refer to the "PS2/GC Game Basics" section for complete explanations of basics such as opening doors and opening doors with stealth.

Hacking Computers and Equipment

To open the encrypted file on a computer or laptop, choose the Security Access folder. Sam's hacking device appears. Displayed on the interface are four columns of rapidly cycling numbers. When a number in any column becomes fixed, move the cursor to highlight that number and press the Interact button to input that digit for the column. If you input a still-cycling digit, the entire column of digits resumes cycling. Once you input a digit in all four columns, the security is broken. Sam may then access the secure folder's files and functions.

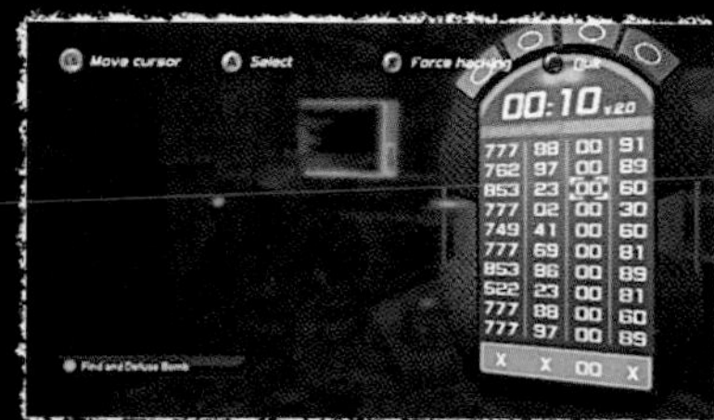

Some doors that are electronically locked by security devices such as keypads, retinal scanners, and voice recognition panels can all be hacked in order to unlock them.

TIP

By completing certain objectives (denoted in the Objectives menu of the OPSAT watch), Sam obtains equipment upgrades and access to new types of launcher projectiles. Upgrades to the hacking device may allow Sam to hack a computer or device automatically, without lifting a finger.

Also, check the upper part of the display while hacking to see if the Force Hacking option is available. Force Hacking inputs the correct code for each column automatically, but without stealth precautions. As a result, Force Hacking could cause an alarm to sound.

Picking Locks

You can unlock locked doors by using Sam's professional set of picks and tension rods. Once the lock picks are inserted, rotate the Move control until the pick begins to wiggle against the tumbler and the controller vibrates. When this happens, you have hit the "sweet spot." Agitate the tumbler by moving the Move control from the center to the sweet spot until the tumbler sticks. Repeat the process for as many tumblers as necessary until the cylinder can be turned to unlock the door.

Picking a lock is quiet and should not alert anyone to your presence. However, the longer it takes to pick a lock, the more Sam grunts and groans, drawing attention to himself.

The electronic lock pick allows Sam to pick locks automatically, without needing to force the tumblers into place. Also, completion of certain objectives may upgrade Sam's lock-picking tools so that he will pick locks automatically, with or without the electronic lock pick.

Special Abilities

Safecracking

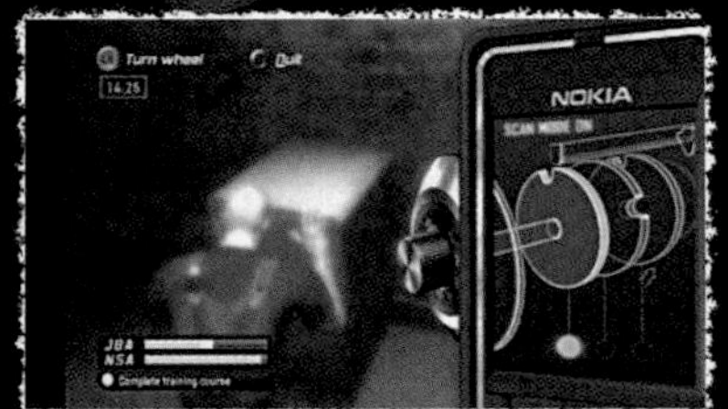

To be a valuable asset to the JBA, Sam must become an expert safecracker. Upon examining a safe, Sam's OPSAT watch displays a 3-D rendering of the inner workings of the combination lock. Tilt the Move control to the outer edge, and then rotate it clockwise repeatedly until the largest disc begins to rotate. Reduce your rotation speed as the niche in the largest disc approaches the pin at the top. When the first red light comes on and the safe makes an audible click, stop rotating the Move control. Now rotate the Move control counterclockwise until the second disc begins to rotate. Align the middle disc's niche with the pin, and then rotate the Move control clockwise again to turn the smallest disc into place. It's just like opening your locker in school!

Climbing Pipes and Ladders

Apart from the many controller functions, Sam Fisher and other splinter cell agents can perform some unique feats.

To begin climbing a ladder, simply move toward the ladder until Sam grabs the rungs and begins ascending.

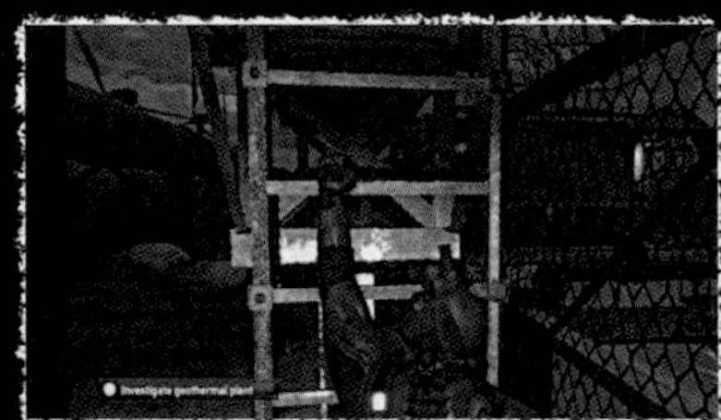

You can climb pipes in a similar fashion to ladders. Sam grabs on to vertical pipes by simply walking into them. When vertical pipes connect with horizontal pipes, Sam automatically changes position and posture at the corners as applicable.

To grab horizontal pipes running along the ceiling, position Sam directly under the pipe and jump up to grab hold. Press the Jump button while Sam hangs from a horizontal pipe to pull his legs up, making him harder to see and enabling him to move through small gaps in walls and fences. From this position, Sam can also grab characters from above and choke them unconscious with a nonlethal attack.

Press the Equip button while hanging from a ceiling pipe to draw the SC pistol. In a hanging position, Sam can aim within 180 degrees in front of himself, but not to the sides or rear.

Grab Ledge

While jumping, Sam grabs hold of any ledge situated less than three feet above his normal height. Sam can hang from a ledge for an unlimited amount of time.

While hanging from a ledge, shimmy left or right using the Move control. To climb onto a ledge or over a railing, tilt the Move control upward until Sam is standing on his feet.

Zip-line

A sturdy rope or a cable at a tilted angle can be used as a zip-line to slide across areas quickly. Position Sam underneath a zip-line and then press the Jump button to leap up and grab hold. Sam automatically slides along the zip-line until he reaches the end. He then automatically drops to the ground.

Swimming

For the first time in the *Splinter Cell* series, Sam Fisher can swim underwater. Use the Move control to control Sam's direction and swimming speed, and use the Camera/Aim control to direct Sam up, down, or sideways. Press the Equip button to briefly swim faster. Press the Crouch button to swim straight down, and press the Jump button to swim up or surface.

To climb out of water, surface and then use the Move control to guide Sam toward a shoreline or dock. When Sam is next to a surface, press the Jump button to climb out.

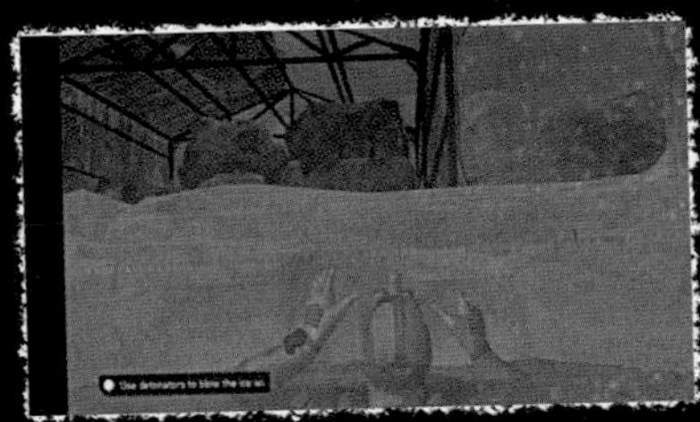

Ice Smash Kill

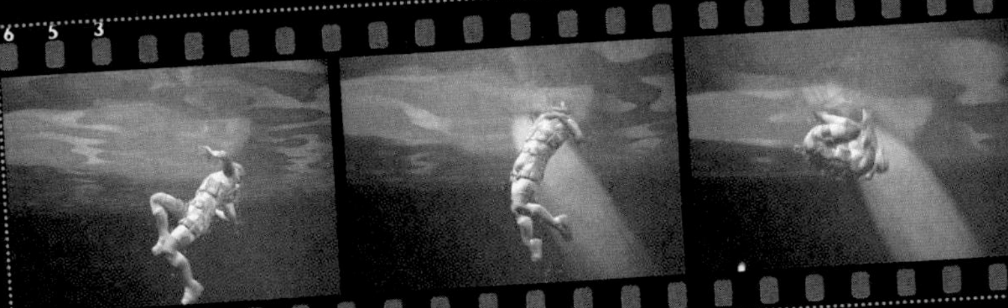

While swimming beneath the surface of frozen lakes, Sam can smash through patches of thin ice, pull a man into the chilly waters, and stab them in the heart. This is a lethal attack and kills the enemy.

TIP

Use thermo vision to see if an enemy is walking toward a thin ice patch. Then swim over to the thin ice patch and wait for the Smash Through icon to change into a Grab Character icon to perform an Ice Smash Kill.

Water Stealth Kill

While swimming below the water's surface near the bank of a stream or near the edge of a floating boat or dock, Sam can leap out of the water and grab characters standing close to the water's edge. You cannot perform a Water Stealth Kill from inside the crater of a thin ice patch Sam has recently broken through.

Inverted Neck Snap

While hanging from the winch attached to a horizontal pipe as described in the next section, Sam can grab characters directly below and strangle them unconscious. This is a nonlethal attack.

Corner Grab

When positioned near a corner with his back pressed against a wall, Sam can lean out and grab a character approaching from beyond the corner. To initiate a corner grab, press Sam's back against the wall and slide out to a corner. Tilt the Move control left or right as applicable in order to peek around the corner. When an enemy moves near to the corner, the Grab Character icon appears. Press the Interact button to perform a corner grab.

After grabbing a character from around a corner, Sam spins the person in a half-circle and slams their face into the wall. He then seizes and twists their arm, and folds them into the usual headlock position. The hostage can then be interrogated, choked unconscious, or murdered at your whim.

XBOX 360 VERSION ACHIEVEMENTS

ACHIEVEMENT	CRITERIA	GAMER POINTS
Agent of the Month	Completed the profiles of all the major members of the JBA	20G
The Collector	In Solo mode, collected all gadgets and upgrades	20G
Getting Technical	In Solo mode, knocked out 5 enemies using nonlethal gadgets	20G
The Human Light Switch	In Solo mode, used your EMP pistol to turn off 20 light sources	20G
The Invisible Man	In Solo mode, completed a mission without being detected	20G
Professional Ninja	Completed Solo mode on Hard difficulty	40G
Save Hisham	In Solo mode, saved Hisham's life	10G
Save Lambert	In Solo mode, saved Lambert's life	10G
Teacher's Pet	In Solo mode, beat John Hodge's score in training	10G
Training Completed	In Solo mode, successfully completed training	40G
Iceland Assignment Completed	In Solo mode, completed the Iceland assignment	30G
Ellsworth Assignment Completed	In Solo mode, completed the Ellsworth Penitentiary assignment	30G
HQ1 Assignment Completed	In Solo mode, completed the first terrorist HQ assignment	30G
Okhotsk Assignment Completed	In Solo mode, completed the Sea of Okhotsk assignment	30G
Shanghai Assignment Completed	In Solo mode, completed the Shanghai assignment	30G
HQ2 Assignment Completed	In Solo mode, completed the second terrorist HQ assignment	30G
Cozumel Assignment Completed	In Solo mode, completed the Cozumel assignment	30G
HQ3 Assignment Completed	In Solo mode, completed the third terrorist HQ assignment	30G
Kinshasa Assignment Completed	In Solo mode, completed the Kinshasa assignment	30G
Defeated the JBA	In Solo mode, completed the main storyline	150G
Hero	In Solo mode, completed the game with the best ending	20G
RECRUIT	Obtain an overall characteristics average of over 1%	10G
OPERATIVE	Obtain an overall characteristics average of over 5%	15G
FIELD AGENT	Obtain an overall characteristics average of over 20%	20G
SPECIAL AGENT	Obtain an overall characteristics average of over 45%	25G
OFFICER	Obtain an overall characteristics average of over 75%	30G
COMMANDER	Obtain an overall characteristics average of over 95%	45G
Bronze Trophy	Complete all the challenges by obtaining at least the bronze medal	15G
Silver Trophy	Complete all the challenges by obtaining at least the silver medal	30G
Gold Trophy	Complete all the challenges by obtaining the gold medal	50G
BLACKWING Expert	Get at least 10 victories as a spy and 10 in the UPSILON FORCE and play 25 sessions in this map	20G
MOTORWAY 90 Expert	Get at least 10 victories as a spy and 10 in the UPSILON FORCE and play 25 sessions in this map	20G
TERMINUS Expert	Get at least 10 victories as a spy and 10 in the UPSILON FORCE and play 25 sessions in this map	20G
SLAUGHTER HOUSE Expert	Get at least 10 victories as a spy and 10 in the UPSILON FORCE and play 25 sessions in this map	20G
RED DIAMOND Expert	Get at least 10 victories as a spy and 10 in the UPSILON FORCE and play 25 sessions in this map	20G
BOSS HOUSE Expert	Get at least 10 victories as a spy and 10 in the UPSILON FORCE and play 25 sessions in this map	20G
DAWN WAVES Expert	Get at least 10 victories as a spy and 10 in the UPSILON FORCE and play 25 sessions in this map	20G
USS WISDOM Expert	Get at least 10 victories as a spy and 10 in the UPSILON FORCE and play 25 sessions in this map	20G

08: 360/PC

EQUIPMENT

SC-20K

Magazine Size: 30
Shotgun Barrel Capacity: 8
The SC-20K is a prototype weapon developed specifically for splinter cell agents of Third Echelon. Designed in a bullpup configuration (magazine located in the stock), the SC-20K fires 5.56 x 45 mm jacketed rifle rounds. The rifle's magazines hold 30 rounds.

The SC-20K is modified with a silencer and electronic reflex sight. The sight allows the user to zoom in on the target 1.5x. While equipping the SC-20K, press the Aiming Mode button to look through the scope. The zoom degree cannot be increased or decreased. The electronic scope is capable of night vision, wave vision, and thermo vision, allowing the user to see through the scope in a special vision mode while the surrounding area is viewed normally. The scope enhancement also allows the user to combine vision types, viewing night vision through the scope while wearing thermo vision goggles, viewing wave vision through the scope while wearing night vision goggles, and so on.

The underside of the barrel is mounted with a combination 12-gauge shotgun and 40 mm gas-powered rocket launcher that has been modified to fire a variety of military gadgets (any device marked "—attachment").

Quickly tap the Primary Attack button to fire a single shot, or hold down the Primary Attack button to release a continuous stream of automatic fire. Press the Secondary Attack button to fire sticky shockers, airfoil rounds, and the other gadgets listed below:

STICKY CAMERA—ATTACHMENT

Sticky cameras function the same as their counterparts in the PlayStation2/GameCube version of the game, with some exceptions in the graphics display format and quality of the image transmitted to the OPSAT watch. Once the video signal is dropped, it cannot be reacquired. Approach a sticky camera that has not been detonated or made to release gas, and press the Interact button to retrieve it.

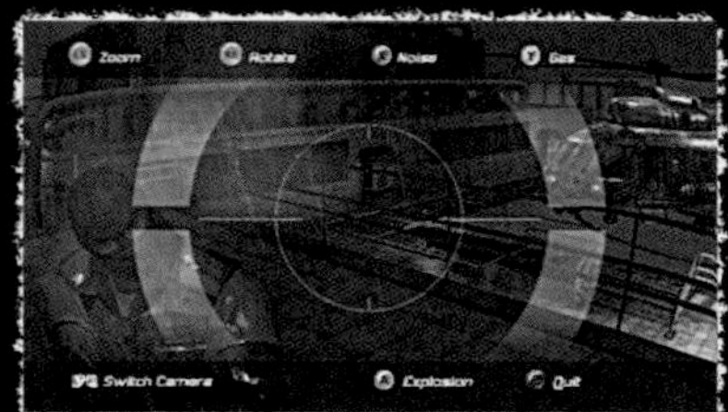

Please refer to the PlayStation2/GameCube Equipment section for a complete rundown of sticky shocker operation.

EXPLOSIVE STICKY CAMERA—ATTACHMENT

Explosive sticky cameras are an upgrade unlocked by completing any special objective marked with a star on the OPSAT watch's objective list. The main difference is that when you press the Interact button while viewing through the sticky camera, the device detonates, creating an explosion that should kill all enemies standing within one yard. Enemies standing just outside blast range may suffer intense damage.

STICKY SHOCKER—ATTACHMENT

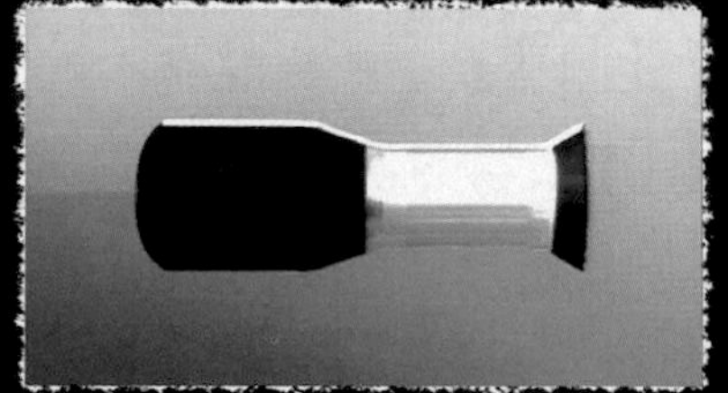

The sticky shockers in the 360/PC versions of the game function identically to the ones used in the PlayStation2/GameCube versions. (Please refer to the other PlayStation2/GameCube Equipment section for a complete description.)

If a sticky shocker is fired into a wall or the ground and does not release its electrical charge, retrieve the device by approaching it and pressing the Interact button.

AIRFOIL ROUND—ATTACHMENT

A launcher-compatible blunt round that can be fired from the SC-20K to stun and immobilize targets. Depending on the target, firing an airfoil round at the target's head may knock them out in a single shot. Stout enemies such as presidential soldiers and enemies wearing helmets may be incapable of being knocked out by an airfoil round, even when struck upon the head. Striking the target anywhere else only stuns them momentarily, allowing you to approach and grab them or knock them out. Firing two rounds anywhere on any target should knock the person unconscious.

Airfoil rounds can be reclaimed near the position of the target hostile. However, if the airfoil is left too long, it may vanish.

SMOKE GRENADE—ATTACHMENT

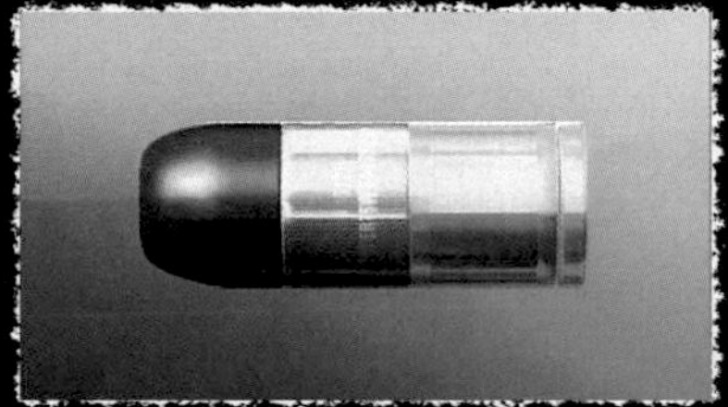

This smoke grenade is identical to the hand-tossed version and can be fired from the SC-20K's launcher attachment. Attachment smoke grenades become available after completing any two special objectives indicated with a star on the OPSAT watch's objectives list.

SONIC GRENADE—ATTACHMENT

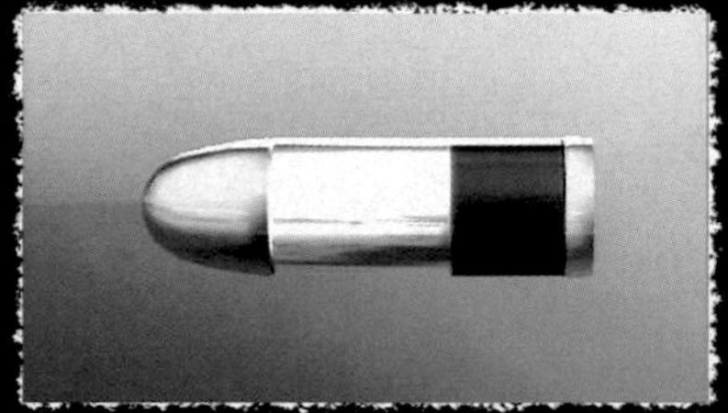

This sonic grenade is identical to the hand-tossed version and can be fired from the SC-20K's launcher attachment. Attachment sonic grenades become available after completing any three special objectives indicated with a star on the OPSAT watch's objectives list.

GAS GRENADE—ATTACHMENT

This knockout gas grenade is identical to the hand-tossed version and can be fired from the SC-20K's launcher attachment. Attachment gas grenades become available after completing four special objectives indicated with a star on the OPSAT watch's objectives list.

EMP GRENADE—ATTACHMENT

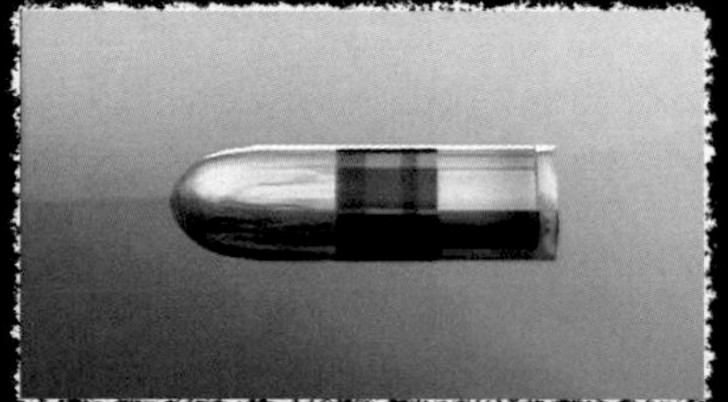

This electromagnetic pulse explosive is identical to the hand-tossed version and can be fired from the SC-20K's launcher attachment. Attachment EMP grenades become available after completing any five special objectives indicated with a star on the OPSAT watch's objectives list.

FRAG GRENADE—ATTACHMENT

This exploding fragmentation grenade is identical to the hand-tossed version and can be fired from the SC-20K's launcher attachment. Attachment frag grenades become available after completing any six special objectives indicated with a star on the OPSAT watch's objectives list.

SHOTGUN SHELL—ATTACHMENT

This is an additional modification to the SC-20K's launcher attachment that allows the user to fire 12-gauge triple-ought loads. Eight shells can be loaded into the barrel. These become available after completing any seven special objectives indicated with a star on the OPSAT watch's objectives list.

SC PISTOL

Magazine Size: 20

This prototype pistol designed specifically for splinter cell operatives of Third Echelon is equipped with a nonremovable sound and muzzle flash suppressor. It fires 5.7 x 28 mm jacketed cartridges. The magazines are extended to carry 20 rounds. The grip is configured for ambidextrous use. A prototype optically channeled potentiator (OCP) is custom-mounted under the barrel.

Press the Primary Fire button to fire a single shot. Even with the suppressor, the rapport is loud enough to be heard by enemies within a three-yard radius.

OCP

When equipping the SC pistol, aim at electronic equipment such as surveillance cameras, laser sensor emitters, and lights. Press the Secondary Fire button to use the OCP to temporarily disable electronic equipment. The jamming effect lasts approximately 30 seconds.

OCP—ENHANCED

This enhanced model OCP recharges at nearly double the rate of the regular OCP. This upgrade is added to the SC pistol after you complete eight special objectives denoted by stars in the OPSAT watch's objectives menu.

SC COMBAT KNIFE

A custom knife employed by splinter cells of Third Echelon. The SC knife is identical to the one used in the PlayStation2/GameCube version of the game. Please refer to the PlayStation2/GameCube Equipment chapter for more information.

FRAG GRENADE

An SC-60 series lightweight fragmentation grenade identical in use to the one utilized in the PlayStation2/GameCube version of the game. Please refer to the PlayStation2/GameCube Equipment section for more information.

SMOKE GRENADE

A SC-81 series smoke grenade identical in use to the one utilized in the PlayStation2/GameCube version of the game. Please refer to the PlayStation2/GameCube Equipment section for more information.

FLASH GRENADE

An SC-54 series flash grenade identical to the one from the PlayStation2/GameCube version of the game. Please refer to the PlayStation2/GameCube Equipment section for more information.

SONIC GRENADE

This SC-82 series nonlethal grenade emits a high-pitched ringing for approximately 10 seconds after detonation. The grenade is useful in distracting enemies, causing them to turn in a different direction. If used properly, the distraction may allow Sam to maneuver behind the enemy and seize him. The ringing allows Sam to run at full speed through areas virtually unheard.

To release a sonic grenade, equip it and then press the Equip button in preparation to throw. Aim the crosshair at the desired detonation location and then press Primary Attack to release.

EMP GRENADE

This hand-tossed SC-66 series nonlethal grenade emits an electromagnetic pulse that temporarily disrupts electronics within the blast range, roughly 10 feet. Equipment such as cameras, laser sensors, and lights remain jammed for approximately 25 seconds.

Press the Equip button to prepare to toss an EMP grenade. Aim the crosshair at the intended landing zone, compensating slightly for physical bounce. Press the Primary Attack button to throw the EMP grenade.

The EMP grenade is a special item unlocked by completing nine of the specially marked objectives in the OPSAT watch's menu.

GAS GRENADE

This is an SC-40 series nonlethal CS knockout gas grenade. Toss this puppy into the midst of enemy groups to knock them unconscious within seconds. Avoid throwing the gas grenade too close to Sam's position, or he suffers minor damage.

Press the Equip button to prepare to throw a gas grenade. Aim the crosshairs at the intended landing zone, raising your aim slightly to compensate for range and bounce. Then press the Primary Attack button to release.

Gas grenades are an equipment upgrade available only after completing 10 of the specially marked objectives listed on the OPSAT watch's screen.

WALL MINE

A motion-sensitive wall-mounted adhesive mine lethal to all enemies within three meters upon detonation. To place a wall mine, select them in the Quick Inventory menu and then face a suitably flat wall. Press the Primary Attack button to place the wall mine on the vertical surface. After placing the mine, back away slowly to avoid detonating the device yourself! Mines can be recollected from walls by pressing and releasing the Interact button when the green light is flashing. Attempting to disable a wall mine while the red light flashes results in instant detonation.

WALL MINE—STUN

A motion-sensitive wall-mounted adhesive mine that emits a chemical stunning agent when triggered. Effective against enemies up to three meters from the mine. Place them on walls and retrieve them in the same manner as regular wall mines.

Stun wall mines are an upgrade unlocked only after completing any 11 specially marked objectives in the OPSAT Watch's objective list.

WALL MINE—FLASH

A motion-sensitive wall-mounted adhesive mine that creates a blinding light, stunning all enemies within three meters of the mine. Flash wall mines are placed and retrieved exactly like regular wall mines.

Flash wall mines are an upgrade unlocked only after completing any 12 specially marked objectives in the OPSAT Watch's objective list.

RIOT SHOTGUN

A custom air weapon that fires nonlethal beanbag rounds to knock out opponents. When fired at a hostile, he becomes stunned for roughly 10 to 12 seconds. Use the opportunity to grab the person from behind or knock them unconscious. The riot shotgun is available only in the Ellsworth Penitentiary mission.

OPTIC CABLE

The optic cable is a flexible fiber-optic cable with a tiny camera affixed to the end that allows the user to see into the adjoining room. The optic cable can be inserted under doors, through trapdoors in floors, through vent covers, and various other portals.

To use the optic cable, approach a door or portal until the Open Door icon appears in the screen's center. Press and hold the Interact button and scroll upward until the Optic Cable icon is

displayed. Then release the Interact button to insert the optic cable. You can utilize the optic cable in conjunction with thermo vision, night vision, and wave vision. While viewing through the optic cable, twist the cable right or left by moving the left analog stick in the appropriate direction.

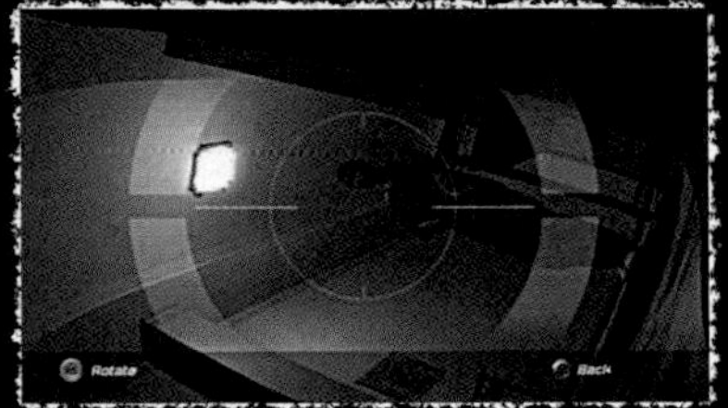

LOCK PICK

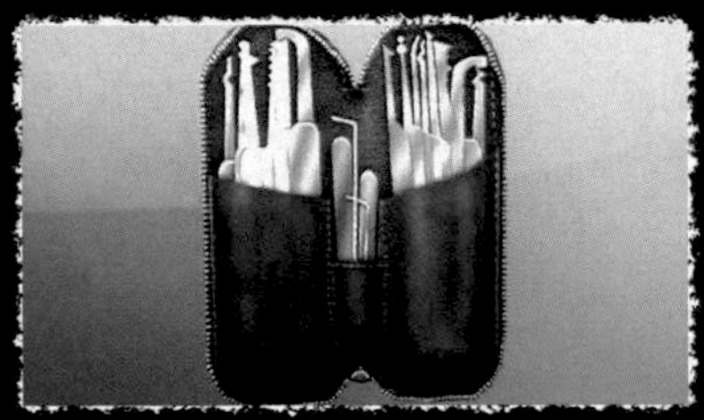

This is a set of professional lock picks consisting of diamond pick and tension wrench sets. Insert them into a lock's cylinder in order to manipulate the tumblers.

To unlock a locked door, insert the lock pick. Rotate the left analog stick in a wide circle until the pick begins to raise the cylinder, a position known as the "sweet spot." Keep the left stick in the sweet spot but gently move it slightly inward and outward from the center to jostle the tumbler. When the tumbler finally locks in place, the pick automatically moves on to the next tumbler. Rotate the left stick again until you find the sweet spot, and jostle the tumbler until it clicks into place. Some door locks require you to break only two or three tumblers, whereas others require you to break all six tumblers before you can rotate the cylinder to unlock the door.

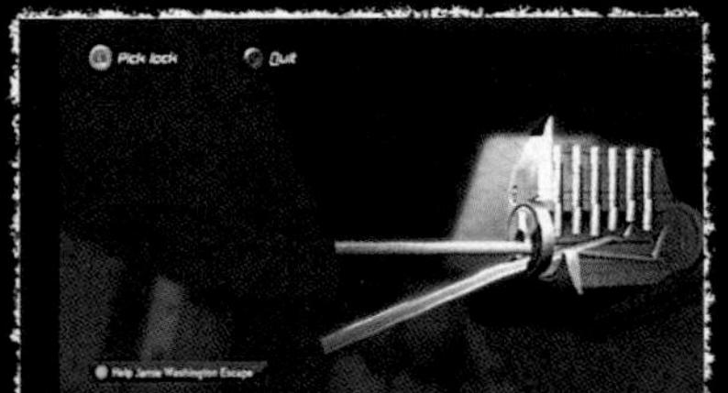

ELECTRONIC LOCK PICK

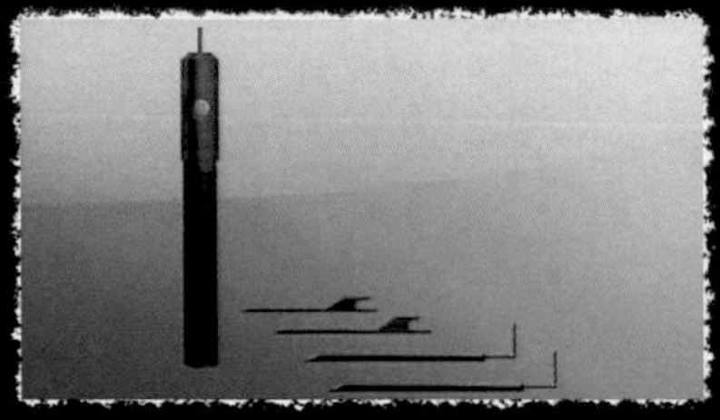

This lock pick upgrade allows Sam to pick locks automatically. Working in conjunction with Sam's multifaceted OPSAT watch, the device allows Sam to affix the watch face to the lock plate and overthrow the tumblers within the lock automatically. Obtain this upgrade after completing 13 of the objectives marked with stars in the OPSAT watch's menu.

HACKING DEVICE

You can attach the OPSAT watch to digital hardware to penetrate security mechanisms and override protection programs. Whenever the Hack icon appears when Sam stands near a computer or device, press the Interact button to enter the Hacking Device screen. Four columns of rapidly cycling digits are displayed. When a digit in any column stops cycling, highlight it with the cursor and press the Interact button to lock in the code. You must accomplish hacking within 30 to 45 seconds to prevent detection by the system. If time runs out before Sam locks in all four code numbers, an alert may sound.

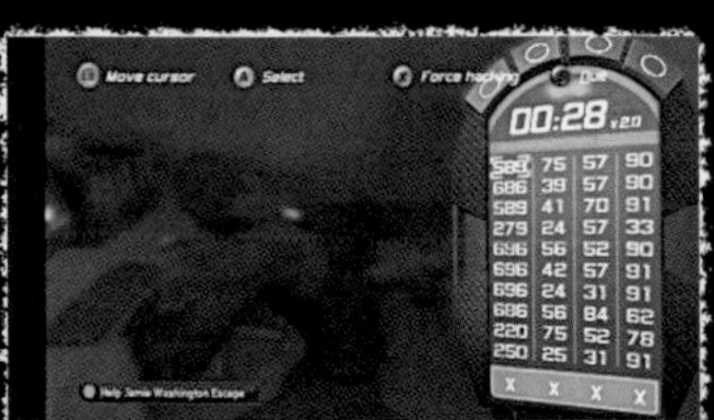

HACKING DEVICE—SOFTWARE UPGRADE

This hacking device upgrade allows the user to faster penetrate layers of electronic security, making code input numbers brighter and easier to read; it also makes them become fixed and suitable for locking in more quickly than the regular hacking device. This upgrade is obtained after completing several special objectives marked with stars in the OPSAT watch menu.

HACKING DEVICE—FORCE HACK UPGRADE

This allows a person using the hacking device to force hacking with the press of a button, overriding electronic security in the most intrusive manner. In most cases, forcing hacking triggers an alarm, which may alert enemies.

Obtain this hacking device upgrade after completing several objectives marked with stars in the OPSAT watch menu.

LASER MICROPHONE

A handheld surveillance device capable of picking up sounds at a distance or sound reverberating through a pane of glass. Important voice samples are recorded automatically. Simply aim the crosshairs at the intended recording target to pick up useful sounds.

ULTRASONIC EMITTER

This handheld projectile launcher shoots a small transceiver. Upon contact with a surface, the transceiver emits a sound in an attempt to draw an enemy's attention. The best use is for drawing an enemy to any location but your own.

GLASS CUTTER

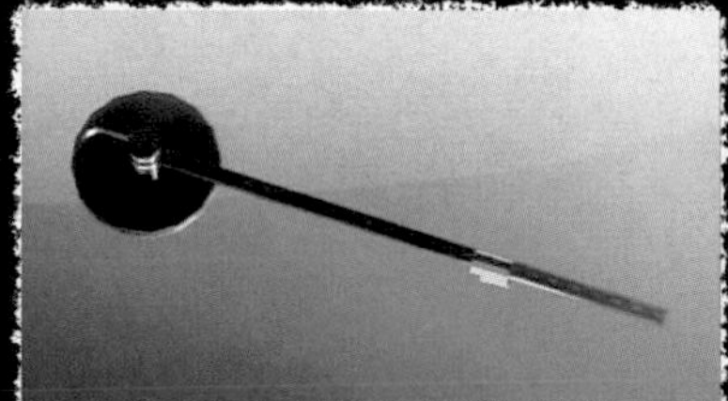

A professional-grade suction cup and rotating rod affixed with a thick diamond-edge blade for cutting glass. When near a vertical glass surface without steel reinforcement, the Cut Glass Interact icon may appear. Press the Interact button to affix the glass cutter to the window and make a circular hole in the pane. Afterward, move toward the hole until Sam climbs through, one leg at a time. The glass cutter allows Sam to penetrate areas that might be otherwise unreachable, and it allows him to follow alternate routes in order to sneak up behind enemies.

WINCH

This titanium alloy winch apparatus connects to a grapnel line in order to extend or retract a rope. While hanging from a pipe, Sam can use the winch in certain locations to descend toward the ground from above. While in this inverted position, Sam can grab enemies from above and choke them unconscious.

To use the winch, shimmy along a horizontal pipe until the Winch icon appears. Press the Interact button to attach the grapnel and winch to the pipe and hang. Then tilt the Move control up or down to rise or descend along the grapnel line. Descend to the floor and Sam automatically drops to his feet.

NIGHT VISION

Night vision enhances the level of ambient light in the environment, allowing the user to see better in the dark. To avoid blindness, disable night vision when moving through brightly lit areas. Because night vision colors everything in greenish tones, Sam suffers a flattening effect, sometimes making it hard to judge the true distances between objects and personnel. Press the Night Vision button to toggle night vision on or off.

NIGHT VISION—ENHANCED

Acquire this night vision goggle upgrade by completing objectives marked with

stars in the OPSAT watch's objectives menu. Enhanced night vision allows the user to see in the dark without the flattening effect or green discoloration common to ordinary night vision. By rendering the area in black and white, objects and enemies stand out strikingly against the background.

WAVE VISION

Wave vision is one of three vision modes available through Sam's goggles. Press the Wave Vision button to toggle wave vision on or off. In wave vision, electronic or sound-emitting devices are highlighted in the environment. Wave vision allows Sam to spot electronic devices that may be hidden in the shadows. Many objects that register highly in wave vision can be jammed or disabled using the OCP attached to Sam's SC pistol. Thus, wave vision is highly recommended for use in conjunction with the OCP.

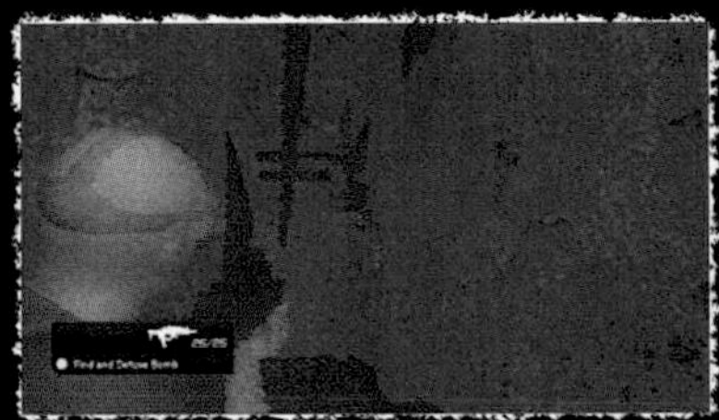

THERMO VISION

Thermo vision highlights heat-registering objects and personnel in an area. Press to toggle thermo vision on or off. In thermo vision, nonheated objects register as blue, whereas people or hot objects register as pink, red, or yellow, depending on the temperature. After a kill, you can ensure your target is dead by watching their body temperature drop in thermo vision.

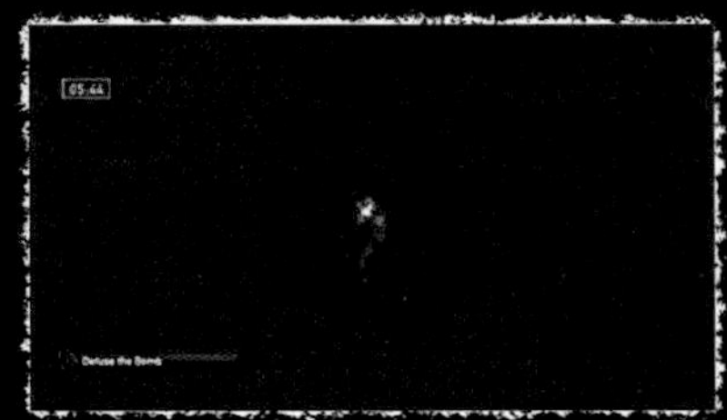

SUNGLASSES

This set of stylish marksman's ultraviolet filtering lens sunglasses cut down on sunlight glare and make the wearer harder to identify. Press the Night Vision button to wear or take off the sunglasses. In interior areas, the sunglasses tend to reduce color and darken rooms unnecessarily. But in outdoor areas, the sunglasses reduce the light onscreen and filter out the glare emanated by objects bouncing sunlight. The sunglasses are only available during the Kinshasa mission.

BREATHING EQUIPMENT

This lightweight underwater breathing apparatus extracts oxygen from water and from exhalation, enabling the user to remain underwater for long periods without surfacing. Sam can swim through even arctic waters without suffering from prolonged exposure.

OPSAT WATCH

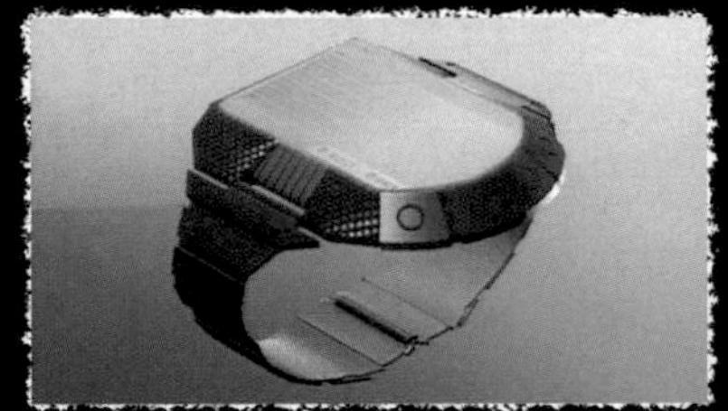

Sam wears a male wristwatch with complete OPSAT (operational satellite uplink) communications functionality. Using the OPSAT watch, Sam can review mission objectives and e-mail data downloaded from computers and laptops, check for new JBA profiles, and peruse equipment descriptions at a glance. The OPSAT also allows Sam to view a 3-D rendering of the stage, with a red arrow marking Sam's position and yellow arrows marking the positions of other characters. The tracker functions of the map enable Sam to keep tabs on enemy whereabouts at all times. Simply exit the map and return in order to view an update. And, yes, the OPSAT watch also tells time. Press the Back button to bring up Sam's OPSAT watch at any time during gameplay. The OPSAT can be upgraded and improved with downloads available from the NSA, delivered

SATCOM

The map function of the OPSAT watch links with the Satellite Communications Network (SATCOM) to pinpoint the approximate locations of Sam and hostiles in the environment. The SATCOM can only refresh the image when Sam is not moving. To display the Quick OPSAT map in the screen's lower left corner, press ⊕↓.

BLUEPRINT SCANNER

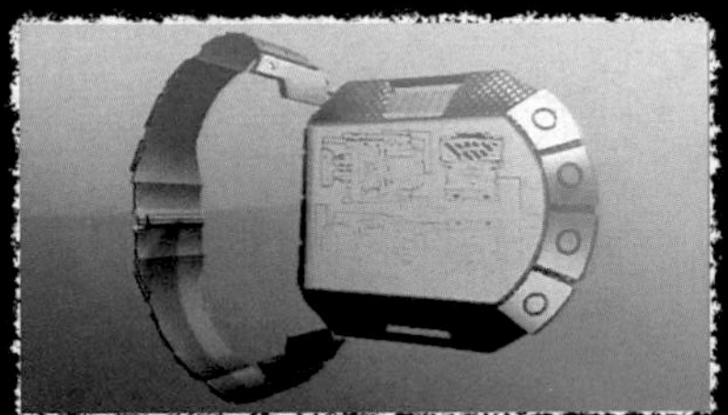

The scanning function of the underside of the removable OPSAT watch face allows the user to scan important blueprint documents at high resolutions for transmission to NSA databanks. When the Scan Blueprint icon appears, press the Interact button to initiate scanning. You use this to scan the blueprints of the red mercury device in Emile Dufraisne's office.

RETINAL SCANNER

You can also use the OPSAT watch as a handheld retinal scanning device designed to reproduce security-grade retinal scans. The high-resolution laser stores retinal scan data and projects it into retinal-scanning devices mounted on walls next to locked doors. To obtain a retinal scan, knock out or kill one of the main JBA leaders. Move over their body until the Scan Retina icon appears, then press the Interact button to scan his or her retinas. Use this data to open retinal-scanner locked doors within the JBA compound.

FINGERPRINT SCANNER

A dual-purpose, handheld ultraviolet fingerprint detection and scanning device. To use the fingerprint scanner, select it in the Quick Inventory menu and press the Equip button. Sam holds the OPSAT watch face near his shoulder and aims a concentrated cone of ultraviolet light. Move the ultraviolet light over flat, horizontal surfaces such as tables and desks until a fingerprint becomes highlighted in green. Then press and hold the Primary Attack button to scan the fingerprint. Fingerprint scanning makes a little noise that can be heard up to five feet away, so use with caution.

SOLO MISSIONS

Training: Test Course A

OBJECTIVES

MAIN OBJECTIVES

> EXIT THROUGH NORTH DOOR: The test will be completed once you step through the north door. Make sure to accomplish secondary objectives first, as they will determine your score at the time you step through the door.

SECONDARY OBJECTIVES

> RETRIEVE PICTURE: Your first task in this test is to retrieve the picture of your daughter from the center of the room. You will be evaluated on the methods you choose to accomplish this task.

> REMAIN UNDETECTED: You will be evaluated on your ability to avoid detection by the cameras in the test area. Remain undetected to score higher on the test.

> COMPLETE THE TEST WITHIN THE TIME LIMIT: This test is timed. Complete the test within the required time to score higher.

LOADOUT: TEST COURSE A

AVAILABLE WEAPONS
SC pistol/40

To learn the basics of infiltration and stealth in *Splinter Cell: Double Agent*, we strongly recommend choosing the "Training" option on the Solo Mission menu. Both of these courses are virtual-reality training missions designed to help you learn some basics of the Splinter Cell world. Test Course A is an introductory mission designed to help you learn how to cover all the bases when infiltrating a secure area.

Spotlights

Sam begins the training mission in a room with blank white walls. He must complete this test course within five minutes. Move forward through the doorway into a dark open area. Avoid the searchlight directly ahead by waiting for it to sweep to one side or the other, and then stand and run beyond the light to avoid detection.

Climbing Pipes

After avoiding the searchlight and moving a few feet farther inward, the room lights up and walls appear. When the walls reach full height, a vertical pipe appears on the nearest wall. Jump and grab hold of the vertical pipe, and then climb on top of the wall.

Another horizontal pipe hovers overhead. Position Sam directly under the pipe, and then press the Jump button to jump and grab the pipe. While holding a horizontal pipe, you may move along it hand over hand.

When you reach the center of the area, the Winch interaction icon appears. However, if you use the winch to descend right now, the security cameras to the left and right will see you. Instead, continue moving along the pipe into the glass enclosure at the far end.

Hacking Security Access

Continue climbing along the pipe until it bends downward inside the glass structure. Climb down to the floor.

Inside the glass room, a laptop rests on a table. Access the laptop and choose the Security Access folder. Sam's hacking device appears onscreen. Hack the security access and then disable the security cameras.

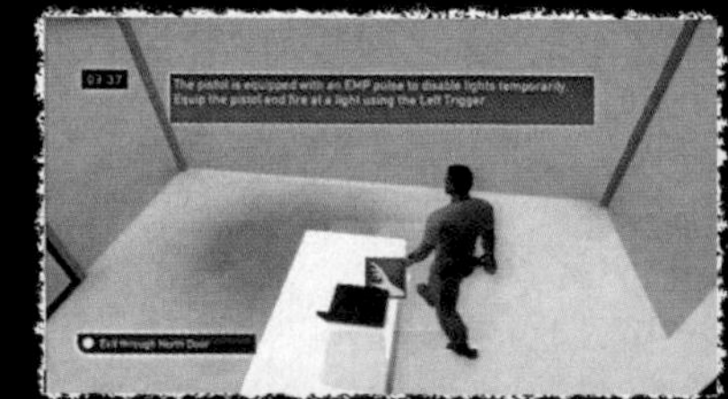

NOTE

To hack the security access, search the columns of rapidly cycling digits. When one of the numbers in the column becomes fixed, highlight it with the cursor and press the Interact button to lock in that column. Lock in all four columns before 30 seconds expires to successfully hack the security access. Then you may disable the security cameras.

Grab the Picture

Climb back up the vertical pipe to the horizontal length. Climb hand over hand back to the center of the area, until Sam is positioned over Sarah's portrait and the Winch icon appears.

Use the winch to descend into the center of the area. When Sam disconnects from the winch in the center of the security zone and the Grab icon appears, press the Interact button to pick up the picture.

A doorway appears at the room's north end. Stand upright and run through the doorway to complete this training exercise.

Training: Test Course B

OBJECTIVES

MAIN OBJECTIVES

> EXIT THROUGH NORTH DOOR: The test will be completed once you step through the north door. Make sure to accomplish secondary objectives first, as they will determine your score at the time you step through the door. (John Hodge's score is three minutes.)

PRIMARY OBJECTIVES

> RETRIEVE INFORMATION FROM HOSTAGE: Your first task in this test is to retrieve information from the hostage. You will be evaluated on the methods you choose to accomplish this task.

SECONDARY OBJECTIVES

> TAKE OUT ALL HOSTILES: The test room contains some hostiles. You will be evaluated on the ways you take them out.

> REMAIN UNDETECTED: You will be evaluated on your ability to avoid detection by the cameras in the test area. Remain undetected to score higher on the test.

> DO NOT USE LETHAL FORCE: The test requires you to refrain from using lethal forces on the hostiles in the room. Killing them will deduct points from your score.

LOADOUT: TEST COURSE B

AVAILABLE WEAPONS
SC-20K/60
Sticky camera/4
Sticky shocker/2
Airfoil round/4
Frag grenade/2
Smoke grenade/3
Flash grenade/3
Sonic grenade/3
Wall mine/3

Now it is time for the nitty-gritty of stealth infiltration work: hostile takedown and hostage escort. In this virtual-reality mission, Sam must neutralize all hostiles without use of lethal force, free the hostage in the center of the second area, and extract.

Takedown Made Easy

Sam begins this virtual mission perched atop a high platform. Stay in position until a security guard emerges from the far door directly ahead. The guard heads to the left and stops in front of a door. As the guard opens the door, slowly move forward and drop from the perch's side. Follow the guard into the small dark room, and grab him from behind. Drag him a few feet away from the door if necessary and then press the Secondary Attack button to perform a non-lethal attack, strangling the guard unconscious.

The Long Stalk

Find the double doors in the area and go through them. Sam stands at the top of a long staircase, overlooking a complex labyrinth. A guard at the bottom of the stairs begins to walk away to the right. Run downstairs to the corridor, and then follow him at a stealthy pace. Crouch to reduce the amount of noise made. Tilt the Move control only halfway to avoid moving too quickly. As you approach the patrolling guard's flank, reduce speed to a stalking pace. Keep following him until the Grab Character icon appears. Press the Interact button to seize the guard, then press the Secondary Attack button to knock him out.

The Hostage

Return to the long staircase and head about halfway up so that you may overlook the maze once again. Use your eyes to trace a path through the labyrinth to the central area, where a terrorist holds a young woman hostage. The quickest route is to descend the stairs, head left to the corner, follow the corner to the right, go through the first opening on the right, and then follow the passage to the far right.

Sneak up quietly behind the terrorist guarding the hostage. Grab him in a chokehold and strangle him, or knock him out by pressing the Secondary Attack button when in extremely close range.

Move behind the hostage and press the Interact button to untie her wrists. A doorway appears in the corner of this area. Go through the doorway to complete the mission.

TIP

Our explanation helps you learn to sneak up behind enemies without having to use gadgets. Most of the guide is written in this manner. To beat John Hodge's time of three minutes, use sticky shockers to take down the police officer and the patrolling terrorist as quickly as possible.

Iceland—Geothermal Plant

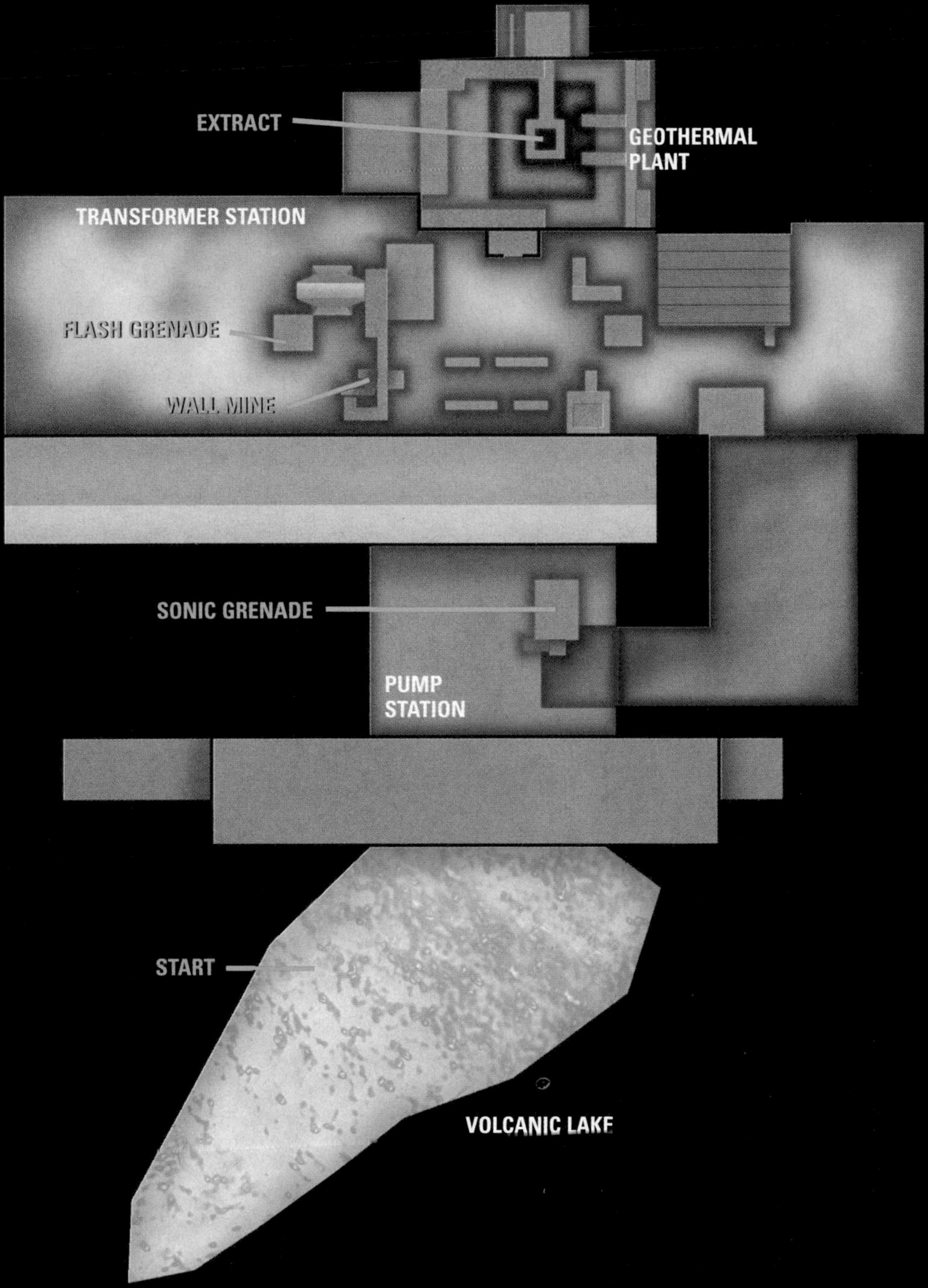

EXTRACT
GEOTHERMAL PLANT
TRANSFORMER STATION
FLASH GRENADE
WALL MINE
SONIC GRENADE
PUMP STATION
START
VOLCANIC LAKE

OBJECTIVES

MAIN OBJECTIVES

> INVESTIGATE GEOTHERMAL PLANT: Intel indicates that the geothermal plant is being used as a base of operations by a terrorist organization, one that may have access to missiles. Investigate any terrorist activity you can find at the site.

> REACH OSPREY FOR EXTRACTION: The crew of the Osprey has dropped a rope for you to climb in order to extract from the geothermal plant. Reach the helicopter before the missile's ignition vaporizes everything around it.

PRIMARY OBJECTIVES

> PREVENT MISSILE LAUNCH: You are now under orders to prevent the missile from launching by any means necessary. Once that bird is in the air, we have no means of bringing it down.

SECONDARY OBJECTIVES

> INFILTRATE PLANT WITHOUT ALERT: You cannot afford to let the terrorists on-site know that you are there or they will scrub their current operations. Infiltrate the geothermal power station without being detected.

> INFILTRATE BASE WITHOUT ALERTS: It is imperative that you reach the terrorists' central facilities and that you are not detected as you do so. Failure may compromise the observation operation.

LOADOUT: ICELAND GEOTHERMAL BASE

AVAILABLE WEAPONS
SC-20K/60
SC pistol/40
Sticky shocker/2
Airfoil round/4
Frag grenade/2
Flash grenade/3
Smoke grenade/3
Sonic grenade/3
Wall mine/3

Sam Fisher and a rookie Third Echelon operative named John Hodge are sent to a geothermal power plant in Iceland from whence terrorists are planning to launch a ballistic missile against England. Sam must work with the overly cocky Hodge to determine whether the terrorists have the capability to launch, and stop them if they do.

Volcanic Lake

Drop from the cargo ramp of the V-22 Osprey into the cold Icelandic waters surrounding the geothermal plant. While underwater, use your left analog stick to swim and use your right analog stick to change direction.

Ice Smash Kill

Continue swimming into a large circular tunnel. Press the Equip button to swim faster. Upon emerging from the tunnel, use the right stick to angle your perspective upward and see Hodge in the process of performing an "ice smash kill." Now it is your turn to try. Press the Jump button to swim up to the ice, and then use your left stick to swim around until you find a weak spot in the ice, as indicated by a Break icon. Wait until the remaining terrorist patrolling the surface walks over this patch of ice. When the Break icon changes into a Grab Character icon, press the Interact button to smash through the ice, pull the terrorist into the water, and stab him in the heart.

Press the Jump button to surface through the opening in the ice. Then swim toward the side and hold the left stick up to make Sam climb out onto the surface.

Pump Station

Rendezvous with Hodge in the corner of the area. Press up on the D-pad to activate wave vision. When viewed through this sound/energy vision mode, the fence near Hodge's position is completely lit up, indicating the presence of electricity. Sam suffers electrocution damage if he touches the fence. You must find the power source and shut it down so Sam can safely climb the fence.

Behind Hodge is a small building. Quietly enter the building through the door on the far right side. Sneak into the next room and notice a guard sleeping in a bunk. To knock him out, move close to his head and press LT. Sam may now freely move around inside the building without fear of waking the guard.

Head into the room's second portion and use the notebook computer to access informative e-mails. E-mails are stored in the Data menu of your OPSAT watch.

Collect the sonic grenade on the desk next to the laptop and head to the room's corner. Cut the wires to the power breaker box. Hodge radios confirmation from outside that the fence is now safe.

Zip-line into the Base

Return to Hodge's position and move toward the fence's center. When a Co-op Move icon appears, press the Interact button to boost Hodge onto a platform above the fence. Then move toward the fence until Sam grasps on. Move the left stick upward to climb over the fence. Press the Crouch button to drop to the ground on the other side.

Head toward the well-lit corner and climb the ladder up to a second platform. Position Sam underneath a cable that leads farther back into the plant. Press the Jump button to leap up and grab the cable. Sam and Hodge zip-line into the next area.

Transformer Station

Turn to Sam's right and notice the terrorist on the catwalk below. When the terrorist stops near the wall, drop on top of him to knock him out. Then head down the stairs nearby.

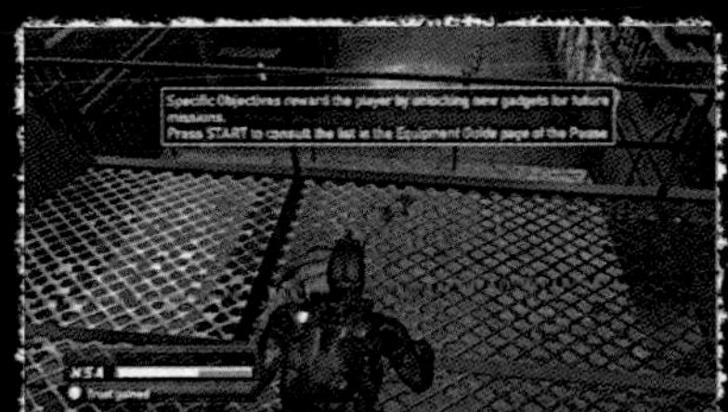

Another set of stairs descending from the platform leads to a well-lit area where two guards are talking. That route is too dangerous, so seek an alternate path. Upon reaching the platform with a control booth, turn to Sam's left and climb over the rail. (To climb over a rail, face it and press the Jump button while moving the left stick toward the rail. Sam should climb over the rail, spin around to grab the ledge, and hang.) Sam is positioned over a cargo container. Press the Crouch button to drop onto the cargo container.

Head to the cargo container's opposite end, drop over the side and to the ground. Inside the open cargo container, a wall mine lies on the box to the right. Sneak through the cargo container, grab the terrorist, and drag him inside the container. Interrogate the guard to learn the code to the nearby gate (1977). Then press the Secondary Attack button to choke him unconscious.

At this point you have two options: either use the code on the keypad to open the gate, or neutralize the two men still in this area.

To take out the remaining guards, exit the dark side of the cargo container and head around the corner to the left. A terrorist patrols the well-lit area between Sam and a small building that controls the gate dividing this area. Hide behind the covered stacks of cargo until the terrorist moves into the shadowy area with a flashlight. Move around the stack of cargo in the area to circle behind him and grab him from behind. If you have trouble seizing him because of his pace, equip the SC-20K and fire a sticky shocker at him instead. Either way, be sure to take him out before he returns to well-lit open ground.

Sneak around the area's dark outskirts toward the small building. Through the window, you see a terrorist inside, staring at a monitor. Enter the building, sneak up behind him, and knock him out. Pick up the flashbang grenade on the desk, and use the laptop to open the gate.

If you learned the code by interrogating the guard, then enter the code into the keypad beside the gate. Use the OCP to jam the bright light beside the gate first so you can enter the code without giving away your position. The barrier slides open, and you may proceed into the next sector.

Evade the Searchlight

Wait outside the newly opened gate until a terrorist patrols near the opening and then stops nearby to the left. Sneak around the fence's corner and head down the dark middle aisle between the power transformers. As you move, notice that a searchlight scans this area. Continue forward until Sam begins to look up to the left and right. This indicates that he is capable of performing a Split Jump. To move into a Split Jump stance, face the vertical surface on either side of you and press the Jump button. Sam leaps off the ground and hovers in midair over the narrow passage, supporting himself with his legs.

Wait for the searchlight to pass on the ground beneath Sam, then drop to the ground and move to the next point where Sam can perform another Split Jump. Continue performing Split Jumps to avoid the searchlight while crossing the area.

At the far end of the aisle of transformers, a guard with a flashlight stands stationary off to the left. Provided that nothing is done to alarm him, you should be able to sneak out of the transformer aisle and over to the ladder beside the guard. Climb up the ladder to the water tank platform.

Reach the Fan Vent

Hodge deactivates a fan in the main building, which should allow Sam access to the plant interior through the vent. At first glance, it seems the only way up to the platform under the vent is via a staircase. The stairs are well lit, and a guard with a flashlight waits at the top. If you deactivate the light with the OCP, the guard moves to investigate. This route is not suitable. Instead, climb the ladder attached to the water tank on the platform. Jump up to grab the horizontal portion of a pipe attached to the tank. Shimmy across the area using the pipe, pressing the Jump button to raise your legs as needed to bypass rails. Upon reaching the other side, shimmy along the rail to the left, and then climb over. Sneak downstairs and go through the fan vent hole.

Geothermal Plant

Terrorists inside the building have spotted the overeager John Hodge, and they quickly machine-gun him down. The terrorists then activate the launch sequence on the massive ballistic in the room's center. Sam must reach the missile and prevent it from launching within six or seven minutes, depending on difficulty level.

Sam climbs out of the fan vent and hangs from a girder. Shimmy to the left and around a corner until Sam is under a crane platform. Then move the left stick upward to climb over the rail onto the crane platform.

Descend the nearby staircase to find the crane platform controls. Press the Interact button to activate the platform.

Go back up the stairs and continue across the platform as it moves. The platform stops and you see a vertical pipe and a bright light at the platform's end. Use your SC pistol's OCP to jam the light, and then climb up the pipe. Connect to a horizontal pipe running along the ceiling, and climb hand over hand across it to the area's center.

Hack the Missile's Computer

Continue shimmying across the horizontal pipe until the Winch icon appears onscreen. Press the Interact button to attach Sam's winch to the pipe. When Sam hangs upside down, use the left stick to lower him or raise him as necessary. Control the speed of Sam's descent by moving the left stick gently.

A technician stops directly below Sam's position. Descend until the Grab Character icon appears onscreen, and then press the Interact button to perform an inverted neck snap. Next, descend to the platform until Sam stands on his feet.

Position Sam in front of the missile's control panel. When the Hack icon appears onscreen, press the Interact button to begin hacking the device. Four columns of numbers appear on the hacking device, indicating that the device is searching for the access code. Whenever a number anywhere in any column becomes fixed onscreen, move the cursor to the number and press the Interact button to lock the column. You must lock all four columns within 30 seconds. Keep a sharp eye roving up and down the columns!

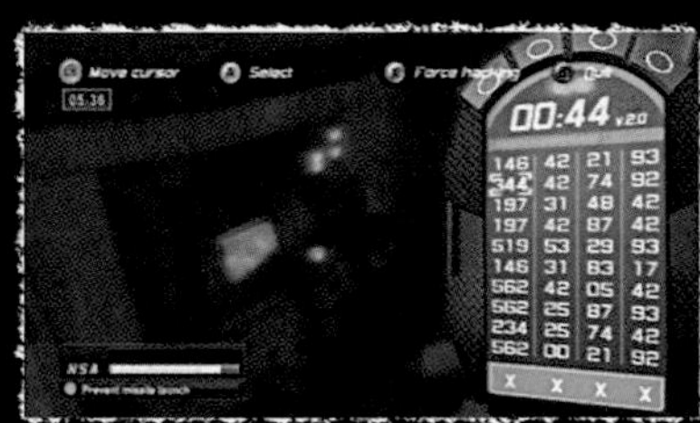

The Rope Hanging from the Ceiling

After you successfully hack the missile, the service platform overhead moves closer, bringing a ladder in contact with the missile platform. Sam has one minute to climb up the ladder and find the rope to the Osprey, which hangs over the circular platform. Grab the rope and climb up to the Osprey for extraction!

Kansas—Ellsworth Penitentiary

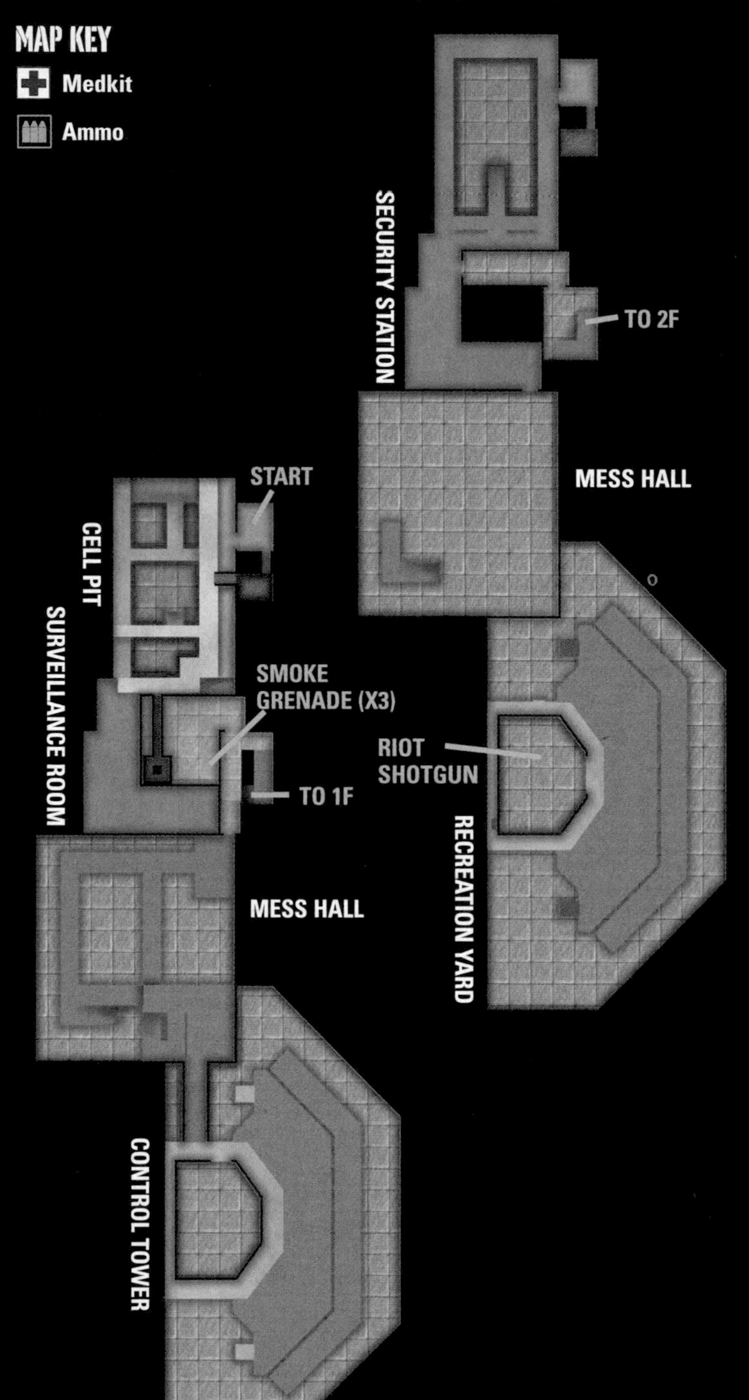

OBJECTIVES

MAIN OBJECTIVES

> (JBA) HELP JAMIE WASHINGTON ESCAPE: Your goal in being imprisoned is to befriend JBA member Jamie Washington and help him escape. By earning his trust and aiding him, you should be able to convince him to lead you to his organization.

> (JBA) HIJACK NEWS HELICOPTER: The news helicopter circling the roof is your ticket out of Ellsworth Penitentiary. Make your way aboard, and hijack it.

PRIMARY OBJECTIVES

> (JBA) RESCUE JAMIE FROM GUARDS: Judging by his last walkie-talkie communication, Jamie has been apprehended by prison guards. Reach his position on the roof, and help him break free.

SECONDARY OBJECTIVES

> (NSA) REACH CENTRAL TOWER WITHOUT ALERTS: To fulfill your role in Jamie's plan to trigger a prison riot, you need to reach the central tower block. Do so without triggering an alert, or you run the risk of being captured and returned to your cell, which puts the entire plan at risk.

> (NSA) AVOID ALL ALERTS: The higher the level of alert, the more likely you are to be prevented from escaping prison. Therefore, extract yourself without raising an alarm and let the chaos of the riot cover your disappearance.

> (NSA) DON'T KILL GUARDS: Fisher has to avoid killing innocent guards. They are not terrorists and are just doing their job preventing him to escape.

> (JBA) OPEN CELLS TO START RIOT: Washington's plan to create a riot depends on you opening the cell doors in the tower block. You must do so, and let the escaping prisoners create cover for your other actions.

Following the death of his daughter Sarah, a despondent and disillusioned Sam Fisher undertakes the mission of a lifetime. His overall objective is to infiltrate the John Brown's Army (JBA), determine their plans for terrorism action in the United States, and sabotage them from within. To do so, he must engender the trust of the terrorists and their leader, Emile Dufraisne. Gaining their trust may require Sam to do horrifying things.

The first step is getting the JBA to let him through the front door. The key is Jamie Washington, a JBA lackey incarcerated in Ellsworth Penitentiary in Kansas. Sam must become Jamie's friend by helping him break out of Ellsworth.

Cell Pit

Sam stands in his cell. Jamie Washington stops outside the door and instructs Sam to sneak inside the prison's central control tower and open the A block cells, helping to stoke a riot that Jamie intends to start.

After Jamie heads off to start a fight, move to the poster on the wall and press the Interact button to tear it away, revealing a tunnel through the wall. Crawl into the tunnel and travel through to the area beyond.

Climb up the vertical pipe to the ceiling, then shimmy to the right. Drop onto the catwalk, and crawl into the open vent.

Emerging from the open vent, Sam can fully view the inmates brawling in the area below. Head to Sam's left along the vent duct. Near the end, follow the snaking vent over to the wall. Press the Interact button to pry the vent cover off the duct. Crawl through into a ventilation junction.

Surveillance Room

Open the trapdoor in the junction's center and drop into the office below. Quietly creep up behind the guard looking out the window, and grab him. Drag him back into the shadows and interrogate him. The guard gives up the code number to the weapon's locker in

To maintain the NBA's trust, Sam cannot kill any of the guards, so press the Secondary Attack button to strangle the man unconscious. Use the computer on the central desk to read e-mails bearing informative clues. Then move to the weapon's locker and input the code 1403 into the keypad to open the door. Pick up the three smoke grenades on the shelf inside the locker.

The exit door has a window, and Sam risks exposure by standing near it. Approach the wall to the window's left and flip the light switch to darken the area so that Sam may pick the lock unseen. This may draw suspicion, so pick the lock quickly.

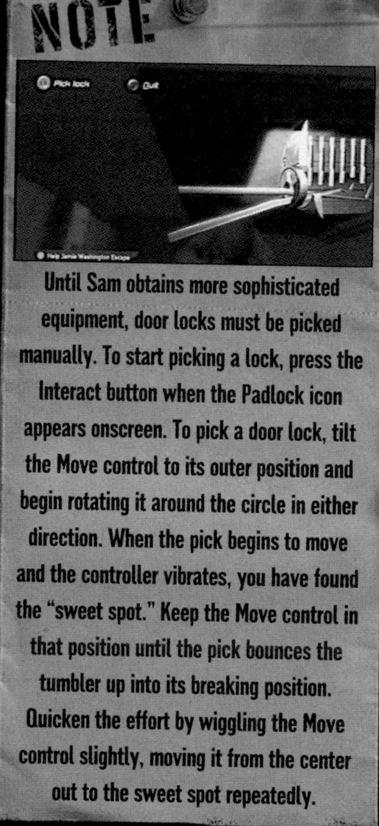

NOTE

Until Sam obtains more sophisticated equipment, door locks must be picked manually. To start picking a lock, press the Interact button when the Padlock icon appears onscreen. To pick a door lock, tilt the Move control to its outer position and begin rotating it around the circle in either direction. When the pick begins to move and the controller vibrates, you have found the "sweet spot." Keep the Move control in that position until the pick bounces the tumbler up into its breaking position. Quicken the effort by wiggling the Move control slightly, moving it from the center out to the sweet spot repeatedly.

Mess Hall

When the door is unlocked, look through the window into the area beyond before proceeding. Make sure that no prison guards are looking through the door on the opposite side of the stairwell prior to opening the door.

If the guards on the balcony in the mess hall become suspicious of the lights being off in the guard station and move in to check it out, retreat to the wall opposite the door and wait for one or both of them to enter. Allow the first guard into the room to move toward the light switch, and grab him from behind. Quickly choke the first guard unconscious in the corner, and then intercept the second guard as he moves for the light switch if necessary. Knock him out with a nonlethal attack delivered from the side or behind.

The Catwalk Route

There are two ways to slip into the mess hall, currently the scene of a shootout between guards and inmates. One method is to take the guard's body from the guard station and carry him toward the sliding security door on the stairwell's upper level. A tracker in the guard's uniform opens the door automatically. Deposit the guard's body in an area where the visibility indicator is green, and then grab and knock out the guards standing near the balcony edge, if they remain. Follow the upper-level catwalk around the room's outer edge. Descend the stairs on the room's far side, and dash for the open doorway in the corner before someone draws a bead on Sam.

The Security Station Route

The alternate path is to descend the stairs outside the guard station and go through the security station. After passing under some windows through which you can see the chaos in the cellblock, use the "Open Door Stealth" option and open the door only far enough to see into the room. Wait a few seconds until a prison guard passes through a metal detector behind the glass dividing the room. Wait for the guard to stand for a moment, then go

To open the glass barrier, enter the code 1403 into the keypad on the wall to the right.

Sneak through the room over to the left side of the metal detector, and hack the security access to deactivate the metal detector. Hide in the dark corner to the left of the hacking point. Wait until the guard comes back through the metal detector, and knock him out.

Turn out the lights in the corridor leading to the mess hall, and pick the lock on the door. Inside the cafeteria, navigate to the back of the room, following the wall to the right. Climb over the serving line counter, and sneak to the room's other corner. Watch the battle in the cafeteria, especially the prison guards' patterns of stepping out from behind cover to shoot. When the guards duck behind cover, sneak out from behind the serving line and head to the open doorway in the corner.

Recreation Yard

After the checkpoint, sneak into the weight-lifting area and hide in the niche to the left of the short staircase. Wait for a guard with a flashlight to descend the stairs. Sneak up behind him and grab him. Drag him behind a bench and quietly choke him unconscious.

Head up the steps and move to the door at the base of the central control tower. No one will be alarmed if you break the lock on the door rather than pick it.

Control Tower

Head upstairs and search the weapon rack to find a riot gun and a pack of additional ammo. This weapon fires a nonlethal round. One shot stuns an opponent, and a second shot knocks them out. However, one shot to the head should knock out a guard instantly. Use the computer on the desk to gain a little knowledge via e-mail, and then head upstairs.

Two high support beams run between the wall and the glass barrier to the left. Jump up to grab either beam and then pull yourself up. This allows you to spy on the guards (if any) inside the cellblock control booth and to formulate your plan

The two guards usually inside the tower should be near the exterior door, and not near the computer, which you can use to open the cell doors. Sneak up to the corner of the stairwell, and move through the shadows to the back corner of the nearby desk. From this vantage point, you can easily toss one or two smoke grenades to prevent the guards from spotting Sam at the computer.

Allow the smoke to fill the room, obscuring the guards' vision; then access the computer. Hack the security access folder to open all the cell doors, thus engendering a little trust with Jamie and the JBA.

After you open the cell doors, the guards are drawn out of the booth. They attempt to shoot the inmates trying to escape. Follow them out to the balcony and knock them unconscious.

Path Choices to the Tower Top

There are three routes to the upper level. The first, and worst, route is going up another level and hacking the elevator's control panel. Then ride the elevator to the upper level, where two prison guards stand ready to gun you down.

Otherwise, climb up the third pipe on the balcony, the one located in the area of heaviest shadows. Hang from the rail's base until the guard typically patrolling the platform moves past. Climb onto the platform behind him, grab him, and quietly choke him unconscious. If the balcony guard is not patrolling, simply sneak up and punch him. At this point, two routes to the level above are available: go up the ladder on the balcony's far side or crawl through the crawlspace under the platform and emerge from a trapdoor in the floor.

If you choose to go through the open vent, navigate through the crawlspace to the end. Open the trapdoor and jump to climb out. Because the trap area is so well lit, you risk detection. We do not recommend this route.

Instead, go up the ladder at the balcony's end. Climb to the upper rung and rotate your view to make sure a guard is not standing nearby or approaching. Then climb onto the platform.

Control Tower Dome

Sneak through the hole smashed in the glass and climb the vertical pipe attached to the wall. Shimmy to the left and climb onto the rooftop platform.

Rooftop

At this time, you should receive a transmission from Jamie. A prison guard has captured him and is escorting him away. You must rescue him from the guard. Quickly but carefully sneak across the narrow gantry to the outer roof edge, and run through the smashed window. A dozen yards ahead, the prison guard is escorting Jamie. If you have any ammo left, knock him out with the riot gun. Otherwise, run halfway over there before crouching and sneaking up behind the guard. Knock him out with a nonlethal attack. If you fail to knock out the guard quickly, Jamie kills him and you fail an objective.

Hijack the Helicopter

A news helicopter refuses to back away from the rooftop. That is your ticket out. Descend the stairs to the roof's lower part and go behind the building beneath the news helicopter. Go inside the building and climb the ladder up to the roof. Move toward the helicopter to escape from Ellsworth Penitentiary.

NYC—JBA HQ 1—Part 1

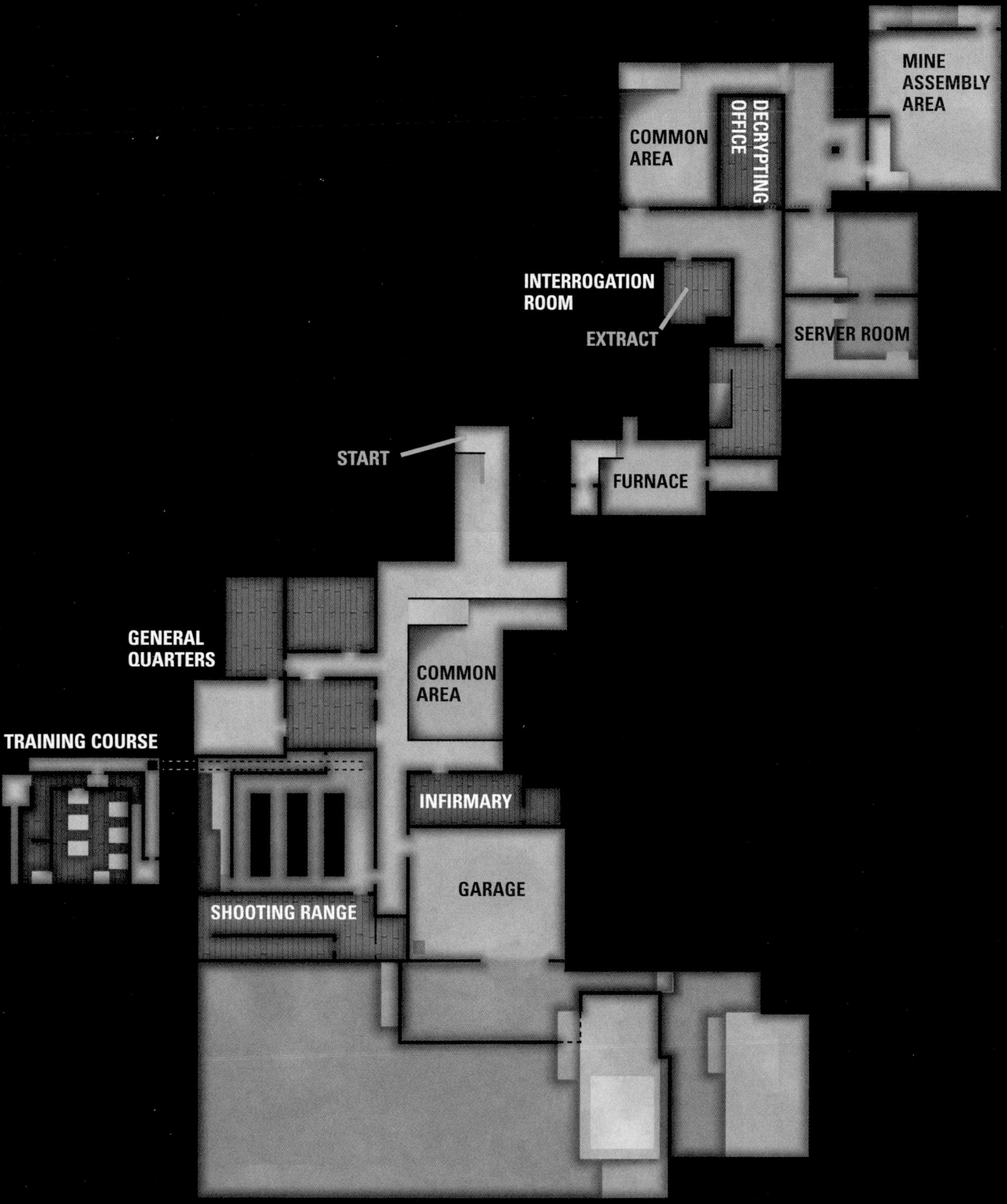

MINE ASSEMBLY AREA

COMMON AREA

DECRYPTING OFFICE

INTERROGATION ROOM

EXTRACT

SERVER ROOM

START

FURNACE

GENERAL QUARTERS

COMMON AREA

TRAINING COURSE

INFIRMARY

GARAGE

SHOOTING RANGE

OBJECTIVES

PRIMARY OBJECTIVES

> (JBA) COMPLETE TRAINING COURSE: Practice your skill at safecracking in the JBA's training area. The skill will no doubt come in handy, both for the JBA and your true mission. To reach the practice safe, you will need to cross the obstacle course successfully. The course is comprised of various challenges. Failing at one challenge will prevent you from continuing, and you will have to backtrack in order to restart.

> (NSA) UPLOAD TROJAN TO JBA SERVER: We need a backdoor into the JBA's servers. Load the Trojan horse application we've sent you onto their main computer network, and we'll be able to tap into their files.

> (NSA) BUG ANTENNA ON THE ROOF: It is vital that we be able to tap into the JBA communications network. Climb up to the roof and plant a listening transceiver on the main communication antenna. This will let us eavesdrop at will.

SECONDARY OBJECTIVES

> (JBA) PRACTICE AT FIRING RANGE: Improve your skills with firearms on the JBA's firing range.

PROFILE OBJECTIVES

> (NSA) GET JBA MEMBER MEDICAL FILES: To complete the agency profiles on the core of the JBA, you're going to need to access their medical profiles and pass that information along. The more we know about them, the better prepared we are to stop them.

> (NSA) GET PROFESSIONAL BACKGROUND INFO: In order to complete the NSA dossiers on the various core members of the JBA, we need you to get data on the group's activities and their roles in it. Uploading this information will help us create a more accurate prediction mode for what they might do next—and will help us plan to stop it.

After helping Jamie Washington escape from Ellsworth Penitentiary, Sam and Jamie fly the stolen helicopter to the JBA's headquarters in New York City. All of the JBA members are immediately skeptical of Sam and his membership in the JBA. While attempting to gain the loyalty of the JBA core members, Sam must also find an opportunity to install surveillance devices and software in the compound so that the NSA can get a lock on the terrorists. One such opportunity arises when thickheaded Carson Moss gives Sam far too much time to complete a simple infiltration training course. However, if Sam is spotted in any of the restricted areas inside the headquarters, the JBA may become suspicious of him. If the JBA Trust meter drops to zero, the mission is over!

Common Area

Jamie stands at the top of the stairs. Follow Jamie into the common area. If Jamie turns around and Sam is not right behind him, trust is lost. Lose too much trust during this mission, and the entire operation is aborted.

Jamie introduces Sam to Carson Moss, the moose-faced security head of the JBA. After exchanging pleasantries, follow Jamie into the general quarters. Moss follows and orders Sam to follow him to the training course.

Training Course

Moss leads Sam past the rifle range to the training course. He orders Sam to navigate through the training course and crack the safe located at the course's end. He gives Sam 17 minutes to complete the course and crack the safe. A 17-minute timer appears onscreen. Moss returns to the training area approximately 10 seconds before the timer elapses. If Sam is not in the training area at that time, the JBA loses major trust in him.

Follow the passage around the corner. Crouch and move under a laser sensor, then momentarily wait for the lower portion of the sensor array to deactivate before proceeding.

Around the corner to the left is a locked door. Rather than pick the lock, climb the vertical pipe attached to the wall. Then climb along the horizontal ceiling pipe into the next area. Continue climbing past a horizontal array of sensors near the floor, then drop to the ground next to the exit and go around the corner to the right. If you touch a sensor, a gate closes and you must backtrack to find another way around.

Climb up the ladder. Stand upright and move out onto the thin ledge. Slide to the left across the thin ledge, and then rappel down to an opening on the lower level.

Drop through the opening and turn right. Squeeze into the narrow gap and continue moving forward until you emerge from the narrow space. Head around the corner to the left and grab a rope. Climb up the rope to a suspended platform. Move to the platform's other end and rappel over the side. Climb down the wall until past the first sensor. Then watch the lower sensor move back and forth. As it moves away from directly beneath Sam, press the Jump button to rappel down the wall quickly.

After detaching from the rope at the bottom, head around the corner to the right. Stop at the first obstacle and check out the motion sensors. If the bottom motion sensor is close, crouch and follow it down the passage. If the upper motion sensor is closer, climb onto the upper surface and follow the laser down the passage. When you reach the middle, drop or jump to the other level. Then continue to the end.

Go around the corner to the left and watch the laser sensor moving across the top of the area. Wait until it is some distance away, and then climb on top of the first obstacle. Drop down on the other side and wait for the laser sensor to pass overhead if necessary. Then climb over the next obstacle, and the next, until clear.

NOTE

Head around the corner to the right and go up the steps to find the safe. Crack the safe using Sam's OPSAT. Leave the safe door open to show Moss your handiwork later. Then turn around and go through the door.

Cracking a combination safe is similar to picking a lock. Press the Interact button to start cracking the safe. Sam's OPSAT watch displays a 3-D rendering of the combination lock's inner workings. Tilt the Move control to the outer edge, and then rotate it clockwise repeatedly until the largest disc begins to rotate. Reduce your rotation speed as the niche in the largest disc approaches the pin at the top. When the first green light comes on and the safe makes an audible click, stop rotating the Move control.

Now start rotating the Move control counterclockwise, until the second disc begins to rotate. Align the middle disc's niche with the pin, and then rotate the Move control clockwise again to turn the smallest disc into place.

Exit the Training Area

Follow the short passage to a ladder, and climb up through the floor vent to return to your starting point. Check the onscreen timer to see how much time is remaining, and determine how many more objectives you can fulfill inside the JBA HQ. Although the shooting range is near the training course, improving your shooting range score is probably the last objective you should try to complete.

Infirmary

Head out to the main area. To your right is the infirmary, and inside is Enrica Villablanca. After meeting her, you must leave the infirmary; then Enrica goes through the door in the corner. Allow her to go into the side room and close the door behind her. Then reenter the infirmary and turn out the lights using the switch by the entrance. Slowly move to the door through which Enrica exited.

Pick the lock on the door and slowly go inside. Enrica sits at the desk to the left, humming a pretty tune. Avoid making any noise inside the room; if she spots Sam, trust will be lost—if the mission doesn't fail entirely. Close the door behind you to avoid someone else outside spotting you inside the restricted area. Quietly move across the tiny office to the other desk in the room. Open the file drawer to retrieve the medical records of all five core JBA members. Then use the computer on the same desk and hack the security access to open a very special e-mail that contains the code to the server room door: 6278.

Use your optic cable to survey the infirmary, then go back outside. Close the door behind you, and leave the infirmary.

Roof

After Sam exits the infirmary, climb the ladder to the right, which leads to the uppermost interior level. On the catwalk's opposite side stand two technicians, laughing. Wait until they both turn to face the wall, and then start heading to Sam's right. Go around the catwalk toward the two guys. At the corner, angle your view downward to make sure no one walking below can spot Sam. Then continue walking toward the two guys, and divert to the right into a circular tunnel.

Climb the ladder at the tunnel's end. Stop on the ladder's top rung and angle your camera to see the man seated on a pile of sandbags just a few feet away. Wait for him to rise and walk off to the right, and then climb up onto the roof.

Turn to Sam's right and follow the man toward the back of the roof. The man stops at the back corner of a skylight. Wait behind the crates until he heads to the right before entering the fenced area on the left, where the communications tower is situated. On

the back side of the tower is a breaker panel. Use your lock pick to open the panel door. Then hack the hardware on the panel to install the bug.

Continue hiding by the breaker panel until the patrolling man passes around again. As he heads away from the entrance of the fenced area, head out to the roof's main portion. Just outside the entrance of the fenced area is a small hatch. Open the hatch and climb down the ladder until you reach a broken part, and then drop to the floor.

Server Room

Climb down to the main floor, and then descend the stairs to the lounge area. To get into the decrypting office with the computer, which is optional, head through the doorway on the right, follow the corridor, and go through the next doorway on the left. The computer in this room contains several important e-mails with vital information for all lower-level JBA members, such as Sam. The corridor beyond this room leads to the furnace, and not much else.

Return to the lounge and head down the hallway across from the stairs. This passage leads to the barred door blocking access to the server room area. Move over to the keypad on the barred door's left side. Wait for a man inside the restricted area to approach the bars, and then turn and walk away. Input the code 6278 into the keypad to open the bars.

Stop behind the partition and wait for the man walking around the room to look in the other direction. Then crouch and quickly creep over to the platform in the corner. Jump up to grab a pipe over the platform, and pull Sam's legs up. The Visibility meter should turn green, allowing Sam to shimmy across the room.

When Sam is positioned above the server room door, Washington emerges from the server room, arguing with another man inside. Wait until he finishes and walks out of the area. Watch the man moving around the room. When he moves far enough away that he won't hear you, drop from the pipe to the left side of the server room door, where the surveillance camera above the door cannot turn.

Stan Dayton argues on the phone inside the server room. While he is talking, quickly move across the room and up the stairs onto a platform. To the left is a trapdoor in the platform. Open the trapdoor, drop through, and crouch.

Move under the platform to the corner, and then head to the right. Find a second hole at the far end, and stand up through it. Jump to climb out of the hole, and quietly move to the server access point.

Hack the access point using your hacking device. If successful, Sam uploads the spyware to the JBA's server.

Dayton's activity data is located in the small filing cabinet next to his desk. You must draw him away from his desk for Sam to have access to the file. Sam has to play a kind of joke on Dayton to accomplish this. Drop through the trapdoor and navigate back to the other side of the server room. Climb out of the trapdoor by the stairs. Equip the ultrasonic emitter and aim at the door. Fire a sound transceiver toward the door, and then holster the emitter and press your back to the wall. Dayton rises from his desk in the corner and goes over to the door. As soon as he passes Sam's position, head over to his desk and open the file drawer. After collecting Dayton's activity data, drop through the trapdoor behind the server access point. Then navigate under the floor back to the trapdoor by the stairs, and leave the server room the way you came in. Avoid the security camera outside the door by exiting quickly as the camera turns to the right.

Shooting Range

Depending on how much time remains, you can explore the rest of the compound or try to set the high score at the shooting range. To find the practice range, return to the training course area.

A sniper rifle is set up on the range. Press the Interact button to take hold of it. Aiming through the scope, try to shoot the moving targets at the room's far end. Hold the Secondary Fire button to hold your breath and steady your aim for brief periods.

Hitting the target on the outer ring scores one point, hitting it on the inner ring scores three points, and hitting a bull's-eye scores five points. Three scoreboards are posted above the target area. The one to the left is your top score, the middle is your current score, and the one to the right is the score you must beat to complete your objective.

Score better than 75 points to complete the firing range practice objective. If you have to reload, your score resets to zero. Completing the firing range objective can help regain trust lost by being spotted in restricted areas.

Interrogation Room

No matter what objectives you complete or fail to complete, make sure you're standing outside the training area entrance at least 20 seconds before the timer elapses. Moss returns to the training area roughly 10 seconds before time is up. If he does not see Sam standing under the big plasma screen mounted on the wall, and if the safe is not cracked, then trust is lost.

Moss orders Sam to follow him. Stay behind Moss as he heads out to the main area, goes downstairs, and stops outside the interrogation room. Inside the room is a bound and savagely beaten Cole Yeagher, the pilot of the helicopter Sam and Jamie hijacked to escape Ellsworth. JBA leader Emile Dufraisne is also in the room, and by way of initiation he wants Sam to execute the poor civilian.

Next thing you know, you stand there with gun in hand, crosshairs trained on Yeagher. Will you shoot an innocent man in order to gain Emile's trust? Or will you stall until a minute elapses, at which point Moss gets impatient and takes care of the poor guy himself? Let the Trust meter be your guide and please the faction that trusts you the least at this point.

Sea of Okhotsk—Ice Floe

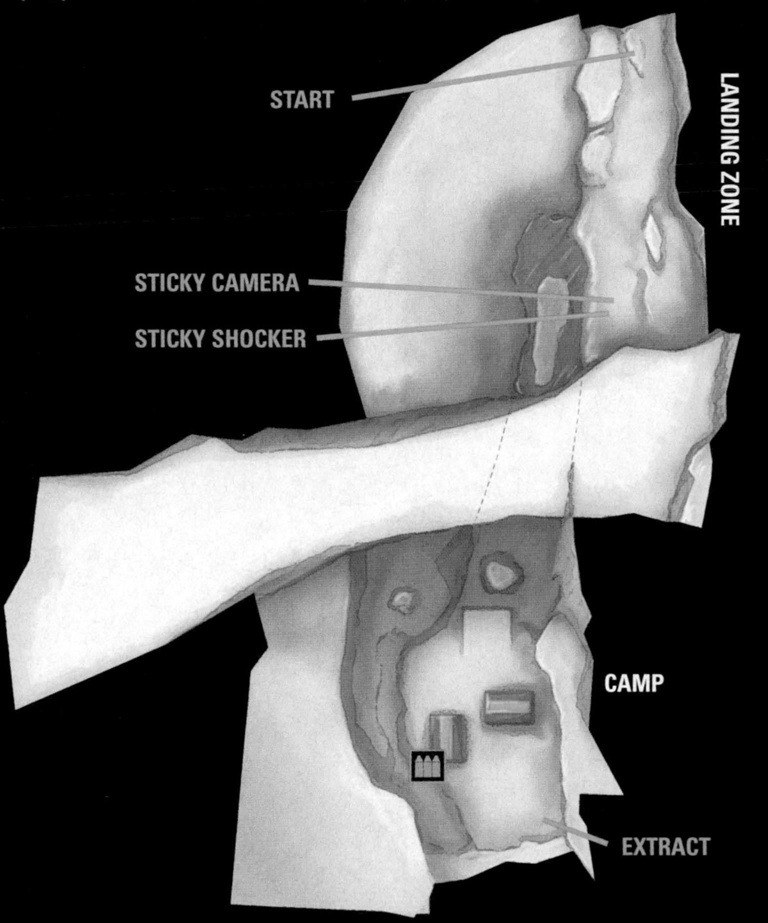

LOADOUT: SEA OF OKHOTSK

AVAILABLE WEAPONS
SC-20K/60
Shotgun attachment/8
SC pistol/40
Airfoil round/2
Frag grenade/2
Flash grenade/3
Sonic grenade/3
Smoke grenade/3
Gas grenade/3
EMP grenade/3
Wall mine/3
Wall mine—stun/3
Wall mine—flash/3
Ultrasonic emitter

OBJECTIVES

ASSIGNMENT

> (JBA) CAPTURE THE SUPERTANKER: Your objective is to take control of the iced-in Russian supertanker *Rublev*. Once you have achieved control of it, you will be told what to do next.

PRIMARY OBJECTIVES

> (JBA) RETRIEVE EQUIPMENT: In order to accomplish your tasks on the *Rublev*, you will need to obtain the equipment that landed on the ice. Get it and you'll be able to start your operation properly.

> (JBA) USE DETONATORS TO BLOW THE ICE WALL: In order to reach the supertanker, you will need to get past the ice wall blocking the way. The crew of the *Rublev* is using explosives to free the ship; you might be able to use some of their detonators to your advantage.

SECONDARY OBJECTIVES

> (JBA) REACH THE *RUBLEV* WITHOUT ALERTS: The first step in taking over the *Rublev* is getting on board without being detected. It is critical to the success of this operation that nobody from the *Rublev* raise a general alarm.

To prove his loyalty to the JBA, Sam parachutes out of a plane over the sea of Okhotsk, Russia. His objective is to board a Russian tanker, the RSS *Rublev*, neutralize the crew, and take control of the ship. But first he must navigate overland to the point where the *Rublev* is trapped in ice. Moving in broad daylight, Sam must employ tactics never before utilized by splinter cell operatives to survive.

Faulty Chute

Sam jumps from the airplane at high altitude. As he descends, press the Interact, Jump, Crouch, and Equip buttons to perform flips in various directions. Tilt the Move control downward to slow Sam's descent, and tilt it upward to increase speed. When the Parachute icon is displayed in the screen's middle, press the Interact button to deploy Sam's chute.

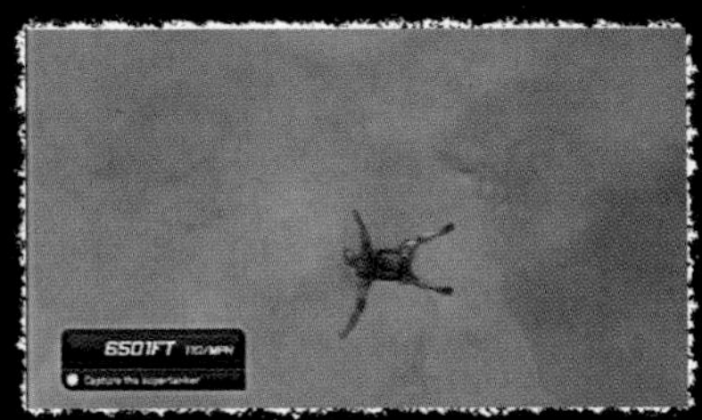

Sam's main chute fails to deploy properly. He must cut himself loose from the tangle. When he is ready, use the Move control to gently guide Sam's left hand onto the emergency chute release. When the Parachute icon appears, press the Interact button to deploy Sam's emergency chute.

Landing Zone

Sam's gear lands several dozen yards away. Unfortunately, a helicopter drops off two mercenaries from the *Rublev*, who find his gear and then begin searching the area.

As soon as you have control of Sam, drop over the side of the raised landing area and move forward. Crouch and hide behind a small ledge at the top of a slope, as shown in the screenshot:

Wait patiently until one of the guards approaches your position. He comes within 10 yards, then turns and moves to the left. Slide down the slope to the left with your back against the wall. Stop under a dark-colored section of the ledge. Wait until the mercenary stops at the top of the wall, and then heads off to the right. Slide along the wall behind him. As he moves away from your ridge, detach from the icy wall and follow him out to a cliff's edge. Sneak up behind him and grab him. Drag him to the left and hide behind a large icy rock face so that the remaining merc cannot see. Then you may interrogate the merc before choking him unconscious.

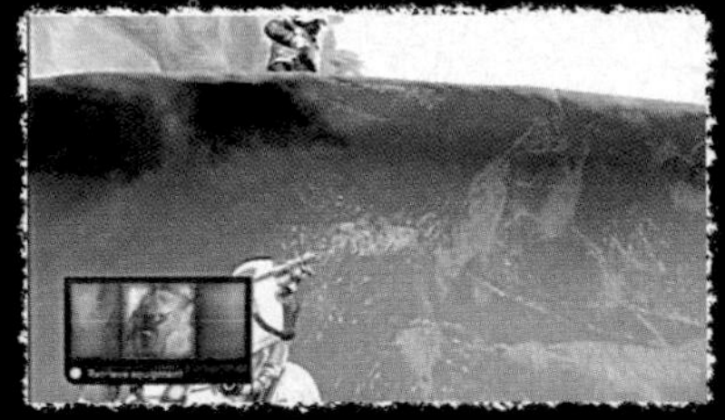

The second merc is just on the other side of the large rock face. Pursue him as he walks back toward the box containing Sam's additional equipment. When he stops, perform a nonlethal or lethal attack to take him out.

Pick up the two sticky cameras and two sticky shockers lying around the equipment box. Then move to the cliff's edge and dive into the waters.

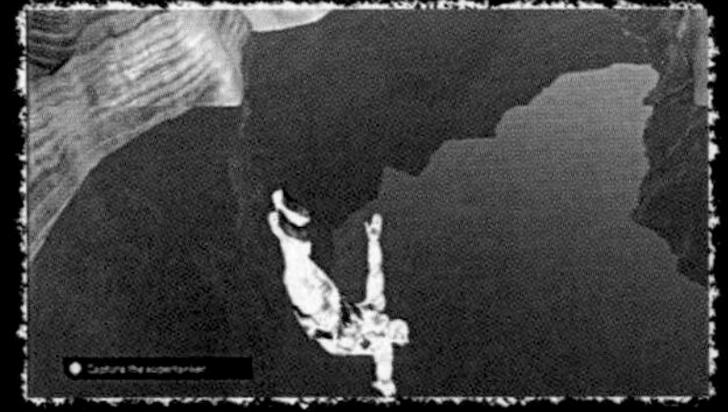

Camp

Under the surface, turn to Sam's left and swim through an underwater cave. Upon emerging, look for a thin patch of ice overhead. Swim up to this thin patch and grab the mercenary standing on it. Pull him down into the water for an icy death.

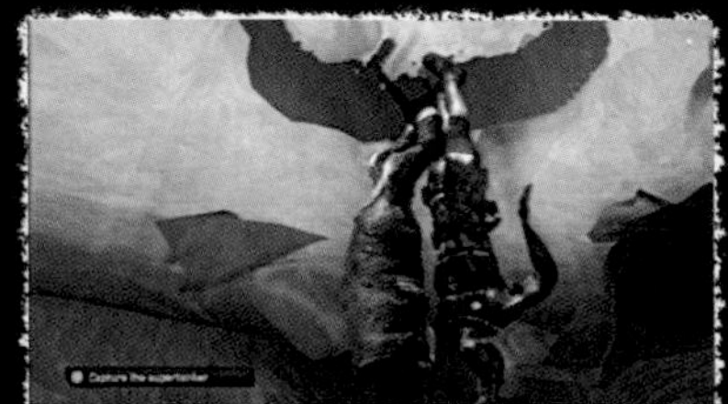

Do not surface here. Instead, swim through another cave to Sam's right into a large lake area. You may surface in the lake to view the mercenary camp area, but you cannot climb out onto land.

Swim toward the camp, diving to swim under the ice. Find the next-closest patch of thin ice, where yet another unsuspecting merc stands. Smash through the ice and drag him into the depths for a meeting with your knife. Surface through the hole you created, and you'll quickly determine that this is not an opportune spot. Instead, dive underwater and continue swimming to the next small hole in the ice. Surface there.

The Mercenary Base

Sam is behind a hastily constructed shelter that houses equipment. On the shelter's other side is another merc, warming himself by a bonfire. He is your next target.

Carefully head around the outer wall of the shelter. From there, sneak over to the lake's edge. Follow the water's edge until you wind up behind the merc standing by the bonfire. Grab him and drag him behind the boxes to either side, and then choke him unconscious.

Inside the shelter is a laptop where you may read some e-mails containing highly informative info regarding the *Rublev*. A box of SC-20K ammo sits on the stack of crates near the bonfire.

Prepare for Explosion

Near the self-warming merc's position is the detonator control panel for some explosive charges the mercs have set on an ice wall blocking access to the supertanker. But the mercs have been twiddling their thumbs, and now Sam must blow it up.

Leave the detonator alone for the moment and head into the tent to the right. Locate more SC-20K ammunition sitting on the table's far end. Exit the tent the way you came in, and go into the other tent. A merc is sleeping on the rear cot. Move up beside the dozing man and press the Nonlethal Attack button to knock him unconscious. This prevents him from rising when the charges go off.

Now return to the detonator control panel and hack the security access folder. Detonate the charges on the ice wall. The remaining two mercenaries are killed in the blast.

Head to the blast site. Slip into the newly revealed pond and descend.

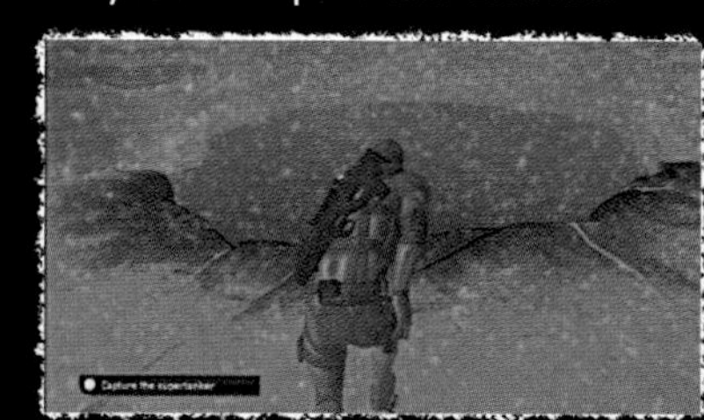

Sea of Okhotsk—RSS *Rublev*

MAP KEY

SC-20K Ammo

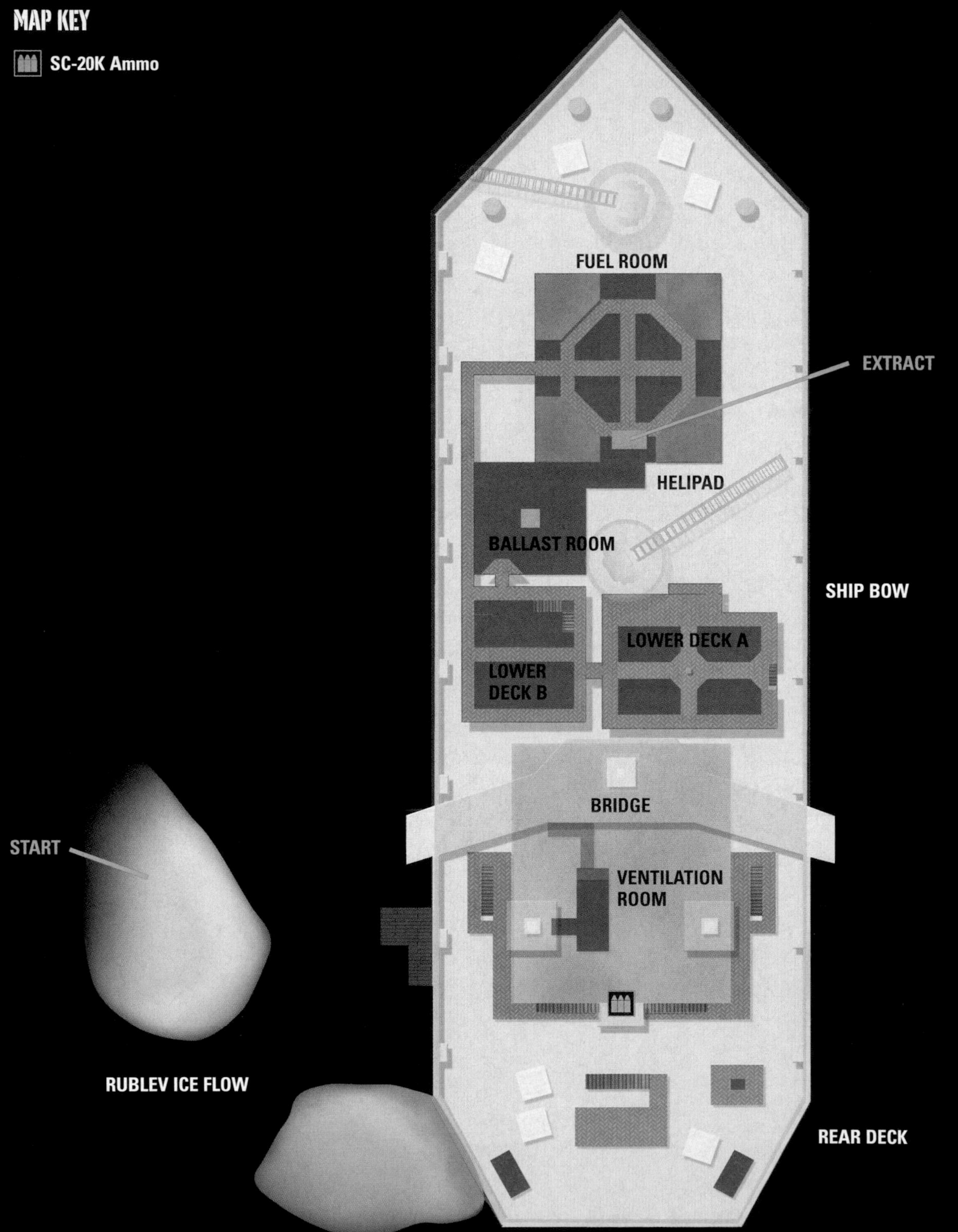

OBJECTIVES

ASSIGNMENT

> CAPTURE THE SUPERTANKER: Your objective is to take control of the iced-in Russian supertanker *Rublev*. Once you have achieved control of it, you will be told what to do next.

> (JBA) DISABLE THE SUPERTANKER'S CREW: In order to secure the *Rublev*, you will have to reduce its crew of mercenaries, by either killing or disabling a significant number of them.

> (JBA) SEIZE THE SUPERTANKER: Your objective is to seize control of the tanker *Rublev*. In order to do so, you will need to subdue the ship's captain at all costs, as he is threatening to blow up the ship to prevent its capture.

> (JBA) REACH THE LANDING PAD FOR EXTRACTION: Massoud's team is on its way to take over this operation. You are no longer needed on board the *Rublev*, and are free to extract. A helicopter is waiting for you on the ship's landing pad. Reach it to extract from the supertanker.

PRIMARY OBJECTIVES

> TAKE OUT BRIDGE CREW: At this point, the entire crew is expendable, including the crew on the bridge. You could use fentanyl on the ventilation system to gas the bridge and disable the crew located there.

> CONTACT LAMBERT: It is vital that Lambert knows what you are doing. Contact him so that he is aware of your position and actions.

SECONDARY OBJECTIVES

> SEIZE THE *RUBLEV* WITHOUT ALERTS: If possible, seize the *Rublev* without triggering a general alert. This will make it easier for you to deal with the guards and crew, as they will be unaware of your presence until it is too late.

> DISABLE COMMUNICATIONS: Disable the ship's communications in order to keep them from calling for help. No one can know that the *Rublev* has been taken, or they just might come looking for it.

After detonating the ice wall, Sam swims into the area surrounding the icebound supertanker. Sam must board the RSS *Rublev* and cut off the ship's communications. Then he must neutralize the crew one by one.

Rublev Ice Flow

Swim upward until Sam is directly under two conversing mercenaries. Wait until one man starts to walk off, then smash through the ice and drag the remaining man into the water and quickly stab him. This draws the remaining merc's suspicion, so swim away from the hole you created. Activate thermo vision and swim under the ice. Follow the suspicious guard over to another thin patch, and smash through to drag him into the depths.

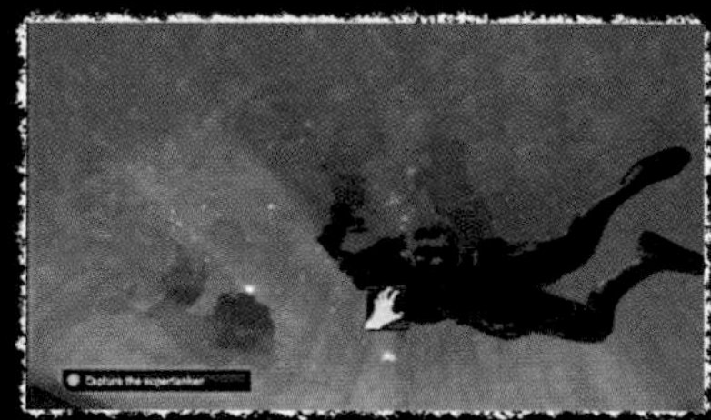

Surface through one of the holes you created. The icebound RSS *Rublev* is visible in the distance. Slip into the icy lake surrounding the tanker, and swim over to a pontoon boat anchored not far away. Steal up to the boat's side and grab the occupant. Sam drags the man into the water and snaps his neck.

There are two ways to board the supertanker: swim over to the dock and use the remote control to lower the crane-operated boat, or swim to the ship's stern and climb up the rope. This guide describes how to infiltrate the ship by using the crane-operated boat.

Once on board, you must neutralize every crew member to please Moss and fulfill your JBA objectives.

Cleaning the Rear Deck: Port to Stern

Board the small boat and press the button on the remote to raise the crane up to the ship's deck level. Run onto the deck and hide behind the nearest boxes. Use thermo vision to locate the two mercenaries arguing a few yards away. When they finish their spat and resume their patrol routes, follow the merc who patrols the deck level. Stay underneath the platform so the merc overhead does not spot you. Slip through the narrow space between the wall and the tanks. Grab the merc and drag him back under the platform. Interrogate him to find out a little about the ship's captain, and then strangle the guy unconscious.

Position Sam under the platform's back corner. Jump to grab the ledge, and wait there until the merc patrolling the upper level moves near and stops, staring over the ship's side. Then climb over the rail and sneak up behind the stationary guard on the platform. Knock him unconscious.

TIP

The weather is taking a turn for the worse. However, Sam can use the occasional flurries to his advantage. When the snow falls more heavily, visibility is greatly reduced. Try to time every movement to changes in the weather so that Sam is moving under minimal visibility conditions. Whenever the wind and snow increase, the mercs brace themselves against the wind, hunkering down and raising their hands against the cold. In this position, mercs are virtually blind.

Cleaning Time: The Stern

Move to the rear corner of the upper level. Use thermo vision if necessary to watch the center of the rear deck. Locate a merc who climbs up and down a set of stairs to a launch platform. When the merc heads up the stairs, climb over the rail and drop back to the deck.

Activate the Quick OPSAT map to help you locate a man who wanders between the equipment and boxes on the rear deck. Sneak up behind him and grab him. Drag him behind the big red anchor winch on the boat's port side.

When the weather kicks up next, head toward the rear deck's raised central platform. Stop behind the barrels at the bottom of the stairs leading up to a central platform. Wait for the man from the platform to descend the stairs. As he moves off the stairs and turns away, sneak up and grab him. Drag him back to your hiding place and strangle him unconscious.

CAUTION

The panels on the central platform control the launch moored to the inclined rails. Avoid releasing the launch or an alert is raised.

Clearing the Stern

At this point, you can do nothing about the two mercs patrolling the starboard side of the rear deck's lower level because another mercenary patrols the upper deck and keeps a good eye on the area below. Therefore, it is time to take out the guard on the upper deck. From the base of the raised central platform, head port side toward a lookout tower with a spotlight. Grab the rope hanging from this tower and climb to the top.

Wait for visibility conditions to diminish, and then jump up to grab the line running from the lookout tower over to the wall of the upper deck. Sam zip-lines over to the wall and grabs a horizontal pipe. Wait until the weather clouds up again if necessary, and then shimmy to the right and around the corner. Drop on top of a green crate at the corner, where a pack of SC-20K ammunition sits.

Move to the center of this balcony and crouch to avoid being seen by the mercs below. Equip the SC-20K and a sticky shocker. When the guard patrolling the upper level moves toward the far corner of his platform, hit him with a sticky shocker.

The next time visibility diminishes, climb over the railing and drop onto the roof of a small piece of machinery below your position. Drop to the lower deck and move under the central platform, squeezing through the narrow gap. Head to the end of the launch rails and around the barrel to the left. Sneak up behind a merc wearing a hood and patrolling the ship's rear portion. Grab him and drag him behind the boxes stacked under the launch craft before knocking him out. Hide behind the boxes under the launch craft.

Wait for the guard patrolling a

large circle around the lower deck to stop nearby, and then turn and start walking away. Exit your hiding spot and sneak up behind him. Leave his body someplace discreet.

When visibility is cloudy, head

toward the raised levels of the rear deck. Ascend the stairs to the starboard side of the upper levels, and head around the corner toward the three-tier stairwell. A mercenary patrols all three levels, and you must modify your strategy to adapt to what he is doing. Rather than sneak up behind him, try taking him out with a well-placed airfoil round.

Cut Off Communications

Climb back to the rear starboard upper level, where a merc formerly patrolled. Use the vertical pipe fastened to the tower's side to climb to the uppermost levels. Stay close to the wall as a merc above, identifying himself as Andrejz, takes a call. As he turns away, jump to grab the ledge and climb over the rail. Sneak up behind Andrejz and knock him unconscious.

Enrica radios Sam and orders him to find the ventilation system and toss in a fentanyl gas grenade to kill the crew. First, head to the front of the top deck and climb the ladder to the communications tower. Pick the lock on the breaker panel and hack the security access in order to inform Lambert what's going on. Exit the computer screen after hacking the security access in order to communicate with Lambert. Lambert doesn't seem too worried about a few dead mercenaries. After the conversation, access the panel again and cut off all communications.

Ventilation Room

Grab the zip-line on the communications tower and slide down to a raised level with a floor hatch. Open the hatch and climb down a rope into the ventilation system. Go through the opening into the next room. Press the Interact button to toss a lethal fentanyl gas grenade into the vent. The entire bridge crew soon falls dead.

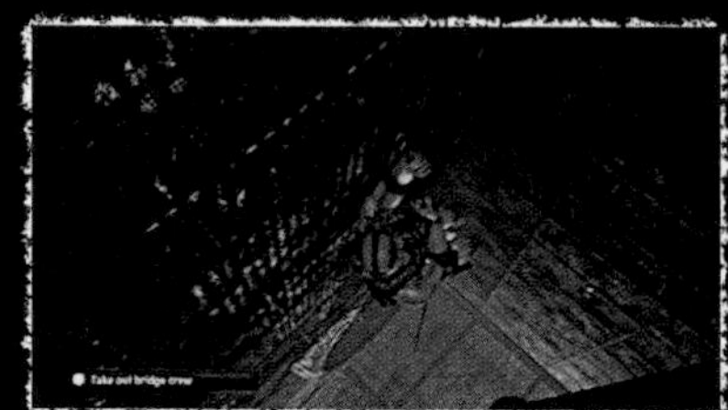

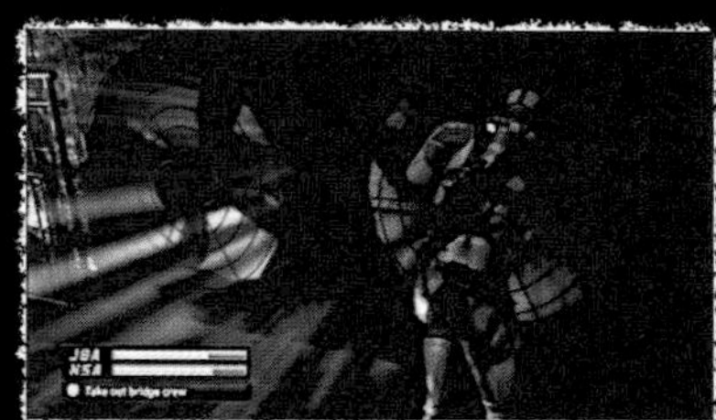

Turn left and move toward the only active fan. Jump to grab the ledge above the fan, and climb up. Crawl through an open vent duct. The duct emerges outside, near one entrance to the bridge. The crew's dead bodies are visible inside. Use the computer inside the bridge to read e-mails (optional).

Ship Bow

Across from the door to the bridge is a vertical pipe. Climb down the pipe to a small ledge, and drop from there to a stairwell's upper platform. The belligerent captain orders the crew to move the cargo container blocking off the bow of the ship.

Descend to the deck and hide behind the small crane with a yellow arm. Wait a long time for the mercenary patrolling the ship's port side to appear. merc and interrogate him to find out what the captain is doing belowdecks. Leave his unconscious or dead body behind the big oil tank.

Behind the large oil tank, a series of black mesh nets prevents the guard in the high central tower from seeing anyone walking underneath. Stay close to the pipes on the right, and move forward to the base of a staircase covered with a tarp. Cut through the tarp and move into the area under the stairs.

Stay under the stairs, close to the pipes on the right, until the two remaining guards finish their conversation. Then check the 3-D map on your OPSAT watch to determine when the merc watching from the tower is facing the area behind the direction Sam is moving. Then cut the canvas on the other side of the stairs. Sneak into an open cargo container to find a pack of SC-20K ammo.

Retreat through the cargo container and under the covered stairs to the area under the black mesh behind the deck fuel tank. Find a clear shot at the tower, and prepare the SC-20K. When the guard on the tower comes into view, fire a sticky shocker to take him out.

"Last Man Standing"

Ascend to the raised platform and sneak toward the ship's starboard side. Use the OPSAT watch's map to get a fix on the last merc patrolling on the ship's starboard side. Stay hidden behind one of the red control stations on the platform near either of the starboard side stairs until the merc passes, and then sneak up behind him and knock him out.

Lower Deck A

Find an open deck hatch on the ship's starboard side, and climb down into the hull. Head to the other end of the venting area and go through the sliding hatch on the left.

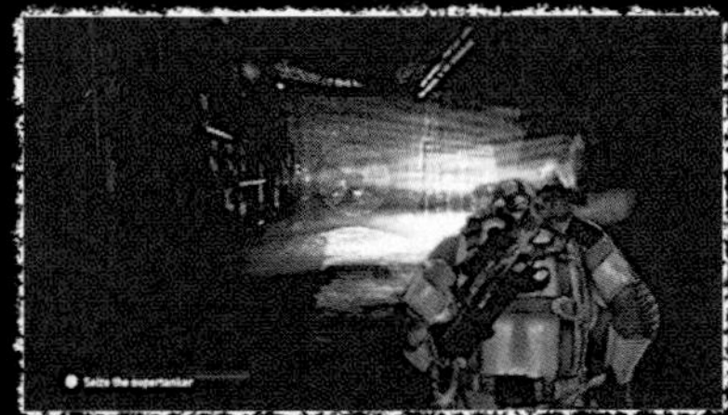

Turn to Sam's left and follow the chain-link fence to the corner. Stop in an area where the visibility meter is green; this allows you to spot a technician working at control panels near the back of the turbine room. When the tech starts to move down the center aisle, sneak up behind him and knock him out.

Lower Deck B

Climb down the ladder in the room's center. Toward the ship's bow is a sliding hatch. Proceed through the short passage beyond the hatch into a two-level room where two crew members are arguing in a panic. Slide the hatch closed behind you and head behind the boiler to the right. Stop behind the boiler and wait for a mechanic with a flashlight to enter the area. Maneuver behind him and grab him. Quietly choke him unconscious to avoid alerting the man still overhead.

A vertical pipe attached to the wall in this area allows Sam to climb up to the catwalk. Climb over the rail and sneak up behind the man patrolling the upper level. Take him out.

Ballast Room and Fuel Room

Cross the catwalk to the room's other side. Go through the sliding hatch in the corner and descend a long slope. Turn right at the corner to spot the captain, searching the fuel room with a flare. If he sees Sam, he drops the flare into the fuel below, destroying the tanker and abruptly ending the game. One solution is to shoot him in the head and just hope the flare doesn't fall into the fuel. The nonlethal variation involves shooting him with an airfoil round. Even if the airfoil round hits him in the head, he won't be knocked out. Quickly run up and perform a nonlethal attack to knock him out. Otherwise, following Enrica's suggestion to sneak up behind him is fairly impossible.

Helipad

Head toward a ladder near the wall. Climb up the ladder to a platform, and continue climbing up a second ladder until Sam reaches a trapdoor. Open the trapdoor to emerge on the helicopter pad on the deck. Soon a helicopter appears. Grab the helicopter's rope and start climbing up to extract.

Shanghai—Hotel

MAP KEY

SC Pistol Ammo

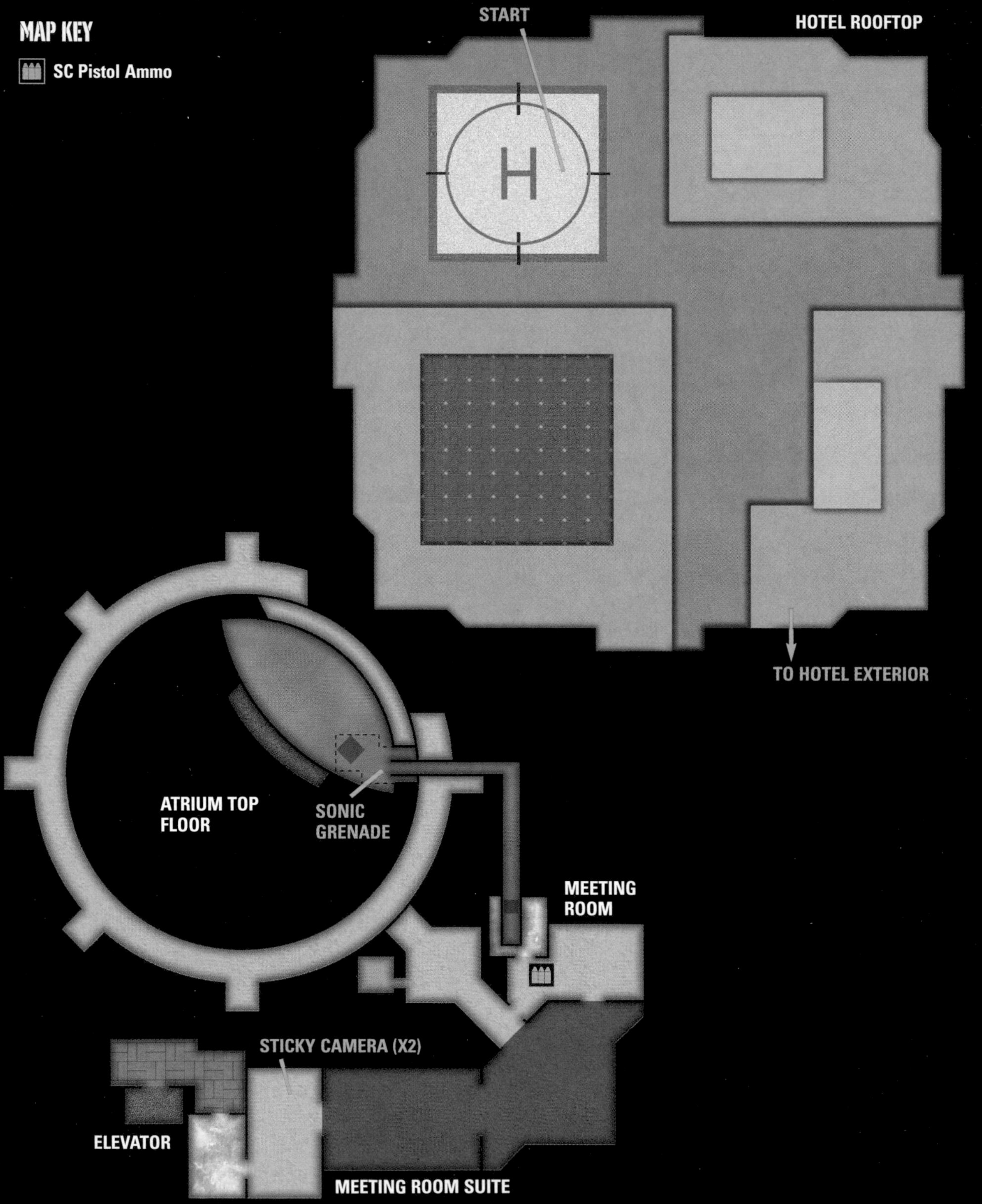

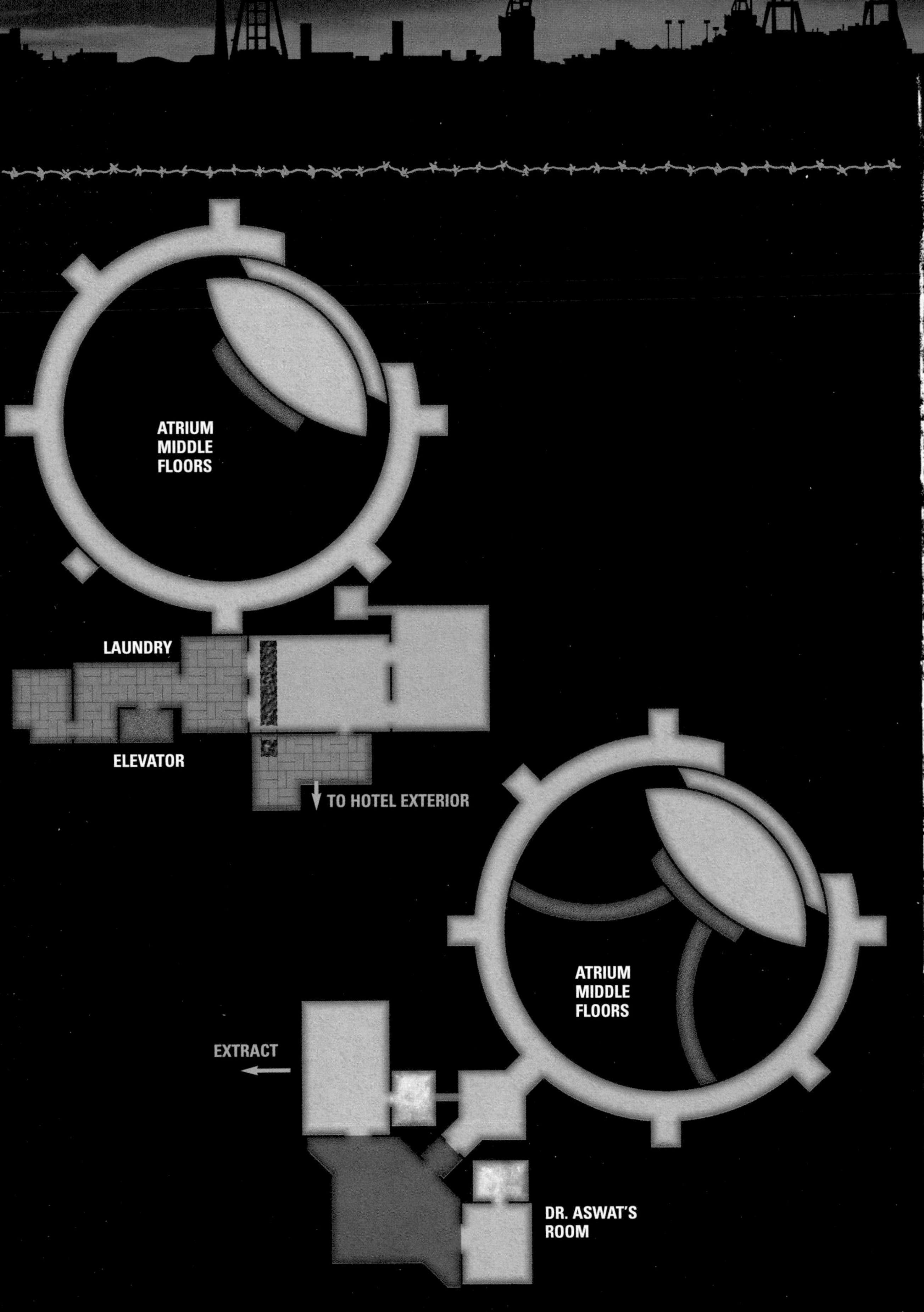
ATRIUM
MIDDLE
FLOORS
LAUNDRY
ELEVATOR
TO HOTEL EXTERIOR
ATRIUM
MIDDLE
FLOORS
EXTRACT
DR. ASWAT'S
ROOM

OBJECTIVES

ASSIGNMENT

> (JBA) REACH ASWAT'S ROOM 2406: The information we need is in Dr. Aswat's hotel suite. Infiltrate his bedroom in order to be in a position to get the data.

> (JBA) EXTRACT VIA EMILE'S HELICOPTER: Emile is waiting for you aboard the JBA's helicopter. Reach it to extract from the hotel.

PRIMARY OBJECTIVES

> (NSA) RECORD THE SECRET MEETING: It is vital that we learn what Dr. Aswat is discussing with Emile. Aswat is suspected of selling Pakistani nuclear secrets, and if he's talking to Dufraisne, that could mean big trouble.

> (NSA) INFILTRATE HOTEL: A helicopter belonging to Dr. Aswat's security forces is patrolling the outside of the hotel, looking for intruders. Avoid detection by making your way inside the hotel.

> (JBA) GET DOCUMENTS FROM THE SAFE: Here's where your safecracking skills will come in handy. Aswat's notes are in the safe in his room. Crack the safe and retrieve the documents.

> (NSA) KILL DR. ASWAT: We cannot allow Dr. Aswat to continue selling his knowledge. It's simply too dangerous. You need to take him out of commission before anyone else gets their hands on his work.

SECONDARY OBJECTIVES

> (NSA) INFILTRATE THE HOTEL WITHOUT ALERT: Aswat is very security-conscious. You'll need to get inside without triggering an alert, or he may get nervous and check out.

> (NSA) DON'T KILL CIVILIANS: The hotel where the meeting is taking place is a public area filled with hotel staff and tourists. Killing civilians would attract too much attention from the authorities and should be avoided at all costs.

> (NSA) COMPLETE MISSION WITHOUT ALERTS: Aswat is very security conscious. You'll need to get inside without triggering an alert, or he may get nervous and check out.

Sam accompanies Emile to a Shanghai hotel, where the JBA leader intends to purchase a mysterious chemical agent from a Pakistani researcher. Emile wants Sam to sneak into Dr. Aswat's hotel room and steal his research. Meanwhile, the JBA wants Sam to record Emile's meeting and sample the chemical compound.

Near-Fatal Experience

The helicopter pilot suffers a coronary and keels over. Sam must take over and pilot the helicopter to the hotel. First, you must steer the chopper out of a dive. Tilt the Move control left or right to raise the chopper to an upright position. The tail rotors respond slowly. As soon as the helicopter begins to tilt, release the Move control and allow the tail rotors to do their job. Continue tilting the helicopter left or right with delayed reaction as needed until the onboard level sensors stop going off. Keep the chopper level for a few seconds to continue.

LOADOUT: SHANGHAI

AVAILABLE WEAPONS
SC-20K/60
Shotgun shell—attachment/8
SC pistol/40
Sticky camera/4
Sticky shocker/2
Airfoil round/4
Frag grenade/2
Flash grenade/3
Sonic grenade/3
Smoke grenade/3
EMP grenade/3
Gas grenade/3
Wall mine/3
Wall mine—stun/3
Wall mine—flash/3
Laser microphone
Ultrasonic emitter

Hotel Rooftop

Emile orders Sam to stay with the chopper. Hisham Hamza, a CIA operative working undercover inside Massoud's organization, contacts Sam. Apparently he is somewhere in the building. He will provide support throughout this mission. The dual agencies want Sam to record Emile's meeting.

At the roof's far side is a crane Sam can use to rappel down the side of the building in order to eavesdrop on Emile. All that stands in his way is a small army of terrorists patrolling the rooftop. Move toward the elevator doors. Climb onto the stack of pallets to the left of the doors. Wait for the terrorist standing on the level above to move away. Then jump up, grab the rail, and climb over.

Stay crouched near the wall until the terrorist on your level finishes conferring with the guy on the level above. Then follow him over to the rail, sneak up behind him, and grab him. Drag him back toward the wall, choke him unconscious, and leave him there.

Climb up the ladder toward the higher level. Stop after stepping off the ladder and watch the terrorist patrol the roof and move over to the ledge on the right. Position Sam under a cable running from this structure to the next. Jump up to grab the cable and zip-line across the roof.

Climb over the vent duct. Move across the planks to the top of the small structure. Attached to the wall on the left is a vertical pipe. Run and jump across the gap to grab the pipe.

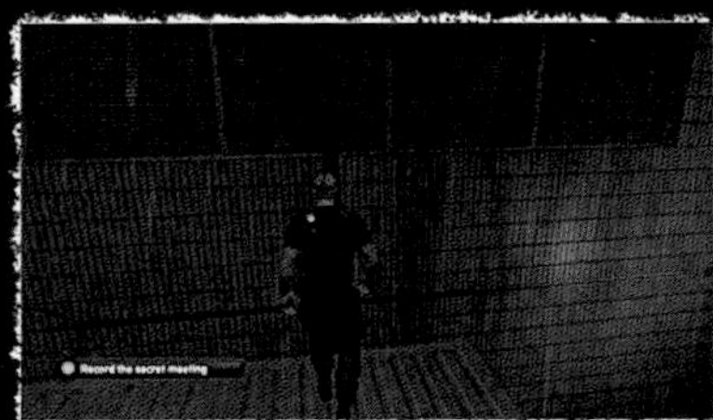

Ascend the vertical pipe to a thin ledge. Shimmy along the wall to the right and around the corner. Drop to the roof near the breaker box. Open the breaker box and access the computer inside. There are two ways to activate the nearby crane. If you choose the normal access, the crane rotates but a bright light comes on. That's no good. Instead, hack the security access in order to rotate the crane and override the safety lights.

Climb the ladder to the crane cabin's roof. Carefully move to the thin crane arm's end, and rappel down the building's side.

Hotel Exterior

To rappel faster, press the Jump button while moving down. Sam eventually arrives on a scaffold. Stand and move to the platform's edge. Sam flattens against the building. Slide across the ledge to the left until Sam reaches the corner. Tilt the Move control downward to make Sam climb down and hang from the ledge. Continue shimmying around the corner to the left until Sam reaches a pipe at the building's edge.

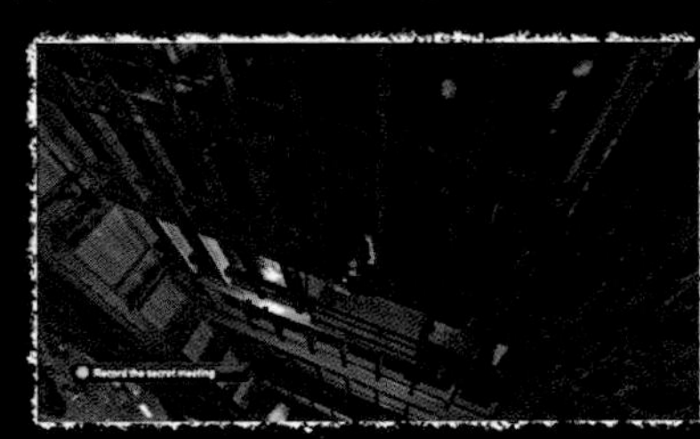

Slide down the pipe until Sam stops, then shimmy to the right and around the corner. Continue shimmying under the lounge area windows until you reach an obstruction that blocks the path. Climb to stand on the ledge and sidestep to the right, past the obstruction. Climb back down and continue to the right. Work your way around a second obstruction but remain standing on the thin ledge.

Record the Meeting

Sidestep along the angled portion of the building and across the ledge until Sam reaches a rappel point. Rappel down the building's side until positioned outside the secret meeting room. Equip the laser microphone and point it through the window to record the meeting.

Dodging the Spotlight

Hisham points out a helicopter in proximity. Quickly put away the mic and continue rappelling down the building's side until Sam stands on a ledge. Start sidestepping to the left. The helicopter shines a spotlight on the building's side. The spotlight first sweeps underneath Sam's ledge. Continue moving left as the helicopter searches. The spotlight then moves up. Climb down to hang from below the ledge, and continue shimmying left as the spotlight sweeps the wall above the ledge.

Continue shimmying left until Sam hangs underneath a vent. Wait patiently until one of Aswat's security opens the vent and leans out. Grab the man and pull him from the hole; he free-falls over the building's side. Climb through the opening.

Laundry

Sam finds himself in a small maintenance room outside of the hotel's laundry facility. The room is well lit, and there's no light switch. Going through the door leads to instant detection. Instead, open the trapdoor in the corner to the left. Drop through the trap into a crawlspace. Move through the crawlspace until you locate a second trapdoor.

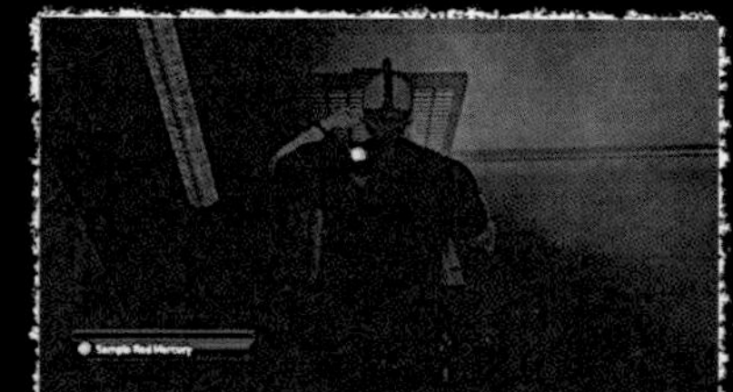

Climb out of the trapdoor into the laundry room. Face into the center of the heavily patrolled room. There are two exits from the laundry area to the floor above.

The First Path out of the Laundry Area

The trapdoor from which Sam emerges is located near a large dividing wall with a tall open window. Climb through the window, sticking to the right to stay in the shadows. Approach the double doors on the other side of the machinery and flatten Sam's back against the wall to the door's right. Look through the windows on the doors. One of Aswat's men stands near the elevator in the next area, and sometimes he stoops to examine the bodies of murdered hotel employees. Another terrorist, one of Emile's, momentarily stands in the room at the far end. He then emerges from the room and moves through the double doors.

When the terrorist with a ski mask emerges from the elevator corridor, go through the door. Sneak up beside the man standing in front of the elevator doors. When the man goes over to examine the dead employee bodies, move to the elevator's other side and press the call button. Then grab the man from behind and drag him into the elevator. Strangle him unconscious

when the doors close. Examine the controls on the left side and press the Up button to ascend.

Deboard the elevator when it stops, and head around the corner to the right. Use the optic cable to check the bathroom next door. Then enter the room.

Creep into the bedroom and sneak up behind the seated man. Grab him and interrogate him to learn that he controls the security cameras in the area. Choke him unconscious. Read e-mails on the laptop and hack the security access to disable the security camera in the main corridor by the elevators. Pick up the two sticky cameras on the desk and go through the double doors into the room where Emile and Aswat are talking.

Second Path out of the Laundry

The other path out of the laundry room requires more stealth, less waiting. After climbing out of the trapdoor, turn until you see a terrorist searching the bright area near the laundry machines. While he searches, sneak over to the wall and cut the power cables to the conduit box on the wall.

Soon, the lights in the washing machine area go out. Switch on night vision and navigate through the dark area, avoiding the terrorist who continues searching in the dark. Head to the end of the row of laundry machines, and then go around the corner to the left. Move through the aisle behind the machines into a maintenance chute. Climb up the ladder and crawl through an open vent into a closet. Turn out the light in the closet and use the optic cable on the door before exiting to the meeting room suite.

Meeting Room Suite

Hide behind the tall screens dividing the room on the opposite side from the windows. Aswat's security man in the meeting room patrols a variable path. Sometimes he stands at the window in the well-lit area, and sometimes he sits in the chair in the dark area. Neither of these locations is a good spot to take him out. However, sometimes he stands near the window in the dark area, and sometimes he stands in front of the thin paper wall dividing the rooms. When he is in either of these locations, sneak up behind him and grab him. Drag him away from the windows and behind the screens dividing the room, and choke him unconscious.

Go through the double doors into the bedroom and grab the man seated at the laptop (if you haven't already). Interrogate him about the hotel surveillance system, and then knock him out. Hack the laptop's security access to deactivate the surveillance camera in the main corridor by the elevators.

Meeting Room

Proceed past the thin paper walls into the living room area. To the left is the meeting area. Moss stands in the doorway to the right, and Emile stands in the doorway to the left. Wait until Emile moves into the meeting area. Then sneak over to the safe and press the Interact button to crack it. Open the safe and sample the red mercury inside, and pick up the SC pistol ammo.

Around this time, Moss leaves the meeting area and orders Sam to head for Aswat's room. The JBA wants to steal the design documents so they can make their own red mercury. Enter the bathroom next to the safe in the meeting area. The ceiling tile at the back of the room is missing. Jump up to grab the ledge, and climb into the ventilation crawlspace. Enter the open vent duct.

Atrium Top Floor

Crawl through the vent duct into a security room. Wait for one of Aswat's men to exit the room; when he does, drop from the vent. The guards outside the room may hear Sam's exit. If so, quickly move to the ladder on the room's other side and climb up. If not, collect the sonic grenade on the desk near the computer, which contains some hotel employee e-mails.

Climb the ladder and emerge onto the roof of the elevator structure. Position Sam in the area's center and jump up to grab a thin cable stretching across the area. Climb out until the Winch icon appears; then descend until Sam lands on a small curving catwalk.

After detaching from the winch cable, move onto the roof of the nearby elevator car. Ride the elevator car down to the next catwalk, and move off the car's roof. Cross the curving catwalk to the center. Equip the SC-20K and sticky shockers. Look for one of Aswat's men, wearing a cream-colored suit and holding a flashlight, patrolling the balcony two levels down. When he stops in a dark spot and stands staring over the rail, fire a sticky shocker to knock him out. You'll thank yourself later.

Continue to the opposite end of the curved platform and wait for another elevator car to rise to your level. Move onto the elevator car's roof and ride the car down to the next level.

In the middle of this curving catwalk, a bodyguard stands looking through an open window. Stay on the catwalk to the window's right and equip the SC-20K with airfoil rounds. Soon, the guard begins coughing and sneezing. Switch the gun to your left shoulder and aim at his head as he leans out of the open window. Strike him with an airfoil round to knock him out, and then search the ground to see if you can reclaim your airfoil round.

With both guards on this level neutralized, move out onto the curving platform that runs under the ornamental dragon and over to the balcony. Wait until the spotlights connected to the catwalk and to the far right move down and up. Cross the catwalk quickly and climb over the rail.

Dr. Aswat's Room

Aswat's room is the suite with the long corridor leading up to the double doors. The room is *filled* with bodyguards. Go through the doors and close them behind you. Wait for a bodyguard to enter from the left and head to the table on the far right. Follow him, grab him, and drag him back to the entrance before strangling him unconscious.

Make sure to tuck the bodyguard in the shadows near the entrance. Wait for another bodyguard to emerge from the den to the right, walk across the area, and stop near the windows. Sneak up behind him and grab him. Drag him back to the dark doorway and strangle him unconscious.

Move over to the doorway of the den to the entrance's right. Press Sam's back against the wall near the doorway, and watch the guard inside the room. As the guard moves toward the doorway, watch for the Grab Character icon to appear. Grab the man from around the corner and pin him to the ground. Then press the nonlethal attack button to knock him out.

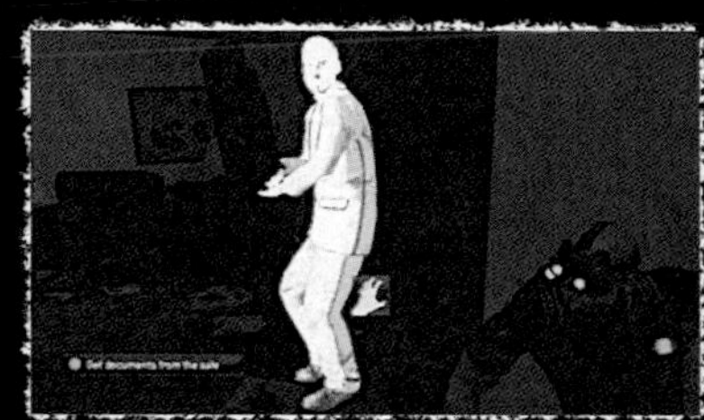

NOTE

Do a little cleanup at this point, in preparation for future objectives. Take the bodies piled by the door and carry them into the bedroom to the entrance's right. Stack them in the bathroom. Also, return to the corridor outside and collect the disabled bodyguard you may have left near the railing, no matter how concealed in shadow he may be. Drop his body in the bathroom as well. These actions help avoid suspicion later if someone else enters the suite.

Crack Aswat's Safe

Sneak over to the bedroom where a flashlight sits on the bed. Inside the room, a bodyguard works on the safe in the corner to the right. Load the SC-20K with an airfoil round. Fire the airfoil round at the man's head to knock him out.

Crack the safe in the corner, and take the notes inside to complete your main assignment. While you work, Emile radios in that the meeting is over and Aswat is returning to his room. Hisham butts in and relays orders for Sam to kill Aswat, whose wholesaling of chemical weapons is dangerous to the public.

Kill Aswat and Extract

As soon as you have the document in hand, Emile and Moss park the helicopter outside the other bedroom in the suite. They shoot out the window and expect Sam to extract immediately. JBA trust is lost for every three seconds Sam remains in the suite. Aswat will enter his suite and into Sam's gun sights in time only if the hotel corridor and suite entrance are clear of suspicious things such as bodies and open doors. To speed things along, open the suite's doors and machine-gun Dr. Aswat as soon as he comes into sight.

Quickly head to the second bedroom and approach the shattered window. Grab the zip-line to glide over to the helicopter and extract.

NYC—JBA HQ 1—Part 2

MAP KEY

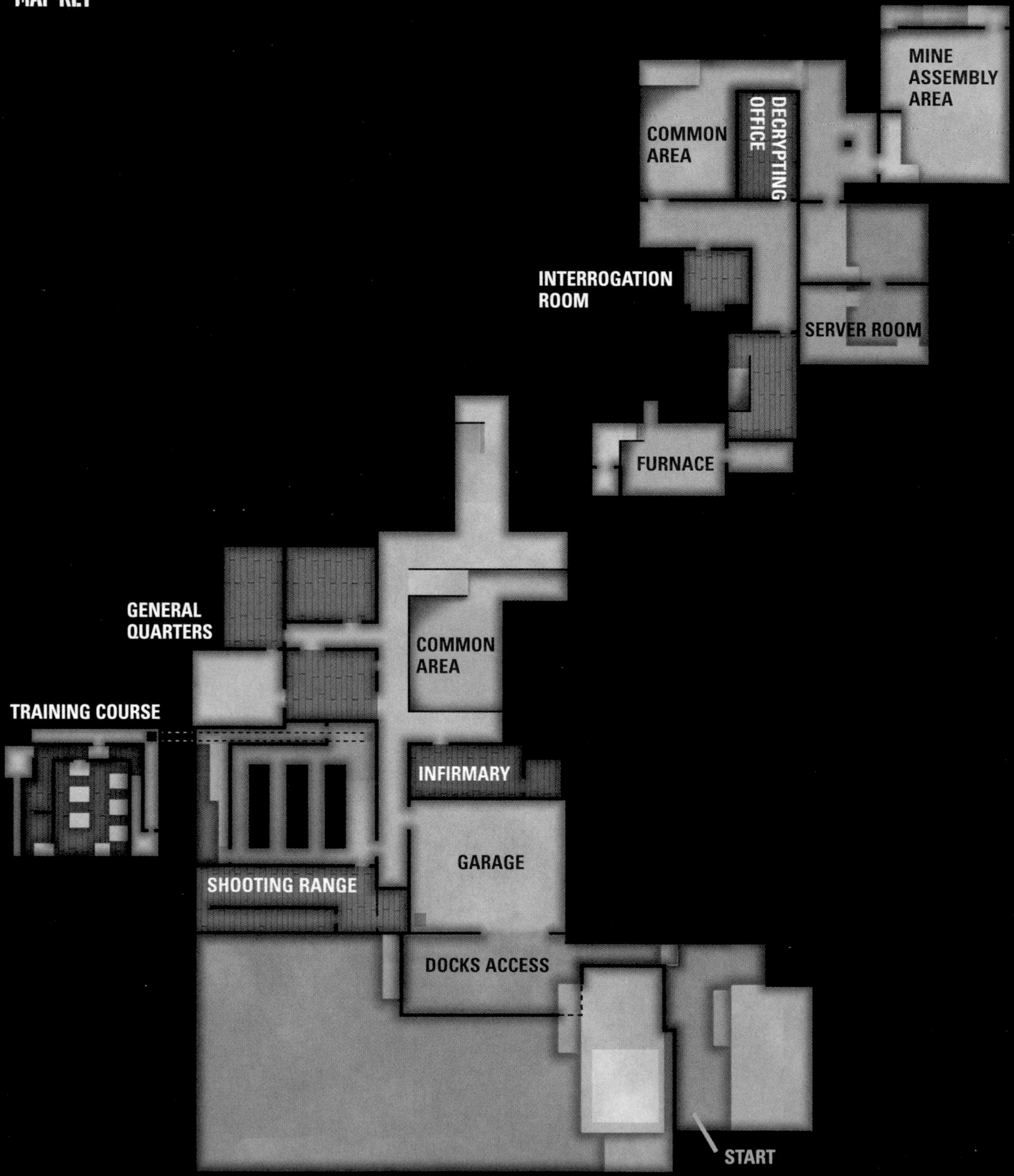

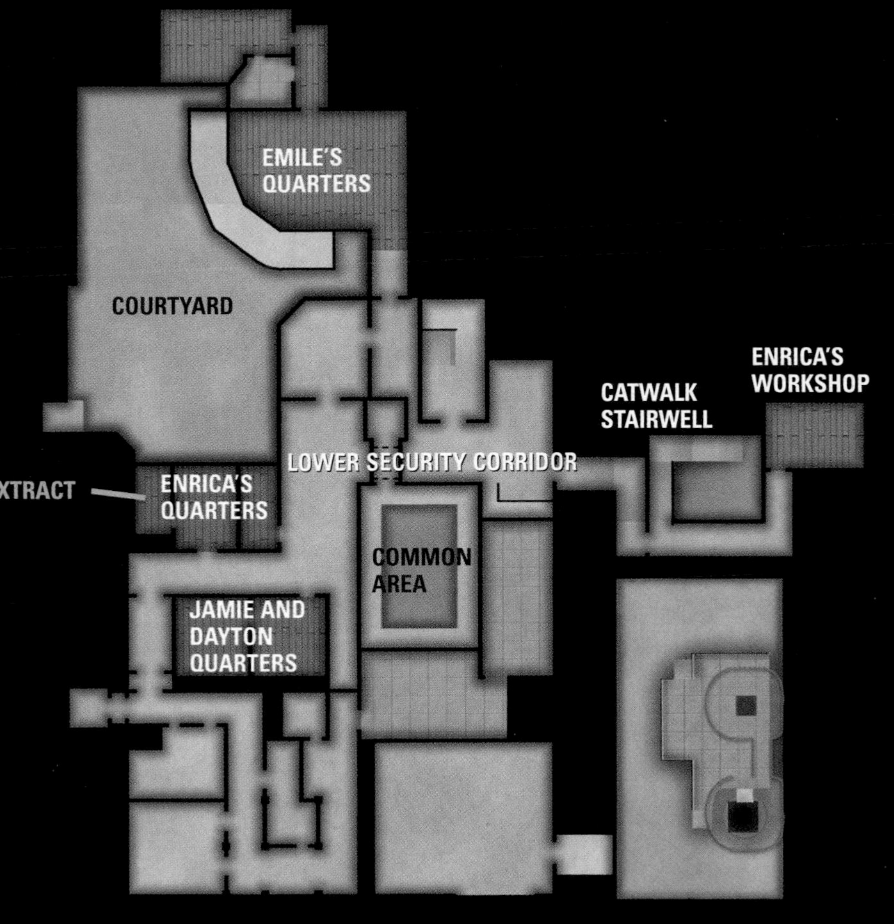

OBJECTIVES

PRIMARY OBJECTIVES

> (NSA) RECORD VOICE TO ACCESS LOCKS: In order to access Emile's office you will need to pass through one of the voice security locks in the compound. Since the conversation in Shanghai was not recorded, you have no voice sample to use to access the lock. It will be necessary to use the laser mic to record a voice from one of the main JBA members to pass through the security lock and reach Emile's office.

> (JBA) ASSEMBLE MINES FOR KINSHASA: Use the micro-manipulators in the workshop area of the compound to assemble the mines that you'll be taking to Kinshasa as part of a weapons shipment.

> (NSA) SCAN BLUEPRINTS IN EMILE'S SAFE: The blueprints for the red mercury device are most likely located in Emile's office. Break in and find those blueprints, then scan them in for transmission. That will give us a good idea of the capabilities of the device he's building.

SECONDARY OBJECTIVES

> (JBA) PRACTICE AT FIRING RANGE: Improve your skills with firearms on the JBA's firing range.

> (JBA) DISPOSE OF THE PILOT'S BODY: The pilot from your trip to Shanghai didn't make it. You can dispose of his body by moving it from the infirmary down to the furnace. Doing so will please Enrica, not to mention making things smell a little better around the compound.

> (JBA) COMPLETE TRAINING COURSE: Practice your skill at safecracking in the JBA's training area. The skill will no doubt come in handy, both for the JBA and your true mission. To reach the practice safe, you will need to cross the obstacle course successfully. The course is comprised of various challenges. Failing at one challenge will prevent you from continuing, and you will have to backtrack in order to restart.

PROFILE OBJECTIVES

> (NSA) SEARCH QUARTERS FOR PERSONAL INFO: In order to complete the NSA dossiers on the various core members of the JBA, we need you to get the personnel files of the core members of the JBA. With this data, the NSA can create a more accurate prediction model for their behavior—and how to stop them.

> (NSA) GET PROFESSIONAL BACKGROUND INFO: In order to complete the NSA dossiers on the various core members of the JBA, we need you to get data on the group's activities and their roles in it. Uploading this information will help us create a more accurate prediction model for what they might do next—and will help us plan to stop it.

> (NSA) GET JBA MEMBER VOICE SAMPLES: The JBA uses voice ID locks on sensitive areas of the compound. To get past them, you'll need to record the voices of the group's core members—the only ones certain to be cleared for all areas. You'll also help complete the profiles the NSA is compiling on the members of the JBA.

Returning from Shanghai, Sam steps outside the JBA compound into a restricted area to meet Lambert face-to-face. Sam's NSA handler wants him to find and scan the blueprints of the red mercury bomb Emile is intent on building. However, Sam must risk exposure by penetrating the JBA head's private quarters to obtain the plans.

Docks Access

Sam meets Lambert in the restricted area outside the compound. If Sam is spotted going back into the compound, you lose the JBA's trust. Head to the back of the alley and climb onto the Dumpster near the wall. Stay crouched behind the wall until a guard comes into view and briefly scans the area near Sam's hiding spot. As the guard turns and walks behind the truck parked in the alley, climb over the wall. Quietly head into the garage while the man works on the truck. As soon as Sam is inside the garage door, he is safe from suspicion.

Garage

Head toward the double doors on the garage's other side to meet with Enrica. Follow her down the passageway. Before reaching the large open portion of the common area, equip the laser microphone and point it at the back of Enrica's head to record her voice. Make sure no one else sees you doing so, or the mission ends abruptly.

Mine Assembly Area

Enrica charges Sam with moving the Shanghai pilot's body to the furnace room downstairs. She also orders him to build land mines as part of a weapon shipment en route to JBA allies in Kinshasa. Enrica leaves Sam in the mine assembly area near the mine machine, with 25 minutes to complete his objective. Sam must report back to Enrica within 25 minutes or risk losing faith with the JBA. Many areas of the compound become off-limits to Sam until he completes his mine quota, so first thing's first.

TIP

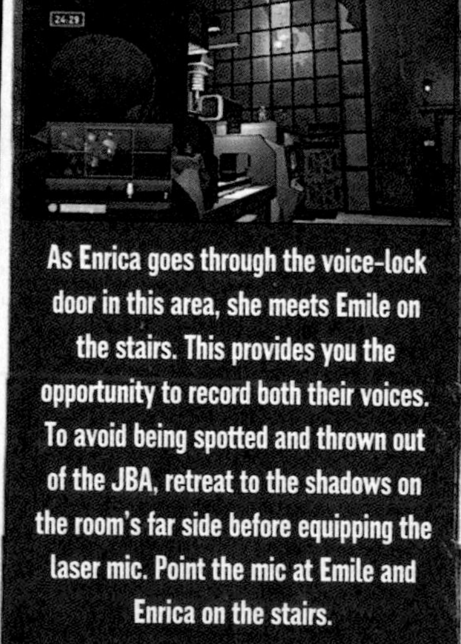

As Enrica goes through the voice-lock door in this area, she meets Emile on the stairs. This provides you the opportunity to record both their voices. To avoid being spotted and thrown out of the JBA, retreat to the shadows on the room's far side before equipping the laser mic. Point the mic at Emile and Enrica on the stairs.

Time to build some mines. The objective is to insert a fragile detonator into the mine's center. If the detonator collides with the mine's interior, the detonator breaks. You must assemble 10 mines to fulfill the objective. If too many detonators are broken and not enough remain to fill the quota, you fail the objective.

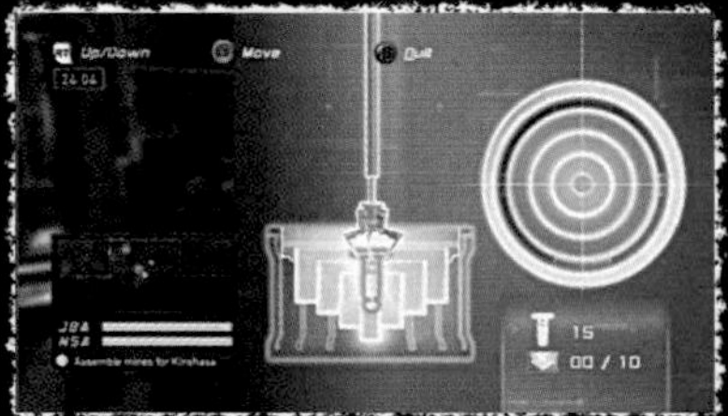

The Primary Attack button controls the detonator's descent into the mine. Press the Primary Attack button very lightly so the detonator slowly descends into the mine. Watch the diagram on the screen's right side, and use the Move Control to guide the detonator into the mine's center. The detonator must be in the center when it reaches the central niche. Upon successfully inserting the detonator into the niche, press the Primary Attack button harder to increase speed and finish the mine.

Secondary Objectives

After successfully building 10 mines, Sam is free to complete all other objectives. Before heading to Emile's quarters to scan the blueprints, try to accomplish as many of the following subordinate objectives as possible:

> Emile is in the server room. This provides an opportunity to record his voice as he screams at the computer. Hide in the shadows above the first trapdoor on the platform. When Emile goes behind the server equipment to the right, sneak over to the PC and hack the security access folder to decrypt an e-mail containing the code to Emile's office: 2701 (there may have been a previous opportunity in HQ1).

> Head out to the common area. As you approach the stairs, Jamie may head through the area. Follow him toward Sam's starting point in the previous HQ mission. Go up one flight of stairs, and let him go up the rest of the way alone. Jamie meets up with a technician who tells him the voice lock on the door is not working right. Aim the laser mic at Jamie's head to record his first sentence. Stand where Jamie's body is blocking the technician's view of Sam, so that "Sully" does not see the recording in progress.

> Stay on the stair landing and let Jamie go back out to the common area. A few minutes later, Moss appears downstairs. After stopping to look around for a moment, he grumbles under his breath about a missing guard. This is your best opportunity during this stage to record Moss's voice. If you need comic relief, watch Moss head to the lavatory in the general quarters area to chew out a guy hiding in a toilet stall.

> The dead pilot is in the infirmary. Take his body to the furnace room to regain a little lost JBA trust. Pick up the body and carry it downstairs past the conference table and chalkboard. Go through the corridor past the interrogation room and around the corner to the right. Go down to the basement level and enter the furnace area. Cole Yeagher's body lies on a platform under the furnace. Approach the platform while holding the pilot's body until the Pick up Body icon appears. Press the Interact button to set down the pilot's body properly. The fastest way back upstairs is to climb the nearby ladder up to the garage and open the trapdoor.

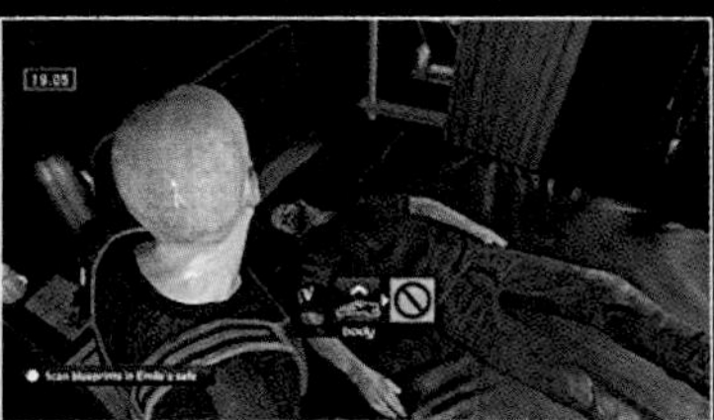

> The JBA wants you to complete the training course again. The course is no different than before. They also want you to improve your sniping skills at the firing range. Enrica recently set a new high score of 92. Score a lot of five point bull's-eyes to beat her.

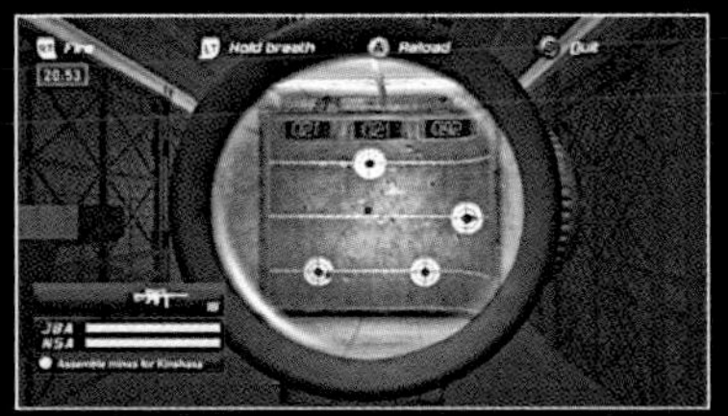

Voice Access

Whenever you complete a mine assembly and record any JBA member's voice, return to the mine assembly area and use the voice recording at the voice lock to open the door in the corner. Crouch and head upstairs quickly to avoid being spotted by the surveillance camera on the top floor.

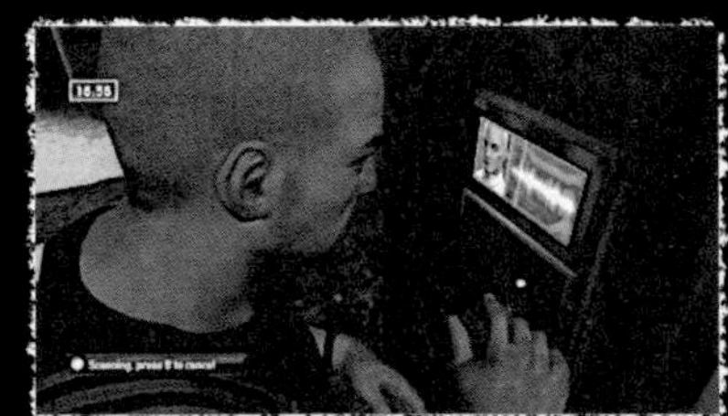

On the top floor, a pipe runs the corridor's length, past the camera. Jump to grab the pipe, pull your legs up, and shimmy down the corridor past the camera. Drop to the ground at the next corner, and continue over to the door of Enrica's workshop.

01: DOSSIERS

PS2/GC

02: GAME BASICS

03: EQUIPMENT

04: SOLO MISSIONS

05: CO-OP MISSIONS

06: VERSUS MISSIONS

XBOX 360/PC

07: GAME BASICS

08: EQUIPMENT

09: SOLO MISSIONS

NYC—JBA HQ 1—Part 2

10: MULTIPLAYER

Enrica's Workshop

Either hack the keypad to gain access to Enrica's workshop, or enter the code 1337 into the keypad. This code is not obtained until later in the stage, but there's no point letting it go to waste.

Inside her workshop, Enrica is busy working at the desk across from the door. Crouch and sneak around the small table to the right. Go behind the double desk and slip through the narrow gap. On the other side, access the computer to read an e-mail about the Cozumel bomb. When finished, turn off the computer so that light from the monitor does not give away Sam's position. Then sneak over to the file cabinet in the corner and open it to obtain Enrica's activity data.

Catwalk Stairwell

Sneak out of Enrica's lab and use the pipe to avoid detection by the surveillance camera as before. Go through the blue door into the catwalk stairwell. Before exiting the stairwell, turn out the lights using the switch by the door.

Low-Security Corridor

A guard is asleep in a chair, facing the voice-lock door on the upper level. Head into the small area to the right and flip the light switch on the wall to plunge the entrance into darkness.

Cross the dark area and pause just outside the next lit area. A technician may approach from the lounge area around the corner to the left, or he may already be sitting in the well-lit area outside the entrance to Emile's office on the right. Depending on the situation, wait for him to pass, or wait for him to stand, stretch, and turn his back in your direction. Then crouch and quickly go to the corner behind the room with a pool table.

Head past the pool table room door and flip the light switch on the wall to darken the lounge area. Head through the lounge area and around the corner to the right. Flip the light switch on the back corner to darken the area in front of Jamie and Dayton's quarters. Use the lock pick to open the door, and close the door behind you.

Jamie and Dayton's Quarters

Equip the laser mic and go into the bedroom, where Dayton is asleep on the first cot. Dayton is prone to nightmares and talks in his sleep. Aim the mic at Dayton until he cries out to get a sample of his voice. Then sneak over to the file cabinet beside his bed and open it to obtain his personal info file.

Sneak around Jamie's cot and open his file cabinet to obtain his personal info data. Then quickly hide under Jamie's bed. Jamie sometimes enters the quarters and turns on all the lights. After rooting through his own file cabinet and chiding Dayton for a few minutes, Jamie turns the lights back off and leaves. Exit their quarters.

Enrica's Quarters

The next door down the corridor outside Jamie and Dayton's quarters leads to Enrica's quarters. Pick the lock on her door and open the file cabinet inside to the right to obtain her personal info data.

To the Boss's Den

Exit Enrica's quarters and head back toward the room with the pool table. Stop just inside the closest door of the pool table room and turn out the lights. This switch also controls the lights in the corridor leading up to the glass doors of Emile's quarters. Hopefully this action does not draw too much attention from the guard posted outside Emile's quarters.

Head through the pool table room and through the other door. Pick the lock on the double glass doors in the corridor. Sneak inside to the right and flip the switch on the wall to extinguish the light on the doors to Emile's quarters. Input the code 2701 into the keypad on the right, and go inside.

Emile's Quarters

Close the door behind you inside Emile's quarters. Head left and find the file cabinet behind the grandfather clock to obtain Emile's activities data. Hack the security access folder on Emile's computer to read an e-mail from Enrica that contains the keypad code to her workshop: 1337. Read two other e-mails in the "Normal" folder.

Emile's safe is built into the far end of his desk. Avoid going anywhere near the safe for the time being. Instead, head through the door in the wall across from Emile's desk and into the bedroom. Access the file cabinet in the bedroom to obtain Emile's personal info data.

Return to Emile's office and approach the safe at the desk's end. A checkpoint is saved, and Emile enters the room with Jamie. Quickly move to the shelves on the wall opposite the desk and hide in the closet. Emile opens the safe and takes out the blueprints Sam needs to scan. Continue hiding in the closet until Emile returns the blueprints to the safe and closes it. After Jamie exits, Emile sits in the armchair near the exit. Looks like Sam cannot leave the way he came in.

Exit the closet, sneak over to the safe, and unlock it. Scan the blueprints inside the safe, and then close the safe again.

Courtyard

Move to the corner and open the balcony doors. Close the doors behind you, and follow the curving balcony to its far end. Climb over the balcony and hang; shimmy to a vertical pipe attached to the wall. Slide down the pipe to the courtyard.

Cross to the open courtyard's opposite side, toward the only other open window. Climb onto the stack of pallets below the window and onto the shanty roof. Climb through the window into the bathroom in Enrica's quarters. Exit the bathroom to encounter Enrica. Fortunately, Sam knows how to handle the situation....

Cozumel—Cruise Ship—Part 1

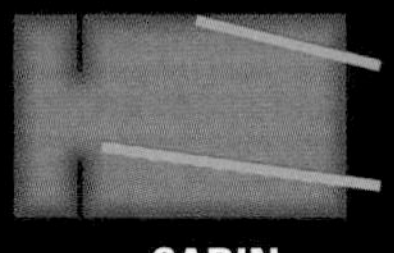

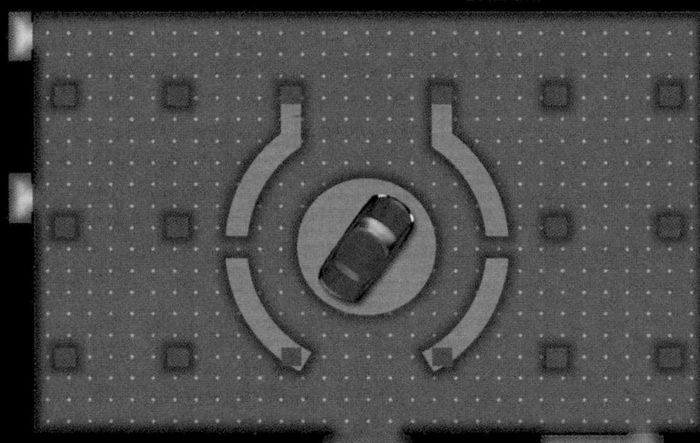

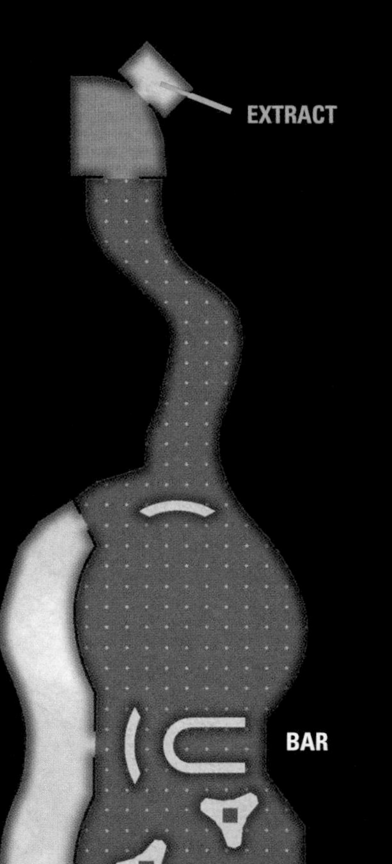

OBJECTIVES

ASSIGNMENT

> (JBA) PLACE THE JBA'S BOMB: In order to preserve your cover, you must plant the JBA's bomb on the ship as they instruct you. If you leave the ship before this mission is carried out, you will compromise your cover within the JBA and lose their trust. Any deviation puts your cover, and thus the entire operation, at risk.

PRIMARY OBJECTIVES

> (NSA) PLACE SMOKE BOMB: In order to evacuate the ship, we're going to need to convince the Mexican coast guard that there's a real threat. That means using a fake one to get the point across. Plant smoke bombs in the ship's vents. When they go off, the tourists will be evacuated, and the potential loss of life will be reduced.

> (NSA) GET DETONATION FREQUENCY: You will be able to defuse the bomb remotely by capturing the detonation frequency and triggering a blocker signal on it. To do that, you'll need to use your watch to record that frequency after you've put the bomb in place. Don't take too long, or Enrica may get suspicious.

SECONDARY OBJECTIVES

> (JBA) REACH POOL DECK WITHOUT ALERTS: In order to carry out your objectives, you need to reach the pool deck. Follow Enrica's directions to get there, and try to avoid raising an alarm. The ship is being patrolled by the local coast guard, so they'll be on you in a hurry if you do.

> (NSA) DON'T KILL CIVILIANS: The cruise ship is crawling with the Mexican coast guards, as well as the occasional tourist. Killing civilians would attract too much attention from the Mexican authorities and should be avoided at all costs.

LOADOUT: COZUMEL

AVAILABLE WEAPONS
SC-20K/60
Shotgun shell/8
SC pistol/40
Sticky camera/4
Sticky shocker/2
Airfoil round/4
Frag grenade/2
Flash grenade/3
Sonic grenade/3
Smoke grenade/3
Gas grenade/3
EMP grenade/3
Wall mine/3
Wall mine—flash/3
Wall mine—stun/3
Laser microphone
Ultrasonic emitter

The JBA is determined to test their newfound weapon system by planting a bomb on board a passenger cruise ship. Sam and Enrica board the ship. But when the NSA tips off the Mexican coast guard about the terrorists' plans, Sam and Enrica become separated. Sam must sneak past Mexican authorities combing the cruise ship and plant the JBA's bomb.

Cabin

After Sam gets off the phone with Lambert, move to the entertainment center and pick up the two sticky shockers. Head out to the balcony.

Climb over the rail and hang from the ledge. Shimmy to the right and grab the vertical beam. Climb up the beam until Sam stops, and then shimmy to the right toward a balcony.

Stop shimmying and hang between the windows of the passenger cabin wherein you see a tourist raiding his minifridge. Wait until the man rises from the fridge, stares out the window vacantly a moment, then returns to the fridge before you continue shimmying toward the balcony. If you move past the window while he's looking, he flees in panic, which could trigger an alert.

A coast guard stands on the balcony. Another soon joins him. Hang from the bottom of the balcony until both men go inside. Then climb over the rail and enter the casino.

Casino

Hide behind the closest banquet table until Enrica hacks the system and organizes a little distraction. When the two guards are pulled away, head across the back of the room toward the shadows.

Continue past a dividing wall that is covered in winner plaques and head right. Move quickly past a pool of light on the ground, and look for a coast guard who starts moving away from a slot machine. Sneak up behind him, grab him, and drag him into shadows near the high wall of the circular central area. Interrogate him about the situation on board, and then choke him unconscious.

Head toward the clearly marked "Counter," but stick to the curving wall to the right. At the back of the casino, two coast guards remain on patrol, unaffected by the lure of free money. Stay by the curved wall until one coast guard stands at the top of the stairs for a long moment, and then turns away. Grab him and drag him down the steps and into the shadows before choking him unconscious.

Then return to the same position near the end of the curved wall. Wait for the other coast guard patrolling in this area to stop near the picture of the hottie on the signboard. Sneak up behind him a bit quickly and grab him. Drag him downstairs and knock him out.

The immediate area is now clear enough for you to enter the Counter. Crack the safe to obtain two sonic grenades. Access the laptop to find out about possibly advantageous situations on board.

At the back of the counter area is a vent. The NSA wants you to place a smoke bomb in the vent to encourage the Mexican Coast Guard to evacuate the cruise ship later. However, Enrica has control of the surveillance camera in the room. If she sees you putting a smoke bomb in the vent, the JBA loses trust. Either turn out the lights in the room or use the SC pistol's OCP to jam the camera before inserting the smoke bomb into the vent.

Access the breaker panel in the Counter if you want to turn out the lights. Unfortunately, this draws attention to your activities rather than provide you with cover.

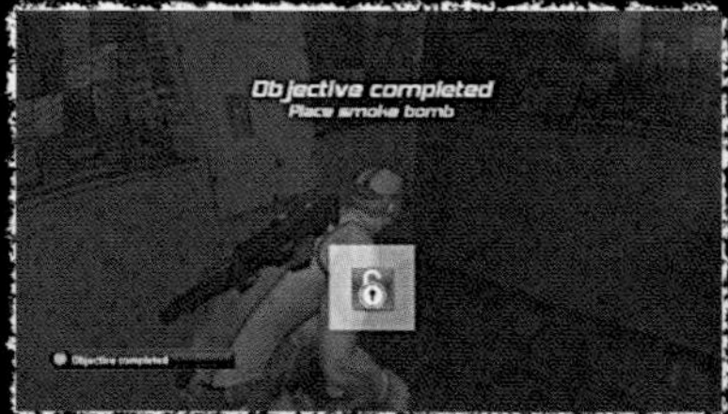

Sneak out to the sets of double doors at the back of the casino, near the spot where you ambushed the two coast guards. Check the area on the casino's opposite side to make sure the two remaining coast guards are not looking toward the doors; pick the lock on the closest door. Exit the casino quickly and close the door behind you.

Stairwell

Quickly move behind the standing screen to the door's left. Wait a long time for a steward to pass by and stop to open the door to the casino. If he goes into the casino, he will find the unconscious coast guards you left there, no matter how well you hid them. Step up behind him and grab him. Drag him behind the screen and knock him out.

Bar

Continue upstairs to the bar. Allow the coast guard to move away from the door. Then go through the door and quickly close it behind you. Move into the bar until Sam is not visible.

Sam should be very close to a counter. Go behind the counter and head right. Move across a space and hide behind the second counter until the guards head into the area's other portion. Quickly head over to the bar's end. Stop in the space between the bar and the small wall, where Sam is not visible. If you have gone undetected thus far, a coast guard should be leaning on the bar to the right. Wait for a coast guard who patrols the bar's length to move past, then head forward and stop by a small round table.

Stay very close to the little round table as the patrolling guard stops near the piano. Allow him to turn away from the piano and head over to the aquarium.

Notice a guard who comes in from the balcony and then goes out again briefly. Move behind the far end of the low wall near his stopping position and press your back against the wall. Stay near the end nearest the aquarium. Wait for the guard to return inside. As he moves to his stopping position, head down the dark corridor toward the elevators.

If you have not yet planted the smoke bomb, search the wall near the aquarium to find a suitable vent. However, before inserting the bomb, use the OCP to jam the surveillance camera on the column across the room to prevent Enrica from witnessing your actions. If you already placed a smoke bomb in a vent, avoid risking exposure and do not approach the vent.

Elevator to the Pool Deck

Head down the corridor past the bar. Stop at the closest end of the last column near two glass doors. Two coast guards are chatting near the elevators. Sam remains unseen behind the first column in the corridor.

Allow both coast guards to come through the double doors and leave the bar area. The second coast guard moves down the corridor in a zigzag pattern. Hold position and watch the guard go to the corridor's end. Then race over to the elevators.

Go through the double doors at the corridor's end. Board the open elevator car.

Cozumel—Cruise Ship—Part 2

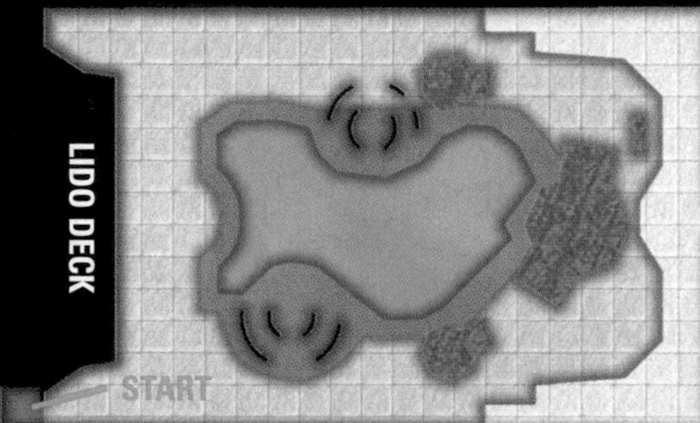

HAMMAM STEAM ROOM

SMOKE GRENADES

NAVIGATION ROOM

CREW'S QUARTERS

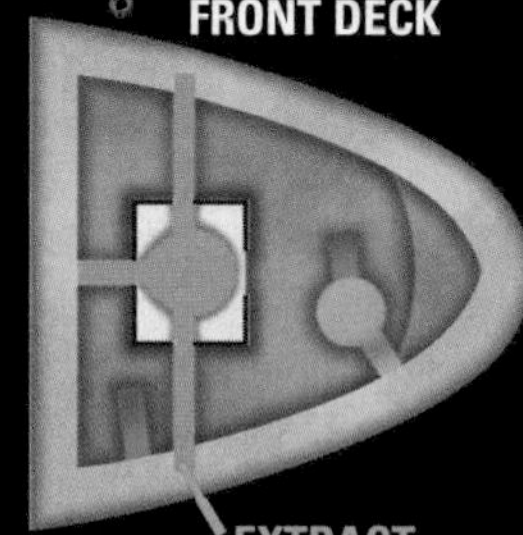

OBJECTIVES

ASSIGNMENT

> PLACE THE JBA'S BOMB: In order to preserve your cover, you must plant the JBA's bomb on the ship as they instruct you. If you leave the ship before this mission is carried out, you will compromise your cover within the JBA and lose their trust. Any deviation puts your cover, and thus the entire operation, at risk.

> DIVE TO EXTRACTION: Now that the bomb is in place, you can leave the cruise ship before you attract unwanted attention. Reach the security hatch, and dive into the sea to leave the ship.

PRIMARY OBJECTIVES

> PLACE SMOKE BOMB: In order to evacuate the ship, we're going to need to convince the Mexican coast guard that there's a real threat. That means using a fake one to get the point across. Plant smoke bombs in the ship's vents. When they go off, the tourists will be evacuated, and the potential loss of life will be reduced.

> GET DETONATION FREQUENCY: You will be able to defuse the bomb remotely by capturing the detonation frequency and triggering a blocker signal on it. To do that, you'll need to use your watch to record that frequency after you've put the bomb in place. Don't take too long, or Enrica may get suspicious.

SECONDARY OBJECTIVES

> PLACE BOMBS WITHOUT ALERTS: The bomb needs to be placed toward the front of the ship. You'll have to travel through the air ducts to get to the foredeck. Do so without triggering an alert.

> DON'T KILL CIVILIANS: The cruise ship is crawling with the Mexican coast guards, as well as the occasional tourist. Killing civilians would attract too much attention from the Mexican authorities and should be avoided at all costs.

Having reached the cruise ship's forward portion, Sam must navigate through broad daylight situations, avoiding detection only by hiding behind minimal cover. Working his way through the ship's spa and the bridge, Sam eventually reaches the foredeck, the target area to plant the JBA's bomb. After triggering the device, Sam must risk the JBA's trust by lingering and capturing the bomb's detonation frequency. Otherwise, the terrorists detonate the device and kill thousands of civilians at any time.

Lido Deck

As Sam's elevator arrives at the swimming pool deck, Enrica warns of impending danger. Face the back of the elevator car and jump to grab the lip of the open hatchway in the ceiling. Crawl into the space above the elevator to hide from a guard. Allow the guard to enter the elevator and move under the hatchway. Drop on top of him to knock him out.

Move to the side of the open elevator door and make sure the area beyond is clear. Then exit the elevator and hide behind the small table to the right. If the area remains clear, move across the opening to the left and hide behind the long buffet table.

As the closest coast guard heads left, move forward and hide behind the stacks of blue and white striped chairs. Move out to the corner of the second stack.

Enrica activates the fountain geysers at the foot of the pool. The coast guards are momentarily intrigued by this, but then walk away. As they walk off, run over and climb into the pool.

Swim underwater across the entire pool. Veer left, and swim over to the wall. The geysers are running here as well, partially covering Sam's exit from the pool.

Head past some stairs to the right, and hide behind a tall metal wall with water painted on it. Climb the pipe behind this wall until Sam reaches a thin ledge. Shimmy left or right around this ledge until Sam hangs from under the balcony.

A lone coast guard patrols the balcony. Hang from the balcony ledge until he patrols past and heads right. Then climb over the rail. Follow the coast guard at a distance until he passes the clear glass doors on the left. Go through the glass doors into the spa area.

Hammam Steam Room

Two corridors go into the spa. Follow the right-hand corridor. Stop at the corner, and press your back to the wall. A coast guard emerges from the sauna room and stands in the opposite corner for a long moment. He then moves close to Sam's position and stops. When he turns his back to Sam, grab him and drag him into the dark passageway. Ask him for directions to the ship's bridge before strangling him.

Head through the doorway on the right. A coast guard soon turns your way and heads down the aisle. Back out of the room and press Sam's back against the wall on the door's left side. When the coast guard draws near to the doorway, the Grab Character interaction appears. Press the Interact button to perform a corner grab. Interrogate the coast guard, and press either the Primary Attack or Secondary Attack buttons to put him out of his misery.

Head down the aisle past the massage booths and around the corner to the left. Approach the doorway cautiously, sticking to the right to avoid the pool of light on the ground. As Sam nears the doorway, he asks Enrica to pump steam into the sauna. If necessary, activate your Quick OPSAT map to locate the guard within the steam room. Allow the steam to build for a moment, and then enter the sauna under cover. Sneak up behind the coast guard wherever he stands in the dark room, and knock him out.

Climb onto the waterfall, and jump up to grab the ledge above. Pull yourself onto the thin ledge and use your knife to remove the vent cover.

Crew's Quarters

Crawl through the vent into a tiny crew cabin. A crew member soon enters. As he flips on the lights and turns his back, grab him from behind. Question him to learn the code to the navigation room: 2112.

Turn out the cabin's lights and slide open the door. Another crew member sits at the nearby table. Sneak up to his side and perform a nonlethal attack to knock him out. Pick up his body and stow him with his buddy in the middle cabin.

Search the right-hand cabin to find two smoke grenades. Use the laptop in the left-hand cabin or on the coffee table in the small lounge area to read e-mails.

Navigation Room

Input the code 2112 to open the navigation room's door. Sneak downstairs and head right, behind the steps. Crouch and move along the row of breaker panels until you reach the end. Press your back against the equipment to hide.

Wait patiently. Eventually two men on the bridge begin conversing. When the short chat ends, two bridge crew members go upstairs, leaving only one man on the bridge. Exit your hiding spot and watch the lone crew member carefully. When he is using the consoles at the front of the bridge, sneak out from behind the stairs and hide behind the central navigation console. Wait for him to stop at another station, and then sneak up behind him and knock him out. Carry his body under the stairs, where it is not likely to be discovered before you leave the ship.

Go through the door to the bridge's balcony. In the balcony's center is a line that runs down to the foredeck. Jump to grab it and zip-line down to the ship's bow.

Front Deck

A crew member stands in the area's center, smoking a cigarette. As the crew member walks to the right and stops, facing inward, head around the rail to the right. Hide behind the red life preservers lashed to the rail. When the crew member's back is to Sam's position, climb over and hang from the ledge, then drop to the lower level. Hide behind the closest covered lifeboat.

Sneak around the lifeboats' left side and slide up behind the crewmember. Grab him before he goes inside to chew out the coast guard patrolling the pump room. Drag him someplace out of sight of the pump room, and quietly choke him unconscious.

Head toward the door leading into the central pump station, and press Sam's back against the wall to the door's right. Wait for the coast guard to emerge from the pump room and head off. Sneak around the door and knock the guard unconscious.

If you have yet to place a smoke grenade to warn the crew of imminent danger, there is a suitable vent on the upper level underneath the bridge.

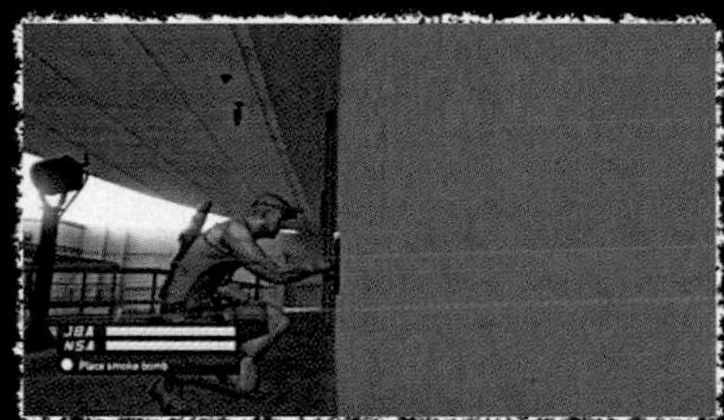

Pick the lock on the glass door at the base of the central hub. Go inside and use the laptop to the right to check e-mails for pertinent info.

Go behind the partition and place the JBA's bomb on the fuel pump. Quickly hack the device to gain the detonation frequency for the NSA. The longer you dilly-dally in the pump room, the more trust you lose with the JBA.

Exit the pump room and head right. On the ship's side wall is an emergency exit hatch. Pick the lock on the panel to the hatch's left, and open the door. Lower the platform, and then move out to the end. Sam dives to extraction.

NYC—JBA HQ—Part 3

MINE ASSEMBLY AREA
COMMON AREA
DECRYPTING OFFICE
EXTRACT
INTERROGATION ROOM
SERVER ROOM
FURNACE
EMILE'S QUARTERS
COURTYARD
ENRICA'S WORKSHOP
CATWALK STAIRWELL
LOWER SECURITY CORRIDOR
ENRICA'S QUARTERS
COMMON AREA
MOSS' OFFICE
JAMIE AND DAYTON QUARTERS
SURVEILLANCE ROOM
MOSS' BEDROOM
HIGH SECURITY CORRIDOR
START
GENERAL QUARTERS
COMMON AREA
TRAINING COURSE
INFIRMARY
GARAGE
SHOOTING RANGE
DOCKS ACCESS

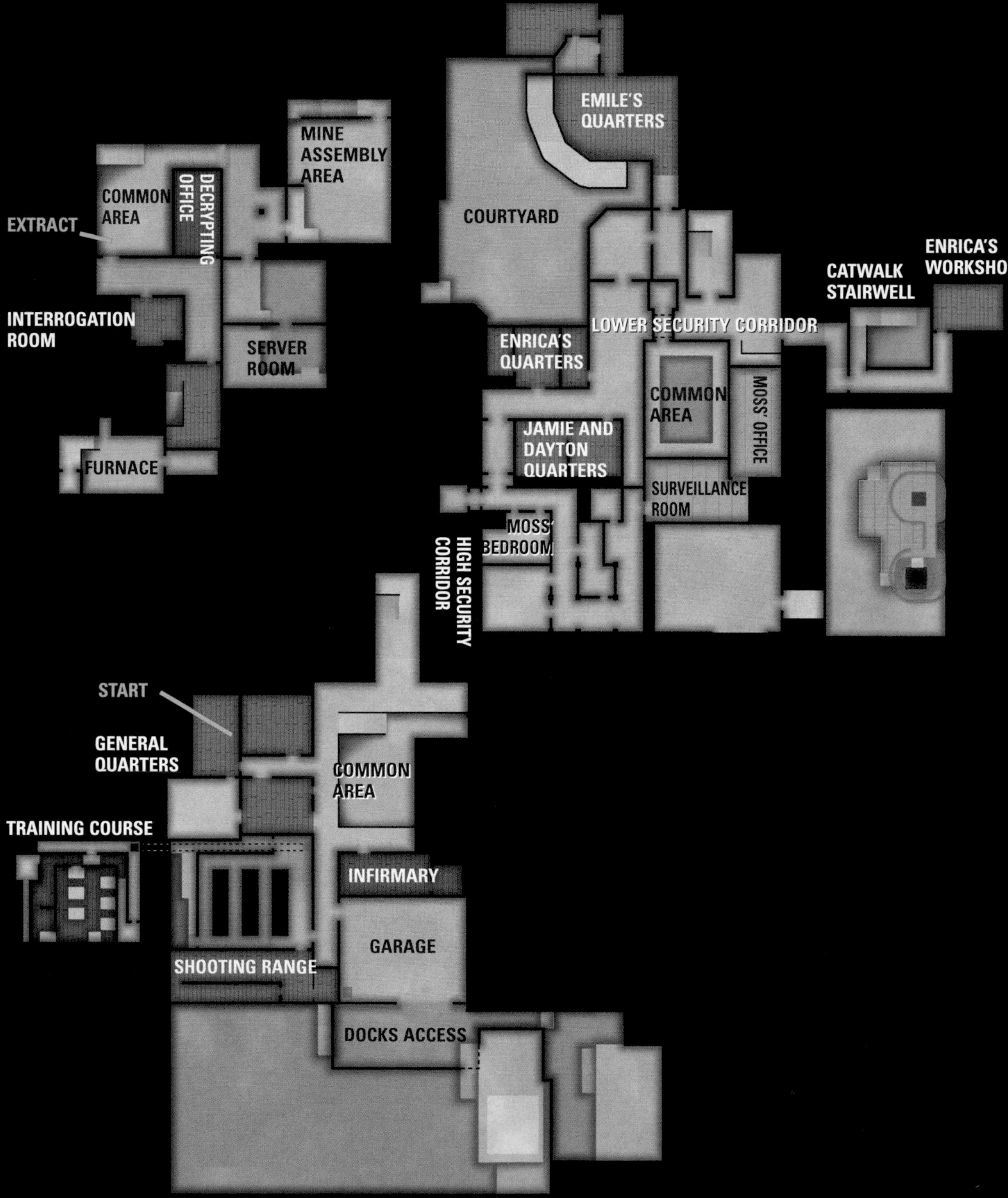

OBJECTIVES

PRIMARY OBJECTIVES

- (JBA) DECRYPT E-MAIL MESSAGE: It is vital to know what information Massoud is passing along to Tawkfir, particularly as it pertains to Emile. Decrypt the e-mail that Emile intercepted in order to produce a more accurate picture of their relationship—and what might be waiting in Kinshasa.
- (NSA) SCAN FINGERPRINT TO ACCESS LOCK: In order to search for the presence of the bomb, it will be necessary to access the next level of security of the compound located beyond the fingerprint lock. Use the fingerprint scanning software uploaded to the watch by Lambert to obtain one from one of the main JBA members.
- (NSA) OBTAIN VISUAL PROOF OF BOMB: It is of paramount importance that we confirm the presence on-site of a red mercury device. As there is no doubt high security on the bomb's location, the camera monitors in the surveillance room seem like the best bet for locating it without having to penetrate all of the JBA's security.

SECONDARY OBJECTIVES

- (JBA) ASSEMBLE MINES FOR KINSHASA: Use the micro-manipulators in the workshop area of the compound to assemble the mines that will be taken to Kinshasa as part of a weapons shipment.
- (JBA) PRACTICE AT FIRING RANGE: Try to improve your skills with firearms on the JBA's firing range.
- (NSA) OBTAIN ENRICA'S DISARM CODE: The bomb the JBA has placed on board the cruise ship cannot be allowed to detonate. However, if you stop it, suspicion may fall on you. Therefore, you must ensure someone else takes the blame. Enrica is the best target. She can be found working in her lab above the Mine Assembly area. You can use the code located in her computer to deactivate the bomb and the action will be traced to her.
- (JBA) COMPLETE TRAINING COURSE: Practice your skill at safecracking in the JBA's training area. The skill will no doubt come in handy, both for the JBA and your true mission. To reach the practice safe, you will need to cross the obstacle course successfully. The course is comprised of various challenges. Failing at one challenge will prevent you from continuing, and you will have to backtrack in order to restart.

CHOICES OBJECTIVES

- (NSA) FRAME ENRICA: Use Enrica's disarm code to prevent the explosion on the cruise ship. All of the blame will fall on her, leaving you in good standing with the JBA.
- (NSA) STOP CRUISE SHIP EXPLOSION: It is imperative that the cruise ship not be allowed to explode and that the JBA not be allowed to test their weapon. You must prevent the explosion.
- (JBA) ALLOW CRUISE SHIP EXPLOSION: As difficult as it is to do so, you must sacrifice the lives on board the ship to maintain your cover. The loss of life is regrettable, but keeping the trust of the JBA will put you in position to prevent an even greater tragedy.

PROFILE OBJECTIVES

- (NSA) GET JBA MEMBER MEDICAL FILES: To complete the agency profiles on the core of the JBA, you're going to need to access their medical profiles and pass that information along. The more we know about them, the better prepared we are to stop them.
- (NSA) SEARCH QUARTERS FOR PERSONAL INFO: In order to complete the NSA dossiers on the various core members of the JBA, we need you to get the personnel files of the core members of the JBA. With this data, the NSA can create a more accurate prediction model for their behavior—and how to stop them.
- (NSA) GET PROFESSIONAL BACKGROUND INFO: In order to complete the NSA dossiers on the various core members of the JBA, we need you to get data on the group's activities and their roles in it. Uploading this information will help us create a more accurate prediction model for what they might do next—and will help us plan to stop it.
- (NSA) GET JBA MEMBER VOICE SAMPLES: The JBA uses voice ID locks on sensitive areas of the compound. To get past them, you'll need to record the voices of the group's core members—the only ones certain to be cleared for all areas.
- (NSA) SCAN JBA MEMBER FINGERPRINTS: You'll need to scan the fingerprints of a core JBA member in order to get past any fingerprint locks in the compound. Use the app we've uploaded to your watch to locate and then scan the prints for later use.

After planting the bomb on the cruise ship, Sam and Enrica return to the JBA Headquarters. As Emile prepares to detonate the bomb in his grandiose style, Sam must prepare to prevent the detonation. However, his ability to do so is hampered when Emile assigns him to a menial decryption task. Further complicating matters is Lambert's demand that Sam access the next level of security in the compound and obtain visual proof that a bomb is being constructed on the property. Sam must obtain a fingerprint scan in order to access the ultrasecure surveillance room.

E-mail Decryption

Following a compound-wide blackout initiated by Lambert, Sam gets a phone call from his old colleague with new objectives. However, Emile appears at the door. Approach Emile to learn that he wants Sam to follow him.

Follow Emile to the main area and down the stairs. In the computer room, Emile leaves Sam at a computer and orders him to decrypt an e-mail from Massoud within 20 minutes. You must break the code as quickly as possible so you may spend the rest of the time infiltrating the surveillance room to obtain visual proof of the bomb. Return to the computer room before the onscreen timer expires.

TIP

The decryption module depicts a cube-shaped encryption block. Each side of the cube is broken down into four squares. Use the Move control to select squares, and press the Interact button to change the binary coding on the square to one of the following codes: 000, 001, 010, 011, 100, 101, 110, and 111. No two numbers in any row or column can be the same. Acceptable numbers appear on the cube in blue and white, while unacceptable or duplicated numbers are highlighted in orange.

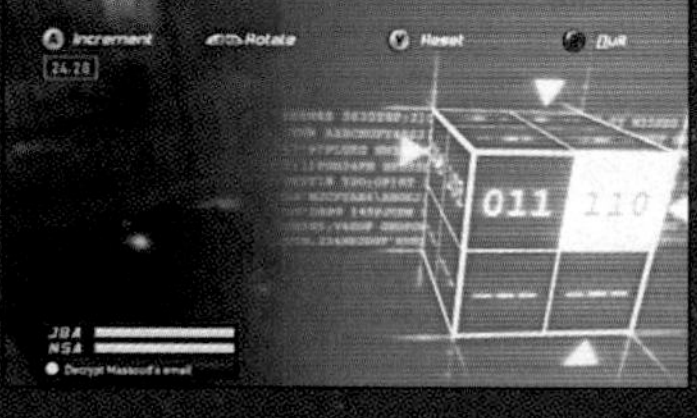

To solve the puzzle, you must use all eight numbers in every row. If a number has already been used in the row running left to right or up to down, then you will not be able to use all eight numbers in the row.

To do this without thinking too hard, use a placement strategy. Start off by filling the top row all the way around the cube. To avoid getting into a jam later, use a low number and a high number on each side of the cube. For instance, on one face you might use 000 and 101. On the next side, 001 and 100. On the next, 010 and 111, and so on.

After you fill the top row all the way around the cube, rotate the cube down so that the top face comes to the front. Fill the two squares on the left column with acceptable digits. As before, make one a low number and the other a high number. Rotate the cube downward twice so that you see the other blank side of the cube. Fill the left column with two acceptable digits, one high and one low.

Now rotate the cube in any random direction. Fill the open squares with the low or high equivalent of the diagonal square. For instance, if the upper-right square on a face has a 000, then fill the lower left square with another low digit such as 000, 001, 010, or 011, if possible. Continue going around the cube filling the empty squares until you have cracked the encryption. If you still can't fill a square on a face, see if you can change any of the other digits on that face to another number.

On to the Main Objective

With the above strategy, you should be able to decrypt the e-mail in roughly three or four minutes. That leaves sixteen minutes to scan a fingerprint sample, access the surveillance room upstairs, and obtain visual confirmation of the bomb. Any other objective is secondary, since none of it is essential and most you can fulfill in a later mission.

Upper Levels

Return to the corridor and go to the stairs where Sam began the first JBA Headquarters mission. Go upstairs and use a voice sample to bypass the voice lock on the door.

Inside the door, move to the left until the Visibility meter turns green, indicating that Sam is hidden. Wait for a man seated to the left to get up and walk off to Sam's right. Then head left, sticking to the shadows to avoid detection. Open the door and go down the stairs.

Enrica's Workshop

Upon emerging into the stairwell above the mine assembly area, jump to grab the horizontal pipe running the catwalk's length. Pull Sam's legs up, and shimmy to the corridor's end before dropping back to the ground. Input the code 1337 to unlock the door to Enrica's workshop. Stealthily open the workshop's door, because Enrica is inside performing some tests.

Go around the small table to the right and slip through the narrow gap between the desk and the wall. On the back side of the second desk is a laptop. Hack the computer's security access to learn the frequency to trigger the Cozumel bomb and to learn the code to the surveillance room door: 1269.

When you exit the computer, Jamie radios Enrica about the bomb. Move a step to the right and hide under the desk. Enrica rises from her seat and explores the room. Remain in hiding until she returns to her seat. Then sneak out quietly.

Enrica's Quarters

Head back to the low-security corridor where you used the voice recording to access the door. Move to the area's center. If a technician approaches, stay in the dark area near the voice-locked door until he moves past, then continue across the room. Head to the left past some couches, and follow the next turn to the right.

If a technician is working on the window at the corridor's end, move to the hall's left side and stand in the shadows until he leaves the area. Then pick the lock on the door on the corridor's right, which leads to Enrica's quarters. The technician is slowly making his way back. Hurry!

Inside Enrica's room, close the door behind you. The file cabinet on the right adds Enrica's personal info to her profile on the OPSAT watch, if you failed to obtain this info in a previous mission.

Equip the fingerprint scanner and move to the nightstand beside Enrica's bed. Hold the Primary Attack button to scan the top of the nightstand and find one of her fingerprints on the right side. Continue holding the Primary Attack button until the scan is complete.

Use the optic cable to check the corridor outside; then exit Enrica's quarters and head to the double doors to the right. Access the security panel on the wall. Enrica's fingerprint gets Sam inside the restricted area.

Surveillance Room

Stop just inside the double doors and wait for Jamie and Moss to finish their little spat directly ahead. Wait another second after Jamie disappears to the right; then go through the doorway and turn left. You see Carson Moss entering the surveillance room on the armory's opposite side.

Follow the passageway to the right past a conference room where two men discuss Moss's sanity. Stay close to the right-hand wall to avoid being identified by a security camera in the corridor.

Move past the room and head to the corner; turn left and continue down the passage, sticking to the right wall. This prevents the techie sitting at the desk inside the armory area to the left from spotting Sam. Avoid making any noise as you pass the door, and he will not look up from his computer monitor.

Visual Proof

Continue down the passage and stop outside the surveillance room door. Enter the code 1269 into the keypad to enter the surveillance room. Stop just inside the door and listen to Moss chew out a techie on your left.

When Moss leaves, the techie gets up and moves from his computer to the monitor on the right. Sneak over to his computer. Access the computer on the same desk to view the bomb staging area.

Exit the surveillance room and move into the shadows to the door's right. Wait for a guy to come out of the ammunition cage and move past your location. Then head down to the corner.

Another man leans against the wall in the passageway. Go through the gate to the right into the ammunition depot. Cross through the caged area and go through another gate on the left.

Continue out to the double doors. Open one and check for the technician working in the corridor. If he is standing by the window, allow him to walk off before moving through the door.

Head up the corridor's left side. Stop at the farthest possible point where the Visibility meter is still green. Wait for a man to enter the bathroom around the corner to the left; then head down the corridor to the vocal-scanner door and return downstairs to the main area.

Time to Play

If you have ample time remaining, raise your JBA Trust level by assembling another 10 mines in the mine assembly area, or by practicing at the firing range. Jamie has set a new high score of 113. The only way you stand to beat that score is by hitting at least 85 percent of the targets directly in the center.

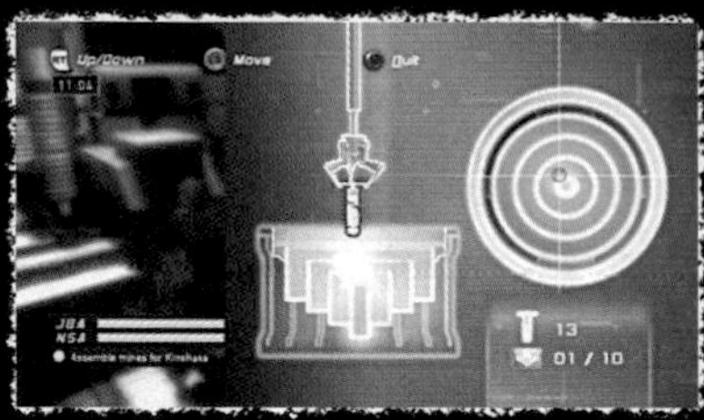

Showtime

You can fulfill all other profile-gathering objectives in an upcoming mission, so do not worry about those objectives now. Watch the timer while you play, and report back to the computer room where you decrypted the e-mail at least 10 seconds before Emile returns to check in.

After Emile checks to see if Sam decrypted the e-mail, the JBA heads gather in front of the big-screen television to watch the Cozumel bomb go off. If you failed to hack the detonation frequency during the Cozumel mission and failed to obtain the frequency from the computer in the lab during the current mission, then there is nothing you can do but watch as thousands die. But if you obtained the frequency, Sam raises his watch. As Emile counts down, press the Interact button if you wish to jam the transmission. Do nothing if you want the bomb to go off. Your action raises trust with one side or the other, depending on the outcome.

CAUTION

SPOILER ALERT! The following information contains story spoilers. Avoid reading this section to prevent ruining enjoyment of the game.

If the Cozumel bomb does not go off, Enrica is blamed for the failure and pays the ultimate price. If the bomb does go off, she remains alive. Don't feel bad about the passengers. Enrica's continued presence could prove useful in future missions...

Kinshasa—Presidential Hotel

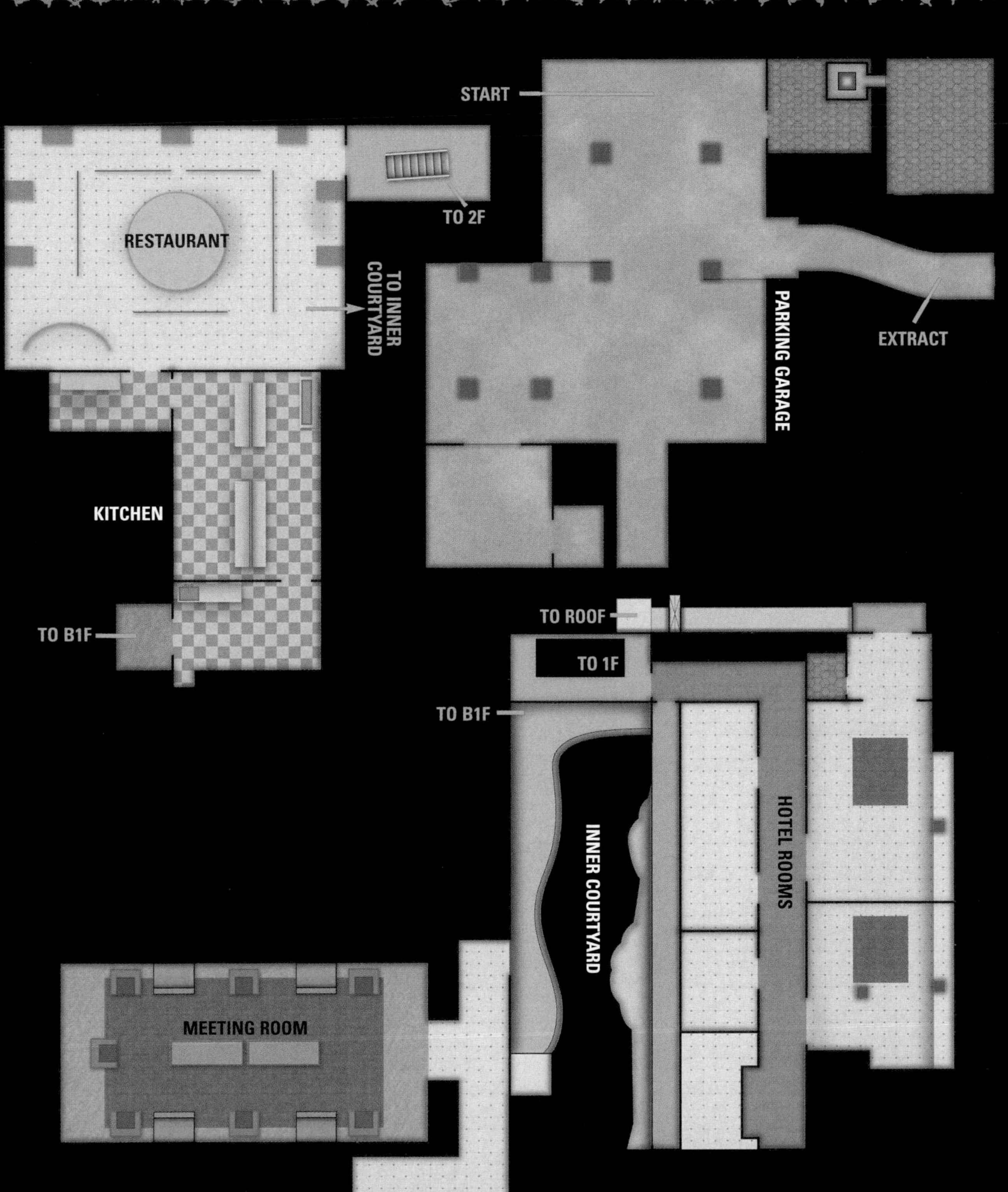

OBJECTIVES

MAIN OBJECTIVES

> (NSA) BUG THE SECRET MEETING ROOM: It is desperately important that we know the content of Emile's meeting with the other terrorist leaders. Plant a miniature microphone in one of the plants of the meeting room, so that the information can be communicated and we can make appropriate preparations. Avoid detection by Emile at all costs: if he notices you in the meeting room, your cover will be blown for sure.

> (JBA) RETURN TO PARKING LOT: Emile is on his way back to the parking lot. You have to reach it before he does, or he will be suspicious of your activities inside the hotel.

> (JBA) FIND CIA AGENT HISHAM HAMZA: You must locate Hisham Hamza. With the terrorist groups hunting for him, it is imperative that you find him first.

SECONDARY OBJECTIVES

> (NSA) AVOID ALL ALERTS: The terrorists are using a secure room at the top of the hotel for their meeting. However, it shouldn't be secure enough to keep you out. Find a way to infiltrate it without raising an alarm, or they may choose to use another site.

LOADOUT: KINSHASA

AVAILABLE WEAPONS
SC-20K/60
Shotgun shell/8
SC pistol/40
Sticky shocker/5
Airfoil round/5
Smoke grenade/3
Frag grenade/2
Flash grenade/3
Sonic grenade/3
Smoke grenade/3
Gas grenade/3
EMP grenade/3
Wall mine/3
Wall mine: flash/3
Wall mine: stun/3
Ultrasonic emitter

Sam accompanies Emile to a meeting in Kinshasa deep in the dark heart of the war-torn Republic of the Congo. The meeting is scheduled to take place at the ravaged Presidential Hotel just a few blocks from the palace. Rebel forces have overtaken the hotel. But in spite of this, Emile is determined to meet with terrorist leaders Massoud and Alejandro one last time. The meeting is set to take place in a high-security room. Sam must infiltrate this area and plant a bug in order to record the meeting.

Parking Garage

In spite of Sam's protests, Emile orders Sam to stay with the truck. After Emile departs, head around the truck's right side. Go around the equipment to the right and move to the chain-link fence. Do not use your knife to cut a hole in the fence, or the rebels in the area may notice the damage. Instead, climb over the fence and drop to the ground. Move around the right side of the crates and hide on the right side of a support column with yellow and black striping.

Hold position until a large truck pulls into the area. As all three men in the area head off to the left, move past the parked forklift and climb onto the low platform. Head diagonally to the left and board the elevator. Move somewhat quickly, or the truck's driver Tawkfir may spot you.

TIP

During the Kinshasa mission, Sam is equipped with one of the greatest high-tech gadgets available: the sunglasses! Press the Night Vision button to take your sunglasses off or put them on. In exterior settings, wearing the sunglasses filters sunlight and glare just like real sunglasses. However, while indoors you may want to toggle them off.

Kitchen

When the elevator arrives, the back doors slide open. Exit the elevator and move into the dark niche to the right. Hide in the niche as two men in the next room finish a conversation in another language. One man enters the room and heads to the shelves on the left. Exit your hiding place and grab him. Interrogate him, and then strangle or kill him, depending on how you feel about cold-blooded murderers.

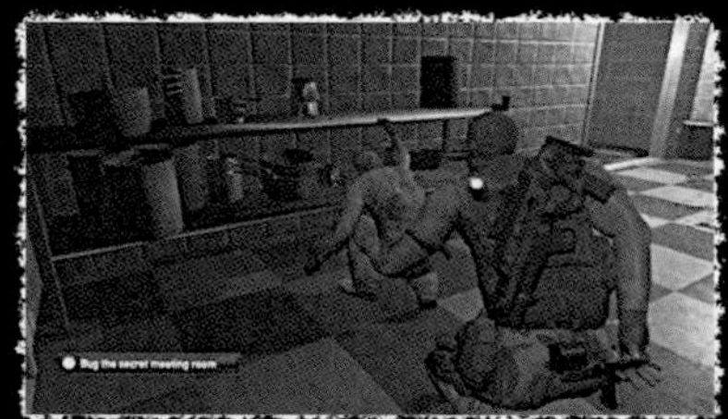

Restaurant

Head diagonally across the empty kitchen and go through the door. Press your back against the wall to the right side of the next doorway, which is adorned with flags. Wait until a helicopter attacks rebel forces in the next room. Watch as two rebels move from the room's right side over to the windows on the left. When both men have passed, go through the doorway and head right.

Follow the wall to a set of windows overlooking a courtyard. One of the windows is shattered. Climb through the open window, drop over the ledge's side, and hang.

Inner Courtyard

Shimmy to the right and around the corner. Ignore the open window, and shimmy around the next corner to reach a vertical pipe. Climb to the top of the pipe. A rebel soon appears on the balcony; before climbing over the rail, wait until the rebel steps through the doorway and moves to the right. Load a sticky shocker into the SC-20k and press the Secondary Attack button to knock him out.

Hotel Rooms

Use the optic cable on the door to view the corridor beyond. Twist the cable hard to the left to spot a rebel patrolling the corridor. Wait until he moves past the door to the right, and then open the door. Follow him down the corridor and grab him. Interrogate him, and then knock him out and hide his body in one of the rooms on the corridor's right side.

The second room on the right down the corridor contains a laptop with some highly informative e-mails regarding the security system on the hotel rooftop.

Presidential Suite

Go through the set of double doors in the corridor. Stay near the closets to the right or hide inside the closet. Wait until two rebels in the suite stop bickering. One man moves to the desk near the entrance and begins rummaging through the drawer. Sneak up behind him, grab him, and then drag him back toward the entrance. Interrogate him to hear some rather amusing excuses, and then choke him unconscious and leave him by the door.

Stop near the entryway's corner and rotate your view to see into the suite. When the guard patrolling the back bedroom moves out of sight, cross the living area and hide on the bedroom door's left side.

Wait patiently until the rebel reappears, searches the bedroom, and then heads left again. Then move around the corner and follow him into the bathroom. Strike him from behind to knock him out or kill him.

Hotel Rooftop

Head to the bedroom patio and turn left. Climb over the balcony rail and follow the ledge to the hotel sign. Climb up the sign as you would a ladder.

After Sam hoists himself on top of the sign, turn to face the wall and jump to grab a ledge. Shimmy right and climb onto the rooftop.

A rebel climbs the ladder to the far right, heading off to shoot at a helicopter circling the hotel. He'll be back soon, so head through the doorway to the left and hide in the empty room. Press your back against the wall near the doorway and peek outside.

After the rebel returns, he adopts a pattern: He stands near the building's edge and fires on government troops below for several seconds. He then retreats to the roof's far side in order to reload. After he reloads and starts heading back toward the ledge, exit your hiding spot and run up behind him. Strike him with a nonlethal attack. If he falls over the building's side, that's *his* problem.

Maintenance Shed

Climb up the ladder to the next section of rooftop and hide behind the air-conditioning unit. Observe the rebel moving back and forth near the wall until you perceive his pattern. Then head left around the air-conditioning unit and stop at the next corner of the air conditioner. Wait until the rebel moves right, then cross the rooftop diagonally, heading toward the far corner of the small building structure.

Press your back to the tall rooftop structure's outside wall and slide forward to the corner. Another rebel fights on this section of the rooftop. Unlike the other guy, he is in your way. Notice how he moves past the building's corner to the left to reload his weapon. Prepare an airfoil round. Switch the SC-20K to your right arm. Allow the lad to move past the corner so you can adjust your aim, and then let him go back to his other position and fire off another clip. The next time he stops in your sights, take him down. Reclaim your airfoil round if possible, then collect his body and hide it behind the building.

Head around the front of the building structure. Stop at the corner near the stairs leading up to the structure's entrance and observe the rebel you left on the rooftop's far side. When the he moves away with his back to Sam, run upstairs and enter the building structure.

Maintenance Access

The trapdoor in the structure's far corner is sealed and protected by laser sensors. Wall mines running down the shaft make it next to impossible to descend without being shredded apart. To overcome these obstacles, use the lock pick to open the breaker panel on the wall to the floor hatch's left. Hack the security device to deactivate the wall mines and open the floor hatch.

Jump to grab a horizontal pipe that runs over the open hatch. Climb out over the shaft until the Winch icon appears. Connect the winch to the pipe and descend to the shaft's bottom.

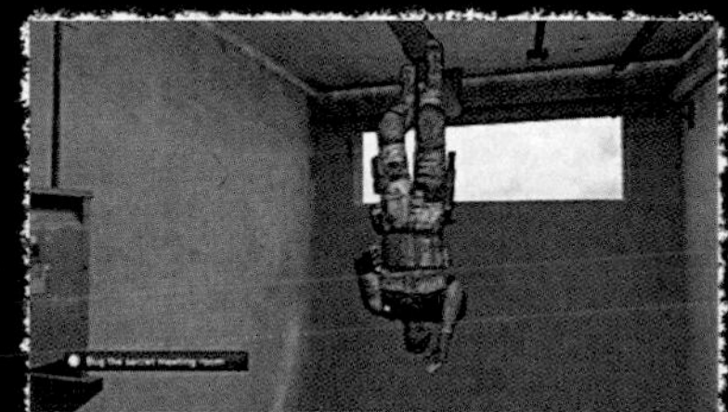

Meeting Room

Sam lands in a space overlooking the meeting room. The meeting area is encased in glass. The floor has laser touch sensors, meaning you must stick to the ceiling's pipe structure.

Climb down the ladder and enter the narrow gap between the barred area and the solid wall. Upon exiting the narrow passage, head to the left and enter a crawlspace under some pipes. Crawl through to the meeting room's other side.

Grab a gray vertical pipe attached to the outer wall and climb to the ceiling. Travel across the pipe's horizontal section and drop on top of the glass chamber. Head to the hatch in the glass ceiling's far corner and use the hacking device to crack the trapdoor's encryption.

Drop through the hatch and grab the horizontal pipe attached to the wall. Shimmy left and around the corner. Climb down a vertical pipe. Stand and press up against the glass wall in order to sidestep across a very thin ledge. After stepping off the ledge, jump to grab the next vertical pipe and climb back up to the ceiling.

Continue shimmying left and around a corner. Sam soon reaches a horizontal pipe that runs up the room's center. Climb hand over hand along the pipe until the Winch icon appears. Attach the winch to the pipe and descend toward the plant on the central coffee table. When the Microphone icon appears, press the Interact button to insert a bug into the plant.

The Meeting

The security sensors suddenly turn off and terrorists begin sauntering into the room. Quickly retract up to the ceiling and grab the horizontal pipe. Stop and do not move throughout the course of the meeting or risk being shot on sight.

Eventually a rebel enters the room and tells Alejandro Tawkfir that there is a mole in Massoud's organization. Everyone leaves. Sam must return to the truck in the underground parking lot before Emile gets there, or the operation is a bust. Use the winch to descend to the coffee table.

Shortcut to the Parking Lot

Exit the room and head to the gaping hole in the wall. Rappel down the wall, pressing the Jump button to descend as fast as possible.

Upon reaching the ground, run toward the door in the wall beneath the ballroom windows on the courtyard's far side. Instead of going through the door into the bathroom, take a shortcut through the vent hidden behind the toppled plant in the corner to the left.

Crawl through the vent into an airshaft. Drop through the central hole into another bathroom in the underground garage. Exit the bathroom and run over to the truck's front end before Emile gets there.

Emile orders Sam to hunt down and kill Hisham Hamza, the CIA mole working inside Massoud's group. Head up the long ramp toward the garage door to enter the streets of Kinshasa.

Kinshasa—Streets

MAP KEY

SC-20K Ammo

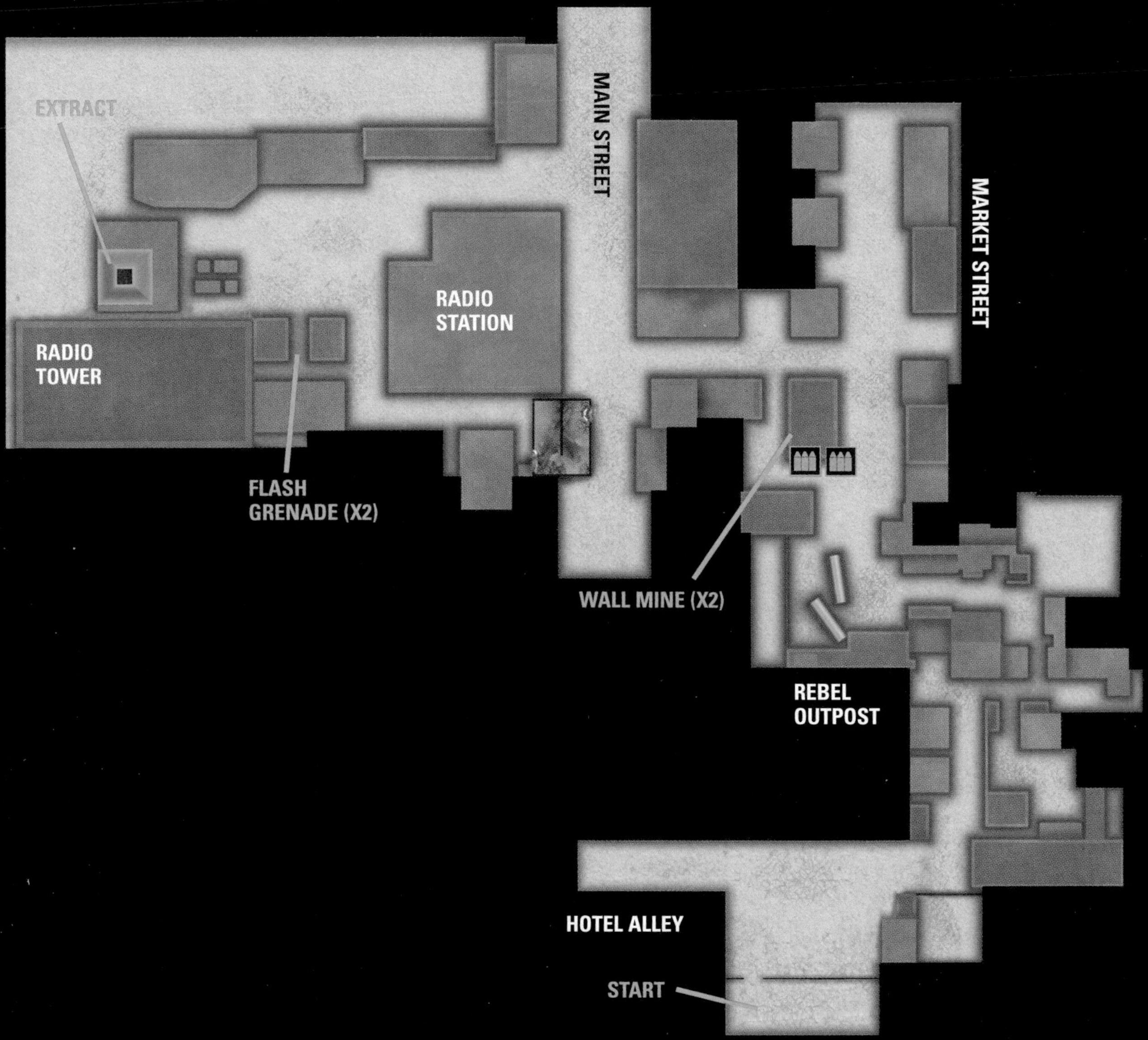

EXTRACT

MAIN STREET

MARKET STREET

RADIO STATION

RADIO TOWER

FLASH GRENADE (X2)

WALL MINE (X2)

REBEL OUTPOST

HOTEL ALLEY

START

OBJECTIVES

MAIN OBJECTIVES

> (JBA) FIND CIA AGENT HISHAM HAMZA: You must locate Hisham Hamza. With the terrorist groups hunting for him, it is imperative that you find him first.

PRIMARY OBJECTIVES

> (NSA) RETRIEVE PLANS FROM THE CAMP: If possible, infiltrate the rebel camp and take their operational plans. Do this while avoiding attention if you can, as the camp is crawling with Presidential forces.

SECONDARY OBJECTIVES

> (NSA) PREVENT THE EXECUTION: If possible, you should prevent civilian casualties. The Rebels will execute three civilians. You should stop them if possible.

> (NSA) SAVE WOMAN ON THE BUS: If possible, you should prevent civilian casualties. A woman is trapped inside the bus: you should try and reach her, and free her if you can.

CHOICES OBJECTIVES

> (NSA) DO NOT KILL HISHAM: Hisham Hamza has been identified as an embedded CIA operative in Massoud's group. Emile Dufraisne has ordered you to kill him, but doing so would deprive the NSA and the CIA of critical information that could lead to the prevention of massive terrorist attacks.

> (JBA) KILL HISHAM: Hisham Hamza has been identified as an embedded CIA operative in Massoud's group. Emile Dufraisne has ordered you to kill him, a move that would fortify your cover within the JBA.

After learning that a mole has infiltrated Massoud's group, Emile wants Sam to hunt down and kill Hisham Hamza. The CIA agent has fled into the streets of Kinshasa, which is in the grip of a rebel uprising. Everywhere Sam goes, rebel troops clash with government soldiers. Sam must navigate through the wholesale bloodshed and mayhem while pursuing Hamza to the presidential palace.

Hotel Alley

If you thought the battle was intense inside the hotel, you haven't seen anything yet. Sam hides behind a compact car. Hold your position and watch what happens to the military truck attempting to pull away. As the rebels run to the left behind the shattered wall, circle around the car to the left and break the lock on the gate. Close the gate behind you and quickly move along the wall. Stop behind the tall box near the corner.

Wait for a rebel to appear from the left, slowly walking to the right. Emerge from behind the box and pursue the young man. Grab him from behind and drag him toward the hodgepodge of crates near the opposite wall. Choke him unconscious.

Move to the wall's end and peer around the corner into the next area. Wait until a bandaged rebel appears from the left and moves to the middle of the street. When he starts speaking with the rebel in the building ruins to the left, run across the street into a small alleyway.

Rebel Outpost

Continue through the alleyway and stop at the next corner. Peek around the corner and watch an armed rebel move to the left out of sight. Then go around the corner and follow the left wall to a gruesome scene.

The rebels are about to slaughter an innocent family. The NSA wants you to prevent civilian deaths. That means killing or disabling the rebels. If you fail to act, the rebels slaughter the civilians one by one. The best strategy is to grab the closest rebel and use him as a human shield while you shoot the other. Then perform a lethal attack to finish off the man you hold.

Climb through the open window in the courtyard, and sneak through the empty apartment. Climb out the next open window to the street.

Battle Zone

Stop at the next corner and peek into the area. A woman runs through a doorway on the right as rebels run down the street to engage in battle. When the street is clear, or when the rebels seem focused on the battle, follow the woman into the house. Ignore her cries of surprise at seeing you and climb through the open window.

As a tank blows up the streets, head to the right down the alley. Find the ladder attached to the building's side and climb up to the balcony.

Government troops on the ground may spot Sam. To them, he is no different than a rebel. Exit and run down the balcony while crouched. Move down to the balcony's corner.

Market Street

As usual, Emile is not happy with Sam's progress. But don't let him rush you. Head from the balcony's corner to the cover of the next chunk of concrete wall to the right. Hold your position and watch a tank blow up and overturn a civilian bus farther down the street. A woman is trapped on that bus, and the NSA wants Sam to save her. Meanwhile, Sam has his own skin to think about.

Exit your cover position, move left, and sneak out to the end of the wooden rooftop. Drop over the rooftop's side and hang, then drop to the ground. The government troops by the tank now behind you may notice. Quickly run over and drop into the nearby ditch. Move into the first broken pipe segment and wait for the Visibility meter to change from red to yellow, if needed.

Run through the broken pipe segments in the ditch. At the end, turn right and climb out. Quickly run over to the bus's end. The window is smashed out, creating an entrance. A woman is trapped halfway down the bus, with her leg caught under a seat. Approach her and press the Interact button to free her leg. A small amount of trust is gained with the NSA. The fire at the end of the bus subsides, allowing you to exit in that direction.

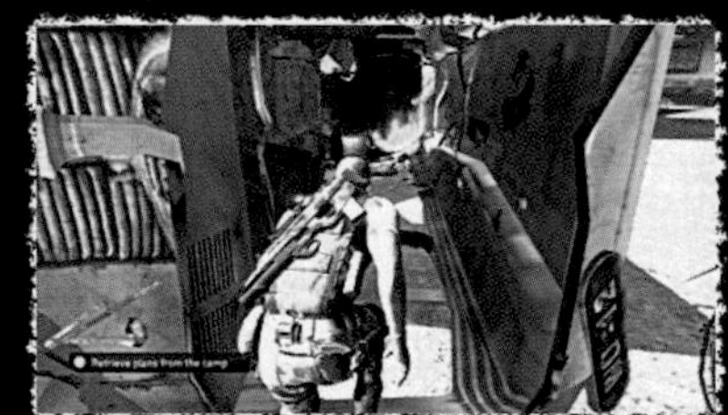

Sniper's Apartment

Head down the street and hide behind the overturned vehicle. Peer around the sides of the car to watch two soldiers as they fix a stalled truck. When the men crawl underneath the truck, race for the alley to the left.

Go down the alley and up the stairs on the left. Ascend the stairs and crouch under the open window. Angle your view to make sure the sniper inside the apartment is shooting through the window and not facing the doorway. Then sneak into the apartment and knock him out. Use the laptop on the table to read important e-mails. Also on the table are two wall mines and two boxes of SC-20K ammunition.

Main Street

Return through the narrow alley to the street. The soldiers are finished working on their truck now. Hide behind cover on the street's left side until the two men board the truck and drive off. Then head to the street's end.

The area to the right is an open-ground war zone. Even a rookie knows better than to take that route. Instead, cross the street, moving behind the destroyed vehicles and tanks to remain hidden. Go through a hole blown in a blue and green wall.

Mined Alley

Follow the twisting corridor until it opens into an alley. A few steps away, a rebel accidentally steps on a mine. Bear that in mind as you head down the alley. Stay as close to the alley's left side as possible. Continue up the side until you reach a box that has fallen on top of some sandbags. From there, head diagonally across the street to the concrete stairs. Follow the concrete stairs around the corner.

Radio Tower

A helicopter lands as Sam approaches a rebel camp at the foot of the destination radio tower. The military has taken control of the base with reinforcements incoming. Five soldiers disembark from the helicopter and begin patrolling the base, in addition to their commander and two other soldiers who were already nearby. This complicates matters, to say the least.

As the helicopter lands, move behind the closest green tent. Cut through the fabric of the tent wall and go inside. The commander sits at a laptop in the far corner. Hide behind the boxes on the room's left side until the commander exits to greet his troops. Climb over the boxes and the file cabinet, and hack the security access on the laptop to download the rebel's plans, thus pleasing the NSA. You have 15 seconds to hack the security access, so spot those fixed digits quickly!

After downloading the plans, exit the way you came in. The rest of this strategy requires a great deal of patience, so prepare to wait while soldiers make long patrols. Move to the outer corner of the commander's tent and wait two or three minutes for a soldier to come around the corner. Move back from the corner as he approaches, since Sam is highly visible even when peeking from a corner.

Load an airfoil round into the SC-20K. As the guard stops across from the alley where Sam hides, fire the airfoil at his head. While the guard attempts to recover from the blow, run up and grab him from behind. Drag him around the corner of the building, in the direction from which you entered this area. Choke him unconscious and leave his body behind the building's corner. Return to your hiding spot behind the commander's tent.

Move to the tent's left corner and peek around the corner. Keep watch on the central area until you see a soldier briskly walking in either direction behind the helicopter. This indicates that the central area is clear enough for you to cross to the area behind the other tent.

Cut through the fabric on the back of the tent. Cross the tent's interior and press your back against the front opening's right side. Survey the scene by the green power transformers outside and to the left. Watch a soldier come around the corner and cross in front of the transformers. This soldier is your target hostile. Beyond him, another soldier walks to the left behind the transformers. When the second man disappears behind the transformers, slip out of the tent and follow the target soldier past the transformers.

Take your time creeping down the aisle between the transformers and brick wall to the left. Hold off on grabbing the target soldier until he turns to his right and starts to go behind the aisle. This should give the other soldier in the area ample opportunity to turn and walk off. Capture the target soldier as soon as possible, and hide his unconscious body between the transformers and the electric fence barring access to the radio tower.

The coast should now be clear enough to cut the power cable to the transformer and deactivate the electrified fence. The power cables are located in the center of the transformers.

Go through the gate and climb the red ladder all the way to the top of the communications tower. Head around to the platform's opposite side to find a sniper rifle. Press the Interact button to grab the sniper rifle and view through the scope. The scope is trained on a window in the presidential palace. Keep it there until Hisham Hamza appears.

Monitor the situation until Emile orders Sam to kill Hisham. Lambert is screaming bloody murder, absolutely forbidding Sam to shoot the CIA operative. Either way, Sam must act fast. The government soldier inside the palace has decided to kill Hisham after speaking to his superior. If you do nothing, the soldier eventually chops him up with a machete. If you choose to protect your cover, shoot Hisham before the government soldier kills him in order to gain trust with the JBA. Should this be your choice, skip ahead in this book to the next JBA Headquarters mission.

To save Hisham, shoot the government soldier. He is easier to hit before he and Hisham get into a scuffle. Press the Zoom button for better aim, and hold the Secondary Attack button to hold your breath. Fire when ready. Just then, rebel forces invade the presidential palace. Have fun sniping the rebels inside the palace until a mortar rocket takes out the tower, knocking Sam unconscious.

Kinshasa—Presidential Palace

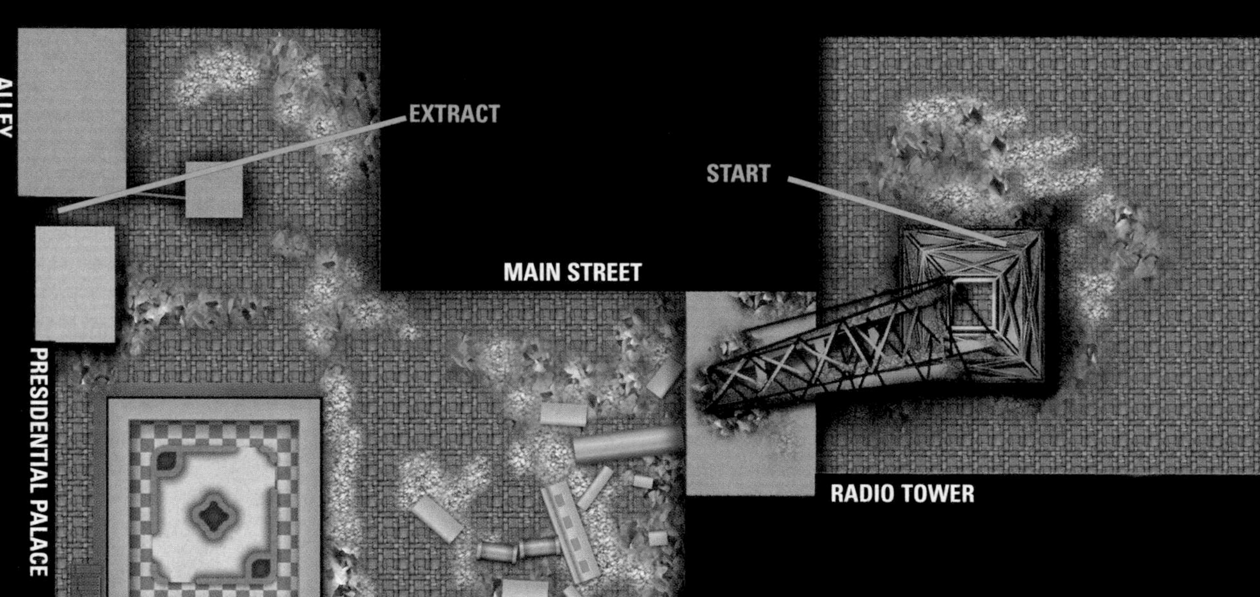

ASSIGNMENT

> (NSA) RESCUE HISHAM: Hisham Hamza is a prisoner of the rebel forces who have overtaken the Presidential Palace, located on the other side of the battle zone from the radio tower. Infiltrate the palace, and help Hisham escape from his captors. Be careful; the rebels are on edge, and if you trigger an alarm, they might begin to execute prisoners.

> (NSA) HELP HISHAM ESCAPE: Despite your orders from Emile, Hisham Hamza is a valuable asset who must be kept alive. Do what you must to help Hamza escape. Escort him to the fence near the docks, so he can regroup with CIA assets on the ground. The fence is near your rendezvous point with Emile.

Having rescued Hisham Hamza from the hands of corrupt government officials, Sam must now head through the scene of a bloody shooting battle toward the presidential palace, just one block away. Ducking machine-gun fire every step of the way, Sam must navigate inside the palace and determine how to free Hisham from the rebels before they execute him.

What a Headache

Sam wakes up on what's left of the communications tower just as a helicopter crashes one block away. Luckily, his sunglasses are still intact. Move to the edge of the tower facing the presidential palace and jump up to grab a zip-line.

Main Street

After dropping into the building ruins, head through the door to the left. In the street outside the building is a massive shoot-out between rebels and soldiers. The chances of being spotted and fired upon by either side are extremely high. If you are targeted, crawl inside a hole or cover until the Visibility meter turns from red to yellow.

Drop through the hole to the ground level. Exit the building and enter the destroyed bus on the left. Move through the bus and drop through the hole on the left side. Hide behind the construction trash bin and watch as a rebel charges forward and steps on a mine.

To the right of the construction bin is an overturned truck with a huge hole in the bottom. Enter the truck and head left.

Another hole near the end of the truck on the right leads into a concrete pipe segment. Toss a smoke grenade at the ground between this pipe segment and the next to prevent the combatants outside from seeing you pass from one tube to another. Drop from the second pipe into a ditch, and quickly head to the left.

As you emerge from the pipe's end, the crashed helicopter falls from above. Climb into the open back of the helicopter and go to the cockpit. Two sonic grenades are located in the cockpit. However, stopping to pick them up may cause you to miss an opportunity to get out of the cockpit without being detected. Drop out of the left side of the open cockpit into the presidential palace yard while the smoke from the last explosion still hangs in the air.

Presidential Palace

Hisham's situation is critical. If even one rebel sees Sam, the rest of the rebels will execute Hisham immediately. That is why you can only watch helplessly as a rebel abuses a soldier in the courtyard. Eventually, the soldier tries to run and the rebel guns him down right next to Sam. Overzealous, the rebel moves to the soldier's body and riddles his body with bullets. Sneak up behind the rebel and knock him out.

Move beside a stack of bricks piled up next to the large open doorway. From here, watch the activity inside the palace interior. Hisham is bound and on his knees in the far left corner. A rebel with a red bandana moves around the central area, soon interrogating a presidential soldier tied to a chair. The rebel with the red bandana then goes to the desk on the left. This is your cue to cross the large doorway and climb the ladder attached to the scaffolding.

A soldier at the far corner on the scaffold's top level is oblivious to all but the targets he shoots at outside the palace walls. Sneak up behind him and punch him in the neck to knock him out. Then turn to face the building and jump up to grab the roof's edge. Climb onto the roof.

Move toward the area's center. Sam is invisible to the rebels pacing the ground below. Use either sticky shockers or well-aimed bullets to take out the three rebels inside the palace in the following order:

1. Take out the rebel to the far right who rummages through the pockets of dead soldiers.
2. Take out the rebel with the red bandana in the central area. Try to hit him before he returns to the center and spots the body of the previous rebel.
3. Take out the rebel with the light blue bandana who patrols near Hisham. Sometimes he sits on a crate near the railing of the central area.

Rescue Hisham

Return to the corner where you climbed up. Notice the ladder attached to the hole in the ceiling. Climb down the ladder to an interior scaffold. Move to the scaffold's other end and drop to the level below. Follow this level of the scaffold to the other end. Drop over the side and hang, then drop to the ground level.

Exit from under the scaffold, head over to Hisham, and untie him. After a few grateful words, Hisham follows Sam. Head through the shattered window to the right, and carefully approach the hole in the back wall in the area behind the presidential palace.

Alley

Equip the SC-20K. A lone rebel patrols the alley behind the presidential palace. When he passes across the hole in the wall, take him down by whatever means remain available. Do it before he spots Sam or Hisham and opens fire.

Lead Hisham through the alleyway. Turn left at the end and head to a large barricade. When the Co-op Move icon appears, press the Interact button to boost Hisham over the barrier to safety.

NYC—JBA HQ—Part 4

MAP KEY

SC-20K/goggles
SC-20K ammunition
Smoke grenade

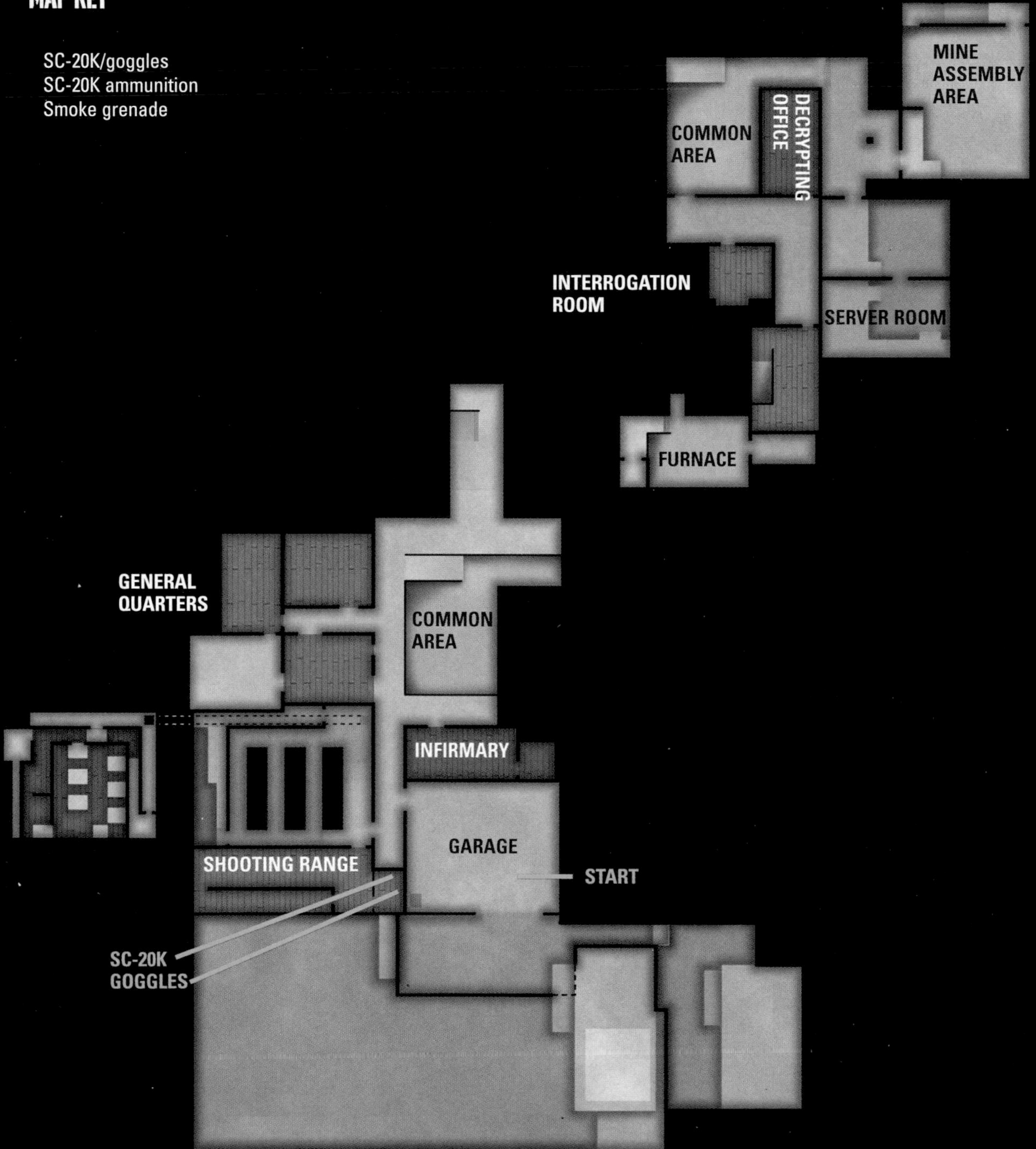

MINE ASSEMBLY AREA
COMMON AREA
DECRYPTING OFFICE
INTERROGATION ROOM
SERVER ROOM
FURNACE
GENERAL QUARTERS
COMMON AREA
INFIRMARY
GARAGE
SHOOTING RANGE
START
SC-20K GOGGLES

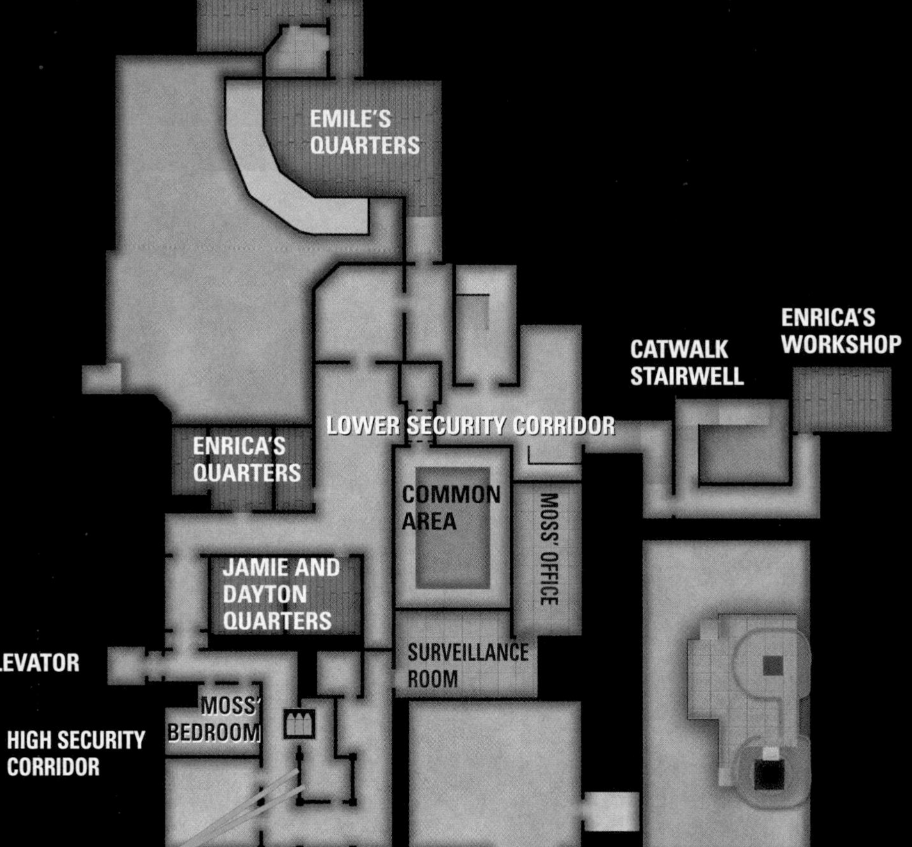

OBJECTIVES

PRIMARY OBJECTIVES

> (NSA) FIND AND DEFUSE BOMB: Thanks to you, we know that the last red mercury device is on-site. You must find it and neutralize it, for if it is triggered, it could devastate the greater New York City area.

PROFILE OBJECTIVES

> (NSA) SEARCH QUARTERS FOR PERSONAL INFO: In order to complete the NSA dossiers on the various core members of the JBA, we need you to get the personnel files of the core members of the JBA. With this data, the NSA can create a more accurate prediction model for their behavior—and how to stop them.

> (NSA) GET PROFESSIONAL BACKGROUND INFO: In order to complete the NSA dossiers on the various core members of the JBA, we need you to get data on the group's activities and their roles in it. Uploading this information will help us create a more accurate prediction model for what they might do next—and will help us plan to stop it.

> (NSA) GET JBA MEMBER VOICE SAMPLES: The JBA uses voice ID locks on sensitive areas of the compound. To get past them, you'll need to record the voices of the group's core members—the only ones certain to be cleared for all areas.

> (NSA) SCAN JBA MEMBER FINGERPRINTS: You'll need to scan the fingerprints of a core JBA member in order to get past any fingerprint locks in the compound. Use the app we've uploaded to your watch to locate and then scan the prints for later use.

> (NSA) SCAN RETINAS OF JBA MEMBERS: The most secure areas of the compound are behind a retina-scan lock. A live group member might help you through. Otherwise, eyes taken from a corpse should open the lock. With these, you'll also help complete the profiles the NSA is compiling on the members of the JBA.

With Hisham Hamza dead or presumed dead, Sam returns to the JBA headquarters in New York City to help Emile Dufraisne and the others finally carry out their sadistic plans for terrorism. As the criminals divide and prepare to conquer, Emile leads Sam into the grizzly interrogation room. There, Sam is confronted by a shocking dilemma. No matter what his decision, the time has come to take down the JBA once and for all.

Lambert's Fate

Follow Emile out of the garage. In the common area, notice that Stanley Dayton runs toward the server room. Keep that in mind as you follow Emile to the interrogation room.

Today's subject of execution is none other than Irving Lambert. Emile hands Sam the familiar Luger and excuses himself. Jamie Washington is in the room as well, and his threats are serious. If Jamie counts down and Sam does not pull the trigger, Jamie will shoot Sam. You must shoot either Lambert or Jamie.

NOTE

Your choice here directly impacts the rest of this mission and the game's ending. If you pull the trigger on Lambert to protect your cover, then the JBA Trust meter fills completely. This allows Sam to walk freely through the compound and complete the rest of his objectives with little interference. If you go this route, the JBA members are not actively searching for Sam and many may appear in different locations. Choosing to shoot Lambert does not allow you to finish the game on board the coast guard boat. This is considered the "bad ending."

If you kill Jamie, Sam's action is caught on the surveillance camera and he is instantly identified as a traitor. Every man in the compound will be out to get you. However, this choice allows Sam to finish the game with the "good ending" and play the Coast Guard Boat mission. This path choice requires a great deal more strategy and skill; therefore, this guide explains how to overcome this path, with a note or two regarding the other path.

Shoot Jamie Washington in the chest. Watch the expression on his face change, let his body drop to the ground, and then move to his corpse and press the Interact button to scan his retina.

Hunting Fisher

Men are on their way to the interrogation room to kill you. Exit to the corridor and move right. Flip the light switch outside the doorway to darken the corridor, and turn off the lights inside the decrypting office to draw the attention of all the enemies in the common area. Head to the door closest to the conference area and wait in the darkness. Press Sam's back against the wall on the door's right side and wait for two or three men to slowly enter the corridor, one at a time. Perform corner grabs on each man and knock out or kill each as they come around the corner.

Head down the corridor past the decrypting office, and go downstairs to the furnace room. If you prevented the detonation of the Cozumel bomb, Enrica's body is lying on the slab below the incinerator. Scan her retina to complete her profile.

Gear Up

Climb up the ladder from the furnace room into the garage. Cross the corridor and enter the shooting range. The cage is open, and the weapon racks have been raided—all but Sam's SC-20K and vision goggles. Equip them both, and return to the common area corridor.

Common Assassinations

If you killed only two men in the corridor outside the interrogation room, then another man may be patrolling the midlevel of the common area. Either snipe him with a single SC-20K shot or wait for him in the shadows and punch his ticket.

Do yourself a big favor and position Sam at the corner at the top of the stairs. Use the SC-20K's scope to survey the surveillance room high overhead. When the lone man inside the surveillance room moves into the opening, giving you a clear shot at his head, take him down. This prevents him from spotting you and warning others several times down the road.

Dayton Dies

Head downstairs and go behind the decrypting office to the server room. Input the code 6278 to enter the server room. Jump up in the corner to grab the horizontal ceiling pipe and shimmy past the surveillance camera over the server room door.

Enter the server room and look right to spot Stan Dayton, hard at work trying to crash the JBA's server. Move up the steps and open the trapdoor in the raised level's corner. Move under the platform to the other trapdoor, and climb out behind Dayton carefully; avoid making any noise. Grab Dayton by the neck and make him tell you where Emile is; then sentence him to death with a lethal attack. Use the retinal scanner on his corpse. If you have not yet obtained his activity data, open the file cabinet on the computer desk's other side. Use the fingerprint scanner on the desk to obtain Dayton's print. That closes the case on poor, misguided Stanley Dayton.

Before exiting the server room, shoot the camera above the door. Then you may exit the server room area without having to avoid the camera.

Last Stop at Enrica's Workshop (Optional)

Head through the mine assembly area and open the voice-lock door. Ascend the stairs quickly to avoid being spotted by the camera. If you missed getting Enrica's activity data earlier, shoot the camera mounted on the wall near the top of the stairs and go to her workshop. Enter the code 1337 to open the workshop door, and examine the file cabinet in the corner to obtain her professional history.

Clearing Low Security

Exit Enrica's workshop and head to the catwalk stairwell. Turn out the lights before exiting to the low-security corridor outside Emile's quarters. Two armed men patrol the area. Head over to the light switch at the corner on the right and plunge the two men into darkness. Since bullets are in short supply at the moment, sneak up on the guys in the dark. Drag them off to the corners of the area for interrogation and strangling or death.

If you only managed to drag off one guy, it means the bald fellow is probably patrolling the area around the couches. As he heads past the wall near the pool table room, follow him to the corner. Allow him to walk off, and turn out the lights on him. He reacts by summoning another terrorist from the corridor near Enrica's quarters, and the two stand amidst the furniture for a moment. Wait until the men resume their patrol routes, and then sneak up on baldy in the dark and quietly choke him unconscious.

The last remaining terrorist in this area runs into the bathroom. Follow him in there and take him out.

Emile's Prints

Head back to Emile's quarters. Enter the code 2701 into the keypad to open the door. A lone technician is boarding up the windows in Emile's office. Sneak up behind him and take him out. If needed, examine the file cabinets in the office and in Emile's bedroom to fill out his profile. Then head over to the sitting area across from the entrance. To obtain Emile's fingerprint, use the fingerprint scanner on the center of the coffee table.

Jamie's Prints

Return to the low-security corridor. Turn out the light at the corner near Jamie and Dayton's quarters. Break the lock on their door and go inside. Two glass desks are situated in the corner across from the entrance. Scan the center of the desk to the right to find Jamie Washington's fingerprints. If necessary, go into the bedroom and open the two

file cabinets to add Jamie's and Stan's personal info to your profiles.

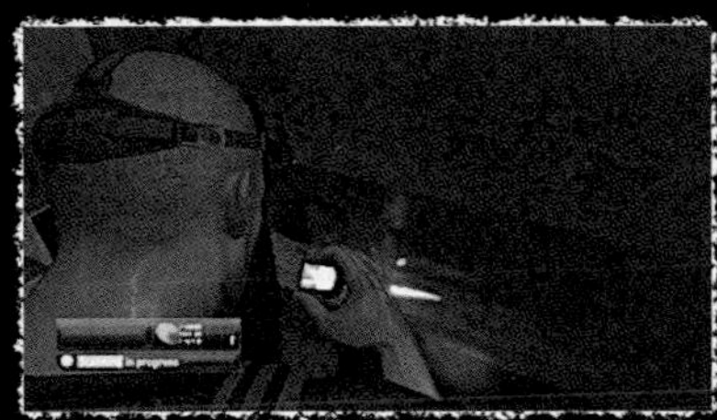

If necessary, break into Enrica's quarters to get her personal info, and then head down to the fingerprint-lock door leading to the high-security corridor.

Rendezvous

Head through the short passage and go through the next set of double doors. If the Cozumel bomb went off as planned and Enrica survived the last JBA HQ mission, then she appears in the corridor. She volunteers to help Sam try to stop Emile from detonating the bomb. You have a couple of sick options at this point. You can grab Enrica in a unique chokehold and interrogate her, then knock her out or snuff her candle. Or, you can shoot her while she's at the retinal scanner by the elevator. Scan her retina and complete her profile.

Moss's Bedroom

Pick the lock on the door near the elevator, which leads to Moss's bedroom. Do not break the lock, or the locals might get rowdy. Inside Moss's quarters, open the file cabinet to obtain his personal data. Use the fingerprint scanner to obtain Moss's print from the desk.

Armory

Return to the high-security corridor and head around the corner to the right. Avoid stepping in the rays of light emanating from the conference room at the corner. Wait for a guy to jog out of the conference room into the corridor, and then back again. Go through the gate on the left into the armory cage.

Check the low shelf just inside the armory cage to find two boxes of SC-20K ammunition. Reload your weapon, then head to the bench on the computer desk's right side to find two smoke grenades. This is all the weaponry available in this mission, so make it count!

Wait until Mr. Bouncy-trots goes from the conference room out to the corridor, and then back to the conference room again. Exit the armory cage via the sliding gate to the computer desk's left, and wait in the shadows around the corner. When Mr. Bouncy-trots stops at the window in the corridor near the corner, grab him from behind and choke him unconscious.

Another guard patrols near the surveillance room door. Sneak up behind him and knock him out. Enter the code 1269 into the keypad to enter the surveillance room.

Moss's Office

If you did not already snipe the man in the surveillance room from the lower level, take care of that now. Then cross the surveillance room and open the door to Moss's office in the corner.

Hack the security access folder on Moss's computer to read an e-mail containing the code to the underground lab: 2112. Open the file cabinet in the corner behind the desk to add Moss's activity data to his profile. Now you just need to find the big man himself and scan his dead eyeball.

Return to the elevator in the high-security corridor. Use the retinal-scan data you've accumulated to override the retinal scanner lock on the elevator door. Enter the elevator car and press the button to descend to the lower levels.

NYC—JBA HQ—Final Showdown

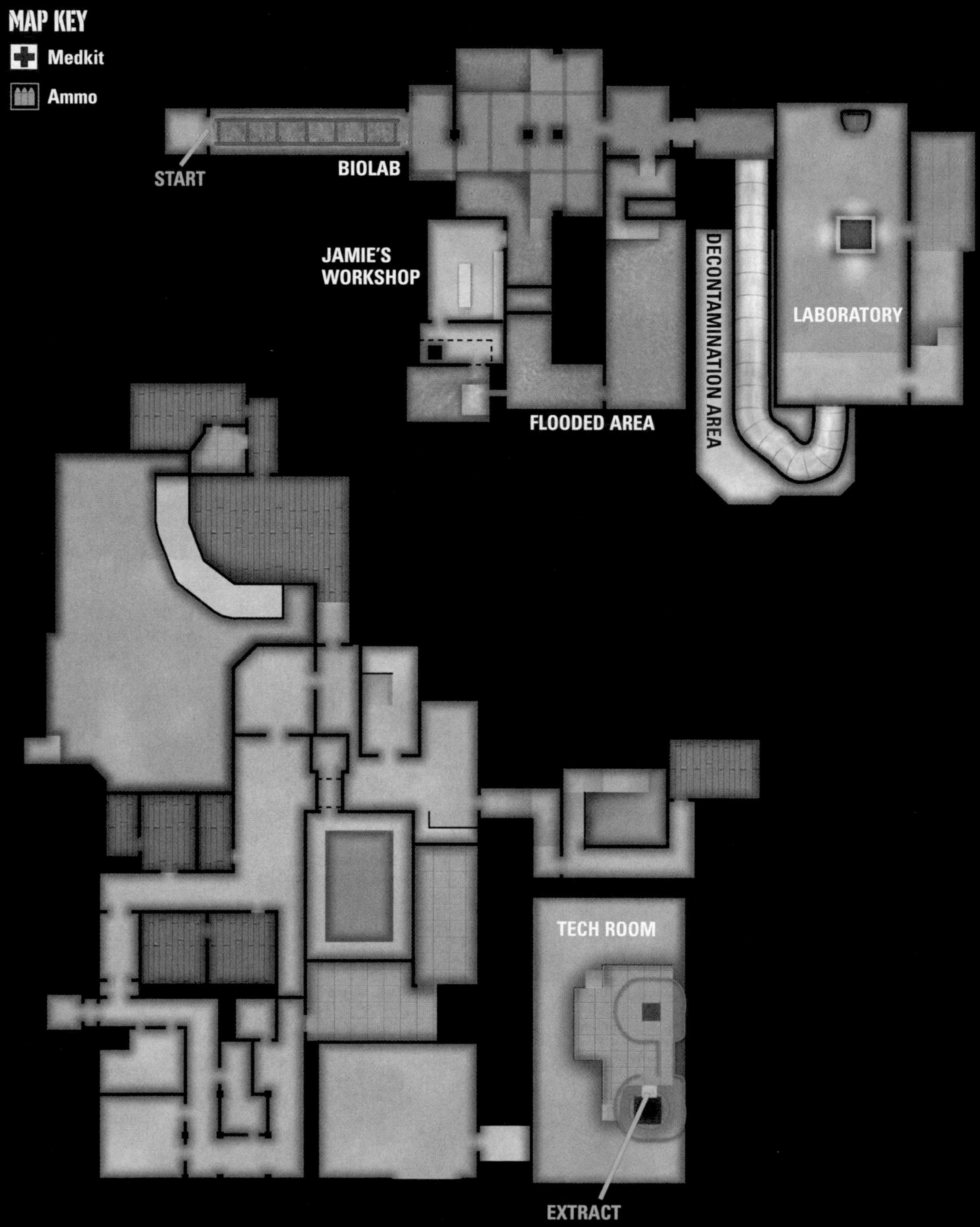

MAP KEY

Medkit

Ammo

OBJECTIVES

PRIMARY OBJECTIVES

> (NSA) FIND AND DEFUSE BOMB: Thanks to you, we know that the last red mercury device is on-site. You must find it and neutralize it, for if it is triggered, it could devastate the greater New York City area.

PROFILE OBJECTIVES

> (NSA) GET PROFESSIONAL BACKGROUND INFO: In order to complete the NSA dossiers on the various core members of the JBA, we need you to get data on the group's activities and their roles in it. Uploading this information will help us create a more accurate prediction model for what they might do next—and will help us plan to stop it.

> (NSA) GET JBA MEMBER VOICE SAMPLES: The JBA uses voice ID locks on sensitive areas of the compound. To get past them, you'll need to record the voices of the group's core members—the only ones certain to be cleared for all areas.

> (NSA) SCAN JBA MEMBER FINGERPRINTS: You'll need to scan the fingerprints of a core JBA member in order to get past any fingerprint locks in the compound. Use the app we've uploaded to your watch to locate and then scan the prints for later use.

> (NSA) SCAN RETINAS OF JBA MEMBERS: The most secure areas of the compound are behind a retina-scan lock. A live group member might help you through. Otherwise, eyes taken from a corpse should open the lock. With these, you'll also help complete the profiles the NSA is compiling on the members of the JBA.

Having penetrated to the heart of the JBA lair in the caves deep under the compound, Sam must now take out the last members of the JBA and defuse the bomb before Emile Dufraisne's evil plans to annihilate New York City are realized. All that stands in your way is Dufraisne, who isn't going out easily.

Biolab

As the elevator doors open, you see a man in a red biohazard suit walking away on patrol. Find the light switch halfway down the corridor on the right, and turn out the lights. Press Sam's back against the support column under the light switch, and wait for the guard to return. As he approaches the corner, perform a corner grab. Interrogate him about the lab before taking him out.

Turn out the lights using the switch at the corner. Then press Sam's back against the wall at the corner and wait. Soon, one of the lab techies notices the lights are out and comes to investigate. Perform a corner grab and choke him unconscious.

Your actions probably failed to pique any interest from the two men remaining in the biolab; sneak into the biolab and steal up behind the guard in the red biosuit. Grab him and drag him out to the corridor, and choke him unconscious.

Taking out the guard in this manner brings out the last remaining techie into the corridor. Hide behind the corner and take him down with a corner grab.

If the last techie does not notice his missing compatriots or the doused lights, do not go after him. Instead, wait for another armed guard to emerge from the decontamination corridor and notice that the lights are out. Wait for him with your back pressed against the wall near the corner, and take him down with a corner grab. Now you may take out the last remaining techie with a knockout attack.

Jamie's Workshop

Head downstairs to Jamie's workshop and enter the code 1234 to open the door. The computer in his workshop contains the lab code 2112. Open the file cabinet against the wall to obtain Jamie's activity data.

Go through the second doorway in Jamie's room and drop through the open floor hatch. Head around the bars to the right and climb onto a small box. Enter an open vent hole high up on the wall and crawl through to the flooded area.

Flooded Area

A mechanic wearing a blue bandana should be moving away from Sam's position, wading through the hip-high waters. The best way to handle him is to snipe him with the SC-20K.

Wade to the flooded area's other side and head up the stairs. Turn out the lights using the switch on the brick wall, and then go through the door back to the biolab area.

If you chose to shoot Lambert, then Jamie Washington is through the door on your right. Otherwise, the route should be clear.

Decontamination Area

If Jamie is standing at the equipment opposite the door, sneak up behind him and grab him. Interrogate him, and then smash his spinal column. Scan his retina to close his profile.

Otherwise, simply head through the decontamination doors and navigate through the plastic tube corridor into the laboratory.

Laboratory

Sam is helpless to watch as Emile activates the countdown sequence on the Red Mercury bomb. The bomb is then raised to the tech room above the lab. Sam has just 10 minutes to reach the bomb and defuse it before New York City is history.

Head down the ramp and to the door on the right. Pick the lock, and use the SC-20K to take out the spotlight across from the door. Move through the darkness into the control room. A guard in a red biosuit stands at the opposite end. Snipe him from the top of the stairs.

Sneak downstairs and head over to the door, keeping to the shadows as much as possible. Enter the code 2112 into the keypad on the lab door to open it. Equip a smoke grenade and toss it into the room, between the doorway and the two guards in biosuits. Quickly equip the SC-20K and switch on thermo vision. Try to take down the two guards with single shots to their heads as they move in to investigate the cause of the smoke.

Now switch to wave vision and shoot the camera above the ladder access booth. Return to the control room and hack the security access on the computer to open the ladder access doors. Unlock the lab door once again, and go up the ladder to the room on the level above.

Tech Room

After climbing two ladders to reach the tech room, dismount the ladder and move quietly through the open doorway. Don't linger too long near the ladder for fear of being spotted by the other men in the room. You can see Emile through thick glass, waiting for his precious bomb to go off.

Climb over the railing outside the door. Move through the shadows directly across the outer area to the wall, and then head left through a narrow gap behind some cargo. Continue following the wall over to the corner, and you should find yourself standing behind a stationary guard. Grab him and drag him into the corner, then quietly choke him unconscious.

Sneak forward along the shadow created by the column at the platform's corner. Watch as one man climbs a ladder to the upper level. This is your cue to sneak around the right side of the nearby column. Jump to grab the platform that runs between the two columns, and pull yourself up.

Sam is now in a prime position to take everyone out. There are no other shadows to sneak through, so it's all about your skill at taking down enemies quickly. Snipe the man on the upper platform. This alerts the men on the ground, including Emile, who emerges from his position near the bomb's fail-safe device. As the men cluster up in front of the door to the bomb room, sweep them with continuous machine-gun fire. Don't worry about conserving ammo anymore; there isn't anyone left.

Find Emile's body among the pile and scan his retina. Then enter the small room in front of the bomb. A panel with a combination lock covers the fail-safe device. Open the lock as you would a safe, rotating the three disks into place. Then hack the security device to gain access to the controls.

Save your game. There are two possible outcomes to your next action. Disarming the bomb is like assembling a Kinshasa mine, but in reverse. The detonator is at the bottom of a long cylinder. Press and hold the Primary Attack button to make the arm quickly descend to the bottom. Then hold the Secondary Attack button to hold your breath, steadying your grip.

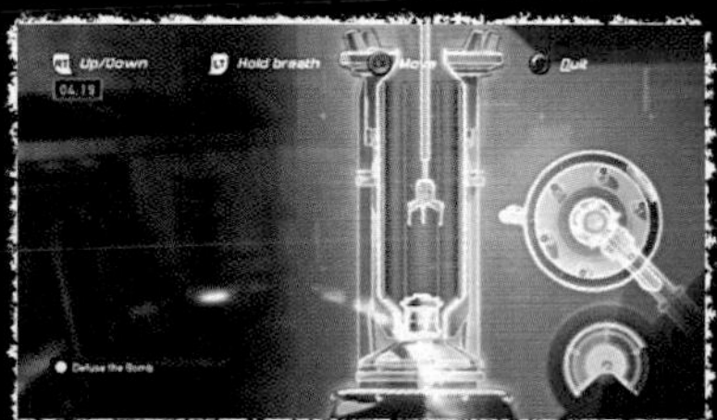

Slowly release the Primary Attack button to lift the detonator out of the bomb. You must avoid striking the sides of the cylinder, or you'll break it and have to start over. Notice that the temperature gauge in the screen's lower right begins to rise as you lift the detonator from the device. You must get the detonator safely out of the bomb before the temperature peaks into the red zone, causing the bomb to go off. If this happens, you'll be able to watch what is known as the "bomb ending."

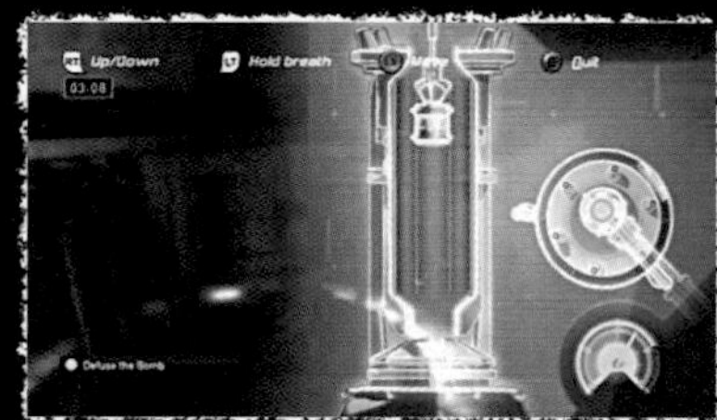

The trick is to let the bomb come out of the cylinder in spurts. Release the Primary Attack button, then press it again to slow down at intermittent points. Hold your breath throughout the ascension, and avoid colliding the detonator with the sides of the device. Do this successfully, and New York is saved—almost.

NYC—Coast Guard Boat

MAP KEY

Medkit

Ammo

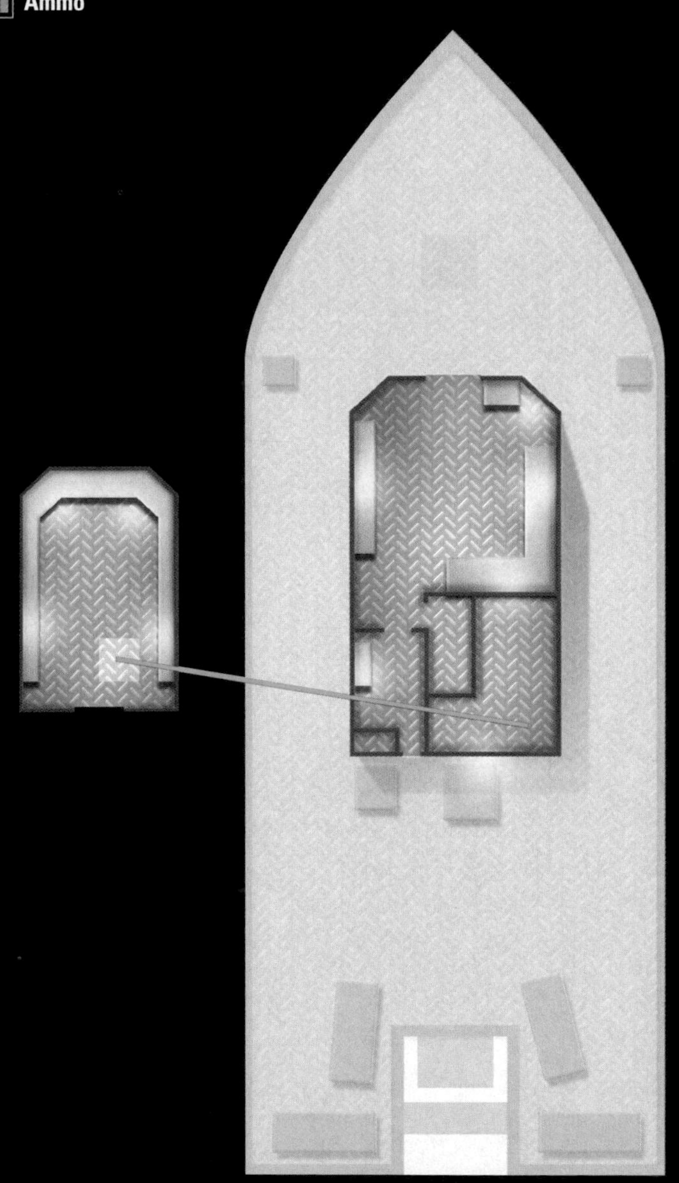

OBJECTIVES

MAIN OBJECTIVES

> DISARM THE BOMB: Emile Dufraisne has entrusted Carson Moss with the final Red Mercury device, and Moss is on his way to deliver it to Massoud. You must reach the bomb and disarm it at all costs.

Choosing to shoot Jamie Washington instead of Irving Lambert, Sam has defused the bomb at the JBA Headquarters and killed the rest of the JBA core members. During the SWAT raid on the compound, Sam overtakes a tactical officer and steals his uniform. Escaping from the scene of the raid, Sam races to the Upper New York Bay and swims out to the coast guard boat Moss has overtaken. Armed with nothing but his knife and his cunning, Sam must disable the entire crew and defuse the bomb before the vessel arrives at the harbor in 10 minutes.

Lady Liberty Watches

The only way Sam can hide on the deck is to hang from its side. After Sam climbs out of the water on the boat's rear ladder, shimmy left and around the corner. Continue shimmying past Moss and his men while they talk.

Blue Bandana

The boat starts moving toward the harbor. A goon with a blue bandana slowly moves up Sam's side of the boat. Continue shimmying toward the boat's bow.

Position Sam between the *o* and *a* of "Coastal Guard" painted on the boat's side. Wait for Blue Bandana to move within range. When he passes near Sam's location and the Grab Character icon appears, quickly press the Interact button to pull the man over the boat's side and fling him into the water.

Navigation Tech

Shimmy to the right until positioned over the "G" and "U" of "Guard" painted on the side of the boat. Continue hanging from the side until a technician moves down the side aisle of the boat. When he passes your position, climb over the rail and grab him. Choke him unconscious and leave his body under the nearest porthole window.

Purple Jumpsuit

Move across the bow of the ship and press Sam's back against the port side of the box just beyond the door to the navigation room. This is the one spot on the deck where the Visibility meter is completely green. Wait here for several minutes and allow the terrorists wearing the purple vest and the purple jumpsuit to patrol the starboard side of the deck. After the two men almost collide near your position, wait for the man in the purple jumpsuit to head around the corner to the right. Then leave your hiding spot, sneak up behind him and grab him. Drag him back to your hiding spot and strangle him unconscious.

Purple Vest

Return to your hiding spot, with your back pressed up against the side of the storage box on the bow. Allow the terrorist to patrol back toward the bow of the ship. As he comes around the corner and moves toward the bow, follow him and knock him unconscious.

Moss

Follow the starboard rail to a door on the side of the ship. Go inside to find a ladder in the cabin. Climb to the ladder's top rung. Watch Moss move back and forth at the helm. When he stops in any position near the controls or near the bomb, climb off the ladder and sneak up behind him. Stab him in the back or slash his throat, and then scan his retinal to complete his profile.

Defuse the Bomb

Pick the lock on the bomb cabinet. As you do so, the ship's deck explodes into flames. Ignore it and focus on defusing the bomb. Hack the security access. All four columns must be locked in within 15 seconds. The numbers take a long time to appear, so you cannot afford to make any mistakes.

When the bomb is defused, Sam has 20 seconds to get off the boat. Exit the cabin's rear door. Sam automatically leaps from the upper deck into the water. Swim away from the boat as its gas tanks explode. The JBA is defeated and the United States is safe. Operation complete.

10: 360/PC

MULTIPLAYER

Spy Basics

SPY DEFAULT CONTROLS

Action	XBOX 360	PC
Move	Left Stick	NOTE: Since every player has their own preferences for multiplayer control schemes, and since PC controls are fully customizable, press Esc to configure the keyboard to best suit your playing style.
View/Aim	Right Stick	
Zoom	Click Right Stick	
HUD Options	START	
Map and Status	BACK	
Interact/Close Action	A	
Crouch/Roll	B	
Jump	Y	
Night Vision	D-pad Left	
Thermo Vision	D-pad Right	
Hacking Unit	RT	
Escape Movement	RB	
Gadget	LB	

Spy Overview

The role of the spy is to infiltrate UPSILON protected facilities and hack information terminals to download vital data. Once the data has been fully downloaded, the spy who completed the download must return to the insertion point and move near to the control drone. At that point, data is delivered to the control drone. Spies win by downloading data twice and returning to the control drone to pass off the information. Spies mainly play from a third person perspective and carry no lethal weapons.

Movement

Spies move quite fast when standing upright. Their movement is a little easier to control when crouched. Ascending or descending stairs in a crouched position slows down the spy a bit. Therefore, stand up in order to traverse stairs more quickly.

Zoom

Press the Zoom button to use the goggles to survey and area from afar. While viewing through the goggles, press the indicated buttons to zoom in and out.

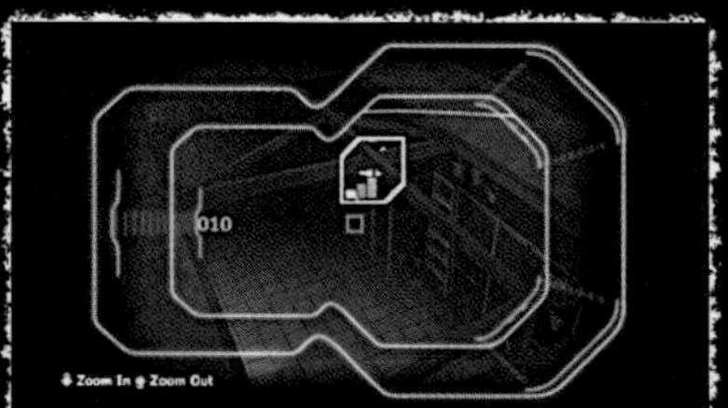

HUD Options

Press the HUD Options button to bring up a mini-diagram of the onscreen display. Press the displayed button to toggle activation of things like the mini-map, game messages, player status, and player name and download status. Press the HUD Options button again to exit this screen.

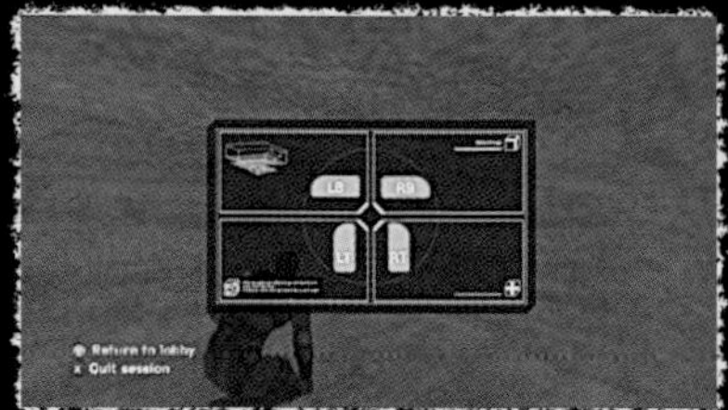

Press the Map and Status button to view a larger and more detailed version of the mini-map, including map zones, spy locations, and data terminal locations.

Map and Status

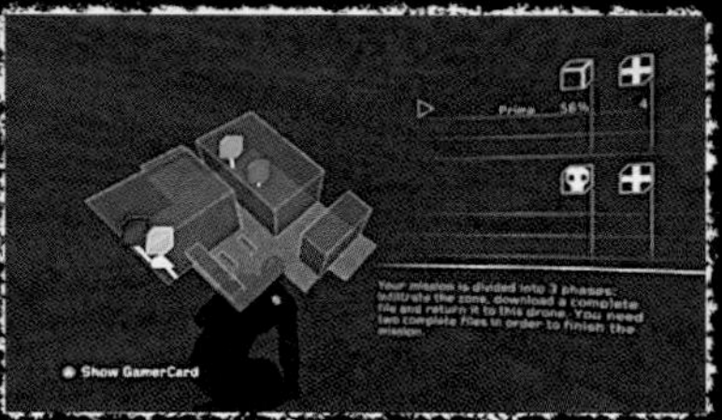

The stats displayed on the right side of the screen show the players according to ranking. Ranking for spies is determined by the amount of data downloaded and the number of lives remaining. The spy with the highest in both categories is listed at the top. UPSILON mercenaries are ranked according to kills and lives remaining. Press the Map and Status button again to exit this screen.

Interact/close action

Press the Interact button to interact with the environment when the Interact button icon is displayed onscreen in association with an environmental object. This function is typically used in conjunction with the spy's hacking unit, which allows the spy to break lights and windows and hack terminals.

To perform a close action against an UPSILON mercenary, sneak up behind the merc and press the Interact button to grab them. Once you have a merc in a chokehold, press the Interact button again to snap their neck.

When hanging from underneath a railing, if a mercenary moves near the railing the Interact button icon may appear. When this occurs, press the Interact button to grab the mercenary and pull them over the railing, possibly to their death depending on the distance fallen.

Crouch/roll

Press the Crouch button to assume a crouching stance. It is easier to hide behind low obstacles and take less damage from gunfire and explosions while crouched. Spies move more slowly while crouched, enabling greater control over movement in areas near ledges.

Press and hold the Crouch button while moving to perform a roll.

Jump

Press the Jump button to leap roughly six feet off the ground. While jumping, a spy may be able to leap gaps, grab and climb onto ledges, or grab on to zip-lines.

Press the Jump button to climb over low obstacles or to climb through open windows.

Night vision

Press the Night Vision button to toggle night vision on or off. Night vision collects available light and uses it to illuminate low-light areas for the viewer. Turn night vision on whenever entering dark areas such as crawlspaces or any place where all the lights have been destroyed.

Thermo vision

Press the Thermo Vision button to toggle thermo vision on or off. Thermo vision registers heat temperatures, allowing spies to locate enemies and other spies more easily.

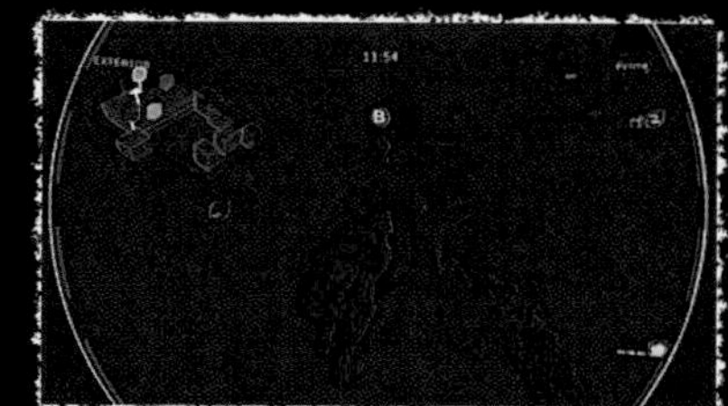

Hacking unit

Press and hold the Hacking Unit button to activate the spy's hacking unit. While the hacking unit is equipped, use the movement control to adjust viewpoint. When an object falls into the center of the screen, the hacking device locks onto it with a green targeting reticule. The Interact button icon appears along with a command, such as "Hack" or "Destroy." When this occurs, press the Interact button to destroy lights, break panes of glass, or to begin hacking data terminals.

Once a spy has started hacking a data terminal, file download begins. Download progress is displayed in the upper right corner of the screen, and also on the hacking device itself. Hacking continues as long as the Hacking Unit button is held. To cease hacking, simply release the Hacking Unit button. While hacking, you can still look to the left or right by moving the View Control.

TIP

File download can be resumed at any time from any data terminal. Download progresses more quickly when two or more spies are hacking terminals at the same time. Therefore, coordinate with your teammates to get into position and hack two or more data terminals simultaneously in order to speed file download and throw the UPSILON forces into chaos.

Escape movement

When near certain locations such as windows, ceiling holes, or low ducts, press the Escape Movement button to perform a fast acrobatic flight movement. This function is especially useful when an UPSILON mercenary is in hot pursuit. Just when the merc seems to have cornered a spy, the spy can jump out the window or into the ceiling to escape death.

Gadget

Press the Gadget button to deploy the gadget currently held. Spies can carry three of one gadget type, whether it be flash grenades, jammers, smoke grenades, or syringes. To restock on gadgets or switch the type of gadget held, visit the item chest near the spy insertion point.

Flash Grenade: The spy tosses a flashbang grenade at his own feet. The device detonates instantly, creating a blinding white flash and a cloud of smoke. Mercenaries using EMF vision in the spy's vicinity at the time of detonation may suffer from temporary blindness (indicated by a white screen) for several seconds afterward. Use the opportunity to flee without giving away your escape route.

Jammer: Creates a false echo to make an UPSILON mercenary believe that the spy is standing in a different location. Allows the spy to infiltrate by an alternate route, or to escape with less likelihood of pursuit.

Smoke Grenade: The spy throws a smoke grenade at their feet, creating a large cloud of sight-obscuring smoke. Spies can use the opportunity to escape, or to slip behind mercenaries that are naïve enough to enter the veil.

Syringe: Can be used to heal yourself or another spy. To heal a teammate, move close to them and press the Gadget button to administer treatment. If one spy agrees to always carry syringes, then the spies can reduce the number of lives lost.

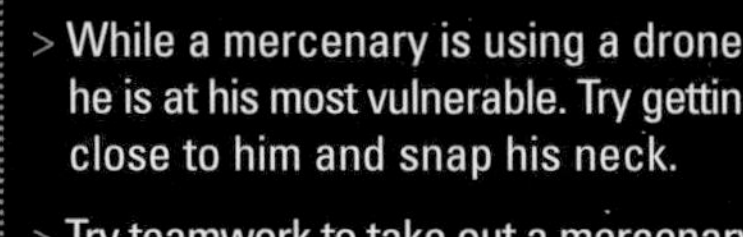

The Frag Dolls are a team of gamers recruited by Ubisoft to represent their video games and promote the presence of women in the gaming industry. Started in 2004 by an open call for female gamers, the Frag Dolls immediately rocketed to the spotlight after winning the *Rainbow Six 3: Black Arrow* tournament in a shut-out at their debut appearance.

The Frag Dolls are known not only for being skilled gamers in multiple titles, but for their advocacy of female gamers. The Frag Dolls have spoken on panels at the Women's Game Conference and two of the Women in Games International conferences. They have stated a desire for more female gamers in multiple interviews and have developed a gaming community friendly to other women interested in trying out video games.

GENERAL SPY TIPS FROM THE FRAG DOLLS

> UPSILON mercenaries are unable to make use of crawlspace ducts, and usually cannot reach the upper levels of an area. Use this to your advantage, and always look for a way to hack terminals from above.

> You cannot hope to hurt a mercenary in a straight-on fight. Don't try.

> Use your speed and agility, and work with the environment, to escape from mercenaries. Jump through windows, climb pipes, duck into vents. These are all places mercenaries can't follow.

> Don't think you're safe by just ducking into a vent. Mercenaries now have drones, which can follow you where the mercenaries can't. Once you're out of sight, keep moving.

> While a mercenary is using a drone, he is at his most vulnerable. Try getting close to him and snap his neck.

> Try teamwork to take out a mercenary. While your teammate draws his attention, you can get behind the mercenary and snap his neck.

> Two spies can hack into the same terminal at the same time. If you're already using the buddy system, don't forget to take advantage of this.

> Knowing the maps is key. Memorize how long it takes you to get from one objective to another, and what routes you can take. You probably won't be able to complete an entire download in one try, so plan ahead for your next destination.

> While you can pick up your file download at another terminal without penalty, dying will lose all your progress. Remember that it's more important to stay alive than to finish the objective. If you run you can continue at another objective. If you die you have to start over.

> Shadow is your best friend. Use your hacking tool to disable any lights you come across. Those lights will stay off, making it harder for a mercenary to see you with a casual sweep of the room.

> Communicate constantly with your teammates. Update them on how many mercenaries you've seen and where. If you can keep tabs on all of them, you'll have a better idea of which objectives will be the least guarded.

> Learn how to use your gadgets. You only get one tool to take with you at a time. Become expert with the tool of your choice, and keep in mind that some tools will be more helpful on some maps than others.

> If you can get close enough to a mercenary, try hacking into his system. It will temporarily neutralize his defensive capabilities.

> You've got a cute bottom and a shiny bald head, but that's not going to help you in combat against a mercenary with a machine gun. Don't try to take down your foe mano-a-mano.

> Controlling a drone takes a lot of

concentration. Should you find yourself spying on a mercenary focused on such a task, why not take the opportunity to snap his neck?

> There's no "I" in "team"—when faced with a mercenary, why not work with your chums to take him down? One spy should run out and distract the first-person foe, while the other sneaks round the back and applies a bit of over-zealous shiatsu. In a match with three spies, it's advisable that two provide the distraction through the medium of modern dance.

> Hacking isn't just for terminals, lights, and doors—you can hack a mercenary's system too, compromising his defensive capabilities.

> Stop admiring the architecture, and start using it to your advantage. Leap through windows, dive into vents, and shimmy up pipes. The mercenaries won't be able to follow.

> Having said that, don't forget that the mercenaries have drones. These pesky little self-destructing menaces can follow you into all sorts of places. So live by this motto: a rolling spy gathers no mercs—keep moving.

> Cartography is win-ography. Learn the maps and plan ahead. You might not always have a chance to finish a download before you're rudely interrupted. Remember that you can pick up where you left off if you make it to another terminal. If you hang around too long and get killed, you won't have the luxury. Be ready to move on if you're discovered.

> Remember that you don't have to be standing in front of a terminal to hack it. You can be in the rafters or under the floorboards. But the further away you are, the slower the hack will progress.

> Two spies can hack the same terminal at the same time. But remember to maintain decorum—you're not pigs round a trough.

> You're dressed in black for a reason (and not just because it goes with everything). Stick to the shadows and the mercs might miss you.

UPSILON Basics

UPSILON FORCE DEFAULT CONTROLS

Action	XBOX 360	PC
Move/Strafe	Left Stick	NOTE: Since every player has their own preferences for multiplayer control schemes, and since PC controls are fully customizable, press Esc to configure the keyboard to best suit your playing style.
Circle Attack	Click Left Stick	
View/Aim	Right Stick	
Sniper Zoom	Click Right Stick	
HUD Options	START	
Map and Status	BACK	
Interact/Close Action	A	
Crouch/Stand	B	
Reload	X	
Jump	Y	
Flashlight On/Off	D-pad Left	
Adjust Flashlight Halo	D-pad Down, D-pad Up	
EMF Vision	D-pad Right	
Fire	RT	
Launch Grenade	LT	
Sprint	RB	
Gadget	LB	

UPSILON Overview

UPSILON mercenaries are the defenders of the realm; their job is to prevent spies from infiltrating their facilities and downloading two files from the data access terminals. Mercenaries play from a first-person perspective and carry a machinegun with a grenade launcher. Although mercenaries are unable to pursue spies into crawlspaces and high areas on the maps, their bullets can reach virtually anywhere!

Movement

Mercenaries operate from a first person perspective. The Move Control allows the mercenary to move forward or backward, or to strafe from side to side. To turn left or right, use the View/Aim Control.

Circle Attack

Press the Circle Attack control to performing a spinning move. The merc spins with the butt of his rifle extended, striking enemies on all sides. Spies within close range are knocked to the ground, if not killed.

Sniper Zoom

Press the Zoom button to view through the machinegun's scope. While zoomed in, firing mode switches from fully automatic to continual semi-automatic fire; hold the Fire button to fire one precision shot after another. Adjust scope distance while zoomed in using the Zoom In button and Zoom Out button. Sniping is more effective against spies concealed in high ceiling areas or standing on building rooftops.

HUD Options

Press the HUD Options button to bring up a mini-diagram of the onscreen display. The menu functions identical to the version available to spies, described previously.

Map and Status

Press the Map and Status button to view a larger version of the mini-map and statistics regarding game ranking. The map and status screen is no different than the spy version, described previously.

Interact/close Action

Press the Interact button to interact with the environment in various ways. When a merc approaches certain railings on high platforms, the Interact button icon may appear. Press the Interact button to fasten the merc's grapnel to the railing and drop to the level below.

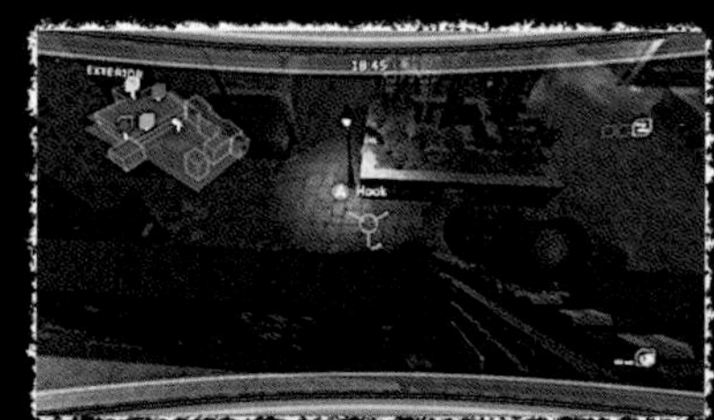

To perform a close action against spy, sneak up behind them and press the Interact button to grab them. Once you have a spy in a chokehold, press the Interact button again to snap their neck.

The Interact button also serves other context-sensitive functions, such as restarting a power generator deactivated by spies and flipping light switches.

Crouch

Press the Crouch button to assume a crouching stance. Mercenaries can penetrate some low crawlspaces while crouched, but they cannot flatten and crawl through ducts or low areas where spies can go.

Reload

Press the Reload button to reload the machinegun magazine after firing a few rounds. Mercs should keep their gun fully loaded at all times in preparation to fire continuously in an emergency.

Jump

Press the Jump button to hop about three feet off the ground. Because of the heavy equipment carried by mercenaries, they cannot jump onto platforms or mantle over obstacles. However, jumping may allow a mercenary to leap from one platform to another if the gap between is small enough.

Flashlight

Press the Flashlight button to activate the flashlight attached to the end of the mercenary's gun. The flashlight lamp can be focused to cast a large halo of dimmer quality or a focused halo of sharp quality. Keep the flashlight active while scouring dark locations for infiltrators.

EMF Vision

Press the EMF Vision button to activate EMF Vision mode. This spectrum highlights electronic equipment in use. If a spy is using Night Vision or Thermo Vision, they may become visible in EMF Vision even through thin walls. Switch EMF vision on and off frequently to locate hidden spies, especially when searching the area around a data terminal for a spy who is attempting to download a file. We do not recommend moving while EMF vision is active, since it makes the user practically blind to all other obstacles and may allow spies to get too close.

Fire

Press and hold the Fire button to release a continuous stream of automatic machinegun fire. Use the crosshairs displayed in the center of the mercenary's helmet visor to aim. Shots may spread slightly during continuous fire. The machinegun holds 40-round clips, and must be reloaded to continue firing. Mercenaries carry unlimited ammunition.

While zoomed in through the sniper scope, the weapon fires semi-automatically. Press and hold the Fire button to fire over and over.

Launch Grenade

The machinegun is equipped with a grenade launcher mounted under the barrel. At the start of a session, each merc is equipped with three grenades. Small icons near the bottom of the crosshairs indicate the number of grenades remaining. Avoid using grenades at close range, or the player may suffer damage or die from the blast. Grenades are best used when teammates are not around, or when attempting to damage spies that are hacking access points from inside ducts or false ceilings. To restock your supply of grenades, visit the chest located near the mercenary insertion point.

Sprint

Press and hold the Sprint button to run forward at twice the normal speed. Mercenaries can sprint for roughly six or seven seconds, at which point they return to normal movement speed out of breath. While sprinting, the Move Control becomes inoperative. The mercenary cannot deploy drones or fire a weapon while sprinting. Use the View Control to turn while sprinting. Employ sprinting whenever you receive word that spies are hacking an access point some distance away, and to pursue spies attempting to flee.

Gadget

Press the Gadget button to deploy the gadget currently held. Mercenaries can carry two of one gadget type, whether it be a drone or a deployable surveillance camera (available only in certain maps). To restock on gadgets, visit the item chest located at the mercenary insertion point.

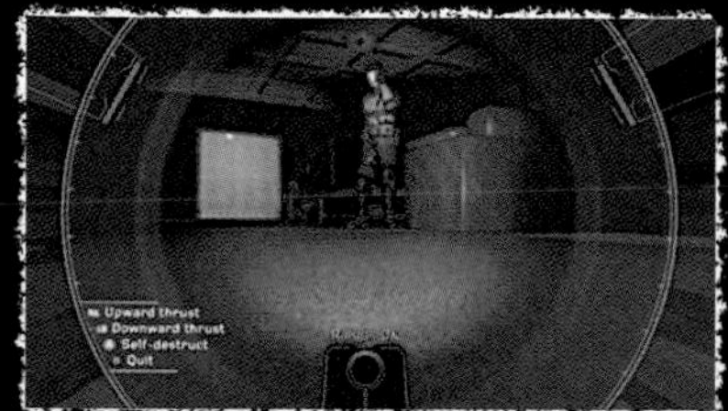

Drone: Press the Gadget button to deploy a drone, which drops to the ground directly behind the mercenary. Use the Move Control to roll the drone forward, backward, or strafe left to right on the ground. Press the Sprint button to raise the drone off the ground with a thruster. Tap the Sprint button repeatedly to cause the drone to float in midair. Press the Gadget button to descend quickly, such as in situations where a spy is attempting to hack the drone. Press the Interact button to make the drone self-destruct, creating a powerful explosion that should kill one or two spies within close range of the drone. Press the Crouch button to exit the drone.

TIP

Employing drones leaves the mercenary vulnerable to attack by spies, so avoid using them too often. While drones can be deployed in most areas, some portions of the map are restricted. If the indicator near the bottom of the drone's screen indicates that you have entered a restricted area or have moved too far out of range, return to an allowed area immediately or suffer losing the drone.

GENERAL UPSILON TIPS FROM THE FRAGDOLLS

> It's as important for mercenaries to know the map as it is for spies. You need to know where a spy can get to from where you just saw him, and how long it will take. Know every in and out.

> Don't under-utilize your EMF vision. If a spy is using night vision or heat vision, he'll light up like the Vegas strip.

> Learn to capitalize on the drone. You can send it into vents after spies. Even if you can't blow them up, you may get a solid idea of where they're headed next.

> While using the drone, keep your back protected. When you're guiding it, you're vulnerable to any spy who sneaks up behind you. Either have another mercenary there or put your back to a wall.

> Identify places on the map that allow you to monitor more than one objective at a time. If you can patrol a specific area, spies have less time to sneak close and hack into one of your objectives.

> If you continue getting proximity signals for a spy in one place, use recent activity to measure whether the signal is a dummy. Spies have a jammer that interferes with your proximity detector.

> Worried there's a spy behind you? Your spin move will knock spies down and make them easy to eliminate.

> Try this stylish finish. After you've knocked a spy down, you can pick them up and head butt them, but not before bragging a little bit while they're helpless. Rubbing it in is what mercenaries do best.

> If you see a spy on a zip-line, it's a perfect time to snipe them right out of the air. They're helpless to do anything until they land.

> Scope out the map for the best patrol routes. You won't have enough team mates to allocate one man to each objective (them's the rules), so try to find fast routes between the terminals and keep them covered.

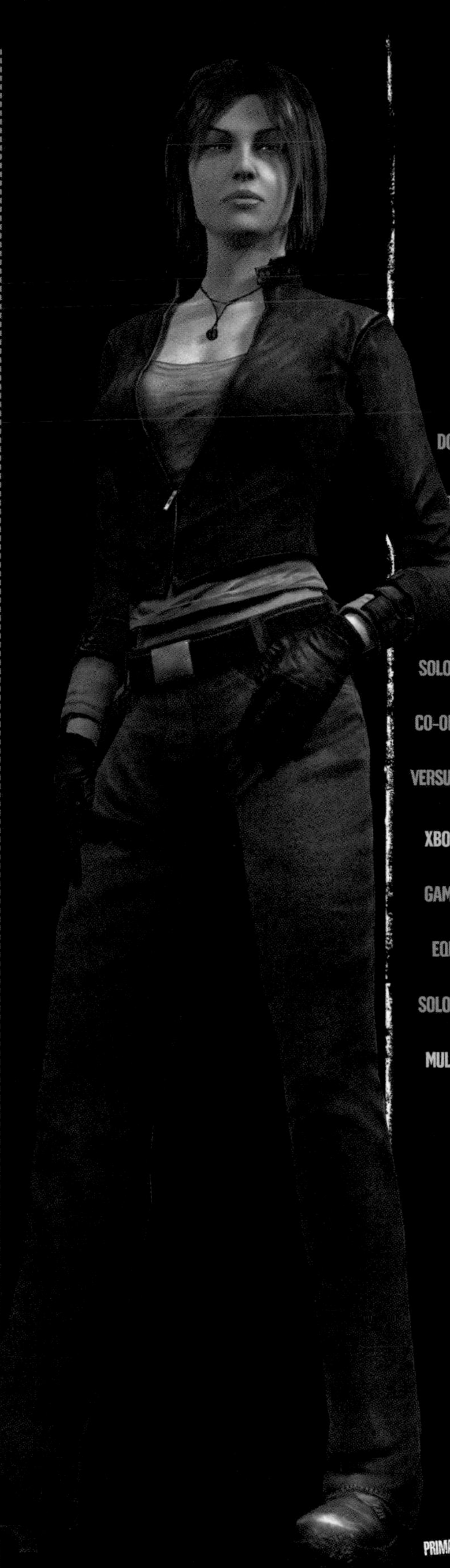

Multiplayer Generalities

Connection Types

Multiplayer games may be played online or by system link; connecting two or more consoles or PCs to a router using ethernet cables. Each player must have a PC or console, a monitor, and a retail copy of *Tom Clancy's Splinter Cell: Double Agent.* Up to six players may join a game session.

Multiplayer Menu

After choosing a connection type, the Multiplayer menu appears. From this screen, players can choose from several options to start up a game or perform other functions:

Home: Allows the player to view their playing statistics, change character skins, view bonuses unlocked, change game options, create a SQUAD and invite others to join, and determine who online has scored the best in the Co-op Challenges mode.

Help Zone: View videos detailing how to play as a spy or an UPSILON Force operative. ***Every player should start here.***

Custom Match: Create or join a custom match for versus mode. Choose a map and whether to play as a spy or UPSILON Force member.

Live Zone: View important messages regarding upcoming events, server changes, etc.

Quick Match: View a list of available matches and join a session.

Co-op Challenges: Play alone or with others to complete missions to earn points and medals. Players play as spies against computer-controlled bots. The basics of the game do not change, but the amount of time allotted or the number of files to download changes from mission to mission.

Match Menu

After creating a custom match session, choose a map to play in. At first, only three maps are available: Blackwing, Boss House, and Dawn Waves. Complete 4 games as a spy and 4 games as an UPSILON mercenary or 12 games total to unlock Motorway 90, Terminus, and Red Diamond. Complete 8 games as a spy and 8 games as a merc or 16 games total to unlock Slaughterhouse and USS Wisdom.

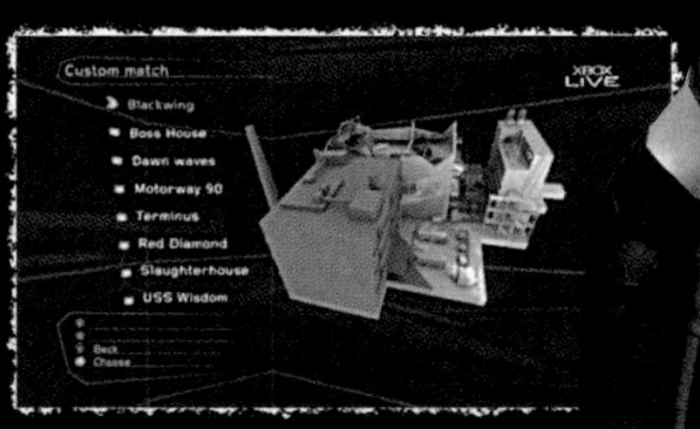

After choosing a map, choose whether to play as a Spy, an UPSILON Force operative, or let the game decide for you. Then choose whether to allow anyone to play, restrict the map to friends, or play with your SQUAD.

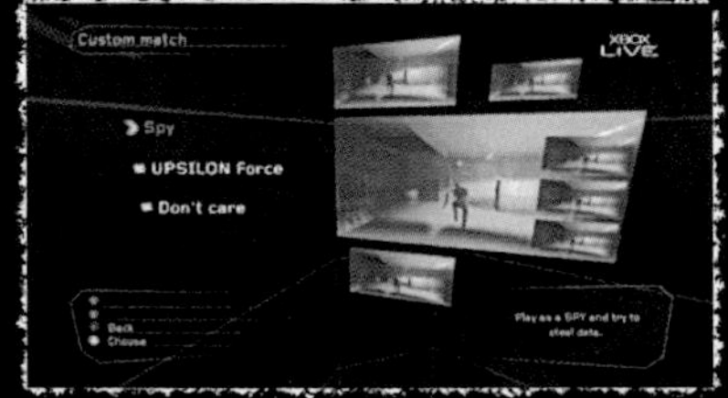

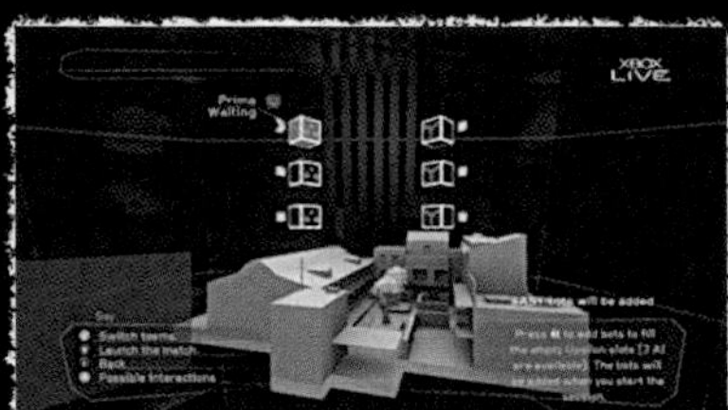

Finally, when the team slots are displayed above the 3D map rendering, choose whether to switch teams, add bots to the UPSILON side, or invite friends to join you from your friends list.

BLACKWING

Blackwing is a stage consisting of an Exterior area where the spies insert, a Headquarters building, and a Detention Zone building. Spies exiting the insertion point should take the stairs up to the third level. At the end of the hallway is a ladder up to the rooftop, where zip-lines can be used to swiftly cross the Exterior area to either the Detention Zone building on the left or the Headquarters on the right.

The zip-line to the Detention Zone arrives on a vertical pipe. Slide down the pipe just a tick and shimmy to the left until you reach an air conditioning unit below an open vent duct. Crouch and move through the vent. Near the end of the vent is an opening on the right. Just outside this opening and directly below is the red terminal. Spies can hide inside the vent duct and hack the terminal. UPSILON operatives can counter this strategy by moving behind the red terminal and sniping the spy inside the vent. After a spy successfully downloads a file from this location, they can follow the vent duct back out to the Exterior area. Jump to grab the zip-line emanating from the wall above the air conditioning unit and slide over to the balconies on the far right. Cross the balconies to an open window on the second level of the insertion point building, and return to the control drone to deliver the file. Mercenaries should head outside and attempt to blast the escaping spy as he slides across the zip-line and crosses the balconies. The spy must be killed before he enters the open window, or it is all over.

The zip-line to the Headquarters building arrives on the roof. At the back of the rooftop is a small vent duct on the right. Drop into this vent duct and follow it into the main room inside the headquarters. The blue terminal is below, but it is hard for a spy to hack without exposing themselves to UPSILON gunfire. Instead, exit the duct and head to the right onto the roof of a small office structure. Drop through the hole into the false ceiling area. From there, you can move to an opening and hack the green terminal. The UPSILON forces can counter this by launching grenades into the ceiling. After spies successfully steal a file from the Headquarters, they should follow the vent ducts back out to the rooftop. Climb down the fire escape platforms on the exterior of the building and leap the gap to return to the insertion point.

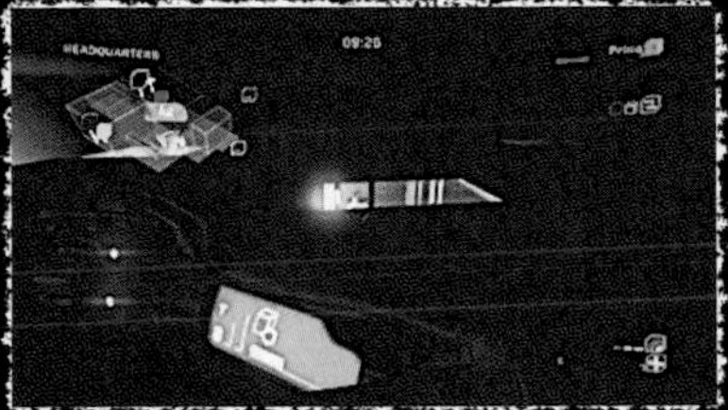

BLACKWING TIPS FOR SPIES FROM THE FRAGDOLLS

- You can get around most of the Blue/Green building via a maze of vents above the room. Use these to move without coming down to the ground level.
- There's a false ceiling above the Green objective. You can hack from the relative safety of this area, and it provides a quick avenue for escape. Be prepared for a long wait if you use this hiding spot though. It's at the outer range for hacking and data downloads much slower.
- Because some of the objectives are so close, it's important to put out as many lights as possible. You'll need to use every shadow to your advantage with mercenaries always so close.
- When returning to the extraction point with your data, stay off the ground! There are plenty of zip-lines and catwalks you can use to stay out of the mercenaries' immediate range.

BLACKWING TIPS FOR MERCENARIES FROM THE FRAGDOLLS

- The objectives are grouped into two buildings. Keep one mercenary in each building and a floater who can run between when help is needed.
- If the spies complete a download, try to get between them and their extraction point. If they flee on the ground level they should be easy to take out, but keep a sniper looking up to stop as they cross the catwalks.

BOSS HOUSE

Boss House takes place in a mansion and the surrounding buildings connected by a beautiful cobblestone courtyard. Spies should climb out of the windows at the top of the insertion point room rather than drop through the hole in the floor. The windows lead to a rooftop where a zip-line can be used to cross the courtyard over to the main building. Two small openings in the roof lead inside to the attic.

From the attic, spies may proceed to the backyard to try to hack the yellow terminal from above. Or, spies can enter the vent duct to the far left and drop down one level. There, from just inside the vent opening, spies should be able to hack the red terminal positioned near the top of a flight of stairs.

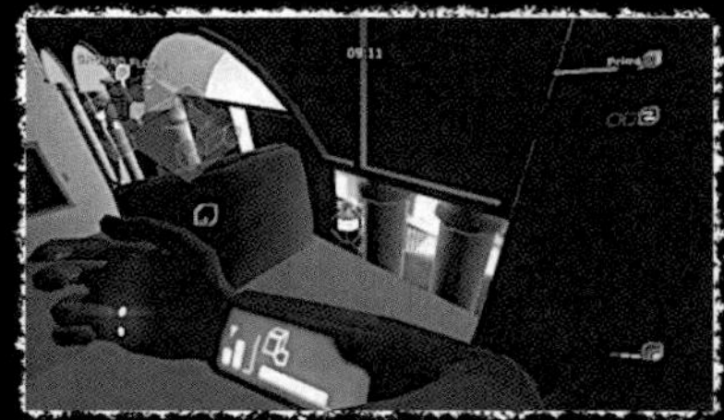

Spies should get to know the vent system within the mansion very well in order to hack the blue and green terminals. The mansion interior is well lit, hacking device to destroy as many lights as possible. One spy on the team should dedicate themselves to extinguishing every light while the other two spies attempt to hack terminals.

Once a file is downloaded, spies can return to the mansion's roof. Head through the attic to the front of the building. Head to the right and use a zip-line to cross the courtyard quickly. Go inside a small room and crawl through a duct. Cross the patio and the rear balcony to find another zip line that arrives near the spy insertion point.

One mercenary positioned on the upper balcony can take out spies attempting to cross the courtyard or glide on the zip-lines above. The other two mercenaries should roam from room to room as needed when spies begin to hack access points.

BOSS HOUSE TIPS FOR SPIES FROM THE

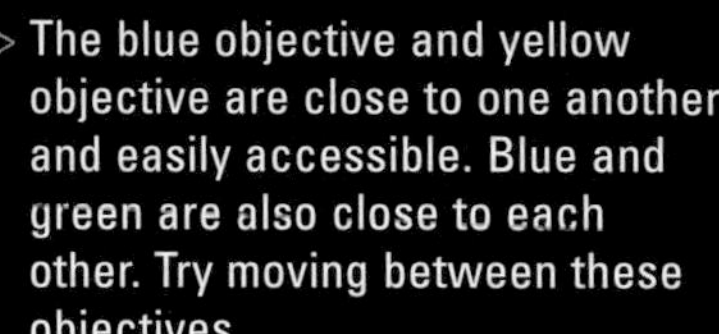

- The blue objective and yellow objective are close to one another and easily accessible. Blue and green are also close to each other. Try moving between these objectives.
- Try extinguishing all the lights in the yellow, red, and green rooms. You can put out most of them without exposing yourself to any potential mercenaries nearby.
- If you use the zip lines to leave your spawn point, you'll be vulnerable to any mercenaries sniping in the large courtyard.

BOSS HOUSE TIPS FOR MERCENARIES FROM THE FragDolls

- You have a quick route from the yellow objective to the red one, from the blue to the yellow, from the green to the blue, and from the red to the green. Establish the routes and assign teammates to patrol the areas to provide the maximum protection for each objective.
- Many spies will try to take zip-lines across the open courtyard. This is a perfect opportunity to snipe them out of the sky.

DAWN WAVES

Dawn Waves takes place in broad daylight at a shipping dock. The map contains a tanker vessel where the spies insert and several storage buildings and warehouses where the data terminals are contained.

Sticking to the high road as usual, spies should follow the action ghosts over to some climbable vertical pulley lines near a stack of cargo containers. Climb the second pulley line up to a horizontal rail connected to a large derrick. Shimmy across the rail and drop onto the derrick platform. Two zip-lines off the right side of the right-hand derrick allow spies to reach the Storage building and Control Tower.

After dropping onto the Control Tower roof, climb halfway down the pipe on the opposite side of the tower. Climb into the open vent and attempt to hack the red terminal from above. Be sure to destroy the light inside the control tower first, and use smoke grenades to help conceal your position. If a file is successfully downloaded from here, the best escape route is to climb back up to the roof and use another zip-line attached to the striped pole to reach the Storage building roof. Climb further up the pole located there to reach a zip-line that delivers a spy back to the derrick near the insertion point.

On the Storage building rooftop, spies can use the hacking device to shatter the glass in the skylight. The green terminal is on the ground floor, and can be hacked from the roof. However, this leaves the spy greatly exposed in the daylight.

At the back of the Storage building, spies can jump from an air conditioning unit up to a high catwalk. To the right is a low vent that leads inside the building. Spies can use this vent to navigate across a series of ducts over to the area above the yellow terminal. Move into the stairwell behind the yellow terminal and hack from the safety of the rear side of the false ceiling. Spies can move back and forth from here over to the hole in the roof of the booth directly above the yellow terminal and eventually hack an entire packet.

This is the strategy good spies typically follow. Therefore, mercenaries need only have one man in the Control Tower near the red terminal, one in the Storage building near the green terminal, and another in the Assembly area near the yellow terminal who can also keep tabs on the blue access point.

DAWN WAVES TIPS FOR SPIES FROM THE FRAGDOLLS

> In this morning map, use terrain to hide from mercenaries. Shadows are too scarce to rely on.

> To escape a mercenary in the outside tower, try diving through the window and jumping from the railing to the crates. You can gain a lot of distance and the mercenaries won't be able to follow.

MOTORWAY 90

Spies would do well to split up and strike in various locations simultaneously in order to take on this challenging map. One spy should attempt to drive the UPSILON forces crazy by repeatedly hacking the power generator located in the trailer of the truck parked in the Courtyard area. For the best route to the truck, climb up the crates stacked to the right of the control drone. Cross the rooftop and climb a pipe that leads to a vent opening. Crouch and move through this low ceiling area. Jump from the ledge onto a zip-line that connects to the building at the back of an alley. As you slide along the zip-line, press the Crouch button to drop onto a large roof beside the power generator. Hack the power generator from this relatively safe spot. Successfully hacking the power generator deactivates many of the lights and also opens many doors that spies would have to hack otherwise. Hide until the mercenaries restart the generator, and then deactivate it again. This strategy means that at least one of the UPSILON team will be continually distracted by the generator problems. The mercenaries can counter this strategy by simply ignoring the power outage.

After this spy hacks the generator, he can move over to the corner of the rooftop and grab the vertical pipe attached to the wall. Climb up this pipe to reach a tunnel that goes into the Yellow Warehouse. Destroy the lights in the vicinity if needed, and start hacking the yellow terminal. If a mercenary gets wise, go back outside and climb down the vertical pipe to another hole that allows the spy to go underneath the semi trailer where the yellow terminal is located. Slip out from under the truck and start hacking it to draw the merc toward the yellow terminal. Then go back to the upper level, then return to the lower level, and so forth.

While one spy is in the process of deactivating the power generator, another spy should take the same zip-line down to a platform near a hole in the wall. Crawl through the hole and look to the left to spot the yellow terminal. Head to the right and jump over onto the top of another duct. Follow this duct over to the far corner, where a hole in the wall opens into another vent. Follow this vent to a small patio overlooking the courtyard. Cross the patio and enter another duct. Follow this duct to the end, and emerge onto a dock directly behind the trailer where the blue terminal is housed. Shatter the windows on the trailer and hack the blue terminal from behind the cover of the pallet stacks until mercenaries arrive to prevent the download. Then head to the other side of the patio and crawl through a hole into a building. Move through the corridor until the red mark is removed from the green terminal inside the nearby building, and the device can be hacked from behind the vent covers. If mercenaries locate the spy, then the spy can simply relocate to another part of the passageway and continue hacking the green terminal until a packet is downloaded. This spy can also confuse the mercenaries by going back to hack the blue terminal. Hacking the green terminal while hidden within the corridor mentioned above is really the best way to download a full file.

Escaping from the building with a downloaded file is not easy, since there are no zip-lines that allow you to fly back to the spy insertion point. If you hacked the green or blue terminals, then the best escape route is to return the way you came in. Upon reaching the Yellow Warehouse, simply drop to the ground and run through the door. Run down the alley and dive under the truck where the power generator is located. Move through the underground tunnel and climb out of the next hole. Climb up one of the pipes on the wall to reach the rooftop, and then run back to the control drone. Mercenaries need only flood the parking lot area and shoot the spies like lemmings as they attempt to return to the insertion point.

TERMINUS

The room next to the spies' insertion point contains several boxes. If you climb onto the first stack of boxes and jump through the hole to the level above, you'll find a zip-line which can be used to reach the far side of the parking lot, near where the power generator is located. Because the generator is out in the open, it is difficult to hack and deactivate. However, doing so is a good way to draw mercenaries out of the Hangar and Offices, where the data terminals are located. While a mercenary is attempting to reactivate the generator, you can drop down behind him, grab him, and choke him unconscious. That is, if he doesn't see you first.

Probably the easiest and safest way for spies to access the terminals is to go through the low vent duct near the insertion point. This leads to an elevator shaft. Slide down the pipe fastened to the wall and drop into the open elevator car. Crawl through the low opening and go through the left passageway. Hack the security lock on the door if necessary, and then enter the subway station that runs below the parking lot area on the level above. Head over to the tracks and follow them up to the back of a stopped subway car. Jump up into the high hold on the left, and follow this low passageway to a ladder. Climb up this ladder to find yourself next to a vertical pipe fastened on the wall. Climb up the pipe to a platform. Use the hacking device to destroy the two lights on the platform, which illuminate the entire parking lot. Head past the lights and enter the open vent duct. This duct emerges inside the Hangar. As you come out of the vent, the floodlight that illuminates the entire Hangar interior is directly to your right. Destroy it, and then proceed carefully across the vent duct to the large duct platform. From here, you can easily hack the blue terminal inside the bus raised on hydraulics. Mercenaries, on the other hand, should be checking the vents for infiltrators.

From this position, a spy can follow the vent duct to the left into a hole in the wall. This short passage emerges into the false ceiling area above the red data terminal. Spies can easily hack it from inside the false ceiling, but mercenaries can just as easily shoot into the ceiling and launch grenades to smoke spies out.

Once you've downloaded a full file from either location, use the ducts to work your way back outside. Move to the opposite side of the platform and slide down the pipe to the ground. If the parking lot is clear, then run across the ground to the vertical pipe attached to the wall. Climb up the pipe and return to the control drone. If a mercenary is searching the parking lot, then climb down the ladder and return to the insertion point through the subway station.

RED DIAMOND

Red Diamond is a huge, New Orleans-style map. If the spies go upstairs to the upper level of their insertion zone, they'll find three zip-lines that lead to paths into the hotel complex where all four terminals are located. If you go under the first shutter to the right, you'll find a zip-line that delivers the spy to the far corner of the map. Head to the far end of the path and climb up the pipe to the upper level of the balcony. Go through the first corridor on the right and jump through one of the open windows. It's possible to catch hold of the roof of the building where the blue terminal is housed. The blue terminal is very difficult to download from, so instead go to the back of the roof and climb into the open vent. Go through the doorway on the left into an elevator shaft, and climb into the false ceiling of the next room. Look down and to your right to spot the yellow terminal.

Hack the terminal until mercenaries arrive and locate you. Then head across the false ceiling and jump into the open vent. Stop at the first opening on the right to see the Dance floor area, encased in a giant red soundproof room. To access the Dance area, go through the vent hole and to the left. Grab onto the vertical pipe and climb up to the ceiling beam. Then shimmy hand over hand over the enclosure, and drop onto its ceiling. Drop through the hole in the roof onto the lighting rig inside the dance room. Move to the side of the lighting rig and download from the red terminal until mercenaries come and blow you out.

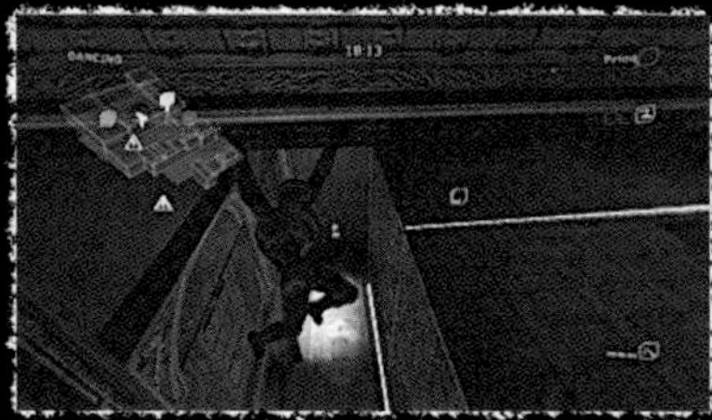

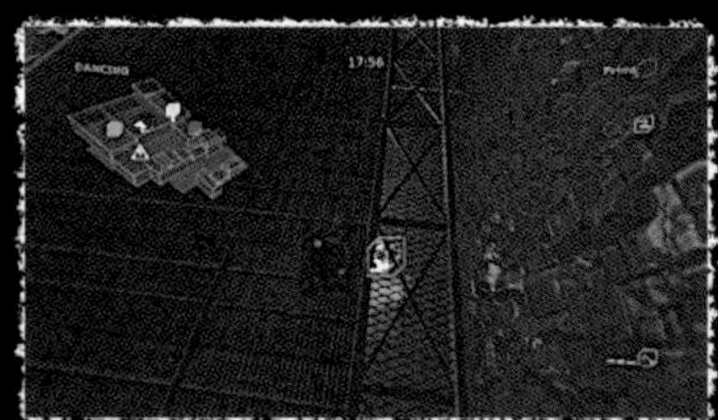

Keep going back and forth between the red terminal and the yellow terminal until a file is downloaded. Then head back to the control drone by one of two routes: if you finished downloading at the red terminal, jump from the enclosure roof into the vent. Head to the left until you find an opening to the courtyard outside the building. Near this opening is a zip-line that you can use to glide over to a raised alleyway. From there, jump up to the highest level and then navigate across the balconies to the insertion point. If you finished downloading near the yellow terminal, climb back out to the rooftop of the building where the blue terminal is housed. Jump from the roof to the open window. Head through the red carpeted corridor back to the street area, and drop over the balcony to the left. Navigate around the balcony above the street level until you reach a sloping rooftop. Run over the roof and climb through the back window into the insertion zone.

Mercenaries need merely prepare to counter this strategy by placing a man near the red terminal who also floats to the green terminal, and another man near the yellow terminal who can also float to the blue terminal. The third man should patrol the courtyard where the power generator is located, and take out any spies attempting to escape with downloaded data.

SLAUGHTERHOUSE

The tables turn in this map which proves sincerely challenging for spies, easy for UPSILON forces. Slaughterhouse presents the first situation where it is better to infiltrate from underground rather than attempt to infiltrate from above. To make the situation easier, one spy must dedicate himself to disabling the power generator in the parking lot so that the slaughterhouse is dark enough to infiltrate. The best way to reach the generator is to climb down the ladder to the left of the control drone and crawl under the fence. Follow this passage along the bottom of the map, toward the power generator's icon displayed onscreen. When you reach the corner, ignore the ladder and climb up the beam in the corner instead. This leads to a duct that runs under the porch on the back building. Emerge from the second to last hole in this duct and hack the power generator.

Meanwhile, the other two spies should follow the same route, except proceed all the way to the end of the vent. Climb out of the top hole in the vent, and drop through the ladder hole in the ground just a foot away. Go through the underground passage and ascend the last ladder. This chute emerges next to the porch of the slaughterhouse. Go under the porch and move to the middle. Drop into the tunnel and follow this all the way through the Dismembering area. At the back, the two spies should split up; one man goes to the right and the other to the left. The spy who goes to the left emerges under the stairs directly behind the blue terminal. Sneak in very close and perform a fast download until a mercenary comes to chase you off. Then dive back under the stairs and move out to the porch area. Wait a few seconds, then return and download some more. Keep repeating this until you have an entire packet.

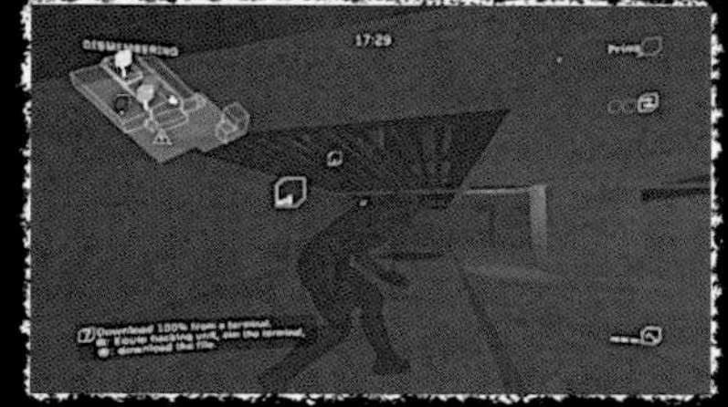

The other spy should go through the first hole on the right. Climb out of the chute here and run directly over to the vent. Press the Escape Movement button to jump up into a vent. Follow this vent over to the middle, and take the first right. Climb up the pipe in this area and crawl through the hole into the room where the yellow terminal is kept. Try to knock out any mercenaries here by dropping onto them. Hack the yellow terminal while standing on top of the vent.

The safest escape route for spies who have downloaded files is to go out the way you came in. Of course, smart UPSILON players will take the initiative to climb down the ladders into the subterranean tunnel, and attempt to stop the spies from returning to the insertion point that way. Spies should check the parking lot, and if the coast is clear then simply take a shortcut directly through the parking lot to reach the control drone as fast as possible.

challenging map for spies to overcome, and an easily defendable hunting ground for UPSILON Force. Two vertical pipes at the spy insertion point can be climbed to reach the next level up. On this level, three vertical pipes can be climbed; two are toward the bow and lead up to zip-lines, and the third is on the wall behind. The three spies should each climb up one of the pipes.

One spy should split off from the other two and climb the lone pipe up into a cable car suspended overhead. Inside the cable car, move to the doorway on the right and jump up to grab a zip-line that allows the spy to slide down to the small building where the power generator is located. The only chance the spies have of winning is to keep power inside the ship cut off. In return, the mercenaries would be better off covering the data terminals inside the main ship body rather than running out to the generator.

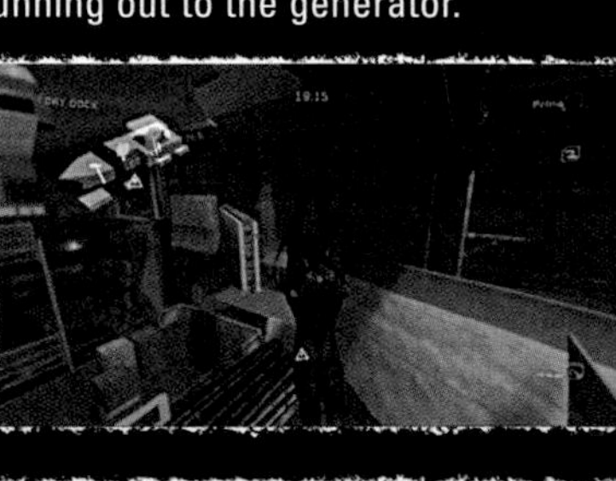

balcony. Move toward the ship and climb over the rail to the right. Head toward the open hold doors and climb over the rail. Drop onto the platform in the Storage area and move onto the false ceiling to the right. Through the hole in the false ceiling, this spy can hack the yellow terminal.

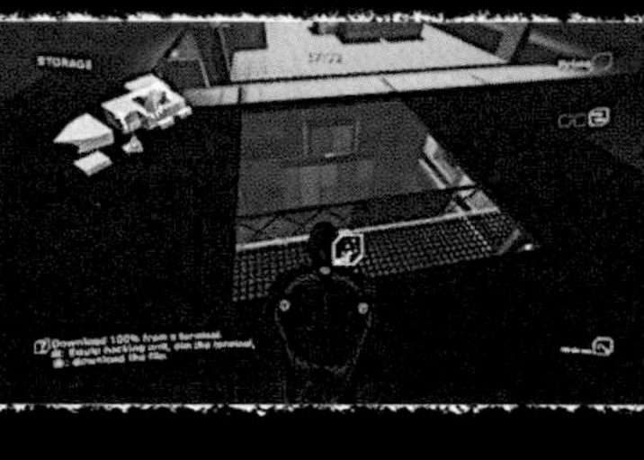

At the same time, the spy who climbed the left pipe to reach a zip-line winds up on a high balcony above the port side of the ship. Head down this balcony and jump up to grab another zip-line, which drops the spy on a hand ledge near a porthole. Shimmy to the left under the porthole and climb up through it. Mercenaries should naturally be alerted by the sound of breaking glass, so quickly move to the right and jump up onto a thin catwalk hanging over the highest interior level. Use this catwalk to navigate over the Engine Room. Position yourself over the blue terminal or the red terminal in the room and hack them. However, it is far too easy for a single mercenary to cover the entire room. The best strategy is to have two spies in the Engine Room, hacking the blue and red terminals simultaneously or intermittently, while a third spy follow the upper catwalk to the rear of the ship. There, he can jump up and climb out of a chute leading to the upper deck. Move to the scaffold left in front of the doorway to the Tech Room and press the Escape Movement button to

through either chute onto a false ceiling above the Tech Room. Hack the green terminal from there.

The mercenaries can still cover these areas quite well, so stay on the move. Download a little, then move to another location. When a file is finally downloaded, head back to the ship's bow as quickly as possible. Be careful of dropping from heights, to avoid damage.

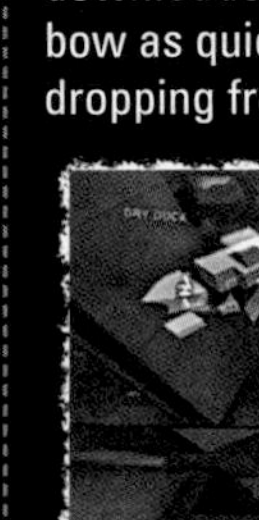

Splinter Cell Double Agent Developer Interview

by UK Frag Doll "Jam"

Three years in the making and the fourth *Splinter Cell* title to grace our control pads (fifth if you include *Splinter Cell: Essentials* on the PSP), much hangs on *Double Agent*. As a Frag Doll, I've had a chance to keep up to date with the development team over the past year.

But how do you evolve one of the most identifiable computer game characters in the world without alienating his massive fan base? How can you break new ground without cracking the foundations a title depends upon? Chris Smith, Lead Designer of the next-generation versions of the game, thinks *Splinter Cell*'s Shanghai team may have found the perfect balance.

"People love *Splinter Cell*. *Splinter Cell* is a massively popular game. But we didn't want to make *Chaos Theory* 2. All of the team were enthusiastic and want to give gamers the best experience—but none of them wanted to make *Chaos Theory* 2. We really took a long look at the forums, what fans thought of the game, and what our friends in the industry and what press thought of the game, and we thought it was time that we did something new for *Splinter Cell*. So we looked at Sam Fisher, and we decided to break him."

Gone are the days when Mr. Fisher could only be found sneaking around in the darkness hiding behind those famous green goggles. In *Double Agent*, Sam is dragged into the open, stripped of his comforts, and sent undercover by the NSA to rediscover himself after the tragic death of his daughter. "Sam's daughter was really his only link to the real world, as fans will know from the game," explains Smith. "A car accident—it happens everyday; we didn't want to be so melodramatic as to have a bad guy that takes out his daughter and you chase him back. We're a little bit better than that."

With Sam thrown into prison to make the contacts that will allow him to infiltrate a terrorist organization, the titular *Double Agent* elements come into play. Trust becomes all important. Julian Gerighty, Senior Producer on the game, elaborates:

"The whole concept was to take Sam Fisher out of his mode of being a soldier, and put him more in an area he was less comfortable with, so we made him a double agent. This was the focal point for all the level design and all the game design issues that we ever tackled. That means that for every single mission that we send you on, you're going to have dual objectives—one set of objectives for the terrorists, and one set of objectives for the NSA. It also means that you're going to have to make choices all the time. So do I do this objective? Do I do that objective? How do I balance my relationship with both the terrorists and the NSA? And that's where the trust meter comes in."

The trust system is something new to *Double Agent*. For Sam to survive his mission, he needs to balance the trust of both the NSA and the terrorists. Two bars represent both parties, and every objective Sam is given will have a trust score linked to it. With certain levels of trust and certain decisions that you take in the game, the player can unlock additional missions.

"Some people asked me 'Does he become a terrorist?'" exclaims Gerighty. "No! Your whole mission is to bring down the terrorists. Now your choice is how far do you take your relationship with the terrorists, and do you need the NSA's support? Sometimes they're going to be asking you to do things that you really don't want him to do. So do you do them just to keep them happy, or do you turn your back on the NSA to complete your real mission?"

It's a difficult task for any developer to carry the torch of one of the most popular video games series. With new features, new game design, and an almost new Sam Fisher, it's a dramatic step for the *Splinter Cell* series. But will it still be the same *Splinter Cell* we all know and love? Smith is pretty confident on this one, stating "I'm a gamer. I refuse to make a game that people will pick out of the box and not love. I am absolutely confident that this will be the best *Splinter Cell* game so far, but don't fear. It's still stealth, it's still Sam Fisher, but a whole lot more."